New Developments in the
Analysis of Market Structure

New Developments in the Analysis of Market Structure

Proceedings of a conference held by the
International Economic Association in
Ottawa, Canada

Edited by

Joseph E. Stiglitz

and

G. Frank Mathewson

The MIT Press
Cambridge, Massachusetts

First MIT Press edition, 1986
Reprinted 1986

First published in 1986 by THE MACMILLAN PRESS LTD

Printed in Hong Kong

Library of Congress Cataloging in Publication Data
Main entry under title:
New developments in the analysis of market structure.
Bibliography: p.
Includes index.
1. Industrial organization (Economic theory)—
Congresses.   2. Vertical integration—Congresses.
3. Oligopolies—Congresses.   4. Competition—Congresses.
I. Stiglitz, Joseph E.   II. Mathewson, G. Frank.
III. International Economic Association.
HD2326.N43   1986   338′8   85-4246
ISBN 0–262–19241–1 (hard)
       0–262–69093–4 (paper)

Contents

v

Introduction

Joseph E. Stiglitz

This volume contains the proceedings of the International Economic Association Round Table Conference on New Developments in the Analysis of Market Structures held in Ottawa, Canada from 10 to 14 May 1982.

The past decade has been marked by a number of important developments in the theory of market structures. These have affected both our views of how markets function and the tools which we use in our analyses. The purpose of the conference was to survey some of these developments, to push forward our understanding of some of the important issues and to give some direction for future research in this area.

In this introduction I do not propose to summarise each of the chapters. They are written with a clarity which is unusual for such technical pieces, and speak for themselves. The excellent summary of the discussion by Frank Mathewson and Michael Peters provides the reader with at least a hint of the lively exchange of views that occurred during the four days of the conference. What I would like to do in this introduction is bring out a few of the major themes that reappeared both in the papers and the discussions, themes which reflect some of these major developments.

My discussion will be organised around six topics:

1. *The determinants of market structure.* What determines the number of firms in an industry, and whether a firm which is in a dominant position in a market remains so.
2. *The determinants of the 'force' of competition.* The behaviour of a market is determined not only by the number of firms in the market. What are other factors determining the effective degree of competitiveness of the market?
3. *The new theory of the firm and the role of competition.* The consequences of alternative market structures obviously depend, in part, on the behaviour of those who manage the firm.

What difference does it make if managers pursue some objective other than maximising the (present discounted value of) profits of the firm?

4. *Decentralisation and co-ordination.* The classical question in industrial organisation, which concerns the consequences of vertical integration, can be placed within a broader context. What is at issue is not only the extent to which various economic activities should be organised through markets rather than hierarchies, but also the scope for a much broader set of contractual relationships not adequately described by these two polar forms of organisation.

5. *Competition and market structure in Socialist economies.* The literature on market structure has primarily developed as an outgrowth of problems facing developed, mixed capitalist economies. Yet similar issues arise in economies in which government enterprises play a more dominant role.

6. *Welfare economics.* The recent developments in the theory of market structure have suggested that the kinds of models underlying traditional anti-trust policy are inappropriate. This has led to some marked changes in views concerning government policies aimed, for instance, at encouraging competition.

I now consider these issues in more detail.

1. *The determinants of market structure.* A central set of questions, around which the conference was focused, concerns the nature of competition and the determinants of market structure. Few markets – particularly for goods produced by the industrial sector – are perfectly competitive. There are few firms that act as price takers – which believe that were they to raise their price by 1 per cent, they would lose all their customers. Yet firms do compete: in most industries, there are several firms; even when there are relatively few firms, there is often the possibility of entry; potential competition *may be* as effective as actual competition. And firms compete not only on price; they compete by their choice of products, the quality of the services they provide, and their advertising; and they compete in R & D, and in the development of new products and new techniques of production.

These ideas are, of course, not new. In the 1930s Robinson (1934) and Chamberlin (1933) each developed their own version of theories of imperfect or monopolistic competition. And Schumpeter developed his own theory, in which one firm succeeds another in a position of temporary monopoly, as each develops inventions which supersede those which have gone before. These ideas remained almost dormant for forty years. In the meantime, there were rapid advances in the economists' tool-kits. When the resulting new techniques were applied to these old problems, new insights were obtained and new questions posed.

While much of the earlier literature took the market structure (e.g. the number of firms) as given, the new theory of market structure begins by asking what determines the number of firms? What are the barriers to entry? To what extent and by what mechanisms can existing firms deter entry? And will they wish to do so?

The objective of this line of research is to identify *exogenous* variables – characteristics of technology (including the technology of innovation and invention) and of demand. These exogenous variables determine the market structure, which is thus viewed to be *endogenous*.[1]

Two general features of technology play a central role in explaining both market structure and the nature of competition: non-convexities and irreversibilities (sunk costs). While many production technologies may exhibit one or both of these characteristics, technological change (whether arising from explicit expenditures on research and development or from learning by doing) and information technologies (both those associated with consumers' learning about products and firms, for example, through advertising or search, and firms' learning about customers and technologies) are characterised by non-convexities and irreversibilities (see for example the chapters by Schmalensee and Dasgupta in this volume.)

Recent research has also attempted to identify *strategies* by which existing firms might deter entry, and to assess whether such *strategies* are ever equilibrium strategies. That is, it must not only be possible for existing firms to deter the entry of new rivals: it must also be in their interests to pursue such strategies. (More precisely, entry deterrence must be shown to arise in equilibrium, in response to the equilibrium strategies pursued by other firms, including potential entrants.)

The tools of game theory have proved of invaluable assistance in clarifying ideas here, though, as research has progressed, it has become increasingly clear that the central problems to be solved are economic and not just mathematical problems. We can analyse the Nash equilibrium, given the strategy spaces of each of the participants; but there are usually many equilibria; the mathematics does not tell us which to choose. And the set of equilibria is likely to differ markedly, depending on the strategy spaces assumed; again, the mathematics does not tell us what is the 'correct' strategy space to assume. Should we assume that firms set their own prices, and take the prices of other firms as given? Or should we assume that firms set quantities, and take the quantities of other firms as given? Or should we consider some alternative strategy space, such as that employed by Grossman (1981)? Should we restrict strategies to depend only on a current pay-off relevant to 'state' variables; or should they be at least allowed to depend on history? What kinds of commitments are feasible? How can they be made binding?

There are two broad approaches to the analysis of the determinants of market structure (the number of firms in equilibrium). In the first, all firms make their investment decisions simultaneously (or there are no sunk costs). The earlier work on monopolistic competition (as well as the Loury and Dasgupta – Stiglitz analyses of market structure and technical change) is of this variety. In the second, the sequential nature of decision making is central: some firm(s) is (are) already in the market. There are some potential entrants. The incumbent firm(s) may undertake some action(s) which may deter entry.

In the following paragraphs, I want to discuss briefly a few of the general *economic* issues associated with entry deterrence.

The recent literature has made use of an important distinction between *state* variables, variables which cannot be instantaneously changed, and variables which *can* be instantaneously changed (see, for instance, Stiglitz, 1981). An entrant, in deciding on whether to enter, must come to some view concerning the nature of the equilibrium which will emerge *after* he has entered. The nature of that equilibrium will depend on the characteristics of the incumbent firms at that time – on their state variables.[2]

A class of state variables that is of particular interest comprises binding pre-commitments. The firm signs a contract that it will produce a given quantity of output, or purchase a given quantity of inputs, with a proviso that if it fails, it must incur a large penalty, a penalty sufficiently large that it pays the firm to live up to its commitment. If there were no restrictions on the kinds of binding contract that could be signed, it would be easy for any firm to deter entry. The firm would sign a contract with all its customers that committed it to deliver its good at an outrageously low price so long as another firm was in the market. Given that the incumbent firm had signed such binding contracts, it would not pay any other firm to enter the market, and so entry would be costlessly deterred. Such contracts do not *seem* to be prevalent. Why? Are there some important contractual arrangements which serve to deter entry (perhaps more subtly than in the above example)? What provides a limit to the use of these contractual arrangements as entry deterrence devices? At present, there are no agreed answers to these questions. (There are some obvious intuitive explanations for why such contracts are not signed; if the event (entry) occurs, it will be very costly to the firm making such a commitment. But in the context of most of the formal models, where all firms are rational, entry *never* occurs if the binding commitment has been made, and hence the costs of enforcement are never incurred.)

A state variable which has been at the centre of discussion since Spence's 1977 paper is the use of *excess* capacity as an entry deterrent. Clearly, in general, the stock of *sunk* capital affects the nature of equilibrium. (If the capital is costlessly mobile, then it is not a state variable, and cannot serve as an entry deterrent.) Spence showed that in his simple model, by increasing the excess capacity, the existing firm could deter entry if the entrant believed that the firm would use the full capacity upon his entry. Dixit (1980) posed the question, was this a reasonable expectation? He postulated that the entrant would assume (a) that his rival was rational, and (b) that once the entrant had entered, and committed himself to a particular sunk capital, his rival would respond in a rational manner. In the equilibrium, the existing firm does not increase its output to use its excess capacity, but accommodates the entrant, in general by lowering its output. Thus excess capacity is not a credible entry deterrent.

This illustrates the central role of beliefs, expectations about what will happen after entry. Much of the recent literature can be viewed as attempting to ask what restrictions can be placed on these beliefs by postulates of 'rationality'. For instance, while the earlier literature suggested that firms would use limit pricing as an entry deterrent – charge a price just low enough to make it unprofitable for a new firm to enter – in the 'new view' at first blush this seems unreasonable: prices are not state variables, and there is no reason for an entrant to assume that the firm will leave its price unchanged in the face of his entry. But Salop, in his important 1979 paper, provided a new interpretation to limit pricing: the prices charged by firms could convey information about these firms' cost functions; low cost firms have an incentive to charge a low price to persuade potential entrants that their costs are low; technology – cost of production – is a state variable, and if the entrant believes that his rivals' cost functions are low, that will affect the post-entry equilibrium; if they are low enough, entry will be deterred. The high-cost firms wish to persuade potential entrants that they too have low costs; this gives rise to a standard 'self-selection' equilibrium. Here, the high cost firm operates at the point where marginal revenue equals marginal cost, while the low cost firm sells at a sufficiently low price that it does not pay the high cost firm to imitate.[3]

Pre-entry prices may affect state variables in other ways. In models of exhaustible natural resources, *raising* prices leads to slower rates of exhaustion, and hence higher stocks of natural resources. In models of learning-by-doing, lower prices lead to more sales, and hence lower costs (see Stiglitz, 1981).

Predation represents another important class of strategies aimed at altering beliefs in such a way as to make entry less likely, and is conventionally said to occur when a firm charges a price below marginal cost;[4] the firm is willing to suffer temporary losses, provided this serves to deter future entry. It does so because if future entry is deterred, long run profits can be higher. Again, though it may be *feasible* for firms to deter entry by this strategy, the question has been posed: Can these strategies be part of an equilibrium? It only pays to take a loss today if it serves to deter *future* entry. In any economy operating over a finite number of periods, it therefore cannot pay to deter predators in the last period; if entry occurs then, the equilibrium in that last period is the standard Nash equilibrium. But now consider what happens in the next-to-last period. It cannot pay to deter entry then, since the entrant firm knows that it will not pay the incumbent to charge a low price in the last period, regardless of what it does in the next to last period. Since it does not serve to deter entry, it does not pay to predate.

There are at least three responses to this seeming paradox: (i) predation does not occur; it turns out to be very difficult to ascertain whether predation has in fact occurred, since it is difficult to ascertain what marginal costs are;[5] (ii) the analysis hinges on there being a finite number of periods; in a world without end (or with no finite date at which the market will end) then predation may be an equilibrium strategy; (iii) assume there are irrational firms, who respond to entry by predating; if potential entrants know about this irrationality, such firms do better than rational firms. Thus, if potential entrants know that there are some irrational firms, but do not know which these firms are, it pays all firms to act as if they were the irrational firms; predation may then be an equilibrium strategy.[6,7]

A final category of entry-deterrence strategies, in a dynamic context, is referred to as pre-emption and is discussed below in the paper by Gilbert. The existing firm takes advantage of its current presence in the market to remove the profitable opportunities available to potential rivals.

Thus, the existing firm may pre-empt a research opportunity, engaging in R & D at a sufficiently fast pace that it does not pay any rival to enter (Dasgupta and Stiglitz, 1980b; Gilbert and Newbery, 1982; Dasgupta *et al.*, 1983): or in a growing market with plants exhibiting indivisibilities, the existing firm may anticipate this future demand and build its current capacity in anticipation of the future demand (Eaton and Lipsey, 1980).

Three questions are addressed:

(1) Is it profitable to pre-empt?
(2) Does pre-emption arise as an equilibrium strategy?
(3) To what extent do the dominant firms in markets in which pre-emption occurs exhibit monopoly power?

These questions were first addressed in the context of R & D. It is easy to show that if it pays an entrant to engage in R & D at a particular level, it pays the incumbent firm to engage in the same R & D project at a slightly faster pace, and win the patent (Salop, 1979). The incumbent could behave in the same way as the entrant, and obtain the same profits; but, in addition, he has the advantage arising from the possibility of co-ordination. He can, in other words, operate his two plants (his old plant with the old technology and his new plant with the new technology) independently, obtaining the standard duopoly outcome. But he has the possibility of co-ordinating the action of the two, thus increasing his profits. This says little more than that it would pay one firm to buy out its rival (at its rival's present discounted value of profits, in the duopoly equilibrium). While buying out one's rival may, however, be interpreted as an anti-competitive move, prohibited by anti-trust laws, pre-empting one's rivals – deterring entry – may not be. An important question which has been addressed in the recent literature has been to see how general is this argument. Under what circumstances is such pre-emption not profitable? For instance, if there is a large number of alternative products which might be developed and which can serve as perfect substitutes, it will not pay the existing firm to pre-empt all entry by obtaining a patent for each (even were it feasible to do so);[8] similarly, some new entrants may have a comparative advantage over existing firms in the development of new technologies (camera companies like Canon might have a comparative advantage in developing photographic reproduction techniques). Or there may be interactions between a potential entrant's current products and an innovation which will result in greater returns to the research project for it than for the existing firm (Dasgupta *et al.*, 1983).

A new class of arguments is provided by Gilbert in his chapter in this volume. Allowing a second firm into the market affects the nature of the equilibrium which would emerge were a third or fourth firm to enter. It may be impossible for the initial firm to make the kinds of binding commitments which serve (costlessly) to deter entry; in that case, allowing one small entrant may turn out to be a low cost way of deterring entry which would have a more deleterious effect on profits.

But even if it is feasible to take pre-emptive action, to do so may not be part of an equilibrium strategy; assume for instance, that the current firm spends enough to make it not worthwhile for any rival to engage in R & D. But if no rival engages in R & D, it does not pay for him to engage in such a high level of R & D. If the strategy space of the participants is taken to be the level of R & D expenditures, then there is no pure strategy equilibrium. There is, however, a mixed strategy (see Gilbert and Stiglitz, 1979). But if the strategy space of the entrant is allowed to be expanded, so that the entrant specifies for any level of R & D expenditure undertaken by the incumbent what his (subsequent) R & D will be, then pre-emption is a Nash equilibrium.

The issue of pre-emption is of particular importance because of its implications for the persistence of dominant firms. While the Schumpeterian vision had one temporary monopolist being succeeded by the next, when pre-emption is an equilibrium strategy, then the current monopolist may remain a monopolist for an extended period of time. On the other hand, the welfare consequences (discussed more fully below) may not be too serious: to maintain its monopoly position, the firm must continue to compete vigorously, by engaging in the same level of R & D as any entrant would have undertaken. (This result, however, is not general, as we shall remark below.)

The chapter by Gilbert provides a general treatment of the theory of pre-emption, focusing on pre-emptive investment. He concludes:

. . . pre-emptive investment, as alleged in the Alcoa case, is not likely to be a credible threat to market performance unless: (i) scale economies are sufficient to allow only a few firms in an efficient market structure; or (ii) an established firm can convince potential competitors that it would compete aggressively against even small entrants.

Though the general principles of entry deterrence have thus become reasonably well understood within the past decade, there remains considerable work to be done in assessing particular entry-deterrence devices. As we have noted, much of the recent literature has focused on two decisions: capacity and R & D. There are other important decisions, such as the durability and flexibility of the capital, which have entry deterrence effects. The chapter by Schmalensee, on advertising, analyses a class of decisions whose effects on entry and market structure are of particular importance. He shows that the strategic implications of investments in introductory advertising may differ dramatically from those of investments in productive capacity.

2. *The force of competition.* A second central issue with which the recent literature has been concerned is what are the determinants of the degree of 'competitiveness' of a market. While, in the older view, a large number of firms in the market seemed both necessary and sufficient for effective competition, the new view has questioned both premises.

For instance, take the recent developments in monopolistic competition (represented in this volume by the chapter by Archibald, Eaton and Lipsey). Here, it is not only the number of firms in the market which matters, but also their relationship with one another. In the one-dimensional spatial equilibrium model (whether firms are located around a circle or along a line), each firm has two neighbours. Thus, though there may be many firms altogether, each firm interacts with only two other firms; the market is more aptly described as a series of local (overlapping) oligopolies. By contrast, this is not true in the Spence and Dixit/Stiglitz models (where all 'products' are equidistant from all other products.) Nor is it in the higher dimensional spatial equilibrium models (where every firm has many neighbours); or in models with costly search (where individuals of a given type may end up at a number of different stores). All of these models capture better the spirit of Chamberlinian monopolistic competition, where strategic interactions may legitimately be ignored. It is an important empirical question to determine which markets are best described by the monopolistically competitive structure, in which strategic reactions are not of first order importance.

There are other circumstances in which there are markets with several firms which do not behave competitively: the firms collude together or act _as if_ they colluded together. While the chapter in this volume by d'Aspremont and Gabszewicz addresses the question of the stability of these collusive arrangements, Salop shows that a number of practices serve to facilitate co-operative behaviour. Some of these practices, such as a promise to match the lowest prices, look very competitive; but they remove the incentive to lower prices, to deviate from the collusive price.

More generally, the theory of repeated games has shown that it is often easy to get collusive solutions out of non-co-operative behaviour. While the history of cartels suggests that explicit collusive agreements seem to be quite fragile, the extent and stability of these more general collusive outcomes is a subject for continuing research.

A quite different context, in which there are many firms but where the equilibrium price is the _monopoly_ price, arises in markets where consumers have imperfect information concerning prices. They obtain information through a process of sequential search, and there are strictly positive search costs. (Diamond, 1971.) Indeed, in these circumstances it can be shown that prices may be lower with two firms in the markets than with many firms (Stiglitz, 1985).

These analyses have provided us with examples of important market structures in which, though there may be many firms, the outcomes are not competitive.

On the other hand, the Theory of Contestable Markets (Baumol, Panzar and Willig) argues that – when there are non-convexities but no sunk costs – there may be important circumstances in which there will be only a single firm in a market, but where the market will behave competitively. The debate over this theory has centred around the issue of the importance of sunk costs, particularly in those technologies for which there are important non-convexities (and which will therefore be characterised by one or a few firms). (See the exchange between Weitzman, 1982 and Baumol, Panzar and Willig, 1982). Even for airlines, where the major asset (aircraft) is not a sunk cost, expenditures to inform customers about their existence and their time schedules may represent important sunk costs.)

Another example illustrating the ambiguity of the relationship between numbers of firms and competitive behaviour, arises with technological change. As we noted earlier, a monopolist could persist in its monopoly position, by pre-empting potential rivals. But in doing so, the monopolist is behaving, at least with respect to his R & D policy, much as competitors would. A slight change in assumptions, however, alters this conclusion in a dramatic way: if the research project is to be undertaken over a number of years, it is possible that the incumbent firm will begin that research project, and push it to the point where the firm has a commanding lead. The firm then can behave like a monopolist, simply threatening potential entrants that if they do attempt to engage in R & D, the firm will respond (as it can, and as it will be profitable for it to do) by increasing the speed of its research to ensure that it captures the patent. This is referred to as ε-pre-emption. It requires that the existing firm be able to observe and to react (possibly with a lag) to potential entrants.[9] The smaller the lags in observation and reaction, presumably the more like a monopolist will the behaviour of the entrant be.

What is important about these examples is that they show that the nature of competition in a market may depend on a variety of factors other than simply numbers, e.g., the presence of sunk costs and the information structure.

3. *New theories of the firm, market structure and competitive behaviour.* The past decade has witnessed not only marked developments in the theory of market structures, but also rapid changes in the theory of the firm. The traditional neoclassical models assumed unitary firms, in which all participants work to maximise the value of the firm and where there is unanimity both among shareholders and managers about this objective and about what it entails (that is, what actions are required to maximise profits). Recent work, however, has questioned all of these assumptions: (i) workers and managers must be motivated by a reward structure to pursue the objectives of the firm; only if it were costless to monitor instantaneously all of their actions would it be possible to ensure that they pursued the policies which the owners might wish. (This problem of incentives is now generally referred to as the principal-agent problem; following Mirrlees, 1971; Ross, 1973; and Stiglitz, 1974 a huge literature has developed – too extensive to treat adequately in this brief introduction.)[10] (ii) Workers and managers work according to certain rules of thumb and routines; though some resources may be devoted to assessing and devising improvements in those routines, many of the improvements are a result of chance discovery and it is not at all clear that the process of 'search' can be well described by models of rational maximisers of expected utility. This theme, stressed in the earlier

work of Simon and March (1958), plays an important role in the evolutionary theories of Nelson and Winter, as exemplified in the chapter by Nelson contained in this volume. Improvements are spread by a similar evolutionary process, with firms which have discovered good techniques of production or good managerial techniques surviving, and inefficient firms disappearing.

These new theories of the firm have several important implications for the theory of market structure and for the role of competition. First, our earlier analysis stressed the role of strategies and beliefs in determining the nature of market structure; most of the work focused on what might be called 'rational' strategies and beliefs: that is, strategies and beliefs which were consistent with optimising behaviour by the participants in the market. But the strategies chosen by firms may not be 'optimising' and their beliefs may be based on some interpretation of historical experience, rather than on an analysis of what the rational behaviour of rivals entails. Thus, a firm may be a predator, simply because its managers believe that that is how one should respond to entry. They may have some limited experiences to support their views, but they certainly do not assess the reasonableness of their views by using the kind of game theoretic analysis introduced earlier.

Second, since managers do not appropriate all the returns accruing to their activities, there is the possibility of 'managerial slack', a theme taken up in the chapters by Selten and Stiglitz in this volume. There is a long-standing conjecture that managerial slack is greater in monopolies than in competitive markets. (The neoclassical model denies the existence of slack, and hence cannot say anything about the relationship between market structure and slack.)

Selten puts forward what he calls the 'strong slack hypothesis', which maintains that slack has a tendency to increase so long as profits are positive. This hypothesis has some strong consequences. Consider traditional Cournot oligopoly theory with fixed costs. Under this theory, welfare may be increased by restriction of entry if fixed costs are sufficiently small; under the strong slack hypothesis, free entry is always best. Though workers may gain from consumption at the working place, their welfare gains are less than the cost in inefficiency. And because slack is reflected in marginal costs, prices are higher and consumers worse off.

Stiglitz attempts to relate the managerial slack associated with monopoly to the optimal incentive structure under monopoly (by comparison with managerial incentive structures in more competitive environments). First, the variability of profits in monopoly will, under certain circumstances, be greater than their variability in more competitive environments; and this means that the optimal managerial contract will make the pay of managers less dependent on profits. But this, in turn, will reduce managerial incentives. Second, and more importantly, the presence of competitors allows pay to be based at least in part on relative performance – or on prices, which will reflect changes in the environment. As a result, incentive contracts (reward structures) can be designed which provide better incentives (particularly for managers) at lower risk than in monopolised sectors.

4. *Firms, decentralisation and co-ordination.* Recent advances in the economics of uncertainty and information, which led to the development of the New Theory of the Firm, have also led to a re-examination of the issues associated with vertical integration. The basic question is: Where should the boundaries of firms be? What transactions should be conducted through the market-place? Oliver Williamson in his chapter shows how his transactions-costs approach provides answers to these questions.

Green points out that when there are limits to the contractual arrangements which firms can make, and where prices do not clear markets, vertical integration may provide a mechanism for firms to assure themselves of a market; the desirability of this depends on the likelihood that firms will be rationed (unable to sell their goods); this, in turn, depends on the 'thickness' of the market (the extent to which transactions occur within the firm, or through the market).

Mathewson and Winter show that the consequences of vertical restraints can be viewed within the context of a principal-agent problem: to what extent do the restraints enhance the ability of the upstream firm to control the downstream firm. They show that these restraints may, in the presence of a variety of kinds of externalities, be welfare-enhancing.

The fundamental issue raised by all of these papers is what it is which firms can do that markets, either through prices or through a broader range of contractual arrangements, cannot do. (Or can do, but at greater cost.)

Among the arguments for vertical integration put forward in the earlier literature, was the argument that it enables the two firms to co-ordinate their actions (including the exchange of information) and thus to increase their profits. It also reduces the risk faced by the two firms, ensuring that the upstream firm experiences a demand for its output (Green). In these views, there are initially, two independent firms; once they are integrated, all workers act to maximise the joint profits of the combined firm. In the New View, each of the workers in each of the firms pursues his own interests. Behaviour will change only as a result of a change in the reward structure. Much of what could be accomplished by vertical integration, for example in risk sharing, assuring markets, etc. could have been accomplished by an appropriate set of contractual relationships. The question is, how can we identify the ways in which contracts differ from 'firms'. For instance, no contract specifies what is to happen in every state of nature; there are always some circumstances in which Pareto efficiency would dictate a change in the terms of the contract. When the contract (reward structure) is 'internal' to the firm, there is some presumption that such changes can be made more easily than between firms. But the difficulties experienced when making institutional changes within a firm suggest that this may not necessarily be the case.

5. *Competition and market structure in Socialist economies.* The behaviour of firms is affected, at least to some extent, by the incentives provided to their managers, and this is as true in Socialist economies as in market economies. The (implicit or explicit) incentives depend in part at least on the market structure in which the firm (enterprise) operates. There can be competition even in a socialist economy, where managers' pay is dependent on the relative performance of different enterprises. The absence of competition may provide part of the explanation of the allegedly high levels of slack and low levels of R & D. Two chapters in this volume, by Horvat and by Roman, address themselves to two aspects of these issues.

6. *Welfare economics and the functions of competition.* In traditional economic theory, competition performs an important role: if all markets are perfectly competitive, resource allocations by those markets will be Pareto efficient. Unfortunately, the standard welfare analysis has little to say about modern industrial economies, where technological change and information problems (explicitly excluded from the traditional analysis) are of central importance. We do not have, nor is there likely to exist, a welfare theorem for such economies possessing the generality of the fundamental theorem of welfare economics. (Perhaps the closest we have to such a general theorem is the Greenwald–Stiglitz, 1983, result, showing that economies with incomplete markets, adverse selection, self-selection constraints, moral hazard, etc. are in general Pareto inefficient.) What we do have is a number of 'insights' and 'examples' which serve more

to make us cautious in applying standard welfare economics than to provide us with a basis for policy prescriptions.

Several of the chapters in this volume show how difficult it is to devise rules which ensure either that a given practice is anti-competitive, or that the prohibition of a particular practice will be welfare enhancing. As Salop pointed out, practices such as matching the lowest price, while appearing competitive, may facilitate collusion. Responding to entry by lowering one's price may be predatory, but need not be so: one may simply be accommodating the entrant. And charging a price below current marginal cost need not be predatory: with learning by doing, the relevant (long run) marginal cost is always lower than the current marginal cost.

We also know that, without some degree of monopoly power, firms will not be able to appropriate returns from innovation, and thus will have no incentive to innovate. Thus, there is a trade-off between static efficiency and dynamic efficiency. Similarly, spill-overs from the research from one firm to another firm, introduce an inefficiency – the firm undertaking R & D fails to appropriate all the returns from his expenditures. Yet, at the same time, they generate a benefit (in the higher productivity in other firms). Spence, in his chapter, explores the interaction of these two effects.

Furthermore, we know that potential competition may actually make everyone worse off. The threat of entry induces firms to engage in entry-deterrent strategies which are socially wasteful (Stiglitz, 1981).

Still, there is a belief among many economists that competition serves a useful function, for instance in promoting efficiency. Such arguments are explicitly excluded from traditional neoclassical analysis, where it is assumed that firms always minimise costs; that is, whether the firm is a monopolist or a competitor, it behaves efficiently. The New Theory of the Firm, discussed briefly above, provides a rationale to explain why firms might not always minimise costs. Thus the chapters by Selten and Stiglitz – attempting to relate competition and slack (managerial incentives) – provide a basis for a welfare analysis of competition which, while consistent with many popular arguments for the virtues of competition, is quite different from the standard analysis.

CONCLUDING REMARKS

The papers of the conference reflect the notable advances in our understanding of market structure during the past decade. We now know, for instance, that the relationship between the number of firms in a market and the effective degree of competition is complex; markets with a few firms may, under certain circumstances, act much more competitively than markets with many firms. We have come to understand much more the determinants of market structure itself, to view it as endogenous rather than exogenous. At the same time, the papers pointed to the many questions to which we do not know the answer. Thus, we know that arguments for anti-trust policy based on traditional competitive analysis are inappropriate. But we do not really know the welfare consequences of the kinds of anti-trust policies pursued by various governments; nor do we have a good basis for judging whether particular modifications to these policies are likely to be welfare enhancing or welfare decreasing. Perhaps, in another decade, another IEA Round Table Conference will assess progress on these fundamental issues.

NOTES

1. See, for instance, Dasgupta and Stiglitz (1980a, b), the chapter by Dasgupta in this volume and the works cited there.
2. It also obviously depends on the nature of the interactions that are postulated to occur after entry, that is, on the assumptions concerning the post-entry game. How these beliefs are formed, or how 'rational' potential entrants would form their beliefs, is a subject of continuing research. See below.
3. For an extension of this idea to the case where there is a whole distribution of costs of firm, and for a formalisation of these ideas in game-theoretic terms, see Milgrom and Roberts (1982).
4. We saw in the previous paragraph that firms might well charge a price below the point where marginal revenue equals marginal cost, in order to convince potential entrants that their cost functions were low.
5. If there are important elements of learning by doing, for instance, the relevant marginal cost is not the current cost of production, but some future cost of production.
6. For an excellent formal development of similar ideas, see Kreps and Wilson, 1982.
7. There are at least two objections to this approach. The first is one of consistency: even if one does not believe in rational behaviour, one might be interested in the kinds of equilibria which might emerge if individuals were consistently rational. Alternatively, one might wish to model equilibrium using the observed behavioural responses, which often do not seem to be in accord with rationality postulates. The approach just described is viewed by some as a curious mixture of the two. The second objection is that the nature of the equilibrium may be

sensitive to the kinds of irrationality postulated; since the kind of irrationality postulated is *ad hoc*, the results are *ad hoc*.

8. A general discussion of this case is provided in Dasgupta *et al.*, 1983.
9. The equilibrium strategies for these dynamic patent races are again characterised by mixed strategies. For a more extended discussion, see Fudenberg, *et al.*, 1983.
10. The assumption that all shareholders of the firm are unanimously in agreement over the objectives which they wish the firm to pursue has also been questioned; see e.g. Grossman and Stiglitz, 1980.

REFERENCES

Baumol, W., Panzar, J. and Willig, R. (1982) *Contestable Markets and the Theory of Industrial Organization* (New York: Harcourt Brace Jovanovich).

Baumol, W., Panzar, J. and Willig, R. (1983) 'Reply: Contestable Markets: An Uprising in the Theory of Industry Structure', *American Economic Review*, vol. 73, June, pp. 491–7.

Chamberlin, E. (1933) *The Theory of Monopolistic Competition*. (Cambridge, Mass: Harvard University Press).

Dasgupta, P.S. and Stiglitz, J.E. (1980a) 'Industrial Structure and the Nature of Innovative Activity', *Economic Journal*, vol. 90, pp. 266–92.

Dasgupta, P.S. and Stiglitz, J.E. (1980b) 'Uncertainty, Industrial Structure and the Speed of R & D', *Bell Journal of Economics*, Spring, pp. 1–28.

Dasgupta, P.S., Gilbert, R. and Stiglitz, J.E. (1982) 'Invention and Innovation Under Alternate Market Structures: The Case of Natural Resources', *Review of Economic Studies*, vol. 49, pp. 567–82.

Dasgupta, P.S., Gilbert, R. and Stiglitz, J.E. (1983) 'Strategic Considerations in Invention and Innovation: The Case of Natural Resources', *Econometrica*, vol. 51, pp. 1439–48.

Diamond, P. (1971) 'A Model of Price Adjustment', *Journal of Economic Theory*, vol. 3, pp. 156–68.

Dixit, A. (1980) 'The Role of Investment in Entry Deterrence', *Economic Journal*, vol. 90, pp. 95–106.

Dixit, A. and Stiglitz, J.E. (1977) 'Monopolistic Competition and Optimum Product Diversity', *American Economic Review*, vol. 67, pp. 297–308.

Eaton, B.C. and Lipsey, R.G. (1980) 'Exit Barriers are Entry Barriers: The Durability of Capital as a Barrier to Entry', *Bell Journal of Economics*, vol. 11, pp. 721–729.

Fudenberg, D., Gilbert, R., Tirole, J. and Stiglitz, J.E. (1983) 'Pre-emption, Leap-frogging and Competition in Patent Races', *European Economic Review*, vol. 22, June, pp. 3–31.

Gilbert, R. and Newbery, D. (1982) 'Pre-emptive Patenting and the Persistence of Monopoly', *American Economic Review*, vol. 72, pp. 514–26.

Gilbert, R. and Stiglitz, J.E. (1979) 'Entry, Equilibrium and Welfare', paper presented at an NBER conference on Theoretical Industrial Organization. Montreal.

Gilbert, R. and Harris, R. (1981) 'Investment Decisions with Economies of

Scale and Learning', *American Economic Review*, vol. 71, May, pp. 172–7.

Greenwald, B. and Stiglitz, J.E. (1983) 'Pecuniary and Market Mediated Externalities: Towards a General Theory of the Welfare Economics of Economies with Imperfect Information and Incomplete Markets', Bell Laboratories, Mimeo.

Grossman, S.J. (1981) 'Nash Equilibrium and the Industrial Organization of Markets with Large Fixed Costs', *Econometrica*, Sept., pp. 1149–72.

Grossman, S.J. and Stiglitz, J.E. (1980) 'Shareholder Unanimity in Making Production and Financial Decisions', *Quarterly Journal of Economics*, May, pp. 543–66.

Kreps, D.M. and Wilson, R. (1982) 'Reputation and Imperfect Information', *Journal of Economic Theory*, vol. 27, Aug., pp. 253–79.

Loury, G. (1979) 'Market Structure and Innovation', *Quarterly Journal of Economics*, vol. 93, pp. 395–410.

Milgrom, P. and Roberts, J. (1982) 'Limit Pricing and Entry Under Incomplete Information: an Equilibrium Analysis', *Econometrica*, vol. 50, pp. 443–59.

Mirrlees, J. (1971) 'An Exploration in the Theory of Optimum Income Taxation', *Review of Economic Studies*, Apr., pp. 175–208.

Nelson, R.R. and Winter, S.G. (1982) *An Evolutionary Theory of Economic Change*, (Cambridge, Mass. Harvard University Press).

Robinson, J. (1934) *The Economics of Imperfect Competition* (London: Macmillan).

Ross, S. (1973) 'The Economic Theory of Agency: the Principal's Problem', *American Economic Review*, May, pp. 134–9.

Salop, S. (1979) 'Strategic Entry Deterrence', *American Economic Review*, Papers and Proceedings, pp. 335–8.

Schumpeter J.A. (1947) *Capitalism, Socialism and Democracy*, 2nd edn. (London: Allen & Unwin).

Spence, A.M. (1977) 'Entry, Capacity, Investment and Oligopolistic Pricing', *The Bell Journal of Economics*, vol. 8, pp. 534–44.

Spence, A.M. (1976) 'Product Selection, Fixed Costs and Monopolistic Competition', *Review of Economic Studies*, vol. 43, pp. 217–35.

Simon, H. and March, J.G. (1958) *Organizations* (New York: J. Wiley).

Stiglitz, J.E. (1974) 'Incentives and Risk Sharing in Sharecropping', *Review of Economic Studies*, Apr., pp. 219–55.

Stiglitz, J.E. (1981) 'Potential Competition May Reduce Welfare', *American Economic Review*, Papers and Proceedings, pp. 184–9.

Stiglitz, J.E. (1985) 'Competitivity and the Number of Firms in a Market: Are Duopolies More Competitive than Atomistic Markets?', *IMSSS Technical Report*, Stanford University.

Weitzman, M.L. (1983) 'Comment on Contestable Markets: an Uprising in the Theory of Industrial Structures', *American Economic Review*, vol. 73, pp. 486–8.

Part One
Address Models

Part One
Address Models

1 Address Models of Value Theory[1]

G.C. Archibald

UNIVERSITY OF BRITISH COLUMBIA

B.C. Eaton

UNIVERSITY OF TORONTO

and

R.G. Lipsey

QUEEN'S UNIVERSITY

I INTRODUCTION

This paper presents an approach to the theory of monopolistic competition which owes a particular intellectual debt to Gorman (1980), Kaldor (1934; 1935) and Lancaster (1966). Our interest is in deriving testable hypotheses from partial equilibrium analysis. Some simple conceptual experiments, in conjunction with some awkward facts, lead us to take strong positions concerning the appropriate demand and cost primitives. The choice of primitives has important implications for the concept and the properties of equilibrium. We hope that the approach presented here is coherent; but it has to be said that the analysis has not been completed, by ourselves or anyone else. Part of our purpose is accordingly to note unsolved problems, and generate an agenda for further research. At some points we are able only to offer a conjecture as to what the results of further research may be. We confine ourselves throughout to the market for consumer goods (Chamberlin's, 1933, problem) and do not consider the markets for capital, labour or intermediate goods.

The remainder of this introduction outlines our argument.

(1) We start by inviting the reader to share in a conceptual experiment. Choose some currently produced good, X: can you specify an

3

arbitrarily close substitute? To paraphrase Eddington[2] (1958, p. 119), 'Hesitate before you answer: much of modern value theory hangs in the balance'. We think that in most cases the answer must be 'yes'. (Clearly we can specify an automobile with a little more acceleration, deceleration, fuel consumption, and so on; indeed, examples are many and obvious.) A 'yes' answer has important implications. First, it would be hard to describe your specified substitute as an *arbitrarily* close substitute for an existing good without operating in some *space of product attributes or characteristics*. Second, natural notions of continuity suggest that there exists a neighbourhood around good X in the appropriate characteristics space such that all goods in the neighbourhood are close substitutes for good X. This suggests to us that the natural way to describe your preferences is in some appropriate *and continuous* characteristics space. Thus a 'yes' answer to the original question suggests that the set of goods considered by the consumer is a continuum in some appropriate characteristics space (or the union of continua in appropriate sub-spaces). Convenience suggests that the set of possible goods be described in the same space. Whether or not the set of *possible* goods should also be assumed to be a continuum is considered in Section II.

(2) Now we invite you to specify the neighbourhood in which you find close substitutes for good X, and we ask other consumers if they too regard goods in this neighbourhood to be close substitutes for X. If they answer 'yes', we conclude that they perceive goods as points in the same characteristics space. We do not expect a 'no' answer, and, indeed, it would be hard to live with: if individuals perceive different spaces, or if the characteristics are as ephemeral as automobile models themselves, we do not know how to specify tractable demand primitives. We do expect a 'yes' answer and, accordingly, adopt the characteristics approach pioneered by Baumol (1967), Quandt–Baumol (1966) and Lancaster (1966).

(3) We take as awkward facts that consumers' tastes over characteristics are diverse and that the number of produced commodities in any 'group' is small relative to the number of consumers. (The definition of a group is considered below.) We argue that product-specific capital inputs are necessary to explain the paucity of produced commodities and are sufficient to explain the range of increasing returns to outlay necessary for the very existence of firms.

(4) Specification of demand primitives in characteristics space, together with diversity of tastes and product-specificity of capital, imply that competition among firms is often localised. (The extent to which competition is localised and, indeed, the necessary conditions

for localisation itself are, however, largely unexplored issues. We return to them below.)

(5) Localised competition and product-specific capital imply the existence of a *range* of free-entry equilibria in which firms may earn profits, even in groups with large numbers of firms. At one extreme of the range, profits are zero so that exit is just avoided; at the other extreme profits are positive but just not large enough to attract entry.

(6) The existence of specific capital inputs implies that entrants into a market have something to lose if their expectations with respect to sitting firms' responses are not accurate. We argue that this rules out 'naive' expectations (for example, the assumption that sitting firms will not respond) and makes it a desirable feature that new entrants should have correct, or consistent, expectations of any equilibrium concept where specific capital is important.

(7) Consistent expectations on the part of new entrants, plus product-specific capital, make it profitable for sitting firms to engage in strategic behaviour with respect to specific inputs. The goals of such behaviour are to bar entry and/or to create asymmetric entry equilibria. Such strategic behaviour may dissipate some or all of the profits in a socially wasteful fashion.

(8) Our analysis of strategic behaviour leads us to the conjecture, contrary to much existing literature, that the market equilibrium will converge on the extreme that yields the largest profits that sitting firms can earn without attracting entry.

In Section II we discuss the set of all possible goods, and identify two distinct characterisations of that set which, we think, differ in important ways. In Section III we discuss demand primitives, and find again that a choice must be made between distinct sets of primitives. In Section IV we discuss cost-technology primitives, paying particular attention to the problems of increasing returns, indivisibility, and specificity of capital. Section V discusses free-entry equilibrium, paying particular attention to expectations and to the possibility that equilibrium profits will be strictly positive. In Section VI we endeavour to assemble results, paying particular attention to strategic behaviour. Section VII briefly considers problems of welfare economics, while in Section VIII we propose a research agenda.

II THE SET OF ALL POSSIBLE GOODS

In models of monopolistic competition, questions about firms' product selection and the optimal diversity of products naturally arise.

These questions require that the set of all possible goods be larger than the set of currently-produced goods. We see two quite different characterisations of the set of possible goods.

Where goods are differentiated by 'quality' (e.g., Prescott–Visscher (1977) 'Example 3', Dorfman–Steiner (1954), Shaked–Sutton (1982)), each good is characterised by an element of a continuum in R^1 and the set of all possible goods is this set. In models of spatial competition (e.g., Hotelling (1929), Losch (1954), Eaton–Lipsey (1978), Salop (1979)), firms sell undifferentiated products but their locations are (potentially) differentiated in a continuum in R^1 or R^2. With costly transportation, undifferentiated products sold at different locations can be regarded as differentiated goods and the set of all possible goods is then a continuum in R^1 or R^2. In models of monopolistic competition in characteristics space (e.g., Baumol (1967), Archibald–Rosenbluth (1975), Lancaster (1975)), a good can be characterised by the ratio of the quantity of one characteristic embodied in a unit of that good to the quantity of a second characteristic similarly embodied (taking the two-characteristics case for illustration). In each of these illustrations, the set of all possible goods is a continuum in the real space of appropriate dimension, and there is an uncountable infinity of possible goods.

The alternative characterisation of the set of possible goods is to specify a finite, or countably infinite, list (e.g., Spence (1976), Dixit–Stiglitz (1977), Perloff–Salop (1982)). In this case the set of possible goods is obviously not a continuum. This characterisation has the obvious advantage that it is the natural extension of the set used in traditional neo-classical theory, but it imposes a severe restriction on the technology: it is discontinuous. *If brand A can be distinguished from brand B (other than merely by their labels), or if it is meaningful to ask if it is possible to produce a good arbitrarily close to brand A, there is implicitly some space of attributes, or characteristics, of goods,* however defined or measured. Then the implication of assuming that the set of possible goods is countable is that, in this space, it is not continuous.

The argument of the last paragraph in some sense replicates the conceptual experiment of sub-section I (1), except that we are now considering technological possibilities rather than consumers' perceptions. We can see no obvious *a priori* reason for assuming that production possibilities, in the appropriate characteristics space, are *not* continuous. Once again, we could obviously offer many examples. (Cost-minimising producers are clearly concerned with properties of goods for which consumers' preferences are not defined, but the analysis of demand must be carried out in the consumers' space.)

It seems to us that the vast majority of produced goods are elements from some characteristics-space continuum and that, other things equal, this is the preferred characterisation of the set of possible goods. Since analysis of such a characterisation may be difficult, we face the important question: can we successfully study behaviour in the continuum by using a countable characterisation of possible goods? We shall argue that the answer is 'no' (but we must first consider demand primitives).

Thus we see a fundamental distinction between the characterisations. The first we refer to as the *address branch*, because goods must be described by their address (co-ordinates) in some continuum. The second we refer to as the *non-address branch*, because the goods constituting the countable set are just goods.

III   DEMAND PRIMITIVES

We use the address, non-address distinction to structure our discussion of demand primitives. In the non-address branch, preferences are defined over a finite or countably infinite set of goods, and in the address branch preferences are defined over the appropriate continuum.

(A)   THE ADDRESS BRANCH

With some loss of generality, economists have usually analysed *either* problems in which otherwise homogeneous consumers and products are distinguished by their locations in physical space, *or* problems in which consumers are not homogeneous and goods are distinguished by their locations in characteristics space. In this section we consider these two approaches and the sense in which they may be analogous.

(1)   Geographic Models

(i) In these models, firms sell products with identical characteristics bundles, but firms and consumers are distinguished by addresses in the continuum of geographic space. For simplicity, we examine the consumer's problem in a one-dimensional geographic continuum, assuming that the prices he faces are simply mill-prices plus transport costs. Define his preferences over quantity of the 'group' good, y, and quantity of a composite good, x, with representation $U = U(y, x)$,

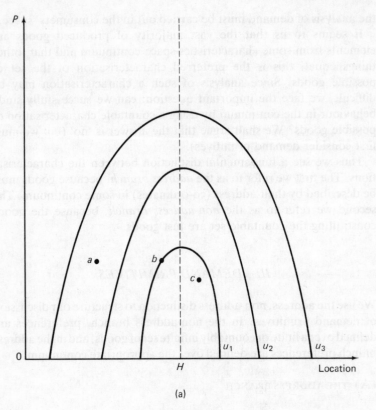

FIG. 1.1(a)

having the standard properties. Let H and L denote respectively the consumer's and a firm's location in the continuum, and let $t(L, H)$ denote the cost to the consumer of transporting a unit of y from L to H. To ensure that competition is localised we assume now that $t(L, H)$ is an increasing and convex function of $|L - H|$. Then we can define an indirect representation of the consumer's preferences:

$$W(L, p) = \max_{y, x} \{U(y, x) \quad \text{subject to } [p + t(L, H)]y + x = B\},$$

where p is price at the mill, and the price of the composite good is normalised to be 1. Figure 1.1(a) presents level surfaces of $W(L, p)$. These level surfaces are necessarily vertical translates of one another, and intersect the horizontal axis as illustrated. Clearly W is decreasing in p.

Goods can then be characterised by points in (L, p) space. The consumer will obviously choose to purchase the good which maximises $W(L, p)$: e.g., good c in Figure 1.1(a).

(ii) From this representation of the problem, it follows immediately that the consumer's cross-price elasticities among goods are discontinuous: they are infinite at crucial prices and zero at all others. The consumer typically purchases a positive amount of only one (or at most two) of the many goods.

(iii) Assume that there is a continuum of consumers along the geographic space. Then competition is localised: cross-price elasticities between a good and its neighbouring goods (of which there are only two in our linear market) are non-zero, but between that good and all others they are zero. (We consider the conditions under which competition is localised in this sense in Section (4) below.)

(2) Characteristics Models

(i) In these models consumers' preferences are defined over characteristics, which are embodied in goods. Either all production and consumption implicitly takes place at one point in geographic space, or transportation is costless. For simplicity, we consider the case in which the goods in a group embody two characteristics. Define the utility of a consumer over the quantity of the two characteristics, z_1 and z_2, and the quantity of a composite good, x (which embodies neither z_1 nor z_2), with the representation $U = U(z_1, z_2, x)$ having standard properties.

For easy comparison with models in geographic space, we again derive an indirect representation of the consumer's preferences. To do so, we need a convention for defining units of 'group' goods. Let L be the angle between a ray through the origin in (z_1, z_2) space and the z_1 axis. For any given L, the functions $g(\cdot)$ and $h(\cdot)$ define the amount of each characteristic in a unit of the specific group good described by that value of L. Now we define the indirect utility function

$$W(L, p) = \max_{y, x} \{U(yg(L), yh(L), x) \quad \text{subject to } (py + x = B)\},$$

where y is the quantity of the group good. Of course, $g(L)$ and $h(L)$ are simply a parametric representation of a line in (z_1, z_2) space. If we choose $g(L)$ and $h(L)$ appropriately, $W(L, p)$ is quasi-concave and we have the level surfaces shown in Figures 1.1(b) and 1.1(c). L is, of course, defined on the interval $[0, \pi/2]$. If the indifference curves of $U(z_1, z_2, x)$ in z_1–z_2 space are asymptotic to the axes, the level surfaces of $W(L, p)$ are as illustrated. If the indifference curves

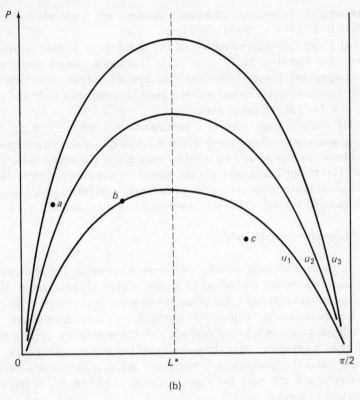

$$(b)$$

FIG. 1.1(b)

intersect one or both axes, the level surfaces intersect one or both of
the vertical axes in Figure 1.1(b) and 1.1(c). Unlike the level surfaces
of Figure 1.1(a), these level surfaces *cannot* intersect the horizontal
axis if the indifference curves have throughout a negative slope in
characteristics space (see Note 5), and, of course, cannot be vertical
translates. Again W is decreasing in p. If z_1 and z_2 are homothetically
separable from x in U, then the consumer has a most-preferred L, L^*
in Figure 1.1(b). L^* is clearly analogous to the consumer's location,
H, in Figure 1.1(a). The consumer is 'located' at L^* in the continuum
of possible goods in the sense that L^* defines his 'most preferred
good'. Marketed goods can obviously be characterised by points in
(L, p) space, such as points a, b and c in the Figure. If we do not have
homothetic separability (Figure 1.1(c)), we cannot define a 'most
preferred good' and there is no direct analogy between *location* in
geographic and in characteristic space.

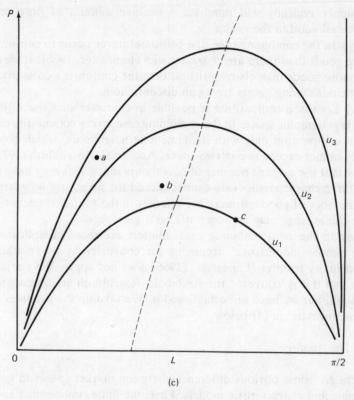

FIG. 1.1(c)

(ii) We have to decide a question about the consumer's techno-logical possibilities: can he combine goods in order to produce characteristic combinations not embodied in any single, marketed good? At the two extremes, combining may be physically impossible or combining may be possible at zero cost. In the latter case, any convex combination of the mixes of characteristics provided by the separate goods is available. In between, combining may be possible at some (objective and/or psychological) cost. We consider the com-bining and non-combining cases separately (but omit intermediate cases of costly combination).

(iii) In the non-combining case, the choice set which the consumer faces is just the set of points in (L, p) space which describe marketed goods (and good c is the preferred good in Figures 1.1(b) and 1.1(c)). As in the geographic model, each consumer's cross-price elasticities are discontinuous: infinite at crucial prices and zero at all others. The consumer typically will purchase a positive amount of only one marketed good in the group.

(iv) In the combining case, the consumer never needs to consume more goods than there are characteristics (Lancaster, 1966). If there are more goods than characteristics, then the consumer's cross-price elasticities among goods are again discontinuous.

(v) Localised competition is possible in characteristics space just as it is geographic space. In the combining case, every commodity can be in competition only with its immediate neighbours[3] which obviously cannot exceed two in two-space. Archibald–Rosenbluth (1975) show that the *average* number of neighbours that goods may have in the three characteristics case cannot exceed six, no matter how large the number of goods, n, may be, whereas in the four-characteristics case the average may approach $n/2$, as n gets large.

(vi) In the non-combining case, matters are more complicated. The simple 'dominance' argument for convexity of the market-opportunity frontier (Lancaster, (1966) does not apply. We conjecture that if it is 'convex',[4] the Archibald–Rosenbluth argument goes through, but we have not established it. We take up the problem of 'non-convexity' in (4) below.

(3) The Analogy

There are some obvious differences between market spaces in geographic and characteristic models. First, the finite, unbounded and, closed geographic space that results when an n dimensional space is curved back on itself in the $(n + 1)$th dimension has few, if any, analogies in characteristics space. Thus we cannot in characteristics space avoid the problems associated with boundaries. Second, the obvious restriction on the dimensionality of geographic space does not apply to characteristics space: it is easy to think of a group of commodities sharing a very large number of characteristics. (On the other hand, we can readily increase the dimensionality of geographical models by adding non-spatial characteristics such as the product range and service quality of stores.)

We have so far taken the group or 'market area' as a primitive which is, of course, essential if we are to engage in partial-equilibrium analysis. In geographic models the market area, defined as the space over which potential customers are distributed, may be taken as a primitive without much difficulty. (The distribution of customers is often taken as exogenous. In the most general models it is, of course, endogenous.)

In characteristics space the problem is more complex. We unambiguously have a group if: (1) we can identify a set of produced goods, each of which embodies non-negative amounts of the same list of characteristics (at least one amount must be positive), and none of which embodies positive amounts of any other characteristic; and (2) no other goods outside the group embody the characteristics supplied by the group. Whether these conditions are satisfied, and thus whether we have an unambiguous group, is in the long run endogenous: it is determined by tastes and technology. We have very little more to say about this interesting problem. It does, however, raise two further questions. To what extent can these conditions be violated while still preserving some useful concept of a group? And, assuming the conditions are violated, to what extent may we still have localised competition between goods? This last question seems to us to be of fundamental importance.

(4) Localised competition

In the previous paragraph we encountered Triffin's problem: is there a meaningful unit of economic activity between the firm and the whole economy? If there is not, of course competition cannot be localised. Much recent literature has been addressed to localised competition; but we need a more careful analysis of the determinants of the extent of localisation. We know sufficient conditions for localisation, and were careful to employ them in (1) and (2) above; but we do not know the necessary conditions, as we may now see.

Consider first geographic address models. If transportation costs are identical for all consumers and convex in distance, then competition is clearly local in nature. Thus in one-dimensional models, each firm is in direct competition with at most two other firms. Suppose, however, that transportation costs are subjective and differ among consumers. Then a low-price firm could be in direct competition with a large number of high-price firms selling identical products. Its market area would no longer be a connected subset of the entire market, and competition would not be localised to the same extent. The analogous problem obviously arises in characteristics space. Lancaster (1975) refers to this phenomenon as 'cross over', and makes assumptions sufficient to rule it out.[5] In the non-combining case, it is possible that the consumer's choice set is not '*d*-convex' (see Note 4) so that cross-over, as in the spatial example, is an obvious possibility. Suppose now that in the spatial model transport costs are a concave function of distance and identical for all consumers. Again, it is possible that a low-price firm may be in competition with several high-priced ones, diminishing the extent to which competition is localised. Indeed, the use of delivered pricing systems clearly raises the possibility that, in some geographical markets, competition is not localised at all. We have to ask what determines the choice of pricing mode in geographic markets, and what are the effects of delivered pricing modes on the extent to which competition is localised.

In the characteristics model the dimensionality of the space itself may be an important determinant of the extent to which competition is localised. Apart from the Archibald–Rosenbluth results, however, we know virtually nothing about how these possibilities may affect the properties of equilibrium. We think that there is an obvious research task here. We should also bear in mind that in more-general models goods would have addresses in both spaces: in characteristics space for the reasons we have argued; and in physical space whenever transport costs are non-zero. At this stage, it can be a conjecture only that in such a model we should find a high degree of localisation to be the most plausible configuration.

(B) THE NON-ADDRESS BRANCH

The seminal papers in this tradition are Dixit–Stiglitz (1977), which can be regarded as a formalisation of Chamberlin's large group case, and Spence (1976). In these models, the set of possible goods is countable. Fixed costs of production, associated with each good, dictate that only a subset of possible goods will be produced.

The demand primitive is a well-behaved utility function of a representative consumer, defined over the set of all possible goods. The representative consumer's problem is the standard choice problem: given prices, he chooses quantities to maximise utility. In any equilibrium, the representative consumer necessarily consumes a non-zero quantity of each of the goods produced, and the cross-price elasticity of demand between any pair of marketed goods is non-zero: competition is not localised.

If we take the notion of a representative consumer literally, then we ignore an important and obvious source of product diversity,

diversity in consumers' tastes. For reasons suggested in sub-section I(3), this approach is not appealing to us. If, instead, we regard the utility function as an aggregate preference relation, we are forced to ask what the implied restrictions on individual's preferences are.

Given our view of monopolistic competition, we accordingly must ask if the utility function of the representative consumer could be derived from some aggregation of individual preferences, drawn from the address branch. In general, the answer is no. In the combining case of the characteristics model, where localised competition is a certainty in the two-characteristics case, every consumer who buys some of commodity L_i buys at most one other commodity. Thus no matter how diverse are the tastes of individual consumers, the cross-elasticity between L_i and all but two other goods in the group must be zero. Thus the representative consumer, with positive cross-elasticities for all goods in the group, cannot be taken as representing the aggregate behaviour of market demand when tastes are defined over characteristics. In the non-combining case, non-localised competition becomes possible. It is then important to know if there exists *some* specification of demand primitives in the address branch which could be aggregated to yield well-behaved preferences of a representative consumer. The model of Perloff–Salop (1982) allows them to aggregate, in order to obtain a representative preference-relation which is symmetric over goods, thus satisfying the necessary condition for a Chamberlinian equilibrium. We think their approach is illuminating, but unsatisfactory.

To see why, recall the question of whether consumers' perceptions of relevant characteristics differ, so that we cannot define demand primitives over a *common* characteristics space or proceed with the characteristics approach as outlined above. We suggested an experiment designed to answer this question in Section I(2), and need not repeat it. If the characteristics space is specific to the consumer (which, although possible, is not what we expect), then tractability may require that we define individual preferences over a countable set of goods.

Perloff and Salop do this. They assume that there is a finite number, n, of differentiated brands available in a given product-class.[6] Each consumer '. . . attaches relative values to these brands according to his *preference vector* . . .' (p. 3) $\theta = (\theta_1, \theta_2, \ldots, \theta_n)$ and each chooses the brand which maximises his surplus, $\theta_i - p_i$ (p. 4) (and consumes zero of $n - 1$ goods).[7] *Diversity is then obtained by the random assignment of θs to consumers*. In the symmetric case, aggregate preferences for each brand are independent and identically distributed: each brand is the best-buy for an equal share of consumers, and all firms' demand curves are identical. It also follows that all consumers who agree that good i is the best buy have their second choice uniformly distributed over the remaining $n - 1$ goods (with obvious implications for non-localised competition).

Perloff and Salop argue that their approach is, in some sense, a synthesis of what we have called the address and non-address approaches to the problem. Although they do capture the address branch phenomenon – that consumers are in corner solutions with respect to most goods in the group – they do this at the cost of implying consumer-specific characteristic spaces. It is not clear what the appropriate primitives are in this approach.

Our rejection of this approach leads us to conclude that a clear *choice* of demand primitives must be made in the study of monopolistic competition. The choice is between the usual goods-approach exploited by Dixit–Stiglitz, and Spence, and the characteristics-approach. This choice must be determined, at least in part, by how we think we should try to account for the diversity of produced goods that we observe. If we take the goods approach, the representative consumer buys at least some amount of everything. Given some initial range of falling costs in production, diversity of produced goods increases as his endowment increases. If we want to account for the observation that most consumers buy a zero quantity of most goods produced, we must proceed otherwise. Diversity of produced goods now follows from the diversity among consumers themselves, and production-diversity increases as this consumer-diversity is increased (more non-identical consumers are added to the model). It seems to us that the characteristics approach accounts satisfactorily for this sort of diversity. Whether or not it 'works', in the sense that consumers do consider the same short list of characteristics to be relevant, is an empirical question not yet resolved.

Also, there is much yet to be done in the way of formulating and testing restrictions on the distribution of preferences. We argued in Section I(2) that agreement on what is a close substitute implies the existence of some common space of characteristics on which preferences are defined. In any case, to avoid making undesirable or even absurd implicit assumptions on the basic primitives, it is imperative to ask what restrictions on tastes in characteristic space are implied by even seemingly very reasonable restrictions on tastes defined over goods.

IV COST-TECHNOLOGY PRIMITIVES

(1) AWKWARD FACTS

It is generally agreed that *in the absence of a range of increasing returns to outlay, or decreasing unit costs of production*, any good for which there is positive demand at minimum unit cost of production (given all other prices) will be produced. First, suppose that each consumer has a unique 'most-preferred good' in the continuum of possible goods. Then, if that good is not offered by some producer at minimum unit cost of production, the consumer can and will produce that good for himself. (There are, in this case, no compelling reasons for the existence of firms.) Second, suppose that there is a continuum of most-preferred goods. There will then be a continuum of produced goods.

Given that the set of possible goods is a continuum (in some space), the awkward fact which we must confront is that the set of produced goods is small relative to the set of consumers. But although the phenomenon of increasing returns to outlay is necessary to explain the awkward fact, it is not sufficient. Imagine, for example, that the production function for a good, written in terms of flows of inputs and output, exhibits an initial range of increasing returns to scale, and that all inputs are perfectly divisible, i.e., can be purchased as flows. Then, again, each consumer has the option of producing his most-preferred good at its minimum unit cost of production. This is because production of an arbitrarily small quantity at minimum unit cost can be achieved by producing at minimum efficient scale for an arbitrarily short period of time.[8] Again, there is no compelling reason for the existence of firms and if there is a continuum of most-preferred goods, there will be a continuum of produced goods.

To sum up, the existence of some degree of increase in returns is not sufficient to explain the awkward facts, so long as that increase is associated only with the flow-rate of output. If it is, an arbitrarily small output can be had at minimum cost by producing at as fast a rate as is needed, for an arbitrarily short interval. Thus, to explain the awkward facts there must be some property of the technology that prevents us from 'getting round' the non-convexity in this way. We think there is; and we shall sketch a model in Section (2). Suppose that there do exist product-specific capital inputs which cannot be dispensed with.[9] Suppose further that they are 'lumpy' in the sense that, once constructed, they embody a *stock* of capital services to be used up over time, and that this lumpiness sets a (strictly positive) lower bound to the total quantity of output that must be produced in order to attain minimum unit cost of production. Now, if there is any positive cost of waiting (an interest rate) it is cheaper to use up the stock of services embodied in the capital good sooner rather than later. It follows that 'home production' at high speed for short intervals is not as cheap as is continuous 'mass production' at high speed: there is a reason for the existence of production-points (firms) selling to many consumers. It also and obviously follows that the existence of such lumpy inputs implies that the existence of a continuum of goods would violate the scarcity constraint.

Production functions for final goods, defined by the flow inputs of capital services and of labour, may exhibit constant returns to scale. Indeed, we shall assume that they do. Even so, the existence of product-specific lumpy capital goods implies increasing returns to outlay. This in turn explains both the existence of firms and the fact that the number of products is small (relative to both the number of consumers and, we conjecture, the diversity of their 'most-preferred goods'). As we shall see specific, lumpy capital is also the vehicle for commitment and thus essential to strategic behaviour.

(2) SPECIFICITY AND INDIVISIBILITY

We confine our attention to the extreme case where the meaning of the product-specificity of capital goods is unambiguous: product-specific capital goods are ones that are useful in the production of a particular good and which have no alternative uses. Although the definition of partial-specificity poses some difficult conceptual issues,[10] it is obvious that transactions costs, set-up costs, re-location costs and costs of training specialised labour contribute significantly to specificity.

We now turn to a simple demonstration that product-specific capital inputs imply increasing returns to outlay in the production of final goods. The presentation is an intuitive but, we hope, comprehensible account of the basic argument made in a forthcoming paper by Eaton and Lipsey.

Suppose that good X can be produced as a flow, using a flow of labour, n, and a flow of product specific capital services, according to

$$x = f(n, v). \tag{1}$$

Assume that $f(\cdot)$ exhibits constant returns to scale (and is quasi-concave) and that the flow of specific capital services, v, is obtained from a capital good which embodies a stock of specific capital services.

We adopt the simplest possible characterisation of the specific capital good: it is characterised completely by the number S which is the stock of specific capital services embodied in the *indivisible* good.[11] Initially we assume that $S = \bar{S}$ and is not subject to choice. Define $C(v)$ as the present discounted cost of obtaining a constant positive flow of capital services, v, over an infinite horizon. Assume for convenience a time-invariant rate of interest, r. We then have

$$C(v) = \frac{\bar{c}}{1 - e^{-rT}} , \quad T = \bar{S}/v, \tag{2}$$

where $\bar{c}$ is the cost of the capital good. $C(v)$ is simply the present discounted-cost of buying the stock $\bar{S}$ every $T = \bar{S}/v$ periods (evaluated at a point in time at which a unit is purchased). The following results can be shown, and are in any case intuitively obvious:

$$C'(v) > 0, \; C''(v) > 0, \quad \lim_{v \to \infty} C'(v) = \bar{c}/\bar{S}r, \tag{3}$$

$$\lim_{v \to 0} C'(v) = 0, \quad \lim_{v \to \infty} \frac{C(v)}{v} = \bar{c}/\bar{S}r.$$

Thus $C(v)$ and $C(v)/v$ are as illustrated in Figure 1.2(a) and (b).

Now consider minimising the present discounted-cost of producing a flow of output, x^1, over an infinite horizon, and let $V(x)$ denote that minimised cost. Let W be the present discounted-cost of obtaining a flow of one unit of labour over an infinite horizon. Let v^1 and n^1 solve the cost-minimisation problem for x^1, and assume that we have an interior solution ($v^1 > 0$, $n^1 > 0$). Consider, now, producing some larger level of output αx^1, $\alpha > 1$. Then we have

$$V(\alpha x^1) < C(\alpha v^1) + \alpha W n^1 < \alpha C(v^1) + \alpha W n^1 = \alpha V(x^1). \tag{4}$$

The first inequality follows from the assumption that f is homogeneous of degree 1 and the fact that, although $(\alpha n^1, \alpha v^1)$ will produce αx^1, it is not the cost-minimising input combination.[12] The second inequality follows from the properties of $C(\cdot)$ given in (3): $C(\alpha v) < \alpha C(v)$. Thus the indivisibility of specific capital implies increasing returns to outlay.[13] The general shape of $V(x)$ and $V(x)/x$ will mirror the shapes of $C(v)$ and $C(v)/v$ in Figure 1.2(a) and (b).

(3) CHOICE OF INDIVISIBILITY

These results are based on our assumption that the capital good is indivisible. Let us then enquire into the conditions which might lead

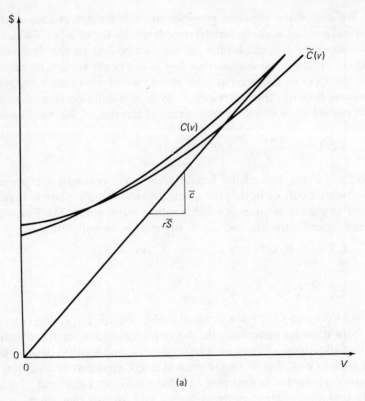

FIG. 1.2(a)

firms to create such indivisibilities. Suppose that the quantity (S) of capital services is produced by embodying a quantity of labour (L) and a quantity of materials (M) into a good according to

$$S = g(L, M),\tag{5}$$

and that L and M are purchased on competitive markets. Let (g) be homogeneous of degree λ, and define $H(S)$ to be the minimum cost of embodying (S) units of capital services in a capital good. Now consider,

$$\bar{C}(v) = \min_s \left(\frac{H(S)}{1 - e^{-rT}}\right), \quad T = S/v.\tag{6}$$

$\bar{C}(v)$ is the minimum cost of obtaining (v) units of capital services forever, when we choose the magnitude of the indivisibility (S). It is

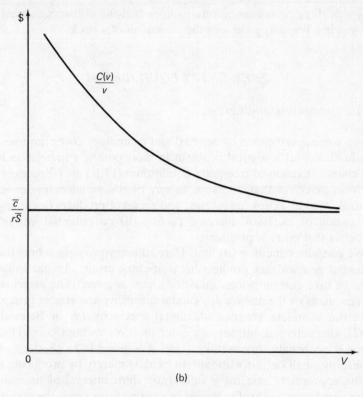

(b)

FIG. 1.2(b)

easy to show, and is intuitively obvious, that the solution to the minimisation problem is degenerate, in the sense that S goes to zero, if $\lambda < 1$. Thus, if we rule out God-given indivisibilities, man-made indivisibilities (capital goods) arise because there are increasing returns to scale (or outlay) in the embodiment of capital services in goods.[14]

According, let $\lambda > 1$. Then $\bar{C}(v)$ is the envelope of $C(v)$ (defined in equation (2)) as S varies. $\bar{C}(v)$ has the same general properties as $C(v)$, and our conclusion that God-given indivisibilities imply increasing returns to outlay is obviously strengthened when we allow for man-made indivisibilities.[15] Thus the age-old question of why there should be scale effects when combining pure flows of input services is answered 'there do not have to be'. The range of falling costs needed to explain the existence of a finite number of firms and products requires only that there be increasing returns in embodying a flow of (capital) services in a (capital) good with the dimension of a stock.

V FREE-ENTRY EQUILIBRIUM

(A) EQUILIBRIUM CONCEPTS

Given some specification of demand and technology-cost primitives, the fundamental analytical problem in monopolistic competition is the characterisation of free-entry equilibrium (FEE) as: (i) no existing firm *perceives* that a change in any of the variables under its control, such as prices, quantities, and range of products (including the option of exit) will increase profits; (ii) no potential entrant *perceives* that entry is profitable.

We consider condition (ii) first. Here, the key problem is how the potential new entrant predicts his post-entry profits. In particular does he take current prices, quantities, etc. as given? The principal determinants of the answer are capital specificity and size of group.

In the complete absence of capital specificity (as in Baumol, 1982), the potential entrant can enter or leave without cost. Thus there is no penalty for mistakes, and it is possible to produce an arbitrarily small output without cost penalty merely by producing it at the appropriate rate for a sufficiently short interval of time. In these circumstances, profits earned by existing firms signal the opportunity for profits to a new entrant. The FEE will then display zero profit and will hold at all points in time.

Now consider the case of specific, lumpy capital in the non-address branch. Here we encounter the well-known *integer problem*. Suppose that market demand is such that n firms make positive profits while $n + 1$ firms would make losses. In the large number case, this problem may not be of great practical significance, but it does raise theoretical issues.[16] When n is small, say 1 for purposes of illustration, a rational, potential new entrant will not take the sitting firm's data as given. A potential entrant who did take the monopolist's price as given would enter and undercut this price, expecting to usurp virtually all the sitting monopolist's pure profits. But the sitting monopolist will prefer to supply a positive output at any price not less than his minimum average variable cost than to shut down. By asking himself what he would do if he were in the sitting monopolist's position, the potential entrant can foresee that result: he cannot take the sitting monopolist's price as given. If we accept the notion that the potential entrant expects the post-entry equilibrium to be symmetric, then we infer that entry will not occur (since, by hypothesis, there exists no price at which $n + 1$ firms can cover costs of production). Thus if entrants are rational, pure profit does not necessarily invite entry: potential entrants do not naively take existing market data as given, at least in small-group situations.

This much foresight is a necessary condition for small-group FEE to exist (and is sufficient for it to exhibit positive profit). It seems imperative therefore to impose some form of rationality on the entrants' expectations. We adopt what we call *consistent expectations:* the new entrants' expectations are consistent with realisations. (The concept of consistent expectations is distinct from that of consistent conjectural variations.)

Now consider condition (i) of our FEE definition. To give (i) meaning requires an equilibrium concept. The Nash concept seems the acceptable one for the non-address, large-group case. But in the small-group cases, in both the address and non-address branch, where we necessarily have localised competition, the choice of an equilibrium concept is more problematic. The argument against the Nash concept is that rational firms in small-group competition know that their competitors will respond to any initiative that they take. Choice of the most plausible concepts will, of course, have to be made in the end on empirical grounds.

In the meantime *we take some equilibrium concept for (i) as given and assume that an equilibrium actually exists.* Consistent expectations then requires the potential new entrant to calculate the post-entry equilibrium and to base his entry decision on the profits or losses that he would then earn.[17]

Consistency of expectations leads logically to the strategic use of specific capital. This appears to us to be one of the key conceptual innovations in the recent literature on imperfect competition. If the post-entry equilibrium is influenced by the quantity of specific capital held by firms, then existing firms can influence the value of entry. They may find it in their interest to deter entry (as in Eaton–Lipsey, 1979, 1980b; Dixit, 1980; Schmalensee, 1978; Salop, 1979a) or to impose asymmetric post-entry equilibria (as in Prescott–Visscher, 1977; Dixit, 1980; Eaton–Lipsey, 1981).

What has emerged over the past few years in the literature on imperfect competition is what might be called a paradigm of *strategic free-entry equilibrium.* The essentials of this approach are the existence of firm-specific capital and the assumption that all actors know the manner in which prices and quantities are determined, given the commitments of specific capital to the market. This assumption allows all actors, existing firms as well as potential entrants, to assess accurately the consequences associated with the commitment of new specific capital to a product group.

The paradigm seems to have evolved in two bodies of literature. One line of evolution arose from misgivings about the limit-quantity (or limit-price) model of oligopoly. The credibility of the implied threat to maintain output in the face of entry was questioned. Spence (1977), drawing on Schelling's (1956) distinction between threats and commitments, observed that it is the *ability* to produce the limit output after entry has occurred (the holding of 'limit capacity'), and not actually producing that output before entry, which influences the credibility of the threat. Dixit (1979) observed that, even if the threat were credible, the entry-deterrence strategy might not be preferred, thus making endogenous the decision whether or not to deter entry. Dixit (1980) imposed consistent expectations by invoking the assumption of 'known rules of the game', which allowed him to assess the credibility of the limit-output threat: the threat is credible if and only if the solution to the post-entry game has the established firm producing at least the limit output. Eaton–Lipsey (1980a) invoked known rules of the game and employed Schelling's distinction. They thereby determine the optimal strategy by which a natural monopolist would deter *predatory* entry, entry with the objective of driving the monopolist out of the market when committed capital was not infinitely durable.

In the literature on differentiated products and spatial competition, Archibald–Rosenbluth (1975) raise the possibility of market preemption (entry deterrence) through product proliferation. Peles (1974), in a model with parametric prices, raises the possibility of entry deterrence by plant proliferation. Prescott–Visscher (1977) invoke known rules of the game, again with parametric prices, to analyse asymmetric market solutions and clearly raise the possibility of entry deterrence through plant proliferation. Schmalensee (1978) uses the notion of brand proliferation to understand the ready-to-eat cereals industry. Eaton and Lipsey (1979) invoke consistent expectations to analyse entry deterrence in a 'small' spatial market.

Another implication of the use of specific capital to deter entry is that capital may be used wastefully in the sense that more than the socially optimal amount may be committed to the industry. Such possibilities are raised in most of the works cited in the previous two paragraphs. Similar results are obtained in the literature on technological change (see, e.g., the chapter by Dasgupta in this volume, and Gilbert–Newbery (1982)).

(B) EXISTENCE

The discussion so far has avoided the troublesome problem of existence of equilibrium, which is particularly difficult in the address models. Suppose we adopt *price-taking behaviour* as our equilibrium concept. Then, as d'Aspremont–Gabszewicz–Thisse (1979 and 1981) demonstrate,[18] price equilibrium does not exist in Hotelling's model if the two firms are too close together. Indeed, this is a general problem in one-dimensional models of spatial competition where transport costs are linear. The source of non-existence is a discontinuity in the firms' (perceived) demand functions. In Salop's (1979) terminology, there exist 'zap prices'. (Let p_1 and p_2 be the mill prices of the two firms, $a < b$ be their locations on the unit line, and t be unit transport cost; then Firm 1's demand function is discontinuous at $p_1 = p_2 - t(b - a)$.) Archibald–Rosenbluth (1975) observe that 'zap' prices exist in characteristics space, at least in the combining case.[19]

Hotelling, who clearly foresaw this problem, appears to invoke what Eaton–Lipsey call the 'no mill-price undercutting' assumption to remove the problem (see Hotelling, 1929, p. 48). Eaton (1972) explicitly invokes this assumption. Archibald–Rosenbluth dismissed as absurd the idea that firm i would assume it could drive firm j out of the market, when j had the option of cutting its own price and thus continuing to sell goods profitably. Eaton–Lipsey (1976; 1978) argue that the most elementary foresight will allow any firm to conclude that it cannot drive a competitor out of the market by charging a price marginally-lower than the zap price, as long as the competitor has the option of selling a positive quantity at a price in excess of unit *avoidable* costs. They therefore introduce the 'no mill-price undercutting assumption'. This can be thought of as an attempt to rule out obviously inconsistent expectations by 'doctoring' the equilibrium concept.[20] Indeed, Novshek (1980) argues that, in the absence of this restriction, FEE will ordinarily not exist in address models.

We would not argue that this is necessarily the correct solution to the problem. We would, however, argue that where the source of non-existence of price equilibrium arises from assumptions about competitors' responses which are grossly inconsistent with competitors' profit maximising responses, and where elementary foresight reveals this inconsistency, the problem is not in any empirically-relevant sense one of the non-existence of equilibrium. The problem is that we have attributed foolish beliefs to economic agents.

(C) SPECIFICITY, COMMITMENT AND LUMPINESS

In our discussion of free-entry equilibrium, we simply assumed that product-specific capital was also firm-specific. Product-specific capital is firm-specific *if there exists no other use for such capital that will increase the value of the firm*. This view of firm specificity is a direct consequence of Schelling's notion of commitment and the view, implicit in our discussion of FEE, that commitments, but *not threats*, are credible. As we saw in Section (A), the importance of specificity is well understood in recent literature on industrial organisation. We wish to argue that specificity must be considered in conjunction with indivisibility and, in particular, that the extent to which product-specific capital is firm-specific depends on its lumpiness. We shall illustrate this argument by examining Dixit's (1980) formulation of the undifferentiated duopoly problem. We shall show that the effect of assuming divisibility is to make product-specific capital non-firm-specific; and, indeed, the possibility that one firm may sell some (necessarily divisible) capital to the other opens up a set of possible solutions which would not be feasible in the indivisible case. (We could make the same point by adapting the Eaton–Lipsey (1981) model in which capital is subject to radioactive decay; but it is seen more easily in Dixit's model in which capital is infinitely durable.)

In Dixit's model, the 'rules of the (post-entry) game' are Nash rules for quantities, based on *avoidable costs*. It is assumed that there are two types of product-specific capital. The first entails a once-for-all 'set-up cost', f, on entry. *Each unit* of output per unit time also requires *one unit* of 'production capital' (k) Choice of (k) thus sets an upper bound to output. Average variable costs are assumed to be constant. Both entry capital and production-capital are completely product specific and infinitely durable. Production capital is perfectly divisible. We assume, for simplicity, that costs are identical for both firms and that both would earn profits in the symmetric Nash equilibrium. Dixit shows that the incumbent firm (first mover) is able to impose asymmetric solutions by his choice of (k), which determines his own avoidable cost reaction function and therefore the post-entry equilibrium.

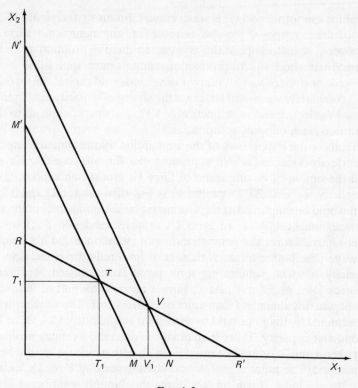

FIG. 1.3

For the incumbent (Firm 1) Dixit defines three reaction functions. The first is the 'full-cost' reaction function, i.e., it takes into account the cost of the capacity k_1 required to produce x_1, as well as the (constant) variable cost. It is illustrated by MM' in Figure 1.3. The second is the avoidable-cost reaction function which takes into account only the constant variable cost. It is illustrated by NN' in Figure 1.3. The third, or 'effective', reaction function, which we will write $g_1(x_2 \mid \bar{k}_1)$, is conditional on 1's choice of capacity, $\bar{k}_1$. For a given $\bar{k}_1$, it is NN' for $x_1 < \bar{k}_1$ (spare capacity) and MM' for $x_1 > \bar{k}_1$ (expansion costs). The potential entrant (Firm 2) has no prior commitments, and accordingly has the full-cost reaction function shown as RR' in Figure 1.3 (where the stable, Cournot case is assumed).

Now Firm 1 chooses k_1 and thus the reaction function $x_1 = g_1(x_2 \mid \bar{k}_1)$ that it will present to Firm 2 in the event of entry. The locus of possible equilibria is illustrated by TV in Figure 1.3. We take the case in which the set-up cost (f) is small enough for entry deterrence to be impossible. Suppose, for the purpose of argument, that Firm 1 chooses $\bar{k}_1$ so as to impose the asymmetric duopoly solution at V. Its capacity is then V_1. If production capital were indivisible once created, or if there was no market in second-hand capital, this would be a completely successful strategy: the choice of capacity determines Firm 1's effective reaction function $N'VV_1$, and thus commits it to the Cournot–Nash duopoly solution, at V.

To show the importance of the assumption that production capital is perfectly divisible (as well as product-specific), suppose that Firm 2 had the option of buying some of Firm 1's production capital. (For simplicity, we assume 1's capital V_1 is less than the total capital $2T_1$ that would be employed at the symmetric Nash-equilibrium point.) If Firm 2 bought $V_1 - T_1$ of Firm 1's capacity (and added $2T_1 - V_1$ itself) it could force the symmetric duopoly solution at T. Firm 1 may, however, be better off at T than at V (and must be if the sale of capacity is to be voluntary). Joint profit is maximised at T, and exceeds joint profit at V. At T, Firm 1 receives his half of the joint profit *plus* any share less than unity of Firm 2's half. This share will be determined by the price paid by Firm 2 for the quantity $V_1 - T_1$ of 1's productive capacity. There is an obvious bilateral bargaining problem between 1 and 2 (or any potential Firm 2), with which we are not here concerned. The point is that, by purchasing some of Firm 1's 'entry-deterring' capital, 2 can, in fact, force the duopoly solution at T on terms advantageous to both. Thus 1's original strategy is not successful, but may be more profitable to 1 than non-strategic behaviour, i.e., the failure to use incumbent advantage and instead, meek acceptance of the symmetric solution, by building T_1 capital in the first place.

Our purpose in exploring this variation in Dixit's model is to show that product-specific capital is not necessarily a vehicle for commitment in a model of undifferentiated oligopoly, if it is *divisible*. If production-capital could be made indivisible after its construction, then 1's choice of capacity, V_1, would be irreversible, and would block entry.

In the address branch, entrants usually choose to differentiate their products from those of existing firms. Product-specific capital is then firm-specific capital – although group-specific capital is not. Thus, in an address model, product-specific capital is a vehicle for commitment regardless of its divisibility, while group-specific capital needs to be lumpy if it is to act as an entry deterrent.[21]

VI   SOME RESULTS

The analysis of strategic behaviour is essentially the analysis of rent-seeking behaviour. In our view the most significant difference between the address and non-address branches is that, in the address branch, there is a presumption that rents will exist in free-entry equilibrium even if firms behave non-strategically: while there is no such presumption in the non-address branch. We must then expect firms to behave strategically, as they attempt to capture such rents. (Firms may, of course, dissipate some or all of these potential rents in their attempts to capture them.) We first consider non-strategic behaviour and then turn to strategic behaviour.

(A) PROFIT IN NON-STRATEGIC FEE

(1) The Non-Address Branch

Consider first an industry in which firms sell undifferentiated products. The potential for pure profit is then essentially determined by the ratio of minimum efficient scale to market demand. If this ratio is large, we have an undifferentiated oligopoly and there exists some potential for⋅ pure profit. As this ratio becomes small, the non-strategic equilibrium rapidly approaches the competitive equilibrium.

Now consider the case of monopolistic competition, in which there is a finite or countably-infinite number of goods. In the absence of further restrictions, each product will attract entrants as long as entry promises some profit. The crucial feature is again the ratio of minimum efficient scale to market demand. If it is arbitrarily assumed that one product can only have one producer (say, in an attempt to catch the 'essence' of monopolistic competition in a non-address branch formulation), then other results are possible. If every good in the group is made a symmetrical substitute for every other good, as in Dixit–Stiglitz (1977), then a Chamberlinian tangency solution is possible. If this symmetry is not assumed, then positive profits can be earned by some firms, since their positions can be assailed only by producing the nearest permissible substitute (as in Spence, (1976). Then, while the marginal entrant earns approximately zero profits, other firms may earn positive profits. But this result seem to us to be an artefact of the arbitrary restriction on the number of producers of each good.

(2) The Address Branch

First, consider geographical location models in which existing firms behave non-strategically with respect to entry. In Eaton–Lipsey (1976 and 1978, Section VI) entrants' profit expectations are consistent, and existing firms can earn a rate of return on specific capital which is up to twice the competitive rate of return. In Eaton (1976), the main model of Eaton–Lipsey (1978), and Novshek (1980), entrants' profit expectations are inconsistent, since they expect existing firms to maintain price. Since existing firms respond to entry by reducing price, their profit expectations are overly optimistic. Despite this, FEE is consistent with pure profit, which may be substantial. In Eaton (1976), the rate of return on specific capital is up to 16/9 times the competitive rate of return.

What is the source of these positive profits in FEE? First, the source is *not* the integer problem. The integer problem arises in a locational model when existing plants (or products) can be costlessly relocated. Then their number can be augmented one at a time, while all relocate to remain in the middle of equally-sized markets. Under such circumstances (in finite-sized markets such as the boundary of a circle) positive profits in FEE depend only on the integer problem. Note, however, that if firms really could relocate costlessly (in money and in time) they would move continuously, producing at each point in space since there would be no reason to transport goods costfully, if firms themselves could be transported costlessly. *Absence of relocation costs in a spatial market implies a continuum of production over that market.*[22]

The source of positive pure profits in FEE is specific, lumpy capital that must take on a specific address, which means fitting this into a slot among existing firms. Thus if, for example, a new entrant expects to be charging the same price as his neighbours, he expects to obtain a market that is discretely smaller than those they enjoyed before his entry. In a one-dimensional market, the ratio of the new entrant's expected market length to the market lengths of existing plants before entry is 1/2, regardless of the number of plants in the market. In a two-dimensional spatial model with some symmetric configuration of plants throughout the market, the ratio is on the order of 1/2 (see Eaton–Lipsey, 1976), and is again independent of the number of plants in the market. In these spatial models, the market structure is one of overlapping oligopolies.

Now consider characteristics models. Lane (1980), develops a model in which FEE is consistent with substantial pure profits. Where the number of characteristics is small, the reason for positive profits in FEE is the same as in geographic models: any new product must fit into a slot in characteristic space between a small number of neighbours, the number of neighbours remaining small even as the number of products increases indefinitely. That a new product must fit into a slot between existing products and therefore expect a significantly smaller market area than that enjoyed by its neighbours before entry, is independent of whether or not products are combined to obtain characteristic mixes not available in any single product.

Shaked–Sutton (1982), drawing on Gabszewicz–Thisse (1980), develop a model in which goods are differentiated by quality. They identify quite plausible cases in which there is an upper bound to the number of firms which can attract a positive market share in equilibrium. Suppose, for purposes of illustration, that a 'large' number of firms have committed specific capital to such a market. Their result says that only a limited number of these firms will make non-zero sales in the non-cooperative price equilibrium. In the terminology of Shaked–Sutton, we have a 'natural oligopoly' and substantial pure profit is clearly possible in FEE.

In spite of these results, a great deal of the literature in the address branch (particularly in geographical-location models) imposes a zero-profit equilibrium condition with, as far as we can see, *no behavioural justification whatsoever*. There seems to be an intuitive feeling that the non-specificity of capital in the long run should lead to a zero-profit result. Some people have envisaged a tatonnement process in which no specific capital is committed to the market until equilibrium is reached.[23] But the real world does not duplicate this 'empty-plain experiment'. For the market as a whole, the closest we get to such a long-run experiment is a *mixed long-run case*. Here, one firm makes a long-run decision (e.g., to replace a depreciated plant or to create a new plant) in a situation in which some specific capital is currently committed to the market.[24]

To see that such mixed long-run decisions do not necessarily lead to a zero-profit equilibrium, consider the following example. Imagine a circular market, one unit in length, with a uniform density of demand of one unit of demand per unit distance (which is independent of delivered price). Let price be parametric at a value of one (resale price maintenance). Firms enter the market by locating an immovable plant, which produces any desired output at a fixed total cost of (K) per unit of time for as long as it exists. Each firm can own

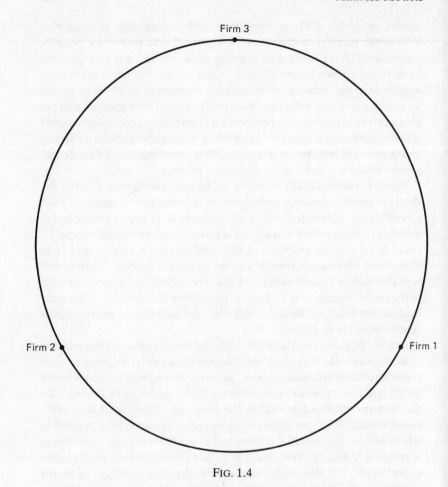

Firm 3

Firm 2

Firm 1

FIG. 1.4

only one plant and all plants are subject to random expiry. If a firm's capital expires, this information is available first to the firm itself so that it can maintain its hold on the market by immediately replacing it. Capital having expired, there is a non-zero but 'small' cost of choosing a different location for the new plant.

Initially, let there be three firms equally spaced around the circular market, as shown in Figure 1.4, and let $1/5 > K > 1/6$ so that the market could sustain four or five equally spaced firms. If existing firms behave *non-strategically*, they will simply replicate their locations when their plant expires. Further, a new entrant must anticipate a market of size 1/6, but requires a market of K, which is greater than

1/6, to cover costs The three-firm locational configuration is thus a FEE when firms behave non-strategically, and there is no tendency for profits to be driven towards zero. A second point is also obvious from this example. If we take as an initial condition four or five equally-spaced firms, we conclude that these are also free-entry equilibria when firms behave non-strategically: FEE is not unique. Thus history, in the form of the specific capital that is in place, affects the mixed long-run decisions taken by each firm, and thus the convergent FEE. (We consider strategic behaviour in this model in Section (B).)

In the address branch, there is a strong presumption that rents do exist in free-entry equilibrium when firms behave non-strategically. These rents will, however, induce firms to behave strategically with respect to specific capital.

(B) STRATEGIC BEHAVIOUR: DEMAND PRIMITIVES AND MARKET STRUCTURE

In the non-address branch, the fundamental determinant of the extent to which FEE is consistent with pure profit and, therefore, the extent to which firms are able and willing to create asymmetry through strategic behaviour is, roughly speaking, the size of the market relative to MES. Schmalensee (1981) argues that strategic behaviour in non-address models is a trivial issue when the market can support even a few firms. His arguments suggest 'the general unimportance of entry barriers erected by economies of scale' (p. 1228) (see also Gilbert's chapter in this volume).

Although the paradigm of strategic, free-entry equilibrium discussed above has not yet been systematically applied to the address branch, the existing literature suggests that the problem is fundamentally different in this branch.

Prescott–Visscher (1977), Hay (1976) and Rothschild (1976) investigate the problem in models of spatial competition in which price is parametric, and the artificial one-plant, one-firm restriction is imposed. The initial conditions are that the market is unserved, and that firms enter sequentially. Lane (1980) extends the sequential entry paradigm to a characteristics model in which price is endogenous. In these models, the convergent FEE is unique: it is the FEE which yields, for sitting firms, the largest profits that will not attract entry.

Schmalensee (1978) analyses the problem of product selection in a model of spatial competition in which the density of demand is growing over time, price formation is co-operative, and the artificial one-plant, one-firm restriction is removed. Given an initial selection of products (or brands) he concludes that existing firms always have an incentive to pre-empt entry by proliferating brands and also that the unique FEE is that FEE which yields, for sitting firms, the largest profits that will not attract entry. Eaton–Lipsey (1979) arrive at the same conclusions in a somewhat more general model.

Two important questions arise from this literature.

(1) Given an unserved market and sequential entry, is monopoly pre-emption always to be expected? (If initial conditions have more then one firm serving the market, some closely related questions arise. When the growth of demand is foreseen, will strategic behaviour by existing firms prevent the subsequent entry of other firms? Do there exist incentives for the whole market to be monopolised?)

(2) Is the result *that the convergent FEE (in the presence of strategic behaviour) yields the maximum profit that sitting firms can earn without attracting entry* independent of initial conditions?

We address these questions sequentially. (The argument in the next two paragraphs is based on a forthcoming paper by Eaton.)

Suppose we have some market in the address branch which is unserved, and consider the problem facing a first mover. Given the equilibrium concept which determines prices (given a vector of products), the first mover could contemplate establishing a sufficient number of products in the continuum to deter entry. It is not obvious that such a 'sufficient number' even exists. What is, however, obvious is that if the equilibrium concept is non-cooperative (in the broad sense that it does not maximise profit given the number of products), the number of products which the monopolist would have to establish to deter entry is larger than the number of products which would deter entry if they were owned by independent firms (since equilibrium prices will be lower when three firms are in the market than when there are only two). This raises the important point that monopoly pre-emption in this circumstance is not necessarily the most profitable option facing the initial mover.

In spite of the above, we must nevertheless expect substantial concentration in this market when we allow a first mover to enter an unserved market. Suppose, for example, that the equilibrium concept is Nash in prices, subject to the no-mill-price-undercutting assumption. Identify the minimum number of one-product firms (n) which will deter entry in a one-dimensional market. The first mover has the option of establishing $n/2$ products, alternating over the continuum, knowing that the second mover will also establish $n/2$ products to deter entry. We then have 'duopoly pre-emption'. Notice that, given this equilibrium concept, *the first mover can do no worse than to adopt this duopoly–pre-emption solution*. Three observations then follow. First, we must always expect substantial concentration to emerge in this first-mover experiment. Second, any measure of this concentration is not easily interpreted. Suppose the first mover chooses the duopoly solution. Then, from an economic point of view, this solution is indistinguishable from the solution which would emerge if we conducted the corresponding sequential-entry experiment with the one-product, one-firm restriction. Yet, in one case, measured concentration is insignificant (assuming n to be large) and in the other the two-firm concentration ratio is 1. The point is obvious (and well known): we must be very careful to define 'markets' in an economically meaningful sense. What is, however, not so obvious is just how difficult this may be in the address branch. Third, the possibility that the first entrant might prefer to create the conditions for a multi-plant duopoly rather than a multi-plant monopoly may be the answer to the worry expressed by many theorists: why do not we see monopoly everywhere that addresses matter? (See, e.g., Prescott–Visscher (1977, pp. 391–2) and Eaton–Lipsey (1979, p. 157).)

The above discussion is clearly related to Markham's (1966) observation that the standard, monopolistically-competitive case seems to comprise a few firms, each producing a wide range of differentiated products. This phenomenon is, we think, more easily understood in the address branch.

We turn now to the second question. Impose the one-product, one-firm restriction. Independent of initial conditions, is the convergent FEE, when firms behave strategically, always the equilibrium which yields the maximal profit which sitting firms can earn without attracting entry? We do not provide a general answer to this question. We simply present a simple example, in which the answer is 'yes'.

Consider the model introduced in the previous section and illustrated in Figure 1.4. We make one alteration: $1/4 < K < 1/3$. Now the market: (i) will not support four firms; (ii) will support three or two firms with positive profit in FEE; and (iii) will not be in FEE with only one firm (since a new entrant could then expect a market of $1/2$).

Now, starting with three firms, suppose Firm 1's capital expires first, and consider the available strategic options. If Firm 1 chooses to relocate at $1/3$, it must expect to serve $1/3$ of the market. If it chooses to locate at 1/2, it will again expect to serve 1/3 of the market until another firm's capital expires. Suppose Firm 1 makes the latter choice. If Firm 2's capital expires second, then Firm 2 will exit, leaving Firm 1 and Firm 3 to serve the market. In this case, Firm 1's 'squeeze play' is obviously successful. If Firm 3's capital expires second, Firm 3 cannot move left, since that would invite entry. Nor will he attempt to squeeze 1, since there is a small added-cost of replacing 1's plant at a different location. Thus Firm 3 sits tight. Eventually Firm 2's capital will expire. Firm 2 then exits, and we again end up with just two firms serving the market.

The above is, if nothing else, a counter-example to the commonly-expressed idea about positive profits in equilibrium of address models. This idea is that it is a result of capital fixity and that, in the long run, when all capital is variable, profits must tend to zero. What is wrong with this idea is, of course, that in the long run all capital does not become *simultaneously* variable.

There remains the question of asymptotic properties: do small groups become large groups as the market grows, and, particularly, is the equilibrium configuration competitive in the limit? In the non-address branch, the answer given has usually been 'yes' (see Hart, 1979). It is easy to see intuitively that a growing demand for a finite number of goods must create a market for each of them in which MES can be made as small as we like, relative to demand. In such a market there is, as we have seen, little room for strategic behaviour. It is our conjecture that, in the address branch, the asymptotic results are, in general, *not* competitive. In this branch, the interesting replication experiment is not cloning the representative consumer, but increasing the diversity of tastes: introducing new utility functions (perhaps 'between' the initial ones in some appropriate, i.e., continuous, function space) or new locations (more consumers between the initial ones in physical space). As we saw in Section III (A)(4), we do not know the sufficient conditions for competition to be localised in address-branch models. Suppose, however, that the necessary conditions are satisfied. It is not then obvious that this replication experiment will reduce the degree of localisation or ensure that pure profit in FEE is zero.

(C) CHOICE OF SPECIFICITY

We observed above that indivisibility of capital goods is not God-given, but is subject to technologically-constrained choice. An analogous observation applies to specificity: it is subject to technologically-constrained choice. In the address branch, which we take to be the 'standard' case, specificity of capital implies the possibility of profits in strategic free-entry equilibrium. This implies that firms have some incentive to create more specificity than cost-minimisation requires.

It is this observation which leads us to be sceptical of the theory of contestable markets (see Baumol (1982) and chapter by Baumol, Panzar and Willig in this volume) as a positive theory of market structure. Although the *sine qua non* of a contestable market is the absence of specificity, firms engaged in strategic behaviour have incentives to create specificity even where cost-minimisation requires none. Our view is that a positive theory of market structure must be driven, on the cost side, by specificity.

This force opposes another well-known force acting on the firm: *ceteris paribus*, in an uncertain world, it is wise to keep one's options open. The discussion of 'flexibility' in Stigler's (1939) classic is addressed to this proposition. Uncertainty provides an incentive for firms to choose less specificity than cost-minimisation requires. There is thus an important unexplored margin: non-specificity has value because it maintains options, while specificity has strategic value precisely because it limits options (it is the vehicle for commitment).

A theory of endogenous market structure must therefore take into consideration the firm's choice of specificity. Are the incentives to create specificity for strategic purposes swamped by the inherent uncertainty of our world? This would seem to be a very important research topic.

(D) THE ANALOGY BETWEEN SPATIAL AND CHARACTERISTICS MODELS

In Sections III (A)(3) and (4), we noted some obvious similarities and dissimilarities between spatial and characteristics models. We make only a further brief remark (since the forthcoming Archibald–Eaton paper is addressed to the subject). From what has been said, it is clear that a pair of models *can* be specified in such a fashion that they are very close (perhaps isomorphic), but they need not be. The models may differ in several ways, among which are: (i) the dimensions of the space, (ii) the existence of boundaries; (iii) the unique-ness of a consumer's address. Further, in the characteristics case, the consumer's choice-set may be continuous or discrete and, if discrete, may not be 'd-convex'. Similarly, the possibility of 'cross-over' arises in the spatial model, if consumers perceive 'distance' differently or the transport-cost function is concave. Thus we cannot agree with Schmalensee (1983) when he writes

> As the analyses of Baumol (1967), Lancaster (1975) and Salop (1979) have shown, the formal correspondence between Lancastrian models with two characteristics and one-dimensional spatial models is almost exact. In particular the same localization of competition is preseved.

It is, of course, *possible* to put sufficient restrictions on a characteristics model to reduce it effectively to the simplest spatial model, as Lancaster attempted[25] in the reference quoted by Schmalensee; but it is false to assume that any characteristics model necessarily 'twins' with all, or indeed any, spatial model, or vice versa. Further, only sufficient conditions for the localisation of competition in these models are presently known.

VII WELFARE

Many investigators have made welfare comparisons of alternative states within address models, by summing consumers' surpluses or using other similar techniques. We are sceptical of all existing attempts, for at least the following reasons.

(1) Even the partial-equilibrium analysis of single markets seems to pose difficult second-best problems. The positive model is one of overlapping oligopolies in which marginal cost does not equal price.

(2) The theory of contestable markets provides one benchmark against which the performance of real markets may be compared. It may be of interest to know how much worse is the performance of some real market than that of a perfect but unattainable market. For policy purposes, however, it seems to us that it is more interesting to compare the performance of some existing market with the best-attainable alternative market structure. This requires that we first have a theory of attainable market structures.

(3) It is at least possible that markets for factors and intermediate goods are fragmented for the same reasons that tend to confine competition to a few neighbours in the address-branch models for final goods considered here. In that case, it cannot be assumed that transactions prices reflect opportunity costs, so that the status of any

partial-equilibrium welfare economics becomes dubious. The implications for general equilibrium theory of an address view of the world have yet to be studied.

(4) Once it is agreed that, thanks to scale effects, only a small subset of the set of possible goods will be produced, the question of which ones should be produced becomes urgent. Lancaster (1975; 1979) has seen correctly that the implication of scale effects, given diversity of tastes, is that efficiency and distributional considerations are inextricably mixed here.[26] The old 'overhead-cost problem', which was thought to be peculiar to the public utilities (the natural monopolies) becomes ubiquitous in the address branch and, we therefore think, in the real world. The problem of the optimal product range is yet to be solved.

(5) Another urgent question follows. If we knew how to characterise the optimal product range, what institutions (market structure) would deliver it? It seems at least a plausible conjecture that the sort of market structure which we expect in the address branch (Kaldorean chains of overlapping oligopolies; positive profit in FEE; pre-emptive proliferation of stores, plants, and products) delivers nothing of the kind. The whole policy problem here awaits exploration.

VIII SOME OUTSTANDING PROBLEMS AND RESEARCH NEEDS

(1) A systematic application of the paradigm of strategic FEE to address models is, we think, an important research task. We suspect that it will produce a theoretical understanding of what seems to us to be the empirically relevant case for monopolistic competition: a multitude of differentiated products produced by a few oligopolistic competitors.

(2) Most of the address-branch modelling has worked with spaces of low dimensionality. This is perhaps not too restrictive in geographic space, but in characteristics space there is no *a priori* restriction on the dimensionality of the space, and we need some empirical work.[27]

Archibald–Rosenbluth have argued that, in the combining case, if there are more than three characteristics, the average number of neighbours which a product may have approaches $n/2$, where n is the total number of products in the group. For us, this raises two key issues. First, does the large number of neighbours of a new entrant mean that the loss of market by each neighbour is small enough, and

diffuse enough, so that something analogous to Chamberlin's symmetry assumption will apply? Second, will the new entrant's market
be of approximately the same size as (say only $1/n$ smaller than) the
pre-entry markets of its neighbours, or will it be discretely smaller
(say one-half the size)? Note that the new entrant can have a very
diffuse effect on its (large number of) neighbours' markets, while
itself picking up only a total market on the order of one-half the size
of the pre-entry markets of its neighbours. We suspect that the
discreteness of entry will in fact produce this result even when the
number of neighbours is large, *thus preserving the possibility of
substantial positive profits in FEE*.

(3) Virtually all of the characteristics models of which we are
aware make assumptions designed to localise competition completely. Yet we know of nothing to suggest that 'cross over' is
unimportant, empirically.

(4) In many ways, the most interesting and potentially rewarding
research task is to develop a theory of endogenous market structure.
We have explained above why we think that the theory of contestable
markets will not do the job. To us market structure is a battle
between attacking potential entrants and defending sitting firms.
Entry and entry prevention seems to us to be driven by the nature of
firm-, product-, and group-specific capital. Thus another potentially-
fruitful research programme seems to be the development of a theory
of endogenous market structure based to a large extent on the nature
(which is itself partly endogenous and partly exogenous) of lumpy,
specific, sunk capital (see Eaton–Lipsey, 1981, Section III for some
discussion).

As one possibility for a theory of endogenous market structure, we
conjecture that the results of several studies we have reviewed will
turn out to be illustrative of a generalization: the FEE consistent with
rational, strategic behaviour and foresighted entry decisions will be
the one that produces the largest profits which sitting firms can earn
without attracting entry.

NOTES

1. The first and third authors are indebted to the Canada Council for the
   opportunity provided by Killam Fellowships in various years. All three
   authors are indebted to the Social Sciences and Humanities Research
   Council of Canada for research support. We are also indebted to Simon

Anderson, Mukesh Eswaran, David McGechie and Gernot Kofler for comments and suggestions.

2. The full quotation is 'Is the bunghole of a barrel part of the barrel? Think well before you answer; because the whole structure of theoretical physics is trembling in the balance'.

3. Since, in some cases to be considered, firms may be in competition with firms that are not their immediate neighbours in the physical sense, we need a potentially wider definition of 'economic neighbours'. We say that two goods are neighbours, at given prices, if it is possible that a consumer with convex indifference curves (in characteristics space) could be indifferent between them and that there exists no intermediate good (mixing their characteristics) which he prefers.

4. The Market Opportunity Frontier in characteristics space is determined, for any consumer, by the set of produced goods, their prices, and his budget. In the combining case, an interior good would be dominated by a convex combination of neighbouring goods and be unsaleable. This does not necessarily follow in the non-combining case. The 'MOF' is a discrete point set. We construct the free-disposal convex hull of this set. If every attainable point lies within the boundary of the convex hull, we say that the set is 'd-convex'. An interior good is not, however, dominated by an (unattainable) convex combination of neighbouring goods (it may be the 'best buy' for some individuals) so that the set is not necessarily d-convex.

5. Lancaster (1979) does this by placing restrictions – symmetry and mutuality – directly on his derived compensating functions. He does not investigate the implied restrictions on his primitives and it seems to us that these are unacceptable – e.g., if the consumer whose most-preferred good is 1/2 has indifference curves that are asymptotic to both characteristic axes, other consumers must have indifference curves that slope upwards over part of their range.

6. 'Product class' is not, in fact, defined; and it is not clear that a useful definition could be formulated in this approach when each consumer perceives a different characteristics space. Also note that, in this approach, 'tastes' cannot be represented as continuous and that the problem of modelling changes in the vector of available goods, so easily dealt with in Lancaster's approach, remains awkward.

7. The preference vector θ is a vector of reservation prices. This, as it stands, means that the demand 'primitives' are not independent of the budget set, which must be known to the consumer before he can compute reservation *prices*.

8. The argument applies only to goods and does not carry over to services that must be consumed at their rate of production. If the consumer's desired rate of consumption of a service is less than the minimum-cost production rate, he is not indifferent between producing it for himself and buying it from a firm that is operating at its minimum efficient scale. Since writing our paper, we have discovered that a similar argument is most lucidly made by Weitzman (1983). Whereas we restrict our argument to goods, he seems to imply it is also applicable to services.

9. There are some interesting issues with respect to product- and group-specific capital that we do not go into here. The identical capital may be able to produce some variations of breakfast cereals or of chocolates, but be unable to produce equally well over the whole range of group characteristics. Experience thus suggests a rich range of product-, sub-group- and group-specific capital. What we need for the argument of the text, however, is that there be some product specificity to the capital; otherwise there would be a continuum of goods produced over the characteristics space that defines the group.

10. Eaton–Lipsey (1981) suggest that the index $1 - R$, where R is the ratio of the value of a capital good, in its best alternative use, to its reproduction cost, is a useful index of specificity. 'Value in best alternative use, presumes, however, at least known properties of equilibrium and perhaps even the equilibrium concept itself, whence the index is not a technological primitive. Moreover, our attempts to define an index of specificity convince us that, except in the extreme case used in the text, any appealing index uses market data and therefore implicitly involves some properties of equilibrium. We cannot now offer a satisfactory technological measure of specificity. None the less, we shall argue that specific inputs can be used strategically and that they are therefore determinants of the properties of equilibrium, so that it seems unwise to use value in alternative use to devise an index of specificity. Moreover, as we argue below, some interesting puzzles involving the equilibrium concept, and the possible use of specific capital as a vehicle for commitment, arise even when capital is completely product-specific.

11. Imposing an upper bound on the rate of which capital services can be extracted from the capital good does not change the *fundamental* result: specific capital implies increasing returns to outlay over some initial range of output.

12. The first order condition for an interior solution to this cost minimisation problem is

$$\frac{W}{C'(v)} = \frac{f_1(n, v)}{f_2(n, v)}$$

Since $C'(v)$ is not constant, it is clear that n/v depends on x. Indeed n/v increases as x increases. A corner solution with $v = 0$ is clearly possible for low levels of output, since the unit cost of (v) goes to infinity as (v) goes to zero.

13. If there is an upper bound on the rate at which capital services can be extracted from the capital good, then we clearly have increasing returns to outlay up to the level of output at which the optimal rate of extraction is equal to this upper bound.

14. The demonstration that the existence of man-made capital goods requires some non-convexity can be thought of as an illustration of the 'round-aboutness' of production in time: we embody capital services today for use in the future. There is, however, another interpretation of 'round-aboutness' which centres on the question: why does production involve specialised inputs (some of which may be capital services)? This

interpretation focuses on the number of arguments in the production function. These are quite separate issues.

15. This analysis implicitly assumes that the firm itself purchases the indivisible capital good. The indivisibility of the good will, in many circumstances, require this. It is, however, conceivable that the capital good could simultaneously yield services to many firms, i.e. although product-specific it is not firm-specific. We can then imagine many final-goods-producing firms purchasing specific capital services from firms which own capital goods. In this, case individual firms in the X industry will be price takers for capital services and they will have constant returns to outlay in X production.

16. There are two approaches to equilibrium in this circumstance. First, assume that potential entrants take existing market data as given. Given n firms, one firm will enter, creating losses for all. As specific capital of firms expires, one firm will leave, creating positive profits for the remainder and the incentive for yet another to enter. We have approximate equilibrium (n firms, $n + 1$ firms, n firms,...), and price is approximately the competitive price. Moreover, although entrants' expectations about profits are incorrect, they are approximately correct. Second, assume that each potential entrant, *knowing how each firm chooses quantity*, calculates the post-entry equilibrium and enters only if its profits in the post-entry equilibrium are positive. Then the FEE is unique (n firms) and is also approximately the competitive equilibrium.

17. This view of the entrant's problem dates at least as far back as Hotelling (1929). The mobile firm in Hotelling (which could just as well be considered to be a new entrant as a relocating existing firm) uses the rules of the game, which are Nash in prices, to calculate its equilibrium profits in each possible location. The choice of location is that which yields the highest post-relocation equilibrium profits.

18. Although they were the first to demonstrate this rigorously, many earlier writers, including Hotelling himself, have noted the possibility. See, e.g., Hotelling (1929), p. 48; Eaton (1972), p. 269, and Prescott–Visscher (1977), p. 380–1.

19. As d'Aspremont–Gabszewicz–Thisse demonstrate, the non-existence problem does not arise when transport costs are quadratic, nor does it arise in a two-dimensional market when the metric is Euclidean. However, the problem remains with the 'block metric' in two space (Eaton–Lipsey, 1980a).

20. Notice that this also rules out Bertrand's price-taking assumption. It was argued to us in the conference that our no mill-price undercutting assumption was inconsistent with the common observation that *ceteris paribus* the more distant is a firm's nearest competitor the higher is its price. We do not see, however, that the irrational behaviour implied by mill-price undercutting is necessary for this result.

21. Although we have not needed the concept of group-specific capital here, it is clearly needed for a more general treatment. Group-specific capital is committed to the group (cars or popsicles) but not to the firm (GM or General Foods).

22. This argument applies to goods, but not necessarily to services. See note 8 above.
23. For example, Mills–Lav write (1964, p. 283, footnote 6)

> It should be emphasised that we consider only static industry equilibriums in this paper. We do not consider adjustment processes, and we make no attempt to ascertain whether any adjustment process will converge to industry equilibrium . . . One way to envisage the adjustment is to assume a *tatonnement* process in which no plants are actually built until equilibrium is reached.

    We doubt that such a tatonnement process would converge on a long-run equilibrium. In any case, the experiment is inappropriate: the relevant experiment relates to the mixed long-run case.
24. When commitment to the market matters and firms make strategic decisions, the behaviour of firms will ensure that all long-run decisions are 'mixed', since firms will choose to replace their capital before it is economically worthless (Eaton–Lipsey, 1980).
25. But cf. Note 5 above.
26. Space prevents us from exploring here the properties of Lancaster's compensation function, or of the distance functions that may be defined by characteristics space. It is in fact possible to define a precise and 'reasonable' measure of the distance between two goods in a group, i.e. to metrise the MOF. This is discussed in a forthcoming paper by Archibald–Eaton.
27. Successful empirical applications have, however, made do with very few characteristics. See, e.g., Quandt–Baumol (1966), Lancaster (1971) and Morey (1981).

REFERENCES

Archibald, G. C. and Rosenbluth, G. (1975) 'The "New" Theory of Consumer Demand and Monopolistic Competition', *Quarterly Journal of Economics*, vol. 80, pp. 569–90.
d'Aspremont, C., Gabszewicz, J. J. and Thisse, J. F. (1979) 'On "Hotelling's Stability in Competition"', *Econometrica*, vol. 47, pp. 1145–50.
Baumol, W. J. (1967), 'Calculation of Optimal Product and Retailer Characteristics: The Abstract Product Approach', *Journal of Political Economy*, vol. 75, pp. 674–85.
Baumol, W. J. (1982) 'Contestable Markets: An Uprising in the Theory of Industry Structure', *American Economic Review*, vol. 72, pp. 1–15.
Chamberlin, E. (1933) *The Theory of Monopolistic Competition*, (Cambridge, Mass.: Harvard University Press).
Dorfman, R. and Steiner, P. O. (1954) 'Optimal Advertising and Optimal Quality', *American Economic Review*, vol. 44, pp. 826–36.
Dixit, A. (1979) 'A Model of Duopoly Suggesting a Theory of Entry Barriers', *Bell Journal of Economics*, vol. 10, pp. 20–32.

Dixit, A. (1980) 'The Role of Investment in Entry-Deterrence', *The Economic Journal*, vol. 90, 95–106.

Dixit, A. K. and Stiglitz, J. E. (1977) 'Monopolistic Competition and Optimum Product Diversity', *American Economic Review*, vol. 67, pp. 297–308.

Eaton, B. C. (1972) 'Spatial Competition Revisited', *Canadian Journal of Economics*, vol. 5, pp. 268–78.

Eaton, B. C. (1976) 'Free Entry in One Dimensional Models: Pure Profits and Multiple Equilibria', *Journal of Regional Science*, vol. 16, pp. 21–33.

Eaton, B. C. and Lipsey, R. G. (1975) 'The Principle of Minimum Differentiation Reconsidered: Some New Developments in the Theory of Spatial Competition', *Review of Economic Studies*, vol. 42, pp. 27–49.

Eaton, B.C. and Lipsey, R. G. (1976) 'The Non-Uniqueness of Equilibrium in the Loschian Location Model', *American Economic Review*, vol. 66, pp. 77–93.

Eaton, B. C. and Lipsey, R. G. (1977) 'The Introduction of Space into the Neo-Classical Model of Value Theory', in *Studies in Modern Economic Analysis*, M. J. Artis and A. R. Nobay, (eds) (Oxford: Basil Blackwell), pp. 59–96.

Eaton, B. C. and Lipsey, R. G. (1978) 'Freedom of Entry and the Existence of Pure Profit', *Economic Journal*, vol. 88, pp. 455–69.

Eaton, B. C. and Lipsey, R. G. (1979) 'The Theory of Market Preemption: the Persistence of Excess Capacity and Monopoly in Growing spatial Markets', *Economica*, vol. 46, pp. 149–58.

Eaton, B. C. and Lipsey, R. G. (1980a) 'Block Metric and the Law of Markets', *Journal of Urban Economics*, vol. 7, pp. 337–47.

Eaton, B. C. and Lipsey, R. G. (1980b) 'Exit Barriers are Entry Barriers: the Durability of Capital as a Barrier to Entry', *The Bell Journal of Economics*, vol. 11, pp. 721–9.

Eaton, B. C. and Lipsey, R. G. (1981) 'Capital, Commitment and Entry Equilibrium', *Bell Journal of Economics*, vol. 12, pp. 593–604.

Eddington, Sir A. (1958) *The Philosophy of Physical Science* (Ann Arbor: University of Michigan Press).

Gabszewicz, J. J. and Thisse, J. F. (1980) 'Entry (and Exit) in a Differentiated Industry', *Journal of Economic Theory*, vol. 22, pp. 327–38.

Gilbert, R. J. and Newbery, D. M. G. (1982) 'Preemptive Patenting and the Persistence of Monopoly', *American Economic Review*, forthcoming.

Gorman, W. M. (1980) 'A Possible Procedure for Analyzing Quality Differentials in the Egg Market', *Review of Economic Studies*, vol. 47, pp. 843–56.

Hart, O. (1979) 'Monopolistic Competition in a Large Economy with Differentiated Commodities', *Review of Economic Studies*, vol. 46, pp. 1–30.

Hay, D. A. (1976) 'Sequential Entry and Entry-Deterring Strategies in Spatial Competition', *Oxford Economic Papers*, vol. 28, pp. 240–57.

Hotelling, H. (1929) 'Stability in Competition', *Economic Journal*, vol. 39, pp. 41–57.

Kaldor, N. (1934) 'Mrs. Robinson's "Economics of Imperfect Competition"' *Economica*, vol. 1, pp. 335–41.

Kaldor, N. (1935) 'Market Imperfections and Excess Capacity', *Economica*, vol. 2, pp. 33–50.

Lancaster, K. J. (1966) 'A New Approach to Consumer Theory', *Journal of Political Economy*, vol. 74, pp. 132–57.

Lancaster, K. J. (1971) *Consumer Demand: A New Approach* (New York; Columbia University Press).

Lancaster, K. J. (1975) 'Socially Optimal Product Differentiation', *American Economic Review*, vol. 65, pp. 567–85.

Lancaster, K. J. (1979) *Variety, Equity, and Efficiency* (New York; Columbia University Press).

Lane, W. (1980) 'Product Differentiation in a Market with Endogenous Sequential Entry', *Bell Journal of Economics*, vol. 11, pp. 237–60.

Losch, A. (1954) *The Economics of Location* (New Haven: Yale University Press).

Markham, J. W. (1964) 'The Theory of Monopolistic Competition After Thirty Years', *American Economic Review*, vol. 54, pp. 53–5.

Mills, E. S. and Lav, M. R. (1964) 'A Model of Market Areas with Free Entry', *Journal of Political Economy*, vol. 72, pp. 278–88.

Morey, Edward R. (1981) 'The Demand for Site-Specific Recreational Activities: A Characteristics Approach', *Journal of Environmental Economics and Management*, vol. 8, pp. 345–71.

Novshek, W. (1980) 'Equilibrium in Simple Spatial (or Differentiated Product) Models', *Journal of Economic Theory*, vol. 22, pp. 313–26.

Peles, Y. (1974) 'A Note on Equilibrium in Monopolistic Competition', *Journal of Political Economy*, vol. 82, pp. 626–30.

Perloff, J. M. and Salop, S. C. (1982) 'Equilibrium with Product Differentiation', Gianini Foundation for Agricultural Economics, Working Paper, no. 179.

Prescott, E. C. and Visscher, M. (1977) 'Sequential Location Among Firms with Foresight', *Bell Journal of Economics*, vol. 8, pp. 378–93.

Quandt, R. E. and Baumol, W. J. (1966) 'The Demand for Abstract Transport Modes: Theory and Measurement', *Journal of Regional Science*, vol. 6, pp. 13–26.

Rothschild, R. (1976) 'A Note on the Effect of Sequential Entry on Choice of Location', *Journal of Industrial Economics*, vol. 24, pp. 313–20.

Salop, S. (1979) 'Monopolistic Competition with Outside Goods', *Bell Journal of Economics*, vol. 10, pp. 141–56.

Salop, S. (1979a) 'Strategic Entry Deterrence', *American Economic Review*, vol. 69, pp. 335–8.

Schelling, T. C. (1956) 'An Essay on Bargaining', *American Economic Review*, vol. 46, pp. 281–306.

Schmalensee, R. (1978) 'Entry Deterrence in the Ready-to-Eat Breakfast Cereal Industry', *Bell Journal of Economics*, vol. 9, pp. 305–27.

Schmalensee, R. (1981) 'Economies of Scale and Barriers to Entry', *Journal of Political Economy*, vol. 89, pp. 1228–38.

Schmalensee, R. (1982) 'The New Industrial Organization and the Economic Analysis of Modern Markets', in W. Hildenbrand (ed.), *Advances in Economic Theory* (Cambridge: Cambridge University Press).

Shaked, A. and Sutton, J. (1982) 'Natural Oligopolies', unpublished manu-
script, London School of Economics.
Spence, A. M. (1976) 'Product Selection, Fixed Costs, and Monopolistic
Competition', *Review of Economic Studies*, vol. 43, pp. 217–35.
Spence, A. M. (1977) 'Entry, Capacity, Investment and Oligopolistic Pric-
ing', *Bell Journal of Economics*, vol. 8, pp. 534–44.
Stigler, George J. (1939) 'Production and Distribution in the Short Run',
Journal of Political Economy, 47, pp. 305–27.
Weitzman, Martin L. (1983) 'Constestable Markets: An uprising in the
Theory of Industry Structure: Comment', *American Economic Review*,
73, pp. 486–7.

Discussion of the Paper by Archibald, Eaton and Lipsey

Lancaster began the discussion by praising the authors for stressing the importance of primitives in models of monopolistic competition. He noted that a large variety of results found in the literature could often be traced to assumptions about primitives in the corresponding models. For example, consider the work related to whether prices in a monopolistically competitive equilibrium converge to the appropriate competitive prices as the economy grows large. In this regard, the model of Oliver Hart (1979) was useful as it was one of the most general of the many papers addressing this question.

Lancaster explained that Hart's results were driven by two assumptions about primitives. In the first of these assumptions, preferences were restricted so that indifference curves cut the axis. This gave rise to what Lancaster called the scarcity paradox: When indifference curves all cut the axis, the demand for any commodity must go to zero at some finite price. As the commodity in question became scarce, the supply curve of a competitive industry or the marginal cost curve of a monopolist, shifted left. In both cases, the price converged to the price at which demand went to zero. In this case, the monopoly and competitive price were the same at the limit. Hence, this simple assumption about primitives (in this case preferences) guaranteed Hart's limit result for the case where output expanded more slowly than demand.

For the case where output grew as fast, or faster than demand, Hart's result came from another assumption about primitives, in this case technology. Hart's assumption was that every firm's output was bounded. This guaranteed that if output expanded as fast as demand, the number of firms must get large, so that the competitive price must result.

Lancaster pointed out that one of the most important primitives was the nature of returns to scale in an industry. Returns to scale were incompatible with freedom of movement into and out of an industry. Returns to scale implied that a firm must commit itself to production of a specific commodity, and this was critical in much of the recent literature. Lancaster disagreed that this implied product-specificity of capital associated with production. To illustrate this point he used the example of spray painting an automobile. It was costly for a firm to switch colours in response to entry since this required cleaning sprayers. However, if the sprayers must be cleaned anyway at regular intervals, the firm could use these intervals to change costlessly to another colour. The capital involved was not product-specific (i.e. colour-specific), yet painting any given colour would involve some commitment.

Lancaster pointed out that monopolistic competition must involve some sort of indivisibility if products were storable. This prevented the possibility that firms might operate at a large scale for a very short interval of time, thereby achieving all scale economies.

Curtis Eaton responded that he did not think that Oliver Hart's model was an address model. In particular, contrary to Hart's claim, it was not a Lancasterian characteristics model, as Hart required consumers to have strictly quasi-concave preferences over the set of *goods*. This could not be true in a characteristics model, at least in a Lancasterian characteristics model. Eaton did not think that it was appropriate to argue about the true model of monopolistic competition. He contrasted the Dixit–Stiglitz (1977) and Spence (1976) models of monopolistic competition with the AEL approach. The former both represented the Chamberlinian approach to monopolistic competition. However, AEL's approach could be classified as an overlapping oligopoly approach, more in the tradition of Kaldor (1935). It was an empirical matter which was correct. For the reasons stated in the paper, AEL believed that their approach was representative of a large segment of the economy.

Pure profits did not disappear in equilibrium because new entrants expected discretely smaller markets than those enjoyed by incumbent firms. This was a property of both geographic and charateristics spaces.

Claude D'Aspremont raised the issue of how potential entrants predicted post-entry profits. He suggested that this was an aspect of a more basic problem, namely the sequencing of moves by firms. He contrasted models where firms moved simultaneously, as in the classic Cournot model, with those where incumbent firms moved first. As a further example, he cited the Hotelling problem where equilibrium would be quite different when firms chose price and location simultaneously, than when firms chose location first and price later, once all locations had been decided. In his view, this aspect of modelling monopolistic competition was critical.

The second issue he raised was that of the existence of equilibrium. The non-existence of equilibrium in Hotelling models was interesting in the sense that it indicated the possibility for price wars. The tendency for competitors to move closer together in order to increase market area was offset by the fact that this was more likely to lead to profit-destroying price wars. He criticised models that assumed away mill-price undercutting for eliminating this potential explanation for location.

Partha Dasgupta responded to D'Aspremont's concerns about existence, by noting that the discontinuities which arose in location models could usually be removed by allowing consumers to random-ise certain choices. In regard to the limit theorem issue raised by Kelvin Lancaster, he speculated that along with heterogeniety of preferences, the necessary condition for establishing such a theorem might be that the space of goods be compact. He suggested that compactness of production sets suggested by Lancaster might not be crucial. He also noted that in the Dixit–Stiglitz model, where the limit theorem did not hold, the space of goods was not compact.

Spence suggested that the literature on monopolistic competition consisted of two parts. The first involved the derivation of demand functions for goods from distributions of preferences over character-istics. The second involved welfare analysis with these demand func-tions. He suggested that the payoff from this research was an understanding of the relationship between preferences for character-istics and demand for goods.

Salop suggested that differences between models should show up in the way that they answered the limit-theorem problem. In his paper with Perloff (1982), the limit theorem rose because demand curves hit the axis, as suggested by Lancaster. If demand curves were asympto-tic to the axis, he explained, perfect competition could never be the outcome – since some firm would always have the option of charging a very high price and attracting only a few customers. He contrasted address models with representative consumer models, noting that limit theorems did not arise in neo-Hotelling models because of localised competition. But he pointed out that the Dixit–Stiglitz representative consumer model was a counter-example. If contra-dicted the notion that address models could be classified according to whether or not they yielded a limit theorem.

Shaked referred to work that he was doing with John Sutton (1982). In their model, firms choose qualities from a continuum and compete in prices. Each quality was produced at a different but constant marginal cost. If all consumers agreed about a preference ranking of qualities priced at this marginal cost, then no more than a finite number of products would be produced in equilibrium. This explained the awkward fact of limited product selection referred to by AEL.

Gabszewicz pointed out the existence of an asymmetry in the typical treatment of demanders and suppliers in address models: Suppliers behaved strategically while demanders always behaved competitively. In his view address models should be extended to the labour market or to explain the nature of investment decisions in human capital where both sides of the market might be expected to behave strategically.

Jacquemin suggested that one unexplored issue in address models was the trade-off between the strategic advantage enjoyed by the incumbent and the flexibility enjoyed by the entrant in a world of uncertainty. In other words, what were the relative benefits to each firm in capturing a share of the market?

Gilbert and *Panzar* both noted that firms tended to cluster in product and geographical space. John Panzar added that at the source of this observation was the efficiency of search from product clustering.

Von Ungern-Sternberg asserted that costs of switching brands gave rise to consumer loyalty which should be incorporated into monopolistic competition. *Laffont* expressed surprise at the fact that limit theorems would be of interest in models where existence had not already been demonstrated.

Stiglitz suggested that his joint model with Dixit was consistent with address models provided one interpreted each good as supplying only one characteristic. He added that when the dimension of the characteristic space was much larger than the dimension of the commodity space, continuous demand curves of the sort used in the Dixit–Stiglitz model were a good representation of reality. When the dimension of the space in which a firm could locate was larger than one, each firm had a large number of neighbours. Then, the Chamberlinian view of monopolistic competition was appropriate. But when the characteristic space was one-dimensional, each firm had at most two neighbours, and Nash equilibrium was not a plausible equilibrium concept. Then, the characteristics approach as formulated so far did not provide a good basis for a theory of monopolistic competition.

Stiglitz pointed out the dimension of the product space could also affect the elasticity of the demand curves. As price changed, the behaviour of buyers on the boundary of the market area was affected. Elasticity was roughly a measure of the ratio of the boundary to the volume of the market area and as dimensions changed, this ratio would change as a consequence in a particular way. In turn, this implied that many of the welfare theorems that applied in one-dimensional space did not hold in higher dimensional spaces.

REFERENCES

Dixit, A. and Stiglitz, J. (1977) 'Monopolistic Competition and Optimum Product Diversity', *American Economic Review*, vol. 67, pp. 297–308.

Hart, O. (1979) 'Monopolistic Competition in a Large Economy with Differential Commodities', *Review of Economic Studies*, vol. 46.

Hotelling, H. (1929) 'Stability in Competition', *Economic Journal*, vol. 39, pp. 41–57.

Kaldor, N. (1935) 'Market Imperfection and Excess Capacity', *Economica*, vol. 2, pp. 35–50.

Perloff, J. and Salop, S. (1982) 'Equilibrium with Product Differentiation', Working Paper, no. 179, California Agricultural Experiment Station, University of California at Berkeley.

Shaked A. and Sutton, J. (1982) 'Relaxing Price Competition Through Product Differentiation', *Review of Economic Studies*, vol. 49, no. 1, pp. 3–14.

Spence, A. M. (1976) 'Product Selection, Fixed Costs, and Monopolistic Competition', *Review of Economic Studies*, vol. 43, no. 2, pp. 217–35.

Part Two
Types of Competition
and their Impact

2 Strategic Competition and the Persistence of Dominant Firms: a Survey

David Encaoua

UNIVERSITY OF PARIS, I, FRANCE

Paul Geroski

UNIVERSITY OF SOUTHAMPTON, UK AND
CATHOLIC UNIVERSITY OF LOUVAIN, BELGIUM

Alexis Jacquemin

CATHOLIC UNIVERSITY OF LOUVAIN, BELGIUM

I INTRODUCTION

In the struggle to create, maintain and expand favourable market positions, firms' actions are intended not only to affect the current conduct of rivals directly, but also to have an indirect effect by altering market structure in a way which constrains the rival's subsequent actions. In this dynamic process, market strategies or conduct (the control variables) interact with market structure (the state variable); and current conduct can become embedded in future market structure through strategic investments made by firms to bar entry and reduce intra-industry mobility. (For an analysis of this view of industry dynamics, see Jacquemin, 1972; Caves, 1976, Part I; Caves and Porter, 1977; Spence 1981a, p. 51; and Stiglitz, 1981, p. 187). Of course, not all investments made by firms have the intended effect on market structure, and the purpose of this survey is to consider a recent body of literature which has devoted itself to precisely this point.[1] This work is of interest because of the new light it has shed on the combined structural and strategic origin of market power; that is, on the hoary question of the persistence and profitability of dominant firms (compare Posner, 1972, p. 130 with Williamson, 1975, p. 218 for contributions to this old debate). The literature seems to have coalesced around two basic types of model. By far the most common approach is to assume an initial asymmetry in favour of incumbent firms: this makes them dominant in the sense that it allows them to make commitments prior to entry (that is, it gives them first-mover advantages). A second type of model treats the entrant and the incumbent symmetrically, allowing each the ability to affect the other's strategy. In equilibrium, a dominant firm, in the sense of having gained a first-mover advantage, may or may not emerge as a consequence of some other asymmetries, such as asymmetry in information.

In Section II, we shall make some general reflections on how strategic investments can affect market structure, and on the nature of the entry process. In Section III, we take up the topic of strategic investments made by first movers to exploit their initial advantages. By way of contrast, in Section IV we highlight models in which a more symmetrical view of strategic aspects of entry is taken. Our conclusion, in Section V, is that this literature gives good reasons for thinking that dominant firms will persist.

II   GENERAL REFLECTIONS ON ENTRY

In this section, we wish to make a few remarks on the nature of those strategic investments which can be expected to have an effect on market structure. To do this, we first need to discuss a fairly general representation of the entry problem (Sub-section (A)). Second, we wish to discuss industry dynamics. To make the transition from static entry equilibrium (that is, theory describing the outcome of entry attempts) to industry dynamics, one must discuss the entry process itself (that is, theory describing the generation of entry attempts) as a source of change (Sub-section (B)).

(A)   PRECOMMITMENT, CREDIBILITY AND THE ENTRY PROBLEM

Consider any competitive weapon, X (price, location, capacity, etc.) which an existing firm can use to discourage entrants. The necessity for, and the profit-maximising extent of these expenditures, depend basically upon the exogenous variables determining demand, costs of production, cost of movement, and so on.[2] Since some expenditures on X will be made in the absence of entry, it is conceptually worth separating out that proportion of such expenditures as would be incurred by profit-maximising firms in the absence of entry from that part which is strategically chosen in order to obstruct entrants (this is the basis of the distinction by Salop, 1979, between 'innocent' and 'strategic' entry barriers[3]); the ratio between them depends upon the various exogenous variables in a way that has been familiar since Bain's distinction (1956) between 'blockaded', 'effectively impeded' and 'ineffectively impeded' entry. Thus, whether or not an incumbent has to incur strategic expenditures (and the extent to which he has to do so) depends on the extent of his own scale economies (relative to market size), those enjoyed by the entrant, and so on.

Since we are concentrating on strategic conduct regarding the choice of X, it is natural to think in game-theoretic terms. Let us commence by distinguishing two time periods, pre-entry ($t = 0$) and post-entry ($t = 1$).[4] Let us consider, first, the simplest possible non-co-operative equilibrium of a post-entry game, the Nash equilibrium. A rationale for such an outcome is that the game is played in secret, with no communication between players at $t = 0$; hence there is no possibility of rivals learning of each other's reaction functions and then using such information. When we introduce the possibility of pre-play communication (and allow firms to make pre-commitments, for example) we introduce the possibility that firms can make threats and can incorporate information about rivals' reaction functions into their maximising decisions. The result is that we have two types of (*two*-person) games: (i) those in which there are no advantages from making the first move and assuming the initiative of leadership ('Stackelberg-rational' solvable games); and (ii) those in which there are such advantages ('non-Stackelberg-rational'). A game is said to be Stackelberg rational if no player has an incentive to change his strategy, to commit himself to another, and to let the other player know. This results in each receiving at least as much as could be gained by maximising, subject to the other's reaction function.[5]

Dominance clearly ought not to be equated with first move (some games give follower advantages because the first move expand the choice set of the second), but we shall concentrate here upon non-Stackelberg rational games. Two possible ways of ensuring a final equilibrium in such games are (i) to put some restrictions on pre-play (period $t = 0$) behaviour, for example, by allowing only one player to make pre-play commitments; or (ii) to alter the context of the game, for example by introducing incomplete information. We shall consider these two types of restriction in Sections III and IV below.[6]

It is clear that when we allow pre-play communication, we introduce the possibility of strategic action through pre-commitment, and so must face the problem of distinguishing between empty and non-empty threats.

We begin by noting that a strategic move is '. . . one that influences the other person's choice in a manner favourable to oneself by affecting the other person's expectations of how oneself will behave . . .' (Schelling, 1969, p. 160). In anticipation of Section III, consider a model with an assumed first mover[7] who, at $t = 0$, makes a strategic choice X, recognising the possibility of entry at $t = 1$. (For an equivalent discussion in the absence of a first mover, see note 28.) The choice of X may affect the pre-entry output choice of the existing firms: $Q = Q(X)$; more importantly, it gives rise to an expectation by the entrant of what the post-entry output of the incumbent will be: $\beta = \beta(X)$. The entrant chooses output q to maximise: $\pi_2(\beta(X), q)$; call the solution to that problem $q^* = q(\bar{\beta}(X))$. The value of which the entrant takes to be implied by choice of a particular X is a credible one if it is that $\beta = \beta^*(X)$ which the incumbent would choose given entry; that is, p^* maximises post-entry profits $\pi_1^1(\beta, q(\beta))$ for the existing firm, given X. Hence an investment strategy (with the incumbent acting as a Stackelberg leader) in which the existing firm chooses X so as to maximise the sum of pre- and post-entry profits, $\pi_1^0(Q(X), 0) + \pi_1^1(\beta^*(X), q(\beta^*(X)))$, is one which can be said credibly to pre-empt the entrant if $p(\beta(X), q) \leqslant c(q)/q$ for all q. (Here $p(\cdot\cdot)$ is the post-entry price and $c(\cdot)$ the entrant's cost function.) Such a strategic investment, if executed, becomes embedded in the structure of the industry and so enhances the persistence of dominance. Notice that X is not a threat, and therefore there is no question of it being credible; it is the beliefs of the entrant, $\beta = \beta(X)$, which are (or are not) credible.[8] To say that the investment strategy derived above credibly pre-empts the entrant is simply something about its power *vis-à-vis* sophisticated entrants.

It follows that an investment (X) must be irreversible if it has credibly to pre-empt entry; if it is reversible, then it will not enter as a parameter (or initial condition) in the $t = 1$ maximisation problems: hence, it will not give rise to a credible belief, $\beta = \beta^*(X)$, by the entrant. Of course, irreversibility is not an inherent property of investments, and thus it is not only a matter of degree, but also of rational calculation (by the entrant) given the circumstances. A second relevant characteristic of the capital created by strategic investments is its durability, which determines the time interval within which pre-emption may credibly occur. For example, investment in plant leads to credible pre-emption of entry, depending (among other things) on its industry specificity[9] (that is, the proportion of it which is sunk; see the results of Baumol and Willig, 1981; or Grossman, 1981; and the not unrelated notion of exit barriers in Caves and Porter, 1976). The degree of industry specificity determines the extent to which entrants can reasonably believe that investment is irreversible; and its depreciation determines for how long it can reasonably keep entrants at bay (see Eaton and Lipsey, 1980, 1981).

The question of how pre-commitment gives rise to credible beliefs by the entrant becomes a good deal more tortuous in a world of incomplete information. From an *a priori* point of view, incomplete information could equally affect both the incumbent and the entrant, and both could devise strategies of deception and bluff (see Easterbrook, 1981). Nevertheless, informational asymmetries have usually been linked to presence in the market: the incumbent is viewed as facing less uncertainty about his own costs, since they are actual rather than potential; and, similarly, the incumbent is assumed to know more about market demand characteristics than is the putative entrant.[10] The main implication of incomplete information seems to be that for a belief to be credible, it does not have to correspond to the actual and *ex post* optimal response by the incumbent; it is sufficient that the probability of it proving to be optimal *ex post* is high enough in the eyes of the entrant. Of course, what the entrant thinks likely to occur depends upon what he knows and can infer. Hence, expenditures on X not only give rise to credible beliefs; they may also generate inferences by the entrant which affect his view of what is, in fact, likely to be a credible belief to hold.

Since rationality is a moot point in such contexts, all kinds of apparently 'irrational' behaviour are likely to appear and to affect the nature of entry equilibria. (For a general discussion of this, see Scherer, 1980, p. 246 and Schelling, 1960.) The distinction between substantive and procedural rationality may be useful in this connection. According to Simon (1978), substantive rationality is the extent to which appropriate courses of action are chosen; procedural rationality is for him the effectiveness (in the light of human cognitive powers) of the procedures used to choose actions. Given the complexity of the problems they face and the limitations of decision makers, it might be more appropriate to shift attention away from substantive and towards procedural rationality. In the light of this, it would seem that some types of substantively irrational behaviour might nevertheless characterise otherwise acceptable entry models.

(B)   THE NATURE OF THE ENTRY PROCESS

Entry models are a necessary part of any discussion of the persistence of dominance, for the process which generates trials is the force which potentially generates strategic investment. However, the lacuna in our knowledge concerning what brings an entrant to a market (as opposed to what determines the outcome of any particular trial) is a major obstacle to the development of dynamic models of industrial structure. To understand the entry-generating process, we must first understand how firms are attracted towards industries and the factors which translate general interest into actual entry attempts.

Not unrelated to this is the problem of what type of entrant will appear. There seems to be a general presumption that entry is likely to be attempted by firms established elsewhere rather than by *de novo* firms; and that entry will occur with less delay and inhibition, in the face of given obstacles, by such firms (Hines, 1957; Farrar and Phillips, 1959; Penrose, 1959; Jacquemin, 1967; Caves and Porter, 1977, use this line of observation to broaden the notion of entry barriers into a theory of intra-industry mobility). 'The already established outsiders could command financial strength, managerial experience, and prestige among customers sufficient to prevent old-timers from frightening them away by threats . . . Their history and their diversified operations would attest their power to survive'. Hines, 1957, p. 142). Entry trials involving firms established in related product, geographical or temporal markets then depend on the type of interrelationship between markets (Klevorick and Joskow, 1979; Porter, 1981; Salop, 1981; Spence 1981a). Even the plausibility of non-cooperative behaviour is not clear, as when two firms which are potential entrants into each other's market 'internalise' the mutual threats by merging. About the most that has been achieved in this regard is to try to relate some or all of these points to stages in the industry's life cycle. The argument frequently encountered here is that entry is rather less of a threat to established firms in their mature stages (Kaysen and Turner, 1959, pp. 73–5; Williamson, 1975, ch. 1), and that such stages are those for which the assumption that first-mover advantages exist are reasonable.

What lies behind these considerations is, *inter alia*, the question of what kind of asymmetry one can reasonably postulate between entrant and incumbent. One could argue that to ignore the rich detail of differences between firms and to assume symmetry in all respects (except, perhaps, first movement) is to deal with the general case. (But see Schelling, 1960, Appendix B and, in a related vein, consider the remarks of Eaton and Lipsey, 1981, p. 603, on product-specific capital). The trouble with this view is that it does lead to some rather unpersuasive generalisations. These arise from a confusion of the convenience of assuming symmetry with the likelihood that symmetry actually is a property of real-world entry processes. We are only now beginning to see models in which asymmetry emerges from prior axioms; in what follows, we shall primarily be exploring the consequences of assuming certain types of asymmetry.

III STRATEGIC INVESTMENTS BY FIRST MOVERS

Of the various types of investment that existing firms can make, much of the literature since Bain (1956) has emphasised limit pricing, developing the proposition that potential competition disciplines pricing decisions in the short run. In Section III(A) we reassess this proposition, assuming the existence of a first mover, and argue that the strategic importance of pricing decisions has been overstated in the Bain tradition. This theme re-emerges in Section IV, but, before that we make a slight digression to consider (Section III(B)) some simple entry processes which open up insights on industry dynamics. Such models are a first step in exploring the familiar distinction between 'immediate' and 'general' conditions of entry (Bain, 1956).

(A) STATIC MODELS[11]

The simplest limit-pricing model assumes homogeneous goods and scale economies, considers price alone as a strategic weapon, and invokes the *Sylos Postulate* (the entrant believes that incumbents will maintain the same output after entry) to establish the entrant's conjecture about the post-entry equilibrium. (Modigliani, 1958; Fisher, 1959; Bhagwati, 1970; and Spulber, 1981 are instructive on the Sylos Postulate in different ways). In the Modigliani model, incumbents are constrained in that they must bar entry. Relaxing this (as in Osborne, 1973 and Dixit, 1979) allows existing firms to tolerate entry if that is in their best interests, and this puts a lower bound on the limit price which one is likely to observe (that is, it will pay to deter entry only when scale economies are 'large'). This means that there is an upper bound on expenditures to deter entry. The difficulty here, of course, is that the Sylos Postulate is not a credible belief for large-scale entrants.[12] Substituting a credible post-entry output conjecture by the entrant (based upon knowledge about the existing firm and the rules of the post-entry equilibrium game) does not suppress entry-barring equilibrium. Rather, since the pre-entry strategic choice (price/output) is reversible, it no longer affects the entrant's computations. Hence, the choice of pre-entry price will no longer be fettered by strategic considerations but will be set at monopoly levels. However, price may have some dynamic effects: through leading to habit formation by consumers (Rosenthal, 1982); by signalling information to entrants (Milgrom and Roberts, 1982); by creating reputations (see Section IV below), and so on. (See also Salop, 1981, p. 16 for similar arguments used against the McGee (1958)–Telser (1966) proposition that predatory pricing will be unlikely.) If price does have dynamic effects, then, because phenomena like those listed above create a link between pre-entry prices/outputs and the post-entry choices of incumbents and the putative entrant, a limit-pricing policy can emerge as a credible strategic investment by a first mover.

While one can contrive circumstances in which limit pricing gains a certain credibility, other strategic investments also command interest. To the extent that it is irreversible, capacity choice is subject to strategic considerations[13] (Pyatt, 1971 and Wenders, 1971b). Constrained, unconstrained, and entry decisions with the restriction of credibility have been considered, respectively, by Spence, 1977 and Dixit, 1979 and 1980. (For extensions of the last model, see Schmalensee, 1981; the continuous time models of Spence, 1979, and Fudenberg and Tirole, 1983, can be thought of as loosening the constraints of these two-period models.) Generally speaking (and unless entry is blockaded) the existing firm will choose more capacity than would be the case in the absence of putative entrants; in the latter two cases, this is done to a smaller extent than otherwise because choosing the excessively high level of capacity which is necessary where there are only small economies of scale may be less profitable than allowing entry, and is in any case unlikely to be credible. Credibility also seems to rule out the possibility of observing that there is idle capacity when marginal production costs are independent of capacity when the post-entry concept is that of Nash (Dixit, 1980 and Spulber, 1981), and where capital is infinitely durable (Eaton and Lipsey, 1981).[14]

The list of other weapons which can be used to discourage entrants is fairly lengthy, and we need mention only a few. Advertising[15] is a pre-commitment with, perhaps, rather high 'depreciation' rates. More substantial are location decisions in geographical or product space.[16] Such types of space exaggerate the natural limits on numbers posed by scale economies; moreover, by localising competition, such space may make the prevention of entry less of a collective good. (On the problem this presents, see Wenders, 1971a; Caves and Porter, 1977).[17] So, perhaps, entry is more likely to occur. However, mere presence at a location is only part of the story; the costs of repositioning the firm determine the credibility of the pre-emption. In any case, it is the extent of presence as much as mere presence itself which discourages would-be entrants. Thus the choice of location does not build up strategic capital so much as facilitate the formation and exploitation of such capital. Other possible investments can be aimed at altering cost functions (whether or not scale economies exist). One possibility is investment in learning (Lee, 1975 and Spence, 1981b). By keeping its price low initially, the incumbent can stimulate a rapid expansion of demand for its product, and so move further down its learning curve before rivals begin competing. Investment in style change (Menge, 1962; see also Scherer, 1980, pp. 398–401) raises the fixed component of costs, and investment in higher wages (when small-scale production is relatively labour-intensive (Williamson, 1968)) are also possible. They are substantive and fairly irreversible pre-commitments which could supplement choices on basic capacity, location and other variables by putting entrants at an absolute cost disadvantage. It is worth recognising that a large part of total labour costs may come into this category, because of the quasi-fixed nature of some (or many) labour inputs. These last possibilities suggest a broader class of pre-emptive strategies based on activity in input markets (Salop and Scheffman, 1983); aside from labour markets, capital markets (Caves *et al.*, 1980, Chapter 13) and activities in R & D (Dasgupta and Stiglitz, 1981; Gilbert, 1981; see the general survey by Kamien and Schwartz, 1982) both open up further weapons.[18] For example, an R & D strategy could create entry difficulties if a competitor's costs of product development and production lagged behind those of an early mover; increases in the size of this gap might enable the dominant firm to reduce its R & D expenditures without increasing the risk of entry. Another familiar example is the securing of control over scarce inputs through vertical integration. These are both instances of the well-known argument that vertical-integration strategies may have important horizontal effects (perhaps even when incumbents' costs rise by as much as those of entrants).

An interesting question that emerges from all of this is which of the many potential weapons at their disposal and what combination of them incumbents will use. *A priori*, it is expected that the larger is their strategy space, the stronger is their position. But in the study of what mix of weapons will be chosen, and which interactions exist between them,[19] little progress has been made (for an exception, see Schmalensee, 1978). The literature goes little beyond the not-entirely-persuasive proposition that the most credible investment(s) will be those most relied upon – thus ranking of weapons by probability of choice according to their 'durability' and inter-industry immobility.

A second interesting question is how different exogenously given concepts of post-entry solution affect the analysis. Dixit (1980) is informative on the implications of differing post-entry game rules for the effectiveness of strategic investment in capacity, as is Spulber (1981). Fudenberg and Tirole (1983) consider how Spence's (1979) model of strategic expansion is affected by alternative solution concepts. And, in a not unrelated vein, Geroski (1981a) considers how variations in the post-entry solution concept affect the incidence of entry in a simple model where credible pre-emption of entry is not possible. It is also possible, empirically, to make some inferences about solution concepts so far as price is concerned (for example, Iwata, 1974; Gollop and Roberts, 1979; Bresnahan, 1981b, Geroski, 1981b; Panzar and Rosse, 1981). But it remains to be seen whether this can also be done for choice of capacity, etc.

(B) SIMPLE SEQUENTIAL ENTRY PROCESSES

In this and the following three paragraphs, we propose (by way of a slight digression) to apply the lessons learned with the static model to a few fairly simple entry processes. This provides us with a kind of backdrop to the dynamic analysis necessary for assessing the likelihood that first movers will continue in business.

Consider a process in which one identical entrant per period

($t = 0,..., \infty$) arrives and tries to enter an industry; let t^* be the number of successful trials.[20] Suppose that we are concerned with 'immobile' location choice (each firm is allowed to move only once and to choose only one fixed-size plant); and that there are some scale economies. As long as commitment to a location is permanent, this represents a credible pre-commitment; as before, we allow the first firm correctly to anticipate the post-entry solution which is conditional on its location choice. However, when scale economies are small relative to market size, the second firm to enter will have a chance to make a similar pre-commitment *vis-à-vis* the third, fourth, and so on. Similarly with each new aspirant in turn. It is thus natural to credit all firms with perfect foresight in this context.[21]

Models which consider geographical (Prescott and Visscher, 1977) or product (Lane, 1980) space suggest a not unsurprising result. This is that the extent of the scale economies available determines both t^* and profits at t^*. Further, if the market supports more than two firms, they will be evenly spaced (at about twice the minimum required distance for a single plant). We may compare this to Eaton and Lipsey (1975), who generate a wide range of equilibria with pairs or clusters of firms dispersed throughout space when plants are mobile. These models also provide predictions about how the space will be filled up, and show clearly that location patterns differ as between a 'fixed numbers' ($T < t^*$) model and a model in which trials continue as long as t^*.[22]

The really interesting feature of these models, however, occurs when we remove the artificial restriction that firms are allowed to choose only one plant when they make their moves, or if, instead, we focus on capacity choice. In either event, it is clear that the first firm could always monopolise the market from the outset. To avoid such an embarrassment, one must appeal to multi-plant diseconomies or (rather more plausibly) attribute significant costs to large-scale expansion.[23] Retaining an expansion rate of one plant per period, but now letting existing firms gradually expand by installing one other new plant in each period, reproduces the same tendency for the model to yield highly-concentrated outcomes. For example, if the market could support ten fixed-size plants, then, after four periods, entry will cease; the first mover controls 40 per cent of the market, the second 30 per cent, the third 20 per cent and the marginal firm 10 per cent.

This tendency towards monopolisation is at least partly due to the artificial restrictions on both the timing and the ordering of movements in the entry process being considered. (For an example showing the advantage of being late, see Guasch and Weiss, 1980; such advantages would further complicate the problem of determining the order of entry.) Let us now suppose that the existing firm has the option of setting up a second plant when it wishes and that entrants are free to choose to enter when they wish. Since the latter are all identical, they will all choose to move at the same time (but see the related discussion in Reinganum (1981) who shows that a Nash equilibrium in the adoption dates of a new technology involves diffusion rather than simultaneous adoption). To avoid the problems that this occasions (Sherman and Willett, 1967; Goldberg and Moirao, 1973; Kalish *et al.*, 1978), we take the case of only one entrant. Suppose that one firm already operates in the market, and that some factor, such as market growth, makes feasible the existence of a second firm. (For a race when the entrant is also free to start at $t = 0$, see Rao and Rutenberg, 1979.) Eaton and Lipsey (1979) suggest that, in this case, the monopolist will move first and pre-empt a move by the entrant, because differential risk arising from the possibility that post-entry price competition will operate unequally between entrant and incumbent. That is, there is always a strong presumption of pre-emption by a first mover, because any possibility of less-than-perfect post-entry collusion makes the move less profitable for the entrant than for the incumbent, who would be free to set monopoly prices if he made a pre-emptive move.[24] This lack of collusion would be a strong incentive for merger if it happened that the entrant did enter, although, obviously, subsequent entrants would be less likely to be deterred if such a merger occurred. Notice that whilst there are many similarities between entry barriers and mobility barriers, this argument about differential risk is not as persuasive in the context of intra-industry mobility as it is in the case of entry.

A rather different race occurs when we consider renewing less than infinitely durable commitments, and when we allow firms to choose when to renew plant, and how durable to make it. Eaton and Lipsey (1980) have offered their model III (1981) in which the existing firm faces the possibility of predatory entry, that is, that entrants may displace it in a market which can support only one firm. (For an interesting study of cycles in the balance of power between host nations and foreign firms determined by just this type of consideration, see Moran, 1974.) The wrinkle here is that, unlike a situation with exogenous market growth, the time when the entrant would like to enter is at least partly determined by actions of the existing firm.

The presumption remains, nevertheless, that (however it is done) the existing firm will pre-empt the rival simply because the expected loss in profit it faces is larger than the gain to the entrant in the absence of perfect post-entry collusion.

These two kinds of model suggest a basic distinction to be made between entry processes. In the one attempt at entry per period model (or the *exogenous* market-growth model), entrants appear exogenously; the actions of existing firms determine the outcome of the attempt at entry but not the likelihood of occurrence of that attempt. Alternatively, the entry process can be considered *endogenous* when the number of entry attempts (either more attempts per period or an increasing frequency of attempts) depends on the action of incumbent firms, whether that action be renewal of durable capital or any other move. In this second sort of model, then, choices are made about strategic variables (X). These determine not only the initial conditions of the post-entry game (that is, the likelihood of successful entry given that an attempt at entry will occur); they also determine the likelihood that the game will be played at all. It seems at least conceivable that the strong tendency towards monopolisation (evident in previous models) may be weakened when entry is made endogenous.

At this stage, it is worthwhile recalling the classical model of Gaskins (1971) which lies squarely in this second tradition. In that model, the rate of entry (that is, the rate of successful attempts to enter) is proportional to the difference between the current price of the dominant firm and the limit price (determined by entrants' costs). The optimal price is such that, in the absence of absolute cost advantages, the output of the competitive fringe will asymptotically approach the output of the total industry.[25] All these optimal control models work easily because of the simple conjectures which the small-scale entrants are assumed to hold (that is, they take existing market data as given). In a sense, the occurrence and the outcome of each attempt to enter is blurred by the small-scale nature of the entrant. When entrants try to enter at a larger scale, however, it is worth considering the entry process as consisting of at least two phases: the generation of players which takes place through agents scattered throughout the economy picking up signals pointing to attractive opportunities for investment; and the generation of outcomes by those players who elect to attempt entry plus incumbents. An intermediate phase is the transformation of some or all players into those willing to attempt entry. It is clear that rational players contemplating possible outcomes before deciding whether to attempt entry will not decided whether or not to enter by pre-entry prices; they will require much more substantial pre-commitment before being deterred. But such rationality depends both on a substantial investment in information about the market by the would-be entrant and on the type of entrant. Price (or profitability) is clearly precisely the kind of signal which may convert a foot-loose agent into a player willing to invest in information. That may be true even if price is not the signal converting such a player into an entrant (Geroski and Jacquemin, 1984).[26]

Let us illustrate this endogenous process, using a sketch of a model in which price can be made to re-emerge as a strategic weapon. From what has been said above, we clearly need some restrictions on movement by the incumbent firm, and we shall suppose that these are limitations required by the need to finance investment.[27] Against his evident and perfectly sensible desire completely to pre-empt the market, the incumbent firm now faces the constraint that his ability to do so (setting high prices, making large profits and so financing high investment rates) is the engine which makes the race all the more intense. By attracting more and more players at exactly the time when he is most vulnerable (having not yet made a pre-emptive move, the incumbent firm risks generating the entry that his actions are designed to discourage. In this model of limited first-mover advantages, price re-emerges as a strategic weapon. It does so because of its role in attracting players (and thus attempts at entry) as well as because of its role in generating the finance needed to make possible the sort of strategic investment and the kind of pre-emptive move which turns such attempt to enter against these entrants. It directly affects the likelihood of trials and indirectly affects their outcomes.

(C) A SUMMING UP

It is now time to sum up what we have said on first movers. First, from the discussion in Section III(A) it would seem that price is unlikely to be used as a strategic weapon, and only when consumer habits, uncertainty or financing needs are important. As a rule of thumb, it would seem that one can thus look to the forces of actual competition as those which primarily determine price. Second, from Section III(B), it seems that, given the existence of a first mover, a wide strategy space including capacity expansion, spatial pre-emption and so on, can (at a cost) convert first movement into monopolisation and can do so fairly easily, even when scale economies are unimportant. The entrenchment of large, dominant firms which stubbornly persist is the likely outcome, it seems, of unbridled strategic competition when there are first movers. This second observation also points up the importance of history in explaining market structure. Finally, it suggests that an interesting question is not so much how a first mover can take advantage of his situation, as why he does not appear always to do so fully in practice. We have suggested that, in addition to phenomena like multi-plant diseconomies or capacity expansion costs, the limitations may lie in the possibility that the sheer act of running as fast as he can will attract the attention of others which weakens his persistent hold in the market.

IV STRATEGIC SYMMETRY IN PRE-ENTRY PLAY

In Section III we have discussed at length entry deterrence and the persistence of positions of market power cases where there is an exogeneously-given first mover. It is now time to relax this assumption. The interesting question then is whether or not the conclusions derived from this assumption in Section III will survive.

Consider, first, the following stylised example involving two players: the second firm must decide whether or not to enter, while the first must choose either to fight or to share the market with the entrant. In extensive form, the pay-off matrix is in Figure 2.1 and we assume that: (i) $\pi_1^M > \pi_1^S > \pi_1^P$, and (ii) $\pi_2^S > \pi_2^0 > \pi_2^P$. (i) reflects the assumption that predation is costly for the predator, and (ii) ensures that the entrant would rather stay out than be preyed upon if he enters. Without communication, the Nash equilibrium is (π_1^S, π_2^S). Allowing for communication and giving both firms the option of making pre-play moves gives relevance to the distinction between Stackelberg and non-Stackelberg rational games. The stability of the

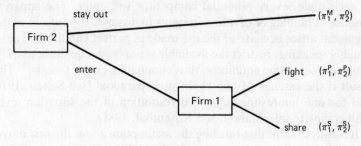

FIG. 2.1

Nash equilibrium is also altered (see Aumann, 1974; d'Aspremont and Gérard-Varet, 1980; and Moulin, 1981). The point is that when players do not move secretly, they can make agreements which, even if not binding, may be enforced by bilateral threats. The next step is to ask whether such threats are credible in this game and the answer is no; that is, the game is not Stackelberg rational and competition for the first move arises.[28] For example; the threat to fight by Firm 1 is not credible because this is not its optimal response to the fact of entry and, moreover, this is known by the entrant. Sharing is the optimal response ($\pi_1^s > \pi_1^p$) as in Nash equilibrium without pre-play communication. Consequently, entry will occur.[29]

Suppose we now imagine that this game is played a finite number of times by the incumbent against different potential entrants. We do this in a manner similar to the sequential entry process discussed in Section III(B) above. We allow all information about past moves to be known, at each stage, by all the players. The problem is to see whether past behaviour may affect current behaviour, and whether this provides conditions for entry deterrence. The same problem emerges in a super-game context where the stage game is repeated infinitely (see Rubenstein, 1979).

Somewhat surprisingly, even in the context of this game, predatory strategies will not be adopted by the incumbent (Selten, 1978). The solution proceeds by backward induction, as with the sequential entry process in Section III. In the last stage, the incumbent will not adopt the predatory strategy because to do so is not in his short-run interest ($\pi_1^p < \pi_1^s$) and because adopting the strategy has no effects on future entry, since there are no more entrants. Given this, the incumbent has no incentive to deter entry in the last stage but one. Given that he has perfect information, the entrant has no reason to expect predatory behaviour at this stage. Thus, by continued backward induction, it emerges that predation will never occur and that, at each stage, every potential competitor will enter. The apparent absence of bluffing or of other attempts to dissuade the entrant in this argument arises because of the use made of perfect equilibria. These, roughly speaking, restrict the available set of Nash equilibria to those which are sub-game equilibria, thus eliminating empty threats.[30] This result is the essence of 'the chain-store paradox' (see Selten, 1978; and for one interesting suggested resolution of the situation, even with complete information, see Rosenthal, 1981).

It is thus evident that relaxing the assumption about the first mover and allowing pre-entry symmetry in the ability of both firms to make threats and to establish pre-commitments makes it hard to see the basis for the conclusions derived in Section III. Such results can re-emerge, however, when we alter the context of the game.

An obvious (and not very interesting) alternative environment is that of an infinite-horizon version of the model just discussed. In this case, there exists an equilibrium in which any attempted entry is met by predation. Unfortunately, there are indeed many equilibria of such a game. (See Dixit, 1982, for an elementary demonstration; and Friedman, 1977 on infinitely repeated prisoners' – dilemma games.) To see this, consider the moves of the two players at some stage (n) in equilibrium. For the incumbent: (i) if there has been no entry before stage (n), or if the incumbent has fought previous entrants, then it should continue to fight at stage (n); (ii) if it has accommodated previous entrants, then it should continue to share at stage (n). For the entrant: (i) if there has been no entry before (n) (or if previous entry attempts have not been accommodated) then it should stay out; (ii) if previous entrants have been accommodated, then it should enter. Clearly, two completely different sequential equilibrium outcomes occur: always fighting, with no entry; or accommodation and entry by all potential competitors.

Returning to finite-stage games, a more promising possibility is to relax the property of common knowledge which has, until now, characterised the game. This common knowledge lies in the fact that each player knows that the other player knows that co-operation is the best response to entry and that entry is the best response to co-operation.[31] It turns out that lack of common knowledge can be sufficient to generate predatory strategies in equilibrium. The basic idea is that no entrant knows whether a profitable commitment to the market exists, because it cannot distinguish 'innocent' from 'strategic' situations. As a simple illustration of this argument, consider a three-state world and a two-stage game (a monopolist confronted by two potential entrants, one entering after the other). In one state of the world, the game is played at each stage in such a manner that entry automatically results in predatory responses by the incumbent; in the other two states, the game is the same as in the first part of Section IV. Let the three states of the world be equally likely but not experienced. Suppose also that the information sets of the players are such that, in the latter two states of the world, the incumbent's aversion to predation is not obvious to the entrants. Then, a sequential equilibrium can involve a strategy of predation. This is because the entrant can no longer clearly distinguish the three states of the world and, in particular, cannot infer them from the actions of the incumbent.

This basic notion underlies the rather different models of Milgrom and Roberts (1982a; see also their 1982b paper) and Kreps and Wilson (1980; see also Kreps *et al.*, 1981 for an application of these ideas to the prisoners'-dilemma game). Let us suppose that the incumbent has perfect information, while the entrants are not so informed.[31] Let us also believe that the incumbent is either in a 'strong' or 'weak' position (this is one of the two cases analysed by Kreps and Wilson). The first entrant in the (finite) sequence has some subjective probability that each possible state applies to the incumbent; and each subsequent entrant has full knowledge of all that occurred in previous stages of the game. What turns out to be essential is that there must exist a non-null probability that the incumbent's pay-offs will be higher if it fights entry than if it accepts entry without fighting. Hence, it is no longer clear to the entrant whether a state of the world in which the incumbent is 'strong' has occurred or whether predation is occurring even though the monopolist is 'weak'. The equilibrium leads to fighting at early stages of the game and the creation of a reputation effect.[33] A rather different type of departure from common knowledge is introduced by Milgrom and Roberts. Here, fighting always gives a smaller pay-off than does sharing, but now there is always some doubt in the minds of the entrants about the characteristics of the incumbent firm. This is represented by the belief (by entrants) at each stage that some simple behavioural rule guides the incumbent's behaviour; all the rules are given a non-null probability of realisation. The point now is that the possibilities expected by an entrant at stage (n) include both predatory and co-operative responses. Consequently, once again, the actions of the incumbent do not permit precise inferences about unknown parameters. When the number of stages is fairly large, predation will occur in early stages, since failure to do so would encourage entry; while preying keeps alive the possibility that future entrants will meet a similar response.

It is thus clear that reputation effects can arise from the lack of common knowledge inherent in each situation, with the corresponding uncertainty giving some rationality to predatory practices. In particular, in the context of a repeated-play game with incomplete information, the threat of predation is credible, even if it is not the *ex post* optimal response. A not dissimilar result can also emerge when it is not a reputation for toughness that matters but a reputation for weakness – that is, where the incumbent tries to persuade the entrant that the market is inherently unprofitable. Easley *et al.* (1981) show that, even when all parties have rational expectations but where all have incomplete information, a multi-market incumbent facing entrants who are not sure which markets are inherently unprofitable can deter entry.[34]

We started Section IV by showing that, when we relax the first-mover assumption of Section III but retain assumptions about perfect information, we lose a rational basis for deterrence strategies. Nevertheless, we wind up with fairly similar looking results when we relax the perfect information assumption. It is important to recognise that the reputation established by an incumbent firm, in these models, is not the result of allowing an incumbent to make a choice first. It is a natural feature of the solution of a non-Stackelberg rational game, in which it matters who has the first move. So it is a consequence of the analysis (and, in particular, of assumptions about information symmetries) rather than an initial assumption: a functional relationship between the actions of the established firms and those of the entrant emerges endogenously from the equilibrium. It is clear that the rigid exogenous sequencing of these multi-stage games must be relaxed (along the lines of Section III(B)). In addition, the arbitrary imposition of the assumption of incomplete information must be justified before one can completely accept the claim that these models provide a persuasive rationale for predation, unless the first movement is assumed.[35] Such modifications should also continue to soften the unacceptably ahistorical tone of many of these models. Without such extensions, the choice between the two approaches – assuming that there is a first mover or allowing strategic symmetry under conditions of imperfect information – can be made only on empirical grounds; for both contain different, but ultimately no less-arbitrary, bases.

V CONCLUSIONS

We have surveyed here what might be thought of as dynamic extensions to the familiar, static structure-conduct-peformance paradigm. We have done so in the sense that we have allowed conduct to become embedded in subsequent market structure. This occurs as firms make strategic investments in order to retard or deter entry. The main conclusion to be drawn from this discussion is that strategic investment, using non-price variables, is likely to be used to provide the necessary pre-commitments to deter entry. When there is strategic symmetry, but a lack of common knowledge, then price may be used strategically; but it is possible that other weapons will dominate, even in such situations. A second conclusion is that when first-mover advantages are present, strong tendencies towards dominance based on strategic pre-emption exist. In a nutshell, much support can be found in this literature for the notion that dominant firms can profitably continue in existence – which is, in fact, what they appear to do. (See Shepherd, 1975; Mueller, 1977; and Scherer, 1980, for a discussion of the evidence.)

The interesting question that remains concerns the normative implications of this analysis. A full discussion is beyond the scope of this survey, but it is worth closing with a few remarks on some recent arguments which suggest that observed market structures constitute reasonable approximations to efficient structures. One argument is that if entry is free, exist is costless and, more generally, if markets are contestable, then no strategic weapon could enable a dominant firm to avoid marginal cost pricing. All the things required for a first-best optimum would be present (Baumol *et al.*, 1982; Baumol, 1982). A second, alternate, argument is that, in a less-than-perfect world, what is called an entry barrier may actually reflect consumers' interests, when broadly considered (Demsetz, 1982; see also von Weiszäcker, 1981, for a less extreme view). Rather than allowing resources to move into high-profit industries, it might be better from the point of view of consumer welfare more generally to take into account the role of externalities, information and transaction costs. One could then consider entry barriers to be a valuable second-best answer to real world frictions:[36]

> existing firms have an advantage insofar as their existence commands loyalty . . . (that is) it reflects lower real costs of transacting, industry specific investments, or a reputable history as, in general, it will . . . A reputable history is an asset to the firm possessing it because information is not free. (Demsetz, 1982, pp. 50–1).

However, entry may not be free (for example, most fixed costs may be sunk, all firms may not be identical, and so on) and a large part of the costs of entry may result from the deliberate creation of asymmetries by existing firms: then one cannot accept such a sanguine view that 'what is, is reasonably efficient'. If, in addition, the costs of monopoly are high (as argued, for example, by Cowling and Mueller, 1978) then one is entitled to view strategic conduct as, at best, a mixed blessing. There are examples of reasonably constestable markets and also cases where entry costs are innocently created. Moreover, the use of some strategic weapons does have ambiguous effects on welfare. But it seems to us[37] that there are no strong normative conclusions in this literature to calm the apprehensions of those who have never been persuaded that the unregulated activity of the large, dominant firms which characterise many modern markets has benign effects on welfare.

NOTES

1. The attention focused on conduct (a reaction to the structuralist school of Bain, 1945) is a hallmark of the 'New Industrial Organisation' (for example, Schmalensee, 1980) and is the common feature of most of the papers to be considered here. It is, of course, a return to earlier methodologies, albeit with more analytic rigour. This same kind of shift of attention has seen a move from inter-industry to intra-industry empirical work; for example, compare the work surveyed in Weiss (1974) with the intra-industry structure-performance work of Gale (1972), Shepherd (1972), Newman (1978), Porter (1980) and those surveyed in Geroski (1981b). Cowling (1976) discusses some of the virtues of intra-industry work relative to inter-industry work.

2. These exogenous variables are not necessarily to be regarded as barriers *per se*, for as was stressed by Caves and Porter (1977), entry barriers are '. . . partly structural but at least partly endogenous' (p. 241). For various definitions of entry barriers, see Bain (1956), Stigler (1968), von Weiszäcker (1981) and Baumol and Willig (1981). Some of this discussion is purely terminological, arising from the alleged pejorative implications of the term 'entry barriers'; in addition to all other papers for which references are given below, see Yamey (1972) and Hay (1981, pp. 162–4). Hay argues that predation can have an undesirable effect, even when the victim is inefficient.

3. The first situation would correspond to the case of an incumbent being superior (because of its technological efficiency and so on) and able to deter entry as a by-product of simple profit maximisation; i.e. deterrence depends only on the exogenous elements of cost and demand.

   The second situation occurs when an incumbent is equally (or less) efficient but enjoys an advantage because of its early committed resources. To a certain extent, however, the distinction is artificial; for example, scale economies may be strategically manipulated by research to perfect larger-scale facilities (Porter, 1981, p. 145) and some investments in advertising and promotion are not strategic, but are an innocent response to the existence of information costs. For a methodological start to untangling these two components, see Salop and Shapiro (1980).

4. Limit pricing is strategic behaviour occurring in period $t = 0$ to affect the $t = 1$, post-entry outcome. Predatory pricing is post-entry behaviour ($t = 1$), which may be threatened in $t = 0$ and whose strategic effects

apply also to later entrants. Much of what follows can be applied (with some modification) to both types of competitive practice.

5. For a formal definition, see Moulin (1981) and Section IV.

6. An equivalent distinction is between situations in which the rules of the post-entry game are exogenous or endogenous (respectively). When we allow the first player only to make a commitment (as in Section III), then it is to his advantage to adopt a Stackelberg strategy; if not, then it is in his interest to adopt another view (such as is described in Section IV).

7. That is, a firm which has actually moved first rather than a firm which rivals know will move faster. Asymmetries in speed of movement open up the possibility that strategic investments do not actually have to be executed to be effective: rivals merely have to accept that they will lose any race they care to initiate because it will be in the interest of faster rivals to block them once they begin it.

8. The common practice of thinking of the beliefs $\beta = \beta(X)$ as threats (and $\beta = \beta^*(X)$ as 'credible' threats) is no more accurate than thinking of the commitment X as a threat. A commitment fixes one's course of action and a threat fixes a course of reaction to the other player: '. . . the commitment is a means of gaining the first move in a game in which the first move carries an advantage; the threat is a commitment to a strategy for the second move . . . it is a credible reclamation of a conditional choice for second move' (Schelling, 1960, p. 124).

9. Product- or firm-specific capital is relevant for a discussion of mobility rather than of entry barriers. Firm-specificity exists if there is no alternative use for such capital which would increase the value of the firm controlling it.

10. In conventional dominant-firm (or Stackelberg) models (Worcester, 1957; Saving, 1970; Gaskins, 1971), the dominant firm knows the fringe's reaction function, but not vice versa. This asymmetry in information is not a necessary consequence of assuming that a first mover has an advantage; indeed, it is not clear at all. (But, see Section IV.) Spence (1959) is an example of how earlier (or faster) movement affects the outcome of an exogenous, post-entry game in a way which makes it look as if informational asymmetries have been introduced.

11. We restrict attention here to private firms. Harris (1978) and Harris and Wiens (1980) discuss the case of public ownership. They suggest that a public firm having a first-mover advantage could announce a reaction function and make this credible to private entrants in a way that privately-owned first movers could not.

12. For a game-theoretic treatment of this point, see Friedman (1979) who shows that limit pricing does not give a Nash equilibrium. Strictly speaking, whether a quantity-taking conjecture is a consistent or credible belief (e.g. Bresnahan, 1981a; Ulph, 1983) depends on the slope of rivals' marginal cost curves and also on demand. (For some interesting interpretations of conjectural variations, see Boyer, 1981; and Grossman, 1981.) However, very small entrants may (not unreasonably) take the incumbent's output (or price) as fixed. (For a defence of the virtues

of entering on a small scale to avoid predation, see Gelman and Salop, 1983.) Also note that the large-scale entry case (in which quantity-taking conjectures are unlikely to be reasonable) may not be empirically important (Bain, 1956; Scherer, 1980, ch. 4; Schmalensee, 1981).

13. Smith (1981) points out that these commitments may help to co-ordinate an industry's responses to altered conditions, a problem likely to be found in moderately concentrated industries (Esposito and Esposito, 1974; Caves *et al.*, 1979). Such commitments may also facilitate collusion among existing firms, and this can conflict with their strategic use against entrants (Spence, 1977, p. 537).

14. If we allow market uncertainty to come into the model, the argument becomes considerably more complex. For example, the excess capacity which a firm may maintain in order to meet demand fluctuations may also (innocently) help to deter entry. There may also be a conflict where durability is required both for making credible commitments and for dealing with uncertainty.

15. For recent discussions on advertising and entry, see Comanor and Wilson (1979); Schmalensee (1980); Cubbin (1981); Spence (1980) and Williamson (1963) are interesting on the interaction between advertising and scale economies.

16. For example, Eaton and Lipsey (1978); Schmalensee (1978); Salop (1979). The latter (pp. 464–6) present an interesting discussion of the reasonableness of entrants' conjectures that existing firms are immobile. Lancaster (1979, pp. 59–61) is informative on the differences in the two types of space. For a geographical model with uncertainty, see Jovanovic (1981).

17. If the established firms act non-co-operatively in the face of entry, it is possible that entry would be less likely than if they co-operated.

18. For not unrelated problems which firms producing durable goods face in second-hand markets for their goods, see Bulow (1982) and references therein; Schmalensee (1979) is a good survey on quality choice restricted to this single dimension.

19. As an example of interaction, when an expansion of capacity reduces marginal costs, the pre-entry marginal costs in monopoly (and so price) are lower if threatened entry leads to pre-emptive capacity expansion than if no putative entrants loom on the horizon. See Spence (1977, Section 3).

20. For a dynamic model of a situation commencing with a steady stream of new ideas – pertinent to product improvement – which are then developed by firms, see Dasgupta and Stiglitz (1981).

21. This leads to solution through backward induction (see Cyert and de Groot, 1970, in a related context). The post-entry solution concept is usually taken to be Nash, but it is in some ways difficult to imagine firms with the foresight to anticipate the behaviour of models contenting themselves with altering only the initial conditions of the post-entry game and not its rules (e.g. becoming co-operative with some or all entrants). A difficulty with empirical application of these models is that, in the circumstances posited, it is not easy to see how an early-entrant firm which

makes an irrevocable mistake would eventually be eliminated, so as to ensure that the equilibrium pattern was robust to miscalculations by firms.

22. Hay (1976, pp. 247–51) considers location in a growing market in which firms must trade off short- and long-run profits by locating closer (or further away) from existing rivals. If all firms have the same discount rate, then presumably even spacing will still occur.

23. This is clearly recognised by Prescott and Visscher (1977, Section 3). For empirical evidence on multi-plant diseconomies, see Scherer *et al.* (1975). It is important not to confuse such expansion costs with the fact that large firms beyond a minimal optimal size do not seem to suffer great cost disadvantage because of decentralisation within the firm (Chandler, 1977; Williamson, 1970, 1975; Marris and Mueller, 1980). Penrose (1959) is the classic source on growth constraints; see Spence (1979) for a model which makes plain their role in avoiding monopoly outcomes. Jovanovic (1981) suggests that when firms have private information which is only revealed in their actual location choices, then an inter-temporal trade-off (acting sooner on the basis of less information) exists which may retard initial moves to monopolise and may help to explain the actual sequence of entry. This model, it should be noted, is in the spirit of those discussed in Section IV in not assuming a first mover but in assuming incomplete information.

24. See also Schmalensee (1978, pp. 316–8) and Gilbert (1981, p. 22) for similar remarks. Eaton and Lipsey (1979) allow the existing firm also to relocate (which gives an added incentive to pre-empt). Schmalensee (1978, pp. 316–8) adds multi-plant economies to the list of inducements, but in the question of natural ready-to-eat cereals, he found that shifts in consumer tastes which opened up this new segment of the market were not well anticipated by existing firms. The oft-alleged sleepiness of dominant firms may be as important a limitation to the formation of monopoly as may multi-plant diseconomies!

25. Extensions to the model include: Ireland (1972) on growing markets; Kamien and Schwartz (1971), Baron (1973), De Bondt (1976), Lippman (1980) on uncertainty, entry lags, etc.; Jacquemin (1972), Jacquemin and Thisse (1972), Encaoua and Jacquemin (1980) on non-price competition; Kamien and Schwartz (1972) on capital stock; Lee (1975) on learning; and Encaoua *et al.* (1981) who consider switches between régimes with dominant price leadership and with monopolistic competition.

26. Obviously, the use of other strategic weapons (hurried capacity expansion or rapid brand proliferation, etc.) may attract attention and so increase the frequency of entry attempts, but we concentrate on price to economise on space. There is, in any case, some dispute over whether price or profits ought to be the signal (Baron, 1972; Caves and Porter, 1977, p. 243).

27. For the literature of finance and capacity expansion, see Nickell (1978) and the note by von Ungern-Sternberg (1980). In view of the possibility that such strategic brinkmanship may lead to bankruptcy, further actors (like bankers) may be involved in strategic decisions; the bankruptcy model of Bulow and Shoven (1978) is suggestive in this context, as are some of the remarks in Shepherd (1976).

28. Let $\Gamma = \{X, Y, f, g\}$ be a two-person normal game form with X and Y the sets of strategies and f and g the pay-off functions. A *deterrence scheme* is a pair of strategies (x, y) and response functions (α, β) which satisfy: (i) $\alpha(y) = x$, $\beta(x) = y$; (ii) $\forall x' \in X$, $f(x', \beta(x')) \leqslant f(x, y)$ and $\forall y' \in Y$, $g(\alpha(y'), y') \leqslant g(x, y)$. Denoting best replies by $B_X(\cdot)$, $B_Y(\cdot)$, a deterrence scheme is *credible* if: (i) $\forall x' \in X$, $\beta(x') \in B_Y(x')$; and (ii) $\forall y' \in Y$, $\alpha(y'), \in B_X(y')$; this is the same definition as in Schelling (1960). An outcome (x, y) is *Stackelberg rational* if: (i) $\forall x' \in X$, $\exists y' \in B_Y(x')$ such that $f(x', y') \leqslant f(x, y)$; and (ii) $\forall y' \in Y$, $\exists x'$ c $B_X(y')$ such that $g(x', y') \leqslant g(x, y)$, where $(x, y) \in X \times Y$. The pay-offs are: $S_X = \max_{x' \in X} \min_{y' \in B_Y(x')} f(x', y')$ and similarly for S_Y. Finally, a game is Stackelberg rational (see also d'Aspremont and Gérard-Varet, 1980) if S_x and S_y are compatible; i.e. if there exist $(x, y) \in X \times Y$ such that: $S_X \leqslant f(x, y)$ and $S_Y \leqslant g(x, y)$. The assertion of the text follows from the following result (see Moulin, 1981, for a proof): the class of two-person normal form games for which there is no outcome which may be guaranteed by a credible deterrence scheme is the same as the class of games which are not Stackelberg rational.

29. Using the definitions in note 28, the pay-offs corresponding to a Stackelberg rational outcome are: $S_X = \pi_1^M$ and $S_Y = \pi_2^S$. They are not, however, compatible; i.e. there does not exist a pair of strategies $(x, y) \in X \times Y$ such that: $f(x, y) \geqslant \pi_1^M$ and $g(x, y) \geqslant \pi_2^S$.

30. The Nash equilibrium concept is appropriate only in static games – taking one's competitor's strategies as given is reasonable only when such strategies concern current moves. Perfect equilibria (Selten, 1973; 1975) are more acceptable for dealing with multi-stage strategies. A proper sub-game of a game in extensive form is a game beginning at some node (there are two in Figure 2.1) and involving all its successors; a set of strategies is a perfect equilibrium if the strategies yield a Nash equilibrium for every proper sub-game. (For a definition in terms of normal-form games, see Myerson, 1978; see also the related concept of sequential equilibria, Kreps and Wilson, 1982.)

31. The definition of common knowledge has been formalised by Aumann (1976) and has been given an axiomatic characterisation by Milgrom (1981a) who writes (p. 219): '...intuitively, an event A is common knowledge among a group of agents if each agent knows A, each knows that all know A, each knows that all know that all know A, . . ., etc. In this case, the 'etc.' encompasses an infinite sequence of conditions each more stringent than the one before.'

32. The obvious cause of this ignorance is their position as outsiders. The other possibility – that such ignorance can be strategically-created by the incumbent – can only occur if we allow for first-movement.

33. If the same firm attempts entry repeatedly, it may also have the opportunity to build a reputation. Alternatively, if the entrant is a large, established firm (see Section II(B) above) then it may bring a reputation into the game.

34. On games of persuasion, see Milgrom (1981b). Rosenthal (1981), in the same decision-analysis, rather than game-theoretic, framework as was used by Easley *et al.* (1981) shows that predatory strategies may occur when potential competitors have *ad hoc* expectations expressed by

assigning, at every move, subjective probabilities to every subsequent choice.

35. A further question is whether the non-co-operative framework is the best one to adopt for treating all entry problems. In virtually all the models using sequential entry processes, the possibility of co-operation – with an entrant arriving at time (*t*) to fight all subsequent entrants – is either ruled out or neglected.

36. Compare this with Stiglitz (1981), who argues that in precisely this case – where markets are incomplete, information is costly and R & D expenditures are important – increases in competition may have adverse effects on welfare.

37. For a rejection of '*per se*' rules one way or the other and for arguments in favour of a cautious case-by-case approach, see Spence (1981a). Certainly, a case-by-case approach has at least the virtue of generating the precise empirical knowledge which will ultimately prove decisive in this matter.

REFERENCES

Aumann, R. (1974) 'Subjectivity and Correlation in Randomized Strategies', *Journal of Mathematical Economics*, vol. 1, pp. 67–96.

Aumann, R. (1976) 'Agreeing to Disagree', *Annals of Statistics*, vol. 4, pp. 1236–9.

Bain, J. (1956) *Barriers to New Competition* (Cambridge, Mass.: Harvard University Press).

Bain, J. (1959) *Industrial Organization* (New York: Wiley).

Baron, D. (1972) 'Limit Pricing and Models of Potential Entry', *Western Economic Journal*, vol. 10, pp. 298–307.

Baron, D. (1973) 'Limit Pricing, Potential Entry and Barriers to Entry', *American Economic Review*, vol. 63, pp. 666–74.

Baumol, W. (1982) 'Contestable Markets: an Uprising in the Theory of Industry Structure', *American Economic Review*, vol. 72, pp. 1–15.

Baumol, W. and Willig, R. (1981) 'Fixed Costs, Sunk Costs, Entry Barriers, Public Goods and the Sustainability of Monopoly', *Quarterly Journal of Economics*, p. 96.

Baumol, W., Panzar, J. and Willig, R. (1982) *Contestable Markets and the Theory of Industry Structure* (San Diego: Harcourt, Brace and Jovanovich).

Bhagwati, J. (1970) 'Oligopoly Theory, Entry Prevention and Growth', *Oxford Economic Papers*, vol. 22, pp. 297–310.

Boyer, M. (1981), 'Strategic Equilibrium with Reaction Threats', Mimeo, CORE, Université Catholique de Louvain.

Bresnahan, T. (1981a) 'Duopoly Models with Consistent Conjectures,' *American Economic Review*, vol. 71, pp. 934–46.

Bresnahan, T. (1981b) 'Departures from Marginal Cost Pricing in the American Automobile Industry', *Journal of Econometrics*, vol. 17, pp. 201–27.

Bulow, J. and Shoven, J. (1978) 'The Bankruptcy Decision', *Bell Journal of Economics*, vol. 9, pp. 437–56.

Bulow, J. (1982) 'Durable Goods Monopolies', *Journal of Political Economy*, vol. 90, pp. 314–32.

Caves, R. (1976) 'The Determinants of Market Structure: Design for Research, in Jacquemin, A. and de Jong, H. (eds) *Markets, Corporate Behaviour and the State* (The Hague: M. Nijhoff) pp. 3–18.

Caves, R. and Porter, M. (1976) 'Barriers to Exit', in Masson, R. T. and Qualls, P. D. (eds), *Essays on Industrial Organization in Honor of Joe S. Bain* (Cambridge: Ballinger).

Caves, R. and Porter, M. (1977) 'Entry Barriers to Mobility Barriers Conjectural Decisions and Contrived Deterrence to New Competition', *Quarterly Journal of Economics*, vol. 91, pp. 241–61.

Caves, R., Jarrett, J. and Loucks, M. (1979), 'Competitive Conditions and the Firm's Buffer Stocks: an Explanatory Analysis, *Review of Economics and Statistics*, vol. 61, pp. 485–96.

Caves, R., Porter, M. and Spence, M. (1980) *Competition in the Open Economy*. (Cambridge, Mass.: Harvard University Press.)

Chandler, A. (1977), *The Visible Hand: the Managerial Revolution in American Business*. (Cambridge, Mass.: Harvard University Press).

Comanor, W. and Wilson, T. (1979) 'The Effect of Advertising on Competition: a Survey', *Journal of Economic Literature*, vol. 17, pp. 453–76.

Cowling, K. (1976) 'On the Theoretical Specification of Structure-Performance Relationships', *European Economic Review*, vol. 8, pp. 1–14.

Cowling, K. and Mueller, D. (1978) 'The Social Costs of Monopoly Power, *Economic Journal*, vol. 88, pp. 727–48.

Cubbin, J. (1981) 'Advertising and the Theory of Entry Barriers', *Economica*, vol. 48, pp. 289–98.

Cyert, R. and de Groot, H. (1970) 'Multiperiod Decision Models with Alternating Choice as a Solution to the Duopoly Problem, *Quarterly Journal of Economics*, vol. 84, pp. 410–29.

d'Aspremont, C. and Gérard-Varet, L. A. (1980) 'Sincere Pre-play Communication and Stackelberg Competitive Games', *Journal of Economic Theory*, vol. 23, pp. 201–17.

Dasgupta, P. and Stiglitz, J. (1981) 'Entry, Innovation, Exit: Towards a Dynamic Theory of Oligopolistic Industrial Structure', *European Economic Review*, vol. 15, pp. 137–58.

De Bondt, R. (1976) 'Limit Pricing, Uncertain Entry and the Entry Lag', *Econometrica*, vol. 44, pp. 939–46.

Demsetz, H. (1982) 'Barriers to Entry', *American Economic Review*, vol. 72, pp. 47–57.

Dixit, A. (1979) 'A Model of Duopoly Suggesting a Theory of Entry Barriers', *Bell Journal of Economics*, vol. 10, pp. 20–32.

Dixit, A. (1980) 'The Role of Investment in Entry Deterrence', *Economic Journal*, vol. 90, pp. 95–106.

Dixit, A. (1982) 'Recent Developments in Oligopoly Theory', *American Economic Review*, vol. 72, pp. 12–17.

Easley, D., Masson, R. and Reynolds, R. (1981), 'A Dynamic Analysis of Predatory Pricing with Rational Expectations', Mimeo., Cornell University.

Easterbrook, F. (1981) 'Predatory Strategies and Counter-Strategies', *University of Chicago Law Review*, vol. 48, pp. 263–337.

Eaton, B. C. and Lipsey, R. (1975) 'The Principle of Minimum Differentiation Reconsidered: some New Developments in the Theory of Spatial Competition', *Review of Economic Studies*, vol. 62, pp. 27–49.

Eaton, B. C. and Lipsey, R. (1978) 'Freedom of Entry and the Existence of Pure Profit', *Economic Journal*, vol. 88, pp. 455–69.

Eaton, B. C. and Lipsey, R. (1979) 'The Theory of Market Pre-emption: the Persistence of Excess Capacity and Monopoly in Growing Spatial Markets', *Economica*, vol. 46, pp. 149–58.

Eaton, B. C. and Lipsey, R. (1980) 'Exit Barriers are Entry Barriers: the Durability of Capital as a Barrier to Entry', *Bell Journal of Economics*, vol. 11, pp. 721–9.

Eaton, B. C. and Lipsey, R. (1981) 'Capital, Commitment and Entry Equilibrium', *Bell Journal of Economics*, vol. 12, pp. 593–604.

Encaoua, D. and Jacquemin, A. (1980) 'Degree of Monopoly, Indices of Concentration and Threat of Entry', *International Economic Review*, vol. 21, pp. 87–105.

Encaoua, D., Jacquemin, A. and Michel, Ph. (1981) 'Stratégies dynamiques de prix et structures de marché', *Cahiers du Séminaire d'Econométrie*, vol. 23, pp. 153–68.

Esposito, F. and Esposito, L. (1974) 'Excess Capacity and Market Structure', *Review of Economics and Statistics*, vol. 61, pp. 188–94.

Farrar, D. and Phillips, Ch. (1959) 'New Developments on the Oligopoly Front: a Comment', *Journal of Political Economy*, vol. 47, pp. 414–17.

Fisher, F. (1959) 'New Developments on the Oligopoly Front: Cournot and the Bain-Sylos Analysis', *Journal of Political Economy*, vol. 67, pp. 410–13.

Friedman, J. (1977) *Oligopoly and the Theory of Games* (Amsterdam, North-Holland).

Friedman, J. (1979) 'On Entry Preventing Behaviour and Limit Price Models of Entry', in Brams, S. J., Schotter, A. and Schwödiauer, G. (eds), *Applied Game Theory* (Vienna: Physica-Verlag).

Fudenberg, D. and Tirole, J. (1983) 'Capital as a Commitment: Strategic Investment to Deter Mobility, *Journal of Economic Theory*.

Gale, B. (1972) 'Market Share and Rate of Return', *Review of Economics and Statistics*, vol. 54, pp. 412–23.

Gaskins, D. (1971) 'Dynamic Limit Pricing: Optimal Pricing under Threat of Entry', *Journal of Economic Theory*, vol. 3, pp. 306–22.

Gelman, J. and Salop, S. (1983) 'Judo Economics' *Bell Journal of Economics*, vol. 14, pp. 315–25.

Geroski, P. (1981a) 'The Incidence of Entry in Three Oligopoly Models', Mimeo., Université Catholique de Louvain.

Geroski, P. (1981b) 'The Empirical Analysis of Conjectural Variations in Oligopoly', Mimeo., Université Catholique de Louvain.

Geroski, P. and Jacquemin A. (1984) 'Dominant Firms and their Alleged Decline', *International Journal of Industrial Organization*, vol. 2, pp. 1–27.

Gilbert, R. (1981) 'Patents, Sleeping Patents and Entry Deterrence', in

Salop, S. (ed.) *Strategy, Predation and Anti-Trust Analysis* (Washington: F.T.C.).

Gilbert, R. and Harris, R. (1984), Competition with Lumpy Investments. *Rand Journal of Economics*, vol. 15, pp. 197–212.

Goldberg, V. and Moirao, S. (1973) 'Limit Pricing and Potential Competition', *Journal of Political Economy*, vol. 81, pp. 1460–66.

Gollop, F. and Roberts, M. (1979) 'Firm Interdependence in Oligopolistic Markets', *Journal of Econometrics*, vol. 10, pp. 313–31.

Grossman, S. (1981) 'Nash equilibrium and the industrial organization of markets with large fixed costs', *Econometrica*, pp. 1149–72.

Guasch, J. and Weiss, A. (1980) 'Adverse Selection by Markets and the Advantage of Being Late', *Quarterly Journal of Economics,* vol. 94, pp. 453–66.

Harris, R. (1978) 'Entry Regulation, Fixed Costs and Dominant Public Firms', Mimeo., Queen's University.

Harris, R. and Wiens, E. (1980) 'Investment in Capacity and a Normative Theory of the Dominant Public Firm', *Canadian Journal of Economics*, vol. 13, pp. 125–31.

Hay, D. (1976) 'Sequential Entry and Entry Deterring Strategies in Spatial Competition', *Oxford Economic Papers*, vol. 28, pp. 240–57.

Hay, G. (1981) 'A Confused Lawyers Guide to the Predatory Pricing Literature', in Salop, S. (ed.) *Strategy, Predation and Anti-trust Analysis*, (Washington: FTC).

Hines, H. (1957) 'Effectiveness of Entry by Already Established Firms', *Quarterly Journal of Economics*, vol. 71, pp. 132–50.

Ireland, N. (1972) 'Concentration and the Growth of Market Demand', *Journal of Economic Theory*, vol. 5, pp. 303–305.

Iwata, G. (1974) 'Measurement of Conjectural Variations in Oligopoly', *Econometrica*, vol. 42, pp. 947–66.

Jacquemin, A. (1967), *L'entreprise et son pouvoir de marché* (Paris: PUF).

Jacquemin, A. (1972) 'Market Structure and the Firm's Market Power', *Journal of Industrial Economics*, vol. 20, pp. 122–34.

Jacquemin, A. and Thisse, J. (1972) 'Strategy of the Firm and Market Structure: an Application of Optimal Control Theory', in Cowling, K. (ed.) *Market Structure and Corporate Behaviour* (London: Gray-Mills).

Jovanovic, B. (1981) 'Entry with Private Information', *Bell Journal of Economics*, vol. 12, pp. 649–60.

Kalish, L., Hartzog, J. and Cassidy, H. (1978), 'The threat of entry with mutually aware potential entrants', *Journal of Political Economy*, vol. 86, pp. 147–53.

Kamien, M. and Schwartz, N. (1971) 'Limit Pricing and Uncertain Entry', *Econometrica*, vol. 39, pp. 441–54.

Kamien, M. and Schwartz, N. (1972) 'Uncertain Entry and Excess Capacity', *American Economic Review*, vol. 62, pp. 918–27.

Kamien, M. and Schwartz, N. (1982) *Market Structure and Innovation* (Cambridge: Cambridge University Press).

Kaysen, C. and Turner, D. (1959) *Antitrust Policy* (Cambridge, Mass.: Harvard University Press).

Klevorick, A. and Joskow, P. (1979) 'A Framework for Analyzing Predatory Pricing Policy', *Yale Law Journal*, vol. 89.

Kreps, D. and Wilson, R. (1980), 'On the Chain-store Paradox and Predation: Reputation for "Toughness"', forthcoming in *Journal of Economic Theory*.

Kreps, D., Milgrom, P., Roberts, J. and Wilson, R. (1981) 'Rational Cooperation in the Finitely Repeated Prisoner's Dilemma,' forthcoming in *Journal of Economic Theory*.

Kreps, D. and Wilson, R. (1982) 'Sequential Equilibria', *Econometrica*, vol. 50, pp. 863–94.

Lancaster, K. (1979) *Variety, Equity and Efficiency* (Oxford: B. Blackwell).

Lane, W. (1980) 'Product Differentiation in a Model with Endogenous Sequential Entry', *Bell Journal of Economics*, vol. 11, pp. 237–60.

Lee, W. (1975) 'Oligopoly and Entry', *Journal of Economic Theory*, vol. 11, pp. 35–54.

Lippman, S. (1980) 'Optimal Pricing to Returned Entry', *Review of Economic Studies*, vol. 47, pp. 723–31.

McGee, J. (1958) 'Predatory Price Cutting: the Standard Oil Case', *Journal of Law and Economics*, vol. 1, pp. 137–69.

Marris, R. and Mueller, D. (1980) 'The Corporation and Competition', *Journal of Economic Literature*, vol. 18, pp. 32–63.

Menge, J. (1962) 'Style Change Costs as a Market Weapon', *Quarterly Journal of Economics*, vol. 76, pp. 632–47.

Milgrom, P. (1981a) 'Good News and Bad News: Representation Theorems and Applications', *Bell Journal of Economics*, vol. 12, pp. 380–92.

Milgrom, P. (1981b) 'An Axiomatic Characterization of Common Knowledge', *Econometrica*, vol. 49, pp. 219–22.

Milgrom, P. and Roberts, J. (1982a) 'Predation, Reputation and Entry Deterrence', *Journal of Economic Theory*, vol. 27, pp. 280–312.

Milgrom, P. and Roberts, J. (1982b) 'Limit Pricing and Entry under Incomplete Information: an Equilibrium Analysis', *Econometrica*, vol. 50, pp. 443–59.

Modigliani, F. (1958) 'New Developments on the Oligopoly Front', *Journal of Political Economy*, vol. 66, pp. 215–32.

Moran, T. (1974) *Multinational Corporations and the Politics of Dependence* (Princeton: Princeton University Press).

Moulin, H. (1981) 'Deterrence and Cooperation: a Classification of Two-person Games', *European Economic Review*, vol. 15, pp. 179–94.

Mueller, D. (1977) 'The Persistence of Profits above the Norm', *Economica*, vol. 44, pp. 369–80.

Myerson, R. (1978) 'Refinements of the Nash Equilibrium Concept', *International Journal of Game Theory*, vol. 7, pp. 73–80.

Newman, H. (1978) 'Strategic Groups and the Structure-performance Relationship', *Review of Economics and Statistics*, vol. 60, pp. 417–27.

Nickell, S. (1978) *The Investment Decisions of Firms* (Oxford: Oxford University Press).

Osborne, D. (1973) 'On the Rationality of Limit Pricing', *Journal of Industrial Economics*, vol. 22, pp. 71–80.

Panzar, J. and Rosse, J. (1981), 'Structure Conduct and Comparative Statics', Mimeo., Bell Labs.

Penrose, E. (1959) *The Theory of the Growth of the Firm* (Oxford: B. Blackwell).

Porter, M. (1080) 'The Structure within Industries and Companies Performance', *Review of Economics and Statistics*, vol. 62, pp. 214–27.

Porter, M. (1981) 'Strategic Interaction: some Lessons from Industry Histories for Theory and Anti-trust Policy', in Salop, S. (ed.) *Strategy, Predation and Anti-trust Analysis*. (Washington: FTC).

Posner, R. (1972) *Economic Analysis of Law* (Boston: Little, Brown and Company).

Prescott, E. and Visscher, M. (1977) 'Sequential Location among Firms with Foresight', *Bell Journal of Economics*, vol. 8, pp. 378–93.

Pyatt, G. (1971) 'Profit Maximization and the Threat of New Entry', *Economic Journal*, vol. 81, pp. 242–55.

Rao, R. and Rutenberg, D. (1979) Pre-empting an Alert Rival: Strategic Timing of the First Plant by Analysis of Sophisticiated Rivalry', *Bell Journal of Economics*, vol. 10, pp. 412–28.

Reinganum, J. (1981) 'Market Structure and the Diffusion of New Technology', *Bell Journal of Economics*, vol. 12, pp. 618–24.

Rosenthal, R. (1981) 'Games of Perfect Information, Predatory Pricing, and the Chain-store Paradox', *Journal of Economic Theory*, vol. 25, pp. 92–100.

Rosenthal, R. (1982) 'A Dynamic Model with Customer Loyalties', *Journal of Economic Theory*, vol. 27, pp. 69–76.

Rubenstein, A. (1979) 'Strong Perfect Equilibria in Supergames', *International Journal of Game Theory*, vol. 9, pp. 1–12.

Salop, S. (1979a) 'Monopolistic Competition with Outside Goods', *Bell Journal of Economics*, vol. 10, pp. 335–8.

Salop, S. (1979b) 'Strategic Entry Deterrence', *American Economic Review*, Papers and Proceedings, 335–8.

Salop, S. and Shapiro, C. (1980) 'A Guide to Test Market Predation', Mimeo., Princeton University.

Salop, S. (1981) 'Strategy, Predation and Anti-trust Analysis', in Salop, S. (ed.) *Strategy, Predation and Antitrust Analysis* (Washington: FTC).

Salop, S. and Scheffman, D. (1981) 'Strategic Interaction in Multiple Markets: a Beginning to a General Theory of Dominant Firm Industries', Mimeo., FTC.

Schelling, T. (1960) *The Strategy of Conflict* (Cambridge, Mass.: Harvard University Press).

Scherer, F. M., Beckenstein, A., Kaufer, E. and Murphy, R. (1975) *The Economics of Multiplant Operation: an International Comparison Study* (Cambridge, Mass.: Harvard University Press).

Scherer, F. M. (1980) *Industrial Market Structure and Economic Performance* (Chicago: Rand McNally).

Schmalensee, R. (1978) 'Entry Deterrence in the Ready to Eat Breakfast Cereal Industry', *Bell Journal of Economics*, vol. 9, pp. 305–27.

Schmalensee, R. (1979) 'Market Structure, Durability, and Quality: a Selective Survey', *Economic Inquiry*, vol. 17, pp. 177–96.

Schmalensee, R. (1980) 'The New Industrial Organization and the Economic Analysis of Modern Markets', Mimeo., MIT.

Schmalensee, R. (1981) 'Economies of Scale and Barriers to Entry', *Journal of Political Economy*, vol. 89, pp. 1228–38.

Selten, R. (1973) 'A Simple Model of Imperfect Competition Where 4 are

Few and 6 are Many', *International Journal of Game Theory*, vol. 2.

Selten, R. (1975) 'Re-examination of the Perfectness Concept for Equilibrium Points in Extensive Games', *International Journal of Game Theory*, vol. 4, pp. 25–55.

Selten, R. (1978) 'The Chain-store Paradox', *Theory and Decision*, vol. 9, pp. 127–59.

Shepherd, W. (1972) 'The Elements of Market Structure', *Review of Economics and Statistics*, vol. 54, pp. 25–36.

Shepherd, W. (1975) *The Treatment of Market Power* (New York: Columbia University Press).

Shepherd, W. (1976) 'The Elements and Evolution of Market Structure', in Jacquemin, A. and de Jong, H. (eds), *Markets, Corporate Behaviour and the State* (The Hague: M. Nijhoff).

Sherman, R. and Willett, T. (1967) 'Potential Entrants Discourage Entry', *Journal of Political Economy*, vol. 75, pp. 400–403.

Simon, H. (1978) 'Rationality as Process and as Product of Thought', *American Economic Review*, vol. 68, pp. 1–16.

Smith, R. (1981) 'Efficiency Gains from Strategic Investments', *Journal of Industrial Economics*, vol. 30, pp. 1–24.

Spence, M. (1977) 'Entry, Capacity, Investment and Oligopolistic Pricing', *Bell Journal of Economics*, vol. 8, pp. 534–44.

Spence, M. (1979) 'Investment Strategy and Growth in a New Market', *Bell Journal of Economics*, vol. 10, pp. 1–19.

Spence, M. (1980) 'Notes on Advertising, Economies of Scale and Entry Barriers', *Quarterly Journal of Economics*, vol. 94, pp. 493–504.

Spence, M. (1981a) 'Competition, Entry and Antitrust Policy', in Salop, S. (ed.) *Strategy, Predation and Anti-trust Analysis* (Washington: FTC).

Spence, M. (1981b) 'The Learning Curve and Competition', *Bell Journal of Economics*, vol. 12, pp. 49–70.

Spulber, D. (1981) 'Capacity, Output and Sequential Entry', *American Economic Review*, vol. 71, pp. 503–14.

Stigler, G. (1968) *The Organization of Industry* (Homewood: Irwin).

Stiglitz, J. (1981) 'Potential Competition may Reduce Welfare', *American Economic Review*, Papers and Proceedings pp. 184–19.

Telser, L. (1966) 'Cut-throat Competition and the Long Purse', *Journal of Law and Economics*, vol. 9, pp. 259–77.

Ulph, D. (1983) 'Rational Conjectures in the Theory of Oligopoly', *International Journal of Industrial Organization*, vol. 1, pp. 131–54.

von Ungern-Sternberg, T. (1980) 'Current Profits and Investment Behavior', *Bell Journal of Economics*, vol. 11, pp. 745–48.

von Weiszäcker, C. (1981) 'A Welfare Analysis of Barriers to Entry', *Bell Journal of Economics*, vol. 11, pp. 399–420.

Weiss, L. (1974) 'The Concentration-profits Relationship and Antitrust', in Goldschmid, H., Mann' H. M. and Weston F. (eds) *Industrial Concentration: the New Learning* (Boston: Little, Brown).

Wenders, J. (1971a) 'Collusion and Entry', *Journal of Political Economy*, vol. 79, pp. 1258–77.

Discussion of the Paper by Encaoua, Geroski and Jacquemin

Michael Katz began his discussion of the paper by Encaoua, Geroski and Jacquemin (EGJ) by listing some of the issues that arose in applications of the theory of strategic competition. First, he pointed out that it was often difficult to identify those firms engaged in strategic competition, as many of the observable implications of the theory were similar to those of perfect competition. Entry deterrence, for example, was costly, and tended to generate low profit rates. However, low profit rates would also be the outcome of free entry. Second, even if strategic competition could be easily and clearly identified, the appropriate policy response remained unclear. Firms made commitments by advertising and investing in capacity. Preventing firms from advertising or setting up advance capacity was not necessarily socially desirable even if such actions to led strategic competition.

Katz argued that game theory might not be the appropriate tool for analysing issues in strategic competition. It relied too heavily on rationality; it attempts to rationalise almost any kind of observed behaviour by firms. As an example, Katz considered current applications for NSF grants in economics. Budget cuts should reduce the expected return to applying, thereby reducing the number of applications. Exactly the opposite result had actually occurred as NSF applications were at record levels. The game-theoretic explanation of this phenomenon was that the award of grants was a contest, which might be costly to enter, where a fixed number of prizes were awarded at random to each entrant. The appropriate equilibrium, Katz suggested, was a mixed-strategy Nash equilibrium where each player in the game chose to enter the contest with some probability. This probability was chosen to maximise an expected pay-off. The current high level of NSF applications occurred as a low-probability event consistent with this mixed-strategy equilibrium. Katz suggested that the game-theoretic explanation of this phenomenon was not very helpful. A more useful approach would rely on the bounded rationality of applicants.

Finally, Katz identified a number of areas worthy of investigation. First, he suggested that it was important to understand how potential firms selected the market and manner for entry. Incumbent firms must use exactly this kind of information to design effective entry-deterrence strategies. An understanding of this entry process should make strategic competition easier to identify. Second, there were only a few industries with a single incumbent firm. Hence, the theory should be extended to 'oligopolistic' entry deterrence. Two special problems arose with many firms. First, there was a free-rider problem: deterrent strategies by one firm benefited all other firms. Second, existing firms must find a way to prevent the use of excessive capacity as a strategic weapon against each other. A final area for future research suggested by Katz involved the implications of firm reputation for deterrence. To illustrate the difficulties that this could pose for incumbent firms, he offered the example of the Weber Grill Company, which produced a high-quality expensive barbecue. The company wished to pre-empt rivals in the production of low-price substitute barbecues. To do this, it produced an unbranded low-price product which was distributed through K-mart. K-mart announced that the barbecue was produced by Weber. The result was that demand was drawn from the high-price barbecue towards, the low-price K-mart product, with a resulting loss of profits for the manufacturer. In this case, the manufacturing firm's reputation actually limited its ability to deter entry in a related area of the product space.

Spence remarked that the problem of entry deterrence was part of a larger problem of how firms interacted in general with their rivals. That rivals happened to emerge from other industries might only be incidental. To Katz's point about oligopolistic entry deterrence, he suggested that competition among firms *in* the industry was the most important force determining their behaviour. While many of the strategic actions taken by existing firms happened to deter entry, this was not the primary motivation for these actions.

Gilbert suggested that the trade-off between strategic commitment and flexibility had not been adequately explored in the literature.

Dasgupta, Brouwer and *Von Ungern-Sternberg* discussed alleged first-mover advantages. Dasgupta pointed out that, especially in the literature on patents and on research and development, circumstances had been identified in which the second mover had the advantage, while von Ungern-Sternberg suggested that any second-mover advantage might stem from provision of the technology by an incumbent.

Selten made three points on the EGJ paper and ensuing discussion. First, he suggested that in those industries where incumbents were many, expectations by potential entrants that firms in the industry behaved co-operatively even after entry to limit quantities and raise prices might actually encourage entry into the industry, since it would raise profit rates. Commitments by firms to behave non-co-operatively after entry would depress the returns expected by potential entrants, limit entry, and possibly raise the profits of incumbent firms.

To Katz's objections about game theory, Selten responded that although one could not always rely on rationality in analysing actual gaming situations, nevertheless, game theory was still useful as it permitted an understanding of the strategic structure of different problems. In the absence of an acceptable theory of limited rationality, game theory provided the appropriate benchmark.

On the issue of testing for strategic competition, Selten agreed that the theory did not lead to strong tests using field data. However, he did suggest that the theory could be tested in the laboratory. Experimental results also indicated appropriate modifications on the assumption of rationality. *Steve Salop* noted that experimental research on repeated prisoner's dilemma games with finite horizons indicated that co-operation was possible between players for short periods of time, but that this cooperation tended to break down as the game proceeded.

Williamson mentioned the issue of diseconomies from multiplant operations. Why did they exist? Only *ad hoc* explanations currently existed in economics. Consequently, he conjectured that a satisfactory explanation might have to come from the other social sciences. On the issue of appropriate organisational form, Williamson suggested that any organisational form had to service both efficiency and strategic aspects. He argued that in general the public policy ramifications of strategic behaviour were important but far from obvious.

3 Pre-emptive Competition

Richard J. Gilbert[1]

UNIVERSITY OF CALIFORNIA, BERKELEY, USA

I INTRODUCTION

Pre-emptive competition occurs in any market where the timing of actions is important. Schmalensee (1978) considers the pre-emptive introduction of brands to deter competitors. Eaton and Lipsey (1979) examine pre-emptive location models, while Gilbert and Newbery (1982) analyse the returns from accelerated investments in research and development. Pre-emptive investment is the theme in Dixit (1979, 1980), Eaton and Lipsey (1980, 1981), Fudenberg and Tirole (1981), Fudenberg, *et al.* (forthcoming), Gilbert and Harris (1981a,b), Rao and Rutenberg (1979) and Spence (1977, 1979). Ware (1981) considers the potential for pre-emptive product differentiation. This is only a partial listing of work where pre-emptive activity plays a central role, and at current rates of output no doubt many more papers will be added to the pre-emption pool.

This chapter reviews certain features common to all pre-emption models in the particular context of entry prevention. The pre-emptive action is capital investment designed to prevent the entry of competitors who, by assumption, are as efficient as any established firm. Pre-emptive capacity investment was addressed explicitly as a US anti-trust policy issue in the case of *United States* v. *Aluminum Company of America* where the Court challenged the view of 'Alcoa' as a passive beneficiary of a monopoly. Presiding Judge Learned Hand stated,

> we can think of no more effective exclusion than progressively to embrace each new opportunity as it opened, and to face every

90

newcomer with new capacity already geared into a great organization, having the advantage of experience, trade connections and
the elite of personnel.[2]

The actions and motives of the Alcoa corporation can be debated at
great length, but that is not the purpose here. Instead this chapter
deals with two questions central to the efficacy of a pre-emptive
investment strategy:

1. Would a manager of an established firm want to deter entry if
   entry deterrence is feasible?
2. Is entry-deterring capital investment a credible activity given the
   economic incentives that exist if entry occurs?

These questions are related; yet they address different issues. The
first asks whether entry deterrence (or prevention) is a desirable
activity for an established firm. Section II shows that the answer is
'yes' under wide (but not all) conditions when entry into an industry
is limited only by the existence of increasing returns in production.
The second question asks whether entry-deterring actions would be
sustained if challenged by a potential competitor. Alternatively, this
question asks whether entry deterrence is the equilibrium of a competitive game. Section III shows that the answer is 'no' in most
circumstances, *provided* managers cannot make binding commitments to entry-deterring strategies.

As an illustration, suppose that to prevent entry an established firm
must build and operate 10 plants. Given free entry, the firm earns
maximum profits by operating these plants at the smallest aggregate
output that makes entry unprofitable. This is just the 'limit' output
defined by Bain (1956) and others. In this sense entry prevention is
desirable, since the alternative is entry with lower profits.

Is entry prevention a credible policy? If potential entrants are
deterred, managers of the established firm would want to exploit the
situation by cutting back production and even closing plants in order
to raise prices. Perhaps managers would want to operate only the
equivalent of five plants. Reducing output would invite entry, but it is
an irresistible temptation if managers cannot pre-commit themselves
to an entry-preventing output level. It is the temptation to act as a
monopolist that destroys the monopoly temporarily enjoyed by the
established firm.

Dixit (1980) identified the importance of credibility in any investment designed to deter competitors. Capital is a credible deterrent

ony if it would be used if firms compete. Section II extends the Dixit model to allow for unlimited entry of potential competitors and shows how entry prevention would be advantageous if an established firm could make binding commitments to entry-deterring outputs. The extent to which capital investment imitates a binding commitment depends on the cost of using capital whose investment cost is sunk. Data on requirements of costs and scale for several industries are assembled in Section III to test the credibility requirement for entry prevention.

One immediate observation is on the typically small share of capital in total costs. If capital were the only fixed cost, the narrow gap between short- and long-run marginal cost would severely limit the scope for strategic entry deterrence. Yet, for many industries, labour costs are at least partially fixed in the short run. Nevertheless, including labour costs as a fixed item makes strategic entry prevention a credible activity for only a small number of industries, characterised by large fixed costs and large scale of production requirements.

A difficulty with static models is their failure to identify the sequence of events that lead to an 'established' firm and to explain why that firm might enjoy a first-mover advantage. Section IV addresses this question in a dynamic context where any firm may invest at any time. Also, the analysis does not permit 'empty threats'; nor does it assume naive expectations of future outputs or prices.

Successful entry deterrence over an extended time period is an unlikely event in this dynamic model. If all new plants are employed at rated capacity, every firm with the same technology (whether an actual or potential competitor) would earn the same return on a new plant and hence has the same incentive to expand. Entry deterrence is impossible in this instance. Some degree of excess capacity is a necessary condition for successful entry deterrence. But a firm with excess capacity would not invest to create more excess capacity.

Entry deterrence can work only if an 'established' firm can hold capacity which is excess before entry, and yet is a credible threat if entry should occur. This is possible if entry triggers a sharp price reduction by the incumbent firm. However, a sharp price reduction is an unlikely response to a small entrant, and in a growing market a monopolist will eventually be large relative to the minimum efficient scale of entry. At least in the long run, successful entry deterrence is an unlikely outcome. Alcoa's dominance of the aluminium industry could have been the result of experience or of the unique advantages of its 'great organization'. Yet without these advantages or evidence of binding commitments to strategies which would thwart the entry of new firms, Judge Hand's concerns about pre-emptive capacity expansion by Alcoa are not substantiated by theory.

II INCENTIVES FOR PRE-EMPTIVE BEHAVIOUR

This Section examines the desirability of pre-emptive actions by an established firm. We begin by supposing that a firm has an initial monopoly in a market and ask whether the firm would exclude competitors by choosing an entry-limiting output, *assuming that the firm has the power to maintain any desired output level.* Desired actions are assumed credible as well. For the case of a single entrant, this is equivalent to asking when a firm would exclude potential competitors if it could act in the manner assumed by Bain (1956), Modigliani (1958), and Sylos-Labini (1962), where potential entrants take as given the pre-entry output of the established firm (hereafter called the B–S–M limit-pricing model).

Any discussion of entry must make specific the process by which entry occurs. This section considers an industry in which firms enter sequentially, but the analysis is otherwise atemporal. The importance of the sequential entry assumption is to define the order in which firms take actions and, for example, to distinguish the analysis from a situation where firms act simultaneously.[3] The importance of time and the existence of first-mover advantages are dealt with specifically in Section IV.

We make the following assumptions about the entry process and the choices available to each firm.

A.1 (Foresight). Each firm chooses an output taking into account the reactions of future entrants to its output.

A.2 (Commitment). A firm that has entered the industry can choose and maintain any output level.

This behaviour follows that described in Prescott and Visscher (1977). Each firm chooses its output with foresight, and established firms can commit themselves to any output level. Only established firms can make commitments, and entrants take as given the outputs of established firms. In other words, firms act as Cournot competitors with respect to those which precede them, and as Stackelberg leaders with respect to those which follow.

Although the very term 'monopoly' suggests pecuniary gain, it is not true that the owners of a firm would always prefer to maintain a monopoly position, even when they have the power to do so. Dixit (1980) reached this conclusion in the analysis of investment by an incumbent with a single potential entrant. Intuitively, if the damage that a single firm could inflict on the incumbent is less than the cost of entry deterrence, an established firm should allow entry. This section extends the analysis in Dixit (1980) to the case of many potential entrants, and shows how incentives for entry deterrence emerge when potential competition increases.

Consider a simple version of the Dixit model. Industry demand is linear, with

$$P(Q) = a - bQ.$$

There is an established firm, $j = 0$ and a single entrant, $j = 1$. The established firm can choose, and maintain, any output q_0. Any incumbent output is a possible equilibrium of the post-entry game. This strong assumption facilitates entry deterrence because the incumbent need not worry about the *credibility* of any pre-entry output. The assumption will be relaxed later, but for the moment it serves to illustrate conditions under which pre-emptive actions are advantageous to an established firm.

The technology is particularly simple. Firms have access to that same technology and can produce any output, q_j at a constant marginal cost C, provided the output is at least $\hat{k}$. The $\hat{k}$ is a minimum efficient scales (MES) of output for any firm: outputs less than $\hat{k}$ are assumed infeasible. We could obtain similar results by assuming a fixed cost for each plant, with more notation.

The entrant takes q_0 as given and enters if

$$P(q_0 + q_1) > C \qquad \text{for any } q_1 \geq \hat{k},$$

which gives a critical entry deterring output

$$\bar{Q} = \frac{\bar{a}}{b} - \hat{k}. \tag{1}$$

Here $\bar{a} \equiv a - C$. The incumbent may either deter the entrant by setting $q_0 = \bar{Q}$, or it may allow entry. Assume that the monopoly output is

$$q^m = \bar{a}/2b < \bar{Q},$$

so that entry is not blockaded (to use Bain's terminology) by the profit-maximising output of the established firm. The incumbent's profit with entry deterrence is

$$\bar{\pi}_0 = \bar{Q}[P(\bar{Q}) - C].$$

If the incumbent allows entry, it should choose output q_0 taking into account the output of Firm 1. Recall that the incumbent can choose and maintain any output. Then, if the incumbent chooses q_0 with foresight, the profit with the entry of one firm is

$$\pi_0(1) = \max_{q_0} q_0[P(q_0 + R_1(q_0)) - C].$$

Here, R_1 is the reaction function of Firm 1, determined as the solution to

$$\pi_1(1) = \max_{q_1} [P(q_0 + q_1) - C],$$

with q_0 taken as fixed, by assumption.

The entrant's output is

$$q_1 = R_1(q_0) = \frac{\bar{a} - bq_0}{2b} \quad \text{for } q_0 < \bar{Q} \tag{2}$$

and it is easily seen that

$$q_0 = \frac{\bar{a}}{2b}. \tag{3}$$

Note the curious result that the established firm which acts optimally, taking into account its impact on the entrant's output, chooses an output equal to the myopic monopoly output. This is a special case brought about by the symmetry of the linear demand schedule.

The incumbent should choose the entry preventing output if

$$\bar{\pi}_0 \geq \pi_0(1),$$

or if

$$\bar{Q}[P(\bar{Q}) - C] \geq q_0[P(q_0 + R_1(q_0)) - C]. \tag{4}$$

Substituting Equations (1), (2), and (3) in (4) gives, as the condition for entry prevention,

$$\bar{Q} \leq \frac{\bar{a}}{2b}(1 + \sqrt{1/2}).$$

If the limit quantity $\bar{Q}$ exceeds this critical level, the established firm is better off allowing entry. In that case, the profits lost from competition are less than the profits lost by choosing a limit-pricing strategy.

This derivation shows that for $n = 1$, there is a critical 'limit output' at which entry prevention and accommodation by the established firm are equally desirable. If the limit output is greater, the incumbent should allow entry, and if it is less the incumbent should limit-price. But this result was derived with the assumption of only one potential entrant. In most industries not protected by government restrictions on entry or by patent rights, we should expect many potential entrants over a reasonable time period, and we should expect a correlation between the limit output and the number of firms that could enter the industry if the incumbent firm (or firms) did not practice entry deterrence.

With no other barriers to entry, both the limit output and the number of firms that could enter an industry depend on the production technology and, in particular, on the minimum efficient scale of production. We shall argue that when all firms have access to the same technology (and there is a sufficiently large number of potential entrants), it is advantageous for an incumbent firm to deter entry (ignoring the important qualifications discussed in the following sections). To see this, first consider the incumbent's best strategy as a function of a specified number of actual entrants, n.

Define

$$Q_n = \sum_{j=0}^{n} q_j.$$

The assumption of sequential entry with foresight, A.1, means that each firm will choose its output taking into account the reactions of future firms; thus

$$Q_n = q_0 + R_1(Q_0) + R_2(Q_1) + \ldots + R_n(Q_{n-1}).$$

In the linear example with sequential foresight, if each firm chooses its optimal output *conditional on the entry of n firms*, then[4]

$$R_j = \frac{1}{2}\left(\frac{\bar{a}}{b} - Q_{j-1}\right) \tag{5}$$

$$q_j = \frac{\bar{a}}{b} 2^{-(j+1)} \tag{6}$$

and

$$Q_j = \frac{\bar{a}}{b}(1 - 2^{-(j+1)}). \tag{7}$$

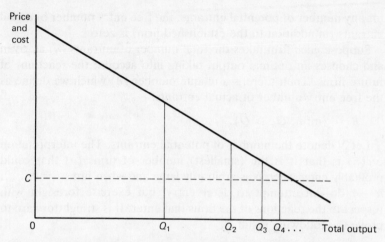

FIG. 3.1 Industry output given sequential entry with foresight. Each firm maximises profit on its residual demand curve.

Each firm acts as a monopolist with respect to the residual demand, and each entrant's output is one-half of the output of the preceding firm. This is shown in Figure 3.1. The result presumes that the number of entrants (n) is given and hence invariant to industry output.

The incumbent firm's profit with (n) entrants is

$$\pi_0(n) = q_0[P(Q_n) - C]$$

$$= \frac{(\bar{a})^2}{b} 2^{-(n+2)}; \tag{8}$$

and this clearly falls as (n) increases. But the number of entrants is not exogenous if entry responds to perceived profits. Although there can be any number of potential entrants, the number of actual entrants is limited by $Q_n \leq \bar{Q}$, or else firm (n) could not enter profitably with the assumed technology. In general if exit is costless, all firms must earn non-negative profits. We say there is *free entry* of (n) firms if

$$\pi_j \geq 0 \qquad j = 0, 1, \ldots, n$$

and

$$\pi_{n+1} < 0 \qquad \text{for all } q_{n+1} > 0.$$

The number of firms (n) in a free-entry equilibrium depends on the outputs of all firms $j = 0, \ldots, n - 1$. For example, if $q_0 = \bar{Q}$, then for any number of potential entrants, the free entry number of actual entrants (in addition to the established firm) is zero.

Suppose each firm takes the total number of entrants (n) as given and chooses an optimal output taking into account the reactions of future firms. Then there is a unique number $(\bar{n})$ which we define as the free entry number of actual entrants:

$$\bar{n} = \{\inf n : Q_n \geq \bar{Q}\}.$$

Let N denote the number of potential entrants. The interpretation of $(\bar{n})$ is that it is the (smallest) number of firms (n) that could profitably enter when N is arbitrarily large and when firms $j = 0, \ldots, n - 1$ do not attempt to deter entry, but exercise foresight with respect to the reactions of the firms that enter. It is straightforward to prove the following result.

PROPOSITION 1

Given the assumed technology, if $N \geq \bar{n}$, and if the monopoly output is less than the limit output $\bar{Q}$ so that entry is not blockaded, then firm $j = 0$ maximises profits with $q_0 = \bar{Q}$.

When firm $j = 0$ deters entry with $q_0 = \bar{Q}$, profits are

$$\bar{\pi}_0 = \bar{Q}[P(\bar{Q}) - C] \geq 0.$$

If the incumbent does not deter entry, and if no other firm acts to deter entry, profits are

$$\pi_0(\bar{n}) = q_0[P(Q_{\bar{n}}) - C].$$

Since $Q_{\bar{n}} \geq \bar{Q}$ and $q_0 < \bar{Q}$, hence $\bar{\pi}_0 > \pi_0(\bar{n})$; it pays to deter all entrants. If any firm $j = 1, \ldots, n - 1$ deters entry, then no matter how many firms actually enter, $Q_n \geq \bar{Q}$. The incumbent firm's profits are

$$\pi_0(n) = q_0[P(Q_n) - C],$$

and this is strictly less than $\bar{\pi}_0$.   Q.E.D

This proof does not depend on the special assumption of a minimum scale of operations, although some economies of scale at small outputs are necessary for the existence of positive profits, when there is entry deterrence. The proof does assume that the incumbent firm has no diseconomies of scale at large outputs; if he does, the costs of entry deterrence may outweigh any revenue gains.

Return, for illustration, to the linear-demand example. Profits with entry deterrence are

$$\bar{\pi}_0 = \bar{Q}[P(\bar{Q}) - C] = b\hat{k}(\bar{a}/b - \hat{k}),$$

while profits with (n) entrants are (if no firms limit entry),

$$\pi_0(n) = \frac{(\bar{a})^2}{b} \, 2^{-(n+2)}.$$

It is a straightforward matter to show from the definition of $\bar{Q}$ (Equation (1)) and Q_n (Equation (7)) that if $n \geq \bar{n}$, and if entry is not blockaded by the monopoly output, then

$$\frac{\bar{\pi}_0}{\pi_0(n)} > 1.$$

When $n \geq \bar{n}$, it pays to defer entry by choosing an entry-preventing output $\bar{Q}$. This is, of course, the B–S–M limit-pricing strategy. Conversely, the incumbent should allow entry *only* if N is less than the free entry number of firms $(\bar{n})$.

The strong incentives for entry deterrence implied by Proposition 1 are subject to certain caveats, among which are:

(i)   the assumed technology has no diseconomies of scale;
(ii) firms can choose and maintain any output level;
(iii) there is a definite ordering of moves, with the established firm moving first; and
(iv) there is no uncertainty.

The ordering of moves and particularly the existence of a first mover advantage are discussed in Section IV, which also briefly mentions uncertainty. Diseconomies of scale may reverse the incentives for entry deterrence if these diseconomies arise at the level of the firm; what are sometimes called managerial diseconomies. Technological diseconomies at the plant level do not alter incentives for entry deterrence. To see this, assume that firms have cost functions $C_j(q_j)$, which may correspond to single or multiplant operation. The absence of managerial diseconomies means that, by using the same technology, any firm can replicate the outputs of any other firm without incurring a cost penalty. In particular, if

$$Q_n = \sum_{j=0}^{n} q_j,$$

then

$$C_0(Q_n) \leqslant \left\{ \sum_{j=0}^{n} C_j(q_j) : \sum_{j=0}^{n} q_j = Q_n \right\}. \qquad (9)$$

In the absence of entry deterrence, the incumbent earns

$$\pi_0(n) = q_0 P(Q_n) - C_0(q_0),$$

while profits with entry deterrence are

$$\bar{\pi}_0 = \bar{Q} \, P(\bar{Q}) - C_0(\bar{Q}) \geqslant Q_n P(Q_n) - C_0(Q_n)$$

(The inequality follows, assuming entry is not blockaded.)
In view of the inequality (9),

$$\bar{\pi}_0 \geqslant \sum_{j=0}^{n} \{q_j \, P(Q_n) - C_j(q_j)\}; \text{ or,}$$

$$\bar{\pi}_0 \geqslant q_0 \, P(Q_n) - C_0(q_0) + \sum_{j=1}^{n} \{q_j \, P(Q_n) - C_j(q_j)\} \qquad (10)$$

Since all entrants make non-negative profits,

$$\sum_{j=1}^{n} \{q_j \, P(Q_n) - C_j(q_j)\} \geqslant 0.$$

Moreover, since the first two terms on the right-hand side of (10) equal $\pi_0(n)$, it follows that

$$\bar{\pi}_0 \geqslant \pi_0(n),$$

and that there is equality if and only if $Q_n = \bar{Q}$ and all entrants make zero profits.

III   IS PRE-EMPTION A CREDIBLE THREAT?

In the derivation of Proposition 1, we allowed firms to choose and maintain any output level (caveat (ii)). This restriction is quite important because it makes any chosen output level credible to potential entrants, and hence a potentially effective entry-deterring threat. But if entrants reason that firms in the industry cannot commit themselves to maintaining their existing outputs, entrants will evaluate profitability on the basis of the output that can be expected to occur if they enter the industry. Existing firms, aware of how rivals evaluate the gains from entry, might as well restrict their choices to equilibrium outputs in the post-entry situation. We shall show that this credibility constraint has profound implications for the viability of monopoly.

Consider again the linear example with the cost function

$$C(q) = Cq \quad \text{for } q \geq \hat{k}.$$

Suppose we refine the commitment assumption, A.2, as follows.

A.2′ (Cournot–Nash) All outputs must be Cournot–Nash equilibrium outputs.

The assumption that firms can maintain any output level is now replaced by the requirement that all outputs must be equilibria of a Cournot–Nash game. If there is no way for firms to commit themselves to specific output levels, then, with $n + 1$ firms in the industry, the Cournot–Nash equilibrium outputs are:

$$q_j = \frac{\bar{a}}{(n + 2)b} \quad j = 0, 1, \ldots, n.$$

All firms produce the same output and the equilibrium number of firms is the largest number for which $q_j \geq \hat{k}$. The incumbent firm cannot deter entry, because there is no way in which a single firm can credibly maintain the requisite output. The incumbent is a victim of its own behaviour. If entry is not blockaded by the monopoly output, the incumbent firm will set $q_0 < \bar{Q}$ in any market equilibrium, even though profits are higher with $q_0 = \bar{Q}$ when there is free entry.

One way to enforce the credibility of outputs is to assume that, when a particular output level is chosen, the cost savings from reducing that output level are less than any loss of revenue resulting from the lower output. Sunk costs are one way in which a firm can make an output commitment. Suppose an established firm chooses a pre-entry output where marginal revenue equals long-run marginal cost. Then, if entry occurs, the cost of reducing output is the short-run marginal cost. Suppose that short-run marginal cost is much smaller than long-run marginal cost (that is, that sunk costs are large). Entry would then have to reduce marginal revenue for the incumbent by a substantial amount before the firm would reduce its output below the pre-entry level.

The extent of the capital commitment depends on the divergence between short- and long-run marginal costs, or on the degree to

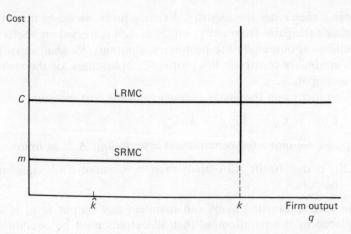

FIG. 3.2 Production cost for each firm, assuming $q \geq \hat{k}$. Installed capacity is k.

which investment is a sunk cost. This divergence is inherent in a fixed-proportions technology with the following cost function:

A.3 (Technology). Let (k) represent installed production capacity and let (q) denote output. The total cost of output (q) with capacity (k) is

$$C(q, k) = mq + rbk \qquad \text{for } q \leq k, \ k \geq \hat{k}.$$

Production is not feasible for $q > k$. Here (m) is short-run marginal cost, (b) is the cost of capacity, and (rb) is interest-cost per unit of capacity. Properties of the function are illustrated in Figure 3.2. This is the same cost function as that used by Dixit (1980), without the minimum capacity constraint $(\hat{k})$. The long run $(q = k)$ marginal cost (= average cost) is, for $q \geq \hat{k}$,

$$\text{LMC}(q) = m + rb \equiv C$$

A firm with this technology can maintain an output level, $q \leq k$, if marginal revenue for outputs less than (q) is larger than short-run marginal cost. However, this ability to make a capital commitment does not guarantee that entry prevention, even with free entry, is either desirable or credible.

Although Proposition 1 suggests that entry prevention is desirable, if not credible, this need not be the case if entry prevention involves having excess capacity. When there is a possibility of excess capacity, inviting entry may be a means for an established firm to pass on the burden of entry prevention to another competitor.

The profitability of allowing entry depends on the way the firms in the industry might compete. If two or more firms act as perfect competitors (as implicitly assumed by Spence (1977)), all capacity will be used, and inviting entry merely invites an erosion of profits. Yet the pursuit by the firm of the policy of allowing entry to pass on the cost of preventing further entry can work in special circumstances. Suppose two firms can be expected to act as a cartel, but that vigorous competition will emerge with three or more firms. (Some evidence for this type of behaviour is reported in Kwoka (1979).) The established firm can choose a capacity that invites entry; the entrant may then choose a capacity that deters further entry, given the expectation of competitive behaviour if entry occurs.

In this example the revenue lost by the incumbent firm when entry occurs can be more than compensated for by the savings in capital costs required for entry deterrence. These costs are borne by the entrant, who then protects the established firm from further competition. Note that when capacity is always fully utilised, the revenue loss from entry exceeds the cost of the extra capital that would be required to limit entry, so that entry prevention, if possible, is also desirable.

Dixit (1980) provided conditions under which excess capacity would not exist in a Cournot–Nash equilibrium. This is assured by:

A.4 (Declining marginal revenue) Marginal revenue for any firm j with output q_j and industry output Q_n, $MR(q_j, Q_n)$, has the property that

$$\frac{\partial MR(q_j, Q_n)}{\partial q_j} < 0 \qquad \text{and} \qquad \frac{\partial MR(q_j, Q_n)}{\partial Q_n} < 0.$$

A direct implication of this assumption is that the Cournot–Nash reaction functions are downward sloping. When the decreasing marginal revenue assumption holds, any increase in output, whether it be from an established firm or from a *de novo* entrant, will be 'accommodated' to some extent by a reduction in the output of competitors. This means that if any capacity is not used before entry, it certainly will not be used after entry. Therefore, excess capacity is useless as a threat to potential entrants and, since capacity is costly, firms would do better by ensuring that excess capacity never occurred.

It is easy to see that A.4 must hold if the magnitude of the demand elasticity does not increase too rapidly when total output increases.[5]

But note that if the expansion or entry of a firm leads a competitor to conjecture that there is a much higher value for industry elasticity of demand, then an accommodating response need not occur.

Proposition 1 did not address the question why the established firm can choose an output before any rival; nor did it determine when the entry-deterring output $(\bar{Q})$ is credible. The first question requires the dynamic analysis in Section IV. The second question can be addressed using an atemporal Dixit-type model.

The entry preventing output $(\bar{Q})$ can be written as $(1 - z)Q^*$, where Q^* is the efficient long-run output, defined by

$$P(Q^*) = C$$

and $z = \hat{k}/Q^*$, the MES expressed as a fraction of the efficient output. Hence, a necessary condition for entry deterrence is the credibility of a capacity

$$k_0 = (1 - z)Q^*.$$

But, given the declining marginal revenue assumption (A.4), if $q_0^M(m)$ is the monopoly output with marginal cost (m),

$$q_0 \leqslant \mathrm{MR}^{-1}(m) = q_0^M(m).$$

That is the case because any output from a competitor will lower the incumbent's marginal revenue curve and cause output to fall below the monopoly level.

Thus credible entry prevention requires that entry be blockaded at the monopoly output $q_0^M(m)$, or

$$z \geqslant 1 - q_0^M(m)/Q^*. \tag{11}$$

Define

$$s_k = \frac{rb}{C},$$

as the capital share of long-run cost. Then, for the special case of linear demand,

$$P(Q) = a - bQ, \text{ and}$$

the credibility requirement is

$$z \geqslant \frac{1}{2}\left[1 - s_k\left(\frac{a}{C} - 1\right)^{-1}\right]. \tag{12}$$

For demand with constant elasticity,

$$P(Q) = \left(\frac{Q}{\alpha}\right)^{-1/\eta}, \text{ and}$$

the requirement is

$$z \geq 1 - \left(\frac{\eta - 1}{\eta}\right)^{\eta} (1 - s_k)^{-\eta}. \tag{13}$$

The results in Equations (12) and (13) imply that credible entry prevention becomes more difficult when demand is more-elastic in the neighbourhood of the limit output. This may seem counter-intuitive. The B–S–M limit pricing model suggests that entry deterrence is *easier* with a less-elastic demand, because an entrant's output then has a more depressing effect on demand. In fact, there is no contradiction here. Equations (12) and (13) are conditions on the *credibility* of the limit output. A less-elastic demand reduces the maximum-credible capacity, corresponding to a higher required MES fraction (z) and that is the binding constraint for entry deterrence. Figure 3.3 shows such a situation. The limit output ($\bar{Q}$) exceeds $q_0^M(m)$ and hence is not credible. A less-elastic demand would increase the limit price ($\bar{P}$) but also exacerbate the credibility problem.

Capital-cost shares can be estimated from Department of Commerce data on payments to factors of production. One result that is evident from the data is that the capital-cost share is typically quite small. A review of twenty two-digit SIC code industries showed a maximum capital-cost share of 0.34 (chemicals), with an average value of 0.20. If the fixed-cost share is 0.34, a MES of at least one-third of demand is necessary to credibly deter entry if the choke price is twice long-run cost in the linear demand case, or if the demand elasticity is two for the exponential case. A higher choke price or a lower demand elasticity requires an even larger MES for credible deterrence of entry.

We can therefore conclude that, if fixed costs are restricted to capital costs alone, credible entry deterrence is limited to quite small markets, where the efficient number of firms is at most a few. Yet this ignores the fact that capital is not the only cost that is fixed (or quasi-fixed) in the short run. In most industries, labour is at least a partially fixed factor in the short run. Managers are reluctant to lay off workers, given both severance costs and the costs of retraining new workers in the event that the desired level of production should

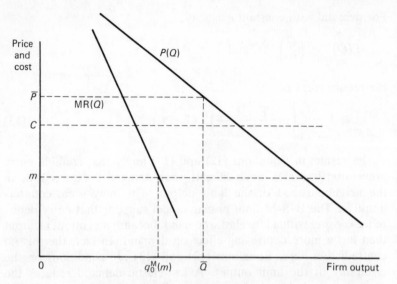

FIG. 3.3 A case where demand is not sufficiently elastic to make the limit output, $\bar{Q}$, credible. ($\bar{Q} > q_0^M(m)$).

increase in the future. Managers can alter the number of shifts and offer paid holidays, but this flexibility is limited. Also, to the extent that morale and hence ultimate productivity is higher when workers are active, managers may choose to maintain output even when marginal revenue falls short of marginal cost. In this way, the economics of the labour force can be an important factor in the ability of an established firm to maintain output in the face of entry.

Although we cannot conclude that labour contracts should be negotiated with the objective of entry deterrence, the characteristics of labour agreements suggest that the relevant share of fixed costs should exceed the capital share. Table 3.1 shows sixteen four-digit SIC code industries, selected on the basis of high MES technologies. Column 3 shows the sum of capital and labour shares that were calculated from Department of Commerce data on the value of shipments and the cost of materials (and energy). Using this figure in place of the capital share in Equations (12) and (13), and substituting the MES figures in column 2, produces the critical demand parameters necessary for credible entry deterrence. For linear demand, the choke price must be *less than* the figure shown in column 4 to credibly deter entry. For exponential demand, the demand elasticity must be *greater than* the figure shown in column 5.

In many, if not most, cases the conditions necessary for credible deterrence of entry appear too restrictive. It is difficult to believe that demand elasticities for intermediate goods are as high as is implied by Table 3.1, or that the choke prices can be so low, although this cannot be rejected in all industries. Also, to the extent that the industry classifications in Table 3.1 ignore differentiated submarkets and local monopoly power, one can expect less-elastic demands and binding credibility constraints, even though MES as a fraction of demand in the submarkets may be much larger.

While these results cast doubt on the credibility of entry deterrence, they depend crucially on the assumptions of the post-entry game (see Salop, 1979). The profitability of entry depends on the post-entry output of the established firm, which in turn depends on the nature of competition. Cournot–Nash behaviour implies that, faced with entry, an established firm will reduce output and thereby tend to accommodate a new rival. In contrast, more vigorous price competition would leave a new entrant with a smaller demand. If consumers incur transactions costs in changing supplies, or if they exhibit significant brand preference, price-matching by the established firm would allow it to keep its old customers. (See Dudley, 1982; and Schmalensee, 1980.) These assumptions fulfil the implied behaviour in the B–S–M limit pricing models, and entry deterrence may be both feasible and profitable with free entry. Gelman and Salop (1982) also study a model of entry with price competition, although they emphasise a potential competitor's strategy for determining its optimal entry size.

We are left with the conclusion that credible entry deterrence is feasible in many realistic situations only if potential competitors anticipate vigorous competition in the post-entry market.

IV DYNAMICS OF PRE-EMPTION

Static models are useful for illustrating the gains from entry deterrence, but they do not show how one firm may gain a first-mover advantage to the exclusion of other firms. Dynamic models can serve this function, but they must be specified with care. For example, a common approach in the dynamic analysis of oligopoly is to choose levels of investment or output that depend on time, holding the actions of others fixed. This is implicit in 'open-loop' control models; it also appears in the intertemporal analysis of sustainability in Willig

TABLE 3.1

Industry		$MES^{(1)}$ (%1967 Demand) z	'Fixed' cost share $s_k + s_L$	Choke price $(a/c - 1)\%$ $(<)$	Demand elasticity η $(>)$
(2082)	Beer brewing	1.0	0.53	54	1.9
(2621)	Paper: unbleached kraft	6.2	0.48	55	2.0
(92631)	Linerboard	4.4	0.52	57	1.9
(2822)	Synthetic rubber	7.2	0.44	51	2.2
(2823)	Cellulosic man-made fibres – rayon staple	18.3	0.58	91	1.6
(2824)	Non-cellulosic man-made fibres – acrylic	8.4	0.43	52	2.2
(2911)	Petroleum refining	1.1	0.23	24	4.3
(3011)	Passenger tyres	$3.8^{(2)}$	0.49	53	2.0
(3241)	Cement	1.6	0.65	67	1.5
(3312)	Integrated steel mills with wide strip mill	2.7	0.44	47	2.2
(3511)	Turbogenerators	$23.0^{(2)}$	0.54	100	1.6
(3519)	Diesel engines, automobile	21.0	0.48	83	1.8
(3573)	Electronic capital goods – computers	$15.4^{(2)}$	0.50	72	1.8
(3621)	Electric motors	$15.0^{(2)}$	0.59	84	1.6
(3632)	Refrigerators	$9.7^{(2)}$	0.43	53	2.2
(3711)	Automobiles	$11.0^{(2)}$	0.27	35	3.4

Source   [1]Weiss (1976), [2]Pratten (1971).

and Baumol (1980) and Baumol (1982), although the latter authors fix prices rather than quantities.

The problem that arises when output- or price-paths are assumed fixed is that the actions taken need not represent equilibria in a sequential game where agents make decisions taking into account credible reactions by others. It is just this problem in the limit-pricing literature that led Dixit (1980) and others to develop credible models of entry deterrence. This section summarises a model of dynamic competition developed in Gilbert and Harris (1983) where expectations *are* fulfilled and firms do not make empty threats. A simplifying assumption is:

A.5 Capital lasts forever.

We assume that markets are growing over time, so that

A.6 $\dfrac{\partial P(Q, t)}{\partial t} > 0.$

Consider, first, a market where no firm has any excess capacity. This is assured by

A.7 $MR(k_j, Q, t) \geq m$: marginal revenue is no less than short-run marginal cost when output (q_j) equals capacity (k_j).

For ease of notation, we normalise capacity so that the MES capacity ($\hat{k}$) equals unity. We assume that firms will build plants of minimum-efficient scale, although this can be demonstrated as a property of a market equilibrium. Let (t_k) be the date at which the kth plant is built. Profits earned on this plant, given an investment sequence $<t_j>$ and the assumption that all plants operate at full capacity, are:

$$\pi(k, t_k) = \sum_{j=k}^{\infty} \int_{t_j}^{t_{j+1}} [P(j, \tau) - m]e^{-r(\tau - t_k)}\, d\tau - b \qquad (14)$$

where b is the cost of the plant, m is the operating cost, and profits are discounted to date t_k.

Define the zero-profit sequence of investment dates $<\hat{t}_k>$, as the earliest sequence for which

$$\pi(k, \hat{t}_k) = 0 \qquad k = K_0 + 1, \ldots.$$

Here (K_0) is the capacity of the existing industry. Define zero-profit capacity $(N(t))$ by

$$N(t) = \max_k \{k : \hat{\imath}_k \leq t\}.$$

This is the capacity level corresponding to the zero-profit investment sequence at date (t).

Now suppose that there are two firms, A and B, each concerned not to miss profitable investment opportunities. Gilbert and Harris (1983) prove the following.

PROPOSITION 2

A Perfect-Nash equilibrium (as defined by Selten, 1975) exists where either firm A or firm B invests at the dates $\langle \hat{\imath}_k \rangle$ and where all new plants earn zero profits.

The assumption in this model – that output equals capacity at all times – has important consequences. It implies that the profits earned on any new investment are the same for *any* firm that makes the investment, because price depends only on total capacity and because all firms have the same technological opportunities. Since the net gain on a new investment is the same for any firm that invests, it follows that market structure is indeterminate in the long run. In particular, *an established firm has no more incentive to invest than does a new entrant, if there is no excess capacity.* The extension to more than two competitors is straightforward.

Relaxing the no-excess-capacity assumption can dramatically alter the implications for market structure. Suppose that along the zero-profit capacity sequence $(N(t))$ there is some date (t) at which

A.8 $\mathrm{MR}(N(t), t) < m.$

Given the declining marginal revenue assumption, this implies that a monopolist would hold excess capacity at (t).

Assume that at time t_0 all industry capacity (K_0) is owned by firm A. The incentives for entry will depend on the price that prevails if a firm chooses to enter the industry. Suppose that two or more firms in the industry would act as perfect competitors. In that case, the output of the industry would equal capacity, as price adjusted to clear the market. Thus there would exist a Perfect-Nash equilibrium, as described in Proposition 2, where all new plants earn zero profits.

The assumption that rival firms act as perfect competitors has profound implications for entry deterrence. Since all new plants built, from the entry date onwards, earn zero profits when rivals act as perfect competitors, an entrant could not expect to earn positive profits. Moreover, an incumbent could guarantee that negative profits could be earned by a potential entrant by investing slightly before the zero-profit dates $<\hat{t}_k>$: the incumbent could finance this strategy from monopoly profits earned in the absence of entry. The entry of rivals is deterred, because new plants would lose money when price fell to equate demand with capacity – which would exceed the zero-profit amount.

These results are summarised in the next proposition.

PROPOSITION 3

Assume there exists an incumbent firm with capacity $k^A = K_0$.

1. If firms act as perfect competitors after entry; and,
2. if A.8 holds so that a monopolist would restrict output below capacity, then there exists a Perfect-Nash equilibrium where the incumbent firm can prevent entry and earn positive profits by investing slightly before the zero-profit dates $<\hat{t}_k>$.

Firm A can afford to pre-empt competitors for two reasons. First, profits are higher with monopoly pricing. Second, and equally important, should a rival firm enter the industry, Firm A can assume that competition in the industries would be as described in Proposition 2; the post-entry price will fall immediately to whatever level is necessary to balance capacity and demand in the industry.

The profit which firm A, with initial capacity K_0, earns by building all new plants at dates $<\hat{t}_k>$ is

$$\pi^M = \sum_{k=K_0+1}^{\infty} \left\{ \int_{\hat{t}_k}^{\hat{t}_{k+1}} [R(Q(k, \tau), \tau) - mQ(k, \tau)]e^{-r\tau}d\tau - be^{-r\hat{t}_k} \right\} \tag{15}$$

(We begin at the investment date for plant $K_0 + 1$, but discount to the initial date). Here $R(Q(K, \tau), \tau)$ is the revenue at date τ when output is $Q(k, \tau)$ given capacity (k).

Without loss of generality, let $m = 0$ for ease of notation. Substituting the defining relation for the pre-emption dates $\langle \hat{t}_k \rangle$ from Equation (14) in (15), gives the profits of Firm A as:

$$\pi^M = \sum_{k=K_0+1}^{\infty} \left\{ \int_{\hat{t}_k}^{\hat{t}_{k+1}} [R(Q(k, \tau), \tau)e^{-r\tau}d\tau \right.$$

$$\left. - \sum_{j=k}^{\infty} \int_{\hat{t}_{ij}}^{\hat{t}_{j+1}} P(j, \tau)e^{-r\tau} d\tau \right\}.$$

After rearranging terms in the second summation, profits may be written as

$$\pi^M = \sum_{k=K_0+1}^{\infty} \int_{\hat{t}_k}^{\hat{t}_{k+1}} \{K_0 P(k, \tau) + [R(Q(k, \tau), \tau)$$

$$- kP(k, \tau)]\}e^{-r\tau}dt. \tag{16}$$

The first term inside the brackets in Equation (16) gives us exactly the profits which firm A would earn on its existing plants, if it did not pre-empt competitors. Pre-emption is profitable if the second term inside the brackets is positive. But this will be positive if firm A can earn monopoly revenues on its plants at any future date, by reducing output below installed capacity. Given Proposition 2, it is not difficult to see that the pre-emption outcome is also a Perfect-Nash equilibrium.

Although pre-emption can be successful in this particular situation, this conclusion rests on quite delicate assumptions. For example, there is no uncertainty in this model: in addition, all firms have identical expectations. But the future is uncertain, and firms will make different assessments about the profitability of entry. Successful pre-emption requires that the established firm always invests before the entry date of every potential competitor. With uncertainty reflected in a range of possible entry dates, pre-emption requires the established firm to dissipate its profits by continually investing *before* any potential competitor, no matter how optimistic that competitor might be about the rewards from entry. Faced with the prospect of throwing away profits to prevent entry, an established firm would do better to gamble and to choose investment dates that pre-empted rivals with some probability less than one. The consequence is that, over time, the probability of maintaining a monopoly position would fall. This is because it would, over time, become more likely that some potential competitor would perceive a profitable investment opportunity and would succeed in entering the industry.

Beyond this, the possibility of successful pre-emption hinges on yet another important condition, namely, the extent of price competition if entry occurs. The assumption that there can be excess capacity (and monopoly profits) before entry, but no excess capacity after entry, provides the driving force for pre-emptive behaviour by the established firm. Firms are assumed to act as perfect competitors if entry occurs. But other strategies are more reasonable as candidates for describing industry behaviour. One would expect, particularly if the entrant is small relative to the incumbent, a much more accommodating response. Since outputs are limited by capacity, the incumbent's profit with entry can be no smaller than the profit it would earn by assuming that the entrant would operate at capacity and by maximising profit from the residual demand. This would be a Cournot–Nash equilibrium if the entrant's output were sufficiently small.

Since Cournot–Nash behaviour appears quite reasonable for a small-scale entrant, let us assume (as in the static model of Section III) that established firms act as Cournot oligopolists rather than as perfect competitors. Let us go on to explore the consequences of this for entry deterrence. We shall see that this change in firm behaviour turns entry deterrence into an unprofitable activity.

Let k_0 be the incumbent's capacity at the initial date. As before, to pre-empt entrants, the incumbent must invest before the dates that yield zero profits to each entrant. Define by $Q(i, t)$ the total industry output when a rival firm enters with one unit of capacity (and output) at date (t) and when the incumbent's capacity is $i - 1$. That is,

$$Q(i, t) = q_0(i - 1, t) + 1,$$

where $q_0(i - 1, t)$ is the incumbent's Cournot–Nash equilibrium output, when the entrant operates at full capacity with one unit. We are assuming that for the entrant,

$$MR(1, t) \geq 0$$

so that the firm would operate at its capacity. The incumbent may or may not operate at full capacity.

Note that if both the incumbent and the entrant are constrained by the size of their existing capacity at all dates, the Cournot–Nash model is equivalent to the no-excess-capacity model which leads to Proposition 2. In this case, the incumbent cannot strictly pre-empt potential competitors, so that entry deterrence is impossible. Thus excess capacity is a *necessary* condition for entry deterrence with the assumed technology, and we shall assume in what follows that

$$\text{MR}(i-1, t) < 0 \qquad \text{for some } (t), \tag{17}$$

so that $q_0(i-1, t) < i-1$ and the incumbent holds excess capacity at date (t).

The 'threat' dates – at which the established firm must invest to deter entry – are defined by

$$b = \sum_{i=j}^{\infty} \int_{\hat{t}_i}^{\hat{t}_{i+1}} P(Q(i,t), t) e^{-r(t-\hat{t}_j)} \, dt, \tag{18}$$

for $j = k_0 + 1, \ldots$. Note that these dates depend on the size of post-entry output and will differ, in general, from the sequence corresponding to full capacity operation. The incumbent must invest at the dates $\langle \hat{t}_j \rangle$ if he is to deter entry, but even that may not be enough. Suppose the incumbent firm holds excess capacity at every future date, so that

$$q_0(i-1, t) < i-1 \qquad \text{for all } (t).$$

Then the addition of another unit of capacity will be of no value to the incumbent firm because the existence of additional capacity will have no effect on its output. Thus a second *necessary* condition for entry deterrence is that

$$q_0(i-1, t) = i-1 \tag{19}$$

for all dates $t = \hat{t}_i$, $i = k_0 + 1, \ldots$. If this condition is not met, capital accumulation will not affect rivals' entry decisions, and entry deterrence would be impossible. This condition constrains the degree to which the incumbent can exercise monopoly power, since the monopoly output must be close to the competitive output, at least at some dates.

Now assume that conditions (17) and (19) are satisfied, so that entry deterrence is credible; suppose also that the incumbent invests at the threat dates. Then the incumbent's monopoly profits (discounted to the initial date) are

$$\pi^M = \sum_{j=k_0+1}^{\infty} \left[\int_{\hat{t}_k}^{\hat{t}_{k+1}} Q^M(k, t) \, P(Q^M(k, t), t) e^{-rt} \mathrm{d}t - b e^{-r\hat{t}_k} \right], \quad (20)$$

where $Q^M(k, t)$ is the monopoly output with capacity (k) at (t).

Substituting Equation (18) and rearranging terms gives

$$\pi^M = \sum_{j=k_0+1}^{\infty} \int_{\hat{t}_k}^{\hat{t}_{k+1}} [Q^M(k, t) \, P(Q^M(k, t), t)$$

$$- k \, P(Q(k, t), t)] e^{-rt} \mathrm{d}t + k_0 b \quad (21)$$

Going from Equation (20) to (21) makes use of the condition that all new plants must break even at the prices that a firm would face if it were to enter the industry. Since only the new plants $(k - k_0)$ must break even, the established firm earns $k_0 b$ on its existing capacity, in addition to the profit from the first term in Equation (21).

The derivation leading to Equation (21) did not make specific use of Cournot–Nash behaviour: as a result, this relation will allow us to make a quick inspection of the gains from pre-emption, with different assumptions about post-entry competition. If entry leads to a perfectly competitive industry output, as assumed in the discussion leading to Proposition 3, then

$$Q(k, t) = k$$

and

$$Q^M(k, t) P(Q^M(k, t), t) \geq k \, P(k, t).$$

This is because monopoly profits are at least as large as the profits earned at full capacity output. The term $k_0 b$ in Equation (21) represents the profit earned on existing capacity when entry occurs with perfectly-competitive behaviour. The remaining term in (21) gives the excess profit earned by investing pre-emptively to deter entry.[6]

Pre-emptive investment yields profits at least as large as the profits yielded when entry occurs, *provided* that entry results in competitive pricing and *provided* that monopoly profits strictly exceed profits at full capacity. On the other hand, if a monopolist would not maintain excess capacity, then $Q^M(k, t) = k$ and the profits earned with pre-emption are identical with the profits earned when entry occurs. That is, if a monopolist would utilise fully all capacity, then the gains from pre-emption would be nil. This is exactly the case assumed in Proposition 2.

The above conclusions depend on the assumption of competitive pricing if entry occurs, and the logic of this assumption already has been questioned. In general we would expect

$$Q^M(k, t) < Q(k, t) < k,$$

so that entry resulted in lower, but not necessarily perfectly competitive, prices. Consider the case where the output of the entrant is small relative to total output, so that $Q(k, t)$ is approximately the monopoly output $Q^M(k, t)$; and assume $Q^M(k, t) < k$ for some (t). Then, monopoly profits with pre-emption are approximately

$$\pi^M = \sum_{k=k_0+1}^{\infty} \int_{\hat{t}_k}^{\hat{t}_{k+1}} [Q^M(k, t) - k] \, P(Q^M(k, t), t) e^{-rt} dt + k_0 b. \quad (22)$$

And this is clearly less than $k_0 b$.

When potential entrants are small, so that their entry has only a negligible impact on price, then profits from pre-emption fall short of $k_0 b$. This does not yet prove that entry-prevention is undesirable, because the relevant comparison is between profits with pre-emption and profits when entry occurs. Profits when entry occurs may exceed $k_0 b$ in the case of Cournot–Nash competition. Suppose the incumbent does not prevent entry, and assume that all entrants operate at full capacity. If $k - k_0$ firms enter, total output is

$$\tilde{Q}(k, t) = \tilde{q}_0(k_0, t) + k - k_0. \quad (23)$$

Here, the first term on the right is the incumbent's Cournot–Nash output, when the firm has capacity k_0 and when competitors produce $k - k_0$.

If all entrants earn zero profits, new plants will be built at dates $<\tilde{t}_k>$ determined by

$$b = \sum_{i=k}^{\infty} \int_{\tilde{t}_i}^{\tilde{t}_{i+1}} P(\tilde{Q}(i, t), t) e^{-r(t-\tilde{t}_k)} \, dt, \quad (24)$$

for $k = k_0+1, \ldots$. Entry drives prices below the monopoly levels and, as a result, $\tilde{t}_k \geq \hat{t}_k$, where $\hat{t}_k$ is the threat date corresponding to pre-emptive investment by the incumbent. Since the initial date of the threat sequence is arbitrary, let $\tilde{t}_{k_0+1} = \hat{t}_{k_0+1}$.

If the incumbent does not deter entry, profits are

$$\pi_0 = \sum_{k=k_0+1}^{\infty} \int_{\tilde{t}_k}^{\tilde{t}_{k+1}} \tilde{q}_0(k_0, t) \, P(\tilde{Q}(k, t), t) e^{-rt} \, dt.$$

This, making use of (23) and (24) gives us

$$\pi_0 = \sum_{k=k_0+1}^{\infty} \int_{\bar{i}_k}^{\bar{i}_{k+1}} [\bar{Q}(k, t) - k] \, P(\bar{Q}(k, t), t) e^{-rt} \, dt + k_0 b.$$

Note that

$$\bar{Q}(k, t) \geq Q^{\text{M}}(k, t),$$

and that

$$\bar{i}_k \geq \hat{i}_{t_k}.$$

This implies that

$$\pi_0 \geq \pi^{\text{M}},$$

with a strict inequality whenever $Q^{\text{M}}(k, t) < \bar{Q}(k, t)$ or $\bar{i}_k \geq \hat{i}_k$. If each entrant has a negligible impact on the total output of the industry, the incumbent earns higher profits by allowing entry. This establishes the main result summarised below.

PROPOSITION 4

Suppose firms would act as Cournot–Nash competitors if entry occurred, and suppose that a firm would enter an industry if expected profits were positive. If the MES for entry were small relative to the capacity of an incumbent firm, *pre-emptive investment to deter entry will not be profitable.*

We have shown that pre-emption is not desirable when entrants are 'small' and when an established firm does not react aggressively to the entry of a small firm. Of course, the incumbent might be better off if it could feign an aggressive price response in order to discourage all entrants, and this rasies issues of threat credibility discussed in Kreps and Wilson (1982).

If we accept Cournot–Nash behaviour as an accurate description of post-entry competition, the case for successful entry deterrence is fragile indeed. Three factors work against the use of pre-emptive capacity investment by the incumbent.

(1) If the incumbent holds excess capacity at every date, additional investment will not affect output and is an empty threat against entry. This is exactly the point made by Dixit (1980) in his discussion of entry deterrence with excess capacity.

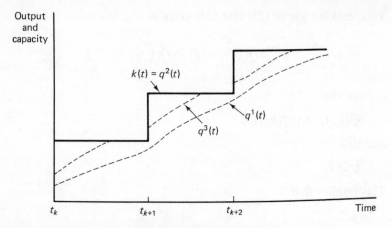

FIG. 3.4 Alternative output paths given capacity $k(t)$. Only path $q^3(t)$ is a candidate for pre-emptive investment.

(2) If all firms operate at full capacity, pre-emptive investment earns no more than the returns which would be earned with competition. Hence, entry deterrence has no value to the incumbent firm.

(3) If entrants are small enough to have a negligible impact on prices, 'successful' entry deterrence yields profits that are strictly lower than the profits earned with entry. The incumbent is better off allowing entry, even when entry deterrence is feasible.

Figure 3.4 shows examples of outputs for incumbents that are not consistent with pre-emptive investment. Here $k(t)$ is the capacity of the incumbent at date (t). The output path $q^1(t)$ implies that there is excess capacity at every date and therefore that pre-emption is not credible. For $q^2(t) = k(t)$ at each date, pre-emptive investment earns no more than the returns earned with competition. Only the output path $q^3(t)$ is a possible candidate for pre-emptive investment, and this is subject to the qualification stated in (3) above.

V CONCLUDING REMARKS

A major result of work on pre-emptive competition is to have identified the importance of behaviour in the determination of industrial structure. Bain (1956) identified the role of economies of scale and of product differentiation in market structure, while others emphasised stochastic factors (e.g., Simon and Bonini (1958), Mansfield (1962), and Nelson *et al.* (1976)). Although economies of scale (as measured by the minimum efficient scale of operations) are positively correlated with measures of the concentration of an industry, markets are typically more concentrated than can be explained by the presence of firms of minimum efficient scale. Both technology and product differentiation may depend on the histories of firms, and stochastic theories do not capture the incentives for firm entry and growth.

An extreme example of the consequences of the behaviour of firms is the possibility of entry deterrence by an established firm. On this subject we have explored whether an established firm would deter entry if it could do so, and whether potential competitors should expect that an established firm would act to make entry unprofitable. The first question concerns the *desirability* of entry deterrence, while the second addresses the *credibility* of entry-deterring threats.

We have shown that, with free entry, an established firm would do well to prevent entry by pre-emptive investment in many although not all circumstances, provided the threat to use capacity if entry takes place is credible. That is, the entry-deterring threat is a good one for the incumbent if the firm can convince competitors that they should take it seriously. In the static model of entry deterrence, an established firm would want to use limit-pricing to exclude competitors. In the dynamic model of capacity investment, pre-emptive investment would be desirable if potential competitors anticipated that existing excess capacity would be used if they entered.

The desirability of pre-emptive activity does not hinge on the absolute magnitude of the profits to be earned, provided that they exceed the profits without entry-deterrence. Schmalensee (1980) argues that successful entry deterrence in the Dixit model implies only modest profits for typical cost functions. But this does not imply that successful entry deterrence is unimportant, particularly if the long-run consequences of market structure are taken into account in such dimensions as technical progress and product differentiation.

Although established firms may be better off with entry deterrence, rational entrants would be deterred by pre-emptive capacity investment only if the incumbent would use the capacity if entry occurred. Generally speaking, the feasibility constraint for entry prevention is weaker the more aggressive is post-entry competition. Assuming a Cournot oligopoly if entry occurs, we examined the feasibility of entry deterrence for a number of industries with substantial economies of scale.

One immediate observation was that entry-preventing outputs are not credible in many circumstances if fixed costs are limited to capital costs, because these are usually no more than 20 to 30 per cent of total costs. With this small differential between short- and long-run marginal costs, an established firm cannot maintain an output much larger than the Cournot output corresponding to its own long-run costs. Adding labour costs to fixed costs increases the scope for entry-deterring behaviour but, even in this case, demand would have to be quite elastic to allow a credible entry-deterring output in all but a very few industries.

The static model illustrates the incentive for pre-emptive capacity investment to deter entry, but it does not explain why an established firm should have a 'first-mover' advantage. This was the subject of Section IV, which examined a dynamic model of firm investment. Explicitly accounting for the dynamics of firm entry and growth introduces further conditions that constrain the feasibility of entry-deterrence. First, given an assumption that marginal revenue is a declining function of industry output, investment is an empty threat against entry if the incumbent firm already possesses excess capacity. Second, with the fixed-proportions technology, pre-emption and competition yield the same profits if all firms operate at full capacity. Hence, entry deterrence has no value. Finally, and perhaps most important, if entrants are small, 'successful' entry deterrence yields profits that are strictly lower than the profits with entry. The incumbent is better off allowing entry, even if deterrence is feasible.

This last result casts doubt on the efficacy of any strategy for pre-emption that is employed during a period of significant growth in an industry. If the minimum scale of entry is small compared to the market size, a competitive response sufficient to deter entry would be very costly to the established firm in terms of current profits foregone. Hence a potential competitor would expect an accommodative response to entry and would not be deterred by pre-emptive investment.

The main conclusion is that pre-emptive investment is not likely, as alleged in the Alcoa case, to be a credible threat to market performance unless: (i) scale economies are sufficient to allow the existence of only a few firms in an efficient market structure; or (ii) an established firm can convince potential competitors that it would compete aggressively against even relatively small entrants. In particular, a Nash–Cournot response to entry is not sufficiently aggressive to deter small competitors.

These results suggest that, in most markets, unless there is a history of hostile behaviour, potential competition should be adequate to bring about workable competition, given enough time for market growth or capital depreciation to make room for entry. In this sense, the results are consistent with the predictions of contestability theory advanced by Baumol *et al.* (1982). But the reason why the two approaches yield similar results are quite different. In contestability theory, an incumbent firm must price at marginal cost (or average cost if that is declining) because not to do so would invite entry and the loss of customers. That is, firms behave much as Bertrand competitors in contestability theory.

In the theory of pre-emptive investment, setting price equal to marginal cost when entry occurs (i.e., acting as Bertrand's competitors), is exactly the type of behaviour that can succeed in deterring potential competitors. Entry is possible because such pricing behaviour is generally not the best response to entry. It is precisely because firms would not try to undercut each other that gives a potential entrant reason for optimism. When an established firm accommodates entry, potential competition can lead to workable competition, although the route to acceptable market performance is not as smooth as is implied by the contestability theory.

NOTES

1. I am grateful to Drew Fudenberg, David Newbery, and Xavier Vives for helpful discussions, and to Alan Berger, Richard Kohl and Jane Haltmaier for research assistance. This chapter includes joint work with Richard Harris.
2. *United States* v. *Aluminum Company of America*, 148 F.2d 416 (2nd Cir 1945).
3. See Vives (1982) for an analysis of the simultaneous entry problem.
4. I am grateful to Xavier Vives for deriving this result. The details are in Gilbert and Vives (1982).
5. A sufficient condition, if $P'(Q) \leqslant 0$, is

$$\frac{\mathrm{d}\ell\mathrm{n}\,\eta}{\mathrm{d}\ell\mathrm{n}\,Q} < \frac{1}{s_j} - \frac{1+\eta}{\eta} \,,$$

where η is the magnitude of the demand elasticity and s_j is firm j's market share.
6. For the case where $Q(k, t) = k$, Equations (21) and (16) are identical. Note that the first term in Equation (16) equals $k_0 b$ as a consequence of the definition of the threat dates.

REFERENCES

Bain, J. S. (1956) *Barriers to New Competition* (Cambridge, Mass.: Harvard University Press).

Baumol, W. J. (1982) 'Contestable Markets: An Uprising in the Theory of Industrial Structure', *American Economic Review*, vol. 72, Mar. pp. 1–15.

Baumol, W. J., Panzar, J. C. and Willig, R. D. (1982) *Contestable Markets and the Theory of Industry Structure* (New York: Harcourt Brace Jovanovich).

Dixit, A. K. (1979) 'A Model of Duopoly Suggesting a Theory of Entry Barriers', *Bell Journal of Economics*, vol. 10, pp. 20–32.

——— (1980) 'The Role of Investment in Entry Deterrence', *Economic Journal* vol. 90, pp. 95–106.

Dudley, W. (1982) 'A Consumer Incentive Model of Entry Deterrence', PhD dissertation, University of California, Berkeley.

Eaton B. C. and Lipsey, R. G. (1979) 'The Theory of Market Preemption: The Persistence of Excess Capacity and Monopoly in Growing Spatial Markets', *Economica*, vol. 46, May, pp. 149–58.

——— (1980) 'Exit Barriers are Entry Barriers: The Durability of Capital as a Barrier to Entry', *Bell Journal of Economics*, vol. 10, pp. 721–729.

——— (1981) 'Capital, Commitment, and Entry Equilibrium', *Bell Journal of Economics* vol. 12, pp. 593–604.

Fudenberg, D. and Tirole, J. (1981) 'Capital as a Commitment: Strategic Investment to Deter Mobility', Mimeo. (University of California, Berkeley).

Fudenberg, D., Tirole, J., Gilbert, R. and Stiglitz, J. 'Preemption, Leapfrogging and Competition in Patent Races', *European Economic Review* (forthcoming).

Gelman, J. R. and Salop, S. C. (1981) 'Judo Economics, Entrant Advantages, and the Great Coupon Wars', Mimeo. (Goergetown University), December.

Gilbert, R. J. and Harris, R. G. (1981) 'Investment Decisions with Economies of Scale and Learning', *American Economic Review* vol. 7, pp. 172–7.

——— (1983) 'Competition with Lumpy Investments', Stanford University Working Paper.

Gilbert, R. J. and Newbery, D. M. G. (1982) 'Preemptive Patenting and the Persistence of Monopoly', *American Economic Review*, vol. 72, no. 2.

Gilbert, R. J. and Vives, X. (1982) 'A Short Note on Sequential Entry', University of California Working Paper.

Kreps, D. M. and Wilson, R., (1982) 'Reputation and Imperfect Information', *Journal of Economic Theory*, vol. 27, pp. 253–9.

Kwoka, J. E., Jr. (1979) 'The Effect of Market Share Distribution on Industry Performance', *Review of Economics and Statistics* vol. 61, pp. 101–109.

Mansfield, E. (1962) 'Entry, Gibrat's Law, Innovation and the Growth of Firms', *American Economic Review*, vol. 52, pp. 1031–1034.

Modigliani, F. (1958) 'New Developments on the Oligopoly Front', *Journal of Political Economy*, vol. 66, pp. 213–32.

Nelson, R. R., Winter, S. G. and Schuette, H. L. (1976) 'Technical Change in an Evolutionary Model', *Quarterly Journal of Economics* vol. 90, pp. 90–118.

Pratten, C. F. (1971) *Economies of Scale in Manufacturing Industry* (Cambridge, Mass.: Cambridge University Press).

Prescott, E. C. and Visscher, M. (1977) 'Sequential Location Among Firms with Foresight', *Bell Journal of Economics* vol. 8, pp. 378–93.

Rao, R. C. and Rutenberg, D. P. (1979) 'Preempting an Alert Rival: Strategic Timing of the First Plant by Analysis of Sophisticated Rivalry', *Bell Journal of Economics* vol. 10, pp. 378–393.

Salop, S. C. (1979) 'Strategic Entry Deterrence', *American Economic Review, Papers and Proceedings* vol. 69, pp. 335–8.

Schmalensee, R. (1978) 'Entry Deterrence in the Ready-to-Eat Cereal Industry', *Bell Journal of Economics* vol. 9, pp. 305–27.

—— (1980) 'Economies of Scale and Barriers to Entry', MIT Working Paper No. 1130.

Selton, R. (1975) 'Re-examination of the Perfectness Concept for Equilibrium Points in Extensive Games', *International Journal of Game Theory* vol. 4, pp. 25–55.

Simon, H. A. and Bonini, C. P. (1958) 'The Size Distribution of Business Firms', *American Economic Review* vol. 48, pp. 607–17.

Spence, A. M. (1977) 'Entry, Capacity, Investment, and Oligopolistic Pricing', *Bell Journal of Economics* vol. 8, pp. 534–547.

—— (1979) 'Investment Strategy and Growth in a New Market', *Bell Journal of Economics* vol. 9, pp. 1–19.

Sylos-Labini, P. (1962) *Oligopoly and Technical Progress* (Cambridge, Mass.: Harvard University Press).

United States v. *Aluminum Company of America*, 148 F2d 416 (2nd Cir. 1945).

Vives, X. (1932) 'A Model of Sequential Entry Deterrence', Mimeo. (University of California).

von Weizäcker, C. C. (1980) 'A Welfare Analysis of Barriers to Entry', *Bell Journal of Economics* vol. 11, pp. 399–420.

Ware, R. (1984) 'Competition with Differentiated Products', Mimeo. (University of Toronto).

Weiss, L. W. (1976) 'Optimal Plant Size and the Extent of Sub-Optimal Capacity', In *Essays on Industrial Organization in Honor of Joe S. Bain.* (eds) Masson, R. T. and Ovalls, P. D. (Cambridge, Mass.: Ballinger Press).

Willig, R. D. and Baumol, W. J. (1980) 'Intertemporal Sustainability', Mimeo. (Princeton University).

Discussion of the Paper by Richard J. Gilbert

In discussing this paper, *Panzar* questioned the assumption used by Gilbert that the game played in the post-entry market be a Cournot quantity-setting game. In particular, Panzar conjectured that a range of potential outcomes in the post-entry market might be possible depending on the nature of conjectures used by players once entry has occurred. In addition, Panzar argued that firms used fixed capital to control variable costs, as well as to establish capacity. He questioned whether Gilbert's conclusions about the necessary conditions for capacity to represent a credible pre-emptive threat could be extended to the case where firms possessed neoclassical production functions.

Richard Gilbert agreed with Panzar that the fixed-proportions assumption was likely critical to his results. He explained that the use of fixed-proportions in production made his model comparable to that of Dixit (1980). Further, he suggested that there were still many important issues that could be explored with relative ease in the context of the fixed-proportions production structure. Gilbert cited the problems that arose when the incumbent firm's capacity choice conveyed information about its objectives as an example of his point. To Panzar's question about the Cournot post-entry game, Gilbert responded that alternative assumptions about post-entry conjectures tended to make entry deterrence more difficult. Since entry deterrence was already relatively difficult for incumbents, exploring other post-entry games was not likely to be a fruitful venture. Gilbert suggested that the implications of the post-entry game for entry deterrence could be understood by examining equilibrium profit rates in the post-entry game. If the post-entry game was Bertrand, then prices would be driven to marginal costs, post-entry profits would be zero, and entry deterrence was very easy. If the post-entry game resulted in a collusive solution, then post-entry profits would be high and entry could be difficult to prevent.

Michael Spence proposed that for extant firms in an industry, the main strategic problem was one of minimising the impact of existing rivals or preventing entry by rivals who were expected to be particularly aggressive. In his view, the current economic literature on pre-emptive competition concentrated excessively on marginal entrants. According to Spence, a more profitable way to view the entry problem for the incumbent firm might assume that existing firms were not concerned with entry *per se*, but rather, they were worried about preventing entrants with specific characteristics from entering the market.

REFERENCE

Dixit, A. (1980) 'The Role of Investment in Entry-Deterrence', *Economic Journal*, vol. 90, pp. 95–106.

4 Elementary Theory of Slack-ridden Imperfect Competition

Reinhard Selten

BONN, FEDERAL REPUBLIC OF GERMANY

I INTRODUCTION

Organisational slack is a central variable in the behavioural theory of the firm (Cyert and March, 1963). Ever since Leibenstein (1966) described organisational slack under the name of 'X-inefficiency', the pervasiveness of the phenomenon has caught the attention of many economists. In his book *Beyond Economic Man* Leibenstein (1976) discusses a number of empirical studies which show the importance of organisational slack. However, present-day textbooks on micro-economics almost ignore the concept, as does most of the literature on formal models of imperfect competition.

Compared with Leibenstein's (1976) attempt at a complete reconstruction of micro-economics, the aim here is much more modest. The theory presented here emphasises organisational slack but, otherwise, it is quite similar to the accepted view. Attention is restricted to the most elementary framework which can be used for the analysis of imperfect competition, the symmetric, linear Cournot oligopoly model. The basic principles can be applied in more general contexts, but no attempt in this direction will be made here.

Traditionally, the firm has been viewed as an organisation under the control of a strong owner whose relentless pressure on costs succeeds in enforcing efficiency of production and administration. At least in the long run, the owner's relentless desire to maximise profits removes the last trace of slack.

126

The pervasiveness of organisational slack suggests that one should look for a different description of reality. The theory presented here will be based on a notion of 'slack-ridden profit maximisation' which maintains that profits are maximised, but on the basis of a cost function which includes slack. This idea must be complemented by an assumption on the behavioural dynamics of slack.

A 'strong-slack hypothesis' will be introduced. This admittedly extreme assumption simply maintains that slack has a tendency to increase so long as profits are positive; slack can be reduced, but only under the threat of losses. Nothing else limits slack but the necessity of non-negative profits. This has the consequence that long-run profits tend to be zero, regardless of market structure.

The strong-slack hypothesis may be described as a theory of weak ownership. In reality, ownership is not quite so weak. It is hard to reconcile empirical findings on the correlation of industrial concentration and profitability (Collins and Preston, 1969, Shepherd, 1972) with the idea of zero long-run profits. In spite of these shortcomings, the strong-slack hypothesis may still be a better idealisation of reality than the hypothesis of profit maximisation without slack.

The strong-slack hypothesis has the virtue of simplicity. It can be used to compare the consequences of extremely weak ownership with those of extremely strong ownership. It turns out that there are striking differences. In the usual theory of the symmetric, linear Cournot oligopoly with fixed costs, welfare can be increased by restriction of entry if fixed costs are sufficiently small. Under the strong-slack hypothesis, the picture is different. Welfare can never be increased by restriction of entry. Free entry is always best.

Organisational slack should not be looked upon as entirely wasteful. It involves some inefficiency, but part of this is enjoyed as 'consumption at the working place'. It is fair to assume that slack has its benefits for the members of the organisation, but the welfare gains are worth less than they cost. (See Figure 4.1.)

The inefficient use of resources is only part of the welfare-loss caused by slack. It is an important feature of the theory presented below that marginal costs contain slack.

Higher marginal costs lead to higher prices and to reduced production, with adverse effects on consumer's rent. The 'marginal-cost effect' of slack is more important for welfare than is the inefficient use of organisational resources.

The gap between the strong-slack hypothesis and profit maximisation without slack can be bridged by a 'general-slack hypothesis',

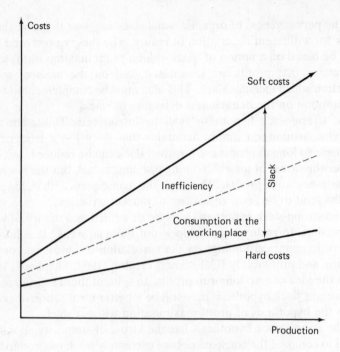

FIG. 4.1

Note: 'Soft costs' include 'hard costs' and organisational slack. Organisational slack is subdivided into 'inefficiency' and 'consumption at the working place'.

which permits a continuum of intermediate cases. It postulates a dynamics of slack, which results in a balance between slack and profits. Under the general-slack hypothesis, an increase in the number of competitors has qualitatively similar effects as in the Cournot theory. Without slack, price and profits decline.

In imperfect markets with slack, competition not only reduces profits; it also puts pressure on costs. It can be expected that the importance of competition will be enhanced by its role as a cost-reducing force. The results obtained here illustrate this point of view.

II   SLACK AND COSTS

Let us assume that there are n oligopolists ($i = 1, \ldots, n$). The following notation will be used:

x_i, supply by firm i;

K_i, costs of firm i;

s_i, slack-rate of firm i;

S_i, total slack of firm i; and

A_i, firm i's 'consumption at the working place'.

Costs are linear in x_i. Slack rates s_i can be described as slack per unit of output. For the sake of simplicity, it is assumed that fixed costs are not affected by slack. One could introduce slack into fixed costs, too, but this would make the computations much more complicated.

$$K_i = F + (c + s_i)x_i \qquad \text{for } i = 1, \ldots, n, \tag{1}$$

with $F > 0$ and $c \geqslant 0$.

The constant c is the level below which marginal costs cannot be reduced. Slack-rates must be non-negative.

$$s_i \geqslant 0 \qquad \text{for } i = 1, \ldots, n \tag{2}$$

The cost function (1) includes slack. One may distinguish 'soft costs' and 'hard costs'. Hard costs are those costs which would arise even without slack, i.e. at $s_i = 0$. Cost functions observed in reality, e.g. in econometric studies, should be thought of as 'soft' or 'slack-inclusive'.

Hard costs may not be observable at all. It is not necessary to assume that anybody in the organisation knows the amount of slack. So long as there is no outside pressure which forces management to reduce slack, there is no reason why anybody should want to know much about slack, since everybody enjoys its benefits. Profits are assumed to be maximised on the basis of soft costs. The necessary computations do not require any knowledge of hard costs.

Total slack is defined as follows:

$$S_i = x_i s_i \qquad \text{for } i = 1, \ldots, n \tag{3}$$

For the sake of simplicity, a constant fraction α of total slack is assumed to be 'consumption at the working place'.

$$A_i = \alpha S_i, \tag{4}$$

with $0 \leqslant \alpha \leqslant 1$.

We refer to α as the 'slack consumption rate'. Maybe it would be more realistic to assume a concave non-linear relationship between A_i and S_i, but this possibility is not investigated here.

III   NORMALISED SYMMETRIC LINEAR COURNOT OLIGOPOLY

It is assumed that cost function (1) is the same for all oligopolists. This is what the term 'symmetric' means. The possibility of different slack rates for different firms is not excluded by assumption: the equality of all slack rates will be obtained as a result. The following notation will be used:

$$x = \sum_{i=1}^{n} x_i \qquad \text{total supply;}$$

$$\hat{p} \qquad\qquad \text{price;}$$
$$p = \hat{p} - c \qquad \text{normalised price; and}$$
$$G_i \qquad\qquad \text{profits of firm } i$$

Consider a linear demand function:

$$\hat{p} = b - ax, \tag{5}$$
for $b - ax \geq 0$ and $\hat{p} = 0$ otherwise.

Equation (5) can be rewritten as follows:

$$p = b - c - ax, \tag{6}$$
for $b - ax \geq 0$ and $p = -c$ otherwise.

Without loss of generality, we can assume $b > c$ since profitable production is impossible for $b \leq c$. The quantity unit and the money unit can be chosen in such a way that we have:

$$a = b - c = 1. \tag{7}$$

With this normalisation, the demand function has the following form:

$$p = 1 - x \tag{8}$$
for $1 - x \geq -c$ and $p = -c$ otherwise

Profits G_i are as follows:

$$G_i = px_i - s_i x_i - F. \tag{9}$$

The normalised model described by (8) and (9) can be interpreted as an oligopoly without variable 'hard' costs. For the sake of brevity p will be called 'price', since $\hat{p}$ will not be important for the analysis.

IV SLACK-RIDDEN PROFIT MAXIMISATION

Slack-ridden profit maximisation optimises on the basis of 'soft' costs. For the normalised Cournot oligopoly, profits are given by (9). The marginal conditions for internal Cournot equilibrium are as follows:

$$\frac{\partial G_i}{\partial x_i} = 1 - x - x_i - s_i = 0. \tag{10}$$

The following notation will be used:

$$s = \frac{1}{n} \sum_{i=1}^{n} s_i \tag{11}$$

The average slack rate s will turn out to be an important variable. Summing up over equations (10), one obtains:

$$n - nx - x - ns = 0 \tag{12}$$

and

$$x = \frac{n}{n+1}(1 - s). \tag{13}$$

In the same way as total supply x, price p is determined by (s):

$$p = \frac{1}{n+1} + \frac{n}{n+1}s. \tag{14}$$

Equation (10) together with (13) yields:

$$x_i = \frac{1}{n+1} + \frac{n}{n+1}s - s_i. \tag{15}$$

Equation (9) can be written as follows:

$$G_i = (p - s_i)x_i - F. \tag{16}$$

This yields:

$$G_i = \left(\frac{1}{n+1} + \frac{n}{n+1}s - s_i\right)^2 - F. \tag{17}$$

For the special case of zero slack rates, one obtains the following formula:

$$G_i = \frac{1}{(n + 1)^2} - F, \tag{18}$$

for $s_1 = s_2 = \ldots = s_n = 0$.

V   THE STRONG SLACK HYPOTHESIS AND ITS CONSEQUENCES

The strong slack hypothesis takes the extreme view that 'slack squeezes out profit'. This means that, in the long run, profits will be zero regardless of the number of competitors:

$$G_i = 0 \qquad \text{for } i = 1, \ldots, n. \tag{19}$$

The long-run equilibrium condition (19), together with the formula (17) for Cournot equilibrium profits at given slack rates, permits us to determine equilibrium slack rates. We must have:

$$\left(\frac{1}{n + 1} + \frac{n}{n + 1} s - s_i \right)^2 = F. \tag{20}$$

Moreover, the expression in brackets on the left-hand side is nothing other than x_i and therefore must be non-negative. Since this is the case, for fixed s the left-hand side is a decreasing function of s_i. Consequently, for given s there is at most one s_i which satisfies (20). This shows that in long-run equilibrium, all slack rates must be equal:

$$s_i = s \qquad \text{for } i = 1, \ldots, n. \tag{21}$$

With the help of (21), condition (20) yields the following equation for s:

$$\frac{1}{(n + 1)^2} (1 - s)^2 = F. \tag{22}$$

In view of (13), we must have:

$$0 \leqslant s \leqslant 1. \tag{23}$$

Considering this, we can conclude:

$$1 - s = (n + 1) \sqrt{F} \tag{24}$$

and

$$s = 1 - (n + 1) \sqrt{F}. \tag{25}$$

Together with (24), equation (13) yields:

$$x = n\sqrt{F}. \tag{26}$$

Hence,

$$p = 1 - n\sqrt{F}. \tag{27}$$

In view of (23) it follows (by (22)) that we must have:

$$\frac{1}{(n+1)^2} \geq F. \tag{28}$$

With the help of (18), it can immediately be seen that (28) can be interpreted as the non-negativity condition for Cournot-equilibrium profits at zero slack rates. In view of (28), an inequality for x follows by (25). It is:

$$x \leq \frac{n}{n+1}. \tag{29}$$

The right-hand side of (29) is nothing other than Cournot-equilibrium supply at zero slack rates. With the exception of the border-case of equality in (28), total supply will be smaller and price will be higher under the strong slack hypothesis than in Cournot-equilibrium without slack.

It is worth pointing out that (27) shows a strong influence of fixed costs on price. In this respect, slack-ridden competition is quite different from competition without slack.

VI CONDITIONS OF ENTRY

The strong slack hypothesis (19) excludes both negative and positive profits. The exclusion of negative profits is based on the usual assumption that long-run losses would eventually force at least one competitor to leave the market.

Let $\bar{n}$ be the maximum number of competitors, such that condition (28) is satisfied for $n = \bar{n}$. Then:

$$\bar{n} = \max_{n=1,2,\ldots} \left\{ n \mid \frac{1}{n+1} \geq \sqrt{F} \right\}. \tag{30}$$

Entry restrictions, such as government regulations, may result in a number of competitors smaller than $\bar{n}$. We shall speak of a *closed oligopoly* if the number n of competitors is exogenously fixed.

Contrary to this, in *open oligopoly* the number of competitors in long-run equilibrium is an endogenous variable; it is assumed that there are sufficient potential competitors (more than $\bar{n}$) who can enter the market if they find this advantageous.

In the framework of a theory of slack-ridden imperfect competition, this description of open oligopoly needs to be complemented by some further assumptions on potential competitors. One has to say something on the slack-rate of new entrants. We shall consider only the case of efficient free entry, where new firms can come in with zero slack-rates. This is quite reasonable if one thinks of new entrants as highly-energetic and hard-working entrepreneurs. However, for some markets the only potential entrants may be old-established firms which operate with considerable slack in highly-concentrated markets. In such cases, there will be a positive minimum slack-rate for new entrants.

Suppose that there are $n-1$ firms $1, \ldots, n-1, n$ on the market and that a potential competitor n with a zero slack-rate considers entry. It is reasonable to assume that he will enter if, and only if, after his entry the sustainability condition $n \leqslant \bar{n}$ is satisfied. For $n > \bar{n}$, he has to expect long-run losses, even if in the short run he may have positive Cournot profits due to his advantage in efficiency. For $n \leqslant \bar{n}$, he need not fear such long-run losses and in view of his efficiency his short-run profits will be non-negative, too.

Admittedly, the argument sketched above is not very precise and needs further elaboration. It implicitly assumes that long-run losses always outweigh temporary gains. In order to justify this assumption one would have to look at the dynamic process which leads to long-run equilibrium in much more detail. However, if it should turn out that competitor n has an incentive to enter even if $n > \bar{n}$ holds, this would mean that no long-run equilibrium can be achieved. Therefore, $n = \bar{n}$ is at least a necessary condition for long-run equilibrium under efficient free entry.

VII WELFARE CONSIDERATIONS

In Sections VIII and IX, we shall look at the question whether welfare might be increased by restriction of entry. This question will be investigated both under the usual assumptions of profit maximisation without slack, and under the strong slack hypothesis.

The following notation will be used:

C consumers rent;

$$G = \sum_{i=1}^{n} G_i \quad \text{total profits;}$$

$$S = \sum_{i=1}^{n} S_i \quad \text{total slack; and}$$

$$A = \sum_{i=1}^{n} A_i \quad \text{total 'consumption at the working place'.}$$

The welfare measure W is defined as follows:

$$W = C + G + A. \tag{31}$$

In spite of the well-known difficulties with such measures, nothing better can be done in the framework of partial analysis. In view of (4), equation (31) can be rewritten as follows:

$$W = C + G + \alpha S. \tag{32}$$

In the present case, consumer's rent is computed as follows:

$$C = \frac{1}{2} x^2. \tag{33}$$

Under the usual assumptions of profit maximisation, total slack S is zero and, under the strong slack hypothesis, (G) is zero.

VIII   WELFARE EFFECTS OF ENTRY RESTRICTION WITHOUT SLACK

We shall first look at the usual theory of Cournot equilibrium without slack. We can rely on the formulæ of Section IV, with $s_i = 0$ for $i = 1, \ldots, n$. The following notations will be used:

W_n the welfare measure for n competitors, and

$D_n = W_n - W_{n-1}$ the first difference of W_n.

The formulæ of Section IV together with (3) and (33), yield the following expression for W_n:

$$W_n = \frac{1}{2} \left(\frac{n}{n+1} \right)^2 + \frac{n}{(n+1)^2} - nF. \tag{34}$$

Entry of the nth competitor does not cause a welfare loss, so long as we have:

$$D_n \geqslant 0. \tag{35}$$

Therefore, we compute D_n as follows:

$$D_n = \frac{n^2 + 2n}{2(n + 1)^2} - \frac{(n - 1)^2 + 2(n - 1)}{2n^2} - F \tag{36}$$

$$D_n = \frac{n^4 + 2n^3 - (n^2 - 1)(n + 1)^2}{2n^2(n + 1)^2} - F \tag{37}$$

$$D_n = \frac{2n + 1}{2n^2(n + 1)^2} - F \tag{38}$$

$$D_n = \frac{1}{2n(n + 1)^2} + \frac{1}{2n^2(n + 1)} - F. \tag{39}$$

Equation (39) shows that D_n is a decreasing function of n. With the help of (38) one can determine intervals for F where a given number $\tilde{n}$ is optimal in the sense that it maximises W_n. Table 4.1 shows intervals for combinations of maximal numbers $\bar{n}$ and of optimal numbers $\tilde{n}$ of competitors in the market (compare (30)). It can be seen that welfare is increased by a restriction on entry if the market is big enough to sustain at least three competitors with non-negative Cournot equilibrium profits.

In order to show that this assertion is generally true, and not only for the range covered in Table 4.1 we observed that, in view of (30), the maximal number $\bar{n}$ of competitors satisfies the following inequality:

$$\bar{n} \geqslant \frac{1}{\sqrt{F}} - 1. \tag{40}$$

In order to obtain an upper bound for $\tilde{n}$, which can then be compared with this lower bound for $\tilde{n}$, we can make use of (38) to obtain:

$$D_n < \frac{2n + 2}{2n^2(n + 1)^2} - F, \tag{41}$$

and

$$D_n < \frac{1}{n^3} - F. \tag{42}$$

TABLE 4.1 WELFARE OPTIMAL NUMBER $\check{n}$ AND MAXIMALLY SUSTAINABLE NUMBER $\bar{n}$ OF COMPETITORS IN COURNOT EQUILIBRIUM WITHOUT SLACK.

Optimal $\check{n}$	Maximal $\bar{n}$	Fixed cost interval
1	1	$0.2500 > F > 0.1111$
1	2	$0.1111 \geq F \geq 0.0694$
2	2	$0.0694 \geq F > 0.0625$
2	3	$0.0625 \geq F > 0.0400$
2	4	$0.0400 \geq F > 0.0278$
2	5	$0.0278 \geq F \geq 0.0243$
3	5	$0.0243 \geq F > 0.0204$
3	6	$0.0204 \geq F > 0.0156$
3	7	$0.0156 \geq F > 0.0123$
3	8	$0.0123 \geq F \geq 0.0112$
4	8	$0.0112 \geq F > 0.0100$
4	9	$0.0100 \geq F > 0.0083$

This shows that we must have:

$$\bar{n} < \frac{1}{\sqrt[3]{F}} \ . \tag{43}$$

Hence, for $F = 0.01$ the lower bound for $\bar{n}$ is 9 and the upper bound for $\check{n}$ is 4.64. With decreasing F, the lower bound for $\check{n}$ decreases more rapidly than does the lower bound for $\bar{n}$. Therefore $\check{n} < \bar{n}$ holds outside the range of Table 4.1, too.

Restriction of entry avoids unnecessary duplication of fixed costs. This is why it gives welfare benefits. Each additional competitor above the optimal number $\check{n}$ decreases price and increases consumer's rent; but it does not do so as much as is needed in order to compensate for the fall in total profits.

IX WELFARE EFFECTS OF ENTRY RESTRICTION UNDER THE STRONG SLACK HYPOTHESIS

Let us now turn our attention to the welfare effects of entry restriction on long-run equilibrium under the strong slack hypothesis. For the sake of simplicity, the symbols W_n and D_n are used here, too, in order to denote total welfare for the closed oligopoly with n competitors and the first difference of this variable. However, W_n is now computed in a different way. The formulæ of Section V must be used, instead of those of Section IV. Total profits are zero. In view of (26) and (33), consumer's rent is as follows:

$$C = \frac{1}{2}n^2F. \tag{44}$$

Total slack, the product of s and x, can be computed with the help of (24) and (26) as:

$$S = n \sqrt{F} - n(n + 1)F. \tag{45}$$

This yields:

$$W_n = \frac{1}{2}n^2F + \alpha n\sqrt{F} - \alpha n(n + 1)F, \tag{46}$$

and

$$W_n = F\left[\left(\frac{1}{2} - \alpha\right)n^2 - \alpha n + \frac{\alpha n}{\sqrt{F}}\right] \tag{47}$$

Hence:

$$D_n = F\left[\left(\frac{1}{2} - \alpha\right)(2n - 1) - \alpha + \frac{\alpha}{\sqrt{F}}\right], \tag{48}$$

and

$$D_n = F\left[(1 - 2\alpha)n - \frac{1}{2} + \frac{\alpha}{\sqrt{F}}\right] \tag{49}$$

In view of (40) and $n \leqslant \bar{n}$ we have,

$$\frac{1}{\sqrt{F}} - (n + 1) \geqslant 0. \tag{50}$$

This fact can be used in order to find out more about D_n, namely:

$$D_n = F\left[(1 - 2\alpha)n - \frac{1}{2} + \alpha(n + 1)\right.$$

$$\left. + \left(\frac{1}{\sqrt{F}} - (n + 1)\right)\right] \tag{51}$$

$$D_n \geqslant F\left[(1 - 2\alpha)n - \frac{1}{2} + \alpha(n + 1)\right] \tag{52}$$

$$D_n \geq F[(1 - \alpha)n - \frac{1}{2} + \alpha] \tag{53}$$

$$D_n \geq F\left[(1 - \alpha)(n - 1) + \frac{1}{2}\right] \tag{54}$$

In view of $0 \leq \alpha \leq 1$ and $n \geq 1$, this yields:

$$D_n \geq \frac{1}{2} F. \tag{55}$$

This shows that the welfare measure W_n is always increased by the entry of a new competitor so long as the maximal number $\bar{n}$ of competitors has not yet been reached. Restriction of entry cannot increase welfare.

The conclusions are very different from those implied by Table 4.1. Whereas under profit maximisation without slack considerable restrictions on entry turn out to be socially beneficial, free entry is always preferable under the strong slack hypothesis.

The effect does not depend on α. Even if all the slack takes the form of consumption at the working place, the conclusion remains valid. The influence of slack on marginal cost is the decisive factor.

In the absence of slack, competition reduces price but does not influence costs. In the presence of slack, competition has an additional role as a cost-reducing force. This explains why slack-ridden imperfect competition may be more in need of free entry conditions than is imperfect competition without slack.

X THE DYNAMICS OF SLACK

Even if, in this chapter, attention is being concentrated on long-run equilibrium, it will be useful to present an explicit picture of the dynamics of slack. The 'general slack hypothesis' mentioned in Section I can best be understood as an equilibrium condition of a dynamical process. This process will be described as evolving in continuous time and the following notation will be used:

$\dot{s}_i$ time derivative of slack rate s_i, and
r_i profit rate of firm i.

It is reasonable to assume that the firm's capital is closely related to its fixed costs. Therefore, the profit rate will be defined as profits divided by fixed costs:

$$r_i = \frac{G_i}{F}. \tag{56}$$

A simple way of modelling the dynamics of slack is as follows:

$$\dot{s}_i = \begin{cases} \mu r_i - \eta s_i & \text{for } s_i > 0 \ \text{ or } \ \mu r_i - \eta s_i > 0 \\ 0 & \text{for } s_i = 0 \ \text{and } \ \mu r_i - \eta s_i \leqslant 0 \end{cases} \tag{57}$$

where μ and η are non-negative constants. Assumption (57) permits the following interpretation: the slack rate will increase more quickly if the rate of profit is high, because the owner's power to put pressure on management will then be weak. Slack will increase less quickly or may even decline if the slack rate is already very high. The higher the slack rate is, the more obvious and the more visible the inefficiency will be. If the profit rate is negative, the slack rate will be reduced regardless how low the slack rate already is. The functional form of (57) guarantees that the slack rate remains non-negative.

The special case $\mu = 0$ leads to a long-run equilibrium without slack. For $\eta = 0$, we obtain the strong slack hypothesis as a long-run equilibrium condition. In the following, we shall always assume $\mu > 0$.

The relationship between profit rate and slack rate in long-run equilibrium depends on η/μ. Therefore, we introduce the following definition:

$$\gamma = \frac{\eta}{\mu}. \tag{58}$$

It is clear that long-run equilibrium with non-negative profits must satisfy:

$$r_i = \gamma s_i. \tag{59}$$

The parameter (γ) may be thought of as reflecting the institutional strength of profit-interests relative to slack pressure. We refer to (59) as the 'general slack hypothesis'.

Ordinary profit maximisation without slack may be looked upon as a limiting case of the general slack hypothesis. The two extremes of (1) the strong slack hypothesis and (2) profit maximisation without slack are bridged by a continuum of intermediate cases.

The general slack hypothesis is a necessary condition for long-run equilibrium. However, it is not yet clear whether the process converges towards long-run equilibrium. A rigorous answer to this question will not be given here. Instead, we shall present a heuristic argument for convergence with fixed n, which might be capable of being worked out into a full-fledged proof.

If, in (17), the average slack rate s is kept constant, $\dot{s}_i$ is a decreasing function of s_i, so long as s_i is positive. The difference between two slack rates s_i and s_j will therefore diminish over time. Finally, all slack rates s_i will be equal. Suppose that all slack rates are equal to s. Then (57) yields for $s > 0$:

$$\dot{s} = \frac{\mu}{F}\left(\frac{(1 - s)^2}{(n + 1)^2} - F\right) - \eta s. \tag{60}$$

Since the right-hand side of (60) is a decreasing function of s, the average slack rate will increase below the equilibrium level and decrease above the equilibrium level. This shows convergence towards long-run equilibrium.

XI SOME CONSEQUENCES OF THE GENERAL SLACK HYPOTHESIS

In view of (56) and (59), the following long-run equilibrium condition holds under the general slack hypothesis:

$$G_i = \gamma F s_i, \tag{61}$$

for $i = 1, \ldots, n$. In view of (17), this is equivalent to the following equation:

$$\left(\frac{1}{n + 1} + \frac{n}{n + 1} s - s_i\right)^2 = F(1 + \gamma s_i). \tag{62}$$

Essentially, the same argument as was applied to (20) in Section V can be used to show that (62) has at most one solution s_i in the relevant range. Therefore, all slack rates s_i must be equal here, too. Of course, this conclusion depends on the symmetry assumption, namely, that the parameter is the same for all firms. Equation (22) is now replaced by the following condition:

$$\frac{1}{(n + 1)^2}(1 - s)^2 = F(1 + \gamma s). \tag{63}$$

It can easily be seen that for $n \leq \bar{n}$, this equation has exactly one solution (s) in the interval $0 \leq s \leq 1$.

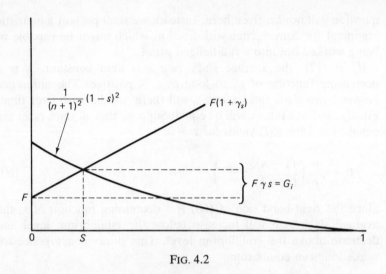

FIG. 4.2

It is not necessary to solve the quadratic equation (63) in order to investigate the influence of the parameters n, γ and F on s, r, x and p, where r is the common profit-rate for all firms. The influences on s can easily be seen if one thinks of both sides of (63) as curves in a diagram showing s horizontally and these expressions vertically (see Figure 4.2). An increase in n causes a downward-shift in the curve representing the left-hand side of this equation and thereby decreases s. An increase in γ or F causes an upward shift of the curve representing the right-hand side of the equation and thereby decreases s, too. In Table 4.2, these effects are represented by minus signs in the first column.

TABLE 4.2   INFLUENCES OF NUMBERS OF COMPETITORS n,
OWNERSHIP STRENGTH γ AND FIXED COSTS F ON SLACK RATE s,
PROFIT RATE r, SUPPLY x AND PRICE p.

	s	r	x	p
n	−	−	+	−
γ	−	+	+	−
F	−	−	+	−

It is an immediate consequence of the general slack hypothesis (59) that a decrease in s is connected to a decrease in the profit rate

r if γ is kept constant. The decrease in s caused by an increase in γ is connected to an increase in $F(1 + \gamma s)$. This has the consequence that, in spite of the reduction in s the expression $F\gamma s$ is increased. In view of (61), this has the consequence that r is increased by an increase of γ. This is plausible in view of the interpretation of γ as a measure of the institutional strength of ownership.

Equation (13) shows that total supply is increased if n is increased and s is decreased or if s alone is decreased. Therefore, an increase of n, γ or F leads to an increased supply and a lower price.

The only influence which may seem to be somewhat surprising is that of F. At a constant slack rate, higher fixed costs would decrease the profit rate. In order to restore the balance, slack rates have to be cut, too. In this way, marginal costs are lowered, with the result that supply is increased and price is decreased.

Even if hard marginal costs c have been normalised away, it is not difficult to see what happens if c is increased. A reduction in the slack rate equal to the increase of c would keep the profit rate constant. In order to restore the balance, the profit rate must fall so that the slack rate has to be cut by less than the increase in c. Soft marginal costs $c + s$ increase, supply is reduced and price goes up.

XII   CONCLUDING REMARKS

If fixed costs are sufficiently small and if entry is free and efficient, long-run equilibrium with slack is not very different from long-run equilibrium without slack. Under such conditions, both profit rates and slack rates must be small. However, if entry is restricted or fixed costs are rather high, it may be quite important what the assumptions on organisational slack are. If slack-ridden competition is a fact of life, policy implications based on models without slack may be very misleading. Under such conditions, one should not disregard the role of competition as a cost-reducing force.

REFERENCES

Collins, N. R. and Preston, L. E. (1969) 'Price-Cost Margins and Industry Structure', *Review of Economics and Statistics*, vol. 54, pp. 271–86.
Cyert, R. M. and March, J. G. (1963) *A Behavioral Theory of the Firm* (Englewood Cliffs, New Jersey: Prentice-Hall).

Leibenstein, Harvey (1966) 'Allocative efficiency versus X-efficiency', *American Economic Review*, vol. 66, pp. 392–415.

Leibenstein, Harvey (1976) *Beyond Economic Man* (Cambridge, Mass.: Harvard University Press).

Shepherd, W. G. (1972) 'The Elements of Market Structure', *Review of Economics and Statistics*, vol. 54, pp. 25–37.

Discussion of the Paper by Reinhard Selten

In discussing this paper, *Okun* directed his attention towards Selten's assumption that organisational slack increased when profits were positive and decreased when profits were negative. In this regard, he made three points. First, he argued that organisational slack was at least partly controlled by the firm's managers. For this reason, Okun believed that it was inappropriate to view slack as simply parametrically related to profits. Second, in Okun's view, slack was larger in public than in private enterprises, as losses for public firms were underwritten (or at least guaranteed) by the government. In this kind of environment, slack might be inversely related to profit levels, i.e. public sector institutions constrained to earn zero profits might have the greatest amount of slack. Finally, he noted that if slack was directly related to profits, then managers of firms would begin to reduce slack when profits fell below some industry norm. In this case, slack would begin to fall well before profits went to zero. Selten responded that he had intended profits to mean the usual pure or economic profits.

Oliver Williamson agreed with Okun's comment that slack should be endogenised. In Williamson's view, much of the evolution of business organisations over time should be understood as attempts by owners to restructure incentives to eliminate such slack. Williamson cited the literature on business history following Alfred Chandler as insightful into this process.

Grossman pointed out that results of models with entry often depend upon assumptions about how entrants could attract customers away from existing firms. He contrasted the simplest Cournot assumption, where sales of the extant firm were assumed by the entrant to be fixed, with the Bertrand model, where price cutting allowed the entrant to attract all the customers of the existing firm. Grossman suggested that one application of the slack concept would be to the buyer–seller relationship. Failure of a buyer to respond to price undercutting by an entrant could be understood as a reflection of slack arising in the relationship between the buyer and the extant firm.

In commenting on Selten's paper, *Horvat* suggested that actions formerly labelled as bribery and corruption could now be euphemistically relabelled as organisational slack. Selten responded by noting that while you could prove that bribery and corruption had taken place, this need not be true for organisational slack. *Roman* suggested that, in addition to organisational slack, there were two additional sources of inefficiency in industries that could be viewed in the manner suggested by Selten, namely the choice of technology by firms, and the employment of inefficient managers by firms. He suggested that, in practice, it might be difficult to separate these three types of inefficiencies.

Part Three
Vertical Integration and Restraints

5 Vertical Integration and Related Variations on a Transaction-Cost Economics Theme[1]

Oliver E. Williamson

YALE UNIVERSITY, USA

I INTRODUCTION

That vertical integration is to be understood in large measure as a transaction-cost economising outcome has been generally conceded since Ronald Coase advanced the argument in 1937.[2] The argument was forcefully restated by Kenneth Arrow as part of his assessment of the market failure literature (1969, p. 48). It was not, however, until 1971 that the underlying mechanics were described (Williamson, 1971). The argument has since been elaborated (Williamson, 1975, 1979; Klein, et al., 1978). Of equal if not greater importance, the same underlying transaction cost reasoning applies broadly – which is to say that vertical integration is a paradigm problem. Such apparently unrelated phenomena as the employment relation, aspects of regulation, vertical market restrictions, and even family organisation[3] are variations on a theme.

This last has a bearing on F. A. Hayek's observation that

whenever the capacity of recognizing an abstract rule which the arrangement of these attributes follows has been acquired in one field, the same master mould will apply when the signs for those abstract attributes are evoked by altogether different elements. It is the classification of the structure of relationships between these abstract attributes which constitutes the recognition of patterns as the same or different (1967, p. 50).

Milton Friedman's remarks about the fruitfulness of a theory are also germane: 'A theory is . . . more "fruitful" the more precise the resulting prediction, the wider the area within which the theory yields predictions, and the more additional lines for further research it suggests' (1953, p. 10).

Thus although transaction-cost economics languished for almost 35 years – to such a degree that Coase observed that his 1937 article was 'much cited and little used' (1972, p. 63) – the past decade has witnessed renewed attention. Much of this, moreover, deals directly or indirectly with the research agenda for industrial organisation that Coase set out at the conclusion of his 1972 essay (p. 72):

> what is wanted in industrial organisation is a direct approach to the problem. This would concentrate on what activities firms undertake, and would endeavor to discover the characteristics of the grouping of activities within firms . . . . In addition . . . , studies should also be made of contractual arrangements between firms (long-term contracts, leasing, licensing arrangements of various kinds including franchising, and so on), since market arrangements are the alternative to organisation within the firm.

Coase contrasts his preferred programme of research with that which prevailed in the early post-war period, which he characterised as the applied-price-theory era. Joe Bain and George Stigler were the leading practitioners (Coase, 1972, pp. 61–2); the study of inter-firm competition, with emphasis on oligopoly, rather than intra-firm organisation or non-standard contracting, was emphasised.

There is no reason, in principle, why the study of transaction-cost issues and work on applied price theory should not proceed in tandem – as, more recently, both have. Coase's concern was that transaction cost economics had been so thoroughly neglected that it was not progressing at all. Two kinds of responses to this condition of neglect have appeared over the past decade. In addition to work of the kind herein described, a mathematical-economics literature has developed in which the study of internal organisation and contracting has come under scrutiny. This second literature deals with the formal analysis of information and incentives and is associated with the research of Robert Wilson (1968), Joseph Stiglitz (1975), James

Mirrlees (1976), Sanford Grossman and Oliver Hart (1980), and the burgeoning principal-agent literature (Ross, 1973; Harris and Raviv, 1976; Holmstrom, 1979).

Assessing this second literature is beyond the scope of this chapter. Accordingly, only two-way comparisons (between transaction cost economics of the comparative institutional kind and the earlier applied price theory tradition) rather than three-way comparisons are attempted.[4]

The rudiments of the transaction-cost economics approach on which I and others have been working are set out in Section II. The vertical integration problem is described in Section III. Applications to regulation are sketched in Section IV. Non-standard contracting practices are examined in Section V. Concluding remarks follow in Section VI.

II TRANSACTION-COST ECONOMICS

Transaction-cost economics is distinguished from mainline price theory in four significant respects:

(1) Organisational man is computationally less competent but motivationally more complex than economic man;
(2) The transaction, rather than a good or service, is regarded as the basic unit of analysis, the dimensions of which are essential to pattern recognition and to efforts at economising;
(3) The firm is regarded as a governance structure rather than a production function;
(4) Contracting and competition are assessed in a comparative institutional way in both *ex ante* and *ex post* respects rather than in once-for-all terms.

Consider these seriatim.

(1) BEHAVIOURAL ASSUMPTIONS

Mainline micro-theory is informed by two behavioural assumptions: men are rational and are reliably given to self-interest seeking. This is a very powerful pair and permits enormous analytic simplification. A natural reluctance to dispute either is understandable. The long gestation period that transaction-cost economics experienced is nevertheless explained in part by a failure to come to terms with what

Frank Knight has felicitously referred to as 'human nature as we know it' (1965, p. 270). As it turns out, the necessary reshaping is not great. Thus rationality notions are preserved, but hyper-rationality excesses are avoided by stating the rationality postulate in terms of bounded rationality: human agents are '*intendedly* rational, but only *limitedly* so' (Simon, 1961, p. xxiv). And simple self-interest seeking is augmented to make allowance for self-interest with guile. Dealings between economic agents are thus complicated by opportunism – on which account parties to transactions recognise that their opposite numbers commonly cannot be relied upon either to disclose fully and honestly all the relevant information needed to reach an informed *ex ante* agreement; or to make convenants self-enforcing, so as to behave in a reliably joint-profit maximising fashion *ex post*.[5]

It is noteworthy that renewed interest in Machiavelli during the past century, in which *The Prince* was recognised as a contribution to political theory rather than a scurrilous handbook of power politics, has had an invigorating influence on political science. In contrast with Aristotle, who imbued his office-holders with virtue, Machiavelli set about to deal with 'men as they are' (Gauss, 1952, p. 14). Knight's reference to 'human nature as we know it' (see above) is the counterpart in economics.

It is instructive that opportunism plays a central role in both positive political science and in transaction cost economics. The assumption of simple seeking of self-interest, on which standard economic analysis relies (Diamond, 1971, p. 31), holds that men will reliably fulfil their promises. The assumption of opportunism disputes this. As Machiavelli puts it, 'legitimate grounds [have never] failed a prince who wished to show colourable excuse for the non-fulfilment of his promise' (1952, p. 93). Standard economic models that suppress this condition miss or misconstrue a great deal of interesting economic behaviour.

Recognition that human behaviour is characterised by bounded rationality and opportunism suggests the following statement of the economic problem: organise transactions in such a way as to economise on bounded rationality while simultaneously safeguarding them against the hazards of opportunism. The first of these purposes can, in principle, be achieved by an appropriate extension of the neo-classical model to make allowance for information costs.[6] Recent concern with 'moral hazard', moreover, discloses an awareness to one manifestation of opportunism. Be that as it may, the basic message is this: the deep and subtle features of both bounded rationality and opportunism need to be plumbed if an understanding of the core purposes of economic institutions – together with their related contracting practices – is to be accomplished. Transaction cost economics is concerned with these issues.

(2) DIMENSIONALISING

A transaction occurs when a good or service is transferred across a technologically-separable interface. Attention is focused on a much more micro-analytic unit of analysis than is characteristic of traditional micro-theory. Ascertaining the factors that expose transactions to differential strain, in respect both of bounded rationality and of opportunism, requires that transactions be given dimensions.

As set out elsewhere (Williamson, 1979), the three dimensions for describing transactions that are of special importance to transaction-cost economics are: (1) the frequency with which they recur; (2) the uncertainty to which they are subject; and (3) the degree to which they are supported by investments in durable, transaction-specific assets. A considerable amount of explanatory power turns on this last.

The crucial investment distinction in evaluating transactions is this: to what degree are durable, transaction-specific expenses incurred. Items that are unspecialised among users pose few hazards, since buyers in these circumstances can easily turn to alternative sources, and suppliers can sell output that was intended for one order to other buyers without difficulty. Autonomous contracting problems arise when the *specific identity* of the parties has important cost-bearing consequences. Transactions of this kind are not faceless or indistinguishable, but are appropriately regarded as idiosyncratic.

Michael Polanyi's remarkable study of 'personal knowledge' includes several illustrations of industrial arts and craftsmanship in which the skills in question are so deeply embedded in the experienced work-force that they can be known or inferred by others only with great difficulty – if at all (Polanyi, 1962, pp. 52–3). Jacob Marschak not only recognised idiosyncrasy but expressed concern over the readiness of economists to accept or employ assumptions of fungibility: 'There exist almost unique, irreplaceable research workers, teachers, administrators: just as there exist unique choice locations for plants and harbors. The problem of unique or imperfectly standardized goods . . . has been indeed neglected in the textbooks' (1968, p. 14).

Although many would concede that Polanyi and Marschak were

formally correct, it was widely believed that idiosyncratic features were rare and/or quantitatively unimportant. Accordingly, the textbooks were seen as soundly grounded and specialists could safely relegate the Polanyi–Marschak nuances to footnotes.

The notion that the idiosyncratic attributes of transactions could not be so easily dismissed but had profound organisational consequences was initially advanced in conjunction with the study of vertical integration (see Williamson, 1971). Transactions that are supported by investments in durable, transaction-specific assets are ones that experience 'lock in' effects, on which account autonomous contracting will commonly be supplanted by unified contracting (vertical integration). Thus, although there may be large numbers of qualified bidders at the outset, if the 'winner of an original contract acquires a cost advantage, say by reason of . . . unique location or learning, including the acquisition of undisclosed or proprietary technical and managerial procedures and task-specific labor skills', bidding parity at contract renewal intervals will be upset. The result is that (comparative or remediable) *ex post* contracting strains predictably develop if autonomous contracting is attempted (Williamson, 1971, p. 116).

The distinction between *ex ante* and *ex post* competition, which had not previously been made, is crucial to the argument. These issues are further developed in Section II (4) below. Suffice it to observe here that others, some of whom once held different views, are now persuaded that asset specificity is the key that unlocks a series of economic/organisational puzzles. As Armen Alchian puts it, 'the whole rationale for the employer–employee status, and even for the existence of firms, rests on [asset specificity] . . . without it there is no known reason for firms to exist' (1982, pp. 6–7).

Although others plainly agree,[7] the contestability literature proceeds on a very different premise. Implicit in the Baumol–Panzar–Willig contribution to the present volume, which emphasises the ease with which markets are contestable, is the assumption that asset specificity is rare or quantitatively unimportant. Transaction-cost economics assumes the opposite. More generally, transaction-cost economics and the contestability literature are to be distinguished in the following significant respects: the former places much more emphasis on: (1) micro-analytic features, (2) comparative institutional choices, and; (3) asset-specificity conditions (the presence or absence of which has crucial organisational ramifications) than does the latter. To the extent that contestability is mainly concerned with very long-run rivalry (a point that Michael Spence makes in his conference comment on Baumol–Panzar–Willig), while many of the contracting issues that are of concern to transaction-cost economics are of shorter duration, the tension is alleviated. But in many respects these two approaches proceed from very different conceptions of the problems of economic organisation. This is particularly evident when issues of strategic behaviour come under scrutiny – which raises issues that are beyond the scope of the present chapter but which have been surveyed elsewhere (Williamson, 1981).

(3) GOVERNANCE STRUCTURES

The notion that the firm is a production function to which a profit-maximisation objective is assigned has served economics well. Such a conception of the firm typically assumes a prior assignment of transactions to firms and markets according to some natural (presumably technological) order. This is not conducive to a study of, or even a sensitivity to, transaction-cost issues.

Supplanting the notion of the firm as production function by one of the firm as governance structure is necessary to advance the argument. By governance structure I refer to the institutional setting within which the execution of transactions is accomplished and their integrity is decided. Firms enjoy potential benefits in relation to markets by harmonising incentives, but whether these benefits will be realised turns crucially on the manner in which internal exchange is organised. Furthermore, the distinctive bureaucratic and other limits of internal organisation also need to be recognised. The upshot is that the economics of internal organisation takes its place on the research agenda. Attention to the decomposition rules within a hierarchy, in both operating and strategic respects, as well as the alignment of the internal incentive and control apparatus, thus come within the purview of transaction-cost economics. Moreover, unified governance (firms) and autonomous contracting (discrete markets) are only two possibilities, indeed polar extremes, on a governance spectrum that includes joint ventures, franchising, and a variety of complex contracting forms (Richardson, 1972). Hence, industrial organisation specialists need to address a much more-extensive set of organisational choices than the applied price theory approach, to which Coase took exception, was prepared to contemplate.

Not only, therefore, does transaction-cost economics require much more micro-analytic knowledge of the detail of the attributes of transactions than does orthodox analysis, but the same is true of the governance properties of alternative structures within which transactions might feasibly be organised. Technology is relevant mainly since it serves to delimit the feasible governance set. Economising on transaction costs[8] is accomplished by effecting a discriminating match between transactions and governance structures within the feasible set. This hitherto neglected strategy is responsible for much of the predictive power of this approach and distinguishes it from other studies of economic organisation.

(4) EX ANTE AND EX POST CONTRACTING/COMPETITION

Although there are many long-term contractual relations in which a supplier is, in effect, continuously meeting bids from fully qualified rival suppliers in the spot market, there are many circumstances where this description fails. Transaction cost economics is largely concerned with contracts where parity-bidding competition breaks down as a consequence of asymmetries between incumbent suppliers and their rivals that develop during contract execution. Orthodox analysis ignores this possibility, which was why the contractual and organisational ramifications of such a condition went unrecognised. Subsequent efforts to extend the reach of applied micro-theory beyond its conventional bounds are likewise culpable.

Thus, consider the interesting and influential treatment by Alchian and Demsetz of what they refer to as the 'classical capitalist firm' (1972); George Stigler's (1951) provocative discussion of vertical integration: and the Demsetz–Stigler–Posner treatments of franchise bidding for natural monopolies. Instructive though each of these is, all suffer an unacknowledged lack of generality. The problem in each case is that technological aspects (non-separabilities; economies of scale) are emphasised while contractual aspects are either neglected or suffer because the authors are excessively sanguine. Given parity among bidders at the outset, the efficacy of competition is uncritically assumed to apply indefinitely into the future. In fact, however, troublesome *ex post* contractual relations predictively develop if, in any of these organisational circumstances, the specificity of assets is at all significant.

Alchian agrees, and now rejects the view that 'long term contracts between employer and employee are not the essence of the organisation we call a firm' (Alchian and Demsetz, 1972, p. 777) in favour of 'Williamson's discussion of the long-term contract in the context of 'idiosyncracies, small numbers, and opportunism" ' (Alchian, 1981, p. 12). Stigler's treatment of vertical integration has been assessed in its *ex ante* and *ex post* contracting respects elsewhere (Williamson, 1975, pp. 16–19). The franchise-bidding issue is discussed in Section IV, below.

The general argument, which applies to long-term contracting in the context of the employment relation, vertical integration, and regulation, takes exception to the conventional view that buyers are assured of efficient supply if non-collusive bids are solicited from large numbers of qualified bidders at the outset. The basic point is this: significant reliance on investments in durable, transaction-specific assets introduces a contractual asymmetry between the initial winning bidder and all others, such that the contractual relation between buyer and seller is effectively *transformed*, during contract execution and at the contract renewal interval, into one of bilateral exchange. The manner in which alternative governance structures implement an adaptive, sequential decision-making process needs to come under scrutiny in these circumstances – which is to say that both the *ex ante* and *ex post* contractual relations matter.

The subsequent discussion will take as given that bounded rationality and opportunism are key attributes of human nature as we know it. Attention will be focused, therefore, on dimensionalising transactions, describing governance structures, and assessing the efficiency consequences of alternative contractual relations in both *ex ante* and *ex post* respects.

III VERTICAL INTEGRATION

The factors that can give rise to vertical integration are legion.[9] Technology is widely believed to be one of them. The transaction cost approach does not deny that technology has a bearing but holds that, contrary to earlier traditions – e.g., Bain (1968, p. 381), technology is rarely determinative.

The main factor that is responsible for vertical integration from a transaction-cost point of view is asset specificity. Take this away, and autonomous contracting between successive production stages has good economising properties in respect both of production cost and transaction cost. As asset specificity increases, however, the balance shifts in favour of internal organisation. A heuristic display of what is at stake is shown in Figure 5.1 where, for convenience, output is

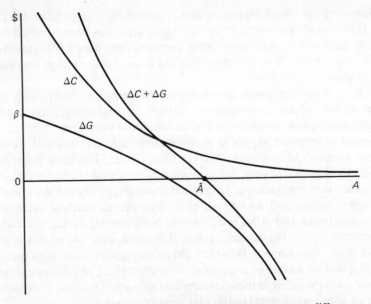

FIG. 5.1 Representative net production and governance cost differences

assumed to be constant. ΔC refers to production cost differences
between internal and market organisation (which is everywhere
positive), ΔG refers to governance cost differences between internal
and market organisation, $\Delta C + \Delta G$ is the vertical sum (which turns
negative at $\hat{A}$), and A refers to the degree of asset specificity.[10]

Several implications immediately obtain:[11]

(1) Market procurement has advantages in respect both of scale
    economy and governance where asset specificity is slight;

(2) Internal organisation enjoys the advantage where asset speci-
    ficity is substantial. Not only does the market realise few benefits
    in economy from aggregation but market governance, because
    of the 'lock-in' problems that arise when assets are highly spe-
    cific, is hazardous;

(3) Intermediate degrees of asset specificity give rise to mixed
    governance in which some firms will be observed to buy, others
    to make, and all to express 'dissatisfaction' with their current
    procurement solution.

Further implications of a transaction cost economising kind can be
derived by recognising that asset specificity takes a variety of forms,
and that the organisational ramifications vary among these. Four

types of asset specificity are usefully distinguished: site specificity – e.g., successive stations that are located in a cheek-by-jowl relation to each other so as to economise on inventory and transportation expenses; physical asset specificity – for example, specialised dies that are required to produce a component; human asset specificity that arises in a learning-by-doing fashion; and dedicated assets, namely, assets that represent a discrete investment in generalised (as contrasted with special-purpose) production capacity. This investment would not be made, but for the prospect of selling a significant amount of product to a specific customer.[12] The organisational ramifications of each are:

(1) Site specificity: common ownership is the preponderent response to an asset-specificity condition that arises when successive stages are located in close proximity to one another. Such specificity is explained by an asset-immobility condition, which is to say that the set-up and/or relocation costs are great. Once located, therefore, the parties are operating in a bilateral exchange relation for the useful life of the assets.

(2) Physical-asset specificity: if assets are mobile and the specificity is attributable to physical features, market procurement may still be feasible by concentrating the ownership of the specific assets (for example, specialised dies) on the buyer and putting the business up for bids. Lock-in problems are avoided because the buyer can reclaim the dies and re-open the bidding should contractual difficulties develop.[13] Thus *ex post* competition is efficacious and internal organisation is unneeded.

(3) Human-asset specificity: any condition that gives rise to substantial human-asset specificity – be it learning-by-doing or chronic problems of moving human assets in teams – favours common ownership, whence an employment relation rather than autonomous contracting characterises the exchange.

(4) Dedicated assets: investment in dedicated assets involves expanding existing plant on behalf of a particular buyer. Common ownership in these circumstances is rarely contemplated. Trading hazards are nevertheless recognised, and are often mitigated by expanding the contractual relation so as to effect 'equilibration' (see Section V).

Yet another implication of transaction-cost reasoning is that where firms are observed both to make and to buy an identical good or service, the internal technology will be characterised by greater asset specificity than will the external technology, *ceteris paribus*. No other approach to the study of vertical integration generates this set of organisational implications.

Not only are distinctions among types of asset specificity useful for making discriminating statements about when and how vertical relations will appear, but much of the confusion that attends the argument that firms must replicate markets in all relevant respects can be dispelled by focusing on 'simple' forms of asset specificity. The mistaken argument is this: markets and firms are indistinguishable in contractual respects because firms must devise transfer-pricing rules and managerial incentive contracts that are in every respect as complicated to write, and as costly to enforce, as are supply contracts between autonomous buyers and sellers.[14]

The argument assumes that the authority relation – whereby bosses instruct workers to 'do this' or 'do that', to which instructions workers are expected to respond in an instrumental way – is of no effect in its application to station managers. Station managers are not only independent agents, but they act as gatekeepers over their respective stations and hence stand in a position to frustrate efforts to effect a co-ordinated adaptation.

I submit that this is true only if station managers are either (1) significantly endowed with specific human capital; or (2) property rights over the station have been assigned so as to provide them with unusual insularity. The first of these is herein assumed away. The second corresponds to an inside-contracting mode of organisation (Williamson, 1975, pp. 95–8) and is likewise assumed away. Accordingly, the station managers in question are fungible – whence they can (and presumably will) be costlessly sacked and replaced for failure to respond as required. The firm's interest in maintaining the continuity of an exchange relation thus turns entirely on physical or other assets, over which the managers have no claim. Incumbent managers in these circumstances are, in effect, continuously meeting outside bids for their jobs so that their employment agreements reduce to little more than a succession of spot contracts. Such agreements are easily distinguishable from sales contracts, where suppliers place specialised physical assets at hazard.

Matters change if the asset specificity that is responsible for a continuity of interest between the parties resides not in site-specificity (or in other physical attributes of a station) but is concentrated in human assets instead. Inasmuch as the termination of employment is then no longer a credible threat, a finely-tuned employment agreement needs to be constructed. Accordingly, the distinction between an adaptable sales contract with an autonomous supplier and an adaptable employment agreement is blurred.[15] These are plainly special circumstances, however. The argument that firms and markets are *less* distinguishable as human asset specificity becomes greater is thus not to be confused with a more general and mistaken proposition. This is that firms and markets are contractually indistinguishable where asset specificity has different origins – as it often does.

IV   REGULATION

Although a tendency toward monopoly supply is indicated where economies of scale are large in relation to the size of the market, it also poses organisational difficulties. As Friedman observes, 'There is unfortunately no good solution for technical monopoly. There is only a choice among three evils: private unregulated monopoly, private monopoly regulated by the state, and government operation' (1962, p. 128).

Actually, a fourth solution has since been proposed, as the result of an imaginative series of papers originating in Chicago. Surprisingly, these papers (and this fourth solution) go unmentioned in Melvin Reder's recent survey of 'Chicago Economics', where he recounts numerous instances in which economic (and even non-economic) issues were reformulated to good advantage within the Chicago tradition (Reder, 1982).

That Friedman characterised private unregulated monopoly as an evil, is because he assumed that private monopoly ownership implied pricing on monopoly terms. The Chicago response – as developed by Harold Demsetz (1968), George Stigler (1968) and Richard Posner (1972) – is that monopoly price is not a *necessary* consequence of a private unregulated monopoly condition. Such an outcome can be avoided by using *ex ante* bidding to award the monopoly franchise to the firm that offers to supply its product on the best terms. Demsetz advances the argument for franchise bidding in natural monopoly by stripping away 'irrelevant complications' – such as equipment durability and uncertainty (1968, p. 57). Stigler contends that 'customers can auction off the right to sell electricity, using the state as an instrument to conduct the auction. . . . The auction . . . consists of . . . [franchise bids] to sell cheaply' (1968, p. 19). Posner agrees and furthermore holds that franchise bidding is an efficacious way by which to award and operate CATV franchises.

Transaction-cost economics recognises merit in the argument but insists that both *ex ante* and *ex post* contracting features be examined. Only if competition is efficacious at *both* stages does the franchise-bidding argument prevail. The attributes of the good or service to be franchised are crucial to the assessment. Specifically, if the good or service is to be supplied under conditions of uncertainty and if non-trivial investments in specific assets are involved, the efficacy of franchise-bidding is highly problematic. Indeed, the implementation of a franchise-bidding scheme under these circumstances essentially requires the progressive elaboration of an administration apparatus that differs mainly in name, rather than in kind, from that which is associated with rate-of-return regulation. It is an elementary conclusion that *a change in name lacks comparative institutional significance*.

This is not, however, to suggest that franchise bidding for goods or services that are supplied under decreasing cost conditions is never feasible. Nor is it to imply that existing regulation, or public ownership, can never be supplanted by franchise bidding with net gains. Examples where it can be include local-service airlines and, possibly, postal delivery. The winning bidder for each can be displaced

> without posing serious asset valuation problems – since the base plant (terminals, post offices, warehouses, etc.) can be owned by the government: other assets (planes, trucks, etc.) have an active second-hand market. It is not, therefore, that franchise bidding is totally lacking in merit, but that those who have favored this mode have been insufficiently discriminating in their endorsement of it (Williamson, 1976, pp. 102–103).

Richard Schmalensee takes a similar position (1979, pp. 68–73). William Baumol and Robert Willig agree with the general argument. 'They also use airlines and postal delivery as examples of industries with 'capital on wheels', whence 'their fixed costs may considerably exceed their sunk costs' (1981, p. 407) so that the economic difficulties that attend non-mobile, fixed-cost industries are greatly relieved. Inasmuch as Baumol and Willig's use of sunk costs corresponds, in the lexicon of transaction-cost economics, to an asset-specificity condition, there appears to be growing agreement over the circumstances where franchise bidding can be presumed to be efficacious, and where it is not. (The fact that I restrict the argument to local-service airlines while they include trunk lines is perhaps noteworthy, but the difference is mainly one of degree.)

V NON-STANDARD CONTRACTING

Regarding the firm as a production function to which a profit maximisation objective has been assigned easily led to the aforementioned view of technological determinism. Transactions either belonged in firms or they belonged in markets. Any effort to tamper with this natural order was accordingly suspect. The inhospitality tradition towards non-standard or unfamiliar contracting practices in the anti-trust field has these origins. As Donald Turner put it, 'I approach territorial and customer restrictions not hospitably in the common law tradition, but inhospitably in the tradition of antitrust law'.[16]

Among the contracting practices that are widely thought to distort the natural and efficient order of markets are reciprocity, product-exchange agreements between rivals, and price discrimination unjustified by production-cost savings. While I agree that each of these practices can be objectionable, I also contend that each may have legitimate transaction-cost origins. The issues are usefully investigated in the context of using 'hostages' to support exchange (Williamson, 1983). Not only is this of interest in its own right; it helps to put vertical integration into perspective. Internal organisation may be unnecessary if contracts can be reshaped so as to mitigate trading hazards.

Thomas Schelling's classic essay on bargaining (1956) mainly deals with tactics by which bargaining advantages are realised by credibly 'tieing one's hands'. But he also addressed himself to the matter of promise and he observed, in this connection, that 'Bargaining may have to concern itself with an "incentive" system as well as the division of gains' (1956, p. 300). To this he added, in a footnote, that the exchange of hostages served incentive purposes in an earlier age (1956, p. 300, n. 17).

Although the offer and acceptance of hostages is widely believed to be a primitive practice, the need for which has long since lapsed, I submit that Schelling's perceptive remarks have widespread application (Williamson, 1983). The argument is somewhat involved, and only the rudiments are sketched here. As might be expected, the attributes of the transactions turn out to be crucial.

(1) THE ARGUMENT

Assume that either one of two production technologies can be used. The first technology uses general-purpose inputs and is variable-cost intensive. The second employs special-purpose inputs of a more durable kind. The costs of production under the second technology are lower than under the first, assuming that plant is utilised to design capacity. Idle plant cannot, however, be economically shifted to other uses. Hence, the producer will be left holding unproductive assets should buyers defect from the agreement under the second technology. If buyers can invoke a technicality and easily defect whenever it suits their purposes, producers will either demand some assurance against such breach or will add a defection premium if the second technology is put in place.[17] Assurance can be provided by offering hostages. Interestingly, hostages can be used both as an *ex ante* screening device and to discourage 'irresponsible' *ex post* breaches.

The *ex ante* screening argument is a variant of the argument by Michael Rothschild and Joseph Stiglitz (1976). This is that it may be possible to offer insurance on discriminating terms, such that good and poor risks sort themselves appropriately across policies.[18] The use of hostages can similarly be used to discourage buyers who have poorer prospects (but who cannot by inspection be distinguished from those who have better prospects) to self-select themselves out of the market.

The *ex post* execution argument is somewhat more involved. Assume that buyers wish to procure product from producers who use the low-cost (asset-specific) technology. Assume, also, that it is not feasible (or perhaps too hazardous) for buyers to make 'up-front' payments that will cover the costs of the dedicated (specific) asset investments which have to be made by producers in support of each buyer's prospective needs. The question is then how to design a contract such that: (1) the efficient technology is selected; and (2) product is exchanged in all states of the world for which demand price (net of marketing costs) exceeds marginal costs of production.

Assume that there are two periods. Dedicated assets are committed in the first. Demand is stochastic and demand is realised in the second. Production, if any, also occurs in the second. Assume that there are many potential risk-neutral suppliers, who will produce to any contract for which an expected break-even condition can be projected. Consider two contracting alternatives:

(a) The producer makes the specific-asset investment himself, and receives a payment of $(\bar{p})$ in the second period if the buyer places an order but otherwise nothing;

(b) The producer makes the specific-asset investment himself and receives $(\hat{p})$ from the buyer if an order is placed; he is paid αh, $0 \leqslant \alpha \leqslant 1$, if no second-period order is made. The buyer, however, pays $(\hat{p})$ upon placing an order and experiences a reduction in wealth of (h) if no order is placed.

The second scenario can be thought of as one where the buyer puts up a hostage that he values in amount (h). This hostage, which the producer values in amount αh, is delivered to him if no order is placed.

Producers will be indifferent with respect to (e.g., will break-even on) each contract, only if $\bar{p} > \hat{p}$. It can furthermore be shown that product will be exchanged on marginal cost terms if (h) is set equal to the amount of the investment in specific assets (say k) and if (α) is equal to one. Indeed, Contract (b) precisely replicates a vertically-integrated supply relation, assuming that there are no problems of valuing and transferring hostages.[19]

(2) APPLICATIONS

Applications of the use of hostages to check *ex post* opportunism include franchising, reciprocal-purchase agreements and product-exchange agreements (Williamson, 1983). The use of hostages to support exchange is also of interest in Robinson–Patman connections.

Thus, assume that there are two types of customers. One type can and will put up a hostage in support of a contract (possibly by making specialised investments of his own, the value of which is negligible if the trade is not completed); the other type is unwilling to make a similar commitment. Suppose that the supplier agrees to service the needs of buyers of the first kind at a price $(\hat{p})$ but will sell to buyers of the second kind for $(\bar{p})$, which exceeds $(\hat{p})$. The Federal Trade Commission conducts a cost-justification enquiry and observes that (steady-state) production, transport, and other expense-differences between the two types of customer-classes do not warrant the price differential. The producer is therefore ordered to equalise prices.

This is not a correct result and will indeed lead to inefficiency. The missing ingredients, plainly, are the differential commitment to buy (as reflected by the willingness to offer hostages); and the differential incentives to breach the contract once hostages have been posted.

The confusion is explained by the propensity to employ conventional (steady-state) micro-economic theory, to the neglect of transaction-cost aspects. Rectifying this entails: (1) assigning dimensions to transactions, with special reference to asset-specificity and the hazards thereby posed; and (2) evaluating alternative contracts in terms to a common reference condition – prospective break-even being a useful standard. Once this is done, a different understanding of many non-standard or unfamiliar contracting practices – which practices are held to be presumptively unlawful under the inhospitality tradition within the anti-trust field – frequently emerges.

VI CONCLUDING REMARKS

This IEA conference celebrates a decade of enormous vitality in the field of industrial organisation. Although some of the developments of the past ten years were anticipated in an NBER conference volume dealing with *Policy Issues and Research Opportunities in Industrial Organization* published in 1972,[20] a scan of that volume quickly discloses that many of the topics on the agenda of the present conference were not even mentioned. Predicting the veritable explosion of interest in the study of incentives, strategic behaviour, competition as a process, information, transaction costs, and related micro-analytic features of industrial organisation would, to say the least, have required remarkable foresight. Plainly, either the field of industrial organisation has undergone a vast transformation, or this conference is a masquerade.

It is noteworthy that Ronald Coase's contribution to the 1972 volume lamented the sorry state of affairs into which, in his judgement, the field of industrial organisation had worked itself. It was not addressing the organisation of economic activity in comparative-institutional terms – whereby firms, markets, non-profits, government agencies and the like could all come under scrutiny and efforts would be made to assign transactions to 'governance' structures in a discriminating way. The study of industrial organisation had, instead, taken these assignments as a datum and was preoccupied with 'the study of pricing and output policies of firms, especially in oligopolistic situations' (Coase, 1972, p. 62).

The transaction-cost approach to the study of economic organisation that is described above attempts to rectify this: by (1) employing behavioural assumptions that are in closer congruence with human nature as we know it; (2) making the transaction the basic unit of analysis; (3) giving dimensions to transactions; and (4) assigning transactions to 'governance' structures with reference to their capacities to economise on transaction costs in respect of both *ex ante* and *ex post* contracting. Empirical studies[20] and public policy formation are both informed by such a perspective.

In addition to the applications to vertical integration, regulation, and non-standard contracting practices sketched here and elaborated elsewhere, the transaction cost approach has a further bearing. This is on the study of the employment relation (including labour-union organisation), the modern corporation (including conglomerate and multinational aspects), strategic inter-firm behaviour (including predation). It may also have application to the study of the family. To be sure, transaction-cost economics is still primitive. Refinements have been occurring, however, and I see no reason why these should not continue. The study of 'bureaucratic failure' is among the leading issues for which further research is needed. As matters stand presently, the market-failure literature is much more-fully developed. As a consequence of this asymmetry, the comparative-institutional study of alternative means of contracting suffers from a limp.

NOTES

1. The writing of this paper was supported by a grant from the National Science Foundation and from Sloan Foundation support to the Transaction Cost Economics Workshop at the University of Pennsylvania. These are gratefully acknowledged. Michael Riordan's comments were especially helpful.
2. As discussed in note 9, below, vertical integration has many sources. Transaction-cost economising is, however, central.
3. For an interesting discussion of family organisation, see Yoram Ben Porath (1978). My colleague, Robert Pollak, is investigating these issues.
4. Both the comparative-institutional approach to transaction-cost economics that characterises this paper, and the mathematical-economics literature referred to above, employ identical behavioural assumptions and are concerned with similar problems. Also the two differ in that the comparative-institutional approach deals with discrete organisational alternatives in greater micro-analytic detail (in which connection the dimensionalising of transactions is central) and employs what Herbert Simon refers to as 'qualitative-institutional analysis' of a relatively-crude kind (1978, p. 6). This apparatus nevertheless appears to be adequate, even suited, to the needs of the task (Simon, 1978, p. 6). Furthermore, it

generates a series of refutable implications yet to be realised from any alternative approach to the study of these same economic phenomena. On these, vertical integration, regulation, and non-standard contracting are examples. The treatment of none of these is, however, exhaustive and, here as elsewhere, parallel study, using other modes of analysis, is apt to be useful.

5. The principal-agent literature commonly uses the term 'moral hazard' rather than opportunism to refer to these contracting difficulties. This is unobjectionable if moral hazard is given an appropriately broad construction and if its sources are explored in a self-conscious way.

Moral hazard has a well-defined (but narrow) meaning in the insurance literature, which is where the term originates. It is appropriately distinguished in this connection from the term adverse selection. The latter refers to an *ex ante* screening difficulty, whereas moral hazard has reference to *ex post* contract execution problems.

To be sure, the term moral hazard may be legitimately extended to reach outside its narrow insurance context – where it refers to the possibility that those insured will fail to take appropriate loss-mitigating actions in the insurance interval and will not candidly accept accountability – to include all failures of 'due care'. But it does not ordinarily elicit sensitivity to the following: whether a party takes advantage of externalities, by free-riding on or by shifting costs on to other members of the system of which he is a part; whether generalised commitments to co-operate are construed narrowly, so that the letter but not the spirit of an agreement is met; deliberate efforts to confuse and obfuscate transactions; active efforts to expropriate investments made by others, by defecting from agreements.

The advantages of the term opportunism are two. First, the purpose, after all, is to describe a basic condition of human nature. The use of a specialised technical term is unnecessary if the condition in question is well described by common language (consult the definition of opportunism and moral hazard in the dictionary; moral hazard plainly has to be *redefined* if it is to have application to the range of practices described above). Second, and more important, opportunism is such a completely general term that users will recognise a need to inquire into the particulars that are responsible for any 'contracting difficulties' that purportedly attend a transaction. The term moral hazard suggests that these difficulties are of a well-defined technical kind, whence analysis can proceed without self-conscious examination of the specifics. This is unfortunate if an understanding of the sources of contractual strain is important in attempting to fashion contractual remedies.

To be sure, use of the term moral hazard need not emphasise technical (at the expense of institutional) features. If it does not, my preference for the term opportunism is merely semantics. To the extent, however, that moral hazard focuses attention narrowly on the analytically more tractable features of contracting, foreshortening can result.

Obviously there are trade-offs. Compare, for example, Okun (1975) and Wachter and Williamson (1978) with Azariadis (1975) and Baily (1976) on implicit contracting.

6. Simon, however, resists restating the maximisation problem in these terms: 'the new theories do nothing to alleviate the computational complexities facing the decision maker' but compound them instead. Hence, to some extent, the impression these new theories deal with the hitherto ignored phenomena of uncertainty and information transmission is illusory (1979, p. 504).

7. Alchian generously goes on to observe that: '*Markets and Hierarchies* [is] by far the most elegant, though abstruse, statement of the principle' (1982, p. 7). Others who are persuaded of the importance of asset-specificity to economic organisation include Benjamin Klein, Robert Crawford and Armen Alchian (1978) and William Baumol and Robert Willig (1981). Klein, Crawford and Alchian develop the argument in the context of what they refer to as 'appropriable quasi-rents', where the quasi-rent value of an asset is the value in its next best use and the 'potentially appropriable specialised portion of the quasi-rent is the portion, if any, in excess of its value to the second highest-valuing user' (1978, p. 298). Baumol and Willig distinguish between fixed costs and sunk costs. The troublesome costs, from a public policy standpoint, are those that are sunk. Also see Klein (1980) and Klein and Leffler (1981), for discussions of asset-specificity in a franchising context, and Goetz and Scott (1981). Applications to regulation and to contracting relations more generally are set out in Williamson (1976, 1979, 1983).

8. Plainly, this oversimplifies. The more general problem is to maximise net benefits – which requires simultaneous attention to demand, production-cost and governance-cost aspects. It is often convenient, however, for purposes of the exposition to hold output constant and focus on governance costs and/or production-cost governance-cost trade-offs.

9. Paul Kleindorfer and Gunter Knieps (1981, p. 1) summarise these as follows:

> The most popular has been that if economies of scope between successive stages due to technological or organisational interrelationships are strong enough, these activities should be provided under joint ownership [e.g., Chandler, 1966]. Other arguments for Vertical Integration have been the avoidance of factor distortions in monopolized markets [e.g., Vernon and Graham, 1971; Warren-Boulton, 1974; Schmalensee, 1973]; uncertainty in the supply of the upstream good with the consequent need for information by downstream firms [Arrow, 1975]; and the transfer of risks from one sector of the economy to another [Crouhy, 1976, Carlton, 1979]. Furthermore it has been pointed out that transaction costs might create important incentives for vertical integration [e.g., Coase, 1937, Williamson, 1971; 1975].

> Omitted from this list is the incentive to use vertical integration as an organisational shell to evade taxes on intermediate products (Stigler, 1968, ch. 12) or as a device which, through judicious use of transfer pricing, can take advantage of differences among tax jurisdictions (that arise, for example, between states).

10. The figure is reproduced from Williamson (1981, p. 560).
11. Comparative-static implications can also be derived by shifting the cost curves in response to changing scale-economy and bureaucratic-cost conditions.
12. See Section V for an illustration.
13. See David Teece (1980) for a related discussion.
14. Although this argument may appear to be a straw man, it was actively advanced by several participants at the conference during the discussion of this paper. I have therefore extended the paper to address it.
15. The study of protective "governance structures" where human assets are highly specific is in the very primitive stages of development. Some of the issues are discussed in Williamson (1975, ch. 4; 1981). Among the areas in which firms and markets differ in non-replicable respects are: (1) incentive differences (where appropriability incentives and bureaucratic disincentives both require scrutiny); (2) constitutional differences (especially with respect to auditing); and (3) stability of the ties (which may depend on legal conventions in the way in which employment contracts and intermediate-product-market contracts are treated).
16. The quotation is attributed to Turner by Stanley Robinson, 1968, N.Y. State Bar Association, Antitrust Symposium, p. 29.
17. The vertical-integration option is arbitrarily assumed to be infeasible.
18. This oversimplifies, in that the good risks are under-insured in relation to the hypothetical ideal.
19. Problems arise, however, if the hostage value is less than the specific-asset commitment or if $\alpha < 1$. Assuming that this is known in advance, the disadvantage accrues entirely to the buyer – since the seller, by assumption, breaks even whatever contracting relation obtains. Thus, *after* the contract has been made the buyer would prefer to offer a lesser-valued hostage and cares not whether the hostage is delivered to or is valued by the producer. At the time of the contract, however, he will wish to assure the producer that a hostage of (k) for which the producer realises full value $(\alpha = 1)$ will be transferred in non-exchange states. Failure to make this commitment will result in an increase in the contract price.
20. The conference was sponsored by the National Bureau of Economic Research as part of its Fiftieth Anniversary Colloquium. The conference volume was edited by Victor Fuchs. Fuchs' Foreword to the volume provides an interesting overview (1972, pp. xv-xvii).
21. Note in this connection that more micro-analytic data is frequently needed, in order to test micro-analytic arguments, than has been characteristic of earlier economic research on firms and markets. Focused case studies are especially useful. See my examination of CATV (Williamson, 1976, pp. 91–101) and petroleum exchanges (Williamson, 1983). Other empirical work of a more traditional kind which, however, also relies on more micro-analytic data than is characteristic of earlier industrial organisation research is illustrated by Teece (1981) and by Monteverde and Teece (1982), including references therein.

REFERENCES

Alchian, A. A. (1981) 'Property Rights, Specialization and the Firm', in Weston, F. (ed.) *Essays in Honor of Neil Jacoby*.
—— (1982) 'First National Maintenance vs. National Labor Relations Board', in *Supreme Court Review*.
—— and Demsetz, H. (1972) 'Production, Information Costs, and Economic Organization', *American Economic Review*, vol. 62, pp. 777–795.
Arrow, Kenneth J. (1969) 'The Organization of Economic Activity," *The Analysis and Evaluation of Public Expenditure: The PPB System*. Joint Economic Committee, 91st Cong., 1st Sess., pp. 59–73.
—— (1975) 'Vertical Integration and Communication', *The Bell Journal of Economics*, Spring, pp. 173–83.
Azardiadis, C. (1975) 'Implicit Contracts and Underemployment Equilibria', *Journal of Political Economy*, vol. 83, pp. 1183–1202.
Baily, M. N. (1974) 'Wages and Unemployment under Uncertain Demand', *Review of Economic Studies*, vol. 41, pp. 37–50.
Bain, J. S. (1956) *Barriers to New Competition* (Cambridge, Mass.: Harvard University Press)
Baumol, W. J. and Willig, R. D. (1981) 'Fixed Costs, Sunk Costs, Entry Barriers, and Sustainability of Monopoly', *Quarterly Journal of Economics*, pp. 405–431.
Ben Porath, Y. (1978) 'The F-Connection: Families, Friends, and Firms and the Organization of Exchange', Report No. 29/78, The Hebrew University of Jerusalem, Dec.
Carlton, D. W. (1979) 'Vertical Integration in Competitive Markets Under Uncertainty', *Journal of Industrial Economics*, vol. 27, pp. 189–209.
Coase, R. H. (1937) 'The Nature of the Firm', Economic N. S., vol. 4, pp. 386–405: and in *Readings in Price Theory* Stigler, G. J. and Boulding, K. E. (eds) (Chicago: R. D. Irwin), 1952.
—— (1960) 'The Problem of Social Cost', *Journal of Law and Economics*, vol. 3, pp. 1–44.
—— (1972) 'Industrial Organization: A Proposal for Research', in *Policy Issues and Research Opportunities in Industrial Organization: Economic Research: Retrospect and Prospect* (eds) Victor R. Fuchs, New York: NBER; distributed by Columbia University Press, New York and London, pp. 59–73.
Crouhy, M. G. (1976) 'Short Run Disequilibria and Vertical Integration.' Discussion Paper, Department of Decision Sciences, University of Pennsylvania.
Demsetz, H. (1968) 'Why Regulate Utilities?' *Journal of Law and Economics*, vol. 11, pp. 55–66.
Diamond, P. (1971) 'Political and Economic Evaluation of Social Effects and Externalities: Comment', in Intrilligator, M. (ed.), *Frontiers of Quantitative Economics*. (Amsterdam: North–Holland Publishing Company) pp. 30–32.
Friedman, M. (1953) *Essays in Positive Economics*. (Chicago: University of Chicago Press).

_____. (1962) *Capitalism and Freedom*. (Chicago: University of Chicago Press).

Gauss, C. (1952) Introduction to the Mentor Edition, *The Prince* (New York: Mentor Books).

Goetz, C. and Scott, R. (1980) 'Enforcing Promises: An Examination of the Basis of Contract', *Yale Law Journal*, vol. 89, pp. 1261–1297.

Grossman, S. and Hart, O. (1980) 'Takeover Bids, the Free-Rider Problem, and the Theory of the Corporation', *Bell Journal of Economics*, vol. 11, pp. 42–64.

Harris, M. and Raviv, A. (1976) 'Optimal Incentive Contracts with Imperfect Information', Working Paper no. 70–75–76, Graduate School of Industrial Administration, Carnegie–Mellon University, April (Revised Dec. 1977).

Hayek, F. A. (1967) *Studies in Philosophy, Politics, and Economics* (London: Routledge & Kegan Paul).

Holmstrom, B. (1979) 'Moral Hazard and Observability', *Bell Journal of Economics*, vol. 10, pp. 74–91.

Klein, B. Crawford, R. A. and Alchian, A. A. (1978) 'Vertical Integration, Appropriable Rents, and the Competitive Contracting Process', *Journal of Law and Economics*, vol. 21, pp. 297–326.

Klein, B. and Leffler, K. B. (1981) 'The Role of Market Forces in Assuring Contractual Performance', *Journal of Political Economy*, vol. 89, pp. 615–641.

Knight, Frank H. (1965) *Risk, Uncertainty and Profit*. (New York: Harper & Row) Republication of 1921 edition.

Machiavelli, N. (1952) *The Prince* (New York: Mentor Books).

Marschak, J. (1968) 'Economics of Inquiring, Communicating, Deciding', *American Economic Review*, vol. 58, pp. 1–18.

Mirrlees, J. (1976) 'The Optimal Structure of Incentives and Authority within an Organization', *The Bell Journal of Economics*, vol. 7, pp. 105–131.

Monteverde, K. and D. J. Teece, (1982) 'Supplier Switching Costs and Vertical Integration in the Automobile Industry', *Bell Journal of Economics*, vol. 13, pp. 206–213.

Nelson, R. R. (1981) 'Assessing Private Enterprise: An Exegesis of Tangled Doctrine', *Bell Journal of Economics*, vol. 12, pp. 93–111.

Okun, A. (1975) 'Inflation: Its Mechanics and Welfare Costs', *Brookings Papers on Economic Activity*, vol. 2, pp. 351-390.

Polanyi, M. (1962) *Personal Knowledge: Towards a Post-critical Philosophy* (New York: Harper & Row).

Posner, R. A. (1974) 'The Appropriate Scope of Regulation in the Cable Television Industry', *Bell J. of Econ. and Management Science*, vol. 5, pp. 335–358.

Reder, M. W. (1982) 'Chicago Economics: Permanence and Change', *Journal of Economic Literature*, vol. 20, pp. 1–38.

Richardson, G. B. (1972) 'The Organization of Industry', *Economic Journal*, vol. 82, pp. 883–896.

Ross, S. (1973) 'The Economic Theory of Agency: The Principal's Problem', *The American Economic Review*, vol. 63, pp. 134–139.

Rothschild, Michael and Stiglitz, Joseph (1976) 'Equilibrium in Competitive Insurance Markets', *Quarterly Journal of Economics*, vol. 80, pp. 629–650.

Schelling, Thomas C. (1956) 'An Essay on Bargaining', *American Economic Review*, vol. 46, pp. 281–306.

Schmalensee, R. (1973) 'A Note on the Theory of Vertical Integration', *Journal of Political Economy*, vol. 81, pp. 442–449.

—— (1979) *The Control of Natural Monopolies* (Lexington, Mass.: Lexington Books).

Simon, H. A. (1961) *Administrative Behavior*. 2nd ed. (New York: Macmillan).

—— (1978) 'Rationality as Process and as Product of Thought', *American Economic Review*, vol. 68, pp. 1–16.

—— (1979) 'Rational Decision Making in 'Business Organization', *American Economic Review*, vol. 69, pp. 499–513.

Stigler, George J. (1968) *The Organization of Industry* (Homewood, Ill.: Richard D. Irwin, Inc.).

Stiglitz, J. (1975) 'Incentives, Risk, and Information: Notes toward a Theory of Hierarchy'. *The Bell Journal of Economics*, vol. 6, pp. 552–579.

Teece, David J. (1980) 'Economics of Scope and the Scope of the Enterprise', *Journal of Economic Behavior and Organization*, vol. 1, pp. 223–245.

—— (1981) 'Internal Organization and Economic Performance: an Empirical Analysis of the Profitability of Principal Firms', *Journal of Industrial Economics*, vol. 30, pp. 173–200.

Telser, L. G. (1981) 'A Theory of Self-Enforcing Agreements', *Journal of Business*, vol. 53, pp. 27–44.

Vernon, J. M. and Graham, D. A. (1971) 'Profitability of Monopolization by Vertical Integration', *Journal of Political Economy*, vol. 79, pp. 924–925.

Wachter, Michael and Williamson, O. E. (1978) 'Obligational Markets and the Mechanics of Inflation', *The Bell Journal of Economics*, vol. 9, pp. 549–571.

Warren-Boulton, F. R. (1967) 'Vertical Control with Variable Proportions', *Journal of Political Economy*, vol. 75, pp. 123–138.

Williamson, Oliver E. (1971) 'The Vertical Integration of Production: Market Failure Considerations', *American Economic Review*, vol. 61, pp. 112–123.

—— (1973) 'Markets and Hierarchies: Some Elementary Considerations', *American Economic Review*, vol. 63, pp. 316–325.

—— (1975) *Markets and Hierarchies: Analysis and Antitrust Implications*. New York: The Free Press.

—— (1976) 'Franchise Bidding for Natural Monopolies – in General and with Respect to CATV', *Bell Journal of Economics*, vol. 7, pp. 73–104.

—— (1979) 'Transaction-Cost Economics: The Governance of Contractual Relations', *J. Law Econ.*, vol. 22, pp. 233–261.

—— (1981) 'Antitrust Enforcement: Where It's Been; Where It's Going'. Discussion Paper No. 102, Center for the Study of Organizational Innovation, University of Pennsylvania, May.

—— (1981) 'The Economics of Organization: The Transaction Cost Approach', *American Journal of Sociology*, vol. 87, pp. 548–577.

_____ (1983) 'Credible Commitments: Using Hostages to Support Exchange', *American Economic Review*, vol. 73, pp. 519–40.

Wilson, R. (1968) 'The Theory of Syndicates', *Econometrica*, vol. 36, pp. 119–132.

Discussion of The Paper by Oliver K. Williamson

Phlips began his discussion of Williamson's paper by underscoring the importance of asset specificity in explaining vertical integration in the paper: the more specific are assets, the more efficient was an internal firm over an external market solution to resource allocation. For example, if a firm's technology used special purpose durable imputs, then it was likely to seek assurance *ex ante* and protection *ex post* against breach of contract or defection by buyers of the output of the firm. As Phlips pointed out, *ex ante* assurance ('hostages' in Williamson's terminology) was a variant of price discrimination with the self-selection by potential buyers of the firm's output into good and poor risks: *ex post* protection guarded against opportunistic behaviour by buyers where states of the world were revealed only after contracts were signed. Phlips made two points on this contractual practice. First, asset-specific technologies where assurance or protection was required by the producer was tantamount to a vertically integrated supply relationship. Second, asset-specific technologies without assurance or protection would yield higher product prices as risk premiums were built into the product prices themselves. Therefore, some observed retail price variability might be cost based. In general, Phlips argued that the desire for upstream firms to price discriminate downstream might provide an even stronger incentive for vertical integration than transactions-costs considerations.

Chaudhuri began his discussion of the Williamson paper by arguing that reliance on transactions-costs explanations of organisational form could cause one to ignore other more important explanations. To illustrate, he argued that in East Asia, the relationship between firms very often took the form of sub-contracts or implicit stable contractual relationships between buyers and sellers, while in Western Europe and North America, these relationships usually led to vertical integration. He suggested that one explanation for this might be that in a labour-intensive economy, small production units economised on monitoring costs. However, he suggested that an understanding of the forces that explained the prevalence of contracts over direct vertical integration, would require a move beyond transactions-costs explanations.

Gilbert cited practices in the US that served as partial substitutes for vertical integration. As an example, he noted that IBM's condition of purchase of microprocessors from Intel was that Intel supplied the technology to a competitor so that IBM would have an established second source of microprocessors.

Schmalensee suggested that the transactions-costs approach did not provide hard testable propositions in the manner of much of the current literature in economic theory. He suggested that if the approach was to be effective, then we required a much more detailed knowledge of empirical facts than was customary. *Salop* felt that the opposite was true, that is, that the transactions-costs approach could be used to provide an efficiency argument for virtually any observed practice. In *Zoltan Roman's* view, insight on organisational form would flow if we had an algorithm that could compute transactions costs and suggest policy. In addition, he noted that in balancing the benefits and costs of vertical integration, we should add a cost in terms of lost flexibility for those who integrate.

Grossman suggested that Williamson had not provided an explanation of the way that vertical integration resolved the incentive problem. Grossman argued that it was incorrect to think that the owner-manager of a firm would have different preferences and incentives to work when he changed from being a sub-contractor to being an employee of the larger company. *Green* responded that the advantage of vertical integration was that it created an irreversible relationship between participants where joint profit-sharing provided sufficient incentives for firms to behave co-operatively. Joint profit-sharing would not work as a voluntary short-term contract since parties would violate the contract and maximise independently whenever this was in their own interest. Green suggested that in the long-term relationship, private information would eventually be revealed in a way that it would not under short-term contractual arrangements.

6 Vertical Integration and Assurance of Markets

Jerry R. Green

DEPARTMENT OF ECONOMICS,
HARVARD UNIVERSITY, USA

I INTRODUCTION

Four incentives for the vertical integration of firms have frequently been mentioned in the literature. Mergers may result from market power in either the primary-resource, intermediate-product or final-product markets.[1] Technological advantages accruing to combination can arise through increasing returns,[2] information advantages[3] or decreased transactions costs, when firms place themselves in a co-operative rather than an adversarial relationship.[4] Tax avoidance provides a third reason for integration.[5] More generally, integration opens up a wider range of strategies in the face of regulation and more flexibility in implementing them. Finally, imperfections in the market for the intermediate product may lead firms to combine in order to bypass these problems by transferring goods internally.[6] This chapter addresses the last of these issues. In particular, it studies the problem of price inflexibility in an intermediate-product market which is beset by stochastic demands, and the temporary shortages and gluts of this product that result. We hypothesise that firms choose to integrate if the expected profit from doing so exceeds that of the separate divisions acting independently. Both descriptive and normative conclusions regarding such an industry are drawn on the basis of the model presented.

The literature concerned with the behaviour of firms in industries with rigid prices has been growing rapidly.[7] However, the effect of imperfect price-flexibility on the structure of markets has not been

177

addressed. General equilibrium models with rigid prices have been explored for the purpose of uniting the Keynesian and Walrasian models.[8] Here also, the scope of activity for each firm has been taken as a datum rather than as a variable of the system.

The lack of treatment received by internal organisation in an explicit equilibrium framework is traceable to the fact that there is no incentive for either integration or divestiture in the static, perfectly competitive model.[9] This allowed the specification of a fixed set of active, or potentially active, firms *ab initio*, describing each only by a set of technological possibilities. As interest developed in various generalisations, the resulting forces for realigning firms in ways other than that permitted by the initial listing were noticed. But a unified treatment that links the results of such actions to the underlying movement of the system towards equilibrium has yet to emerge. This chapter is an attempt to construct such a model, and it is hoped that the techniques and framework employed will find application beyond the narrow question addressed here.

The complexity and multiplicity of forces favouring or opposing alternative forms of internal organisation for the firm, make a general theory of vertical integration intractable. In concentrating on the effect of market imperfections on integration, we shall deliberately abstract from the first three of the incentives for mergers mentioned above. Firms in our model will behave competitively, will operate in unregulated, untaxed industries, and will produce according to a constant-returns-to-scale technology. Such firms, will derive an advantage from integration in the absence of some adverse technological consequences of this action. Since they always have the option of duplicating the behaviour they would have followed separately, integration can hardly be harmful to such firms. Therefore, a theory of integration in the absence of taxes on the organisational form of firms must at some stage rest on the existence of decreasing returns to a expansion of the scope of activities carried out by a single firm – or else integration will always be complete. In the relatively simple model presented below, the market advantages accruing to integration face countervailing forces in the shape of the decreased technological efficiency of the larger enterprise.[10]

The issue of vertical integration, at least in the USA, has arisen largely as a policy question. Should a vertical merger be permitted between two firms who actually desire to take such an action? This rather obvious fact has implications for public policy in the analysis of such cases. Although previous market-oriented studies of vertical integration trace out its effects on prices, quantities, inventory levels and productive efficiency, they hypothesise the merger of two firms without relating that hypothesis to the value which such a move has to the firms in question.[11] Neither do they explore whether the factors causing the initial integration persist and will cause other similar firms to take the same step. In this chapter, we shall treat the integration–divestiture process as the result of an explicit equilibrating mechanism. We therefore focus on the issue of permitting or disallowing those mergers which are actively being pursued by firms in the industry, rather than on whether merger *per se* is socially valuable under arbitary circumstances.

In Section II the basic model is presented. Section III is concerned with characterising the equilibria that can arise in this industry. Welfare and policy implications are developed in Section IV. Section V discusses some generalisations of the model, and a brief conclusion follows.

II THE MODEL

(1) STRUCTURE OF THE INDUSTRY

We construct a model in which there are three types of firm, called upstream, downstream and integrated. Upstream firms transform labour into an intermediate product using capital services in the process, according to the fixed-coefficient technology

$$x = \min \left(\frac{L}{a_L}, \frac{K}{a_K} \right). \tag{1}$$

Here, x is the output of intermediate product and L and K are the amounts of labour and capital used, respectively. Downstream firms use the intermediate product to produce a final output according to the production function

$$v = \min \left(\frac{y}{b_y}, \frac{K}{b_K} \right). \tag{2}$$

Here, y is the quantity of intermediate product used in this process, K is the quantity of capital used, and v is the quantity of final product produced.

Integrated firms use labour and capital in a two-stage production process. This yields final product as an output, but may involve the intermediate product as either a net input or a net output. The production function is

$$
v = \min \left(\frac{z + \min \left(\dfrac{L}{a'_L}, \dfrac{K^1}{a'_K} \right)}{b'_z}, \frac{K^2}{b'_K} \right) . \tag{3}
$$

Here, z is the input of intermediate product in excess of the quantity the firm produces for its own use, which is given by the second term in the sum, and K^1 and K^2 are the quantities of capital allocated to the two stages of the production. We assume that the integrated firms have a technology inferior to their non-integrated counterparts, that is

$$
a_L \lesseqgtr a'_L; \quad a_K \lesseqgtr a'_K; \quad b_y \lesseqgtr b'_y; \quad b_K \lesseqgtr b'_K.
$$

Without a condition ensuring decreasing returns to integration, there is no reason for any producer to remain non-integrated. An analysis of equilibria in the form of organisation of firms in this industry can therefore be non-trivial only under such circumstances.

Since our concern is vertical integration of firms, attention will focus primarily on the market for the intermediate product. We suppose that prices are fixed. The price of labour will be taken to be unity; final product has a price p; and the price of the intermediate product is q. The intermediate product market is subject to stochastic fluctuations in exogenous excess demand, and these lead to rationing of one side of the market or the other.

The industry we study is perhaps not the only user of the intermediate product. The random factors impinging upon this market result in a stochastic net demand (Z) for the intermediate product. Let

$$
Z_+ = \max (0, Z) \text{ and}
$$
$$
Z_- = \min (0, Z)
$$

and the distribution of Z be $f(\cdot)$.

The total demand for the intermediate product is given by the sum of the demand by downstream firms, by integrated firms (if they are net demanders), and the demanders outside this industry. These outside demands are comprised of non-stochastic components (D)

and (S), and the stochastic net demands Z_+. Let this aggregate be denoted

$$\Delta(Z)$$

and let

$$\Sigma(Z)$$

represent total supply, similarly obtained.

Rationing of the product will be assumed to be in accordance with the following simple, and extreme, mechanism:

If $\Delta(Z) < \Sigma(Z)$, the fraction $\Delta(Z)/\Sigma(Z)$ of suppliers can sell their product at the price (q): the remainder lose their sales and receive nothing. The intermediate product is assumed to be non-durable. Similarly, if $\Sigma(Z) < \Delta(Z)$, then $\Sigma(Z)/\Delta(Z)$ have their demands met exactly and the remainder receive nothing. Though very severe, this rationing scheme captures the idea of temporary shortages and loss of sales. More moderate rationing methods probably temper the sharpness of our results but not the broader qualitative features of the model.[12]

We suppose that the capital installed in the two production modes (upstream and downstream) is fixed and not transferable between them. The total quantities of capital are denoted as

$$\bar{K}^1 \text{ and } \bar{K}^2,$$

for the production of the intermediate product and the final product respectively.

To avoid technical problems (like the indivisability of firms) and because the size of firms is indeterminate as a result of our constant-returns-to-scale assumption, we identify 'firms' with infinitesimal quantities of capital. Upstream firms are infinitesimals dK^u, where K^u is that part of $\bar{K}^1$ in the hands of upstream firms. Similarly, dK^d is the capital of a downstream firm. Integrated firms are to be thought of as combinations of infinitesimal units of capital of both types, linked together in the following way. Non-integrated firms must express their desired sales and purchases on a market where rationing is a possibility. Integrated firms, however, can pass the output of their upstream divisions directly to their downstream branches without running the risk of being rationed. The proportions of the two kinds of capital in an integrated firm is one of the variables determined by the model.

In any situation, the state of the industry is described by the organisational structure of the market – how much of each type of capital is owned by each class of firms – and by the actions of each of these firms. This determines the expected profits per unit of capital in the upstream and downstream categories and the expected profits accruing to the mixture of capital in the integrated firms. If all categories of firms are active, we shall say that the system is in equilibrium: (a) if the expected profits per unit of capital of the disintegrated firms (weighted by the proportions of the capital-types in integrated firms) equals the expected profits accruing to the corresponding quantity of capital in integrated firms; and (b) if no different proportions fo capital-types for integrated firms (with the same yield in the non-integrated sector), would lead to higher expected profits. For states in which one or two of the categories of firms are empty, equilibrium requires, in addition, that the capital used in this mode would not earn a greater return than it does in the ongoing situation.

(2) BEHAVIOUR OF FIRMS

Each firm must decide how much of the intermediate product to demand or supply. In addition, upstream and integrated firms must choose an amount of labour. After making these decisions, the amount of exogenous demand becomes known, and rationing takes place as described above. If upstream or downstream firms are rationed, sales or output are zero respectively. Integrated firms, if rationed, carry out their downstream production using only their internally-generated supply of intermediate product. If the integrated firm was participating as a seller in the intermediate product market, the unsold quantity is added to his inputs.[13]

From the structure of the rationing process and of production, it is clear that the net demands per unit of capital by upstream and downstream firms are fixed at the levels corresponding to the efficient operation of their activities. There is no advantage in distorting desired sales or purchases since, by assumption, the probability of being rationed is independent of the firm's actions. Any divergence between stated desires and the efficient level can only decrease profits in the event that rationing does not affect the firm.

In the case of the integrated firm, however, the optimal level of excess demand for the intermediate product for it to present to the market is not independent of the choice of the optimal-integration proportions. The optimal-integration proportions are those which maximise the excess of the total return to the capital of the integrated firm over the return that this capital would have earned if it had been used in non-integrated production processes. Let r^u and r^d be the expected returns per unit of K^u and K^d, in upstream and downstream firms respectively. Thus the optimal-integration proportions are determined by seeking the maximum expected profit for an integrated firm subject to;

$$r^u K^1 + r^d K^2 = 1. \tag{4}$$

Let the K^1 and K^2 satisfying (4) be fixed temporarily. Efficient operation of the firm requires that:

$$L = \frac{K^1 a'_L}{a'_K}. \tag{5}$$

The level of net demand (z) on the intermediate product market that would lead to efficient production in the downstream stage is given by

$$z = \frac{K^2 b'_z}{b'_K} - \frac{K^1}{a'_K}, \tag{6}$$

and the corresponding level of final product is

$$v = \frac{K^2}{b'_K}. \tag{7}$$

If purchases of the intermediate product exceed this level of z, no additional (v) is produced. For lower levels of purchases (or higher levels of sales) the final output is given by

$$
\begin{aligned}
v &= \frac{K^1}{a'_K b'_z} + \frac{z}{b'_z} &&\text{if } z > \frac{-K^1}{a'_K} \\
&= 0 &&\text{if } z \le \frac{-K^1}{a'_K}
\end{aligned}
\tag{8}
$$

The opportunity loci for (v) and (z), at various integration proportions satisfying (4) are depicted in Figure 6.1.

It follows from the above, that the slope of the locus of efficient points is

$$\frac{dv}{dz} = \frac{\dfrac{dv}{dK^2}}{\dfrac{dz}{dK^2}} = \frac{1}{b'_z + \dfrac{r^d b'_K}{r^u a'_K}} \tag{9}$$

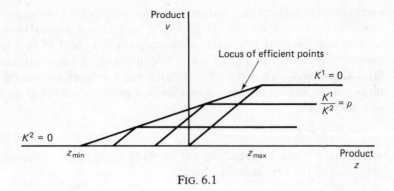

FIG. 6.1

and the maximal and minimal levels of (z) consistent with efficient-firm operation are

$$z_{max} = \frac{b'_z}{r^d b'_K}$$

(10)

$$z_{min} = \frac{-1}{r^u a'_K}$$

At these extreme points, the integrated firm is acting as if it were a purely downstream or a purely upstream produce, though with a different technology.

We shall now argue that, given the assumptions made thus far, the optimal configuration for an integrated firm is such that it operates efficiently, without any participation in the intermediate-product market. It will choose K^1 and K^2 so that the upstream division produces precisely the amount of intermediate product required downstream. Any other choice of K^1/K^2 requires *either* some inefficiency *or* some probability of the rationing of sales or purchases, with consequent economic losses.

Intuitively, the reason for this result is that the inferior input requirements of the integrated firm are independent of the proportions of capital it chooses to employ. Therefore, once it has decided to adopt the integrated form, the only remaining consideration is the minimisation of rationing possibilities.

A rigorous demonstration of this proposition is given in the Appendix. For the subsequent development of this chapter it suffices to note that the efficient mixture of the types of capital is given by

$$\rho^* = \frac{K^1}{K^2} = \frac{a'_K \, b'_z}{b'_K}.$$

We shall also refer to this ratio as the *balanced proportions* of integration.

III EQUILIBRIUM

(1) PROFIT AS A FUNCTION OF INDUSTRY STRUCTURE

In order to determine whether a particular structure of the firms in this industry is in equilibrium, we must compute the expected-profit levels for each type of firm, as it depends on the parameters of the equilibrium. Let

$$k^A(Z) = \min \left(\frac{\Delta(Z)}{\Sigma(Z)}, 1 \right), \text{ and}$$

$$k^B(Z) = \min \left(\frac{\Delta(Z)}{\Sigma(Z)}, 1 \right)$$

be the proportions of suppliers and demanders of intermediate product who are able to realise their desired quantities. Let E^A and E^B be the means (averages) of these two random variables, namely, the expected quantities realised by participants in this market. These, it has been argued above are, respectively, the upstream and downstream non-integrated firms.

Profits of the upstream firms per unit of K^u are

$$E^A \, \frac{q}{a_K} - \frac{a_L}{a_K} = r^u. \tag{11}$$

Profits of downstream firms per unit of K^d are

$$E^B \left(\frac{p - qb_y}{b_K} \right) = r^d. \tag{12}$$

Profits of integrated firms will be independent of rationing since they chose balanced proportions. If we consider such an integrated firm, with capital K^1 and K^2 satisfying

$$K^1 = \frac{a'_K b'_z}{b'_K} K^2, \tag{13}$$

the excess of revenues from the sale of final product over labour costs is

$$K^2 \left(\frac{p - a'_L b'_z}{b'_K} \right). \tag{14}$$

In any equilibrium in which both integrated and non-integrated firms are operating,

$$\left(\frac{p - a'_L b'_z}{b'_K} \right) = r^d + \frac{a'_K b'_z}{b'_K} r^u.$$

or, using (11) and (12)

$$E^A \left(\rho^* \frac{q}{a_K} \right) + E^B \left(\frac{p - q b_y}{b_K} \right) = \frac{p}{b'_K} + \left(\frac{a_L}{a_K} - \frac{a'_L}{a'_K} \right) \rho^* \tag{15}$$

This defines the class of rationing frequencies consistent with mixed equilibria of this type. The right-hand side of (15) is constant, whereas the left-hand side will vary with the extent of vertical integration in the industry, because of the induced changes in $k^A(Z)$ and $k^B(Z)$ and consequently in E^A and E^B. If the left-hand side of (15) is greater than the right-hand side, then integrated firms will tend to dissolve into separate enterprises in order to take advantage of the superior technologies available to these firms. Likewise, the reverse inequality sets up forces favouring integration as firms attempt to avoid the stochastic rationing on both sides of the market.

In any situation that is potentially an equilibrium one, the amount of capital in the three types of firms is given by K^u (upstream), K^d (downstream) and $(\bar{K}^u - K^u, \bar{K}^d - K^d)$ (integrated), where

$$\frac{\bar{K}^u - K^u}{\bar{K}^d - K^d} = \rho^*.$$

The expected values of the rationing-parameters depend on the degree of integration because the total demand and supply for intermediate product varies with the size of the upstream and downstream parts of this industry. The supply of intermediate product is given by

$$\sigma = \frac{K^u}{a_K}, \tag{16}$$

and the demand by downstream firms is

$$\delta = \frac{b_y K^d}{b_K}, \tag{17}$$

in accordance with the discussion at the beginning of Section II(2).

Total demand and supply are defined by

$$\Sigma(Z) = \sigma + S - Z_-$$

$$\Delta(Z) = \delta + D + Z_+. \tag{18}$$

Using (18), the changes in rationing frequencies for non-integrated firms with respect to changing conditions in the intermediate product market are given by

$$dE^A = \int\limits_{\{Z|k^A<1\}} \frac{\Sigma(Z)d\delta - \Delta(Z)d\sigma}{[\Delta(Z)]^2} f(Z) \, dZ \tag{19}$$

$$dE^B = \int\limits_{\{Z|k^B<1\}} \frac{\Delta(Z)d\sigma - \Sigma(Z)d\delta}{[\Delta(Z)]^2} f(Z) \, dZ$$

when integration takes place in the balanced proportions

$$\frac{dK^u}{dK^d} = \rho^* \tag{20}$$

and hence

$$d_o = \rho^* \frac{b_K d\delta}{a_K b_y} = \frac{a_K' b_K' b_z'}{a_K b_K' b_y} \, d\delta. \tag{21}$$

Substituting in (19)

$$dE^A = d\delta \int\limits_{\{Z|k^A<1\}} \left[\frac{1}{\Sigma(Z)} - \frac{\Delta(Z)}{[\Sigma(Z)]^2} \frac{a_K' b_K b_z'}{a_K b_K' b_y} \right] f(Z)dZ$$

$$dE^B = d\delta \int\limits_{\{Z|k^B<1\}} \left[\frac{a_K' b_K b_z'}{a_K b_K' b_y} \cdot \frac{1}{\Delta(Z)} - \frac{\Sigma(Z)}{[\Delta(Z)]^2} \right] f(Z)dz \tag{22}$$

Consider the two terms in the integrand of the expression for dE^A. Whenever Z is in the range of integration,

$$\frac{1}{\sigma + S + Z_-} > \frac{\delta + D + Z_+}{(\sigma + S + Z_-)^2} \ . \tag{23}$$

As the industry becomes more integrated, $d\sigma$ and $d\delta$ are negative. Hence

$$dE^A < d\delta \int\limits_{\{Z|k^A<1\}} \frac{\Delta(Z)}{[\Sigma(Z)]^2} \left(1 - \rho^*\frac{b_K}{a_K b_y}\right) \ f(Z)dZ \tag{24}$$

and

$$dE^B < d\delta \int\limits_{\{Z|k^B<1\}} \frac{\Sigma(Z)}{[\Delta(Z)]^2} \left(\rho^* \frac{b_K}{a_K b_y} - 1\right) \ f(Z)dZ. \tag{25}$$

Let $M = \max(\sigma + S, \delta + D)$ and $N = 1 - \rho^* b^K/a_K b_y$.

The parameter (N) is central to the analysis. When $N = 0$, the technological disadvantage faced by integrated firms is neutral in the following sense. When firms integrate in balanced proportions, the decreased demand for intermediate product by previously downstream firms exactly offsets the decreased supply due to there being a smaller upstream sector. When $N > 0$, integration absorbs more of the demand than it does of the supply. Both decrease, but the net effect on excess demand is negative. Therefore the sign of (N) is a key benchmark for ascertaining the effects of integration on rationing frequencies. At $N = 0$, we can be sure that integration causes rationing more frequently on both sides of the market; in general, the answer will depend on the sign of N and on the distribution of Z, as developed below.

If $N > 0$, we have that as the degree of integration increases,

$$dE^B < -d\delta \ \frac{N}{M} \ \text{Prob}(k^B < 1)$$

$$dE^A < d\delta \ N \int \frac{\Delta(Z)}{[\Sigma(Z)]^2} \ f(Z)dZ. \tag{26}$$

Let $\Delta_{\min} = \delta + D + \min Z_+$

$$\Sigma_{min} = \sigma + S - \min Z_- \, ,$$

where the minimum of Z_+ and Z_- is taken over all Z that occur with positive probability under the distribution F.

We have that

$$dE^A < -d\delta\, N \frac{\Delta_{min}}{\Sigma^2_{min}} \, \text{Prob}(k^A < 1) \tag{27}$$

using the facts the $d\delta < 0$ and $N > 0$.

Therefore an upper bound on the total derivative with respect to increasing integration of the left-hand side of (15) is given by

$$- \left(\frac{p - qb_y}{Mb_K} \, \frac{\Delta_{min}\rho^*q}{\Sigma^2_{min}\, a_K} \right) N d\delta \, \text{Prob} \, (k^B < 1)$$

$$+ N d\delta \frac{\rho^*q}{a_K} \frac{\Delta_{min}}{\Sigma^2_{min}} \tag{28}$$

Similarly, if $N < 0$, we calculate this upper bound as

$$- \left(\frac{p - qb_y}{b_K} \, \frac{\Sigma_{max}}{\Delta^2_{max}} + \frac{\rho^*q}{a_K M} \right) N d\delta \, \text{Prob}(k^B < 1)$$

$$+ N d\delta \frac{\rho^*q}{Ma_K} \tag{29}$$

Expressions (28) and (29) are useful for deriving the qualitative properties of the equilibria in the degree of integration in the industry. Recall that the equality (15) describes the co-existence of integrated and non-integrated firms in equilibrium. If the left-hand side of (15) is decreasing with integration, such an equilibrium is unstable and the qualitative characteristics of the industry are as asserted in Section I. Note that, when $N = 0$, this basic instability result is valid because (28) and (29) – which are upper bounds on this derivative – are both zero. This accords well with intuition. The case $N = 0$ implies the $d\delta = d\sigma$, and hence k^A and k^B both decrease for each value of Z because subtracting equal small quantities from each of two positive numbers with a ratio below one causes this ratio to decrease. Therefore both E^A and E^B will decrease in this situation, and both types of non-integrated firms become less profitable.

Consider $N > 0$. By (21) that this feature

$$0 > d\sigma > d\delta \tag{30}$$

as integration increases.

Let $\bar{Z}$ be the value of the stochastic exogenous excess demand that satisfies

$$\delta + D + \bar{Z}_+ = \sigma + S - \bar{Z}_- \tag{31}$$

Since $Z = Z_+ + Z_-$,

$$\bar{Z} = \sigma + S - (\delta + D) \tag{32}$$

when (30) holds

$$d\bar{Z} = d\sigma - d\delta > 0$$

and hence, since

$$\text{Prob}(k^B < 1) = \int_{\bar{Z}}^{\infty} f(Z)dZ \tag{33}$$

$\text{Prob}(k^B < 1)$ decreases with increasing integration in this industry. If $N < 0$, the opposite result obtains.

Referring to (28) and (29), this implies that both upper bounds on the slope of the weighted disintegrated profits function decrease with the extent of integration. This is the principal result of this section. Sufficient conditions for the slope of the weighted disintegrated profits function to be everywhere negative can be obtained from (28) and (29) as

$$\text{Prob}(k^B < 1) < \cfrac{\cfrac{\rho^* q}{a_K} \cfrac{\Delta_{\min}}{\Sigma_{\min}^2}}{\cfrac{p - qb_y}{Mb_K} + \cfrac{\rho^* q_{\min}}{a_K \Sigma_{\min}^2}} \tag{34}$$

when $N > 0$, and

$$\text{Prob}(k^B < 1) > \cfrac{\cfrac{\rho^*}{Ma_K} q}{\cfrac{p - qb_y}{b_K} \cfrac{\Sigma_{\max}}{\Delta_{\max}^2} + \cfrac{\rho^* q}{Ma_K}} \tag{35}$$

when $N < 0$.

Although the possibility of a rising portion of the weighted disintegrated profits function may lead to stable equilibrium at intermediate levels of integration, the fact that this is impossible when $N = 0$ and unlikely when $|N|$ is small makes the study of this unstable case useful as a benchmark.

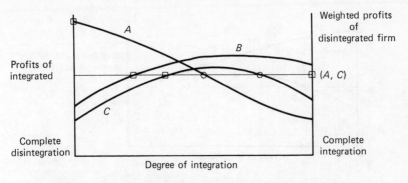

□ Denotes stable equilibrium   ○ Denotes unstable equilibrium

FIG. 6.2

(2) THE STRUCTURE OF EQUILIBRIA

The above analysis indicates how the structure of equilibria in this industry relates to the change in technology when integration takes place. Some possibilities are shown in Figure 6.2.

Let $K_{max}^1 = \min (\bar{K}^u, \rho^* \bar{K}^d)$.

We may then regard the degree of intergration as $K^1/(K_{max}^1) \; \partial \; [0,1]$. Suppose, as Stigler (1951) and a variety of empirical studies suggest, that new industries are 'born' vertically integrated, perhaps because they use intermediate products that are specially tailored for their technology and for which alternative suppliers are not yet reliable producers. Only cases A and C are possible if complete integration is an equilibrium. If the industry grows proportionately by expanding $\bar{K}^u$ and $\bar{K}^d$ at the same rate, at which D and S are growing while $f(Z)$ remains the same, it is clear that E^A and E^B are increasing over time, viewed as functions of K^1/K_{max}^1. Thus, weighted expected and disintegrated profits are rising for each fixed value of K^1/K_{max}^1. At the point at which complete integration ceases to be an equilibrium, we have situation A^* or C^* as shown in Figure 6.3.

In either instance, the system experiences a qualitative discontinuity, arriving either at complete disintegration or at a substantially-reduced level of integration, according to whether the profit functions are of the form A or C respectively. This economic 'catastrophe'[14] seems worthy of empirical testing. The theoretical implication of a reduction of integration as the market grows is identical with Stigler's proposition

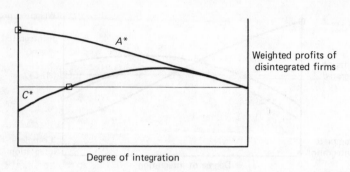

FIG. 6.3

(which is based on assumptions about returns to scale). But the dynamic implications of this model should allow one to discriminate between these theories.

A similar phenomenon is predicted when an initially non-integrated industry experiences increasing fluctuations in the inter-mediate product market. A discontinuous shift to complete vertical integration is indicated in this case.

IV WELFARE CONSIDERATIONS

The model we have presented is fraught with externalities. Each organisational decision to make an incremental in the quantity of capital exerts a real effect on the profitability of every firm in the disintegrated state. It is natural to study the welfare implications of this model. What is the optimal degree of vertical integration? What is the social cost of the price rigidity that generated the incentive for integration? Should integration and divestiture be encouraged or discouraged by public policy?

To approach these issues, we must first calculate the net social contribution made by the sector under examination. The value of the labour input is a non-stochastic quantity given by

$$L = \frac{a_L}{a_K} \left(\bar{K}^u - K^1 \right) + \frac{a_L'}{a_K'} K^1$$

$$= \frac{a_L}{a_K} \bar{K}^u - K^1 \left(\frac{a_L}{a_K} - \frac{a_L'}{a_K'} \right). \tag{36}$$

Output of the final product is stochastic, however, due to the impact of the rationing process on non-integrated firms. Expected output is given by

$$Ev = \frac{\bar{K}^d - K^2}{b_K} E^B + \frac{K^2}{b'_K} = \frac{\bar{K}^d E^B}{b_K} - \frac{K^1}{\rho^*} \left(\frac{E^B}{b_K} - \frac{1}{b'_K} \right). \quad (37)$$

To evaluate the net contribution of the industry since its participation in the market for the intermediate product, we must consider several cases. If the net demand of this industry, $\delta - \sigma$, has the same sign as the exogenous net demand $D - S + Z$. The industry is of no social value in this respect, for it does not satisfy any needs in the economy; nor does it use resources that would otherwise have been employed elsewhere. If $\delta - \sigma$ is positive and $D - S + Z$ is negative, the net social contribution is also zero, since this industry is utilising resources that would otherwise have been wasted. On an overall basis there is a gain, but it will appear in the form of an increase in the amount of final product produced.

However, if $\delta - \sigma$ is negative and $D - S + Z$ is positive, the industry is fulfilling a need elsewhere in the economy. The extent to which it is adding to total social benefits may be limited by the size of the exogenous demand to be filled, if this is smaller than the supply forthcoming. Thus the expected net contribution in the intermediate product market is:

$$E\min_{\{Z|D-S+Z>0\}} (\sigma - \delta, D - S + Z) \quad \text{if } \sigma - \delta > 0,$$

$$0 \quad \text{if } \sigma - \delta > 0. \quad (38)$$

The total expected social value of this sector $[W(K^1)]$ can therefore be written as

$$W(K^1) = W_+(K^1) = \frac{p\bar{K}^d E^B}{b_K} - \frac{a_L \bar{L}^U}{a_K} + K^1 \left[\frac{p}{\rho^*} \left(\frac{1}{b'_K} - \frac{E^B}{b_K} \right) \right.$$

$$\left. + \left(\frac{a_L}{a_K} - \frac{a'_L}{a'_K} \right) \right], \quad (39)$$

if $\delta - \sigma > 0$;

or

$$W(K^1) = W_+(K^1) + qE\min_{\{Z|D-S+Z>0\}} (\sigma - \delta, D - S + Z), \quad (40)$$

if $\delta - \sigma < 0$.

Here, we have valued each commodity at its *fixed* price, an admittedly imperfect approximation.

The evaluation of $W(\cdot)$ is in general quite complex. If equilibria are generated by a profit function for which only the extreme organisational forms represent equilibria, then the relevant consideration is the comparison of $W(O)$ and $W(K^1_{max})$. If the weighted non-integrated profit function is decreasing and both complete disintegration and complete integration are stable equilibria, we have:

$$E^A(0) \left(\frac{\rho^* q}{a_K}\right) + E^B(0) \left(\frac{(p - qb_y)}{b_K}\right) \geqq \frac{p}{b'_K} + \left(\frac{a_L}{a_K} - \frac{a'_L}{a'_K}\right)\rho^*$$

$$\geqq E^A(K^1_{max}) \left(\frac{\rho^* q}{a_K}\right) + E^A(K^1_{max}) \left(\frac{(p - qb_y)}{b_K}\right). \tag{41}$$

Here, we have written E^A and E^B as functions of the degree of integration.

It will again be simplest to treat the case in which $N = 0$ so that $\sigma - \delta$ is a constant with respect to the degree of integration. Hence,

$$W(K^1_{max}) - W(0) = \frac{p\bar{K}^d}{b_K} \left(E^B(K^1_{max}) - E^B(0) \right)$$

$$+ K^1_{max} \left[\frac{p}{\rho^*} \left(\frac{1}{b'_K} - \frac{E^B(K^1_{max})}{b_K}\right)\right.$$

$$\left. + \left(\frac{a_L}{a_K} - \frac{a'_L}{a'_K}\right) \right] \tag{42}$$

Suppose that the industry is in stable equilibrium with complete integration and that the environment of the industry is changing so that weighted disintegrated profits are rising relative to integrated profits. We can ask whether the switch to the disintegrated mode occurs too early or too late in this process. That is, should integration be encouraged or discouraged in the course of the process? At the switch point, the last of the inequalities (41) is an equality.

Solving this for $(a_L/a_K - a'_L/a'_K)$, substituting the result in (42) and using the fact that $N = 0$, we have:

$$W(K_{max}^1) - W(0) = \frac{pE^B(K_{max}^1)}{b_K} \left(\bar{K}^d - \frac{K_{max}^1}{\rho^*} \right)$$

$$+ \frac{qK_{max}^1}{a_K} \left(E^A(K_{max}^1) - E^B(K_{max}^1) \right)$$

$$+ \frac{p}{b_K} \left(\frac{K_{max}^1}{\rho^*} E^B(K_{max}^1) - \bar{K}^d E^B(0) \right). \quad (43)$$

We can divide the possibilities into two cases:

Case I: $\rho^* \bar{K}^d = K_{max}^1$;

Case II: $\rho^* \bar{K}^d > K_{max}^1$; $= \bar{K}^u$.

In Case I, the change in welfare reduces to:

$$W(K_{max}^1) - W(0) = \bar{K}^d \left[\frac{p}{b_K} \left(E^B(K_{max}^1) - E^B(0) \right) \right.$$

$$\left. + \frac{\rho^* q}{a_K} \left(E^A(K_{max}^1) - E^B(K_{max}^1) \right) \right] \quad (44)$$

In Case II we have:

$$W(K_{max}^1) - W(0) = \frac{p}{b_K} \left(\frac{\bar{K}^u}{\rho^*} E^B(\bar{K}^u) - \bar{K}^d E^B(0) \right)$$

$$+ \bar{K}^u \left[\frac{q}{a_K} \left(E^A(\bar{K}^u) - E^B(\bar{K}^u) \right) \right]$$

$$+ \frac{pE^B(\bar{K}^u)}{b_K} \left(\bar{K}^d - \frac{\bar{K}^u}{\rho^*} \right). \quad (45)$$

The first term in each of the expressions (44) and (45) is negative when $N = 0$, because E^B is a decreasing function. The implication of this is that divestiture will tend to occur *too late*, from a social point of view. This is so in the sense that complete disintegration will be the superior organisational form when complete integration could still persist as a stable equilibrium.

The sign of the second term in each is ambiguous, indicating that the first effect will be mitigated if sellers are rationed less heavily than buyers, and will be reinforced in the opposite instance.

Finally, the last term in (45) is positive; there is a force operating in favour of postponing divestiture if the downstream sector is larger than the upstream one.

Turning now to the instance in which integration is about to take place in the industry, we have an exact equality in the left-hand relation of (41). Following a procedure similar to that above, one obtains the result that in Case I,

$$W(K^1_{\max}) - W(0) = \frac{\bar{K}^d \rho^* q}{a_K} \left(E^A(0) - E^B(0) \right); \qquad (46)$$

and in Case II,

$$W(K^1_{\max}) - W(0) = \frac{K^1_{\max} q}{a_K} \left(E^A(0) - E^B(0) \right)$$

$$+ \left(\bar{K}^d - \frac{K^1_{\max}}{\rho^*} \right) \left(E^B(K^1_{\max}) - E^B(0) \right) \frac{p}{b_K}. \quad (47)$$

The first term in (46) and (47) is of ambiguous sign. It indicates that integration will occur too early from a social point of view if sellers are rationed more heavily than buyers in the disintegrated state, and conversely. The second term in (46) is unambiguously negative. This implies that integration will occur *too early*, other things being equal.

Comparing the results of the Section in the cases of integration and disintegration, we note that the socially-preferred equilibrium will be biased toward disintegration if sellers are rationed more severely than buyers; and that there are further forces favouring disintegration due to the differential rationing frequencies in the two potential equilibria.

Now consider the more general situation where $N \neq 0$, but still under the assumption that only complete integration and complete disintegration are potential stable equilibria. We must now add a term representing the change in the supply of the intermediate product to the exogenous market.

The change in welfare when integration gives way to disintegration is given by:

$$W(K^1_{\max}) - W(0) = \frac{pE^B(K^1_{\max})}{b_K} \left(\bar{K}^d - \frac{K^1_{\max}}{\rho^*} \right)$$

$$+ p \left(\frac{K^1_{\max}}{\rho^* b'_K} - \frac{\bar{K}^d E^B(0)}{b_K} \right)$$

$$+ K^1_{\max} \left[q \left(\frac{E^A(K^1_{\max})}{a_K} - \frac{E^B(K^1_{\max}) b_y}{\rho^* b_K} \right) \right.$$

$$\left. + \frac{p}{\rho^*} \left(\frac{E^B(K^1_{\max})}{b_K} - \frac{1}{b'_K} \right) \right] + X, \quad (48)$$

where $X = q\,[E \min (\max (\sigma^{\max} - \delta^{\max}, 0), \max(D - S + Z),$
$0) - E \min (\max (\sigma^0 - \delta^0, 0), \max(D - S + Z), 0)]$.
Here, $\sigma^0, \delta^0, \sigma^{\max}$, and $\delta^{\max}$ are respectively, the supplies and demands of this industry in its extreme organisation structures.

If integration is about to take place, we have

$$W(K^1_{\max}) - W(0) = \frac{pE^B(K^1_{\max})}{b_K} \left(\bar{K}^d \; \frac{K^1_{\max}}{\rho^*} \right)$$

$$+ p \left(\frac{K^1_{\max}}{\rho^* b'_K} - \frac{\bar{K}^d E^B_0}{b_K} \right)$$

$$+ K^1_{\max} \left[\frac{p}{\rho^*} \left(\frac{E^B(0)}{b_K} - \frac{1}{b'_K} \right) \right.$$

$$\left. + \frac{qE^A(0)}{a_K} - \frac{qE^B(0) b_y}{\rho^* b_K} \right] + X. \quad (49)$$

Note that, by definition, $N > 0$ implies:

$$\rho^* < \frac{a_K b_y}{b_K} \quad \text{and,} \quad (50a)$$

$$\sigma^m - \delta^m > \sigma^0 - \delta^0 \quad (50b)$$

Therefore the effect of N having a positive value is seen in (48) and (49) in two ways: The next to the last term becomes smaller in each, due to (50a); but $X > 0$, by (50b). Conversely, $N < 0$ also leads to two conflicting influences on the net change in social welfare. Therefore we can say that although $N \neq 0$ may modify the results above, it introduces no unambiguous systematic bias in the system.

In cases where changes in slope of the weighted disintegrated profits function induce equilibria other than with the extreme organisational forms, the planner must be able to compute the stable equilibrium to which the system will coverge. Only then can he carry out the analysis. Having done so, however, the welfare considerations will parallel those above.

Finally, we should remark on the rigidity of prices which is the source of the incentives for vertical integration discussed in this chapter. We have assumed that the prices (p and q) which relate to products for which the demand is fluctuating over time cannot respond at all to these variations. In the analysis above, we assumed that they did not vary with the organisation of the industry as well. However, it is natural to suppose that the level of these prices *do* respond to the average excess demand in their respective markets over time. Therefore, when the degree of integration varies, prices will adjust to the new distribution of excess demands and this will induce changes in the social product attributable to this industry.

On the intermediate-product market, as we have seen, the distribution of excess demand shifts upward with increasing integration if $N < 0$, and falls if $N > 0$. Thus the consumers' surplus will increase with integration in the latter case, and this must be taken into account in deciding whether to permit such mergers.

In the market for final product, we may suppose that price will vary in response to shifts in the expected value of this output, demand conditions being treated as exogenous. From (37) we have the result that when integration replaces disintegration as the equilibrium, the change in output is given by:

$$\Delta(Ev) = \frac{\bar{K}^d}{b_K} \left(E^B(K^1_{max}) - E^B(0) \right)$$

$$- \frac{K^1_{max}}{\rho^*} \left(\frac{E^B(K^1_{max})}{b_K} - \frac{1}{b'_K} \right). \tag{51}$$

In Case I ($\rho^* \bar{K}^d = K^1_{max}$), this becomes:

$$\Delta(Ev) = \bar{K}^d \left(\frac{1}{b'_K} - \frac{E^B(0)}{b_K} \right); \tag{52}$$

and in Case II we have

$$\Delta(Ev) = \frac{\bar{K}^u}{\rho^* b'_K} - \frac{\bar{K}^d E^B(0)}{b_K}$$

$$+ \frac{E^B(K^1_{max})}{b_K} \left(\bar{K}^d - \frac{K^1_{max}}{\rho^*} \right). \tag{53}$$

Therefore, consumers' surplus in the final product market will increase more with the switch to complete integration, *ceteris paribus*, if the rationing of buyers in the disintegrated state is severe. In Case II, we see that the second term induces a bias in favour of integration through the resulting fall in price. This would have to be offset against the opposing effect, as indicated in equations (45) and (47).

V REMARKS ON THE MODEL

The results in this chapter hinge crucially on two properties of the model; the non-participation of integrated firms in the market for the intermediate product, and the insensitivity of offers to buy and sell this good as the frequency of rationing changes. These are a consequence of the nature of the technology assumed and of the rationing rule. Below, we discuss the generalisation of each of these specifications in turn.

Suppose that, instead of a fixed-coefficients technology, we assume that production functions per (incremental) unit of capital are concave in the other input relevant to that stage of fabrication. Two differences from the analysis in Section II now appear. First, the set of efficient production plans for an integrated firm (given a fixed quantity of labour input) is non-linear in the composition of capital of the firm. Second, the optimal mode of operations given the proportions of integration is not determined independently of the extent of rationing.

Nevertheless, rationing affects an integrated firm adversely should it choose to enter in the intermediate product market on either side. Hence, the optimal action will be constant at $z = 0$ throughout a non-degenerate range of values of p and q, just as in the fixed-coefficient case. Neo-classical production functions do lose the property that no other form of integration can ever be optimal, as a consequence of the non-linearity mentioned above. However, if prices are in the range mentioned, this range will be large when shortages are relatively severe. Our analysis, which depends only on the balanced nature of integrated firms, will go through essentially unchanged.

The robustness of our results to assumptions concerning the rationing rule is on less-certain ground. The problem is that if the extent to which any firm is rationed is responsive to its own actions, then firms will not have the incentive to transmit their technologically-optimal quantities to the market as desired transactions. This complicates the model considerably. But what is worse is that it may tend to destabilise the stochastic equilibrium with a fixed configuration of firms in the industry, rendering an analysis of the equilibrium industry-structure meaningless. In the extreme case of proportional rationing, which is the polar opposite of the allocation mechanism we have used, it is in the interest of downstream firms to exaggerate their demands for the intermediate product, balancing the expected gain in productive inputs received against occasional receipts of excessive quantities. An even more troublesome phenomenon arises with respect to sellers of the intermediate product. They have a natural incentive to promise deliveries in excess of production under any rationing scheme other than the one treated. The necessary legal structure for adjudicating contract violations would then have to be specified before any definitive analysis of their problem could be made; and this would lead us hopelessly far afield.

VI CONCLUSION

This chapter has attempted to study vertical integration in response to imperfect price flexibility. The model used is shown to possess an inherent instability for equilibria in which the industry is only partially integrated. The extremes of market structure are generally the only stable equilibria.

In evaluating whether mergers or divestitures desired by firms are socially advantageous, this property of the nature of potential equilibria was utilised. When divestiture is desired in a completely-integrated situation there are essentially three effects to consider. Vertical disintegration should be discouraged by public policy (1) if the difference in the rationing frequency for sellers will not be greatly improved in the completely disintegrated equilibrium, (2) if buyers are being rationed more heavily than sellers, or (3) if the downstream sector is large relative to the upstream. When integration is desired, it should be discouraged if sellers are rationed more heavily than buyers in the existing equilibrium, or if the frequency of rationing will increase markedly after integration becomes complete.

APPENDIX

In this Appendix, we demonstrate that the integrated firms will choose to constitute themselves so that they do not participate in the intermediate product market at all. This involves comparisons of profitability at $Z = 0$, where the firm is insulated from rationing, from rationing, with $Z \neq 0$, in which case rationing would affect expected profits. Let

$$k^A(Z) = \min \left(\frac{\Sigma(Z)}{\Delta(Z)} 1, \right) \text{ and}$$

$$k^B(Z) = \min \left(\frac{\Delta(Z)}{\Sigma(Z)}, 1 \right) \tag{A.1}$$

and let E^A and E^B be the expected values of these random variables, respectively.

For K^1 and K^2 fixed, and any feasible chosen level of v and z, the firm's expected realised net outputs are given by

$$\begin{aligned} \bar{v} &= vE^B + v^0(1 - E^B) \\ \bar{z} &= zE^B \end{aligned} \tag{A.2}$$

if $z > 0$, and

$$\begin{aligned} \bar{v} &= vE^A + v^0(1 - E^A) \\ \bar{z} &= zE^A \end{aligned} \tag{A.3}$$

if $z > 0$, where v^0 is the net output of final product associated with $z = 0$ and the specified choices of K^1 and K^2.

For any fixed K^1 and K^2, the optimal quantities to register on the product markets, v and z, will be at the efficient level given by (6) and (7) due to the nature of the rationing process. Expected profits, therefore, are

$$p \bar{v} - q \bar{z} \tag{A.4}$$

where $\bar{v}$ and $\bar{z}$ specified in (A.2) or (A.3).

The following diagram depicts the equivalent profit locus ($\bar{v}$, $\bar{z}$) for various integration proportions.

The optimal integration proportions are those which maximise expected profits on the equivalent profits locus. The integration proportions giving rise to $z = 0$ given by (8) as

$$\frac{K^1}{K^2} = \frac{a'_K b'_z}{b'_K} \equiv \rho^*. \tag{A.5}$$

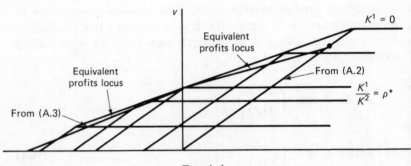

FIG. A.1

The ratio ρ^* will be called *balanced proportions* of integration. For K^1/K^2 above the balanced level, the equivalent profit locus has a slope of

$$\frac{1}{E^A b'_z} \left(\frac{1}{1 + \dfrac{r^d}{r^u \rho^*}} \right) \tag{A.6}$$

since $z < 0$ for such firms and therefore $v^0 = v$[15].

For $K^1/K^2 < \rho^*$, the equivalent profit locus has a slope of

$$\frac{1}{E^B b'_z} \left(\frac{E^B \left(\dfrac{r^u \rho^*}{r^d} \right) - (1 - E^B)}{\dfrac{r^u \rho^*}{r^d} + 1} \right) \tag{A.7}$$

since $z > 0$ and $v^0 = \dfrac{1 - r^d K^2}{r^u a'_K b'_z}$.

It is clear that if there is never any rationing, so that $E^A = E^B = 1$, the equivalent profit locus is linear, i.e. (A.6) and (A.7) are equal. As the former is decreasing in E^A and the latter is increasing in E^B, the equivalent profit locus has the general shape as indicated in Figure 6.2.

Suppose that K^1 and K^2 are varied in accordance with (4), from

$$\frac{K^1}{K^2} = \rho^*$$

to

$$\frac{K^1}{K^2} = 0$$

so that $z > 0$. We see that the change in the profit per unit change in K^2 is then given by

$$\frac{1}{b'_K} \left[p \left(E^B \left(1 + \frac{r^d}{r^u \rho^*} \right) - \frac{r^d}{r^u \rho^*} \right) \right.$$
$$\left. - qE^B \left(b'_z - \frac{r^d b'_K}{r^u a'_K} \right) + \frac{r^d a'_L b'_K}{r^u a'_K} \right] \qquad (A.8)$$

Proceeding in the direction of a more-intensive downstream mode of operation as K^1/K^2 decreases towards ρ^*, the slope of the profit function is now given by

$$\frac{1}{b'_K} \left[p - qE^A \left(b'_z - \frac{r^d b'_K}{r^u a'_K} \right) + \frac{r^d a'_L b'_K}{r^u a'_K} \right].$$

The important thing to notice about (A.8) and (A.9) is that they are constants. Therefore, from the point of view of the (infinitesimal) firm, they are independent of the partitioning of K^1/K^2 within their respective ranges. If (A.8) is negative when (A.9) is positive, the optimal integration proportions are the balanced value, ρ^*. If their signs stand in any other configuration, we know that the optimal integration-proportions lie of one of the extremes – that is, the firm should behave as if it were actually a purely upstream or purely downstream operation. However, under these conditions, the firm would be better off to constitute itself as one of the pure varieties, thereby having access to a superior technology.

Summarising our results, we reach the conclusion that the only mode of operation ever observable for an integrated firm is the balanced one, in which it does not participate in the market for the intermediate product. This will happen whenever (A.8) < 0 < (A.9) which can be rewritten as linear inequalities relating the prices (p) and (q). The sharpness of these results is dependent crucially on the form of the production function, but the general qualitative property concerning the superiority of balanced integration for a broad class of prices and rationing frequencies is robust to the technological specification. Further discussion of this point has been postponed to Section V. For the remainder of the chapter we have assumed that p, q E^A and E^B are always such that (A.8) < 0 < (A.9). Thus, the issue of vertical integration is not an empty question.

NOTES

1. Theoretical studies of the feasibility and results of vertical integration in the presence of monopoly elements include Wu (1964), Edwards (1953), Machlup and Taber (1960), Vernon and Graham (1971), Schmalensee (1973) and Warren-Boulton (1974). In the public policy literature, Bork (1969), Mueller (1969) and Peltzman (1969) have made contributions to the understanding of the way in which various types of vertical control, among which outright merger is only one, are view under the law. Specific studies of industries with imperfectly competitive characteristics that have undergone vertical expansion are carried out in Adams and Dirlam (1964) and Dennison (1939), steel; Crandall (1968), automobile repair parts; Frankel (1953), de Chazeau and Kahn (1959), and McGee (1960), oil; and Peck (1960), aluminium, among others.
2. Adelman (1949), takes the view that integration is likely to increase output of the final product and reduce price. Stigler (1951) qualifies these remarks heavily.
3. See Arrow (1975) for the case in which vertical integration is used as a source of information by the downstream division. Other methods by which such information can be acquired or traded are discussed therein.
4. Williamson (1971) gives the most complete treatment of these issues. The basic problems were first pointed out by Coase (1937) and later explored in Malmgren (1961).
5. Irwin (1971) and Dayan (1972) have modelled this problem; less formal discussions are found throughout the business literature.
6. See Williamson (1971) and Allen (1971). In the case of the cement industry, the FTC study (US Federal Trade Commission, 1966) documents the market foreclosure thesis, though the industry structure has several aspects that complicate the picture – particularly increasing returns and high transportation costs that limit the extent of competition among both integrated and non-integrated firms in any region.
7. See Foley and Hellwig (1973), Leviatan (1971), Whitin (1974), Walters (1960), Rothschild (1969), Smith (1968) and Weitzman (1974) among others.

8. Representative of these models we have Barro and Grossman (1971), Benassy (1982), Clower (1965), Drèze (1975), Iwai (1972), Grandmont and Laroque (1976), Malinvaud (1976) and Younes (1975).
9. This point was first made by Malmgren (1961).
10. The validity of this assumption can certainly be called into question. We adopt it for the reason stated and because it corresponds in some sense to the usual condition of decreasing returns to scale. In the widely analysed case of cement–concrete mergers, industry opinion seems divided on the empirical facts. See Allen (1971, footnote 19) and Wilk (1968, footnote 47).
11. See Allen (1971), and the theoretical studies mentioned in Note 1.
12. Further discussion of this point is found in Section V.
13. This assumption is for concreteness only. It is also possible to treat the case in which the unsold intermediate input is not available for production.
14. Catastrophe theory, a branch of mathematics, was first used in economics by Zeeman (1974), and may fruitfully be applied to models of the structure of industries in more general contexts than that treated here.
15. A corresponding expression can be derived if it is assumed that unsold intermediate product is lost.

REFERENCES

Adams, W. and Dirlam, J. B. (1964) 'Steel Imports and Vertical Oligopoly Power', *American Economic Review*, vol. 54, pp. 626–55.
Adelman, M. A. (1949) 'Integration and Anti-trust Policy', *Harvard Law Review*, vol. 63, pp. 27–77.
Allen, B. T. (1971) 'Vertical Integration and Market Foreclosure: The Case of Cement and Concrete', *Journal of Law and Economics*, vol. 14, no. 1, pp. 251–74.
Arrow, K. J. (1975) 'Vertical Integration and Communication', *Bell Journal of Economics*, vol. 6, pp. 173–83.
Barro, R. and Grossman H. (1971) 'A General Disequilibrium Model of Income and Employment', *American Economic Review*, vol. 61, no. 1, pp. 82–93.
Benassy, J. P. (1982) *The Economics of Market Disequilibrium*, (New York: Academic Press).
Benassy, J. P. (1978) 'A Neo-Keynesian Model of Price and Quantity Determination in Disequilibrium' in *Equilibrium and Disequilibrium in Economic Theory*, vol. 6.
Bork, R. H. (1969) 'Vertical Integration and Competitive Processes', in Peltzman and Weston, (eds), *Public Policy Towards Mergers* (Goodyear, Pacific Palisades, California) pp. 139–49.
Clower, R. W. (1965) 'The Keynesian Counterrevolution: A Theoretical Appraisal', in Hahn, F. H. and Brechling, F. R. R. (eds), *The Theory of Interest Rates, Proceedings of an IEA Conference* (London: Macmillan).
Coase, R. H. (1937) 'The Nature of the Firm', *Economica*, vol. 4, pp. 386–405.

Crandell, R. (1968) 'Vertical Integration and the Market for Repair Parts in the U.S. Automobile Industry', *Journal of Industrial Economics*, pp. 212–34.

Dayan, D. (1972) 'Vertical Integration and Monopoly Regulation', Princeton University dissertation.

de Chazeau, M. G. and Kahn, A. H. (1959) *Integration and Competition in the Petroleum Industry* (New Haven: Yale University Press).

Dennison, S. R. (1939) 'Vertical Integration and the Iron and Steel Industry', *Economic Journal*, pp. 244–58.

Drèze, J. (1975) 'Existence of an Exchange Equilibrium under Price Rigidities', *International Economic Review*, vol 16, pp. 301–20.

Edwards, C. D. (1953) 'Vertical Integration and the Monopoly Problem', *Journal of Marketing*, no. 4, pp. 404–10.

Foley, D. and Hellwig, M. (1973) 'Asset Management with Trading Uncertainty', MIT Working Paper no. 106.

Frankel, P. H. (1953) 'Integration in the Oil Industry', *Journal of Industrial Economics*, pp. 202–11.

Grandmont, J. M. and Laroque G. (1976) 'On Temporary Keynesian Equilibria', *Review of Economic Studies*, vol. 43, pp. 53–67.

Irwin, M. R. (1971) *The Telecommunications Industry: Integration versus Competition.*

Iwai, K. (1972) 'Towards Keynesian Micro-Dynamics of Price, Wage, Sales and Employment', University of California, Berkeley, Working Paper IP-174.

Machlup, F. and Taber, M. (1960) 'Bilateral Monopoly, Successive Monopoly and Vertical Integration', *Economica*, new series, vol. 27, no. 106, pp. 101–19.

Malinvaud, E. (1976) *The Theory of Unemployment Reconsidered* (Oxford: Basil Blackwell).

Malmgren, H. B. (1961) 'Information, Expectations and the Theory of the Firm', *Quarterly Journal of Economics*, vol. 75, no. 3, pp. 339–421.

McGee, J. S. (1960) 'Conservation, Integration and Pricing in the Oil Industry of the U.S.: A Review Article', *Journal of Industrial Economics*, pp. 63–82.

Mueller, W. E. (1969) 'Public Policy Toward Vertical Mergers', in Peltzman and Weston, (eds), *Public Policy Towards Mergers* (Goodyear, Pacific Palisades, California) pp. 150–67.

Peck, M. J. (1960) 'Marginal Analysis and the Explanation of Business Behavior Under Uncertainty: a Case Study of the Output-Inventory Behavior in the Aluminum Industry', in *Expectations, Uncertainty and Business Behavior*, ed. Bowman, M. J., Social Science Council, pp. 119–33.

Peltzman, S. (1969) 'Issues in Vertical Integration Policy', in Peltzman and Weston, (eds), *Public Policy Towards Mergers* (Goodyear, Pacific Palisades, California) pp. 167–79.

Peltzman, S. and Weston, J. F., (eds), (1969) *Public Policy Towards Mergers* (Goodyear, Pacific Palisades, California).

Rothschild, M. (1969) *Essays in Economic Theory*, MIT dissertation.

Schmalensee, R. (1973) 'A Note on the Theory of Vertical Integration', *Journal of Political Economy*, vol. 81, no. 2, pp. 442–9.

Smith, K.R. (1968) 'Risk and the Optimal Utilization of Capital', C.O.R.E. Discussion Paper no. 6818.

Stigler, G. (1951) 'The Division of Labor is Limited by the Size of the Market', *Journal of Political Economy*, vol. 59, pp. 185–93.

US Federal Trade Commission, Staff Report (1966) *Economic Report of Mergers and Vertical Integration in the Cement Industry*.

Vernon, J. M. and Graham, D. A. (1971) 'Profitability of Monopolization by Vertical Integration', *Journal of Political Economy*, pp. 924–5.

Walters, A. A. (1960) 'Marginal Productivity and Probability Distributions of Factor Services', *Economic Journal*, vol. 70, pp. 325–30.

Warren-Boulton, F. R. (1974) 'Vertical Control, and Variable Proportions', *Journal of Political Economy*, vol. 82, no. 4, pp. 783–802.

Weitzman, M. (1974) 'Prices versus Quantities', *Review of Economic Studies*, vol. 41, pp. 471–92.

Whitin, T. M. (1974) 'The Marginalist Principle in Discrete Production: Comment', *Quarterly Journal of Economics*, vol. 88, no. 1, pp. 139–40.

Wilk, D. (1968) 'Vertical Integration in Cement Revisited', *Antitrust Bulletin*, vol. 13, pp. 619–47.

Williamson, O. E. (1971) 'The Vertical Integration of Production: Market Failure Considerations', *American Economic Review*, papers and proceedings, pp. 112–23.

Wu, S. Y. (1964) 'The Effects of Vertical Integration on Price and Output', *Western Economic Journal*, vol. 2, no. 2, pp. 117–33.

Younes, Y. (1975) 'On the Role of Money in the Process of Exchange and the Existence of a Non-Walrasian Equilibrium', *Review of Economic Studies*, vol. 42, pp. 489–501.

Zeeman, E.C. (1974) 'On the Unstable Behavior of Stock Exchanges', *Journal of Mathematical Economics*, vol. 1, no. 1, pp. 39–50.

Discussion of the Paper by Jerry Green

Grossman began his discussion of this paper by pointing out that Green presented an equilibrium theory of industrial structure, in the sense that he defined and computed an equilibrium fraction of vertically integrated firms. Grossman noted the possibility, described in the paper, that this equilibrium might be unstable. He suggested that this was due to an odd externality that arose in Green's model. If a pair of firms integrated this might make rationing more probable for the remaining non-integrated firms. Grossman contrasted this feature with the usual externality that arose in the search literature (e.g., Salop and Stiglitz, 1977) and the literature on information acquisition (e.g., Grossman and Stiglitz, 1980). In this literature, an individiual agent who decided to switch cohorts conveyed a positive externality on the cohort left behind. For example, a buyer who decided to purchase information about prices, made the industry more competitive; in turn, this drove down prices, which increased the expected pay-off to those who chose not to purchase information but to purchase the product randomly, i.e., for those who purchased the product randomly, the expected price fell as more consumers decided to search. This process limited the number of individuals who tended to switch cohorts. In Green's paper, on the contrary, a pair of firms who decided to integrate convey a *negative* externality on the remaining firms which encouraged further integration. This externality generated the instability that Green found in his model.

Grossman put Green's paper in historical context by noting that it had originally been written shortly after the imposition of wage and price controls in the US. Grossman suggested that the benefits of vertical integration under price controls were clear, since integration allowed internalisation of the price system. In the absence of controls, he wondered how one could justify the existence of an allocation scheme involving fixed prices and positive rationing probabilities. Since it was the possibility of avoiding rationing that created the incentive for vertical integration, one must explain rationing first to see this as a possible explanation for vertical integration. As a potential explanation for the existence of fixed prices and rationing, Grossman cited his recent work with Oliver Hart (1981). In this work, he explained, an efficient *ex ante* contractual relationship betwen upstream and downstream firms involved a price for the intermediate product that depends upon the value of the downstream firm's output. If the upstream firm was uniformed about this value, such a contract was not feasible. The second-best efficient contract would require the price of the intermediate product to depend on the downstream firm's demand for this product, which was observable by both firms. Grossman and Hart showed that if the downstream firm was risk averse, and the upstream firm was risk neutral, then the efficient contract would have the intermediate product price varying less and the downstream firm's demand varying more than it would if both parties could observe the value of the downstream firm's output. It would appear to an outsider as if the downstream firm were being rationed.

Vertical integration, Grossman suggested, would circumvent the rationing problem if it allowed both firms to observe the value of the downstream firm's output. It was not obvious that this would occur. He suggested that better auditing procedures in an integrated firm might make this sharing of information possible. He concluded that to draw a strong policy conclusions from Green's result, especially from the instability result, one should provide some rationale for sticky prices, and some more explicit reason why vertical integration allowed one to get around this price stickiness.

Sanchez stated that he thought that the results in Green's paper that the industry moved to one extreme or the other depended upon (1) the choice of a rationing scheme and (2) that there was only a small cost disadvantage associated with integration. He speculated that a large cost disadvantage associated with integration might lead to intermediate solutions. He also found it odd that equilibrium in the Green model did not depend on the distribution of the random shock to excess demand in the intermediate product market.

Martin Perry suggested that one might view the vertical integration in a different way to get intermediate solutions. He referred to a paper he had been working on (Perry, 1981) in which the integrated firms had a cost advantage over the non-integrated firms. The intermediate product market was subject to random fluctuations in demand, as in Green's paper. But this gave rise to fluctuations in the price of the intermediate product. The advantage to disintegration came from the fact that firms' profit functions were convex in prices, so that these price fluctuations tended to increase expected profits. When two firms integrated, the non-integrated sector was subject to larger price fluctuations, which increased the expected profits of non-integrated firms. This was the usual positive externality. It limited the tendency towards vertical integration which arose from the cost advantage. And this led to solutions where both vertically integrated and non-integrated firms co-existed.

Selten suggested that in situations where random fluctuations in demand or prices were prevalent a dual market structure would arise with downstream firms negotiating advance contracts. Spot markets would take care of random fluctuations. He doubted that, with such a dual market structure the assurance of markets could be an important motiviation for vertical integration.

Gabszewicz suggested that the profits of integrated firms might depend on the extent of integration in a more subtle way. As firms integrated, the number of buyers and sellers on the intermediate market would change, changing the *structure* of the market. In particular, as the number of buyers and sellers on the intermediate product market got smaller, the market became less competitive, leading to higher prices and larger profit rates for non-integrated firms. This was exactly the sort of positive externality that would limit the extent of vertical integration in an industry.

Finally *Williamson* suggested that a possible source of the cost disadvantage associated with vertical integration could be the cost associated with a large bureaucracy. He suggested that understanding the sources of organisational failure was as important as understanding the sources of market failure.

REFERENCES

Grossman, S. and Stiglitz, (1980) 'The Impossibility of Informationally Efficient Markets', *American Economic Review* vol. 70, no. 3, pp. 393–408.

Grossman, S. and Hart, O. (1981) 'Implicit Contracts, Moral Hazard and Unemployment', *American Economic Review*, vol. 71, no. 2, pp. 301–307.

Perry, M. (1981) 'Vertical Equilibrium in a Competitive Input Market', Bell Laboratories Economic Discussion Paper, no. 206.

Salop, S. and Stiglitz, J. (1977) 'Bargains and Ripoffs: a Model of Monopolistically Competitive Price Dispersion', *Review of Economic Studies*, vol. 44, no. 3, pp. 493–510.

7 The Economics of Vertical Restraints in Distribution[1]

G. F. Mathewson
and
R. A. Winter

UNIVERSITY OF TORONTO, CANADA

I INTRODUCTION

Anti-trust policy in the United States and other countries towards vertical restrictions on distribution (restrictions placed by manufacturers on retailers' prices and quantities), has been fragmented and unsettled. This is, in part, because of a lack of consensus on what these restraints represent. On the one hand, vertical restraints have been explained as devices of monopolistic control of cartel co-ordination. On the other, restraints have been viewed as devices that can be used as purely vertical instruments to implement 'efficient' forms of distribution.

This chapter synthesises the alternative explanations of vertical restraints, identifying the circumstances under which each explanation is relevant. Where the restraints serve to co-ordinate a cartel, the appropriate public policy is generally clear. Where they serve as purely vertical devices, the appropriate anti-trust policy is less clear. Even if restraints form part of efficient contracts between manufacturers and retailers, i.e., even if they improve the joint profits of a manufacturer and retailers, it does not follow that they are socially efficient, since social welfare includes consumers' interest as well as profits. That a manufacturer is willing to trade-off (*via* vertical restraints) a higher price at the retail level for greater retailer information or services does not, for example, imply *a priori* that society should accept the trade-off. In a model capturing the efficiency reasons for restraints, we analyse the restraints' impact on social welfare. (Positive features are analysed in a companion article (Mathewson–Winter (1984).) The welfare analysis undertaken here involves comparisons of equilibria under two feasible institutional arrangements: legality and legal prohibition of restraints.

Section II of this chapter sets out the menu of constraints we wish to consider, together with a synthesis of previous analyses of these restraints. Section III sketches our model of restraints as efficient contracts and summarises briefly the heuristics of the positive results. Section IV evaluates the welfare impact of the restraints. Finally, Section V summarises our results and highlights the policy conclusions from our work, as well as some unresolved issues on the use of restraints.

II ECONOMICS AND PUBLIC POLICY OF VERTICAL RESTRAINTS

Vertical restraints are contractual limitations placed on downstream distributors or retailers of products by manufacturers or wholesalers. These limitations restrict the products offered for sale by the retailers, the prices set by the retailers and the potential clients of the retailers. Specifically, vertical restraints can include:

(1) *Vertical price restrictions*: Resale price maintenance (RPM) is the establishment of a floor to the retail price. Price ceilings are a possibility as well, although they are observed less frequently in practice.

(2) *Vertical territorial arrangements*: These restrictions protect to some degree a retailer's territory or location against intra-brand competition. The extreme form of this restraint is closed territory distribution (CTD), the assignment to each retailer of exclusive rights to all consumers within a territory. (A more general class of restraints restricts each retailer to supplying a set of consumers defined by some characteristics, e.g., size.)

(3) *Quantity forcing or volume requirements*: Forcing establishes minimum quantities in wholesale transactions with retailers.

(4) *Franchise fees*: Such fees are lump-sum transfers from the retailer to the manufacturer.

(5) *Full-line forcing*: This restraints the dealer to carry the full line (as opposed to selected partial lines) of the manufacturer's products.

(6) *Exclusive dealing*: Exclusive dealing requires the retailers to carry only the manufacturer's brand of the product.

This chapter considers RPM, CTD, quantity forcing and franchise fees. Why would manufacturers impose these restrictions on decisions taken by retailers? The restrictions have been explained both as 'purely vertical' devices used by a manufacturer to control retail prices, product quality, product information and availability at the retail level: and as devices used to co-ordinate the activities of horizontal cartels. A distinction must be made between the source of monopoly power and the practices of firms with such power. Whether monopoly power occurs at the upstream or downstream level or at both levels, firms should seek to maximise joint profits provided there are appropriate tools to divide the spoils. The critical issue on horizontal cartels is whether the restrictive practice(s) in question facilitate a cartel which would otherwise fail should the practice be declared illegal. If the answer is no, then we shall maintain that the cartel issue is irrelevant. Eventually, we shall examine the welfare effects of permitting an upstream monopolist to achieve the benefits of integration through vertical restrictions. We argue that our results are widely applicable. Nevertheless, considerable insight is gained if we first attempt to delineate the issues contained in each of the arguments.

(1) VERTICAL RESTRAINTS AS EFFICIENCY-ENHANCING

A necessary condition for the profitability of vertical restraints is price-setting power. But market power alone is not sufficient: If demand in a competitive retail sector depends only on price (and if technology at the retail level involves fixed factor-proportions) then it is well known (e.g., Warren-Boulton, 1978; p. 53) that an incentive for vertical control does not arise. The common element in most efficiency explanations of vertical control is the recognition that the demand for a manufacturer's product at the retail level may depend upon more than the price.

The classic explanation of resale price maintenance, discussed by Telser (1960) and more formally by Mathewson–Winter (1983b) assumes that demand depends upon product information provided at the retail level. Because of a free-rider problem, the provision of this information may be inadequate. Discount stores can free ride on the information provided elsewhere, offering no information themselves and cutting price so low as to attract informed customers (with low search-costs for price).

By foreclosing discount houses, RPM prevents this informational free-riding and supports retail price margins to increase retailers incentive to provide information. If the positive impact of the additional point-of-sale information more than offsets any detrimental impact of an increase in average retail price, RPM will be profitable. (In fact, with a price floor, the pre-RPM price-dispersion equilibrium will collapse to a single price that may be *less* than the average pre-RPM price (Mathewson–Winter 1983b).)

The potential for RPM to counteract horizontal externalities is not limited to the dimension of product information. For many products, quality is determined at the retail level, especially through retail servicing of the product, but cannot be identified precisely by consumers prior to purchase. In this case, retail demand will depend upon the reputations of the manufacturer and individual retailers for product quality. When an individual retail outlet increase the quality of its service, it contributes not only to its own reputation but to the reputation of the manufacturer's product. This is especially true when the consumer cannot identify precisely the contribution of the retailer to product quality, as in automobile retailing and servicing. Because not all of the benefits from any increase in quality are appropriated by the retailer, the incentive to set high quality-standards is inadequate. By supporting high retail-price margins, RPM can increase retailers' incentive for high-quality retail service.[2] Arguments similar to this formed part of the defence in the Schwinn case in the US (Williamson, 1979, pp. 975–80) and the Raleigh case in the UK (Sharpe, 1982, pp. 25–82).

Demand for a product may depend not only on the price- and quality-decisions of retail outlets selling the product, but also on the *number* of outlets choosing to stock the product. In Gould and Preston (1965), the hypothesis, labelled the 'outlets hypothesis' – that such a dependence could lead to resale price maintenance – is investigated in a model with a perfectly-competitive downstream retail market. The dependence of demand upon the number of outlets (e.g. because of increased availability with more stores) is, however, suggestive of a spatial model. In this case, the appropriate equilibrium concept for the retail market is monopolistic competition. The profitability of vertical price restrictions in spatial markets, where retailers have price-setting power but earn only competitive returns, are investigated in Bittlingmayer (1983), Dixit (1983) and Mathewson and Winter (1983a). These studies suggest that the profitable price-restraint in spatial markets is a price ceiling (which results in retail firms producing at lower average cost) rather than a price floor, which would increase the availability of the product. The price ceiling counteracts the effect of a double mark-up of prices (above the marginal production-cost upstream and then above the wholesale price downstream); as Spengler (1950) first noted, vertical control may reduce prices.[3]

A traditional explanation of resale price maintenance, that is less persuasive than those discussed above, is the 'product image' or 'loss leader' argument.[4] Price-cutting is said to damage the quality reputation of a product to the extent that consumers base their expectations of quality on price. Restraints against price-cutting are therefore said to be profitable. The single instrument of the wholesale price, however, is sufficient to determine the retail price of a product, rendering the vertical price-restraint unnecessary.

Some of these explanations for vertical price restraints have been offered for territorial restraints as well. Where retailers' incentives for quality (retail servicing) or product promotion are insufficient, the assignment of retail territorial monopoly power may improve retailers' incentives, by protecting a high retail margin against intra-brand competition. For example, in a major anti-trust case involving closed territory distribution, the White Motor Company argued that CTDs provided sufficient incentive for the dealers to contact customers and to promote the product (Warren, 1975, pp. 147).

The White Motor case also serves to illustrate the price discrimination incentive for customer restrictions. White Motor reserved all state and government accounts for itself, forbidding dealers to sell to these customers. If the demand from new accounts was relatively elastic, White Motor profited from charging them a lower price (at a given size of sale). Finally, in situations where conditions for price discrimination at the retail level hold, CTD increases the profits of manufacturers and retailers by allowing discrimination which would be impossible in a competitive market.

'Forcing' is a vertical restraint that has received less attention. It is a practice historically used by US automobile manufacturers. (Restrictions on forcing in the automobile industry are discussed in Smith (1982).) Where the only retail decision is on pricing, a minimum-quantity restraint is clearly equivalent to a price floor. Where sales effort or service quality influences the quantity demanded at the retail level, a forcing restraint also has the effect of increasing these non-pricing variables, and may be profitable where levels of these variables are insufficient without the restraint.

(2) HORIZONTAL EXPLANATIONS OF VERTICAL RESTRAINTS

Are vertical restraints helpful practices for manufacturer- or dealer-cartels? RPM, in particular, has been explained as an instrument to co-ordinate a cartel at either the manufacturers' or the dealers' level. In the case of a manufacturers' cartel, the standard collusive practice would be the co-ordination of wholesale prices. But where wholesale contracts are complex or where cheating at the wholesale level is difficult to detect, the manufacturers' cartel may co-ordinate through retail prices.

Contrary to common argument, the desire to fix retail prices is not a *sufficient* reason for a manufacturers' cartel to profit from RPM. With a competitive retail market and stable retail-cost conditions, manufacturers could assume agreed-upon retail prices by appropriately fixing their wholesale prices. Vertical price floors would *not* be necessary. However, fixed wholesale prices do not necessarily produce fixed retail prices. Variation in the costs of other retail inputs could cause retail prices to vary. In this case, the stability of a cartel could suffer, since cartel members would have difficulty in distinguishing changes in retail prices that flowed from a variation in retail costs from those changes that would flow from cheating on the cartel. RPM enhances the stability of a cartel here, by eliminating any retail price variation (albeit at a cost to the cartel) and by easily communicating retail prices.

The mere existence of a manufacturers' cartel, or the use of RPM by manufacturers of close-substitute products, does not imply that the price floor is necessarily co-ordinating the cartel. A cartel acting as a multi-plant monopolist may be using vertical price-restrictions for any of the efficiency reasons that we have discussed. Alternatively, competing manufacturers may each be forced to use restraints in order to achieve the most-efficient distribution system. In each of these cases, appropriate public policy towards vertical price restraints must follow from the efficiency explanation, rather than the cartel explanation, of the practices.

Resale price maintenance has also been seen as a means of co-ordinating price-fixing among retailers with market power. According to this argument, retailers can circumvent the anti-trust restrictions against explicit horizontal price-fixing by persuading manufacturers to impose a floor on retail prices of their products. The horizontal price-fixing agreement is camouflaged as a vertical price restriction, to the benefit of retailers. (Thus, retailers' associations were strong supporters of the US Fair Trade Laws.) The retail cartel would have to put pressure not only on existing manufacturers but on all entrants as well if it were to fix retail prices at the cartel level. A retailer cartel that successfully co-ordinated a restrictive price-policy through an upstream market characterised by some competitive element, would produce a higher retail price than would otherwise prevail. This result would have the usual negative welfare consequences. Whatever its plausibility, this argument clearly requires the absence of a successful cartel upstream. (A successful manufacturers' cartel would seek efficient contracts to maximise joint profits independently of the competitive nature of downstream retail markets.)

Sometimes, vertical restrictions orchestrated by downstream trade groups do not seek to achieve cartel rents, but to impede new market equilibria harmful to the members of the group. The support of Fair Trade Laws by independent retailers' associations such as the National Druggists' Association may be explained as an attempt to retard the growth in the market share of more-efficient (and thus lower-price) chains of retail outlets.

(3) CURRENT LEGAL AND ECONOMIC LITERATURE

Most policy analyses of vertical restraints by economists appear in discussions of anti-trust law. Currently, many economists advise the courts that selected *vertical* market restrictions that do not promote oligopolistic interdependence should be either legal *per se* (Posner, 1981) or else assumed to improve social welfare, provided that these non-cartel, vertical restrictions do not promote strategic purposes, i.e., activities that disadvantage small rivals and potential entrants (Williamson, 1979, especially pp. 960–8). The current position of the US Supreme Court, as stated in the Sylvania case, is that vertical restrictions of price are still *per se* illegal (in accordance with Section 1 of The Sherman Act) but that non-price restrictions of the type we discuss in this chapter are subject to a 'rule of reason'. The relative leniency of the court on territorial restrictions is based on a free-rider justification, along the lines of the classic service argument used to justify resale price maintenance (Posner, 1981, pp. 6–9).[5]

Posner has moved from his earlier position on the application of rules of reason to vertical restrictions (Posner, 1976, pp. 171–217) to a stronger position that the court should adopt a rule of *per se* legality on restricted distribution. In his view, the currently-applied rules of reason are ill-advised on three accounts. First, the continuing application of *per se* illegal rules on price restrictions distorts the judicial approach to non-price competition. From the perspective of the manufacturer, rules that restrict retail prices are similar in principle to rules that assign retail territories: they are alternative devices used to rationalise distribution practices for manufacturers. Further, price and non-price instruments are sometimes imposed on retailers simultaneously by manufacturers, e.g., RPM and minimum-quantity restrictions. At the very least, the asymmetrical legal treatment of restrictive devices motivates an economic analysis of the complementarity and substitutability between price and non-price restrictive instruments.

Second, according to Posner, the application of a rule of reason on non-price restrictions places a costly burden on the court. The rule is poorly-articulated and requires application by judicial tribunals poorly equipped to understand and apply it. The replacement of such rules of reason by *per se* rules, whatever the judicial costs of application, is reinforced if economic analysis indicates a preponderance of evidence that such vertical restrictions, whether they involve price or non-price competition, are either welfare-increasing or reducing.

Finally, the court in the Sylvania case refers to a balancing of intra-brand and inter-brand competition, a reference that has subsequently been elevated to a rule of reason, by some judicial tribunals (Posner, 1981, p. 18). In this balance, vertical restraints are thought to restrict intra-brand competition (an allegedly negative effect) and, by underwriting the provision of product information or service to increase the chances of a brand's survival, to enhance inter-brand competition (an allegedly positive effect). Porter (1976, p. 60) argues that exclusive selling and territorial restrictions, as well as reducing intra-brand competition, enhance manufacturers' power through greater product differentiation.

In our model (developed in Section III) there is a single upstream firm and so inter-brand effects disappear. Yet we produce examples, in Section IV of this chapter, where welfare increases in the presence only of allegedly-negative intra-brand effects. For example, CTDs at the retail level generate local monopoly power and eliminate intra-brand competition completely. However, while the package of CTD's, together with efficient wholesale prices (set at marginal cost) and fixed (franchise) fees remitted by retailers to manufacturers, restricts the number of retail outlets, these restrictions permit manufacturers simultaneously to collect rents through incentive-neutral lump-sum transfers and to set efficient transfer prices to their retailers.

Efficient transfer prices, in turn, avoid 'double marginalising' of marginal costs. The net effect of fewer outlets and lower retail prices may well be that these intra-brand restrictions are not welfare-reducing but welfare, and possibly even Pareto, improving. The inter-brand versus intra-brand rule of reason is inappropriate.

An evaluation of these offsetting effects, which are the consequence of vertical restrictions, is possible only in a more-complete model of consumers' and firms' behaviour. Section III develops the heuristics of such a model, although we have already hinted at the role of restrictions in internalising vertical and horizontal externalities.

III SPECIFICATION OF THE BASIC MODEL AND AN OUTLINE OF THE POSITIVE RESULTS

Our objective in this section is to outline an explanation for the use of vertical restrictions by manufacturers to control decisions by retailers, a basic principal-agent problem. (The formal results are developed elsewhere (Mathewson and Winter, 1984.) The positive analysis sketched here sets the stage for the welfare analysis in Section IV. Why do such restrictions improve joint manufacturer–retailer profits? How are these restrictions packaged together, i.e., which instruments are complements and which substitutes?

While a complete list of the assumptions of our model appears in our Appendix, we set forth here two critical assumptions, which are intended to capture the important elements of markets where restraints are used: (1) demand depends upon the availability of the product and (2) retailers have a role in influencing consumers' purchase choices.

(1) SPATIAL RETAIL MARKETS

Potential consumers are uniformly distributed along a circle or line of infinite length; retail outlets incur a fixed cost and buy one product of known-quality from a single manufacturer (wholesaler) at a whole-sale price; retailers have local price-setting powers, form conjectures on price strategies of their rivals, but earn zero rents as there is free entry into the retail market.[6]

(2) ROLE FOR LOCAL ADVERTISING OR SALES EFFORT

A consumer must be informed of the existence of the product through local advertising or sales effort that is *not* directly monitorable (and therefore cannot be contractually-specified) by the manufacturer. Because of the monitoring problem, indirect means must be found to control local advertising. A proportion of the local-advertising messages potentially spills over into neighbouring retail markets (a spatial analogue to retailer free riding). Once informed of the existence of the good, the consumer has free access to information on retail prices and outlet locations and buys from the store where the delivered price is the lowest, whether or not the store informed the consumer.

We define (P) to be the retail price, (R) to be the market radius, (A) to be local advertising expenditure for each (symmetrical) retailer; define (P_w) to be the wholesale price, (c) to be the (constant) marginal production costs, Π to be the manufacturer's level of profits and Π^R to be each retailer's level of profits. Free entry at the retail level means that $\Pi^R = 0$. Knowledge of (P, R, A) is sufficient to determine total retail-demand and costs, both upstream and downstream, and therefore combined upstream and downstream profit. As $\Pi^R = 0$, obviously all of these profits accrue to the monopolist; hence, Π can be written as a function of P, R and A.

Can a manufacturer using the wholesale price alone induce (P^*, R^*, A^*) (the first-best or joint-profit-maximising levels of these variables)? The answer is no, which means that an incentive exists for vertical control. If packages of vertical restrictions, together with the wholesale price, can achieve (P^*, R^*, A^*), then these packages are alternatives to vertical integration. The nature of the alternative restraint packages follows from an understanding of the insufficiency of P_w alone to achieve (P^*, R^*, A^*). At the source of the insufficiency of wholesale price as a single instrument are three potential externalities, which are the consequence of market conditions:

(i) *Vertical externality*. In attracting demand by lowering (P) or increasing (A), the retail firm does not appropriate additional profits flowing upstream through the $(P_w - c)$ wedge. As a result, from the viewpoint of joint maximisation, (P) will be too high and (A) will be too low, other things held constant.

(ii) *Information externalities*. (Define α to be the proportion of local advertising messages that spills over into neighbouring retail areas). Any increase in profit accruing to either neighbouring retail outlets, or through neighbouring retail outlets to the upstream firm (when $\alpha > 0$), are not appropriated by the advertising retailer. As a result, A is too low. Provided retail price-elasticities are independent of A (i.e., the selection of consumer tastes captured by any retailer is independent of the level of advertising), (P) is unaffected. (Again, other variables are held constant).

(iii) *Horizontal conjectural externality*. A useful separation of potential retailer conjectures is into Loschian and non-Loschian (e.g., Nash) categories. Retailer conjectures are Loschian when each outlet assumes that its market area is invariant to changes in its price, i.e., that price changes by any one retailer are matched by neighbouring retailers; non-Loschian conjectures involve price changes by neighbouring outlets that do not match a price change by a retailer. For example, if a retailer conjectures that neighbouring retailers do not respond to his price change, his conjectures are of the Nash type.

When a non-Loschian firm considers raising its price, it perceives that this would cause consumers at the geographical margin of its market area to switch to neighbouring retail outlets, thus increasing demand at these outlets. This would be a positive (pecuniary) externality. The increase in other retailers' and the manufacturer's profits resulting from a price increase is not appropriated by the non-Loschian retailer. The effect is that (P) set by such retailers is too low. Since (P) is too low, the marginal value-product of local advertising is also too low and (leaving aside the impact of any information externalities), (A) is too low. (Other variables are again held constant.)

The Loschian retailer, by contrast, believes that neighbouring retailers would match any price rises and therefore reciprocate the positive externality. Offsetting externalities mean that Loschian retailer conjectures do not act to the profit detriment of upstream manufacturers.

How do restraints work to remedy these externalities? In this chapter, we shall illustrate only selected packages of restraints, from possible sets of instruments that are just sufficient to achieve (P^*, R^*, A^*). (The full set are listed in Table 7.1 and formal proofs appear in Mathewson and Winter, 1984.)

(3) THREE EXAMPLES OF MINIMALLY SUFFICIENT RESTRAINTS

(1) Set $\alpha = 0$ and invoke Loschian retail conjectures. This is the simplest case, since there is only one (vertical) externality at work.

TABLE 7.1   MINIMALLY-SUFFICIENT SETS OF INSTRUMENTS

	Retailer conjectures			
	Loschian		*Non-Loschian*	
Local advertising spillovers				
Absent	(1*)		(1),	(2)
	FF		CTD,	FF
	QF		CTD,	QF
			FF,	RPM
			QF,	RPM
Present	(1),	(3)	(1),	(2), (3)
	FF,	RPM	FF,	RPM
	QF,	RPM	QF,	RPM

CTD $\equiv$ Closed Territory Distribution
FF $\equiv$ Franchise Fees
QF $\equiv$ Quantity Forcing
RPM $\equiv$ Resale Price Maintenance

*Numbers in parentheses refer to externalities present, as follows:
(1) Vertical externality through $(P_w - c)$ wedge;
(2) Horizontal pecuniary (conjectural) externality; and
(3) Local advertising spillover.

Either (fixed) *franchise fees* or *forcing*, together with P_w, is just sufficient.

If we set $P_w = c$, then transfer prices are efficient in the usual sense and incentive-neutral franchise fees may be used to transfer all rents to the upstream firm. Therefore franchise fees and P_w are just sufficient.

The vertical externality between the Loschian retailer and the manufacturer means that the retailer appropriates only a proportion of the total benefits from pricing and advertising decisions. As the proportion of these benefits appropriated by the retail firm is the same in both the retailer's pricing and advertising decisions, the marginal rate of substitution between (P) and (A), for a given demand by the retailer, is identical to that required to maximise joint profits. In this setting, forcing pushes the outlet to the appropriate demand level, where the retailer uses (P^*, A^*) to sell the product. Meanwhile, P_w is set to elicit R^* (at $\Pi^R = 0$) and acts to transfer rents back to the manufacturer. (Freed from the task of setting the levels of (P) and (A), P_w becomes here an incentive-neutral channel for rent transfer.)

In this setting, RPM would *not* be used. If retail price were set at

P^* (via RPM), then P_w would have to be used to achieve A^*. However, there would then be no instrument to elicit R^* by transferring rents to the manufacturer.

(2) Set $\alpha = 0$, and invoke non-Loschian retail conjectures (i.e., from (1), permit only retailer conjectures to change). Imposing *CTDs*, effectively rationalises Loschian conjectures, so that CTDs – in addition to either franchise fees or forcing (together with the wholesale price) – would be just sufficient (minimally-sufficient) instruments in this case.

(3) Set $\alpha > 1$, and invoke Loschian retail conjectures (i.e. from (1), permit advertising to spill over into other retail areas). In this case, one possibility involves the upstream manufacturer setting directly the retail price P^* (via RPM) and reducing the wholesale price below marginal production cost $(P_w < c)$, to provide the appropriate retailer incentive to advertise the optimal amount A^*. Finally, in this package franchise fees, as usual, could be used to transfer rents to the upstream manufacturer (i.e., to set R^* via $\Pi^R = 0$). Then, RPM and franchise fees (together with the wholesale price) would be minimally-sufficient instruments in this case.

Arguments for the remaining members of the set of minimally-sufficient instruments (noted in Table 7.1) proceed in a similar fashion. All of these packages of instruments are potential substitutes for vertical integration. In actual markets, those candidate restraints that achieve maximum joint profits at the lowest transactions costs will be used by manufacturers. We recognise that issues of shirking or monitoring (Alchian and Demsetz, 1972) and measurement (Barzel, 1982) loom large in any evaluation of the relative cost effectiveness of contractual arrangements. These are not, however, issues we deal with here.

Contracts that maximise industry profits need not be welfare-improving. The willingness of the manufacturer to trade-off a higher price for greater product information or availability does not give an *a priori* signal of the social desirability of the restraints; for the restraints to be socially-efficient, the movement from the equilibrium *without* restraints to the equilibrium *with* restraints must increase the total surplus, including consumers' surplus, and not only the manufacturers' profit. Section IV conducts a welfare evaluation of the use of restraint within the framework developed.

IV   WELFARE ANALYSIS

To answer the question of whether society should tolerate vertical restraints, even if they represent jointly-efficient contracts, we define welfare improvement alternatively as *either* a Pareto improvement (in the absence of side payments among economic agents) *or* an increase in the sum of consumers' and producers' surpluses. While the Pareto definition is stronger, it provides only a partial ordering of alternatives. From our results on the sufficiency of vertical restraints, it is clear that the evaluation of the welfare impact of minimal-efficient sets of restraints involves the comparison of the non-integrated equilibrium, where the wholesale price is the only instrument, with the integrated solution.

To accomplish our welfare task, we are forced to turn ultimately to specific functional forms and pseudo-empirical evidence. In the meantime, however, some insight and progress is possible at the theoretical level. We begin by considering the welfare impact which vertical control has through its effect on retail prices and advertising.

(1)   WELFARE IMPACT OF RESTRAINTS: AN EFFICIENCY COMPARISON

From the viewpoint of social efficiency, holding constant the density of retail firms means that the non-integrated retailer sets too high a price and advertises too little. The source of the retailer's inefficiency involves two social benefits that are not appropriated by the retailer and therefore fail to affect retailer decisions.[7] First, the retailer fails to consider the increased profits that flow to the upstream manufacturer from retailers' decisions; second, the retailer fails to weigh in his assessment the increased surplus accruing to consumers from any actions by retailers that increase demand for the product. Integration (or equivalently in this model, vertical restraints) aggregate retailers' and producers' profits. Hence, they internalise the first of these external benefits and – where these are the only two externalities – bring each retailer's pricing and advertising decisions closer to the socially-efficient levels. (As the second externality is not internalised with integration, the integrated monopolist, holding constant the density of retail firms, continues to set too high a price and advertises too little to be first-best efficient; our welfare comparison of integrated and non-integrated equilibrium is a 'second-best' welfare problem.)

Even in a second-best world, we need to distinguish differences between Loschian and non-Loschian retailer conjecturers, because they lead to different welfare results. Loschian conjectures involve a pro-rationing of the industry demand curve across individual retailers. Therefore, the sole effect of integration with Loschian conjectures involves the internalisation of the first of the two externalities discussed above, and not the re-evaluation of price elasticities, so that the impact of integration on both price and advertising in this case improves welfare. This is not true for the case of non-Loschian retailer conjectures. In the non-Loschian case, retailers perceive a price elasticity for the individual firm that is too large relative to the aggregate downward curve (because of the horizontal, pecuniary externality discussed above). Consequently, retail price may rise or fall with integration, depending on the net effect of (a) falling price-elasticities that favour higher prices and (b) the internalisation of an externality that favours lower prices. Any rise in the retail price would be welfare-decreasing, *ceteris paribus*. Thus the welfare impact of vertical control, through its effect on the retail price, is ambiguous in the case of non-Loschian retailers. The welfare impact of integration through advertising for this case is, however, identical to the Loschian case. All of these evaluations are conditional on a given density of retail firms.

Finally, we consider the welfare impact of integration through changes in the number of retail outlets or (its equivalent), in retail market areas (R). The welfare effect of integration through changes in (R) is ambiguous even in the case of Loschian retailers, since there is no *a priori* prediction of the impact of integration on (R). Even so, one possible effect is clear. Since the monopolist does not appropriate the gain in consumer surplus as (R) decreases, but does incur the full social costs, the integrated monopolist's density of retail outlets falls short of the socially efficient level (conditional upon the monopolist's (P) and (A)). If the density of retail firms decreases with integration, the impact on welfare from market-area changes may be negative. This is because delivered prices will rise for some consumers in this case (irrespective of any effects of integration on (P) and (A)).

(2) WELFARE IMPACT OF RESTRAINTS: PARETO-COMPARISON

Integration is Pareto-improving only when every consumer is at least as well-off, and some are made better-off, with integration. In particular, the consumers who are the most fortunate in the non-integrated equilibrium must not be harmed by integration: these are the consumers located at an outlet, i.e., paying the lowest delivered price. If the retail market is an infinite line, there are always consumers located directly at an outlet in the non-integrated equilibrium who are located arbitrarily close to a market boundary in the integrated equilibrium – i.e., who pay the highest delivered price.[8] Therefore, if we measure each consumer's welfare by expected utility,[9] we have the necessary and sufficient condition for integration to be Pareto-improving. It is that the expected utility of consumers located directly at an outlet in the non-integrated equilibrium shall be no greater than the expected utility of consumers located at a market boundary in the integrated equilibrium. Letting $V(P)$ be the indirect utility corresponding to the average demand (of an informed consumer) at retail price (P), this condition is

$$h(\hat{A}) \cdot V(\hat{P}) \leqslant h(A^*) \cdot V(P^* + tR^*).$$

Here, ^ denotes the non-integrated equilibrium value and $h(A)$ measures the proportion of the population informed by (A) at each location. The general model does not yield an analytical determination of this condition.

(3) PSEUDO-EMPIRICAL ANALYSIS OF THE MODEL

We proceed, employing specific functional forms and using numerical methods, to investigate the welfare effects of integration for ranges of the relevant parameters. We first need to select a consumer-demand function. One functional form that is used in the spatial-economics literature (Eaton and Lipsey, 1976; 1978) yields tractable results for our problem. That is the exponential demand function $ae^{-d \cdot (P+ts)}$, where (s) represents the distance from the consumer to the nearest retailer and (t) represents the consumer's travel cost per unit distance. Without consequence, we may normalise $a = d = 1$. Further, we adopt a particular specification of the advertising mechanism, first used by Butters (1977) and then Balcer (1981). This assumes that the advertising messages disseminated at any retailer location reach consumers independently and with equal probability across the relevant consumers. In this case, the density of informed consumers is given by $1 - e^{-A/v}$, where (v) is the density of potential consumers and (A) is the density of advertising (Butters, 1977, p. 468).

With the addition of these two assumptions, numerical calculations are posssible (although closed-form solutions are not). The equilibrium values of (P, R, A) for the non-integrated market and the first-best (integrated) equilibrium (P^*, R^*, A^*) can then be determined. This is done via the equilibrium equations for non-integrated retailers controlled by the manufacturer through P_w alone, and for retailers controlled by one of the appropriate (perfectly-substitutable) packages of instruments. These equations are outlined in the Appendix. The exogenous parameters are: fixed retailer costs (F), marginal production costs (c), density of potential consumers (v), consumer's travel cost per unit distance (t), cost of advertising per unit distance (b) and advertising spillover (α). These parameter values are chosen as follows: F can be normalised to 1 without consequence; c is set equal to 0; values of (v) and (t) are chosen to range at one extreme, from the margin where retail markets are just viable. That is, where consumers are spread sufficiently thinly and have sufficiently-high travel costs that, given the fixed costs imposed on retailers, retail markets are just viable). At the other extreme, they range to a close approximation to non-spatial competition (v is 'large' and t is 'small'). α is set so that there are either no retailer-information spillovers ($\alpha = 0$) or 'significant' retailer-information spillovers ($\alpha = 0.5$); (b) which is bounded above by a value that yields non-negative profits for retailers given our other parameter extremes ($b < (1/e)$), is set equal to either 0.01 or 0.1; retailer conjectures are either Loschian or Nash (non-Loschian). A summary of our numerical results appears in Table 7.2.

The numerical calculations yield both positive and normative insights as parameter values change and approach interpretable limits. These may be listed:[10]

(1) With (a) high travel costs (high t); and (b) low densities of consumers (low v) where the market is 'just' viable (manufacturer's profits are near zero); but (c) with low advertising costs (small b), the non-integrated and integrated equilibria converge. In this case, the optimal wholesale price (P_w) is close to the marginal production costs (c) and, since $b \simeq 0$, the equilibrium market-radius (R) is very large. So, both the Nash and Loschian equilibria approximate to the integrated equilibrium. The private and social benefits of vertical integration are small in this region.

(2) With high densities of consumers (high v) and high advertising costs (high b) but with retail markets still viable ($b < (1/e)$), the equilibrium market-radius (R) is small. The Nash retailers' price elasticity is therefore large, with the consequent retail margin so low that the incentive to advertise is also very low. For example,

TABLE 7.2 EQUILIBRIUM VALUES OF (P, A, R, Π, W) FOR SELECTED VALUES OF (b, α, v, t) FOR $c = 0$ AND $F = 1$

	α		*0*									*0.5*								
		t	*0.01*			*0.10*			*1.0*			*0.01*			*0.10*			*1.0*		
b	v		I	N	L	I	N	L	I	N	L	I	N	L	I	N	L	I	N	L
0.01	1.0	P	1.00	0.99	1.90	1.00	1.14	1.69				1.00	1.11	1.65	1.00	1.11	1.65			
		A	3.52	1.96	2.68	3.29	2.64	2.70				3.52	1.98	2.06	3.25	1.98	2.06			
		R	17.70	12.07	4.59	6.56	4.79	4.49		NV		6.56	4.76	4.32	6.56	4.76	4.32		NV	
		Π	0.26	0.24	0.12	0.15	0.14	0.10				0.15	0.13	0.09	0.15	0.13	0.09			
		W	0.59	0.54	0.26*	0.41	0.38	0.23*				0.41	0.35	0.23*	0.41	0.35	0.23*			
0.01	10.0	P	1.00	0.90	1.93	1.00	1.00	1.90	1.00	1.14	1.69	1.00	0.77	1.87	1.00	0.93	1.85	1.00	1.11	1.65
		A	35.78	12.02	26.75	35.18	19.61	26.78	32.95	26.44	26.97	35.78	6.31	20.38	35.18	13.22	20.42	32.95	19.79	20.56
		R	5.44	4.44	0.46	1.77	1.21	0.46	0.66	0.48	0.45	5.44	4.43	0.44	1.77	1.20	0.44	0.66	0.48	0.43
		Π	3.03	2.27	1.25	2.64	2.37	1.23	1.51	1.39	0.96	3.03	1.46	1.16	2.64	1.99	1.14	1.51	1.26	0.88
		W	6.51	5.06*	2.61*	5.91	5.36	2.58*	4.11	3.76	2.39*	6.51	3.57*	2.50*	5.91	4.70*	2.48*	4.11	3.53	2.25*
	100.0	P	1.00	0.80	1.93	1.00	0.90	1.93	1.00	1.00	1.90	1.00	0.60	1.88	1.00	0.77	1.87	1.00	0.93	1.85
		A	359.72	61.30	267.30	357.87	120.23	267.49	351.78	190.05	267.83	359.72	18.22	203.60	357.87	63.11	203.78	351.78	132.19	204.21
		R	1.59	2.15	0.05	0.53	0.44	0.05	0.18	0.12	0.05	1.59	2.30	0.04	0.53	0.44	0.04	0.18	0.12	0.04
		Π	31.59	15.46	12.57	30.31	22.69	12.54	26.37	23.67	12.25	31.59	5.04	11.67	30.31	14.57	11.64	26.37	19.87	11.38
		W	67.08	35.80*	26.05*	65.14	50.64*	26.05*	59.08	53.56	25.82*	67.08	14.04*	24.99*	65.14	35.74*	24.99*	59.08	47.02*	24.79*
0.10	1.0	P																		
		A																		
		R		NV			NV			NV			NV			NV			NV	
		Π																		
		W																		
0.10	10.0	P	1.00		1.53							1.00	0.58	1.28						
		A	12.85		7.68							12.85	0.16	3.28						
		R	3.47	NE	1.24		NV			NV		3.47	30.96	1.12		NV			NV	
		Π	1.19		0.61							1.19	0.01	0.21						
		W	3.80		1.77*							3.80	0.09*	0.99*						
	100.0	P	1.00	0.56	1.53	1.00		1.53				1.00	0.56	1.28	1.00	0.58	1.28			
		A	129.28	0.11	76.99	128.53		76.81				129.28	0.17	33.29	128.53	1.59	32.79			
		R	1.97	29.23	0.13	0.35	NE	0.13		NV		1.97	29.29	0.11	0.35	3.10	0.11		NV	
		Π	13.25	0.01	6.17	11.86		6.10				13.25	0.01	2.18	11.86	0.12	2.14			
		W	39.68	0.06*	17.77*	38.02		17.66*				39.68	0.09*	10.08*	38.02	0.88*	9.90*			

I ≡ Value of variable in integrated (first-best) equilibrium.
N ≡ Value of variable when retailer conjectures are Nash.
L ≡ Value of variable when retailer conjectures are Loschian.
NV ≡ Retail market is not viable.
NE ≡ Retail market is non-existent.[13]
* ≡ Pareto inferior to integrated equilibrium.

at ($\alpha = 0.0$, $t = 0.01$, $b = 0.10$ and $v = 100$), the Nash (A) equals 0.11 whereas the Loschian (A) equals 76.99 in comparison to a corresponding integrated (A) of 129.28. Consequently the incentive for the manufacturer to integrate is here greater for the Nash than for the Loschian retail market.

(3) In the integrated equilibrium, retail prices *always* fall for Loschian retail markets. (This can be proven analytically for the exponential-demand case.[11]) Retail prices *may* fall in the integrated equilibrium-even for Nash retail markets with their relatively high perceived price elasticities (e.g., $\alpha = 0.0$, $t = 0.10$, $b = 0.01$ and $v = 100$). We have argued that CTDs may be imposed to force Loschian conjectures on retailers. In this case, even when intra-brand retail competition is completely eliminated via CTDs, retail prices may fall.

(4) As measured by the sum of consumers' and producers' surpluses, welfare always increases with the use of a minimal sufficient set of restraints or vertical integration.

(5) For the values of exogenous variables in Table 7.2, the integrated equilibria are Pareto-superior to the respective Loschian non-integrated equilibria, with one exception. For $\alpha = 0$, and where the integrated equilibria are sufficiently near the boundary of retail-market viability, the integrated equilibria cannot Pareto-dominate the Loschian equilibrium. This is because two equilibria converge near this viability boundary.

(6) In this case there is a high density of consumers (high v) and low advertising costs (low b); which lead to a low equilibrium market-radius (low R) and hence low Nash retail margins. Here, the integrated equilibria are also Pareto-superior to the respective Nash non-integrated equilibria. This suggests that the conjectural and vertical externalities that motivate the private incentive to set integrated solutions are strong. Indeed, they are sufficiently strong to control the welfare outcome; consumer welfare is also increased by the internalising of these retailer externalities.

V CONCLUSIONS

This chapter has reviewed and synthesised alternative explanations for vertical restraints (such as closed-territory distributions, franchise fees, quantity forcing and resale price maintenance) imposed by manufacturers on retailers. The objective has been to develop the appropriate public-policy stance towards these restrictive practices. If vertical restrictions serve *only* to facilitate a cartel at the level of either the dealer or the manufacturer, then public policy should seek to foreclose the restrictive practices. Vertical restrictions can, however, serve exclusively to permit manufacturers to rationalise various aspects of the retail-marketing of their products. (This potential exists in spite of any monopoly power at either the manufacturing or retail level; vertical restrictions themselves are never a source of monopoly power.) While vertical restrictions, in this setting, are necessarily privately-efficient, the policy question is whether they are socially-efficient. The answer requires an identification of the role of vertical restrictions.

On the basis of previous studies by the present authors and others, we identify a number of settings where vertical restrictions, as efficient contracts, seek to counter externalities. In particular, RPM can serve to prevent discount houses from free-riding on information provided by high-price retailers; as such, RPM can improve welfare and therefore, *per se* rules against RPM are inappropriate. Price ceilings, minimum-quantity restrictions and franchise fees can counter vertical, together with conjectural, externalities among retailers in spatial retail settings where individual dealers have price-setting power. In these settings, these particular restrictions are perfect substitutes. Finally, when combinations of the informational, vertical and conjectural externalities are permitted, contracts, undergo a significant change. A rich set of possible restraint packages exists to counter combinations of these externalities. This chapter has analysed the social-desirability of permitting such efficient restraint packages.

As a general welfare analysis of this problem leads only to limited results, we have resorted to welfare comparisons, using specific functional forms and pseudo-empirics. Given the conditions imposed on our parametrisation, the results indicate that vertical restrictions not only improve welfare but can be Pareto-improving as well. These results flow from a model with monopoly at the manufacturing level and, therefore, with a complete absence of inter-brand effects. They counter the anti-trust 'rule of reason' approach to non-price restrictions (from the Sylvania case) which holds that the effect of vertical restrictions, through a reduction in intra-brand competition, is necessarily harmful.

Several issues on restraint use remain. Which of the restraint-packages that are equivalent in our analysis are also transactionallyefficient? Do restraints in any way benefit incumbent firms to the detriment of entrants? Is there empirical evidence to discriminate between the use of restraints for efficiency reasons and against either cartel-facilitation or entry-deterrence?[12] If risk-sharing is an objective of retailers' contracts (retailers are frequently non-diversified, small entrepreneurs), how does this alter restraint packages and instrument levels? And can the idea of efficient contracting explain practices of exclusive dealing or of full-line forcing (restraints not treated in this chapter)?

APPENDIX

This appendix sets forth a complete list of those assumptions and equations of our model which are critical for the welfare calculations.

ASSUMPTIONS

(A1) Consumers are uniformly distributed, with density (v), along a circle or a line of infinite length.

(A2) Consumers have a common travel cost (t) per unit distance, and per unit quantity purchased.

(A3) Retail outlets buy at a wholesale price P_w. Each incurs a fixed (but not location-specific) cost (F) and no variable costs other than the wholesale price.

(A4) A consumer must be informed of the existence of the product before buying.

(A5) Information on the product's existence is provided locally only by the retail firms. Product characteristics are readily verifiable by consumers prior to purchase, so that there is no opportunity to induce consumer misperceptions. Information disseminated by a retail firm takes the form of advertising messages or sales effort disseminated through local sales personnel (all labelled as advertising). These have a constant density over a chosen market area. The total cost of advertising at a density (A) over at interval (ds) is $(bA\,ds)$.

(A6) If the density of advertising at a particular location is (A), then the proportion of consumers informed at that location is a function $h(A)$. The number of consumers informed at each location is $vh(A)$.

(A7) A proportion (α) of the advertising messages disseminated by any retail outlet reaches consumers outside the outlet's market area. This occurs: if consumers migrate to other retail markets, once informed of the product (or were outside their normal shopping area when informed); or if retailers at each location cannot target their advertising exclusively to their local market area.

(A8) Once informed of the product's existence, consumers have access at zero cost to information on the prices and locations of all retail outlets.

(A9) The demand per informed consumer is $f(P + ts)$ where (P) is the retail price paid by the consumer (called the 'mill' price) and (s) is the distance travelled to the outlet. Each consumer buys from the outlet whose 'delivered' price $(P + ts)$ is the lowest, even if informed of the product by a different outlet.

(A10) There is free entry into the retail market, so that outlets continue to enter the market until profits are driven to zero. (A9) and (A10) mean that a retail equilibrium is Chamberlinian.

(A11) The wholesale market is supplied by a monopolist who incurs a constant of production (c), and maximises profit per distance. The manufacturer incurs no transport costs in distributing products to outlets.

(A12) The manufacturer cannot advertise directly. Nor can he, without prohibitive cost, monitor retailers' levels of advertising. These excessive monitoring costs foreclose direct contractual control of retailer-advertising by the manufacturer.

(A13) Vertical integration into the retail market by the manufacturer is (prohibitively) costly.

(A14) Retail conjectures are characterised by *either*:

(a) *Nash conjectures (Hotelling–Smithies competition)*. Each retail outlet assumes its neighbours' prices to be invariant to its price changes; *or*

(b) *Loschian conjectures*. Each outlet assumes that its market area is invariant to changes in its price; equivalently; each outlet assumes that neighbouring outlets will match its price changes.

(Many of these assumptions are standard in the literature on spatial economics.)

MODEL

With the specific functional forms (outlined in the text) used in the welfare evaluation, the critical sets of profit-maximising and equilibrium conditions (developed in Mathewson and Winter, 1983b) are as follows:

Non-integrated retailers (under symmetry of retail outlets):

Nash retail price (retailer profit maximising):

$$- [P - P_{\mathrm{w}}] \left[\int_0^R e^{-(P+ts)}ds + e^{-(P+tR)}/2t \right]$$
$$+ \int_0^R e^{-(P+ts)}ds - bA/2t = 0$$

Loschian retail price (retailer profit maximising):

$$- (P - P_{\mathrm{w}}) \int_0^R e^{-(P+ts)}ds + \int_0^R e^{-(P+ts)}ds = 0$$

Advertising (retailer profit maximising):

$$(1 - e^{-A/v})(P - P_{\mathrm{w}}) \int_0^R e^{-(P+ts)}ds - Rb = 0$$

Zero retail profit (retail-market equilibrium):

$$v(1 - e^{-A/v})(P - P_{\mathrm{w}}) \int_0^R e^{-(P+ts)}ds - RbA - F/2 = 0$$

Integrated (first-best) conditions:

Retail price: $\quad -(P - c) \int_0^R e^{-(P+ts)}ds + \int_0^R e^{-(P+ts)}ds = 0$

Advertising: $\quad (1 - e^{-A/v})(P - c) \int_0^R e^{-(P+ts)}ds - Rb = 0$

Market radius: $\quad Re^{-(P+tR)} - \int_0^R e^{-(P+ts)} ds + F = 0$

NOTES

1. We wish to thank Nancy Gallini, Yehuda Kotowitz, Marty Perry, Jim Rosse, Julio Segura Sanchez and members of seminars at the Federal Trade Commission, Stanford University, and the University of Western Ontario for helpful comments on an earlier draft of this chapter.

2. The argument normally presented is that high retail margins leave rents (or funds) at the retail level to be used for service (quality). In fact, the retail margin is relevant because it determines the retailer's marginal benefit from quality not because it 'increases the availability of funds'.

3. Gallini and Winter (1983) provide simple elasticity conditions for the profitability and welfare effects of vertical price ceilings and floors, when the product is differentiated (symmetrically) at the retail level.

4. This argument is also criticised by Scherer (1980, p. 592) and by Porter (1976, p. 64).

5. In fact, in our model (Mathewson and Winter, 1984), territorial restrictions (such as CTDs) are used only in the *absence* of informational spillovers.

6. Our analysis of the motivations for restrictions (Section II), suggests that our treatment of restraints as efficient contracts extends beyond the monopolist-manufacturer/Chamberlinian retail setting.

7. These externalities imply only that the retail price is too high *given* local advertising (service, quality) and the density of retail stores: and that local advertising (service, quality) is too low given the retail price and the density of retail stores. However, it is a straightforward matter to prove the global statement made in the first sentence of this paragraph.

8. Actually, this statement requires that the ratio of the integrated equilibrium radius to the non-integrated equilibrium radius must be an irrational number. This requirement will be satisfied 'generically' (for all exogenous parameters, except on a negligible set).

9. Thus we are measuring the consumer's welfare *ex ante* to the event of being informed (or not), where the probability of this event depends on (A). If we measured welfare *ex post* to this event, Pareto comparisons would not be possible.

10. These results were verified over a wide range of exogenous-parameter values.

11. Comparison of general, relevant first-order conditions on (P) and (A) between the Loschian retailer and the manufacturer shows that, in general, the Loschian price is higher than the manufacturer's optimal price *conditional upon* (A) *and* (R). With the exponential demand curve, the manufacturer's optimal (P) conditional upon (A) and (R) equals ($1 + c$), i.e., (P) is independent of (A) and (R); therefore, for exponential demand, the condition in italics can be ignored.

12. Posner (1981, p. 26) proposes an output or market-share rule: if the allegedly restrictive practice causes the defendant's output or market share to rise; 'then, on balance, the restraint must promote consumer welfare and economic efficiency'. Whether changes in output and welfare are perfectly correlated remains an open question.

13. The Nash equilibrium does not exist when the radius consistent with the first-order conditions and the zero-profit condition is so small (when (v) and (b) are large) that the Nash outlet perceives a positive profit from undercutting a neighbour's delivered price at the neighbour's location. (For details, see Salop, 1979.) The non-existence problem here is an artefact of our simplifying assumption that the advertising density is constant over the market radius, and so is ignored.

REFERENCES

Balcer, Y. (1981) 'Equilibrium Distributions of Sales and Advertising Prices Over Space', *Journal of Economic Theory*, vol. 25, no. 2, pp. 196–218.

Barzel, Y. (1982) 'Measurement Cost and the Organisation of Markets', *Journal of Law and Economics*, vol. 25, no. 1, pp. 27–48.

Bittlingmayer, G. (1982) 'A Model of Vertical Restriction and Equilibrium in Retailing', *Journal of Business*, vol. 56, no. 4, pp. 477–96.

Butters, G. (1976) 'Equilibrium Distribution of Sales and Advertising Prices', *Review of Economic Studies*, vol. 44, no. 3, pp. 465–92.

Dixit, A. (1983) 'Vertical Integration in a Monopolistically Competitive Industry', *International Journal of Industrial Organization*, vol. 1, no. 1, pp. 63–78.

Eaton, B. C. and Lipsey, R. G. (1976) 'The Non-Uniqueness of Equilibrium in the Loschian Location Model', *American Economic Review*, vol. 66, no. 1, pp. 77–93.

Eaton, B. C. and Lipsey, R. G. (1978) 'Freedom of Entry and the Existence of Pure Profits', *Economic Journal*, vol. 88, pp. 455–69.

Gallini, N. and Winter, R. (1983) 'On Vertical Control in Monopolistic Competition', *International Journal of Industrial Organization*, vol. 1, no. 3, pp. 275–86.

Gould, J. and Preston, L. (1965) 'Resale Price Maintenance and Retail Outlets)', *Economica*, vol. 32, pp. 302–31.

Mathewson, F. and Winter, R. (1983a) 'Vertical Integration by Contractual Restraints in Spatial Markets', *Journal of Business*, vol. 56, no. 4, pp.497–518.

Mathewson, F. and Winter, R. (1983) 'The Incentives for Resale Price Maintenance Under Imperfect Information', *Economic Inquiry*, vol. 21, no. 3, pp. 337–48.

Mathewson, F. and Winter, R. (1984) 'An Economic Theory of Vertical Restraints', *The Rand Journal of Economics*, vol. 15, no. 1, pp. 27–38.

Porter, M. (1976) *Interbrand Choice, Strategy and Bilateral Market Power*, (Harvard University Press).

Posner, R. (1981) 'The Next Step in the Antitrust Treatment of Restricted Distribution: Per Se Legality', *The University of Chicago Law Review*, vol. 48, pp. 6–26.

Salop, S. (1979) 'Monopolistic Competition with Outside Goods', *Bell Journal of Economics*, vol. 10, no. 1, pp. 141–56.

Scherer, F. M. (1980) *Industrial Market Structure and Economic Performance*, (Rand McNally).

Schwartz, M. and Eisenstadt, M. (1982) 'Vertical Restraints' Discussion Paper EPO 82–8 Antitrust Division (US Department of Justice).

Sharpe, T. (1982) 'Refusal to Supply', Centre for Socio-Legal Studies, Wolfson College, Oxford University.

Smith, R. L. II (1982) 'Franchise Regulation: an Economic Analysis of State Restrictions on Automobile Distribution', *Journal of Law and Economics*, vol. 25, no. 1, pp. 125–58.

Spengler J. (1950) 'Vertical Integration and Antitrust Policy', *Journal of Political Economy*, vol. 68, pp. 347–52.

Telser, L. (1960) 'Why Should Manufacturers Want Fair Trade?', *Journal of Law and Economics*, vol. 3, pp. 86–103.

Warren, R. G. (1975) *Antitrust in Theory and Practice* (Grid Press).

Warren-Boulton, F. (1978) *Vertical Control of Markets* (Ballinger Publishing Company).

Williamson, O. (1979) 'Assessing Vertical Market Restrictions: Antitrust Ramifications of the Transactions Cost Approach', *University of Pennsylvania Law Review*, vol. 127, pp. 953–93.

Discussion of the Paper by G. Frank Mathewson and Ralph Winter

In response to some of the discussion at the conference about the relationship between spatial and representative consumer models, *Martin Perry* in discussing this paper presented some simulation results that he had done jointly with Robert Groff. Mathewson and Winter ask a set of questions about restrictions improved by an upstream supplies on the downstream retailer in the context of a spatially-differentiated retail consumer market (address model). Perry and Groff (1983) asked the same questions in an extended representative consumer model (a single 'typical' consumer buying all of the products) similar to the model discussed in Spence (1976) and Koenker and Perry (1981). Groff and Perry's results were derived by computing the•Cournot and competitive equilibrium among downstream firms for various strategies of the monopolist. They use the benefit function.

$$V(X) = [\, \Sigma_j \, \alpha X_j^\beta]^\theta$$

In this welfare function, $X = (X_1, \ldots, X_m)$ was the vector of outputs of all firms in the industry, $\alpha > 0$, $0 < \beta \leq 1$, and $0 < \theta < 1$ were parameters. The integrated monopoly solution could be achieved by using any of the restraints suggested by Mathewson–Winter. Perry and Groff then compared final price, product diversity, and welfare from integration with that which arose under either unit pricing of franchise fee pricing. Unit pricing resulted in a high unit price but high diversity; a franchise fee resulted in low diversity but a low price; and integration resulted in some compromise between these two extremes. For competitive downstream behaviour, integration yielded the lowest welfare. This was contrary to the traditional insight that vertical integration generally improved matters when there was imperfect competition at one or more stages. Unit pricing was best when differentiation was strong (β low) because it resulted in the highest product diversity. And a franchise fee was best when differentiation was weak (β high) because it resulted in the lowest price. When downstream behaviour was Cournot, unit pricing seemed to be uniformly the best alternative and the integrated solution now dominated the francise fee alternative for all but very strong differentiation ($\beta > 0.5$). In conjunction with the results of Mathewson–Winter, these results indicated that different models of product differentiation could affect the nature of policy recommendations.

Perry suggested that one interesting extension of this research on vertical restrictions would be to consider imperfect competition in the upstream part of the industry as well as the downstream part. Perry (1977) posed a simple model to indicate possible results. Imagine an industry with two manufacturers and two retailers. In this case there were then two marketing alternatives: either products were sold in both stores (multi-product retail outlets), or each store carried a single product (exclusive dealing). With integration, consumers who preferred one of the products should be willing to travel a longer distance to visit the store carrying the product that they prefer. Hence, even though retail prices would tend to be lower with integration, increased travel costs would tend to reduce welfare.

Sanchez suggested that the welfare results derived by Mathewson and Winter depended on three assumptions in their model: the functional form chosen for the relationship between advertising expenditures and the probability that a message reached any particular consumer; the symmetric location of retail firms; and the nature of the conjectures that firms made about the responses of their rivals.

Reinhard Selten pointed out that the issue of appropriate conjectural variation might better be viewed by formulating the extensive form game that was actually being played by market participants. He noted that different conjectures might correspond to equilibria of different extensive form games. If so, the appropriate conjectures could be more easily identified. Both Martin Perry and John Panzar responded that conjectural variations provided a very convenient way to analyse questions about welfare, or to see the relationship between collusive and non-co-operative behaviour. *Thomas von Ungern-Sternberg* asked whether address models and transaction cost approaches to vertical issues were reconcilable.

Oliver Williamson saw no contradiction between his transactions-costs approach to vertical integration and the approach taken by Mathewson and Winter. He found them complementary since different approaches to the same question were often useful. In any case, as the schemes studied by Mathewson and Winter were perfect substitutes in their model, transaction-cost consideration of the type analysed by Williamson might be necessary to explain why industries chose one scheme over another.

REFERENCES

Koenker, R. W. and Perry, M. K. (1981) 'Product Differentiation, Monopolistic Competition, and Public Policy', *Bell Journal of Economics*, vol. 12, no. 1, pp. 217–31.

Perry, M. K. and Groff, R. H. (1983) 'Forward Integration by a Monopolist into a Monopolistically Competitive Industry'.

Perry, M. K. (1977) 'Product Differentiation and Vertical Integration',

Spence, A. M. (1976) 'Product Selection, Fixed Costs and Monopolistic Competition', *Review of Economic Studies*, vol. 43, no. 2, pp. 217–36.

Part Four
Collusion and
Oligopoly

8 On the Stability of Collusion

C. d'Aspremont
and
J. Jaskold Gabszewicz[1]

I INTRODUCTION

The literature on oligopolistic competition abounds with various implicit statements about the 'stability' of collusive arrangements. A well known example is provided by comments on price arrangements between the sellers in a given industry. It is asserted that any oligopolistic configuration must be unstable with respect to monopolistic collusion: 'the combined profits of the entire set of firms in an industry are maximised when they act together as a monopolist, and the result holds for any number of firms' (Stigler, 1950, p. 24). At the same time however, it is recognised that 'when the group of firms agrees to fix and abide by a price approaching monopoly levels, strong incentives are created for individual members to chisel – that is, to increase their profits by undercutting the fixed price slightly, gaining additional orders at a price that still exceeds marginal cost' (Scherer, 1980, p. 171). On the other hand, in the recent literature on the core of an exchange market, it has been shown that, sometimes, monopolistic collusion can be disadvantageous to the traders involved when compared to the competitive outcome (Aumann, 1973). As for the collusive price–leadership model, it is stressed that the outsiders of a merger agreement may be better off than the insiders:

> the major difficulty in forming a merger is that it is more profitable to be outside a merger than to be a participant. The outsider sells at the same price but at the much larger output at which marginal cost equals price. Hence the promoter of a merger is likely to receive much encouragement from each firm – almost every encouragement, in fact, except participation (Stigler, 1950).

243

All these statements reveal implicitly the existence of two opposite tendencies in the co-ordination of group decision processes. The first tendency comes from the recognition by individual participants of the collective advantage of co-ordination. The other comes from the evidence that this co-ordination may not be immune against advantageous recontracting by some of these participants. However, it seems that no attempt has been made to provide a unified theoretical framework for analysing the effectiveness of collusive co-ordination. As a first step in this direction, this chapter aims to define some alternative stability concepts for collusive arrangements and to illustrate, in the light of these concepts, how collusive co-ordination can be effective in two different economic contexts.

To illustrate the first stability concept we deal with the problem of imputing the output resulting from a productive activity, between the owners of the factors involved in this activity. We assume that some of the factor owners collude so as to orient the choice of the imputation to their own advantage. We show that, under a constant returns-to-scale technology, they cannot succeed in this endeavour if the imputation is chosen in the core of the market.

The second illustration is devoted to an alternative concept of stability which we use in the context of the price–leadership model. A (dominant) group of firms collude to quote a price which a competitive fringe accepts. We examine the extent to which, with such an arrangement, it is to the advantage of an individual member of the group to move outside it, or of a single member of the fringe to join the group. We show, using an example, that there is always a division of the firms between a cartel and a competitive fringe where no such individual advantage exists.

II   THE STABILITY OF COLLUSIVE ARRANGEMENTS: AN ABSTRACT FRAMEWORK

The departure point of our analysis is a given list of individual decision-makers involved in a group decision process – where they have partially parallel, and partially conflicting, individual interests. The collusive mechanism operates when these individuals, instead of acting independently, tend to guide the results of the process, by forming *groups*. These groups delegate to a single decision unit the task of representing their economic interests. The formal effect of this mechanism consists, first, in reducing the initial set of individual decision-makers to a new set of decision units, which now consists of the groups formed through collusion. Second, the bias in the outcome of the decision process is introduced by the substitution for its expected outcome (when the original decision units are acting independently) of a new outcome, or a new class of outcomes: namely, those which are expected to prevail if groups are effectively acting in place of the individuals themselves. Given a set $N = \{\ldots, i, \ldots, n\}$ of individual decision-makers, we call a *collusive scheme*, denoted C, a partition of N into subsets N_k, with all individuals in N_k acting in unison; N_k is called a *group*. The simplest example of a collusive scheme is the finest partition of N, namely

$$C_0 \underset{\text{def}}{=} \{\{1\}, \ldots, \{i\}, \ldots, \{n\}\};$$

C_0 is the scheme resulting from a collusive process where no collusion has been successful, or even initiated; accordingly, we call C_0 the *disagreement collusive scheme*. At the opposite extreme, if a single decision unit is substituted for the n initial ones, total agreement is reached through the collusive process and we obtain $\bar{C}$ defined by

$$\bar{C} = \{N\}.$$

We call $\bar{C}$ the *total agreement collusive scheme*. An economic example of a total agreement collusive scheme is of course provided by a set of ostensibly independent firms which collude to determine jointly the output or the price which is to prevail in a given industry. All intermediate forms of collusion, like collusive oligopolies or 'leadership' situations, consisting of one 'big' collusive cartel and many small independent firms, can easily be captured by a particular collusive scheme. In the latter case, for instance, if the cartel groups firms 1 to k, and the 'competitive fringe' consists of firms $\{k + 1, \ldots, n\}$, the corresponding collusive scheme is $C = \{\{1, \ldots, k\}, \{k + 1\}, \ldots, \{n\}\}$.

Given a particular group decision process, either institutional factors, or the very nature of the process, impose self-evident restrictions on the class of collusive schemes which are feasible.[2] The most extreme example is the case of an 'anti-trust law' which would forbid any explicit or implicit oligopolistic co-ordination between the firms in a given industry: no other collusive scheme than C_0 is then feasible. Other examples of such restrictions are provided by negotiations involving trade unions, professional associations, bidders at auctions, syndicates of property owners, etc. Such 'groups' share the property that the individual members of the group are all of the same 'type': a trade union includes only workers, and no other type of economic agent. Consequently, the very nature of the decision process excludes any collusive scheme which would embody a group consisting of individuals of different types. Let us formally capture this idea. Let N be subdivided into m disjoint subsets, or *types*, i.e. $N = \{N_1, \ldots, N_i, \ldots, N_m\}$, with all individuals ij in N_i identical. Let A_i be a subset of N_i, $i = 1, \ldots, m$. We call A_i *the syndicate of type i* and $A = \{A_1, \ldots, A_i, \ldots, A_m\}$ a *syndicate structure*.[3] Thus a syndicate is a group involving only identical decision units. A *syndicate collusive scheme* is defined by

$$C = \{A_1, \ldots, A_i, \ldots, A_m,$$
$$\{1j\}_{1j \in N_1 \setminus A_1}, \ldots, \{ij\}_{ij \in N_i \setminus A_i}, \ldots, \{mj\}_{mj \in N_m \setminus A_m}\},$$

where the notation $\{ij\}_{ij \in N_i \setminus A_i}$ represents the set of singletons of $N_i \setminus A_i$.

Intuitively, a syndicate collusive scheme is simply a partition of the m types of decision-makers into m syndicates of different types and the 'isolated' individuals of the various types who are *not* members of their corresponding syndicates. To provide an economic illustration, which will be developed below, consider the group decison process, involving a given set N_1 of workers and a given set (N_2) of capital owners. The process consists of choosing collectively an imputation of the output resulting from their joint activity (imputation of social output). If, in this process, a trade union is formed (call it A_1), and if some capital owners collude (say, in A_2) we obtain a syndicate collusive scheme embodying: (i) the trade union A_1; (ii) the 'unorganised' workers; (iii) the syndicate of capitalists A_2; (iv) the 'unorganised' capital owners. A simpler illustration is also provided by the leadership model, described above, when all the n firms are identical. Then, the number of types reduces to one, and the collusive scheme $\{A, \{i\}_{i \in N \setminus A}\}$, where A denotes the cartel (or the syndicate) and $\{i\}_{i \in N \setminus A}$ the competitive fringe, is a syndicate collusive scheme.

As was stated earlier, collusion is intended to guide the collective decision process, by enforcing outcomes which would not otherwise prevail. The outcome, or class of outcomes, to be taken into consideration in a given collusive scheme, depends on the nature of the collective decision process. Either the process is designed to bring about a non-co-operative outcome, like a Nash equilibrium among the 'players', or it envisages a leadership solution analogous to a Stackelberg point. Or a co-operative outcome must be expected, like an imputation in the core. As soon as a particular solution concept is selected to describe the outcome, or class of outcomes, of a given decision process, it is easy to specify how collusion guides the mechanism of collective choice. To illustrate, let us consider again the example of an industry consisting initially of a large number of identical firms. If no collusion occurs, i.e. if the disagreement scheme C_0 is realised, then it is natural to take as outcome relative to this scheme the vector of competitive pay-offs. By contrast, if all the firms collude in a single cartel, i.e. if $C = \bar{C}$, we may take as the class of outcomes relative to $\bar{C}$ the set of all possible imputations of the monopoly profit between the firms, or its uniform imputation. Now, suppose this set of firms 'splits' into two cartels, C_1 and C_2, then $C = \{C_1, C_2\}$. We can then pick as outcomes relative to C the set of pay-offs corresponding to the Nash equilibrium pairs of strategies of the game with two players C_1 and C_2 (recall that all firms in C_1 and C_2 act in unison). In the price leadership model, for the collusive scheme $\{\{1, \ldots, k\}, \{k + 1\}, \ldots, \{n\}\}$, we may take as the outcome the uniform imputation of the price leadership profit inside $\{1, \ldots, k\}$ and, for each firm in the competitive fringe, the profit level resulting from profit maximisation at the price chosen by the cartel. If we want to consider co-operative outcomes, it may be natural to use the concept of core.[4] Given a set N of decision units, the core is usually defined as the set of imputations feasible for the 'grand' coalition N, which cannot be blocked by any coalition S, where a coalition S is simply defined as a subset of N. However if a collusive scheme $C = \{C_1, \ldots, C_h, \ldots, C_m\}$ that is different from C_0 becomes effective, any coalition which would include a *proper* subset of any element C_h of the corresponding partition can no longer be considered: such a coalition would 'split' an indivisible decision unit, and is thereby forbidden. Consequently, to each collusive scheme, there corresponds the core relative to C, namely the set of imputations which is not blocked by any *permissible* coalition, i.e. a coalition S in the set $\{S \mid \forall h \text{ either } S \cap C_h = \varnothing, \text{ or } S \cap C_h = C_h\}$. With this terminology, the core relative to C_0 is the core as usually defined, where *any* coalition is permissible.

All the above examples show that the cohesiveness of collusive agreements must be evaluated by the outcome, or class of outcomes, which must be expected from a particular collusive scheme. Moreover, to achieve the cohesiveness of the groups observed in this collusive scheme, collusion must bring about outcomes which are, loosely speaking, 'advantageous' to their members: otherwise they might, for instance, be tempted to 'cheat' by secretly recontracting with individuals outside their own group, and thereby breaking the effectiveness of the collusive scheme. Intuitively, one can think of two sorts of requirement of the resulting outcome, which may protect the stability of a given collusive scheme. The first sort refers to comparisons between individual outcomes for a *given* collusive scheme $C = \{N_1, \ldots, N_i, \ldots, N_m\}$, in particular, individual outcomes of N_h-members compared with individual outcomes of N_k-members, $k \neq h$. Such comparisons are particularly relevant in the context of a syndicate structure $\{A_1, \ldots, A_i, \ldots, A_m\}$, $A_i \subset N_i$, for outcomes across the *same* type. Then comparisons are made, for a given collusive scheme, between the pay-offs received by the members of the syndicate, A_i, and the pay-offs of those who remained 'unorganised', and are of the same type (in $N_i \smallsetminus A_i$). The second sort refers to a comparison of the individual outcomes accruing to the decision makers if a collusive scheme C is formed, with the outcomes they would face if some alternative collusive scheme were formed.

These two types of comparisons lead to the following stability concepts for collusive schemes (C) relative to a given class of outcomes. Denote by

$$\Pi(C) = \left\{ \pi(C) \mid \pi(C) = (\pi_1(C), \ldots, \pi_i(C), \ldots, \pi_n(C)) \right\}$$

the class of outcomes associated with the collusive scheme C, where $\pi_i(C)$ denotes the pay-off to individual i if outcome $\pi(C)$ is selected.[5] The first definition refers to the stability of syndicate collusive schemes. Let N be subdivided into m types, i.e. $N = \{N_1, \ldots, N_i, \ldots, N_m\}$; let $A = \{A_1, \ldots, A_i, \ldots, A_m\}$ be a given syndicate structure, and C be a particular syndicate collusive scheme.

(1) INTERNAL STABILITY OF SYNDICATES

The syndicate collusive scheme C is internally stable if

$$\forall \pi(C) \in \Pi(C), \ \forall ij \in A_i \quad \text{and} \quad ik \in N_i \smallsetminus A_i, \ \pi_{ij}(C) \geqslant \pi_{ik}(C),$$

with strict inequality for some ij and ik.

If a syndicate collusive scheme is internally stable, there may be no tendency for the syndicate members to break the agreement which binds them to the syndicate i: they enjoy a more favourable treatment than do their similar companions, who remained outside the syndicate.

By contrast we may consider stability concepts for a given collusive scheme which refer explicitly to the outcomes received under one, or several, alternative collusive schemes. From this viewpoint, our first definition is a strong stability concept, but relative to a given class of collusive schemes.

(2) UNANIMOUS STABILITY

Given a class $\{\hat{C}\}$ of collusive schemes, a particular scheme $\tilde{C}$ is *unanimously stable relative to* $\{C\}$ if $\tilde{C} \in \{C\}$ and if

$$\forall \pi(\tilde{C}) \in \Pi(\tilde{C}), \quad \forall C \in \{C\}, \quad \forall \pi(C) \in \Pi(C),$$
$$\forall i \in N, \quad \pi_i(\tilde{C}) \geqslant \pi_i(C),$$

with strict inequality for at least some i.

The concept of the 'unanimous stability' of a collusive scheme $\tilde{C}$ in a given class of schemes thus asserts that the pay-offs to the agents under this collusive scheme are at least as high as for any other in the class, and unambiguously higher for at least one agent. Generally, there exists no collusive scheme which is unanimously stable in the class of all collusive schemes. Collusive schemes may, however, be stable in restricted, but 'natural', reference classes of collusive schemes. Given a collusive scheme C, consider for instance the class $\{C, C_0\}$. If C is stable in this binary class, the pay-offs to the agents, if C forms, dominate their corresponding pay-offs under the disagreement scheme C_0. This property motivates the following definition.

A collusive scheme C is *unanimously stable relative to the disagreement scheme* C_0 if it is unanimously stable in the class $\{C, C_0\}$. By analogy we define: a collusive scheme C is *unanimously stable relative to the agreement scheme* $\bar{C}$ if it is unanimously stable in the class $\{C, \bar{C}\}$.

Given a collusive scheme $\tilde{C} = \{\tilde{C}_1, \ldots, \tilde{C}_n, \ldots, \tilde{C}_m\}$, another 'natural' reference class obtains by considering *individual moves* across the elements of the partition $\tilde{C}$. To be more precise, assume that some individual i leaves an element $\tilde{C}_h$ to join $\tilde{C}_k$. Then a new collusive scheme obtains, namely $C = \{\tilde{C}_1, \ldots, \tilde{C}_h \setminus \{i\}, \ldots, \tilde{C}_k \cup \{i\}, \ldots, \tilde{C}_m\}$. It is, loosely speaking, a 'neighbour' of $\tilde{C}$.

More formally, consider a class $\{C\}$ of collusive schemes and a given collusive scheme $\tilde{C} = \{\tilde{C}_1, \ldots, \tilde{C}_h, \ldots, \tilde{C}_k\}$ in $\{C\}$; we may then define $V_i(\tilde{C})$ as the set of all collusive schemes $C = \{C_1, \ldots, C_h, \ldots, C_{k'}\}$ in $\{C\}$ such that, for every h, we have either

$$\begin{aligned}
&\quad C_h = \tilde{C}_m, && \text{for some } \tilde{C}_m \text{ in } \tilde{C}, \\
\text{or} \quad &\quad C_h = \tilde{C}_m \setminus \{i\}, && \text{with } \tilde{C}_m \text{ the element of } \tilde{C} \text{ that } i \text{ leaves,} \\
\text{or} \quad &\quad C_h = \tilde{C}_m \cup \{i\}, && \text{with } \tilde{C}_m \text{ the element of } \tilde{C} \text{ that } i \text{ joins,} \\
\text{or} \quad &\quad C_h = \{i\}.
\end{aligned}$$

If we consider, for some individual i, a collusive scheme C in $V_i(\tilde{C})$, we see that there is only an individual, unilateral change between $\tilde{C}$ and C. It seems natural to introduce the following concept of stability for a given collusive scheme relative to its 'neighbours'.

(3) INDIVIDUAL STABILITY

Consider a class $\{C\}$ of collusive schemes. A collusive scheme $\tilde{C}$ is individually stable relative to $\{C\}$ if, for some $\pi \in \Pi(\tilde{C})$, there is no individual i and no collusive scheme $C \in V_i(\tilde{C})$ such that

$$\pi_i(C) > \pi_i(\tilde{C}), \qquad \text{for some } \pi(C) \in \Pi(C).$$

Under a collusive scheme ($\tilde{C}$) which is individually stable, no individual move is desired. It is clear that, because Π is a correspondence, several alternative definitions can be given. However, where Π is a function, then this concept, which involves only individual unilateral moves, may be seen as a Nash equilibrium in a non-co-operative game. In that game, the choice by every player of some strategy would determine a particular collusive scheme C, where the resulting pay-offs would be given by $\Pi(C)$. Hence, a 'strong equilibrium' notion, for which no subgroup could find an advantageous unilateral move, could also be considered. With this framework, that would amount to comparing collusive schemes which are not necessarily 'neighbours'. However, we shall not introduce these alternative concepts in this chapter.[6]

To illustrate individual stability, consider n identical firms, with zero production cost, facing a market-demand function $P(q) = 1 - q$. If the n firms collude, then $\pi_i(\bar{C}) = 1/4n$. Assume that k firms, say firms $\{1, \ldots, k\}$ leave the cartel, resulting in the formation of two cartels, then the new collusive scheme is $C = \{\{1, \ldots, k\}, \{k + 1, \ldots, n\}\}$. If both cartels act non-co-operatively, we obtain the Cournot–Nash equilibrium pay-off for each firm:

$$\pi_i(C) = \frac{1}{9k} \qquad 1 \leq i \leq k,$$

$$\pi_i(C) = \frac{1}{9(n - k)} \qquad k + 1 \leq i \leq n,$$

Putting $k = 1$, shows immediately that $\bar{C}$ is not individually stable for $n \geq 3$. For such cases it is easily seen that the individually-stable collusive schemes are such that

$$k \geq \frac{n-1}{2} \text{ and } (n-k) \geq \frac{n-1}{2}.$$

Another illustration of individual stability can be obtained in the context of the theory of local public goods as formulated by Tiebout (1956) and others.[7] Consider a set of individuals who have to be 'allocated' among a number of distinct 'communities'. The resulting partition would create an individually-stable collusive scheme, whenever no individual would gain from moving from his assigned community to another, taking into account the adjustment in the local provision of public goods.

Equipped with the above framework, we may now turn to detailed illustration of our stability concepts.

III TWO ILLUSTRATIONS

(1) COLLUSION AND THE IMPUTATION OF SOCIAL OUTPUT

The first illustration is devoted to an application of our concepts of stability in the context of a co-operative decision process: the solution concept selected to describe the outcome from a given collusive scheme C is the core, $\Pi(C)$. This example is borrowed from Hansen and Gabszewicz (1972). We consider an economy in which a single output is produced under a constant-returns-to-scale, differentiable production function $F(z_1, z_2)$, where z_1 is labour and z_2 capital. Labour (or capital) is distributed among r labour owners (r capital owners), each labourer (capitalist) owning exactly one single unit of labour (or capital). We denote by N_r the set of factor owners; thus $N_r = N_{1r} \cup N_{2r}$, with $N_{1r} = \{11, \ldots, 1j, \ldots, 1r\}$ and $N_{2r} = \{21, \ldots, 2j, \ldots, 2r\}$. We normalise the production function (F) in such a way that $F(1, 1) = 1$. Total output is thus equal to $F(r, r) = rF(1, 1) = r$. An *imputation* is a $2r$-tuple of numbers $\pi = (\pi_{11}, \ldots, \pi_{1r}; \pi_{21}, \ldots, \pi_{2r})$, with $\sum_{i=1}^{2} \sum_{j=1}^{r} \pi_{ij} = r$. A *coalition* is a subset of N_r. The aggregate factor-endowment of a coalition S is equal to $|S \cap N_{1r}|$ units of labour and $|S \cap N_{2r}|$ units of capital.[8] Accordingly, a coalition S can produce, by its own means,

$$F(|S \cap N_{1r}|, |S \cap N_{2r}|) \underset{\text{def}}{=} F(S).$$

Consider then a proposed imputation π of the total output r among the factor owners. If, for some coalition S, $F(S) > \sum_{ij \in S} \pi_{ij}$, then the coalition *S blocks* the proposed imputation. The *core* is the set of all unblocked imputations.

We denote a particular collusive scheme by C^r if there are r factor owners of each type. If no collusion takes place, i.e. if $C^r = C_0^r$, then *any* coalition S which is a subset of N_r may form. However, if a syndicate A_{1r} (or A_{2r}) forms among the labour owners (capital owners), then the syndicate collusive scheme $C^r = \{A_{1r}, A_{2r}; \{1j\}_{1j \in N_r \setminus A_{1r}}, \{2j\}_{2j \in N_r \setminus A_{2r}}\}$ obtains, and any coalition (S) which would include a proper subset of A_{1r} or A_{2r} is forbidden. The class of *permissible* coalitions is thus reduced to the set:

$$\{S \mid \text{either } S \cap A_{ir} = \emptyset, \text{ or } S \cap A_{ir} = A_{ir}, i = 1, 2\}.$$

The core, $\Pi(C^r)$, is the set of all imputations which are not blocked by any permissible coalition. Denote by k_1 (or k_2) the fraction of factor owners of type 1 (type 2) which are members of the syndicate A_{1r} (A_{2r}), i.e. $k_1 = |A_{1r}|/r$ (or $k_2 = |A_{2r}|/r$). We study now the internal stability of the syndicate collusive scheme (C^r) under the assumptions that: (i) both k_1 and k_2 are unambiguously smaller than one (no type is 'fully organised'); (ii) the amount of output obtained by each syndicate A_{ir} is uniformly distributed among its members.

PROPOSITION 1   No syndicate collusive scheme C^r is internally stable.

Proof   Let $\pi \in \Pi(C^r)$. First, let us show that, $\forall ij, ik \in N_{ir} \setminus A_{ir}$, $i = 1, 2$,

$$\pi_{ij} = \pi_{ik};$$

namely the core does not discriminate among the 'unorganised' factor owners of type i (notice that $N_{ir} \setminus A_{ir}$ is non-empty, by the assumption $k_i < 1$). Define

$$\pi_{i\min} = \operatorname*{Min}_{ij \in N_{ir} \setminus A_{ir}} \{\pi_{ij}\}; \quad \pi_{i\max} = \operatorname*{Max}_{ij \in N_{ir} \setminus A_{ir}} \{\pi_{ij}\}.$$

First, we must have $\pi_{1\min} + \pi_{2\min} \geq 1$: otherwise the coalition S consisting of a single, unorganised factor owner of each type receiving $\pi_{i\min}$ would block the arrangement, since they can produce together one unit of output. (This coalition is permissible, since it does not intersect either A_{1r}, or A_{2r}). On the other hand, $\pi_{1\max} + \pi_{2\max} \leq 1$; otherwise the coalition consisting of all factor owners, except the labourer receiving $\pi_{1\max}$ and the capitalist receiving $\pi_{2\max}$, would block the imputation. This coalition can indeed produce $F(r - 1, r - 1) = r - 1$, and would receive *less* than $r - 1$, if $\pi_{1\max} + \pi_{2\max} > 1$. Futhermore this coalition is permissible, since it includes both A_{1r} and A_{2r}. Consequently,

$$(\pi_{1\max} - \pi_{1\min}) + (\pi_{2\max} - \pi_{2\min}) \leq 0,$$

which implies

$$\pi_{1\max} = \pi_{1\min} \quad \text{and} \quad \pi_{2\max} = \pi_{2\min},$$

and the desired conclusion follows. Thus, any imputation π in $\Pi(C^r)$ is represented by 4 numbers, namely π_{11} (or π_{21}): the amount received by each syndicate member of A_1 (A_2) and π_{12} (π_{22}): the amount received by each 'unorganised' factor owner of type 1 (type 2). Now we prove that no syndicate collusive scheme C^r is internally stable. Suppose on the contrary that there exist C^r and $\pi \in \Pi(C^r)$, such that $\pi_{11} \geq \pi_{12}$, $\pi_{21} \geq \pi_{22}$, with strict inequality for at least one i, $i = \{1, 2\}$. Since π is an imputation, the equality

$$k_1 r \pi_{11} + (1 - k_1)\, r \pi_{12} + k_2 r \pi_{21} + (1 - k_2)\, r \pi_{22} = r$$

must hold. This equality may be rewritten as

$$k_1(\pi_{11} - \pi_{12}) + k_2(\pi_{21} - \pi_{22}) = 1 - (\pi_{12} + \pi_{22}) > 0,$$

where the last inequality follows from the fact that $\pi_{11} \geq \pi_{12}$, $\pi_{21} \geq \pi_{22}$, with strict inequality for at least one i. But then consider a coalition S consisting of a single unorganised worker and a single unorganised capitalist. This is a permissible coalition which can produce $F(S) = 1$, and this coalition receives $\pi_{12} + \pi_{22}$, and is strictly less than one, which is a contradiction. Q.E.D.

According to the above proposition, for all values of r, no syndicate collusive process is internally stable. *A contrario*, any imputation in $\Pi(C^r)$ which would discriminate between syndicate members and non-members, must necessarily give privilege to the non-members of at least one type. Does this mean that the syndicates' cohesiveness must necessarily slacken off? This is not certain: if the syndicate members are better treated at $\Pi(C^r)$ than they would be at $\Pi(C_0^r)$, i.e., in the core if no collusion exists, it might be advantageous for them to keep collusion running. This would be so despite the fact that some syndicate members are worse off than their similar companions who have remained outside the syndicate. But we are then led to study the *external* stability of C^r in the class (C^r, C_0^r). To proceed in that way, let us show that, *as r becomes large*, only the imputation which assigns their marginal product, i.e. the competitive pay-off, to the unorganised factor owners can remain in the core $\Pi(C')$. To that end, denote by π^r an imputation in $\Pi(C')$ and by π_i^r the amount assigned by this imputation to the unorganised factor owners of type i, $i = 1, 2$.

PROPOSITION 2   Let $\pi^r \in \Pi(C')$ for all r. Then

$$\lim_{r \to \infty} \{\pi_i^r\} = \frac{\partial F}{\partial z_1} \bigg|_{(1,1)}$$

Proof   First, for all r,

$$\pi_1^r + \pi_2^r \geq 1. \tag{1}$$

Otherwise, a coalition consisting of a single labourer and a single capitalist would block, contrary to the assumption that $\pi^r \in \Pi(C')$. Furthermore, consider for all r the coalition S consisting of all factor owners, except for a single, unorganised factor owner of type 1. This coalition can produce exactly $F(r - 1, r)$, and is a permissible coalition. Furthermore, it receives an amount of output equal to $r - \pi_1^r$. Accordingly, if $r - \pi_1^r < F(r - 1, r)$, the coalition S would block, contrary to the assumption that $\pi^r \in \Pi(C')$. Thus, for all r,

$$F(r - 1, r) \leq r - \pi_1^r,$$

or by homogeneity of degree one of F,

$$\frac{F(1, 1) - F(1 - \frac{1}{r}, 1)}{1/r} \geq \pi_1^r.$$

Moving to the limit we would obtain

$$\frac{\partial F}{\partial z_1} \bigg|_{(1, 1)} \geq \lim_{r \to \infty} \{\pi_1^r\}. \tag{2}$$

By a perfectly symmetric argument, using the coalition consisting of all factor owners except a single unorganised factor owner of type 2, we would get

$$\frac{\partial F}{\partial z_2} \bigg|_{(1,1)} \geq \lim_{r \to \infty} \{\pi_2^r\}. \tag{3}$$

Accordingly, by Euler's theorem,

$$1 \geq \frac{\partial F}{\partial z_1} \bigg|_{(1,1)} + \frac{\partial F}{\partial z_2} \bigg|_{(1,1)} \geq \lim_{r \to \infty} \{\pi_1^r + \pi_2^r\} \geq 1 \tag{4}$$

where the last inequality follows from (1). Consequently, combining (2), (3) and (4), we obtain

$$\frac{\partial F}{\partial z_i} \bigg|_{(1,1)} = \lim_{r \to \infty} \{\pi_i^r\}, \, i = 1, 2.$$

Q.E.D.

Thus, combining Propositions 1 and 2, we can conclude that, if r is large enough, *no syndicate collusive scheme C^r is unanimously stable relative to the disagreement scheme C_0^r*. Indeed, by Proposition 2, applied to the case $k_1 = k_2 = 0$, $\Pi(C_0^r)$ consists asymptotically of the sole competitive imputation. By the same proposition the unorganised factor owners approximately get their competitive pay-off at an imputation in $\Pi(C^r)$ for an r which is large enough. Since, by Proposition 1, there is at least one syndicate whose members are worse off under this imputation than the corresponding unorganised factor owners (and since not all factor owners can receive more than their marginal product), the members of one syndicate must receive *less* than their marginal product, which is the amount they would receive in the collusive scheme C_0^r; the conclusion therefore follows.

(2) AN EXAMPLE OF COLLUSIVE PRICE LEADERSHIP

In this section, we return to the price–leadership model which was called to mind above. The price–leadership arrangement in an industry has been formulated (see Markham, 1951) as a particularly useful practice of tacit co-ordination among business firms. As emphasised by Scherer (1980), it appears to be compatible with most anti-trust legislation. The particular form of this kind of arrangement that we want to illustrate is the one where a dominant group of firms act as a 'leader' in the choice of the industry price, and the other firms are supposed to react competitively to this given price. The usual argument in favour of this type of arrangement is that the set of firms outside the dominant cartel forms a 'fringe of competitors' and that each one of them is too small individually to expect to have any influence on the price. However, the stability analysis must be carried out when the possibility that a firm may quit (or join) the dominant group is introduced. We examine this question through a simple example, which we developed in common with Jacquemin and Weymark (1981).[9]

Suppose we are given an industry for an homogeneous product, in which each of a set N of n firms faces the same total cost

$C(q) = q^2/2$ for a quantity produced q. The firms are partitioned according to the following collusive scheme:

$$C_A = \{A, \{i\}_{i \in N \setminus A}\}, \qquad |A| = a \geqslant 2,$$

where the set A represents the dominant cartel. We see that, by varying a, we may vary the size of the dominant cartel – and hence generate a whole class of collusive schemes $\{C_A; a \geqslant 2\}$. The stability analysis which will follow the presentation of this example, will be relative to this class. For simplicity, again, we assume that total demand at price p is $D(p) = n(1 - p)$. Furthermore, we suppose that for a price chosen by the cartel A the firms in $N \setminus A$ maximise their individual profit, taking this price as given (they equate marginal cost to price). On the other hand, the dominant cartel is assumed to choose the price (p) which maximises the joint profit of its members given the quantity produced $S(p)$, at that price, by every firm in the competitive fringe. Hence, for every price p, they face only a 'residual' demand, which depends on the collusive scheme C_A, and is given by

$$D(p) - (n - a) S(p) = n - (2n - a)p,$$

since $S(p) = p$. Because all firms in the cartel are identical, maximising joint profit amounts to maximising profit for each firm in the cartel, which is

$$\pi_i(C_A, p) = \frac{p}{a} \, [n - (2n - a)p]$$
$$- \frac{1}{2} \left[\frac{n - (2n - a)p}{a} \right]^2, \qquad i \in A.$$

The optimal price can easily be computed as being

$$p^* = \frac{2}{4 - \left(\dfrac{a}{n} \right)^2}.$$

Finally, the maximum profit for each firm outside the cartel (for a given price p) is simply $p^2/2$. So we get the following outcome function:

$$\pi_i(C_A) = \frac{1}{2 \left(4 - \left(\dfrac{a}{n} \right)^2 \right)}, \qquad i \in A$$

$$\pi_i(C_A) = \cfrac{2}{\left[\; 4 - \left(\cfrac{a}{n}\right)^2 \;\right]^2}, \quad i \in N \backslash A.$$

Under the disagreement scheme (C_0) the outcome $\pi(C_0)$ is assumed to be the competitive outcome, which is obtained by letting $a = 0$ in the above expressions (or $\pi_i(C_0) = \frac{1}{8}$, $i = 1, \ldots, n$).

Three points are to be stressed with respect to this outcome function:

(i)   The profit of a firm outside the cartel is larger than the profit of a firm inside the cartel;
(ii) The profit of any firm (outside or inside the cartel) is increasing in a, the size of the cartel;
(iii) For $a \geq 2$, the profit of any firm is larger than the competitive profit.

These facts allow us to prove the following proposition, concerning cartel stability.

PROPOSITION 3   *In the price–leadership example,*
(a) *No (syndicate) collusive scheme C_A is internally stable.*
(b) *There exists a collusive scheme $\check{C}$, in the class $\{C_A\}$, which is individually stable relative to this class.*

Proof   The first statement is a direct consequence of (i). For statement (b), let us denote by (A_a) any cartel of size a, $a = 2, 3, \ldots, n$, and suppose that none of the corresponding collusive schemes is individually stable. Since, by (iii) no firm would gain by leaving a cartel A_2, we must have the result that one firm, and hence all firms, outside A_2, would gain by joining the cartel. But, then, by the same token, no firm would gain by leaving a cartel A_3. We must therefore have the result that some firm, and hence all firms, outside A_3 would gain by joining the cartel. Continuing in this fashion, we reach the conclusion that no firm would gain by leaving $A_n = N$, and hence that C_N is individually stable. The result follows by contradiction.   Q.E.D.

The proof given for statement (b) above is based on a general argument.[9] In fact, with the present, particular example, a sharper result may be demonstrated.

PROPOSITION 4   *In the price–leadership example, and for all $n \geq 3$, the collusive schemes C_A with $a = 3$ are the only individually-stable collusive schemes relative to the class $\{C_A\}$.*

Proof To be individually stable, a collusive scheme C_A should satisfy:

(1) $$\frac{n^2}{2[4n^2 - (a + 1)^2]} \leq \frac{2n^4}{(4n^2 - a^2)^2}$$

or, equivalently, $4n^2(a^2 - 2a - 1) \geq a^4$;

(2) $$\frac{2n^4}{[4n^2 - (a - 1)^2]^2} \leq \frac{n^2}{2[4n^2 - a^2]}$$

or, equivalently, $4n^2(a^2 - 4a + 2) \leq (a - 1)^4$, where (1) should hold only if $a < n$ and (2) only if $a > 1$.

It is easy to verify that (1) holds for $a = 3$ and $n \geq 4$ and that (2) holds for $a = 3$ and $n \geq 3$. Hence if $a = 3$, C_A, is individually stable for all $n \geq 3$.

Moreover (1) is not satisfied for $n \geq 3$ and $a < 3$, since then $(a^2 - 2a - 1) < 0$. Finally, let us analyse (2) when $n \geq a \geq 4$. Since $(a - 1)^4/(a^2 - 4a + 2)$ is positive and increasing in a (with $a \geq 4$), we have to show only that, for all $n \geq 4$, condition (2) is violated with $a = n$, i.e.,

$$4n^2 > \frac{(n - 1)^4}{(n^2 - 4n + 2)}$$

or, equivalently,

$$n(3n^2 - 12n + 2) > \frac{1}{n} - 4.$$

Because $(3n^2 - 12n + 2) > 0$, for $n \geq 4$, this last inequality holds for all $n \geq 4$.   Q.E.D.

It is interesting to consider this result in the case where we allow n to be very large: that is the case for which the assumption concerning the reaction of the competitive fringe seems more reasonable. Indeed, in that case, for any dominant cartel A representing a sufficient proportion of the total industry (i.e., $a/n > 3/n$), a firm inside the cartel would gain by leaving.

This conclusion is to be compared with the statement of Proposition 3, asserting the non-existence of an internally-stable (syndicate) collusive scheme (C_A).[10] This statement was based on the fact that the profit of a firm outside the cartel was larger than the profit of a firm inside the cartel, for any collusive scheme (C_A). Similarly here, when n is large enough, the negative impact of one firm leaving the dominant cartel on the profit of every firm (and especially every outsider) is negligible in comparison to the advantage of leaving. This is so whenever the size of the given cartel is sufficient to maintain the proportion of dominant firms almost unchanged. Under such conditions, the violation of individual stability almost coincides with the violation of internal stability. On the other hand, consider the individually- stable collusive schemes, those C_A for which $a = 3$. Then, examining the individual profits where 3 is substituted for a, we see that those profits all converge to the competitive profit $1/8$ when we let n grow. In other words, the advantage of price–leadership co-ordination vanishes when the number of firms becomes large.

IV CONCLUSION

In this chapter, we have presented, in a general form, some alternative stability concepts for collusive arrangements, based on two kinds of pay-off comparison: 'internal' comparisons for a given collusive scheme, and 'external' comparisons to different collusive schemes. Of course, one can imagine another conceptual basis and, indeed, other criteria to explain the stability of particular schemes: the existence of threats, the value of commitments, etc. We think, however, that the present approach provides a unifying framework for existing contributions on the subject. Hopefully, it could stimulate new applications. One can think, for instance, of alternative situations or models where these concepts would fit, and for which stability properties would be established. In particular, interesting phenomena, like entry, can be captured, using our framework. In many market situations, indeed, it turns out that, even if 'at the start' a large number of individual decision makers are involved in the group decision process, only a small subset of them could be considered as 'active' decision units. That happens because the others have no interest in entering the market. More specifically, the partitioning between 'active' or 'non-active' individual decision units leads to stability considerations of the kind discussed above.[11]

An essential element in these considerations is the introduction of a two-stage sequence of moves by the individual decision units. At the first stage, their decisions result in the determination of a particular collusive scheme: at the second stage, other kinds of decisions are made taking into account the chosen collusive scheme. This sequential element, and the deterrent implications that it has for individual behaviour, is common to all the numerous analyses of different types of pre-emptive strategies that can be used in industrial competition. They are treated elsewhere in this volume.

NOTES

1. We are grateful to A. Shaked for his comments and suggestions.
2. This kind of admissibility restriction on the set of feasible collusive schemes is also at the root of the Ψ-stability concept (see Luce and Raiffa, 1957, Chapter 10).
3. This terminology is borrowed from J. Jaskold Gabszewicz and J. H. Dréze (1971).
4. It is clear that the core is only one possibility. Other solution concepts like the bargaining set, or the Shapely value, might be more appropriate in other contexts.
5. $\Pi(\cdot)$ is defined here as a *correspondence*; in some applications, Π is a function, i.e., the set $\Pi(C)$ reduces to a single element $\pi(C)$. This remark is important, since most of the stability concepts proposed below may be given alternative (stronger or weaker) definitions based on the multiplicity of outcomes. For simplicity of exposition, we do not consider all such variations.
6. For such considerations, in the context of an extension of the Shapley value, see Hart and Kurz (1981).
7. See, for example, Westhoff (1977).
8. For any set T, $|T|$ denotes the cardinal of T.
9. For the application of this argument in a more general framework and for further analysis of the present example, the reader is referred to d'Aspremont *et al.* (1981). An extension of this example, where conjectural variations are introduced, is analysed in Donsimoni *et al.* (1981).
10. It is also to be compared with the assertions in Postlewaite and Roberts (1977).
11. For instance, assume that n identical firms are candidates to enter the market, but that only a subset of k of them, $k < n$, can make a positive profit under some outcome function. The collusive scheme $\{\{1, \ldots, k\}, \{k + 1\}, \ldots, \{n\}\}$ is individually stable since no excluded firm has an interest in entering, and no active firm has an interest in leaving. For an analysis of entry in this spirit see Selten and Güth (1982)

REFERENCES

Aumann, R. J. (1973) 'Disadvantageous Monopolies', *Journal of Economic Theory*, vol. 6, pp. 1–11.

d'Aspremont, C., Jacquemin, A., Gabszewicz, J. and Weymark, J. (1981) 'On the Stability of Collusive Price Leadership', *Canadian Journal of Economics*, vol. 16, no. 1, pp. 17–25.

Donsimoni, M. P., Ekonomides, N. S. and Polemarchakis, H. M. (1981) 'Stable Cartels', Working Paper, 8112 ENSAE, France.

Hansen, T. and Jaskold Gabszewicz, J. (1972) 'Collusion of Factor Owners and Distribution of Social Output', *Journal of Economic Theory*, vol. 4, pp. 1–18.

Hart, S. and Kurz, M. (1981) 'On the Endogenous Formation of Coalitions', Technical Report No. 328, IMSSS, Stanford University, USA.

Jaskold Gabszewicz, J. and Dréze, J. H. (1971) 'Syndicates of Traders in an Exchange Economy', in H. W. Kuhn and G. Szegö (eds), *Differential Games and Related Topics* (Amsterdam, North-Holland), pp. 399–414.

Luce, R. D. and Raiffa, H. (1957), *Games and Decisions*, (New York: John Wiley).

Markham, J. W. (1951) 'The Nature and Significance of Price-leadership', *American Economic Review*, vol. 41, pp. 1877–8.

Postlewaite, A. and Roberts J. (1977) 'A Note of the Stability of Large Cartels', *Econometrica*, vol. 45, pp. 1877–8.

Scherer, F. M. (1980), *Industrial Market Structure and Economic Performance*, 2nd edn, (New York: Rand McNally).

Selten, R. and Güth (1982) 'Equilibrium Point Selection in a Class of Market Entry Games', in M. Deistler, E. Fürst and G. Schwödiauer (eds), *Games, Economic Dynamics, and Time Series Analysis*, (Wurzburg-Vienna, Physica-Verlag).

Stigler, G. J. (1950) 'Monopoly and Oligopoly by Merger', *American Economic Review, Papers and Proceedings*, vol. 40 pp. 23–34.

Stigler, G. J. (1964) 'A Theory of Oligopoly', *The Journal of Political Economy*, vol. 72, pp. 44–61.

Tiebout, C. M. (1956) 'A Pure Theory of Local Expenditures', *The Journal of Political Economy*, vol. 64, pp. 416–24.

Westhoff, F. (1977) 'Existence of Equilibria in Economies with a Local Public Good', *Journal of Economic Theory*, vol. 14, pp. 84–112.

Discussion of the Paper by d'Aspremont and Gabszewicz

In discussing this paper, *Shaked* made a number of comments. First, he pointed out that stability in this paper required that no individual player in the game be better off in any new equilibrium that might arise should that player move between syndicates, or from a syndicate to the fringe group. The pay-off to player movement then depended critically on the solution concept used to describe the nature of the game after the movement had occurred. This solution concept should depend on the structure of the syndicate. For example, with many small syndicates, a non-co-operative concept would be appropriate, while if the structure consisted of a few large syndicates, a co-operative solution would be more appropriate. Shaked added that he understood the difficulties associated with attempting to resolve this problem. Next, Shaked commented that individual stability ignored the possibility that a group of players might jointly make themselves better off by leaving a syndicate. He wondered whether a stability concept could be usefully defined that was more closely related to the notion of a strong Nash equilibrium. Further, Shaked thought that some attention should be paid to the question of whether a syndicate would accept a new member, should someone decide to move. Finally, Shaked suggested that the concept of internal stability could best be applied when the agents in an economy were small. Otherwise, stability was best directed towards determining whether a coalition would disband completely if there was some better alternative available for the individual players.

Reinhard Selten proposed that the determination of co-operation within a game was an important issue that had not been analysed properly by game theorists. He praised this paper as a first step in this process. He suggested, however, that it might be inappropriate to apply co-operative solution concepts like the core to the second stage of a game when the analysis of stability in the first stage assumed non-co-operation. Selten added that the title 'internal stability' should be changed to something like 'syndicate advantage'. The reason was that 'internal stability' was not a stability concept in the usual sense, so that this title was misleading.

Dasgupta responded to Shaked's suggestion by noting that strong Nash equilibria need not always exist. A stability concept based on that notion might be of limited usefulness, since a stable syndicate structure could never be found.

Jacquemin suggested that oligopolies worked very hard at devising practices that would make co-ordination of strategies easier. He questioned whether the framework of the paper would allow one to analyse these issues. *Gabszewicz* replied that the paper did not analyse these issues directly, but that these problems could be incorporated into the analysis by enlarging the strategy spaces open to firms, or specifying the rules of the game more precisely.

Stiglitz proposed that players in an economic game were not intrinsically interested in co-operation, rather they co-operated because of the losses that they would suffer if they engaged in non-co-operative behaviour. This idea, he suggested, had been captured in the literature on repeated games, where co-operative solutions were achieved as the non-co-operative equilibria of games when players used appropriate threat strategies. Stiglitz wondered why d'Aspremont and Gabszewicz had taken the approach to the problem embodied in their paper.

Gabszewicz responded that he and d'Aspremont had wished to exploit the kind of structure suggested by the entry-deterrence literature, where the pre-entry equilibrium was conditional on the knowledge of players and that the post-entry equilibrium occurred as a result of their own actions. In the d'Aspremont–Gabszewicz paper, players foresaw the equilibrium that would occur after they deviated from the co-operative solution. This concept was in the entry-deterrence spirit since the deviator was similar to the first mover in any entry-deterrence game.

Stiglitz suggested that this specification did not prevent members of the cartel from making threats against firms who deviated. In repeated games, he suggested, these threats could even be made credible. For example, supergame strategies might involve commitments to punish firms who did not punish firms who violated agreements. In infinitely repeated games, such strategies could become Nash equilibria.

Gabszewicz responded that he had recently written a paper with Claude d'Aspremont looking at a related story. In this paper, they began with a continuum of firms all having unit capacity. If the entire market formed a cartel, then these firms would set a monopoly price. Of course, it was always possible for some small sub-set of all firms to deviate from this monopoly solution. The question then became whether the reduction in the cartels' profits would be large enough to cause them to respond. Since firms had limited capacity, however, their supply would not depress the cartel price very much. Under some conditions, the cartel would not find it profitable to respond to this deviation.

Curtis Eaton suggested that any coalition structure that was individually stable in the sense of the d'Aspremont–Gabszewicz paper, would be stable with respect to threats.

Spence suggested that the best way to view the problem of cartel stability was to consider competition on two levels – competition in the formation of groups and competition in the determination of prices once these groups had been formed. The ways that firms interacted on the first of these competitive levels was unspecified, and as a consequence, allowed threat strategies. Individual stability, then, constituted a necessary but not sufficient condition for equilibrium in the first level of competition.

Selten referred to the example given in the paper of the dominant-firm competitive-fringe and asked why the only stable syndicate structure involved only three firms, and in particular, why this number should be independent of the number of firms in the market. d'Aspremont responded that the example was from a more general paper with Jacquemin and Weymark (1982) where the existence of a stable cartel was established. There was no reason to expect the number of firms in this cartel to be 3, or to be independent of the number of firms in the market. Shaked explained that this particular result flowed from a specification of market demand which was linear in prices and multiplicative in the number of consumers.

REFERENCE

d'Aspremont, C., Jacquemin, A., Gabszewicz, J. and Weymark, J. (1982) 'On the Stability of Dominant Cartels' *Canadian Journal of Economics*, vol. 14, no. 1, pp. 17–25.

9 Practices that (Credibly) Facilitate Oligopoly Co-ordination[1]

Steven C. Salop

GEORGETOWN UNIVERSITY LAW CENTER, USA

I INTRODUCTION

It is now well established in both the economic and legal literature that successful price co-ordination (either express or tacit) is not inevitable – even in highly concentrated industries protected by insurmountable barriers to entry. The key to this insight is the recognition that even though oligopolists' fates are interdependent, individual self-interests are not perfectly consonant. As a result, oligopolists may find it difficult to agree on a mutually acceptable co-operative outcome, achieve that outcome smoothly, and maintain it over time in the face of exogenous shocks and private incentives to deviate. In the current language of industrial organisation, the joint profit-maximising point may not be a Nash equilibrium.

The likelihood of successful co-ordination may be increased by the adoption of industry practices that increase oligopolists' incentives to co-operate and reduce their incentives to compete, despite their divergent interests. Contractual provisions can add credibility to such tacit agreements, because they will be enforced by courts. Anti-trust commentators refer to such practices as 'facilitating devices'. Some courts have called them 'plus factors'. Economic theorists can model these practices as profit penalties and pricing constraints that have the effect of altering the oligopoly equilibrium point. Analysis of these practices is the subject of this chapter.

The rest of the chapter is organised as follows. Section II briefly

265

reviews the analytic approaches to strategic interaction in oligopolistic industries. The material in this section is not new, but it provide a useful foundation for analysing facilitating practices. The practices are introduced in Section III. Sections IV and V discuss two examples of contractual provisions that can function as facilitating devices – 'most favoured nation' clauses and 'meeting competition' clauses. A number of other practices are also discussed briefly in these two sections. Section VI discusses the role of 'meeting competition' clauses in credible entry deterrence. Rationales for considering the practices in terms of their effects on efficiency are taken up briefly in the concluding Section VII.

II   THE SIMPLE ANALYTICS OF TACIT CO-ORDINATION: REVIEW

Successful oligopolistic co-ordination consists of three elements – *agreement* about the co-operative outcome, *achievement* of that outcome, and *maintenance* of the outcome over time, in the face of changing conditions and private incentives to 'compete.

Agreement is difficult whenever firms' interests do not exactly correspond. It may be true that raising prices may increase the industry's joint profits. However, unless there is a binding profit-sharing arrangement, higher profits for one rival may come at the others' expense. When non-price variables such as product design, delivery schedules and customer service must also be set, the agreements become unavoidably complex. The desire to indulge in price discrimination also complicates the agreement. Moreover, in a dynamic context, the agreement must be constantly renegotiated or must be made contingent on changing conditions. Otherwise, the agreement will become less profitable when changes occur. Of course, the difficulties in reaching an agreement are compounded when laws prohibit the negotiation of express agreements. In place of open negotiations, the oligopolists then rely instead on tacit understandings subtly signalled through newspaper interviews and at trade association meetings.

Once agreement is reached, the co-operative outcome must still be achieved. This may be a trivial matter for a legal cartel that can openly rely on a court-enforced contract. However, this is not the case for illegal price fixing schemes and for tacit co-ordination. Without such contracts, agreements may not be 'binding'.

The familiar model of a repeated Prisoners' Dilemma game illustrates these difficulties. Suppose the industry consists of two firms – call them Ethyl and DuPont – which produce differentiated products at identical costs.[2] Suppose that as a result of government regulation or some other insurmountable barrier to entry, additional entry is impossible. To eliminate the additional analytic complexity created by asymmetric positions in the industry, assume that consumer demands for the rivals' products are symmetric.[3] Consider the 'strategy space' for each rival to be the set of its prices over an infinite time horizon, or $(p_1, p_2, . . .)$.

Our analysis focuses on the *relative credibility* of possible dynamic equilibria. A *credible equilibrium* is an outcome that can be achieved and maintained over time by firms that exhibit foresight, but which are unable to commit themselves in advance to future prices. That is, in every time period each firm is assumed to select a price that maximises the present discounted value of its profits, taking into consideration its rivals' likely best responses to its price choice. The simple Nash–Cournot equilibrium point may or may not also be a credible equilibrium outcome, as will be discussed below. The term *relative* credibility emphasises that an outcome may be a credible equilibrium (or not) with respect to some information sets and to some degrees of strategic sophistication but not to others. Because some firms may be more or less informed and sophisticated than others, the analysis is not restricted to a single definition of credibility. It should also be emphasised at the outset that many of these results can also be derived as simple Nash equilibria in analogous static models.

(A) TACIT CO-ORDINATION AND THE PRISONERS' DILEMMA

To facilitate the exposition, we shall illustrate these concepts with simple examples. In these examples, each duopoly firm chooses its price in each period from among a finite set of prices (generally two). Table 9.1 illustrates the simplest 2×2 structure for the Prisoners' Dilemma. In this example, each firm can select either a high price (p_H) or a low price (p_L).

The entries in Table 9.1 give the firms' profits in a single period for different pricing combinations in that period. The particular numbers are chosen for illustrative purposes only. We denote a pricing outcome by the specific pair of prices chosen by the rivals. Ethyl's price is entered first. Thus, the price pair (p_H, p_L) indicates that Ethyl

TABLE 9.1   THE PRISONERS' DILEMMA

		DuPont			
		p_H	p_L	p_H	p_L
Ethyl	p_H	100	−10	100	140
	p_L	140	70	−10	70
		Ethyl's pay-offs		DuPont's pay-offs	

charges p_H and DuPont charges p_L. However, joint profits for the price pair (p_H, p_H) exceed joint profits both for the off-diagonal pairs (p_L, p_H) and (p_H, p_L) and for the diagonal price pair (p_L, p_L). We therefore denote (p_H, p_H) as the joint profit maximising (or *co-operative*) point. A co-operative agreement would require that Ethyl and DuPont each charge the high price p_H. We denote (p_L, p_L) as the *competitive* point.

Inter-seller price setting contracts generally violate the anti-trust laws. Lack of a binding contract may make it difficult for DuPont and Ethyl to co-ordinate their behaviour even temporarily, even if they reach a meeting of the minds on the mutual desirability of the co-operative strategy p_H. Beginning from the competitive outcome (p_L, p_L), if the dates of the rivals' price increases to p_H are not co-ordinated, then the price leader's profits are reduced during the transition period. In Table 9.1, if Ethyl raises its price first, its profits fall to −10 until DuPont follows with its own price increase. Of course, DuPont's profits rise to 140 during the transition. Thus, DuPont has every incentive to delay its price increase. Fear of further delays may convince Ethyl that it should return to p_L or should forego the price increase to begin with. As a result, the process of attaining the joint profit point may be interrupted.[4]

It may appear that the 'transitional' difficulties of achieving the co-operative outcome are only a one-time problem. However, this view overlooks the dynamic elements of oligopoly interaction. As cost and demand parameters change over time, the joint profit-maximising point changes as well. Thus, oligopolists face repeated transitional problems. As we demonstrate below, certain industry practices can facilitate the transitions and so make co-operation more credible, allowing the price pair (p_H, p_H) to be achieved repeatedly.

Once achieved, we have the familiar Prisoners' Dilemma – the co-operative outcome must be maintained, despite the oligopolists' incentives to compete. Of course, this problem is similar to the difficulties faced in reaching the joint profit point initially. The co-operative point $(p_H\ p_H)$ is not a simple Nash equilibrium for the single-period Prisoners' Dilemma game. For example, if Ethyl lowers its price to p_L, its profits rise in the short run to 140.

Following Stigler (1968) by viewing the model as a repeated game complicates the analysis as follows. Given the pay-off structure of Table 9.1, once DuPont detects Ethyl's price reduction, it has an incentive to match the price cut; this strategy raises its profits from -10 to 70. Assuming that there is a sufficient time lag between Ethyl's price cut and DuPont's response, a price cut by Ethyl is profitable. This destabilises the co-operative outcome. DuPont's incentive to cut price and Ethyl's incentive to match that cut, are symmetric, of course. In short, in the repeated game, unless detection lags are sufficiently short, each oligopolist has an incentive to cheat. Thus, the co-operative outcome may not be a credible dynamic equilibrium for the repeated game.

It is well known that the incentive of one firm – say Ethyl – to deviate from the co-operative solution depends on its relative profits in the four states (p_H, p_H), (p_L, p_H), (p_L, p_L), and (p_H, p_L) and the relative time intervals spent in each state. The time intervals are themselves endogenously determined by the likelihood, and also the speed of detection of price changes and of the response by one's rival as well as by the dynamics by which the joint profit point might be reached again if and when co-operation breaks down. Formally, denoting the profits to Ethyl at the price pair (p_i, p_j), as V_{ij}, and assuming that the joint profit outcome can *never* be achieved again once it is lost, Ethyl will deviate from p_H if

$$V_{HH} < bV_{LH} + (1 - b)V_{LL} \tag{1}$$

Here the weight b is endogenous and depends upon all the relative time intervals and on Ethyl's time and risk discount rates. The expected relative time intervals depend in turn on Ethyl's expectations about DuPont's behaviour and, hence on DuPont's own incentives.[5]

Most formal analyses of tacit co-ordination have focused on the issue of detecting deviations from the co-operative strategy. Stigler's (1968) model is the classic work, followed by Orr and MacAvoy (1965) on the profitability of cheating given exogenous detection lags. Osborne (1976) analyses a set of oligopoly decision rules that induce stability. More recently, Green and Porter (1981) have erected a stochastic demand model in which both false positive and false negative signals of cheating can occur, and in which the length of price wars (i.e., the time interval spent at (p_L, p_L)) is endogenously determined.

In most formal models, a retaliatory response occurs immediately, once deviations away from the joint profit point are detected.[6] Indeed, this incentive to retaliate has been explicitly built into the Table 9.1 pay-off matrix. On the other hand, if the strategy space is expanded to include *selective discounts* and other limited cheating tactics, retaliation may not be inevitable even after discounts have been detected.[7] First, Ethyl's discount may be offered to a marginal DuPont customer, that is, one to which DuPont had been charging a price approximately equal to marginal cost (including service costs). Even more germane for our purposes is the fact that some contractual provisions can make retaliation more costly. As discussed in detail in the following sections, *meeting competition* and *most favoured nation* clauses in sales contracts can affect both the incentives to discount and the incentives to retaliate against discounts that are detected.

Before turning to an analysis of these contractual provisions, we first examine cases in which tacit co-ordination is successful.

(B) PURE TACIT CO-ORDINATION

Despite all the difficulties, successful tacit co-ordination is not impossible. Pay-offs may have a structure that permits the co-operative outcome to be a credible (or even a simple Nash) equilibrium. This can occur in two ways. First, as was discussed in the context of the Table 9.1 pay-off structure, if the detection lag and the discount rate are small enough and if Vp_{HL} and Vp_{LH} are sufficiently small relative to V_{LL} and Vp_{HH}, then the co-operative point (p_H, p_H) may be a credible dynamic equilibrium.

Alternatively, if V_{LH} is less than V_{HH}, then we can also have (p_H, p_H) as a simple Nash equilibrium. This is illustrated in Table 9.2 below, where Ethyl and DuPont's respective off-diagonal pay-offs are reduced from 140 to 90.

Given this pay-off structure, the co-operative outcome (p_H, p_H) can both be achieved and maintained, if firms are sophisticated strategists. Beginning at (p_L, p_L), if Ethyl raises its price to P_H, its profits fall to -10. However, unlike the position in the standard Prisoner's Dilemma, DuPont now has an incentive to raise its price immediately in order to increase its profits from 90 to 100. Knowing this, it is in Ethyl's interest to raise its price openly. Thus, the competitive equilibrium outcome (p_L, p_L), can be avoided; it is not a credible equilibrium. Of course the competitive point (p_L, p_L) remains a simple Nash equilibrium.

TABLE 9.2   THE PURE TACIT CO-ORDINATION

		\multicolumn{4}{c}{DuPont}			
		p_H	p_L	p_H	p_L
Ethyl	p_H	100	–10	100	90
	p_L	90	70	–10	70
		\multicolumn{2}{c}{Ethyl's pay-offs}	\multicolumn{2}{c}{DuPont's pay-offs}

The analysis for maintaining the co-operative outcome is analogous. In contrast to what happens with the standard Prisoner's Dilemma, if Ethyl lowers its price to p_L, its profits fall from 100 to 90; its incentive to discount is therefore eliminated. Not even an unsophisticated Ethyl will lower its price. DuPont's incentives are identical. Thus, in Table 9.2, (p_H, p_H) is a simple Nash equilibrium as well as a credible equilibrium. It can be both achieved and maintained if DuPont and Ethyl are sufficiently sophisticated.

III   PRACTICES THAT FACILITATE OLIGOPOLISTIC CO-ORDINATION

Unfortunately for potential colluders, pay-off matrices do not always satisfy the pure tacit co-ordination structure of Table 9.2. Nor are detection lags always short enough to make a credible equilibrium out of the repeated version of the Prisoners' Dilemma game in Table 9.1. Therefore, as an alternative, the oligopolists must consciously or fortuitously discover and implement some means of restructuring their pay-offs, so as to facilitate the achievement and maintenance of the co-operative outcome. We refer to these as *facilitating practices*.[8]

There are two distinct effects of facilitating practices, namely *information exchange* and *incentive management*. Although particular practices often combine elements of both roles, it is useful to distinguish between them. Because the information exchange effect is better understood, we shall discuss it only briefly and focus instead on incentive management.

Information exchange facilitates both explicit and tacit co-ordination by eliminating uncertainty about rivals' actions. Classic examples of information exchanges are inter-seller verification of price quotations and advance notice of price changes. In each case, the exchange of information shortens or eliminates detection lags and, therefore, the time interval spent in off-diagonal price-pair states. By decreasing the transitional losses from price rises and the transitional gains from price discounts, incentives are altered in such a way as to make the joint profit outcome easier to achieve and maintain.[9]

The incentive management role of facilitating practices functions by *directly* altering the structure of the pay-off matrix, rather than by working through the medium of information exchange. By restructuring pay-offs, the incentives for a firm to offer price discounts or to raise prices may be directly affected.[10] Similarly, a firm may change its incentives in order to match price changes initiated by its rivals, thereby affecting its rivals' incentives to initiate such price changes. In this way, the adoption of facilitating practices can convert competitive oligopoly outcomes into simple Nash (or credible) equilibria at the co-operative point.

For example, consider the following static model. Let $V_i(p_1, p_2)$ denote the profit function for firm i ($i = 1, 2$), given the prices p_1 and p_2 respectively for the two firms.[11] Profit-maximisation by each firm implies a simple Nash equilibrium (p_1, p_2) satisfying the respective first-order conditions, or

$$\frac{dV_i}{dp_i} = 0 \qquad i = 1, 2 \tag{2}$$

If $V_i(p_1, p_2)$ is altered, say by the adoption of an incentive management device, the Nash equilibrium changes.

Perhaps the purest example of an incentive management device is a monetary penalty on price discounts. For example, beginning from the Table 9.1 pay-off matrix and an equilibrium at (p_L, p_L), suppose that DuPont and Ethyl each contract with separate third parties. Suppose these contracts require a payment to the third party of a penalty equal to 50 if the firm charges any of its customers a price below p_H, and if that price cut is not matched by the rival seller. These penalties transform the rivals' pay-offs into the Table 9.2 pay-off matrix which has a credible (and simple Nash) equilibrium at (p_H, p_H). The penalty scheme successfully raises industry joint profits, relative to Table 9.1.

Incentive management devices can also be created by the provision of purchase contracts between an oligopolist and his customers. Embedding an incentive management device into a sales contract has a number of advantages. First, the use of a contract (with a purchaser or a third party) allows the oligopolist to make a binding commitment to transform his pay-off matrix. If necessary, a public court will enforce the contract. Thus, the credibility of the promised behaviour is increased.[12] Moreover, the ability to collect damages gives the buyer an incentive to ensure performance of the contract and to bear the costs of enforcing it. If the buyer is better situated than rivals or third parties to detect price discounts, this can increase the efficiency of enforcement. Of course, more efficient enforcement increases the credibility of a promise.

The obvious question is why rational buyers would be willing to act as accomplices in achieving this possibly anti-competitive conduct. To the extent that the contractual provision makes price discounting less desirable or price increases less risky, it is difficult to see why buyers would agree to clauses that have such an effect.[13] The answer lies in the possibility of designing contractual provisions that are valued by each buyer individually even while they create an external cost to all other buyers. If such clauses can be developed, though each buyer willingly accepts (or even purchases) the clause, the collective acceptance of the clause by all buyers eliminates the individual benefit by stabilising the sellers' joint profit outcome. A court might characterise this impact as a 'free rider effect in reverse'.

We now turn to a number of examples of practices that can transform incentives in this way. It should be noted that these practices sometimes have procompetitive and efficiency benefits as well as potential anti-competitive effects. For the present, we focus on the latter and discuss some of the efficiency benefits in the final section. This choice of emphasis does not reflect a belief that the anti-competitive effects are always larger or more important, or that courts should take a *per se* approach to these practices. Rather, it implies that the subject of this chapter is strategic interaction and oligopoly equilibrium, a careful balancing of benefits against their likely anti-competitive impact is necessarily beyond the scope of the analysis.

IV MOST-FAVOURED-NATION CLAUSES

A *most-favoured-nation* (MFN) clause in a sales contract provides the buyer with insurance protection against the contingency that the seller may offer a lower price to another customer. These clauses may prevent price discrimination when the seller offers a discounted price to another buyer, either in the future (a 'retroactive' MFN) or in the present (a 'contemporaneous' MFN). Although all MFNs change the seller's incentives in the same general way, the argument is clearer if we illustrate some issues with the case of a retroactive MFN and others with a contemporaneous MFN.

(A) RETROACTIVE MFN

Consider an industry – for example, that produces large scale steam-turbine generators[14] – in which customers that are public utilities contract for the purchase of custom manufactured generators. Because delivery occurs many months after the contract is made, increased competition, reduced demand, or a reduction in costs during the intervening time period may reduce the average price paid by later buyers for comparable generators. By placing the following MFN clause in the sales agreement, early buyers may share that price decrease:

> If at any time before [buyer] takes delivery of said generator, [seller] offers a lower price for a generator of comparable size and quality to any other purchaser, [seller] will also offer that lower price to [buyer].

That is, any future price decreases must be rebated to the buyer.[15] This rebate mechanism effectively creates a penalty system similar to the one discussed in Section III and illustrated in Table 9.2. The MFN requires the seller to pay a monetary penalty if he reduces his price.[16] Because price decreases are penalised, they are discouraged. Thus, if all rivals provide all buyers with MFN protection, the co-operative outcome (p_H, p_H) can be stabilised, once it is achieved.[17]

Cooper (1981) has shown that following Schelling (1960), provision of an MFN *by even one rival* only may be advantageous to all sellers, including the one that institutes the MFN. This is a strong result, because a seller's unilateral adoption of an MFN also places it at a competitive disadvantage – it is deterred from matching selective discounts offered by its rivals. However, as demonstrated by Cooper, this competitive disadvantage may be more than offset by the effect of the clause in stabilising a higher price.

This outcome is illustrated in the Table 9.3 pay-off matrix below. Beginning from Table 9.1, this matrix adds the possibility of charging a third price p_M, where $p_L < p_M < p_H$. Relative to Table 9.1, it also assumes that one rival, Ethyl, offers an MFN which requires it to pay a penalty of 50 for any price decreases below an initial price, whether matched by DuPont or not. Since the penalty is paid only for price decreases, the matrix is constructed contingent on these being a particular initial price pair. In Table 9.3, the assumed initial point is the asymmetric price pair (p_H, p_M).

We may illustrate the possibility of a credible equilibrium exising at the asymmetric price pair (p_H, p_M) as follows. DuPont has no incentive to raise its price to p_H. The penalty provision of the MFN eliminates Ethyl's incentive to lower its price to p_M or p_L. Assuming detection and retaliation can be carried out swiftly, DuPont has no incentive to lower its price to p_L; for if it does Ethyl will quickly respond by lowering its price to p_M. By contrast, without the MFN, (p_L, p_L) might be the equilibrium, because the short term gains from cutting price are relatively larger if the MFN is eliminated.[18] If the equilibrium is altered in this way, Ethyl's profits rise from 70 (without the MFN) to 80 (with the MFN), in spite of its induced competitive disadvantage. DuPont's profits rise from 70 to 130. These results illustrate Cooper's proof of existence.

TABLE 9.3   RETROACTIVE MFN

			DuPont				
		p_H	p_M	p_L	p_H	p_M	p_L
	p_H	100	⃝80	–10	100	⃝130	140
Ethyl	p_M	80	40	30	80	90	125
	p_L	90	75	20	–10	80	70
		Ethyl's pay-offs			DuPont's pay-offs		

(B) CONTEMPORANEOUS MFN

Most-favoured-nation clauses are also found in long-term requirements contracts governing the sale of repeatedly purchased industrial supplies. These clauses insure buyers against contemporaneous price discrimination in favour of other buyers.[19] Consider the following standard form:

> If [seller] should, during the term of this contract, offer or sell goods of equal quality and quantity to any other buyer at a price lower than that provided for herein, [buyer] shall receive the benefit of such lower price on all shipments made hereunder for which such lower price is effective.

This clause differs somewhat from the retroactive MFN. Whereas the retroactive MFN penalises all price reductions made at some date, this contemporaneous MFN penalises and deters only *selective discounts*, that is, price cuts that are restricted to a limited number of customers.[20] General price cuts are not penalised or deterred. Thus, selective discounts are made relatively less profitable than general price cuts. In that oligopoly competition takes the form of selective discounts, the MFN may serve to stabilise the co-operative outcome.

Since general price cuts are not penalised by a contemporaneous MFN, adjustments to a *co-operative* outcome at a lower price are not deterred if they become necessary.[21] Similarly, the ability to retaliate through a general price reduction against rivals' secret discounts is not constrained. Only selective discounts are penalised.

Gelman and Salop (1982) construct a formal model in which an oligopolist does not respond to the limited selective discounts initiated by his rival. Assuming that the existence of secret discounts is detected, but that the identity of the customers offered the discounts is not, then selective matching of secret discounts is clearly impossible. At the same time, retaliation through a general, matching price cut may not be in the oligopolist's own interests if the selective discounts were not offered widely.[22]

As this analysis shows, a contemporaneous MFN constrains the oligopolist's response in the same way as would its inability to identify the customers who were offered discounts. For example, suppose that DuPont offers a selective discount to a limited number of Ethyl's customers and suppose that Ethyl can identify these customers. However, suppose that due to the MFN, it is only feasible for Ethyl to respond with a general price cut to all its customers. In this case, Ethyl will compare the profit reduction from this customer loss to the alternative of offering a general price cut to all its customers, including those not approached by DuPont. The bigger is DuPont's discount and the fewer the customers that are approached by DuPont, the relatively more costly is a matching response by Ethyl. Hence, the more likely it is that Ethyl will accommodate the discounts rather than respond with a general price cut. In short, if DuPont restricts its secret discounting, it is more profitable for Ethyl to accommodate this rather than touch off a price war.

At the same time, the contemporaneous MFN also prevents Ethyl from offering its own selective discounts to DuPont's customers. Thus, if Ethyl has an MFN and DuPont does not, a credible equilibrium may exist at the point where Ethyl offers the high price (p_H) to all its customers, and DuPont offers the price (p_H) to most customers and a discount price (p_L) to the rest. If both rivals offer an MFN, elimination of all selective discounting may stabilise the co-operative outcome (p_H, p_H).

An example of this analysis is provided in Table 9.4. Denoting a selective discount strategy as p_H/p_L, Table 9.4 is constructed by expanding the strategy space of Table 9.1 to include the possibility of a selective discount strategy (p_H/p_L) for either rival.[23] Of course, an MFN will prevent a firm from offering selective discounts.

TABLE 9.4   CONTEMPORANEOUS MFN

		DuPont					
		p_H	p_H/p_L	p_L		p_H	p_H/p_L	p_L
	p_H	100	80	−10		100	130	140
Ethyl	p_H/p_L	130	(85)	20		80	(85)	60
	p_L	140	60	70		−10	20	70
		Ethyl's pay-offs				DuPont's pay-offs		

Three cases must be considered: (i) No MFN; (ii) MFN by one rival only (e.g., Ethyl); and (iii) MFN by both rivals.

No MFN   If neither rival is constrained by an MFN, the co-operative solution (p_H, p_H) represents a credible equilibrium only for sufficiently rapid rates of detection, as was discussed earlier. Because selective discounts are more difficult to detect than general price cuts, (p_H, p_H) may be immune only to general cuts – not to selective discounts. In this case it is usually argued that the selective discounting price pair (p_H/p_L, p_H/p_L) is more likely to represent the credible equilibrium than (p_H, p_H).[24] Assume that is the case here.

MFN by Ethyl only   If Ethyl unilaterally institutes a contemporaneous MFN, it effectively commits itself to eliminate the strategy p_H/p_L. In this case, as was discussed earlier and illustrated in Table 9.4, it is not profitable for Ethyl to match DuPont's selective discounts with a general price cut to p_L.[25] Assuming that general discounts are deterred by rapid detection and retaliation, the outcome (p_H, p_H/p_L) is the credible equilibrium.[26]

MFN by both rivals   If both rivals institute an MFN, only general discounts are feasible. As was discussed above, if rivals always match detected general price cuts but do not match detected selective discounts, then, if detection is sufficiently rapid, neither rival will deviate from p_H. Thus, the co-operative outcome (p_H, p_H) may become a credible equilibrium.

This demonstrates how the adoption of an MFN can improve the likelihood of the co-operative outcome being a credible equilibrium. The mutual or unilateral adoption of most favoured nation clauses can be in the self-interest of the oligopolists.[27]

In spite of this anti-competitive effect, buyers may be willing to 'purchase' the 'protection' of an MFN for two reasons. First, insurance protection against price reductions may have value to risk-averse buyers. The MFN provides this insurance.[28] Of course, broad MFN protection reduces the probability that a lower price will ever materialise because it induces an adverse incentive (a 'moral hazard') for sellers who provide it. However, for any individual buyer, this effect may be small relative to the insurance benefit. Instead, the adverse incentive is mainly an 'external' effect that injures other buyers. The profit-maximising purchaser does not include this external effect in his calculus. Thus, the more buyers there are in the market, the more likely it is that the price stabilising effect will be ignored by buyers.[29]

In addition, a buyer who does add this potential injury to other buyers into his profit calculus may count that injury as a benefit, not as a cost. If rival buyers are also his downstream product market competitors, then his profitability is enhanced when his rivals' costs rise.[30] Looking at the problem in this way, a buyer may be willing to pay more for an MFN, because the MFN acts as a type of bribe to the seller aimed at inducing him to forego deeper discounts to rival buyers.

(C)   PRICES POSTED, RELATIVE VALUE SCALES, AND PRODUCT
      STANDARDS

The provision of a most-favoured-nation clause would appear to require a long-term supply contract. However, this is unnecessary. In fact, a number of common pricing conventions have effects similar or even equivalent to those of an MFN.

Whenever a seller deals in a market in which all transactions are consummated at an identical (posted) price, the analysis of the MFN is applicable. Indeed, the making of transactions only at a single list price is the essence of an MFN.[31] The only difference is that an MFN is a binding contractual clause, whereas price posting (with no discounts permitted) is normally adopted unilaterally and voluntarily.[32] One way a firm might effect a binding commitment without a contract is rapidly to make all of its transactions prices public. Then, those buyers who discover they have paid more than some other buyers may have a powerful tool for negotiating a matching discount.

A similar analysis can be applied to *relative value scales* and other multiproduct pricing formulæ. A relative value scale is a pricing system in which there is a fixed relationship among the prices of a number of products, which thereby restrict price movements to proportional changes in all prices. For example, a car repair shop might set an hourly rate and apply a standard job completion time table from a private or trade association publication (a 'flat rate manual').[33] In this case, the job completion times in the flat rate manual define the relative value scale. Insurers like Blue Cross sometimes use relative value scales for setting reimbursement levels for medical services.[34] Hay (1979) notes the similar effect of the 'price simplification' scheme used by GE and Westinghouse.

Product standardisation can also be analogised to an MFN. By setting the product attributes that define the standard, product standardisation eliminates some non-price competition: no seller can offer more or less of the standardised product attributes in an individual product. As a result, all competition must be in the price dimension. Given the large efficiency benefits of product standardisation, it is likely that the efficiency benefits will normally swamp any anti-competitive effects. However, *National Macaroni* suggests a possible anti-competitive use of product standardisation. This case concerned standardisation of a grain mix. Following a shortfall in the harvest of Durum wheat (semolina), the grain purchaser defendants agreed to fix the ratio of semolina and farina in macaroni. By preventing competition for the scarce supplies of the more expensive and preferred semolina variety, total costs could have been reduced at the expense of wheat farmers.[35]

V MEETING COMPETITION CLAUSES

A *meeting competition clause* (MCC) in a long term supply contract or advertisement provides the buyer with insurance protection against a lost opportunity in the contingency that the buyer is offered a lower price by some other seller.[36] The level of protection offered by an MCC depends on the exact form the provision takes. One common variant is the *meet or release* (MOR) clause, as illustrated by the following example.[37]

> If the [buyer] should be offered by a responsible manufacturer anti-knock compound of equal quality and in a quantity equivalent to or less than that remaining as a commitment hereunder, at a lower delivered cost to the [buyer], and [buyer] gives [seller] satisfactory evidence thereof before the date on which any shipment is required, [seller] shall either supply such quantity of compound at the lower cost or permit [buyer] to purchase elsewhere. Any quantity so purchased shall be deducted from the quantity deliverable under this contract.

The meet or release clause serves mainly as an information exchange device. If the buyer discovers a lower price elsewhere, he cannot escape from his obligation to purchase from his original supplier without informing that supplier of the lower price.[38] By requiring this flow of information, the clause eliminates any detection lag. Thus, the seller is protected against the possibility of losing sales to a rival offering an undetected discount to a current customer. In this way, an MOR facilitates the selective matching of otherwise secret discounts. Assuming that the seller wishes to match the discount, the rival's strategy is countered. As a result, the joint profit outcome is made relatively more credible.

(A) NO-RELEASE MCC

It is unlikely that a seller would choose to *meet* rather than *release* in all cases. For example, if a rival offers a price below the seller's marginal cost, the seller has no direct incentive to match.[39] Likewise, the seller has no incentive to match a discount which he suspects the buyer will reject. For example, if the rival's product is of lower quality or otherwise unsuitable, the buyer might be suspected of using the lower bid simply as a bluff in order to obtain a better deal.[40]

In these cases, an MOR clause offers no protection to the buyer. The buyer prefers, *ceteris paribus*, a contractual provision that allows the seller no escape. This can be accomplished by deleting the *release* language from the provision. Of course, such a *no-release* MCC may lead to allocative inefficiencies.[41] However, if the seller's primary interest is in deterring rivals' discounts, the losses entailed by this inefficiency may be small relative to the anti-competitive benefit of the clause. For, by deleting the *release* option, the clause is made a more credible deterrent. Now, the seller must meet all rivals' offers.

Formally, in the 2×2 example, the co-operative outcome is stabilised as follows. If both rivals provide *no-release* MCCs the off-diagonal price pairs (p_L, p_H) and (p_H, p_L) are made unattainable. Given the remaining choice between the two diagonal price pairs (p_H, p_H) and (p_L, p_L), neither oligopolist wishes to deviate from the joint profit outcome.

An MCC also facilitates the successful achievement of the co-operative outcome. For example, a seller who provides a *no-release* MCC to current customers can raise price to p_H without losing any sales to a lower priced rival. Buyers are automatically given the rival's lower price until all firms raise their prices. This eliminates the transitional losses that might otherwise deter price rises. It also eliminates the rival's transitional gains and with it the incentive to delay a matching price increase. In this sense, when a duopoly seller who has an MCC raises his price to p_H, his rival is automatically transformed into a *de facto* price leader, with the ability to set prices for both firms.[42]

(B) MCC PLUS MFN

When a *no-release* MCC is provided jointly with an MFN,[43] oligopoly co-ordination is further facilitated. As was discussed in Section IV(B), the unilateral provision of a contemporaneous MFN places the provider at a competitive disadvantage against rivals not burdened with the clause. This is because the MFN prevents him from selectively matching discounts that are detected. The joint provision of a *no-release* MCC together with the MFN counters this disadvantage somewhat.

By *requiring* himself to match, the seller eliminates the source of his disadvantageous incentive to accommodate selective discounts. This incentive is disadvantageous because it raises the profitability and, hence, the likelihood that his rival will offer such selective discounts. Of course, if the rival is not deterred by the MCC, his discount must be matched with a general price cut, and the seller bears a larger loss.[44] On the other hand, because of the credibility added by the clause, the need actually to carry out the threat may be reduced.

A complex variant of these contractual provisions is a *marketwide* MFN–MCC combination. The following example of such a combination clause is taken from a contract governing the sale of natural gas from a particular field. Unlike the previous contracts discussed, this particular clause offers MFN–MCC 'protection' to the (natural gas) *seller* rather than to the buyer.

> In the event [buyer] or any other gas purchaser shall pay for any gas delivered . . . under conditions comparable to those provided herein, a price higher than that provided here, to any seller, then the price of all gas delivered hereunder shall be increased to an equivalent price. [Buyer] shall have the right to require under the provisions of this paragraph reasonable proof of the delivery of gas to any other gas purchaser and the price thereof.[45]

Analysis of this clause is left as an exercise for the interested reader.

VI PREDATION, ENTRY DETERRENCE AND MEETING COMPETITION CLAUSES

The focus of the analysis so far has been oligopoly co-ordination. It has been assumed throughout that the industry is protected by insurmountable barriers to entry. In this section, we discuss the role of 'meeting competition' clauses in facilitating deterrence to entry.[46]

Recall the usual critique of the Bain/Sylos-Labini models of limit pricing as a rational deterrent to entry. It is argued that it would be irrational for an incumbent and dominant firm to deter entry by *setting* a low 'limit' price before entry occurs. Instead, the incumbent could increase his profits by setting the higher 'monopoly' price before entry and *threatening* to reduce its price in the event that entry actually occurred. Given the threat, it is argued, no actual entry would occur, because the entrant would anticipate earning insufficient profit at the lower post-entry price. Hence, the incumbent could always get the benefit of charging the monopoly price even while deterring entry.[47]

This argument is usually countered in turn by the observation that the incumbent's threat actually to lower the price after entry lacks credibility. Once entry actually occurs, it is generally in the incumbent's interest to accommodate the entrant by behaving co-operatively.[48] Knowing this, a rational entrant would not be deterred. A similar argument demonstrates the lack of credibility in threats to carry out below-cost 'predatory' pricing.

By providing a *no-release* MCC, an incumbent can add needed credibility to its threat. Even if the incumbent would otherwise prefer to accommodate a rational entrant, the MCC requires him to match the entrant's price.[49] Similarly, even if below-cost pricing is unprofitable, it must be carried out. Knowing that the threat will be carried out, a rational entrant will be deterred. Although the appropriate language of the MCC depends on the details of the industry,[50] the benefit of the MCC to the incumbent is clear. An MCC can deter entry by allowing the incumbent to make credible threats to lower his price in the event of entry, even to a below-cost, 'predatory' level. As Richard Gilbert emphasised during the conference reported on in this volume, the MCC makes Sylos' Postulate credible.

VII CONCLUSIONS

In this chapter, the role of buyer–seller contracts in facilitating credible oligopoly co-ordination has been explored. It has been shown that a number of common contractual provisions can restructure oligopolists' pay-off matrices in such a way that the Nash equilibrium is altered. This may occur for either simple Nash or credible dynamic equilibria.

This brief survey is not a definitive treatment of the area. All the practices would benefit from additional rigorous analysis in standard oligopoly models. However, it seems clear that the main results can be generalised. When contractual provisions add constraints to oligopolists' profit-maximisation calculus, the equilibrium changes.

Some experimental evidence on this point has recently been generated by Grether and Plott (1981).[51] These authors compare the pricing performance of an industry with MFNs, public price posting, and advance notice of price increases with that of the same (experimental) industry but without these practices. Their results confirm that if the three practices are applied in combination prices are raised significantly.[52]

Although this survey has shown how these contractual provisions can raise prices in oligopolistic markets protected by entry barriers, it has clearly not attempted a welfare analysis of the practices. Such an analysis must balance the benefits received by buyers and sellers against any anti-competitive effects of the contractual provisions. Some of the possible benefits have already been discussed in the context of the analysis of specific practices. It is worth reviewing them here.

First, both MFN and MCC clauses provide buyers with insurance against certain contingencies. Risk-averse buyers desire insurance protection. There are significant limitations to the size of this benefit, however. First, a buyer may overestimate the value of this insurance if he ignores the price rigidity that may be induced by the clauses. Similarly, a buyer will be likely to ignore the externality he inflicts on other buyers, that is, the effect of its clause on the price paid by other buyers. As stated earlier, inserting an MFN into one buyer's contract is tantamount to bribing the seller to refuse to offer larger discounts to other buyers.

Although buyers may benefit from insurance, it is not clear that the seller is always best situated to provide this insurance, as opposed to an independent insurance company or some other third party. First, the seller may be more risk-averse than either buyers or insurance companies. Second, a seller is not generally well situated to spread the risk of a decrease in his own selling price, relative to some other firm unaffected by the price change. On the other hand, the seller probably has an informational advantage in providing this insurance. Even if the seller did not provide insurance, he would require information about future prices in order to plan his business.[53]

A second possible benefit of the clauses is that they allow a buyer to purchase before completing his search process. Eliminating this delay can benefit both the buyer and the seller offering the clause. Third, the MCC allows the seller to indulge in price discrimination whereas the MFN prevents discrimination.[54] Thus, industry-wide adoption of either type of clause can benefit some buyers and harm others.[55]

It should be clear that these benefits may be more likely in some industry settings than in others. According to the characteristics of the product sold, the terms of the sales contract, the degree of industry concentration, the height of entry barriers, the structure of competition among buyers, etc. the relative sizes of the efficiency and facilitation of co-ordination effects of particular clauses may tip the welfare balance in one direction or the other. More research is needed on this issue. For now, anti-trust analysis of these clauses must clearly proceed on a case-by-case basis.

NOTES

1. This work reflects the research and litigation skills of a number of my former FTC colleagues with whom I worked on the *Ethyl* case: Robert Burka, Paul Pautler, Margaret Slade and David Scheffman. I have also

benefited from the comments of Bill Dudley, Richard Gilbert, Charles Holt, Jack Kirkwood, Warren Schwartz, Joe Simons, and my discussant, Thomas v. Ungern-Sternberg. Many of the ideas considered here have come out of joint work with Judith Gelman and are discussed more formally in Gelman and Salop (1983). Financial support for this research has been provided by the Bureau of Economics of the Federal Trade Commission.

2. Although the rivals' names are taken from the FTC's recent *Ethyl* (1981) case, the facts assumed in these examples do not correspond exactly to those in the case. For example, the real-life domestic lead-based anti-knock compound industry also includes two fringe firms, PPG and Nalco. In addition, costs may have been different while rivals' products were considered homogeneous by purchasers. Obviously, real life is far richer and more complex than theory. See Grether and Plott (1981) and Carlton (1983) for other economic analyses of *Ethyl*.

3. Formally, assume that the demands for Ethyl (E) and Dupont (D) satisfy the symmetry condition $X^E(p, q) = X^D(q, p)$ for all price pairs (p, q) for the two rivals.

4. It has been argued by the economist-lawyer Donald Turner (1962) that sophisticated oligopolists will easily overcome this problem. Each will recognise his mutual interdependence with his rivals, his long-run interest in raising price quickly, and his rivals' likely identical view. However, this position may underestimate the divergence of firms' interests during the transition period. This issue is taken up in more detail below in the discussion of the maintenance of the joint profit point. For a law review answer to Turner's arguments, see the interesting article by the lawyer-economist Richard Posner (1969).

5. Richard Posner (1969) has pointed out that the easier it is to achieve (and reachieve) the co-operative outcome, the greater is the incentive to deviate from that outcome in order to obtain higher short run profits. That is, $1-b$ might be small because (p_H, p_H) can be quickly reattained. Thus, ease of achieving co-operation increases the incentive to cheat. Green and Porter (1984) and Porter (1983) explore this issue by analysing how a cartel will determine the optimal punishment period.

6. In the Green and Porter (1984) model, this issue is more complicated because cheating is not determined with certainty.

7. See Gelman and Salop (1982) and d'Aspremont *et al.* (1982) models with this property.

8. For the purposes of analysing the economic effects of these practices on strategic interaction, it makes no difference whether or not the oligopolists adopt the practices in the belief that they will stabilise the co-operative outcome. Of course, the intent may be an issue in a legal challenge to a practice.

9. Reaching an agreement can also be facilitated by the exchange of information among rivals.

10. In terms of equation (1), information exchanges directly alter b whereas incentive management devices alter the pay-offs V_{ij} which in turn alter b.

11. Each of the prices can denote vectors of prices and/or other strategy variables, of course.

12. This point is also made by Posner (1979 at p. 1198.)
13. Of course, a buyer would clearly be willing to accept the clause for a compensatory payment in excess of his loss $p_H - p_L$, for each unit purchased. However, compensation at this high level eliminates any benefit to the oligopolist.
14. The Justice Department alleged that GE and Westinghouse had MFN clauses that facilitated tacit co-ordination. See the *General Electric Competitive Impact Statement* (1977) and Hay (1979).
15. Variants of this contract could provide for a rebate even of price cuts made even after delivery was taken, or for a partial rather than a full rebate. The contract might also ease enforcement of the clause by providing the buyer with the right to inspect the seller's books.
16. The total penalty equals the price decrease times the number of outstanding orders. It is paid even if the discount is matched.
17. Of course, the MFN makes it more difficult to achieve a lower price co-operative outcome, if changed conditions warrant a lower price. This is a cost to the oligopolists of adopting such a plan. In contrast, the Table 9.2 penalty scheme does not share this problem because only *unmatched* price cuts are penalised.
18. This can be seen as follows. Given the MFN, if DuPont lowers its price from p_M to p_L, it will obtain a short-run gain of 10 (i.e., 140–130) and suffer a long-run loss of 5 (i.e., 130–125) when Ethyl retaliates by cutting its price to p_M. In contrast, without the MFN, beginning at (p_H, p_H), DuPont gains 30 (i.e. 130–100) from a cut to p_M and loses 10 (100–90) from a matching cut by Ethyl. In this case, DuPont's short-run gain rises by more than its long-run loss rises. Similarly, beginning at (p_M, p_M), a DuPont cut from p_M to p_L gives a short-run gain of 35 (i.e., 125–90) and a long-run loss of 20 (i.e., 90–70) when Ethyl matches. Again, the gain rises by more than the loss. See Cooper (1981) for a more general model.
19. These other buyers may be downstream competitors as well.
20. It should be noted that buyers who are well informed about the prices paid by other buyers may induce a *de facto*, if not explicit, MFN policy. See the discussion of posted prices in Section VI, C below.
21. If costs fall, for example, then the joint profit-maximising price may decline.
22. In addition, as discussed earlier, it may be unprofitable to match discounts to marginal customers. The following analysis applies to this case as well.
23. Note that Table 9.4 is constructed with the property that if your rival offers selective discounts, then selective discounts are more profitable than offering a low price to all customers, even if this low price is not matched (i.e., 85 > 60). This assumption is necessary to make selective discounting a simple Nash equilibrium.
24. See Gelman and Salop (1983) and for d'Aspremont *et al.* (1982) for technical analyses of this point.
25. If DuPont offers selective discounts, Ethyl's profits fall to 80. However, if it retaliates with a general price cut to p_L, its profits fall further to 60.
26. Of course, in a model with a continuous strategy space, the level of the

high and low prices may also change, relative to the case of no MFN.

27. As was discussed in the case of a retroactive MFN, unilateral adoption of a contemporaneous MFN may be in each rival's self-interest even if the clause is not also adopted by rivals. This benefit to a firm from the unilateral adoption of an MFN is independent of any increased efficiency or buyer preference for the MFN. Instead, it derives from its effect of stabilising a more co-operative outcome. Of course, on the other side, *unilaterally* adopting a MFN gives a competitive advantage to rivals.

28. Even without increased oligopolistic competition, prices could also fall if costs or aggregate demand decrease, if barriers to entry were reduced, etc.

29. The possibility that the buyers' cost-minimising outcome of 'no MFN' will be achieved for a market characterised by an oligopsony among buyers depends on an analysis analogous to the one carried out here for oligopolistic sellers.

30. Indeed, if the downstream industry demand is sufficiently inelastic and barriers to entry are sufficiently high, then the buyer's (and his rivals') profits will increase from MFN-induced, *industrywide* increases in input prices. See Nelson (1957), Salop and Scheffman (1981) and Maloney and McCormick (1981) for models of this phenomenon.

31. The analysis of 'secondary' line violations of the Robinson–Patman is analogous.

32. Of course, the efficiency benefits of posted prices may also differ from those of a standard MFN.

33. Of course, the car repair industry probably has too few entry barriers to make a relative value scale able to effectively raise prices for very long.

34. See Kass and Pautler (1979), Eisenberg (1980) and *Arizona* v. *Maricopa County Medical Society* (1982).

35. The Court did not carefully compare efficiency benefits with the postulated anticompetitive effects.

36. Although our analysis focuses on the case of an MCC in a long term contract, much of this analysis applies directly to the case of binding 'We will not be undersold' advertising claims as well.

37. MOR clauses were offered by all of the *Ethyl* defendants but were not included in the Complaint. They have been litigated in other contexts, however. For example, see Peterman's (1979) analysis of the *International Salt* case.

38. Unless the supply contract includes an *exclusive dealing* provision, the buyer can purchase *extra* supplies at the lower price without informing his original supplier.

39. Of course, by requiring the seller to price below marginal cost, an MCC can increase the credibility of threats to become predatory. This is taken up in Section VI below.

40. By an analogous argument, it would not be sufficient to simply *meet* the price of a higher quality product. Instead, the seller would need a *beating competition* clause.

41. The clause may require the seller to provide units at prices below his marginal costs. Thus, the buyer may be consuming beyond the point where his marginal benefit equals the seller's marginal cost.

42. This price leadership is restricted to prices no greater than p_H, of course.

43. The following analysis applies to industries where an effective MFN is entailed by posted prices as well as by contracts that specify MFN protection explicitly.
44. For example, the rival may wish to cut price because of a reduction, in order to generate greater demand by current and new customers, rather than to divert customers from competitors.
45. Adapted from *Louisiana-Nevada Transit Co.* v. *Woods*, 393 F. Supp. 177, 178–9 (W.D. Pa. 1975).
46. See Modigliani (1958), Salop (1979) and Dixit (1982) for surveys of this literature.
47. By assuming that the incumbent can rapidly lower his price after entry, this argument obviously assumes that the incumbent is not paralysed by regulation, not unaware of entrants' existence, or otherwise catatonic.
48. Of course, this counter-argument implicitly assumes that tacit co-ordination will be successful. This may not be obvious, as shown earlier.
49. An MCC merely requires that matching price cuts should be given to the incumbent's current customers. An MFN–MCC combination would extend the discount to all potential customers.
50. For example if, at equal prices, some consumers strictly prefer the entrant's product the incumbent can strengthen his threat by offering a *beat or release* or *beating competition* clause instead. A beating competition clause might offer an x per cent discount off competing bids. Of course, this could lead to 'self-predation' if a more efficient entrant threatens entry.
51. For a survey of some earlier experimental work, see Plott (1981).
52. Given the limited number of experiments run, their preliminary study was unable to measure significantly the individual effects of each practice.
53. Of course, one aspect of the seller's informational advantage – the fact that it controls somewhat the probability of a price cut – is the very adverse incentive ('moral hazard') induced by the clauses, not an efficiency benefit.
54. See Salop (1977) and Weismeth (1982) for analyses of price discrimination based on informational differences.
55. It should be added that the elimination of buyers' price competition for *inputs* entailed by adoption of an MFN, may harm final consumers.

REFERENCES

d'Aspremont, C., Jacquemin, A., Gabszewicz, J. J. and Weymark, J. (1982) 'On the Stability of Dominant Cartels', *Canadian Journal of Economics*, vol. 14, pp. 17–25.

Carlton, D. (1983) 'A Re-examination of Basing Point Pricing', *Journal of Law and Economics*, vol. 26, pp. 51–70.

Cooper, T. E. (1981) 'Price Protection Policies and Tacit Collusion', unpublished manuscript, University of Florida.

Dixit, A. K. (1982) 'Recent Developments in Oligopoly Theory', *American Economic Review*, vol. 72, pp. 12–17.

Eisenberg, B. S. (1980) 'Information Exchange Among Competitors: the

Issue of Relative Value Scales For Physicians' Services', *Journal of Law & Economics*, vol. 23, pp. 441–60.

Gelman, J. R. and Salop, S. C. (1983) 'Judo Economics: Capacity Limitation and Coupon Competition', *Bell Journal*, vol. 14, pp. 315–25.

Green, E. J. and Porter, R. H. (1984) 'Noncooperative Collusion Under Imperfect Price Information', *Econometrica*, vol. 52.

Grether, D. M. and Plott, C. R. (1981) 'The Effect of Market Practices in Oligopolistic Markets: an Experimental Examination of the Ethyl Case', unpublished manuscript, California Institute of Technology.

Hay, G. A. (1979) 'The Oligopoly Problem: Theory and Policy', unpublished manuscript, Cornell University.

Kass, D. I. and Pautler, P. A. (1979) *Physician Control of Blue Cross Plans*, Federal Trade Commission, USA.

Maloney, M.T. and McCormick, R. E., 'A Positive Theory of Environmental Quality Regulation', *Journal of Law & Economics*, vol. 25, pp. 99–124.

Modigliani, F. (1958) 'New Developments on the Oligopoly Front', *Journal of Political Economy*, vol. 66, pp. 215–32.

Nelson, R. (1957) 'Increased Rents from Increased Costs: a Paradox of Value Theory', *Journal of Political Economy*, vol. 65, pp. 387–93.

Orr, D. and MacAvoy, P. (1965) 'Price Strategies to Promote Cartel Stability', *Economica*, vol. 44, pp. 185–97.

Osborne, D. K. (1976) 'Cartel Problems', *American Economic Review*, vol. 66, pp. 835–44.

Peterman, J. L. (1979) 'The International Salt Case', *Journal of Law & Economics*, vol. 22, pp. 351–64.

Plott, C. R. (1981) 'Theories of Industrial Organization as Explanations of Experimental Market Behavior', in S. C. Salop *et al.*, *Strategy, Predation, and Antitrust Analysis*, (Washington D. C.: Federal Trade Commission).

Porter, R. (1983) 'Optimal Cartel Trigger Price Strategies', *Journal of Economic Theory*, vol. 29, pp. 313–38.

Posner, R. A. (1969) 'Oligopoly and the Antitrust Laws: a Suggested Approach', *Stanford Law Review* vol. 21, pp. 1562–1606.

Posner, R. A. (1979) 'Information and Antitrust: Reflections on the *Gypsum* and *Engineers* Decisions', *Georgetown Law Journal*, vol. 67, pp. 1187–1203.

Salop, S.C. (1977) 'The Noisy Monopolist: Imperfect Information, Price Dispersion and Price Discrimination', *Review of Economic Studies*, vol. 44, pp. 393–406.

Salop, S. C. (1979) 'Strategic Entry Deterrence', *American Economic Review*, vol. 69, pp. 335–8.

Salop, S. C. and Scheffman, D. T. (1981) 'Strategic Interaction in Multiple Markets', unpublished paper, Federal Trade Commission.

Schelling, T. C. (1960) *The Strategy of Conflict* (Cambridge, Mass.: Harvard University Press).

Scherer, F. M. (1980) *Industrial Market Structure and Economic Performance* (2nd Edn) (Chicago: Chicago University Press), pp. 160–64.

Stigler, G. J. (1968) 'A Theory of Oligopoly', reprinted in Stigler, *The Organisation of Industry* (Homewood, Illinois), pp. 39–66.

Turner, D. F. (1962) 'The Definition of Agreement Under the Sherman Act: Conscious Parallelism and Refusals to Deal', *Harvard Law Review*, vol. 75, pp. 655–706.

Wiesmeth, H. (1982) 'Price Discrimination Based on Imperfect Information: Necessary and Sufficient Conditions', *Review of Economic Studies*, vol. 49, pp. 391–402.

CASES CITED

Arizona v. *Maricopa County Medical Society*, No. 80-419, U.S. Sup. Ct., 18/6/82.
International Salt Co. v. *United States*, 332 U.S. 392 (1947).
In re Ethyl Corp., No. 9128 (FTC Initial Decision 5 Aug. 1981) 729 F.2d 128 (2d. Cir. 1984).
Louisiana-Nevada Transit Co. v. *Woods*, 393 F. Supp. 177 (W.D. Pa. 1975).
National Macaroni Mfrs Assn v. *FTC*, 345 F. 2d 421 (7th Cir. 1965).
United States v. *General Electric Co.*, Competitive Impact Statement, 42 *Fed. Reg.* 17003 (30 March 1977) (consent decree).

Discussion of the Paper by Steve C. Salop

Von Ungern-Sternberg argued that Salop's paper constituted a set of examples that could not be easily generalised. To demonstrate this point, he provided a set of counter-examples to Salop's arguments. To begin with, he attacked the argument that an agreement to provide low prices to customers who had purchased earlier at high prices would facilitate oligopoly co-ordination. He agreed that such an action would increase the cost of cutting price, since the price cut would have to be extended to some previous buyers through rebates. But he argued that this implied that the demand for a firm with a reputation as a price cutter would rise at every price, just because of the possibility of rebates. This made price cutting more attractive. It was not clear which of these two effects would dominate.

Next, Ungern argued that agreements to extend price cuts made to other buyers by issuing rebates would not be a common practice. Again, he agreed that in a duopoly it was possible that one of the sellers could make himself better off by unilaterally offering a rebate clause. But he pointed out that in such a situation, being a first mover was disadvantageous, so that both sellers would likely wait around for the other to extend the rebate clause first.

Finally, he argued that meeting competition clauses would not work against new entrants. In the absence of strong entry barriers, monopoly would not be stable. Rebate clauses might have perfectly legitimate efficiency enhancing purposes. The net consequence of these considerations was that it was very difficult to use the results of the paper as a guide to policy.

Salop agreed that it was always important to examine each case on its own merits to determine whether the kind of arguments suggested by Ungern might be correct and whether legitimate efficiency arguments could be used to defend the practices. Salop added that when firms compete with prices, facilitating practices would always be attractive. To demonstrate this, he offered an argument that was illustrated in Figure 4.9.1, drawn from a paper by Thomas Cooper.

The figure corresponded to a model where firms made Nash conjectures, but competed in prices. The horizontal axis measured the price charged by firm 1 while the vertical axis gave the price charged by firm 2. Suppose that R_1 was the reaction curve of firm 1 and R_2 was the reaction curve of firm 2. By the definition of the reaction curve, firm 2's iso-profit curve must be vertical at the Nash equilibrium, while firm 1's iso-profit curve must be horizontal. Hence there must be a set of prices where both firms were better off. If firm

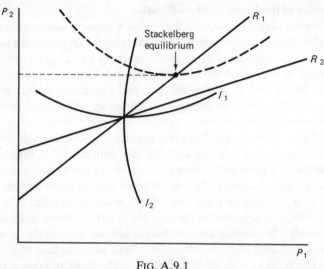

FIG. A.9.1

2 committed itself to a price slightly above the Nash equilibrium price, firm 1 would respond by moving to its reaction curve, and both sellers would be better off. This was in sharp contrast to the Cournot quantity-setting game, where the follower was worse off than he would have been in a Nash equilibrium.

Commitment to a price above the Nash equilibrium price could be brought about by using a 'most-favoured nation' clause, where the firm promised to extend future price cuts to current buyers. This promise made price cutting costly and made firm 2's commitment credible. It was easy to convince oneself that it was possible to construct examples where each player would prefer to be a follower in the price-setting game. Salop agreed that this might make each participant reluctant to move first, as had been suggested by Ungern. Alternatively, one firm might be willing to sacrifice the advantage for a certain smaller gain. This problem might also be overcome by adding a generalised 'meet-the-competition' clause. Firm 2 might commit itself to the desired price, then promise to respond along its reaction curve to any price offer by firm 1. This kind of clause would effectively turn firm 1 into the leader, to firm 2's benefit.

Ungern added that 'meet-the-competition' clauses could give rise to additional demand modelling problems. He suggested that the firm offering the lowest price in the market should get the lion's share of demand, even if all other firms have 'meet-the-competition' clauses.

He commended Salop's use of lexicographic buyer preferences as a potential way of modelling this.

Michael Katz suggested that 'meet the competition' clauses might be difficult to enforce if it were costly for buyers to search out the lowest price available in the market. Salop agreed that this was so but that firms offering the clauses might supply the information themselves to buyers to lower the enforcement costs. Salop referred to Texas International Airlines who, in addition to offering a 'meet-the-competition' clause, also promised to supply a toll-free number for consumers to call. This number would provide the lowest price in every market.

Curtis Eaton, suggested that problems associated with deterring entry and enforcing 'meet-the-competition' clauses required that these issues be modelled in an explicit temporal framework. It was well known that neither entry deterrence, nor contract enforcement would arise in finitely repeated games since recursive arguments suggested that if it were profitable to violate contracts in the last period of the game, it would *always* be profitable to violate them. Eaton suggested that these difficulties might lead consumers and potential entrants to discount such clauses.

In response to a question by *Spence*, Salop explained that certain contractual arrangements might allow firms to overcome the usual informational problems that led to cartel instability. In the Stigler model of cartel stability, for example, the benefit to a deviant firm was the extra profit that it earned before its competitors retaliate. The amount of profit then depended on the time it took other members of the cartel to detect price cuts. Cartels would tend to be stable when this detection lag was short. A 'meet or release' clause in a contract would tend to reduce the detection lag, since it created an incentive for buyers to report sellers who offered price cuts. This shifted the costs of detection from sellers to buyers. *Reinhard Selten* suggested that sellers might be able to neutralise 'meet or release' clauses by disguising price cuts. For example, they could pay buyers rebates at the end of the year that were not related specifically to any single transaction that occurred during the year. Salop responded that the same sort of phenomena occurred when sellers, like car dealers, refused to make price offers in writing. The odd implication of this was that sellers only made a firm price offer once the buyer agreed to purchase the product.

To illustrate further the informational issues associated with facilitating practices, Salop referred to competition between the Giant and

Safeway Supermarket chains in Washington DC. Giant had started to publish a price index which gave the relative cost of buying a common basket of groceries at Giant and Safeway. Salop explained that to make this index into a 'meet-the-competition' clause, Giant could have promised to pay a rebate to buyers based on the differences in these published indices.

Willig pointed out that facilitating practices were defined as conduct that have the effect of altering the pay-off matrix associated with the price game played by sellers. He felt that this definition of facilitating practices was not specific enough for an analyst to conclude that any practice by a firm was necessarily facilitating by looking only at the changes in the pay-off matrix in response to the practice. Salop responded that, broadly speaking, a practice was facilitating if it raised the Nash equilibrium price in the sellers' game without providing an offsetting benefit to consumers such as higher quality.

Schmalensee and *Waverman* suggested that it was usually possible to find an efficiency rationale for facilitating practices. The concept in and of itself, added Schmalensee, would not make anti-trust practices any easier, since it did not determine the *net* benefits associated with any of these facilitating practices.

Gilbert suggested that with entry, it would be difficult for any facilitating practice to raise the industry price much above the Bain limit price without some inertia on the part of the buyers of the products of incumbent firms. *Grossman* added that if buyers moved to the lowest-price seller, simultaneous 'meet-the-competition' clauses, offered by both the incumbent and the entrant, would lead to Bertrand equilibrium.

Larry White suggested that facilitating practices illustrated two well-known paradoxes in industrial organisation. First, in competitive markets, more information made competition work better whereas in non-competitive situations, more information might facilitate collusion and make things worse. Second, long-term arrangements, to the extent they provided insurance, are beneficial, but with imperfect competition long-term contracts, might, again, facilitate collusion.

Part Five
Market Structure and Planned Economies

10 Workers' Management and the Market

Branko Horvat

UNIVERSITY OF ZAGREB, YUGOSLAVIA

THE THEORY OF THE FIRM: AN ATTEMPT OF CLASSIFICATION

I MODELS OF THE FIRM

If the firm is maximising an objective function, its behaviour will depend on the type of that objective function. Basically, we can distinguish three simple cases which, of course, can be further elaborated. The firm maximises either a residual, usually called profit, or one or two ratios, namely, income per worker or profit per unit of capital. I shall denote the three cases as: the *entrepreneurial firm*, the *Worker-Managed* (or *Illyrian*) *firm* and the *capitalist firm*. In order to simplify the analysis, only two factors of production are assumed (labour and capital), and joint products are absent.

(1) THE ENTREPRENEURIAL FIRM

Best known is the *entrepreneurial firm* since it is described in all neo-classical textbooks. The entrepreneur hires two factors of production, labour (x_1) and capital (x_2), pays for them the market prices (p_1) and (p_2) and maximises the residual (Π), subject to the technological constraint of the production function $f(x_1, x_2)$. We have:

$$\max \Pi = pf(x_1, x_2) - (p_1 x_1 + p_2 x_2 + c), \tag{1}$$

where pf is the value of output, $(p_1x_1 + p_2x_2 + c)$ are the variable costs of production and c is some fixed cost (tax, rent, or whichever part of cost does not vary with output).

It is well known that the entrepreneurial firm reaches equilibrium when the value of each factor's marginal product is equalised with its price:

$$pf_1 = p_1, \ pf_2 = p_2 \tag{2}$$

By holding constant one of the elements in (2) and varying one other, we easily find what happens to the third element. Assuming diminishing returns (which guarantee stability):

(a) An increase in product price increases output and employment;
(b) An increase in factor prices reduces output and employment;
(c) A change in fixed cost produces no effects (since c does not appear in the equilibrium conditions);
(d) Labour is treated as is any other resource;

there is complete symmetry.

(2) THE WORKER-MANAGED FIRM

Capital is nationally-owned, if capital-finance is external and if firms are managed by workers, one may assume that workers will maximise residual income per employee, after the market price has been paid for non-labour factors of production. This is the case of a *worker-managed firm* or, as its inventor Benjamin Ward (1958) called it, an *Illyrian firm*, we now have

$$\max y = \frac{pf(x_1, x_2) - (p_2x_2 + c)}{x_1} \tag{3}$$

Here, y is income per worker. Since one factor of production, labour, is exempt, costs of production are not defined. The first-order conditions of equilibrium are easily found to be:

$$\frac{\partial y}{\partial x_1} = 0 \qquad pf_1 = y, \text{ and} \tag{4a}$$

$$\frac{\partial y}{\partial x_2} = 0 \qquad pf_2 = p_2. \tag{4b}$$

For the non-labour factor of production, the equilibrium condition is the same as in (2). For the exempt factor, labour, the equilibrium condition has changed, and that changes radically the behaviour of the firm. In order to see that, let us transform (4a) into:

$$f(x_1, x_2) = f_1 x_1 = \frac{c}{p} + \frac{p_2 x_2}{p}. \tag{5}$$

It is now easy to see that the following is true:

$$\frac{\partial}{\partial x_1}(f = f_1 x_1) = -f_{11} x_1 > 0, \tag{6}$$

if, as we assume for stability $f_{11} < 0$.

A similar analysis now produces the following results:

(a) An increase in p reduces the right-hand side of equation (5); in order to preserve equilibrium, the left-hand side must also be reduced. According to (6), this means reducing employment x_1 and, consequently, output;

(b) An increase in the factor price of the other resource has the same effect as in the neo-classical firm;

(c) An increase in the fixed cost c increases output and employment;

(d) Factors are not treated symmetrically, since wages do not occur in (4a) and the two conditions are differently structured.

The results are somewhat strange. Whatever the entrepreneurial firm does, the Illyrian firm does the opposite. When the market price of the product increases, the firm reduces output. The economy is thus hopelessly unstable. When the government wants to increase employment, it must levy a lump-sum tax. The higher the tax, the higher are output and employment. If, as may happen, $y > p_1$, f_1 (Illyrian) $> f_1$ (entrepreneurial) then this implies lower output and reduced employment. It also implies that, for the same output (given the technology), the capital – labour ratio will be higher. The Illyrian firm uses more capital than necessary. If there is unemployment, and the government provides subsidies in order to create new jobs, the Illyrian firm will reduce employment. Thus the efficiency of the economic policy is reduced. Lower employment and higher capital-intensity implies, for a given time-preference, a smaller rate of growth.

The Illyrian firm appears to be inefficient. Additional assumptions may eliminate some of the defects. More-realistic production functions with several variable factors (Domar, 1966) considerably reduce the undesirable effects. Limited labour supply may generate correct responses to price changes (Domar, 1966). In the long run, with free entry, the Illyrian firm behaves as does the entrepreneurial one

(Vanek, 1970). Risks of dismissal and unemployment may be introduced (Parinello, 1971). If workers dislike dismissing their fellow
workers, and even more being dismissed themselves, and are not
eager to employ new workers because these may change the preference map of the collective in an undesirable way, some of the
perverse reactions will be mitigated. Similar assumptions and results
are obtained by Steinherr and Thisse (1979). Conte (1979) combines
Ward's model and the decision rules of Domar and Horvat and
arrives at stable solutions. Yet, with all these cosmetics, the Illyrian
firm works at reduced efficiency.

(3) THE CAPITALIST FIRM

If workers maximise their incomes, then capitalists may maximise the
rate of profit. Thus the *capitalist firm* may be treated as a symmetrical
counterpart to the Illyrian firm (Dubravčič, 1968; 1970). The Illyrian
firm operates under complete national ownership of capital with
fully-external financing of capital; the capitalist firm operates under
complete private ownership of capital, with fully-internal financing of
capital. The objective function to be maximised is now:

$$\max \pi = \frac{pf(x_1, x_2) - (p_1x_1 + c)}{x_2}, \tag{7}$$

and the equilibrium conditions are

$$pf_1 = p_1, \ pf_2 = \pi \tag{8}$$

Changes in product price and in fixed cost generate perverse reactions, as in the worker-managed firm. But factor intensity is now
reversed: while workers employ more capital than is necessary,
capitalists employ more labour than necessary: the worker-managed
firm is capital-intensive; its capitalist counterpart is labour-intensive.

The results of the analysis may be summarised in Table 10.1.

TABLE 10.1   EFFECTS ON OUTPUT AND EMPLOYMENT

Type of change	Type of firm		
	Entrepreneurial	*Illyrian*	*Capitalist*
Increase in product price	+	−	−
Increase in wages	−	0	−
Increase in the interest rate	−	−	0
Increase in the fixed cost	0	+	+

It may be of some historical interest to point out (a) that the analysis of Illyrian and capitalist firms was anticipated by Wicksell[1] (1893); and (b) that both inventors of the respective models, Ward and Dubravčič, seem to be unaware of this. Wicksell examined the case where 'the workers . . . (who) themselves are entrepreneurs merely strive to attain . . . the greatest possible subsistence or wages' (p.96) and then shows that the equilibrium is the same as when the capitalist firm maximises profit. The three Wicksellian equations in our notation are as follows:

$$x_2 = x_1 p_1 t, \tag{9}$$

$$q = f(t), \text{ and} \tag{10}$$

$$q = p_1(1 + \pi t). \tag{11}$$

Here, x_2 is the amount of (circulating) capital, x_1 the number of workers, p_1 the wage rate, t the average period of production, q output per worker and π the rate of (simple) interest. The first equation is the subsistence fund definition of capital; the second represents the Austrian production function; and the third is the distribution equation. For an individual capitalist, x_2, p_1 and $f(t)$ are given and π is to be maximised, that is:

$$\max \pi = \frac{f^1(t) - p_1}{p_1 t} . \tag{12}$$

The first-order condition is

$$\frac{d\pi}{dt} = 0 \rightarrow \pi = \frac{f(t)}{p_1} . \tag{13}$$

On the other hand, an Illyrian firm will maximise

$$\max p_1 = \frac{f'(t)}{1 + \pi t}, \tag{14}$$

and the first-order condition is again the same as in (13). This should not be surprising since capital is here defined in terms of wages and there is only one independent variable in the maximising equation.

Suppose that the equilibrium condition (13) is added to the initial set of equations (9)–(11), and that the new set, namely,

$$x_2 = x_1 p_1 t,$$

$$f(t) = p_1 (1 + \pi t), \text{ and}$$

$$\pi = \frac{f'(t)}{p_1}, \tag{15}$$

is totally differentiated, we may then examine the reaction of the firm to changes in the market parameters. The reaction is the same for the worker-managed and the capitalist firm. A higher interest rate will lead to an increase in employment; to a decrease in the wage rate and in the period of production; output per man will be reduced but that will be more than compensated by increased employment. Total output will increase (Milanović, 1982).

II   CHOOSING THE APPROPRIATE MODEL

The criterion for choosing a theoretical model is its empirical relevance. Since the Yugoslav economy is so far the only fully worker-managed economy in existence, it will provide us with empirical evidence. And the evidence is reasonably clear: the Yugoslav firm does not behave in the Illyrian fashion (just as the 'capitalist firm' is not a very plausible model for existing capitalist economies). Besides, although productive capital is socially-owned, a significant part (one-third) of capital investment is financed internally within the firm.

The simplest approach to an analysis of the worker-managed firm is to assume that managerial entrepreneurship (representing share-holders interests) is replaced by collective-worker entrepreneurship. (This is the case under conditions of social ownership; collective ownership would produce a co-operative which behaved differently.) Thus, the entrepreneurial type of firm is a likely candidate for a suitable model.

My own managerial experience in worker-managed firms led me to postulate the following hypothesis (Horvat, 1967). At the beginning of the accounting period, the workers' council sets aspiration wages which are valid for that period and which function as accounting costs. These aspiration wages consist of personal income in the last year (or some standard personal income) w and a change in this, normally an increase (Δw) to be achieved in the current year. This aspiration income is a function of:

(a)   Expected sales;
(b)   Incomes in other firms;
(c)   Incomes in the previous (and earlier) years;
(d)   Labour productivity;
(e)   The cost of living;
(f)   Taxation policy; and perhaps of some other factors.

Wages being fixed, what remains to be done is to maximise the residual surplus: that is,

$$\Pi = pf(x_1, x_2) - [(w + \Delta w)\, x_1 + p_2 x_2 + c]. \tag{16}$$

The increment Δw can, of course, be either positive or negative. At the end of the period, aspiration wages are revised upwards or downwards, depending on the commercial success of the firm. Thus, we must distinguish between two types of wages: accounting wages $(w + \Delta w)$ and the wages actually-paid-out $(w + \Delta w + \Delta w^*)$. Only the former enter the objective function.

A glance at (16) suffices to show that the mathematical properties of the equation are the same as in (1): a worker-managed firm will behave like an entrepreneurial firm and will be equally efficient. The only distinction – yet socially an extremely important one – is to be found in the fact that labour is no longer a commodity; it is no longer sold to an employer. The objective function may be described as: maximise total income, subject to the constraint that accounting wages be $w + \Delta w$. Wages in the various firms will tend to converge towards a market wage under the same conditions as in the capitalist market, namely, under competition and free entry.

Equation (16) is intended to approximate to observed behaviour. It is a behavioural, not a normative, equation. It is, however, reasonable to ask whether it is rational to follow an objective function like (16). The answer is positive. We may imagine a workers' council adopting a long-term plan which maximises the incomes of employed workers over a collectively-chosen time horizon. In a situation of uncertainty, such a plan can be only very roughly determined. It is then broken down into a certain number of short-term plans, one for each accounting period. The current short-term plan is fully elaborated, while the others are frequently revised, as new information comes in. The resulting wages (in the current period) represent aspiration wages.

Every theoretical hypothesis needs empirical testing. Several attempts have been made so far, but the most ambitious was undertaken by Janez Prašnikar. He tested two hypotheses, those of Ward and of Horvat, and his preliminary report on 40 Slovenian firms is already available. Prašnikar was also interested in other characteristics of the firm's behaviour and I shall present his main results.

Prašnikar divided his sample into more-and-less efficient firms and again into smaller and larger firms. Three-quarters of the more efficient firms (and two-thirds of the larger ones) reported that they primarily tried to capture as large a part of the market as their abilities and resources would allow. Virtually all of them would try to keep their volume of output unchanged even if material costs, fixed costs or wages changed. Only a change in prices might induce some of them to change the quantity they produced. The determination of wages was influenced by the following factors – in diminishing order of importance: (1) the available income of the firm; (2) the cost of living; (3) the rise in the firm's labour productivity; (4) wages in other firms; (5) cross-industry or cross-national agreements; (6) wages in the previous year; and (7) public opinion. Employment was influenced by the following factors: (1) labour turnover, resulting from workers leaving to search for higher wages and better working conditions; (2) increases in capacity; (3) shortages of particular categories of labour; (4) rises in income per worker; (5) a high level of sales; (6) whether there were unemployed workers. The short-term goals of the firm (according to their managerial staff) in decreasing order of importance were: (1) desire to accumulate funds; (2) level of income per worker; (3) degree of economic power; (4) the full use of productive capacity; (5) a larger income; (6) a larger market share; (7) the level of personal income; (8) meeting a larger demand. On the other hand, workers see their main goals as raising income per worker (64 per cent) and accumulation (13 per cent). Twenty-eight out of the 40 firms in the sample 'accumulate as much as they can after paying out personal income' and 14 firms in the same sample 'prefer investing out of their own resources'. Price formation is determined by the following factors, in decreasing order of significance:

(1) a rise in the price of inputs;
(2) a rise in wages;
(3) an increase in taxes;
(4) an increase in demand.

After a detailed analysis of the behavioural traits of the firms in his sample, Prašnikar concludes that the Yugoslav worker-managed firm is more resistant to market changes than is its capitalist counterpart. On the whole, it behaves like an entrepreneurial firm, maximising its residual income.

III CONCENTRATION OF OUTPUT IN THE YUGOSLAV ECONOMY

Competition in entry to the industry had not, so far, been analysed in any detail, but a recent and extensive study on concentration ratios in the Yugoslav economy has been made by one of my doctoral students (Petrin, 1981).

When studying the worker-managed economy, one must distinguish the common characteristics inherent in all such economies from those specific to the country in question, in our case, Yugoslavia.

One common characteristic stands out clearly: that is, social ownership precludes the buying and selling of firms. Capital markets do, of course, exist, and capital goods may be bought and sold, but not firms. Firms can be amalgamated only if the constituent workers' collectives find that to be advantageous. When the advantages cease to exist, workers may decide to break the firm up again, into its original parts or in some other fashion. Assuming efficient national planning and an orderly financial market, there is no particular advantage in being large. On the other hand, there are clear disadvantages; the larger the firm, the less possible it is for individual workers to influence its running. Self-managers like Schumacher prefer smallness.

The worker-managed firm will grow until technological and organisational economies of scale have been exploited. Beyond that, such firms establish various types of association and business link but do not amalgamate. Consequently, a typical worker-managed firm will be a one plant or several plant firm. Since collusion is impossible – one cannot keep secrets if they are discussed at workers' council meetings – and since being large is not desirable, workers' management is substantially more conducive to competition than is the alternative economic system.

Features specific to Yugoslavia change the picture presented in some important ways. Since planning is in disarray and financial markets are extremely poorly organised, it pays the firm to build-up economic power: thus, being large makes sense. Besides, the governments – eight regional and one federal – can more easily influence bigger units than smaller ones if economic policy is poorly understood; if the country is one where in the main administrative measures are used. What is typically observed in Yugoslavia is that the governments press for amalgamation, while the workers resist that pressure as strongly as they can.

The second feature of the Yugoslav situation is the relative absence of small firms, that is, those with less than 100 employees. This is explained by the fact that entry into the market is more difficult for small firms than for larger ones. An established firm is unlikely to create a small subsidiary: a bank is not eager to finance workshops; a development plan is not likely to go into the detail of small-scale production – which represents an area for individual initiative. Artisans can employ up to five workers. Such firms can grow if they are transformed into co-operatives or, under certain conditions, they can even continue to grow under the management of the original owner (as co-called Contractual Organisations of Associated Labour). But the administrative procedures are not well-elaborated; proper finance is lacking; the authorities, despite political proclamations to the contrary, look askance at such 'hybrid' firms; and taxation is often arbitrary. Since incentives and money are lacking, small firms fail to appear in the numbers which are required by the economy and which are possible under different arrangements.

The third characteristic of the Yugoslav economy is a legal requirement for breaking up firms into smaller units called Basic Organisations of Associated Labour (BOAL). Firms, called Work Organisations (WO), appear as federations of BOALs. WOs are further federated into Composite Organisations of Associated Labour. Self-management requires small groups. Thus the basic self-managed unit is not a firm, but a shop or department.[2] This (valid) observation has been misleadingly extended into a thesis that every shop should be financially and organisationally independent, have its own bank account, etc. Thus the market is introduced into the firm, which tends to disintegrate into a number of smaller firms (BOALs).[3] Fans of competition may argue that this helps to develop competition, which is indeed the case since BOALs tend to compete – even within the same firm. But this is competition in the wrong place, because it destroys the internal organisation, lowers efficiency and adversely affects human relations. Markets and competitions are appropriate outside the factory gate; inside, a very different organisation ought to prevail – that of co-operation.

BOALs have been mentioned because the functioning of the Yugoslav market cannot be understood without considering the changes generated by that issue BOALs introduced in 1974. Neither can the statistical data be properly interpreted without taking into account the existence of the BOALs.

TABLE 10.2 PERCENTAGES OF TOTAL EMPLOYEES IN THE FOUR
LARGEST FIRMS

	Yugoslavia 1973	France 1963	Italy 1963	Netherlands 1963	Belgium 1963
The meat industry	26	24	17	28	18
Breweries	46	24	49	64	20
Woollen textiles	41	14	19	20	20
Cotton textiles	18	19	15	27	25
Leather footwear	27	13	4	31	16
The paper industry	35	26	22	59	56
Basic chemistry	51	35	29	30	62
Cosmetics	68	15	16	33	53
The glass industry	54	39	14	49	61
Steel mills	77	54	30	71	48
Agricultural machinery	71	34	14	29	59
Electric machinery	70	42	12	46	77
Electric bulbs	100	75	60	32	56
Bicycles	100	43	55	31	50

Sources Petrin, 1981, pp. 151–2; Phlips, 1971, pp. 184–94.

Tea Petrin (1981, pp. 151–2) studied degrees of concentration, in terms of employment, in the four largest firms in Yugoslavia for 40 industries, and compared the results with those for four West European countries and she concluded that, on the whole, concentration was greater in Yugoslavia than in any of the other countries. Table 10.2 gives the data for the selected industries.

The data in Table 10.2 refer, of course, to firms, i.e. to Work Organisations in Yugoslavia.[4] If BOALs had been taken into account, the results would have been different. The data are also indicative of market structures. Petrin estimates that in two-thirds of industries (and in 60 per cent of the wholesale and retail trade) oligopoly prevails; that one-third of industries are competitive and that a complete monopoly has been established in copper production.

As to the comparative size of the firms, the relevant data are given in Table 10.3.

In terms of the shares of small and large production units, the worker-managed Yugoslav economy finds itself between the Eastern statist economies and the Western capitalist economies. Differences in industrial structures are not likely to change this conclusion.

TABLE 10.3   THE SHARES OF EMPLOYMENT IN INDUSTRY
(MANUFACTURING) IN PRODUCTION UNITS OF VARIOUS SIZES

	Production units		
	Small *16–125*	*Medium* *120–1000*	*Large* *over 1000 employed*
Yugoslavia: production units, 1963	11.3	50.5	38.2
firms, 1973	12.8	38.7	48.5
BOALs, 1976	10.0	71.5	18.5
Romania, 1967	0.5	29.1	70.4
Hungary, 1973	2.0	22.2	75.8
Bulgaria, 1970	4.9	49.8	45.3
Poland, 1970	14.0	36.1	49.9
Austria, 1973	37.6	41.9	20.4
Netherlands, 1963	40.9	39.6	19.5
Sweden, 1972	32.3	43.2	24.6
Italy, 1971	39.8	38.1	22.1
Canada, 1968	30.4	47.8	21.8
Japan, 1972	43.4	36.1	20.5

Source   Petrin, 1981, pp. 53–4 and 237.

IV   CONCLUDING REMARKS

Yugoslav economic organisation is still in a state of flux. Although
some basic features and tendencies are visible, economic processes
are still very much influenced by frequent administrative changes.
Thus, it is still too early for economic modelling or, at least, this is
still not very rewarding. Models can be built, but this cannot be
verified because the environment is frequently being changed arbitrarily by administrative fiat. At any rate, one thing is certain: the
worker-managed economy behaves substantially differently, when
compared with the two alternative contemporary economies.

NOTES

1. I was reminded of that by Branko Milanović (1982) a participant in my
   research seminar.
2. For an appropriate organisational theory of worker management, see
   Horvat, 1982, ch. 8.
3. Prašnikar (1982) finds that between 22 and 35 per cent of BOALs
   engage in buying, selling, exporting, price setting, financing R and D.

Further, between 73 and 86 per cent of BOALs independently deal with the ôrganisation of production and the income distribution.
4. It is of some interest to note that the data refer to producers' concentration. If sellers'-concentration data were available – various holdings, concentration in export sales, etc. – Yugoslavia would turn out to be comparable to the Benelux countries. I am grateful for this observation to A. Jacquemin.

REFERENCES

Conte, M. (1979) 'Short Run Dynamics of the Labour Managed Firm', *Economic Analysis and Workers' Management*, pp. 3–22.
Domar, E.D. (1966) 'The Soviet Collective Farm', *American Economic Review*, vol. 66, pp. 734–57.
Dubravčič, D. (1968) 'Mogućnosti uopćavanja modela', *Ekonomska analiza*, pp. 120–7.
Dubravčič, D. (1970) 'Labour as Entrepreneurial Input', *Economica*, vol. 37, pp. 297–310.
Horvat, B. (1967) 'Prilog zasnivanju teorije jugoslavenskog poduzeca', *Ekonomska analiza*, pp. 7–28.
Horvat, B. (1979) 'Autogestion: efficacité et theorie néo-classique', *Revue économique*, pp. 361–69.
Horvat, B. (1982) *The Political Economy of Socialism* (New York: Sharpe).
Milanović, B. (1982) 'The Austrian Theory of the Cooperative Firm', mimeo., Jugoslav Research Seminar on Economic Theory (JUNASET), p. 20.
Parinello, S. (1971) 'Un contributo alla teoria dell' impresa jugoslava', *Est-Ovest*, no. 3, pp. 43–66.
Petrin, T. (1981) *Analiza vzrokov koncentracije organizacijskih epot v industriji in trgovini Jugoslavije v litih 1954–76*, unpublished doctoral dissertion, Ljubljana University.
Phlips, L. (1971) *Effects of Industrial Concentration* (Amsterdam: North-Holland).
Prašnikar, J. (1980) 'The Jugoslav Self-Managed Firm and Its Behaviour', *Economic Analysis and Workers' Management*, pp. 1–32.
Prašnikar, J. (1982) 'Samoupravno združeno delo in položaj samoupravnega podjetja v njem', mimeo., JUNASET, p. 27.
Steinherr, A. and Thisse, J.F. (1979) 'Is There a Negatively-Sloped Supply Curve in the Labour-Managed Firm', *Economic Analysis and Workers' Management*.
Vanek, J. (1970) *The General Theory of Labour Managed Market Economies* (Ithaca: Cornell University Press).
Ward, B. (1958) 'The Firm in Illyria: Market Syndicalism', *American Economic Review*, vol. 58, pp. 566–89.
Wicksell, K. (1893) *Über Wert, Kapital and Rente* (Jena: Fischer).

Discussion of the Paper by Branko Horvat

Laffont observed that Horvat's aspiration wage provides[*] a convenient way around the troublesome tendency for labour-managed firms to reduce output as output price rises. He suggested that this propensity might again become important once more attention was paid to the choice of the appropriate aspiration wage. To clarify this, he suggested a simple model with an endogenous aspiration wage. Suppose that firms had random outputs, fixed costs of K dollars, and employment equal to L workers. Suppose further that workers had agreed upon a level of investment I^*. Define P to be output price, X to be labour input and ϵ to be a random variable. Workers chose an 'aspiration' level of output to maximise

$$\frac{P \cdot \sum_\epsilon f(X, \epsilon) - K - I^*}{X}$$

which is equal to expected profit per worker. Let X^* (the 'aspiration' level of employment) be the solution to this problem; then the corresponding aspiration wage was

$$W^* = \frac{P \cdot \sum_\epsilon f(X, \epsilon) - K - I^*}{X^*}$$

However, this was precisely the Ward (1957) model of a labour-managed firm amended to include stochastic output. As a consequence, the same unusual comparative statistics with respect to changes in price still arose. This model only described behaviour in the long run, for suppose that managers learnt ϵ before they performed their maximisation. Taking the aspiration wage, W^*, as given, they maximised *ex post*:

$$P \cdot f(X, \epsilon) - K - W^*$$

This procedure yielded an employment function $X(\epsilon)$; a wage bill equal to $W^* X(\epsilon)$; and actual investment equal to planned investment plus the difference between planned and actual wage payments. This was similar to a classical model so that in contrast to the traditional model of the labour-managed firm, planned output would rise with price. The important point was that, in the short run, the firm would behave like a profit-maximising firm, while, in the long run, the usual problems associated with labour-managed firms arose. Laffont added that the aspiration wage approach might find its best application in large firms, where the objectives of workers and managers were likely to diverge. In small firms, he suggested, managers would be very likely to have the same objectives as workers. Managers would, therefore, prefer to maximise residual profit per worker.

Laffont went on to question whether Prašnikar's empirical results (1980) could be cited as conclusive evidence that the aspiration wage provided a way of formulating the firm's objective function. Laffont quoted from Prašnikar to show that the conclusion of the empirical research must be that firms maximised income per worker, at least in the long run.

Laffont then questioned the 'folk' theorem in the research on labour-managed firms, which stated that free entry would lead to efficiency. He cited his own work with Moreaux (1983) as an attempt to examine this issue. In their paper, they used Novshek and Sonnen-schein's (1978) approach to see whether Cournot quantity setting equilibria in labour-managed economies would converge to the competitive outcome. The unusual short-run behaviour of the labour-managed firm could lead to a situation where equilibrium did not exist. This argument was illustrated in Figure A.10.1.

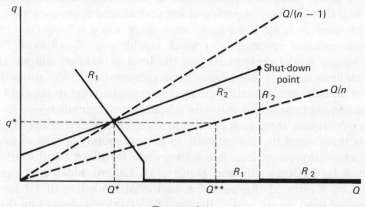

FIG. A.10.1.

The horizontal axis gave the output produced by all the existing firms in an industry (Q). The new entrant into the industry took this output to be fixed. The vertical axis gave output by an individual firm (q). Let R_1 be the reaction curve for a profit-maximising firm. The curve would be downward sloping and there would be some minimal level of output below which the firm would not be able to cover its variable costs. The firm's optimal reaction to large industry outputs would be to shut down conditionally. Roughly speaking, the reaction curve was downward sloping because an increase in output by the existing firms caused price to fall. A profit-maximising firm would tend to respond by reducing output. The only possible symmetric equilibrium occurred when all n firms in the industry produce q^* units of output, i.e. at the point where its reaction curve crossed the line $Q/n - 1$. In this case, each of the n firms in the industry was, on its reaction curve against the other $(n - 1)$ firms in the industry. A firm considering entering the industry would be faced with n competitors producing $n \cdot q^* = Q^{**}$ units of output. Since its reaction curve run along the axis at this point, the new firm would not enter.

In the labour-managed economy, an increase in output by existing firms in an industry would depress price, causing potential entrants to *expand* their outputs. Reaction curves would be *upward* sloping, like R_2 in the figure. Suppose that (q^*, Q^*) was a potential equilibrium with n firms in the industry. A potential entrant facing output Q^{**} would and it profitable to enter. If R_2 remained above Q/n to the shut-down point, there would be no symmetric equilibrium at all with $n + 1$ firms, hence no equilibrium at all. Laffont and Moreaux showed that for every sequence of labour-managed economies along which fixed costs for firms go to zero, there was a subsequence of labour-managed economies for which equilibrium did not exist. In the simple model presented here, the level of industry output at which firms found it best to shut down increased. The discontinuity point on each firm's reaction curve then moved up and to the right. Exact equilibrium would only exist when the discontinuity lay on the line Q/n. It was, then, easy to see that a sequence of decreasing fixed costs that caused the discontinuity to move smoothly up and to the right must involve at least one subsequence for which the discontinuities lay between Q/n and $Q/n(n = 1)$. Laffont added that this difficulty illustrated the need for additional modelling of labour-managed firms, in particular, the need for additional thought on the objective function to be used by labour-managed firms.

Mrinal Datta Chaudhuri took issue with the idea that economies should be distinguished by the different objectives possessed by participants. He suggested that a more important distinguishing characteristic was the manner in which that equilibrium was established among firms. The literature on labour-managed firms that had followed Ward had been exclusively partial equilibrium, at least until the paper by Laffont and Moreaux. This had prevented the literature from considering critical issues like the role of the state, and the potential for co-operation among different agents.

Von Ungern-Sternberg suggested that in a labour-managed economy where income per worker was to be maximised, there would be a tendency toward underemployment. Horvat responded that contrary to this prediction of Ward's model, there tended to be over-employment in Yugoslav industries.

Ungern and *Walroos* suggested that an appropriate response to the difficulty of formulating an objective function for firms was to study firms in more detail, identifying separate interest groups within the firm and studying their interactions. In their view, this was the motivation behind the current literature on incentives. Walroos argued with Horvat's view that a socially-owned industry would be better from a welfare viewpoint, than a privately-owned industry. The main distinction between the two, according to Walroos, was that shares could not be traded with social ownership. Such restrictions on trade should make people worse off. Horvat responded that free exhange was efficient only in highly stylised theoretical economies. In the real world, such restrictions on exchange were often seen to lead to welfare improvements. As an example, he noted that unemployment was typically much lower in socialist economies.

Phlips asked whether interest should be paid for the use of social capital. Horvat responded that to prevent waste there must be an interest charge for the use of social capital. These interest payments could be reinvested in the firm. To the extent that private capital was used in production, it would earn interest in the usual way.

In response to a question by *Nelson* concerning incentives for research and innovation in socialist economies, Horvat responded that very little empirical work had been done to explore the determinants of technological advance in socialist countries. He suggested that empirical work that he had done with his graduate students suggests that technological advance in Yugoslavia followed, rather than led, rates of growth.

Stiglitz suggested that one way to get around the unusual short-run behaviour of the labour-managed firm would be to dynamise the problem. Workers objectives would then be to maximise the discounted utility of their lifetime wage stream, subject to appropriate bankruptcy and investment constraints. Then, at any instant of time, firm choices would have to satisfy the usual marginal conditions. The difficulties associated with the odd objective function would disappear. Horvat responded that this approach had been taken by Conte (1979) in his study of the stability problem. He was able to show that dynamising the workers problem removed the instability that was usually associated with upward sloping supply curves.

REFERENCES

Conte, M. (1979) 'Short-Run Dynamics of the Labour-Managed Firm', *Economic Analysis and Workers' Management*.

Laffont, J.J. and Moreaux, M. (1983) 'The Nonexistence of a Free Entry Cournot Equilibrium in Labour Managed Economies', *Econometrica*, 51(2).

Novshek, W. and Sonnenschein, H. (1978) 'Cournot and Walras Equilibria', *Journal of Economic Theory*, 14.

Prašnikar, J. (1980) 'The Yugoslav Self-Managed Firm and Its Behaviour', *Economic Analysis and Workers' Management*.

Ward, B. (1957) 'Workers Management in Yugoslavia', *Journal of Political Economy*, 65.

11 Competition and Industrial Organisation in the Centrally Planned Economies

Z. Roman

RESEARCH INSTITUTE OF INDUSTRIAL
ECONOMICS OF THE HUNGARIAN ACADEMY OF
SCIENCES, HUNGARY

I COMPETITION

'Competition: the condition prevailing in a market in which rival sellers try to increase their profit at one another's expense. . .' (McGraw-Hill, *Dictionary of Modern Economics*, 1965, p. 102). 'Competition enters all major areas of man's life and generally connotes rivalry between two or more men or groups for a given prize.' (*International Encyclopædia of the Social Sciences*, vol. 3, 1968, p. 181).

In this paper the term 'competition' will be used in its broader sense to mean a phenomenon which predominantly characterises market economies, but it is always present and significant in economic life though in the various types of economic system this is to different extents and in different contexts and forms.

This paper considers competition as a general category manifesting itself in all areas of human activities (and in the non-human organic world too). Competition is evoked by: (i) the scarcity of goods or the limits on other variables (e.g. the purchasing power of buyers); and (ii) the instinct for rivalry. Since these two factors prevail in all societies and in all economic systems, some forms of competition appear everywhere. Competition cannot be eliminated,

315

but it can (and as a rule will) be regulated in order to utilise its driving forces while limits are put on its undesirable consequences (which can be conceived very differently).

Competition goes on between individuals, groups, organisations, nations and systems. It occurs in different fields and in the pursuit of different goals. Individuals, groups, organisations and institutions have multiple goals; while competing with each other for goal A they may co-operate or compete with others for goal B. Therefore competition both separates and connects simultaneously.

Competition might, but seldom does, exclude co-operation between the actors even in seeking to achieve the same goal, and vice versa: behind co-operation, almost always weaker or stronger competition is hidden. Competition can crush co-operation for a time and then revitalise it; co-operation can successively relax and strengthen competition, as environment and power relations change. Competition and co-operation are largely complementary, particularly if they are not considered at a single point of time or isolated in a single dimension.

II   CENTRALLY-PLANNED ECONOMIES

This paper deals with the group of seven European CMEA member countries. They are: Bulgaria, Czechoslovakia, the German Democratic Republic (GDR), Hungary, Poland, Romania and the Union of Soviet Socialist Republics (USSR). These countries call themselves socialist but so does Yugoslavia; they are often described as communist countries or given other names. Since in this short chapter I cannot discuss and clarify these notions adequately, I prefer to use the neutral UN term: centrally-planned economies (CPEs).

These seven countries show both fundamental common features, namely, the social ownership of the overwhelming proportion of the means of production, and the central planning of the economy. But they show significant differences as well, in their area and size of population, level of development, historical traditions, institutional arrangements, and system of economic guidance.

Some of these characteristics can be illustrated statistically, as in Table 11.1; others cannot. On the share of the socialist sector, it should be noted that this includes: (i) state-owned enterprises; (ii) co-operatives; and (iii) auxiliary activities of the population (the 'second economy'). Component (iii) is less significant in industry –

TABLE 11.1 SOME CHARACTERISTICS OF EUROPEAN CENTRALLY-PLANNED ECONOMIES, 1980

Indicator	Bulgaria	Czechoslovakia	GDR	Hungary	Poland	Romania	USSR
Area (000's of sq.km)	111	128	108	93	313	238	22402
Population (millions)	8.9	15.3	16.7	10.7	35.6	22.2	265.5
Relative per capita GDP*† foreign trade turnover*	129	114	133	168	60	64	31
Per cent share of employment:							
in agriculture	24	13	10	21	25	29	20
in industry	35	38	43	33	32	36	30
Per cent share of the socialist sector:							
in net material product	99.9	99.5	96.4	97.6	84.4	95.5	100.0
in industrial output	98.8	100.0	99.0	99.6	85.5	99.5	100.0
in agricultural output	99.9	97.6	95.5	98.9	22.7	85.6	100.0

*Unweighted average of CMEA countries = 100. † Estimates for 1973, from the *Economic Bulletin for Europe*, vol. 31, no. 2, p. 15.
Source *CMEA Statistical Yearbook.*

the major subject of this chapter – but is quite important in agriculture, and not negligible in house construction and some services.

The two common basic features of these countries – the social ownership of the overwhelming part of the means of production and the central planning of the economy – are closely related; but, on the basis of historical experience, they should not necessarily be linked in a uniform way. These two characteristics, in combination, first appeared when the Soviet Union was established. After the Second World War this model was taken over, with some variation, by a number of other European and non-European countries. Yugoslavia, with its system of self-management, produced an example which shows that, on the basis of the social ownership of the means of production, another alternative model can be realised and developed.

On the basis of longer experience, the idea that uniform solutions are both possible and necessary has been dropped; needs and measures for making improvements in the economic systems have been reinforced. Now, within the group of centrally-planned economies there are marked differences of opinion on whether individual enterprises should be obliged to follow indicators derived from the central plan, how many of these and of what type. Furthermore, there are similar differences over the actual role of directives, markets, prices and profits. For example, frequently, direct and indirect systems of economic guidance are distinguished, while other theories think rather in terms of a continuum – with a number of variants existing between the two extreme poles. This makes modelling more complicated, but actually corresponds more closely to reality. At present, Hungary's system has the fewest direct and the most indirect elements in all CMEA countries, next comes Bulgaria and, given the changes planned there, Poland follows.

III INDUSTRIAL ORGANISATION

Industrial organisation is (i) the complex of organisations and institutions active in the economic system; and (ii) a discipline for analysing the interrelationships between markets and the structure, conduct and performance of enterprises; or for dealing, beyond these topics, with industrial economics in a broader sense.

Under conditions of private ownership, production can be organised exclusively in independent enterprises. After a short period of transition, an important historical lesson learned in the Soviet Union was that the production of commodities with efficient management necessitated also the establishment of conditions, under social ownership, which made it possible to organise and manage individual technologically-separate units as economic entities and with 'independent accounting' (*hozraschot*). As in all economic systems, so in centrally-planned economies there are large numbers of 'actors', enterprises, institutions, etc. on the scene. There is also interaction of structure, conduct and performance, with roles and outcomes foreseen (or taking unawares) central planning and control.

The development of industrial economics in the Soviet Union dates back to the early 1930s. The first large-scale federal conference on industrial economics was in 1929; the first widely used textbook, edited by I. A. Granovski and D. L. Markus, was published in 1940. A number of issues treated under 'Industrial Organisation' in the West are dealt with in the centrally-planned economies under 'The Economics of Industry'. Of course, not all these issues are covered, and they are linked with other approaches, emphases, value judgements – and terminology. Some other aspects of 'Industrial Organisation' are considered and developed in the CPEs under the twin-discipline of the 'Planning, management and organisation of industrial enterprises'.[1]

The differences in these disciplines between West and East originate from the different characteristics of the economic systems, industries and enterprises they describe and analyse. Partly, also, they arise from the different demarcation of the topics covered within their framework. Without alluding to convergence, it may be observed that these differences have somewhat diminished. Several phenomena and methods which used to play a vital role only in either the market or the centrally-planned economies have attained greater importance in the other group of countries too. Examples are: corporate and macroeconomic planning; state intervention; the existence of state-owned enterprises in market economies; autonomous decisions on sales, marketing and pricing by individual enterprises in centrally-planned economies.

IV INTERFACES

Usually planning, state ownership and centralisation are associated with socialism and centrally-planned economies; markets, private ownership and decentralisation with capitalism and market economies. Basically this is true, but a closer look reveals that in many respects both systems are mixed and that individual countries within both groups show remarkable differences in this regard. Quite a number of other variables, including those of the political system, are needed to characterise a country accurately.

Competition is not explicitly included in this grid of notions but is usually dealt with implicitly as a corollary of markets. This holds for market competition, but not for the other forms of competition met with under a broader interpretation, as in this paper. Valuable contributions to comparative economics describe and explain the characteristics of the system and functioning of centrally-planned economies. They do so from many angles and with deep insight. This paper attempts to add something to our understanding from the aspects of competition and industrial organisation.

Competition fulfils two basic tasks in market economies: it stimulates and regulates performance. In fact, any competition in any field may perform these two basic roles. In market economies, market competition is the core of competition, although – in the real world of imperfect competition – its non-market forms are also of significance.

The traditional system for the economic guidance of CPEs aims to eliminate market competition entirely: central planning takes over the role of regulation, while performance should be stimulated by other components of the system and by the socialist competition of workers and enterprises. Other kinds of competition are not recognised and, as against competition, common interests and co-operation will be emphasised.

The long discussions on the feasibility and efficiency of such systems are well known. Now, more than six decades of experience in the Soviet Union and more than three in Eastern Europe prove the feasibility of these systems, but with growing indications that they suffer from associated efficiency losses. These indications, together with impulses resulting from the growth of trade with market economies, have led the centrally-planned economies to reconsider the role of market (and non-market) competition and to make changes in their theory and practice. These are reviewed in the following paragraphs.

Industrial organisation was for long studied in the centrally-planned economies almost exclusively as an outcome of the objective processes of specialisation, co-operation, concentration and combination. The organisational pattern was seen as an important variable of the economic system – the impact of structure on conduct and performance could be, and has been, identified only on the basis of a more critical analysis of the functioning of this system, of the sources of loss and the needs for improvement. The structure – conduct – performance paradigm, if properly adapted and transplanted (which is very much needed) might also have great explanatory power for the centrally-planned economies.

V STRUCTURE IN THE CPEs

Industrial organisation in CPEs can be characterised, first, by high concentration (relatively small numbers of enterprises) and by the limited freedom of action permitted to these enterprises. The second feature is the direct consequence of the system of central planning: the first has some other motives. The preference for large enterprises can be traced back to two factors. The first is a traditional overestimation of the economies of scale accruing to large enterprises, through ignoring possible diseconomies of scale and paying too little attention to product-specific economies. Second, as also happens in market economies in the case of state-owned enterprises, control institutions like to simplify their job by dealing with a relatively small number of subordinate units.

In the CPEs, industrial activities are performed by (i) state-owned industrial enterprises; (ii) industrial co-operatives; (iii) as auxiliary activities of non-industrial, state-owned enterprises and co-operatives, the two main examples being food processing in agriculture and the production of building materials in the construction industry; and (iv) private firms (as a rule only handicrafts). As Table 11.2 indicates, in each centrally-planned economy the state-owned sector dominates although, when measured by other indicators (see Table 11.3) the relative shares are somewhat different.

The shares of state-owned enterprises and of co-operatives are not the same when one looks at branches. We can assume that in this respect the rough relative importance in terms of branches (sectors), but not the actual proportions, in Hungarian industry are more or less typical: there are no co-operatives at all in mining or electricity. Their contribution is negligible in the production of basic materials, but is substantial in a number of other, mostly consumer goods, branches. These branches (percentage share of employment in parentheses) are those like fabricated metal products (17), processing of plastics (34), furniture (35), leather and footwear (35) and clothing (46). Non-state-owned enterprises could not be promoted to the same extent in all branches, and not at all in those of strategic

TABLE 11.2 INDUSTRIAL OUTPUT BY SOCIAL SECTORS, 1980 (%)

Social Sector	Bulgaria	Czechoslovakia	GDR	Hungary	Poland	Romania	USSR
State-owned enterprises	95.6	98.4	92.6	93.8	85.6	95.7	97.5
Co-operatives	4.2	1.6	4.9	5.5	12.4	4.0	2.5
Private handicrafts	0.2	0.0	2.5	0.7	2.0	0.3	0.0
Total	100.0	100.0	100.0	100.0	100.0	100.0	100.0

Source CMEA Statistical Yearbook.

TABLE 11.3   SHARES OF THE SOCIAL SECTORS IN HUNGARIAN
INDUSTRY, VARIOUS INDICATORS, 1980 (%)

Indicator	State-owned enterprises	Co-operatives	Private handicrafts	Total industry
Gross value of output	93.7	5.6	0.7	100.0
Net value of output	89.3	9.0	1.7	100.0
Employment	83.8	13.4	1.8	100.0

Source   Hungarian Statistical Yearbook.

importance. Nevertheless, the question of which branches are most appropriate for the promotion of activity by non-state-owned enterprises is a valid one and worthy of consideration in CPEs. In Hungary in general those branches/activities will be put into this category where factors associated with economies of scale do not exclude or endanger the prospects of small-sized units and a strong need is felt for greater flexibility.

All state-owned enterprises in CPEs are responsible, legal persons, and liable to give an account of their activities in a 'statement of balance'. However, their statutes, rights, obligations and other responsibilities can be and are variously defined, in accordance with the actual national system of economic guidance. Within any one system the biggest differences originate from differences in hierarchic arrangements. A public enterprise can be subordinated to an economic unit supervising public enterprises are: (i) ministries or other state agencies with similar duties; and (ii) local or regional authorities. These exert control through special departments, sections or directorates.

Economic units, which have a right and duty to control a certain number of enterprises, can have various names: national enterprises, combines, concerns, trusts, associations. These economic units are legal persons, with complete accounts and balance sheets, but they are also charged with control functions over other enterprises. Usually, enterprises subordinated to administrative units have more autonomy than do enterprises controlled by larger economic units. (I disregard here such mixed forms as, for example, enterprises subject to administrative units with some elements of business accounting.) Below this, in the hierarchical structure within plants and administrative units, the major types of subordination are as follows:

1. An enterprise with a single plant may be; (a) subordinated to an administrative unit; or (b) subordinated to a larger economic unit.
2. A factory which is part of a multi-plant enterprise may be (a) subordinated to an administrative unit; or (b) subordinated to a larger economic unit.

The larger economic units are, of course, controlled by an administrative unit. This means that between the factory and the administrative unit exercising supreme control and supervision there is: in case 1(a) direct contact, in case 1(b) and 2(a) a single intermediate link, and in case 2(b); two intermediate links.

By tradition, the typical form of organisation is the multi-plant enterprise and, except in Hungary, case 2(b) is increasingly found. this means, on the one side, some centralisation *vis-à-vis* formerly independent enterprises, but, on the other side, some decentralisation *vis-à-vis* the ministries.

The main characteristics of the present system of industrial organisation in Hungary reflect the longstanding preference for large enterprises. Table 11.4 indicates an impressive growth in concentration in the Hungarian state-owned industry. The greatest changes took place in two periods; in the early 1950s and in the early 1960s. In the first wave, as part of a process of rationalisation, small plants

TABLE 11.4   CHANGES IN ENTERPRISE CONCENTRATION IN HUNGARIAN STATE-OWNED INDUSTRY

Year	Numbers of enterprises					
	Number of workers					
	Less than 50	51–100	101–500	501–1000	More than 1000	Total
1950	498	210	474	142	101	1425
1960	108	139	644	250	197	1338
1965	46	86	343	111	254	840
1980	32	4		159	303	699
Percentage distribution of numbers of workers						
1950	2.2	3.1	24.2	20.1	50.4	100.0
1960	0.4	1.2	18.9	21.21	58.3	100.0
1965	0.1	0.6	9.0	7.9	82.4	100.0
1980	0.1	0.1	5.3	11.0	83.5	100.0

Source   Hungarian Statistical Yearbook.

TABLE 11.5   ENTERPRISES IN HUNGARIAN STATE-OWNED
INDUSTRY, BY NUMBER OF PLANTS, 1975

Sector	Number of plants per enterprise						
	1	2	3–5	6–10	11–20	21–	Total
Mining	7	2	8	9	3	1	30
Electricity generation	7	5	4	4	1	—	21
Metal production	17	5	—	3	1	—	26
Fabricated metal products	22	23	68	41	7	5	166
Building materials	2	4	8	9	8	3	34
Chemicals	11	9	17	6	3	—	46
Wood, paper and printing	25	20	21	5	3	1	75
Textiles	6	8	13	10	4	—	41
Leather, shoes and clothing	6	9	25	10	3	1	54
Food manufacturing	36	19	52	40	25	1	173
Other industries	21	9	10	8	1	—	49
State-owned industry	160	113	116	145	59	12	715

Source   Unpublished calculations of the Hungarian Central Statistical Office.

were concentrated; in the second, mergers were directed towards medium-sized and larger enterprises aiming to establish huge multi-plant (in many branches omni-plant) firms.

In considering the size distribution of establishments or enterprises for international comparisons, as a rule employment data are used. Where there are significant differences in the relative levels of productivity of the countries under review, however, such measurements characterise only the concentration of employment and not the concentration of production. For adequate comparison, the use of adjusted employment figures is to be recommended: the employment figures should be rearranged into size classes, adjusted on the basis of relative levels of productivity. When one compares these adjusted figures with those for the developed market economies the share of small establishments seems somewhat lower in Hungary, but that of large plants not exceedingly high. On the other hand, in 1975, of the 715 enterprises in Hungarian state-owned industry, only 160 had a single plant; 216 had more than six plants (see Table 11.5). In other words, among the 5387 plants (establishments) only 3 per cent were autonomous enterprises; the overwhelming majority operated as sub-units of large enterprises.[2] This absolute dominance of multi-plant firms is the basic reason why, by any measure, the enterprise concentration ratio is much higher both in Hungary and in all other CPEs than it is in the market economies.[3]

According to the latest data available (see Table 11.6) Czechoslovakia and Romania show the highest degree of concentration among CPEs, but this judgement is somewhat arbitrary because of different terminology and classification for large economic units.

VI RECENT CHANGES AND SOME QUALIFICATIONS

In the 1970s in most CPEs, the trend was towards the establishment of large economic units with control functions. In the USSR, for example, of 43 954 state-owned industrial enterprises, 7366 belonged to associations (data from the *USSR Statistical Yearbook*, 1979). Together, the 3947 associations had 17 516 production units; 7366 enterprises with and 10 150 without 'independent accounting' and balance sheets. The largest enterprises were attached to associations which represented nearly 50 per cent of total industry, both in output and employment.

There are two types of association in the Soviet Union. In the so-called 'production associations', production and economic activities dominate, and they embrace both enterprises with and units without 'independent accounting'. The so-called 'industrial associations' embrace only enterprises together with organisations (institutes, bureaux, etc.) engaged in R & D activities; in their case, the control functions should help with integrating R & D and production.

In the federal system of the Soviet Union there are: federal (all-Union); federal-republican; and republican ministries. The federal-republican ministries are subordinated to the Council of Ministers of the Republic but are also controlled by the corresponding federal ministry. The situation of an enterprise or association superintended by a federal ministry (for example, a large steel mill or car factory) or by a federal-republican ministry (for example, in the textile or food industries) is not identical. Fifty-three per cent of total industrial output in 1979 originated in enterprises and associations attached to federal ministries and 47 per cent from those attached to other types of authority. In the CPEs, as well as in other countries with a large number and/or a high share of state-owned enterprises, the control institutions – governmental, functional, sectoral, regional, etc. – together form a special sub-system of industrial organisation which is worthy of separate study.

In the GDR, the establishment of associations and combinations had already begun in the 1960s and now these organisational forms

TABLE 11.6 ENTERPRISE CONCENTRATION IN CPEs, 1978

(A) The percentage distribution of numbers of enterprises

Size classes Number of workers	Bulgaria	Czechoslovakia	GDR*	Hungary	Poland	Romania	USSR†
0–500	65.5	10.8	86.5	60.4	61.5	28.6	77.?
501–1000	18.8	21.5	6.4	15.2	18.3	23.2	10.?
1001–5000	14.9	61.7	6.5	21.3	18.5	42.6	10.?
5001–	0.8	6.0	0.6	3.1	1.7	5.6	1.?
Total	100.0	100.0	100.0	100.0	100.0	100.0	100.0

(B) The percentage distribution of numbers of workers

	Bulgaria	Czechoslovakia	GDR*	Hungary	Poland	Romania	USSR†
0–500	23.1	1.7	29.6	13.6	16.9	4.9	20.8
501–1000	21.6	7.8	15.0	11.3	16.7	10.6	13.5
1001–5000	44.1	64.2	41.1	46.3	49.2	56.6	37.5
5001–	11.2	26.3	14.3	28.8	17.2	28.0	28.2
Total	100.0	100.0	100.0	100.0	100.0	100.0	100.0

*Data for 1977. †Data for 1975.
Source CMEA Statistical Yearbook.

dominate. The combination is, as a rule, a more or less closed complex of related enterprises. The associations can also have some control functions over enterprises not directly subordinated to them. A third form, the *Leitbetrieb* (leading enterprise) renders assistance to a particular group of enterprises, but with looser legal links. In Bulgaria, associations began to be organised in 1971; in Czechoslovakia the 'concern' form is most common; Poland and Romania have different types of 'large economic unit'.

In Hungary, the term association denotes a legal framework for the voluntary co-operation of completely independent enterprises, though this is not widespread. Associations operate, for example, in the electronic and pharmaceutical industries. More than one quarter of state-owned enterprises were controlled by trusts, up to the end of 1980, in industries like coal, oil, aluminium and food processing where the need for closer co-ordination and control was supposed to be of primary importance. Resolutions of associations are legitimised by a consensus of their member enterprises; trusts are also authorised to intervene directly in financial matters.

According to prevailing opinion in Hungary, the present pattern of industrial enterprises is too centralised and does not conform to the system of economic guidance. The predominance of multi- or omni-plant enterprises means that there is a considerable internalisation of the buyer-and-seller relations. It also restricts or eliminates real competition. To increase flexibility, and curb the rivalry in obtaining subsidies and exemptions, the necessary rationalisation and divestment also seem to be more difficult in large enterprises than with small- and medium-size firms. In 1980 the Hungarian government ended the system of centralisation in industrial organisation. Seven trusts have been dissolved and others are under investigation. A number of large, multi-plant enterprises have been partly or totally disintegrated. The establishment and growth of small undertakings, as well as of different forms of co-operative agreement, joint venture and profit-sharing devices will be stimulated. Within limits, these will also include foreign enterprises.

For state-owned enterprises, organisational forms (in the sense dealt with above) can be easily changed. This possibility often stimulates rapid and uniform change in order to accelerate or implement tendencies which seem general, favourable and promising. But it will not necessarily have this result in all conditions or in every branch of industry. For the administration, direct contact with production units offers more insight and greater possibility for intervention; but where there is a considerable number of enterprises, this will overburden its staff. One or more intermediate links restricts the autonomy of the primary production units, but is favourable for internal economic co-ordination in respect of economies of scale, entry into the market, etc.

These differeı.t organisational forms can be dealt with as 'alternative means of co-ordinating production', to use Coase's (1951) formulation, or analysed by the 'transaction–cost approach' which Williamson (1975) has elaborated. In the CPEs, the traditional alternatives are not market or enterprise but central planning (and management) or enterprise. In this context, the increasing role of large economic units means greater delegation of the powers and responsibilities of central planning and management – a process in the opposite direction to that described for market economies by Chandler (1977). Of the six types of enterprises set out in Williamson's (1975) classification, all can be found in the CPEs: in general, some multi-divisional form will be suggested. At the same time, the need for a wider use of the categories: market, money, prices and profits, has also be emphasised, particularly in Hungary. And, since their role will be limited (internalised) where there are large economic units, current Hungarian moves are now towards decentralisation.

VII ON CONDUCT AND PERFORMANCE IN THE CPEs

Before turning to specific issues in the CPEs, I revert to some of the general problems of performance and evaluation with particular reference to public (state-owned) enterprises in whatever economic system.

1. Performance should, and as a rule will, be evaluated against the goals and tasks of the enterprise. These can and will be formulated, in practice, with different degrees of accuracy – whether *ex ante* or only *ex post*. These goals, tasks, targets, are, with negligible exceptions, multiple. Even where profitability is taken as the only objective, the question arises: over what time horizon? Often difficulties emerge in making operational and in quantifying goals, tasks, targets, and this also leads to uncertainty in assessing the extent to which they have been met.

2. The criteria of performance evaluation can differ – not only in their content, but also in the base-values selected. These base-values can be indicators: of the part performance, of other enterprises in the

same period; or norms, standards and potential calculated *ex ante* or *ex post*; or targets either fixed *ex ante* or adjusted to take account of changing environmental and other conditions.

The problem of multiple goals does arise with private enterprises, but in the performance evaluation of public enterprises it becomes a central issue, and for two reasons. First, although private enterprises do have social obligations and responsibilities, these are, as a rule, treated only as constraints to be met in striving for commercial goals; but in public enterprises, macroeconomic and social objectives can be directly addressed. Second, in private firms different goals are usually represented by different persons or groups; in public enterprises these persons or groups can be very powerful, with authority to act as principals. These two circumstances not only sharpen goal-conflicts but also aggravate problem 2 above.

Moreover, bureaucratic systems never work as smoothly and efficiently as they are designed to do, or as is described in theory. Subordinate organisational units – in our case, state-owned enterprises – follow and validate their own interests, and they have many. First, they have two powerful instruments for this purpose: facilities for information handling and for performance adjustment. An opportunity is given for their effective use (or abuse) in handling information, for example, in discussions of targets or plans, or in project evaluation; in fact, in the whole process of planning and of preparing decisions. This is particularly the case in small countries, since there experts in the enterprises necessarily take part in these activities. The mechanism of 'performance adjustment' was observed and described by sociologists mainly for individuals and groups; its process is similar, but more complex, for the sub-units of an enterprise or for an enterprise as a whole. Nor is it possible to assume that the control institutions in this mostly large and strongly-departmentalised sub-system represent national goals without differences in interpretation or emphasis, or without redefining and adjusting some goals in order to suit their own ends.[4]

The following further points should help towards an understanding of conduct and performance, and of the conditions of competition in the CPEs. First, almost all consumer and producer prices are determined or regulated by state authorities, except in Hungary.[5]

Second, the freedom of action of enterprises is limited by several constraints, in addition to those of price determination. These include: (i) the mandatory performance indicators included in their plans and approved by the supervisory authorities; (ii) the statutes of enterprises which strictly define their 'profiles'; and (iii) the way in which the central allocation of investment funds is carried out. The number of mandatory indicators used has been reduced in all CPEs in the last decade. This has increased the enterprise's share of autonomous decision but only to a limited extent, and only in their operations. On the other hand, it should be noted that planning is an iterative process, including negotiations where enterprises can influence the targets and development prospects set for them. Hungary is again an exception: the central agencies are there entrusted with certain compulsory duties derived from the macroeconomic plan. State-owned enterprises, however, prepare their plans without mandatory directives, though as a rule with some consultation with supervisory authorities.[6]

Third, due to high enterprise concentration, monopolistic and oligopolistic market situations are typical and even where there is a large number of sellers, competition in the market is ruled out when total capacity cannot meet demand; prices are rigid; and entry into the market is impossible or very difficult. Because this is frequently the case in CPEs, the seller's market and shortage situations analysed in depth by Kornai (*The Shortage*, North-Holland (1980)) often arise.

Fourth, the rapid growth of foreign trade in CPEs, even though below the world average, should be mentioned. East–West trade has also increased until recently at rapid rates. Intra-CMEA trade now amounts to 50–60 per cent of the total turnover of these countries, so that their trade with the rest of the world is significant too. In foreign trade they encounter competition both on export markets and, via limited imports, on domestic markets as well.

VIII COMPETITION IN CENTRALLY-PLANNED ECONOMIES

Market competition in the CPEs is very limited and, of course, does not work as a regulatory system. Nevertheless, there are two areas where it has significance: (i) on the free market for agricultural and food products; and (ii) in foreign trade. In (i) the main conditions for market competition are met: large numbers of producers (with freedom for action); flexible prices; easy entry into the market; and little product differentiation. Though different CPEs have different regulations, constraints and areas, this is a sector in all CPEs where the functioning of the market mechanism is at least accepted or (in order to improve supply for the population) even promoted. (In Hungary this system has also been extended to industrial and service activities.)

In their foreign trade with market economies, CPEs enter into real markets and have to act as competitors. Whether their enterprises perceive the impact of this competition directly or only at several removes is difficult to say, but in the end this competition forces them into better performance and greater structural adjustment. Intra-CMEA foreign trade is based partly on long-term agreements and partly on short-term negotiations both about volumes and prices. This does not, however, exclude the need for taking into account actual and potential competition in foreign trade too, and it influences conduct, performance and, especially, investment decisions. Among the centrally-planned economies, Hungary has the highest per capita foreign trade turnover (see Table 11.1). In addition, a series of further measures strengthen the direct links in Hungary between production and foreign trade, domestic and foreign-trade prices, ties between organisations, etc.

Though the role of the market mechanism is limited, market signals are important in CPEs in all sectors, both for the producers and for planners at higher levels. An increasing need is recognised for transmitting these signals as directly as possible to the enterprises to enable them to make proper adjustments. Through these signals and adjustments some elements of market competition appear and gain ground. These primarily concern quality and product-mix rather than prices or resource allocation; thus they have more impact on performance and less on regulation. It should not be forgotten, however, that these signals are later taken into account, both in the evaluation of the performance of the enterprises and managers and (in the planning process) in negotiations about future needs and prospects for growth – also a major goal for enterprises and managers in the CPEs.

The system of central planning consists of an iterative integration of plans drafted by a large number of enterprises and institutions and covering all different aspects of economic development: material, financial, sectoral, regional, R & D, investment, etc. Similarly, enterprises and institutions, as planning agencies, draft their plans on the basis of proposals from their sub-units. This also is an iterative process, with subsequent evaluation and improvement of the aggregate plan. This process of optimalisation should substitute (foresee, forecast, in some sense imitate) actual market competition, as was explained first by Oscar Lange and Fred M. Taylor in the 1930s. Their ideas have been widely discussed, criticised and, later, further elaborated and refined. In the huge literature on this topic, some studies give more emphasis to the role of prices than of quantities; to the interactions of planning at different hierarchical levels; to the new possibilities of using large-scale computers. Studies emphasise the need for more flexibility; the use of elements of market mechanism; the sociological and behavioural aspects of planning; and growing uncertainty, due to faster technological progress; a bigger share of foreign trade and more unpredictable impulses in small countries.

Historical and comparative studies have attempted to evaluate how this system operates under the conditions prevailing in different stages of industrialisation, of development, etc. In the last two decades, all CPEs have introduced some improvements in their systems of central planning, aiming at flexibility and decentralisation in non-strategic issues. In this respect, Hungary has moved furthest, Bulgaria has started to move and Poland plans to move in this direction. In the other CPEs only small changes have occurred.

In this system of central planning, co-operation and cohesion are stressed, but there are many elements of non-market competition too, both formal and informal. What I call formal competition within the planning process occurs when different projects are evaluated, ranked, some of them approved, some remitted for improvement, and others rejected; and when the enterprises or other institutions submitting their projects for decision compete with each other. Enterprises preparing drafts of their annual or medium-term plans for the higher authorities, together with output targets and input requirements, must take into account the fact that these drafts will be assessed comparatively and, during this process, there will be a certain degree of competition between them. I define informal competition as that occurring when enterprises or other institutions try to influence this kind of decision by using several types of connection, including unofficial channels and indirect instruments. As in all competition, to fix the rules-of-game precisely without gaps and to exclude any improper form of influence is a difficult task in this process too. An increasing awareness of these problems must lead all CPEs to changes and improvements in their systems of planning, economic guidance and industrial organisation. Due to divergences in their expectations and preoccupations and in their interpretations of past experience in judging their present situations, they look for different, mostly mixed solutions.

The selection of adequate 'success-indicators' and of the establishment of adequate bases for performance evaluation are invariably central themes. This is because, in the system of compulsory planning indicators and of performance evaluation based on the assessment of these indicators in the current, as compared to the preceding, period and to the plan, these factors are indeed of utmost importance. The search for ways and means for increasing moral and material incentives, for increasing the intensity and proper direction of motivation as well as for stimulating healthy rivalry is centred around this problem. On the other hand, the limited impact of such minor changes and the need for stronger driving forces is increasingly recognised. The closure of factories is (and probably will be) a rare exception in CPEs. This means that there is a correspondingly greater need for radical structural adjustment and/or for urgent improvement in competitiveness, as well as making practical the idea of inducing competition for survival.

In my view, improvements in the system of indicators, the computerisation of planning, the establishment of large economic units, are only partial measures which alone cannot bring about the desired progress in efficiency. The appopriate 'product-mix' of the system's components should be elaborated and introduced by each country, according to its specific characteristics in a learning-by-doing process. One can recommend, as a general guideline, a requirement for more-open, fairer, more-transparent competition, and for a system of industrial organisation conforming with this requirement.

NOTES

1. See Z. Roman, 'L'economia industriale all' Est ed all' Ouest', *Rivista di Economia e Politica Industriale*, no. 1, 1978.
2. The average plant/enterprise ratio was 6.9. Similar data based on calculations for the three largest enterprises in each sector were: US 6.8: UK 6.4; FRG 5.1; Canada 4.2; Sweden 2.6 (see Scherer, 1974) 'The Determinants of Multi-plant Operation in Six Nations and Twelve Industries', *Kyklos*, vol. 17, p. 126). See also Z. Roman (1981) 'Industrial Organization in Hungary', in *"Economic Planning and Management"*, eds New Delhi.

   Quoting another calculation: the Minimum Efficient Scale found in the literature, in 17 out of 29 products exceeded the total Hungarian output.
3. This can also be corroborated for Hungary by using comparative data on the share of the largest enterprises. In 1975, of the 61 sectors in

Hungarian state-owned industry, the three largest enterprises accounted for more than three-quarters of output in 24 sectors; the four largest in 31; the six largest in 44; and the eight largest in 49 sectors. Fifty per cent of total output was produced by one enterprise in 19 sectors, and by less than five enterprises in 43 sectors out of the 61. The comparison of Hungarian and West German data on 29 sectors shows a higher share for the three largest companies in FRD only in three sectors (coal-mining, sugar, tobacco). See Roman (1981) 'Industrial Organization in Hungary'.

4. 'Industrial Policy in Hungary – Today and Tomorrow', in Z. Roman (ed.), *Industrial Development and Industrial Policy* (Budapest, 1979).

5. Here the share of free producer prices in 1980 was estimated to be 67 per cent (see B. Csikos–Nagy, *Economic Policy* (in Hungarian) (Budapest, 1982) p. 327). In 1981 in the industry special rules had been introduced making changes on the domestic market dependent on price changes on export and import markets which limit free price movements significantly.

6. Financial incentives and regulators, as well as a constant flow of information, should induce them to draft (and fulfil) their plans in harmony with the targets of the national plan. Hungarian enterprises also have more freedom in diversification and in investment decisions. The separation of the owner's and the sector's controls is now under discussion.

REFERENCES

Chandler, A.D. (1977) *The Visible Hand: Managerial Revolution in American Business* (Cambridge, Mass.–London: Harvard University Press).

Coase, R.H. (1952) 'The Nature of the Firm', in G.J. Stigler and K.E. Boulding (eds), *Readings in Price Theory* (Chicago: University of Chicago Press) p. 333.

Williamson, O.E. (1975) *Markets and Hierarchies: Analysis and Antitrust Implications: a Study in the Economics of Internal Organisation* (New York – London: Free Press (Macmillan)).

Discussion of the Paper by Z. Roman

Chaudhuri observed that many socialist economies had tended to move away from price-guided incentive systems. He speculated that at the source of this was a tendency in socialist economies toward a greater concentration in industrial structure. This change in structure might lead planners to feel that price-guided incentive systems that rely on competition might be less effective.

Tu Tu argued with Roman's attempt to apply competitive theories to centrally-planned economies. He agreed that the theory of behaviour in socialist economies tended to ignore important difficulties like incentive problems and divergence of goals. He argued, however, that these difficulties should be incorporated into the theory used to formulate socialist plans. If this could be done, an emphasis on competition would not be required.

Richard Nelson suggested that socialist economies might be subject to biases in the choice of research and development projects. This would arise because of the tendency, reported by Roman, for socialist economies to encourage large economic units to form. These large units would tend to concentrate R & D funds on a few key projects thus reducing the likelihood of success. Roman replied that beside centrally selected key projects in the socialist countries there was a growing awareness of the need for a general increase in the innovativeness of the enterprises. The approach to R & D in Hungary was to set aside a fund for R & D, half of which was given over to the central authorities, and half of which was allocated by the relevant unit. The centrally-controlled fund was used to promote research into a variety of projects, partly on a competitive basis.

Branko Horvat suggested that Roman's work suffered from a serious terminological problem. This involved the distinction between socialist, state and public enterprises. Horvat suggested that public enterprises were a Western phenomenon while state enterprises were more common in centrally-planned economies. Especially crucial was the distinction between socialist enterprise, where managers were elected by the workers, and state enterprise where managers were appointed by the state. Horvat argued that these terms should not be used interchangeably. Roman accepted that each country interpreted these ideas differently and they always needed clear explanation. Nevertheless it could not be stated in general that state-owned enterprises were not, or could not be called socialist enterprises.

Part Six
The Perfectly
Contestable Market –
A Benchmark

12 On the Theory of Perfectly-Contestable Markets

W. J. Baumol

NEW YORK UNIVERSITY AND PRINCETON
UNIVERSITY, USA

J. C. Panzar

NORTHWESTERN UNIVERSITY, USA

and

R. D. Willig[1]

PRINCETON UNIVERSITY, USA

I INTRODUCTION

The purpose of this chapter is to provide an overview of the theory of perfectly-contestable markets.[2] The treatment here is deliberately schematic in order to focus on the logical structure of the theory.

Perfectly-contestable markets can be viewed as a benchmark for the study of industry structure – a benchmark based on an idealised limiting case. In this limiting case, potential entry imposes the strongest possible symmetric constraint upon incumbents: entry is without disadvantage and is perfectly reversible. As a result, no role is played by the sunk costs, precommitments, asymmetric information and strategic behaviour that characterise many real markets and that are the subject of much penetrating current research in industrial organisation. With irreversibilities and the inducements for strategic behaviour assumed away, industry structure in perfectly-contestable markets is determined by the fundamental forces of demand and of production technology.

Of course, this is also true of perfectly-competitive markets. However, this most-familiar idealised limiting case is not a satisfactory benchmark for the study of industry structure in general, because it is intrinsically inapplicable to a variety of significant cases. In particular, where increasing returns to scale are present, perfectly-competitive behaviour (with its marginal-cost pricing) is logically inconsistent with the long-run financial viability of unsubsidised firms.

Thus, in place of perfect competition, we propose perfect contestability as a general standard of comparison for more-complex and (usually) more-realistic models of industrial organisation. However, this alteration in general standard does not always produce a change in implications because, as is shown below, perfectly-competitive behaviour is necessary in perfectly-contestable markets in certain specifiable circumstances. In other words, perfect contestability is a generalisation of perfect competition – a generalisation that can be used where returns to scale are increasing, as well as where returns are decreasing or constant.

Section II defines perfectly-contestable markets, compares them with perfectly-competitive markets, derives some of the basic properties of sustainable prices and industry structures, and examines the implications of perfect contestability for industries that produce a single, homogeneous output. In that case, only outcomes that are Ramsey optimal (i.e., welfare maximising subject to the financial viability of unsubsidised firms), can be sustained in a perfectly-contestable market. Section III sketches a model in which profit-maximising potential entrants may or may not exhibit the aggressive behaviour required for perfect contestability, depending on the relative values of structural parameters which characterise the degree to which costs are sunk. The analysis reveals that a market is contestable if entrants can reverse their investments without loss and suffer no other disadvantages relative to incumbents. Section IV outlines some of the implications of perfect contestability for the structure of multi-product industries that are not perfectly competitive. The analysis identifies some qualitative properties of multi-output production costs that are significant determinants of industry structure in these circumstances and examines some normative properties of the equilibria. Section V concludes the chapter by indicating the relevance of the analysis for positive economics and empirical work.

II PERFECTLY CONTESTABLE MARKETS: DEFINITIONS AND BASIC PROPERTIES

The theory presented here lies in the realm of partial equilibrium. It deals with the provision of the set of products $N = \{1, \ldots, n\}$, some of which may not actually be produced, and which is a proper subset of all the goods in the economy. The prices of these products are represented by vectors $p \in R^n_{++}$, and other prices are assumed to be exogenous and are suppressed in the notation. $Q(p) \in R^n_+$ is the vector-valued market demand function for the products in N and it suppresses consumers' incomes, which are assumed to be exogenous. For any output vector $y \in R^n_+$, $C(y)$ is the cost at exogenously-fixed factor prices when production is efficient. The underlying technology is assumed to be freely available to all incumbent firms and to all potential entrants. Where necessary, $C(y)$ and $Q(p)$ will be assumed to be differentiable.

Definition 1 A *feasible industry configuration* is composed of m firms producing output vectors $y^1, \ldots, y^m \in R^n_+$, at prices $p \in R^n_{++}$, such that the markets clear, $\Sigma^m_{i=1} y^i = Q(p)$, and that each firm at least breaks even, $p \cdot y^i - C(y^i) \geq 0$, $i = 1, \ldots, m$.

Thus, the industry configuration is taken as comprised of m firms, where m can be any positive integer, so that the industry structure is monopolistic if $m = 1$; competitive if m is sufficiently large, or oligopolistic for intermediate values of m. The term 'feasibility' refers to the requirements (a) that each of the firms involved selects a non-negative output vector that permits its production costs, $C(\cdot)$, to be covered at the market prices, p, and (b) that the sum of the outputs of the m firms satisfies market demands at those prices.

Definition 2 A feasible industry configuration over N, with prices p and firms' outputs $y^1, \ldots, y^m$, is *sustainable* if $p^e \cdot y^e \leq C(y^e)$ for all $p^e \in R^n_{++}$, $y^e \in R^n_+$, $p^e \leq p$, and $y^e \leq Q(p^e)$.

The interpretation of this definition is that a sustainable configuration affords no profitable opportunities for entry by potential entrants who regard incumbents' prices as fixed (for a period sufficiently long to make $C(\cdot)$ the relevant flow-cost function for an entrant). Here, a feasible marketing plan for a potential entrant is comprised of prices, p^e, that do not exceed the incumbents' quoted prices, p, and a quantity vector, y^e, that does not exceed market demand at the entrant's prices, $Q(p^e)$. The configuration is sustainable if no such marketing plan for an entrant offers a flow of profit $(p^e \cdot y^e - C(y^e))$ that is positive.

Definition 3   A *perfectly-contestable market* (PCM) is one in which a necessary condition for an industry configuration to be in equilibrium is that it be sustainable.

A PCM so defined may be interpreted, heuristically, as a market subject to potential entry by firms that have no disadvantage relative to incumbents, and that assess the profitability of entry on the supposition that incumbents' prices are fixed for a sufficiently-long period of time. Then, since one requirement for equilibrium is the absence of new entry, an equilibrium configuration in a PCM must offer no inducement for entry; i.e., it must be sustainable.

In Section III, we explore in more detail the basic economic elements that make an industry perfectly-contestable by analysing the sort of entrant-behaviour that gives substance to the definition of sustainability. We shall argue that the key to the contestability of non-competitive markets is reversible entry and the absence of sunk costs. However, before focusing on that subject, we proceed to describe some of the properties of PCMs and the implications of sustainability.

Definition 4   A feasible industry configuration over $N, p; y^1, \ldots, y^m$, is a *long-run competitive equilibrium* if $p \cdot y \leqslant C(y) \ \forall y \in R^n_+$.

So defined, a long-run competitive equilibrium has precisely the characteristics usually ascribed to it. Together, $p \cdot y^i \geqslant C(y^i)$ and $p \cdot y \leqslant C(y), \ \forall y \in R^n_+$, imply that $p \cdot y^i = C(y^i)$ and that the $y^i \in \arg \max_y (p \cdot y - C(y))$. Thus, each firm in the configuration takes prices as parametric; chooses output to maximise profits; earns zero profit; and equates marginal costs to prices of produced outputs. It is now easy to show

Proposition 1[3]   *A long-run competitive equilibrium is a sustainable configuration, so that a perfectly competitive market is a PCM.*

Proposition 2   *Sustainable configurations need not be long-run competitive equilibria, and a PCM need not be perfectly competitive.*

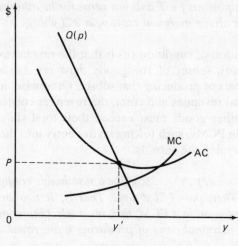

FIG. 12.1

The simplest example sufficient to prove this second proposition is described in Figure 12.1. Here, the feasible configuration, comprised of one firm producing and selling y^1 at the price p, is sustainable. This follows because, at a price equal to or less than p, sale of any quantity on or inside the demand curve yields revenue no greater than production cost; in this range, price does not exceed average cost (AC). Yet, this configuration is not a long-run competitive equilibrium, as defined above. This is because $py - C(y) > 0$, for $y > y^1$ and, at y^1, p exceeds marginal cost (MC). In fact, because the only intersection of the demand and average cost curves occurs in the range of increasing returns to scale, there is no possible long-run competitive equilibrium. However, this intersection point does correspond to a sustainable configuration.

Hence, Propositions 1 and 2 show that the sustainable industry-configuration is a substantive generalisation of the long-run competitive equilibrium, and that the PCM is a substantive generalisation of the perfectly-competitive market. The following propositions summarise some characteristics of equilibria in PCMs.

Proposition 3[4]   Let p; $y^1, \ldots, y^m$ be a sustainable industry configuration. Then each firm must (i) earn zero profit by operating efficiently, $p \cdot y^i - C(y^i) = 0$; (ii) avoid cross-subsidisation, $p_S \cdot y_S^i \geq C(y^i) - C(y_{N-S}^i)$, $\forall S \subset N$ (where the vector x_T agrees with the

vector x in components j ∈ T and has zeros for its other components);
(iii) price at or above marginal cost, $p_j \geq \partial C(y^i)/\partial y_j$.

The interpretation of condition (ii) is that the revenues earned from the sales of any subset of the goods must not fall short of the incremental costs of producing that subset. Otherwise, in view of the equality of total revenues and costs, the revenues collected from the sales of the other goods must exceed their total stand-alone production cost. In PCMs, such pricing invites entry into the markets for the goods providing the subsidy.

Proposition 4[5]   Let $p; y^1, \ldots, y^m$ be a sustainable configuration with $y_j^k < \Sigma_{h=1}^m y_{j'}^h$. Then $p_j = \partial C(y^k)/\partial y_j$. That is, if two or more firms produce a given good in a PCM, they must select input–output vectors at which their marginal costs of producing it are equal to the good's market price.

The implications of this result are surprisingly strong. The discipline of sustainability in perfectly-contestable markets forces firms to adopt prices just equal to marginal costs, provided only that they are not monopolists of the products in question. Conventional wisdom implies that, generally, only perfect competition involving a multitude of firms, each small in its output markets, can be relied upon to provide marginal-cost prices. Here we see that potential competition by prospective entrants, rather than rivalry among incumbent firms, suffices to make marginal-cost pricing a requirement of equilibrium in PCMs, even in those containing as few as two active producers of each product. The conventional view holds that the enforcement mechanism of full competitive-equilibrium requires the smallness of each active firm in its product market, in addition to freedom of entry. We see that the smallness requirement can be dispensed with almost entirely, and exclusive reliance put on the freedom of entry that characterises PCMs.

Proposition 5[6]   Let $p; y^1, \ldots, y^m$ be a sustainable configuration. Then, for any $\hat{y}^1, \ldots, \hat{y}^k$ with $\Sigma_{j=1}^k \hat{y}^j = \Sigma_{j=1}^m y^j, \Sigma_{j=1}^k C(\hat{y}^j) \geq \Sigma_{j=1}^m C(y^j)$. That is, a sustainable configuration minimises the total cost to the industry of producing the total industry output.

This proposition is a generalisation to PCMs of a well known result for perfect competition. It can be interpreted as a manifestation of the power of unimpeded potential entry to impose efficiency upon the industry. For example, the proposition implies that if a monopoly occupies a PCM it must be a *natural* monopoly: production by a single firm must minimise industry-cost for the given output vector. Thus, Propositions 3, 4 and 5 are powerful tools for the analysis of industry structure in PCMs. Proposition 5 permits information on the properties of production costs to be used to assess the scale and scope of firms' activities in PCMs. Then, Propositions 3 and 4 permit inferences to be drawn about the corresponding equilibrium prices.

In particular, this analytic approach leads to very strong results in the single-product case. Propositions 3 to 5 show that there are only two possible types of sustainable configuration in single-product industries. The first type, represented in Figure 12.1, involves a single firm which charges the lowest price that is consistent with non-negative profit. The firm must be a natural monopoly when it produces the quantity that is demanded at this price. And, in this circumstance, the result maximises welfare, subject to the constraint that all firms in question be viable financially without subsidies. Such a second-best maximum is referred to as a 'Ramsey optimum'.

The second type of sustainable configuration involves production, by one or more firms, of outputs at which both marginal cost and average cost are equal to price. Here, in the long run, all active firms exhibit the behaviour that characterises perfectly competitive equilibrium. And, of course, the result involves both (first-best) welfare optimality and financial viability. Hence, in this case, Ramsey optimality and the first-best coincide. This establishes the result that, in a single-product industry, any sustainable configuration is Ramsey optimal.

However, in general, because of the 'integer problem', sustainable configurations may generally not exist. This problem arises, for example, where there is only one output at which a firm's marginal and average costs coincide, and where the quantity of output demanded by the market at the competitive price is greater than this, but is not an integer multiple of that amount. Then, no sustainable configurations exist.

There is, however, a plausible assumption, supported by empirical evidence, at least to some degree, that eliminates the integer problem. Suppose that a firm's average cost curve has a flat-bottom (as in Figure 12.2), rather than being 'U'-shaped. In particular, suppose that the minimum level of average cost is attained not only at one output, but (at least) at all outputs between the minimum efficient scale, y_m, and twice the minimum efficient scale. Then any industry

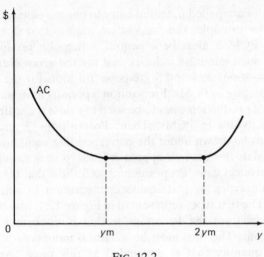

FIG. 12.2

output, y^I, that is at least equal to y_m can be apportioned among an integer number of firms each of which achieves minimum average cost. Specifically, y^I can be divided evenly among $\lfloor y^I/y_m \rfloor$ firms (where $\lfloor x \rfloor$ is the largest integer not greater than x), and each firm's output, $y^I/\lfloor y^I/y_m \rfloor$, must lie in the (half-open) interval between y_m and $2y_m$. Hence, in this case, the Ramsey optimum can either be a sustainable configuration of two or more firms performing competitively, or a sustainable natural monopoly. Such a monopoly may either produce an output at which there are increasing returns to scale, when it will price at average cost. Or it may produce an output between y_m and $2y_m$ with locally constant returns to scale, when it will adopt a price equal both to average and marginal cost. This, together with the preceding argument, establishes the following result.

Proposition 6[7]   In a single-product industry in which the firm's average cost curve has a flat-bottom between minimum efficient scale and twice minimum efficient scale, a configuration is sustainable if and only if it is Ramsey optimal.

This result shows that, under the conditions described, there is equivalence between welfare optimality and equilibrium in PCMs. This extends the corresponding result for perfectly-competitive equilibria to cases of increasing returns to scale. Moreover, since the behavioural assumptions required for a PCM are weaker than those underlying perfectly-competitive markets, the equivalence result is more sweeping. In particular, Proposition 6 implies that PCMs can be expected to perform well, whatever the number of firms participating in equilibrium. It is the potential competition of potential entrants, rather than the active competition of existing rivals, that drives equilibrium in PCMs to welfare optimality.

Because of the strength of this result, it seems appropriate to examine its behavioural underpinnings more closely before moving on, in Section IV to the richer multi-product situation in which the normative implications of PCMs are less clear.

III PERFECT-CONTESTABILITY AS THE ABSENCE OF SUNK COSTS[8]

In this Section, we construct and analyse an explicit model of entry behaviour. We show that, in the limiting case without sunk costs, only sustainable industry configurations can withstand the threat of entry: i.e., the market is perfectly-contestable.

Since entry takes place over time, we must construct a model with a modicum of dynamic structure. At time zero, there is assumed to be an incumbent monopolist operating in the market with an initial capital stock, K_i^0, providing an instantaneous flow of output (y_i) via a technology whose flow of variable costs is given by the function $V(y, K)$. The (representative) potential entrant has access to the same technology and can purchase capital equipment at the price β per unit.

The key to the dynamic structure of the model is a *contract period* of length τ. The potential entrant can compete *for* the market by quoting a price p_e and, *if it is not matched* (or beaten) by the incumbent, make a *firm* contract with consumers for delivery of the flow of output $y_e \leq Q(p_e)$, at that price, for the period $[0, \tau]$. If the incumbent matches the potential entrant's price, the latter simply stays out of the market and incurs no costs. Should the entrant actually contract for delivery, it would be saddled with a capital outlay of βK_e^0. However, this investment may be only partially *sunk*, since we assume that at time τ, the end of contract period, the entrant may, if it chooses, 'scrap' its capital for a salvage price of α per unit, with $0 \leq \alpha \leq \beta$. If $\alpha = 0$ all capital costs are sunk, while if $\alpha = \beta$ no costs are sunk since all investments can be reversed fully at time τ.

(*Physical* depreciation of capital can be subsumed into $V(\cdot)$.) The amount of capital chosen by the entrant will depend upon both the properties of the variable cost function and on the prices α and β.

We shall not attempt, here, to provide a detailed model of the nature of the rivalry between the incumbent and a successful entrant once the initial contract period is over. However, it may plausibly be assumed that the present values, at τ, of future profits are functions of the *state variables* of the system at τ. Thus, the discounted future profits of the entrant and the incumbent can be expressed as $\pi_e^f(K_e^0, K_i^0)$ and $\pi_i^f(K_e^0, K_i^0)$. While the forms of these functions depend upon the behavioural model of future market rivalry, generally applicable lower bounds are yielded by the fact that either firm always has the option of selling its plant for salvage at time τ. Therefore,

$$\pi_e^f(K_e^0, K_i^0) \geqslant \alpha K_e^0 \tag{1}$$

$$\pi_i^f(K_e^0, K_i^0) \geqslant \alpha K_i^0. \tag{2}$$

We are now in a position to examine the entry decision at time zero. The first issue is whether or not there exists any set of contracts (entry plan) which the entrant can offer and which, if *not* matched by the incumbent, would justify the expectation of positive *total* profits. In the simplest case, such 'contracts' consist of an offer price p_e less than the incumbent's posted price p_i^0 and a flow rate of output y_e no larger than the (instantaneous) quantity demanded $Q(p_e)$. Anticipated total profits are thus given by:

$$\pi_e^T = \gamma_\tau[p_e y_e - V(y_e, K_e^0)] - \beta K_e^0 + \pi_e^f e^{-r\tau}, \tag{3}$$

where r is the discount rate and $\gamma_\tau = (1 - e^{-r\tau})/r$. Formally, an *entry offering* will be made if and only if:

$$\pi_e^* \equiv \max_{\substack{K_e^0 \geqslant 0, \\ p_e \leqslant p_i^0, y_e \leqslant Q(p_e)}} \pi_e^T > 0. \tag{4}$$

In order to shed some light on the conditions under which (4) will hold, we use the lower bound (1) to obtain,

$$\pi_e^T \geqslant \gamma_\tau[p_e y_e - V(y_e, K_e^0) - \rho_e K_e^0]. \tag{5}$$

Here ρ_e, the effective rental cost of capital to the potential entrant, is given by:

$$\rho_e = (\beta - \alpha e^{-r\tau})/\gamma_\tau = r\beta + (\beta - \alpha)r e^{-r\tau}/(1 - e^{-r}). \tag{6}$$

This enables us to rewrite (5) in terms of an instantaneous cost function that is fully minimised for the given output vector:

$$\pi_e^T \geq \gamma_\tau [p_e y_e - C^e(y_e, \rho_e)] \tag{7}$$

where $C^e(y, \rho) \equiv \min_K(V(y, K) + \rho K)$. Equation (7) tells us that the total profit is bounded from *below* by what the entrant can earn during the initial contract period, when the effective instantaneous rental rate of capital ρ_e takes into account asset liquidation at the end of that period. If that value is positive for *any* allowable p_e and y_e, an entry offering will be made. Therefore, a *necessary* condition for *no* entry offering to be made at time zero is that

$$p_e y_e - C(y_e, \rho_e) \leq 0 \quad \forall p_e \leq p_i^0, y_e \leq Q(p_e). \tag{8}$$

The only difference between (8) and Definition 2 (of sustainability) is that the effective rental rate of capital faced by the entrant may exceed that of the incumbent, namely $r\beta$, the interest on a unit of invested capital. The difference is attributable to the possibility that the entrant may find itself forced to write off its capital fully over the contract period. This possibility arises because nothing in our model precludes the incumbent from driving any entrant out of business at time τ. Yet, from (6), we see that if $\alpha = \beta$ so that there are no sunk costs, then $\rho_e = r\beta$. Also, note that $\lim_{\tau \to \infty} \rho_e = r\beta$. Thus, in view of (8), we have proven

Proposition 7   If there are no sunk costs (or if the contract period is sufficiently long), then the incumbent firm(s) will be immune from entry offerings only if *the industry configuration is sustainable.*

While we have built our model so that the incumbent always has the option of matching an entry offering, thereby preventing actual entry from occurring, to do so it must lower its price to a sustainable level for the *entire* period $[0, \tau]$. If the basic technology is freely available and potential entrants are sufficiently numerous, the incumbent faces a similar entry threat at *every* instant. Therefore, we have an immediate Corollary to Proposition 7:

Proposition 8   In the absence of sunk costs, entry deterrence requires the industry to operate in a sustainable configuration at all times.

Our model also permits an analytic derivation of an upper bound upon the rate of excess profits attainable by the incumbent. For example, in the single product case, the highest price (p_i^0) that the incumbent can charge without provoking an entry offering is given (in

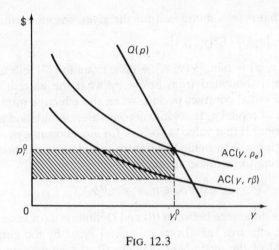

FIG. 12.3

Figure 12.3) by the intersection of the demand curve and the *entrant's* average cost curve $AC(y, \rho_e)$. The shaded area depicts the instantaneous rate of excess profit which the incumbent can earn by virtue of the fact that its effective rental rate of capital is less than the entrant's. (This assumes, of course, that p_i^0 is less than the simple monopoly price.)

To consider a simple example, suppose that $C(y, \rho) = \rho\bar{K} + cy$ for $y > 0$. Then p_i^0 is determined by the condition.

$$(p_i^0 - c)\, Q\,(p_i^0) = \rho\bar{K}_e = r\bar{K}(\beta + (\beta - \alpha)/(e^{r\tau} - 1)) \qquad (9)$$

This bound may be particularly useful because it is based on the actual capital stock employed by the incumbent.

To sum up briefly, this section provides a rather general model of the entry process. This makes it possible to derive a substantive upper bound on the economic value of any 'first-mover' advantages that accrue to an incumbent as a result of the need to sink costs *and* yields, as a readily-interpretable limiting case, precisely the same equilibrium conditions that characterise PCMs. In this model, the approach towards perfect-contestability is also 'continuous'. That is, as long as $\tau > 0$, if the degree to which costs are sunk, as measured by $\beta - \alpha$, declines smoothly towards zero, so does the upper bound on monopoly profits. Thus, in addition to providing a plausible model of the entry process resulting in perfect contestability as a limiting case, the analysis of this section also sheds some light on the 'robustness' of the theory. A small departure from the world of no sunk costs leads, via (9) or (13), only to a similarly small increase in the associated equilibrium price.[9]

IV MULTI-PRODUCT PERFECTLY CONTESTABLE MARKETS

In industries that produce two or more goods, a rich variety of industry structures becomes possible, even in PCMs. Here, while the constraints imposed upon incumbents by perfect contestability are not nearly as effective in limiting the range of possible outcomes as they are in single product industries, they nevertheless provide a helpful basis for analysis. In particular, Propositions 3 to 5 indicate connections among various qualitative properties of multi-product cost functions and various elements of industry structure in PCMs. These connections constitute one theme of this section. The other theme is the normative evaluation of the industry structures that arise in multi-product PCMs.

Before proceeding, it may be useful to provide definitions of some of the multi-product cost properties that are used in the analysis.

Definition 5 Let $P = \{T_1, \ldots, T_k\}$ be a non-trivial partition of $S \subseteq N$. There are (weak) *economies of scope* at y_S with respect to the partition P if $\Sigma_{i=1}^{k} C(y_{T_i}) > (\geqslant) C(y_s)$. If no partition is mentioned explicitly, then it is presumed that $T_i = \{i\}$.

Definition 6 The *degree of scale economies* defined over the entire product set, $N = \{1, \ldots, n\}$, at y, is given by $S_N(y) = C(y)/y \cdot \nabla C(y)$. Returns to scale are said to be increasing, constant, or decreasing as S_N is greater than, equal to, or less than unity. This occurs as the elasticity of ray average cost with respect to t is negative, zero, or positive; where *ray average cost* is $\text{RAC}(ty^\circ) \equiv C(y^\circ)/t$.

Definition 7 The *incremental cost* of the product set $T \subseteq N$ at y is given by $IC_T(y) \equiv C(y) - C(y_{N-T})$ The *average incremental cost* of T is $AIC_T(y) \equiv IC_T(y)/\Sigma_{j\epsilon T} y_j$. The average incremental cost of T is decreasing, increasing, or constant at y if $AIC_T(ty_T + y_{N-T})$ is a decreasing, increasing, or locally constant function of t at $t = 1$. These cases are labelled respectively, increasing, decreasing, or constant *returns to the scale of the product line T*. The degree of scale economies specific to T is $IC_T(y)/\Sigma_{i\epsilon T} y_i (\alpha C(y))/xy_i$.

Definition 8   A cost function $C(y)$ is *trans-ray convex* through some point $y^* = (y_1^*, \ldots, y_n^*)$ if there exists at least one vector of positive constants $w_1, \ldots, w_n$ such that for every two output vectors $y^a = (y_1^a, \ldots, y_n^a)$ and $y^b = (y_1^b, \ldots, y_n^b)$ that lie on the hyperplane $\Sigma w_i y_i = w_0$ through point y^*, $C[ky^a + (1 - k)y^b] \leq kC(y^a) + (1 - k)C(y^b)$ for $k \in (0, 1)$.

In view of the general result that sustainable configurations minimise industry-wide costs (Proposition 5), these cost properties permit inferences to be drawn about industry structure in multi-product PCMs. The first issue that arises is when multi-commodity production is characteristic of equilibrium in a PCM.

Proposition 9[10]   *A multi-product firm in a PCM must enjoy (at least weak) economies of scope over the set of goods it produces. When strict economies of scope are present, there must be at least one multi-product firm in any PCM that supplies more than one good.*

The second basic question that arises is whether there can be two or more firms actively producing a particular good in a PCM. If there are, then, by Proposition 4, marginal-cost pricing must result. The answer depends upon the availability of product-specific scale economies.

Proposition 10[11]   *Any product with average incremental costs that decline throughout the relevant range (i.e., that offers product-specific increasing returns to scale) must be produced by only a single firm (if it is produced at all) in a PCM. Further, such a product must be priced above marginal cost, unless the degree of product-specific scale economies is exactly one.*

Thus, regardless of the presence or absence of economies of scope, globally-declining average incremental costs imply that a product must be monopolised in a PCM. It is an immediate corollary that if all goods in the set N exhibit product-specific scale economies, and if there are economies of scope among them all, then the industry is a natural monopoly that must be monopolised in a PCM.

Another route to this result is provided by the 'weak invisible-hand theorem of natural monopoly'.

Proposition 11[12]   *Trans-ray convexity of costs together with global economies of scale imply natural monopoly. If, in addition, certain other technical conditions are met, a monopoly charging Ramsey-optimal prices is a sustainable configuration.*

In general, there may exist natural monopoly situations in which no sustainable prices are possible for the Ramsey optimal product set. Further, even where sustainable prices exist, the Ramsey optimal prices may not be among them. However, under the conditions of the weak invisible hand theorem, the Ramsey optimal prices for the Ramsey optimal product set are guaranteed to be sustainable, so that PCMs are consistent with (second-best) welfare optimal performance by a natural monopoly.

PCMs will yield first-best welfare optimality if there exist sustainable configurations with at least two firms actively producing each good. For, in this case, Propositions 4 and 5 guarantee industry-wide cost efficiency and marginal-cost pricing of all products. Here, two issues must be resolved: Does industry-wide cost minimisation require at least two producers of each good? And if so, do sustainable configurations exist?

The existence problem can be solved in a manner analogous to its solution in the case of single-product industries: by assuming that ray average costs remain at their minimum levels for output vectors that lie (on each ray) between minimum efficient-scale and twice minimum efficient-scale. And the presence of at least two producers (or one operating in the region where constant returns prevail) of each good is assured if the quantities demanded by the market at the relevant marginal-cost prices are no smaller than minimum efficient-scale (along the relevant ray) and if the cost function exhibits trans-ray convexity. Under conditions that represent these ideas formally, we have demonstrated the existence of a first-best sustainable configuration; i.e., one with competitive properties.[13]

(A) FIRMS ACTIVE IN BOTH MONOPOLY AND COMPETITIVE MARKETS

We have briefly discussed the equilibrium requirements and welfare implications which perfect contestability holds for markets in which industry cost minimisation requires either that one firm market all products (natural monopoly) or that each product be produced by two or more firms. In this sub-section we consider the 'mixed case' in which product 1 is characterised by globally-decreasing average incremental costs and is linked by economies of scope to product 2, which, in stand-alone production, is 'naturally competitive'. What

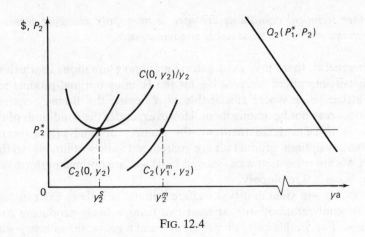

FIG. 12.4

does the theory of perfectly-contestable markets tell us about equilibrium in such cases?

We know from Propositions 5 and 10 that good 1 must be monopolised and that good 2 must be priced at marginal cost, if the market demand is large enough to require two or more active firms. But what role, if any, will the product 1 monopolist have in the market for product 2?

Figure 12.4 depicts the situation there. The equilibrium price in market 2 (p_2^*) is determined by the level of average costs at y_2^s, the minimum efficient scale in stand-alone production. Now the assumption of economies of scope guarantees that the average *incremental* cost curve of the (product 1) monopolist, $(C(y_1^m, y_2) - C(y_1^m, 0))/y_2$, lies everywhere below the average cost curve of specialty firms, $C(0, y_2)/y_2$. So, for example, at an output of y_2^s the revenues from participation in market 2, $p_2^* y_2^s = C(0, y_2^s)$, exceed the associated incremental costs. Thus, industry cost-minimisation requires participation in market 2 by the product 1 monopolist. Its level of output (y_2^m) will be that which equates its marginal cost to price. If, as may well be the case, economies of scope arise, in part, from *cost complementarities*, $C_{12} < 0$, then, as depicted in Figure 12.4, the monopolist's marginal cost curve for product 2 must lie to the right of that of the specialty firms, and its rate of output must be greater. The analysis is completed by the (simultaneous) determination of y_1^m, via the overall zero-profit condition for the product 1 monopolist. More specifically, the six endogenous variables y_1^m, y_2^m, y_2^s, p_1^*, p_2^* and (ignoring the integer problem), the number of specialty firms n_s, are determined by the following system of equations:

$$n_s y_2^s + y_2^m = Q_2(p_1^*, p_2^*) \tag{11}$$

$$y_1^m = Q_1(p_1^*, p_2^*) \tag{12}$$

$$p_2^* y_2^s = C(0, y_2^s) \tag{13}$$

$$p_1^* y_1^m + p_2^* y_2^m = C(y_1^m, y_2^m) \tag{14}$$

$$p_2^* = C_2(0, y_2^s) \tag{15}$$

$$p_2^* = C_2(y_1^m, y_2^m). \tag{16}$$

Comparative-statics analysis can be performed on equations (11)–(16) in order to derive testable implications of the contestability hypothesis in such situations.

In addition, the foregoing analysis sheds light on the important current issue of the proper policy approach to be taken towards regulated or public natural monopolies, whose products or services are technologically-related to those of structurally-competitive industries. It is clear that, under the conditions postulated, the monopoly firm should have a larger share of the market for product 2 than should the representative specialty firm. A policy of precluding it from such markets (or restricting it to producing y_2^s) would leave p_2^* unchanged, but would result in a higher price for product 1. Thus, participation in competitive markets by such firms *benefits* rather than burdens consumers of the monopoly product. Note, however, that such participation does have the effect of forcing *some* specialty providers out of market 2, and this may well be the source of political opposition to such participation by regulated or public enterprises.[14]

(B) MONOPOLISTIC COMPETITION[15]

The standard scenario of Chamberlinian monopolistic competition can be summarised in our terms. It is the case in which a multitude of products (actual or prospective) that are substitutes in demand are included in the product set, each such product having a U-shaped average cost curve, and in which there are no economies of scope among them.

The equilibrium concept which Chamberlin called the 'large group case' entails the adoption by each of the single-product firms of the price that maximises its profits, given the prices of its rivals – which offer differentiated, substitute products. Free entry of firms marketing additional product varieties then continues, until the maximal profit of each active firm is driven to zero, as shown in Figure 12.5.

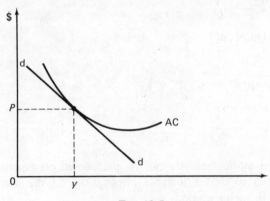

FIG. 12.5

Simultaneously, potential entrants are offered no profitable opportunity for entry, given the prices and product designs already supplied in the market. In this equilibrium, each active firm, of necessity, equates its price to its average cost in the region of increasing returns to scale, because of the requisite tangency between its downward-sloping demand curve, dd, and the average cost curve.

Plainly, then, by its very definition, this Chamberlinian equilibrium is a sustainable configuration over the set of potential products. However, other sustainable configurations are also compatible with the very same scenario. One such type, depicted in Figure 12.6, involves average-cost pricing (point A) by each single-product firm, but not the selection of those prices that maximise its profit on the (not always plausible) assumption that the prices of other active firms are given. Rather, each firm may choose to maximise its profit given the behaviour of potential entrants, who would undercut it if it were to raise its price above average cost. Of course, such a configuration would not be sustainable if an entrant could earn a profit by supplying a new product variant, given the prices and designs of those already offered for sale. However, a large number of sustainable configurations of the form illustrated will generally exist in monopolistically-competitive markets, with an industry-wide trade-off being made between the number of available varieties and the price of each. Notice that a sustainable solution (such as A) does not exhibit excess capacity. That is, excess capacity in a monopolistically-competitive market is not necessary for sustainability.

Another type of sustainable configuration in such a market would arise if the quantity of a particular product-variety that was de-

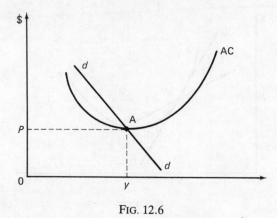

FIG. 12.6

manded in equilibrium were sufficiently large, relative to the minimum efficient scale, to require production by two or more firms for industry efficiency. Then, it is required that any such product variant should coexist with any less-popular variants (characterised by Figure 12.5 or 12.6) in equilibrium. Of course, the price of the popular variant must simultaneously equal marginal and average cost, while the others may conceivably be priced at average cost and above marginal cost. This type of sustainable configuration can be consistent with Chamberlin's assumption that firms choose prices to maximise their profits, given the decisions of the other active firms. As such, these configurations can perhaps provide the foundation for a substantive and relevant generalisation of Chamberlinian monopolistic-competition theory.

Chamberlin and his successors apparently never dealt with the incentive of a firm, in the standard framework, to produce *several* product varieties in order to co-ordinate their prices. In general, the profit-maximising prices for a pair of substitute products are both higher than the prices that comprise a Nash-equilibrium between two non-co-operating price-setting vendors. However, in contestable markets, such co-ordinated prices are not sustainable in the absence of economies of scope, so that in the absence of such economies Chamberlin's disregard of the incentives for co-ordinated pricing can be justified.

Chamberlin suggested that outside the 'large group case', firms can usefully be assumed to set their own prices on the basis of the anticipated price reactions of their rivals, rather than on the basis of the dd demand curve that takes rivals' prices to be fixed. The former yields what he called the high-tangency equilibrium, pictured in

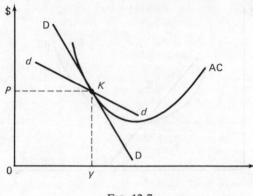

FIG. 12.7

Figure 12.7. Here, the demand curve DD is based on the assumption that rivals are expected to react to any one firm's price moves by changing their own prices in exactly the same way. Hence DD must be less elastic than the dd curve. The situation depicted in Figure 12.7 is purportedly a free-entry equilibrium of this kind, because the DD curve is tangent to the average-cost curve, yielding zero profits that are maximal given the assumed price reactions of rivals.

However, such a position cannot be an equilibrium in a contestable market. An entrant can duplicate closely or exactly the product design of the firm depicted, and enter at a lower price. Since dd is more elastic than the DD curve that is tangent to the AC curve, the dd curve necessarily cuts into and above the AC curve, as illustrated. Consequently, there exist (temporarily) profitable entry opportunities, and so 'high-tangency equilibria' cannot be equilibria in contestable markets. It should be noted that Chamberlin's discussion implies strongly that the markets of which he was thinking satisfied the free-entry requirements of contestability. Thus, it is of some significance for his analysis that his high-tangency solution turns out to be unsustainable.

It should be noted that, recently, important work on monopolistic competition by Spence and by Dixit and Stiglitz has assumed Cournot quantity-behaviour among rivals supplying differentiated products. The resulting 'free-entry equilibria' are analogous to those depicted in Figure 12.7. The assumption that rivals are expected to leave their outputs unchanged is equivalent, in a case of substitute products, to a conjecture that price decreases will induce rivals to respond by decreasing their prices, and to behave analogously when price increases occur. Thus, the corresponding demand curve is, like Chamberlin's DD curve, less-elastic than the dd curve which takes rivals' prices to be fixed. It follows then, by the preceding argument, that quantity Cournot equilibria are unsustainable under free entry, and are not truly equilibria in contestable markets.

Finally, where economies of scope hold for some or all (potential) products, sustainable configurations in monopolistically-competitive markets necessarily entail the presence of multi-product firms. These are discussed later.

(C) NORMATIVE ANALYSIS

Now that we have determined some of the types of industry structure for which sustainability is possible, so that they are consistent with equilibrium in contestable markets, it is appropriate to subject them to a normative analysis which studies their consequences for economic welfare. Should we find any sustainable oligopolistic or monopolistically-competitive structures that necessarily produce optimal results, given the relevant economic circumstances and feasibility constraints, we could infer that in those cases the invisible hand holds, far outside its normal domain. On the other hand, where sustainable solutions are not necessarily optimal, or are even inconsistent with optimality, some degree of market failure must be expected. Such cases of market failure are not those attributable to entry barriers or to friction, because in our analysis they occur in the world of frictionless and reversible free entry that characterises contestable markets. Rather, such market failures must be ascribed to the very nature of production technology, consumer preferences (as described by market demands) and, perhaps, to the system of non-discriminatory simple prices which are taken throughout the analysis to constitute the only form of prices available.

One of the principal lessons of PCMs is that monopoly does not necessarily entail such welfare losses. Rather, the weak invisible hand theorem shows that under certain conditions sustainability and Ramsey optimality are consistent. Hence, the total of consumers' and producers' surpluses may well be maximised (subject to the constraint that firms be self-supporting) in the equilibrium of a monopoly which operates in contestable markets.

Even stronger results follow from the discussion in earlier portions of this section and in Section II. We showed that, under certain conditions, sustainability and a first-best solution are consistent in an oligopoly with a small number of firms. When minimisation of industry cost requires that each good be produced by at least two firms, sustainability requires that any equilibrium should satisfy the necessary conditions for a first-best allocation of resources. Thus, in these cases, the invisible hand has the same power over oligopoly in contestable markets that it exercises over a perfectly-competitive industry.

However, in the other cases discussed in this section, there are systematic reasons indicating that unsustainability may plague the industry configurations that are Ramsey optimal. Industry configurations involving firms that are partial monopolies, as well as those that constitute generalised Chamberlinian structures, may be such. They may lie outside the set of market forms in which decentralised decision making, guided by the price system, can attain results as desirable as those achievable, in theory, by a perfectly-informed and beneficent planner, even if he is constrained to permit firms to break even.

Examination of the requirements of contestability in the 'mixed case' discussed above readily brings out the difficulties, though it is well known that (sustainable) Chamberlinian equilibria may not be even 'second-best'. Suppose the planner were given the task of maximising aggregate consumers' surplus in markets 1 and 2, subject to the constraint that, in aggregate, the *industry* (i.e., the product 1 monopolist and all the specialised firms) at least break-even: this is the case we have referred to as the *viable-industry Ramsey optimum*. Even without characterising this programme formally, it is easy to discern the qualitative properties of the solution. As long as the products are substitutes with finite own-price elasticities of demand, the usual Ramsey inverse-elasticity rule will require that there be a positive mark-up over the relevant *social* marginal cost for *each* product. For product 2, this social marginal cost is given by $C_2(0, y_2^s) = C_2(y_1^m, y_2^m) = p_2^*$. Thus, the viable-industry Ramsey optimum would require $p_2 > p_2^*$, which is clearly unsustainable because of the profit inducement thereby offered to entering specialty firms.

It is also easy to see that unsustainability remains a problem in this example. This is so even if we lower our sights a bit and instruct our planner to seek what we have called a *viable-firm Ramsey optimum* involving the maximisation of consumer's plus producers' surplus and subject to the constraints that *each* active firm earn a non-negative profit. For the solution to this programme, too, would require a $p_2 > p_2^*$, rendering it unsustainable.

It is far from clear that the failure of either type of Ramsey optimum to meet the requirements of sustainability should be viewed as a form of market failure. For it can be shown that contestability can still claim an achievement in such cases, ensuring what we have called 'autarkic Ramsey optimality'. Under this, each firm acts so as to maximise the welfare of its customers, subject to its own financial viability *given the behaviour of other firms*. It is not difficult to show that the achievement of a result superior to this would require intervention that, in effect, directed some firms to undertake actions harmful to their own interests and to those of their customers, in order to benefit other firms in the industry. This may be interpreted to mean that here contestable markets perform as well as one could hope with any decentralised markets employing the pursuit of self-interest and a price system in order to guide the allocation of resources.

V CONCLUDING COMMENT

Our book, *Contestable Markets and the Theory of Industry Structure*, began as an attempt at systematic exploration of the properties of multi-product cost functions that are crucial for the determination of market structure. However, we feel that, in addition, it makes two contributions to value theory. It provides a static (partial) equilibrium theory of industry structure, conduct and performance more generally applicable than what was available before. This static theory is, itself, replete with the kind of testable implications and refutable hypotheses required to satisfy the methodological tastes of Milton Friedman or the Samuelson of the *Foundations of Economic Analysis*. We hope others will continue to join us in drawing them out. The model in Section IV(A) provides one starting point. Second, we have gone further and offered another meta-hypothesis: i.e., that the theory of perfectly-contestable markets will yield good predictions for cases in which sunk costs are unimportant. This, too, is subject to empirical testing and refutation. Thus, in addition to the provision of normative benchmarks, we hope to have offered grist for the mill of positive economics.

NOTES

1. We are grateful for their generous support to the Economics Program of the Division of Social Sciences of the National Science Foundation, the Division of Information Science and Technology of the National Science Foundation, the Sloan Foundation, and to the organisers of the IEA Conference on New Developments in Market Structure. The views

     expressed are those of the authors and do not necessarily reflect those of the institutions with which they are affiliated.

2. Much of the material presented here is a summary of the analysis in Baumol, Panzar and Willig (1982). This work builds upon published writings by authors too numerous to list here. The book includes an extensive list of references that is, inevitably, incomplete.

3. *Proof* $p \cdot y \leqslant C(y)$, $\forall y \in R_+^n$, implies that $p^e \cdot y \leqslant C(y)$, $\forall y \in R_+^n$, for $p^e \leqslant p$. Then $p^e \cdot y \leqslant C(y)$ for $p^e \leqslant p$ and $y \leqslant Q(p^e)$.

4. *Proof* (i) Otherwise, $p^e = p$ and $y^e = y^i$ would be a profitable entry plan. (ii) Otherwise, if $p_S \cdot y_S^i < C(y^i) - C(y_{N-S}^i)$, $p \cdot y^i = C(y^i)$ would imply that $p_{N-S} y_{N-S}^i > C(y_{N-S}^i)$. Then $p^e = p$ and $y^e = y_{N-S}^i$ would be a profitable entry plan. (iii) Otherwise, $p^e = p$ and $y^e = y^i - \epsilon u^j$ would be a profitable entry plan, for some $\epsilon > 0$, where u^j is the jth unit co-ordinate vector.

5. *Proof* Suppose $y_j^k < \sum_{h=1}^m y_j^h = Q_j(p)$ and $p_j > C_j(y^k)$. Consider this function of the scalar t: $\psi(t) = p \cdot (y^k + tu^j) - C(y^k + tu^j)$, where u^j is the vector with zeros for each component except for the jth, which is unity. $\psi(t)$ is the profit earned by an entry plan replicating all of the activities of firm k with the exception of an increase by amount t in the output of good j. Evaluating it at $t = 0$, $\psi(0) = p \cdot y^k - C(y^k) = 0$, since a firm in a sustainable configuration must earn exactly zero profit. Differentiation yields $\psi'(t) = p_j - C_j(y^k + tu^j)$, and, at $t = 0$, $\psi'(0) = p_j - C_j(y^k) > 0$ which is positive by hypothesis. Thus, the profit earned by the entry plan increases from zero as t is increased from 0. Hence, there exists some $\bar{t} > 0$ such that $\psi(t) > 0$ for $0 < t < \bar{t}$. Moreover, the entry plan is feasible for $0 < t \leqslant Q_j(p) - y_j^k$ so that the entrant's output of good j, $y_j^k + t$, remains no greater than the amount demanded by consumers, $Q_j(p)$. Consequently, for $0 < t \leqslant \min(\bar{t}, Q_j(p) - y_j^k)$, the entry plan is both feasible and profitable, which contradicts the hypothesis that the industry configuration is sustainable. Our result follows: p_j must be equal to $C_j(y^k)$ for firm k's output vector to be part of a sustainable configuration in which firm k is not the sole producer of good j.

6. *Proof* The proof is by contradiction. Suppose there were another group of firms with output levels, $\hat{y}^1, \ldots, \hat{y}^k$, that could produce the same total output ($\sum_{i=1}^m y^i$) as that offered by a given sustainable configuration at lower cost. Thus, $\sum_{j=1}^k \hat{y}^j = \sum_{i=1}^m y^i$ and $\sum_{j=1}^k C(\hat{y}^j) < \sum_{i=1}^m C(y^i)$. Then at the original prices, p, the profits of the new group would, in total, be positive; i.e., $\sum_{j=1}^k (\hat{y}^j \cdot p - C(\hat{y}^j)) = \sum_j (\hat{y}^j \cdot p) - \sum_j C(\hat{y}^j) = p \cdot \sum_j \hat{y}^j - \sum_j C(\hat{y}^j) = p \cdot \sum_i y^i - \sum_j C(\hat{y}^j) > p \cdot \sum_i y^i - \sum_i C(y^i) = \sum_i (p \cdot y^i - C(y^i)) \geqslant 0$. Consequently, to some firm j in the new group, the old prices would have yielded a positive profit, $\hat{y}^j p - C(\hat{y}^j) > 0$. Hence, $p^e = p$ and $y^e = \hat{y}^j \leqslant \sum_i y^i = Q(p)$ would have constituted a profitable entry plan that rendered the given configuration unsustainable.

7. This result is extended in our book, in Proposition 2D3, to cases in which the minimum level of average cost extends over a smaller range of outputs.

8. While the *analytics* of this section are based upon those of Section 10H of our book, we are indebted to Sanford Grossman for pointing the way to the richer interpretation presented here.

9. The present analysis yields contestable behaviour as a consequence of less-stringent sufficient conditions than the assumptions of costless and instantaneous entry and exit and an incumbent's price adjustment lag implicit in the informal discussion of Baumol (1982). Thus, it provides us with an opportunity to clarify two issues raised by Martin Weitzman (1983) and by Marius Schwartz and Robert Reynolds (1983) in their critiques of the theory. (For a more complete discussion, see our 'Comment on the Comments'.) Both arguments are based on the mistaken belief that those strong sufficient conditions are also *necessary* for the theory of perfect contestability to be applicable.

Weitzman argued that our theory is incompatible with anything but constant returns to scale and thus is not a generalisation of perfect competition at all. For if entry and exit are perfectly costless and instantaneous, there can never be any economies of scale because a firm can produce as small a quantity of output as it desires by entering a market, producing at minimum efficient scale, however large it may be, but doing so for only a very brief period. If minimum efficient scale yields an output of 10 000 units per hour, the firm can produce 2500 units at the same unit cost by effecting production for only 15 minutes and then disbanding the production facilities, without incurring any exit cost. The firm can then sell the 2500 units over the course of the hour by storing it until customers materialise. Thus, a steady flow of demand at a rate of 2500 units per hour can be met at the same unit cost as the 10 000 unit flow of demand sufficient to keep a firm's production facilities continuously occupied at the cost-minimising output level.

Many outputs and production processes may fit this parable as a limiting case, but many do not. First, some items, notably services, cannot be stored at all. They perish the instant they are produced, and one cannot get around this problem by taking the time they are held in inventory to be very brief, approaching zero in the limit. Second, fixed investment does not always take the form of capacity capable of turning out a continuous steady flow of output. Rather, some types of processes require an irreducible amount of production *time* to be effective and in that time they yield some fixed minimum batch of output. More generally, the minimal average cost per unit produced may be achievable only if the production process is run at a particular intensity over a particular span of time. In these cases the technique of 'substituting' the perfect divisibility of time to compensate for other indivisibilities is inapplicable.

The Weitzman argument against the applicability of perfect contestability to non-constant returns to scale suffers from another more fundamental problem – a mischaracterisation of contestability resulting from a confusion between *economic* and technological notions of sunk costs. As we have just seen, to produce its results, even the limiting case of perfect contestability does *not* require entry and exit to be instantaneous. Rather, it is sufficient that the process be rapid enough so that the entrant does not find his investment vulnerable to a retaliatory response by the incumbent. The length of this time period is not exclusively a technological datum, but is also the result of business practice and opportunities in the market in question. This period can be as long as the longest period for which it is credible for buyers to commit their patronage to the entrant. Thus, perfect contestability can survive the technological imposition of a minimum production-time requirement $t^* \leqslant \tau$, while the Weitzman parable cannot.

The issue raised by Schwartz and Reynolds is very different and more significant. They point out, correctly, that the conditions required for *perfect* contestability are certain to be violated in reality, at least to some degree. It then becomes important to ask whether small deviations from such conditions are likely to alter substantially the conclusions of the analysis. Focusing on the incumbent's price adjustment lag, they argue that relaxing that assumption moves the market outcome far from the contestable equilibrium. Of course the model of this section has revealed that perfect contestability does *not* require such a lag. However, this issue is relevant in the case of the absence of sunk costs: an assumption that is necessary for perfect contestability in our current formulation. The moral of the analysis of this section is that models of behaviour under imperfect contestability in which behaviour converges continuously towards that under perfect contestability are possible and can be extremely plausible. In the model discussed above, and no doubt in others as well, where there are almost no sunk costs, markets are almost perfectly contestable.

It should be emphasised that models which support the robustness of contestability analysis follow a relatively long tradition going back at least to the work of J. S. Bain. This tradition holds that increased ease of entry and exit improves the welfare performance of firms and industries. On this subject, the theory of contestability has only sought to contribute insights on the underpinnings of that judgement. Certainly it is a view widely accepted on the basis of casual observation, though compelling empirical testing still remains to be carried out. One step in this direction is the recent empirical work by Ioannis Kessides (1982), which shows that among 4-digit US manufacturing industries, entry increases with the profit levels of incumbents, holding fixed the expected losses from the possibility of exit. These expected losses are greater, Kessides finds, the greater are the sunk costs (as measured by several proxies) that must be committed by an entrant. Sunk costs deter entry and also diminish the rate at which entry responds to incumbents' profits. In Kessides' estimated model, these effects are statistically significant and they behave in a continuous and monotonic manner. They lend some support to the hypothesis that market performance depends continuously on the degree of imperfection in their contestability.

10. A multi-product firm with diseconomies of scope cannot constitute part of a sustainable configuration, by Proposition 5. With strict economies of scope, a configuration comprised solely of single-product firms cannot minimise industry costs and so cannot be sustainable, again by Proposition 5.

11. It is shown as Lemma 7D1 in our book that with decreasing average incremental costs of product i either $C((y_i^a + y_i^b) + y_{N-i}) + C(y_{N-i}^b) < C(y^a) + C(y^b)$ or $C((y_i^a + y_i^b) + y_{N-i}^b) + C(y_{N-i}^a) <$

$C(y^a) + C(y^b)$. Thus, no configuration with more than one firm producing good i can minimise industry costs. The price of such a good must exceed marginal cost in PCMs because, by Proposition 3, price cannot be less than average incremental cost, and this is greater than marginal cost, except in the knife's-edge case of a locally unitary degree of product-specific scale economies.

12. See the text of Chapter 8 and its Appendix II in our book for a complete statement, proof, and citations.
13. See Proposition 11D2 in our book.
14. However, in markets that are not contestable, monopoly firms may have incentives to extend their operations into related lines of business in a manner that does not serve the public interest. See J. Ordover and R. Willig (1981).
15. This subsection and part of the next essentially reproduce the discussion in Section 11F and 11G of our book, pp. 329–34.

REFERENCES

Baumol, William J. (1982) 'Contestable Markets: An Uprising in the Theory of Industry Structure', *American Economic Review*, vol. 72, no. 1, Mar., pp. 1–15.
Baumol, William J., Panzar, John C. and Willig, Robert D. (1982) *Contestable Markets and the Theory of Industry Structure* (San Diego: Harcourt Brace and Jovanovich).
——, (1983) 'Comment on the Comments', *American Economic Review*, vol. 73, no. 3, Jun.
Kessides, Ioannis (1982) 'Toward a Testable Model of Entry: A Study of the U.S. Manufacturing Industries', Princeton University, unpublished thesis.
Ordover, Janusz and Willig, Robert (1981) 'An Economic Definition of Predation: Pricing and Product Innovation', *Yale Law Journal*, vol. 90, no. 473, Dec., pp. 1–44.
Schwartz, Marius and Reynolds, Robert (1983) 'Comment', *American Economic Review*, vol. 73, no. 3. Jun.
Weitzman, Martin (1983) 'Contestable Markets: An Uprising in the Theory of Industry Structure: Comment', *American Economic Review*, vol. 73, no. 3, Jun.

Discussion of the Paper by W. J. Baumol, J. C. Panzar and R. D. Willig

Spence began his discussion of the paper by Baumol *et al.* by delineating the general features of this paper and other recent work by the same authors. In Spence's view, this material (i) was an important generalisation of conventional competition, (ii) included a set of welfare criteria for assessing the performance of the market (in both price and output mix), (iii) provided a set of operating tools for understanding multi-product cost structures (for both technical efficiency and Ramsey (constrained) pricing), (iv) provided a descriptive theory of markets in the absence of irreversibility in the market (sunk costs).

In commenting on this paper, Spence first presented and then interpreted the basic definitions and results that appeared in each section of the paper (Propositions 1–11). Comments on this material by Baumol *et al.* advanced by others and the reactions of the authors appear elsewhere (*American Economic Review*, June 1983). Spence argued that what was relevant for the applicability of this theory was whether the time required for an entrant to enter and leave an industry was smaller than the time required for incumbents to react. (These relative times probably exhibited considerable variability across industries.) Further, in this work, demand had no intertemporal aspect – only current prices matter. Spence further pointed out that in the model as it stood there were no cost externalities across firms, e.g. shared learning.

Spence maintained that the concept of industry equilibrium in this work (i) meant that it was most applicable to industries without an irreversibility problem and therefore without complicated forms of interaction – history should not matter very much in these industries, (ii) was driven principally by cost or technological considerations, (iii) was applicable to analysing cost structures and pricing rules in all markets, (iv) was most applicable as a descriptive device in the long run to industries producing perishable products (e.g., services) where sunk costs were minimal.

Spence concluded that survival could be a powerful concept in economics. If we put downward pressure on demand, what firms could survive?

Grossman began by noting the importance in these models of both strategy and first-mover advantage. In perfectly contestable markets, entrants were assumed to behave as if existing firms did not alter prices in response to their entry. Grossman contended that in general this work was not so much 'revolutionary' as 'counter-revolutionary'

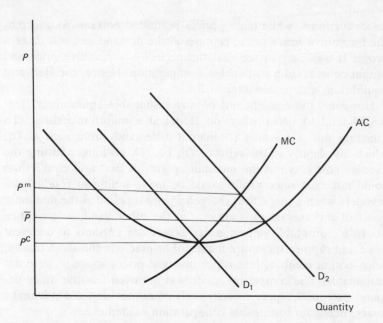

FIG. A.12.1 Relationship between Bertrand equilibrium and sustainability

against game theory and strategic models. Instead, this work represented a revival of the idea of finding a mapping from tastes and technology into outcomes. Grossman was sympathetic to this message. The problem with game theory was that it was possible to choose the rules of the game to produce any outcome. As a result, economists were transformed from scientists to advocates (lawyers).

Instead with this work, the substitution of tastes and technology into the model yielded sustainable allocations (hopefully not empty). While this had a benefit, it also had a cost – we could not do analysis in settings where we were convinced strategic interactions were important. Grossman argued that it was important to analyse the kinds of strategic behaviour that led to the outcomes predicted by Baumol *et al.*

To illustrate the feasibility of this task, Grossman considered the simplest partial equilibrium model with a single commodity. This model is outlined in Figure A.12.1. Aggregate demand was chosen so that it cut the minimum point of a single firm's average cost curve, as did the curve D_1 in the diagram.

The Bertrand equilibrium in this special case occurred when a single firm produced at the competitive p^c. Lower prices yielded only losses for firms, while higher prices permitted entrants to undercut the incumbent firm's price, capture all the demand and still make a profit. It was easy to see that the perfectly competitive price and output constituted a sustainable configuration. Hence, the Bertrand equilibrium was sustainable.

However, there might not be any sustainable equilibrium. This would tend to occur when no Bertrand equilibrium existed. To illustrate this, Grossman considered a demand curve such as D_2, which lay slightly to the right of D_1, i.e., D_2 no longer cutting the average cost curve at the minimum point. A Bertrand equilibrium could not exist since profits could be made selling to residual demanders when a single firm charged p^c and supplied at the minimum point of the average cost curve. On the other hand, at any price above p^c, profitable opportunities existed for entrants to undercut price and capture the entire market. For precisely the same reason, price–output combinations which involved prices above p^c were not sustainable. The competitive price was not even feasible, since demand exceeded supply for all levels of output that did not make losses, hence no sustainable configuration existed either.

Grossman then suggested that it might be possible to use strategic considerations to construct equilibria even when sustainable configurations did not exist. As an example, he suggested that sellers strategies might consist of supply functions rather than simple price–quantity strategies. A supply function implied a commitment to match price cuts by new entrants since with supply functions, incumbent firms were willing to supply different quantities at different prices. This suggested the possibility that equilibria might exist with price above average cost, since entrants would anticipate their price undercutting to elicit responses from existing firms. In the example given in Figure A.12.1, suppose the incumbent firm offered to supply along its marginal cost curve above its average cost curve. Suppose that the market price was adjusted so that offered supplies at every price were just equal to demand at that price. The price of output rose to p^m, when demand was given by D_1, and the incumbent firm made profits.

Any potential entrant perceived the supply *function* of the incumbent firm to be fixed. Entry would drive the price below p^m, but because all firms charged the same price, the entrant would only be able to capture residual demand. In other words, at any price below p^m, the output of the entrant would be the difference between demand at that price and the incumbent firm's supply at that price. If the average cost curve was U-shaped, it might well be that the average associated with producing the residual demand for the entrant was above the price at all possible levels of output open to the entrant. Hence, a price at p^m might not give rise to any entry. Of course, if the average cost curve were flat over initial output levels, this argument did not work. However, this did provide an instance where additional strategic considerations led to potential equilibria that were not sustainable in the sense of Baumol, Panzar and Willig.

Equilibria that were apparently not sustainable might arise for somewhat different reasons. In a perfectly contestable market, all participants were allowed access to the same production technology. All firms adopted the most efficient technology; hence it was reasonable to assume that costs were the same. However, incumbent firms might have sunk costs into an industry so that even though firms were identical *ex ante*, some firms might have cost advantages once they had entered. Again equilibria might arise with some profits because of this first-mover advantage.

Laffont suggested that an appropriate terminology for sustainable configurations might be an 'average-cost pricing equilibrium with free entry'. He agreed with Grossman that these 'equilibria' might not exist, and suggested that conditions for the existence of sustainable points should be established. He also suggested that the relationship between the set of sustainable configurations and Ramsey-constrained Pareto optima should be studied in more detail than they had been in the paper.

Selten suggested that economies of scope was a concept that had been around for some time under the alternative name 'cost complementarities'. It had long been argued that firms were organised around cost complementaries. The concept of a sustainable configuration gave substance to this conjecture. As an empirical fact, organisation around cost complementaries yielded downstream firms located close to supplies of raw materials. It was also true that firms that located close to markets organised around demand complementaries: Retailing firms sold products that were complementary. Selten suggested that sustainability analysis left little room for study of this sort of issue. Willig responded that one might interpret retailing as the provision of a service. Demand complementarities might then be thought of as cost complementarities in provision of the service. Panzar added that cost complementaries could arise as an important phenomenon even in retailing. As an example he pointed out that certain products could not be stored together.

Schmalensee suggested that one of the important contributions of the theory of contestable markets was that it forced one to think about modelling production costs in a dynamic framework, and to worry about the dynamics of entry. He suggested that an especially important difficulty that had not been adequately studied was the way that new entrants attracted customers. If the entrants were required to inform customers of their existence and the prices that they charged, it would be very hard for them not to inform incumbent firms as well. In turn, this information should reduce the costs of retaliation against entrants by incumbents.

Part Seven
Competition and
Market Structure:
Special Issues

13 Advertising and Market Structure[1]

Richard Schmalensee

MASSACHUSETTS INSTITUTE OF TECHNOLOGY, USA

I INTRODUCTION

Manufacturers take many actions designed to enhance the demand for their products. They generally deal with product design and packaging, price structures at wholesale and retail levels, training and deployment of sales personnel, and the economic and contractual dimensions of the distribution channels they employ. They may also engage in media advertising. Retailers generally engage in most of these same activities. Consumer purchase decisions are affected by many external stimuli. Consumers may take into account their own experience, the experiences of friends and relatives, conversations with sales people and other experts, data on relevant prices, and information about product attributes, obtained from a variety of public sources. Purchase decisions may also be affected by media advertising.[2]

Despite the complexity of firms' marketing policies and consumers' purchase decisions, industrial economists have generally limited their attention to two of the variables involved: price and media advertising.[3] It is not clear that the economic significance of advertising generally justifies this allocation of effort. In aggregate, media advertising expenditures are impressive in most developed countries, particularly in the USA. Media advertising in the USA is estimated to have been about $61 billion in 1981, for instance (Coen, 1982); this amounts to about 2.1 per cent of GNP that year and to about 3.3 per cent of personal consumption expenditures. But these percentages are lower in most other countries, typically much lower in developing nations.[4] Similarly, while advertising/sales ratios are high for a few US manufacturing industries, they are quite low for many others, and

373

other selling expenses often equal or exceed outlays for advertising.[5]

Perhaps reflecting the traditional distaste for advertising in the intellectual community, early discussions of advertising by economists were generally critical, describing it as wasteful, manipulative and intrinsically anticompetitive. (Kaldor (1950) is a leading example.) That part of the modern literature of industrial economics concerned with advertising really began with Telser's (1964) response to such critics. He portrayed advertising as a valuable mechanism for providing costly information and thus tending to enhance competition. Most of the subsequent literature has concentrated on choosing between these two diametrically opposed viewpoints.

In what follows, I present a selective overview of theoretical work on the industrial economics of advertising. In Section II, I discuss models in which advertising appears as a form on non-price competition among rivals selling differentiated products. Section III considers the question of the optimality of advertising levels produced by such competition. Finally, in Section IV, I discuss the effects of advertising on market structure, and particularly on conditions of entry.

II ADVERTISING AS NON-PRICE COMPETITION

Given the basic conditions of tastes and technology, and given the key elements of market structure, what does theory permit us to say about the intensity of advertising and its competitive effects? For the purpose of dealing with this question, it is probably sensible to treat advertising simply as a demand-increasing expenditure; it does not seem necessary to make specific assumptions about how advertising induces changes in buyer behaviour. Such analysis thus has fairly direct application to at least some other forms of non-price competition.

Two specific issues seem to be of particular interest in this context, and they are the focus of the rest of this section. First, how does competition through advertising affect profits? Do its effects differ in any basic way from those of price competition? Second, how does such advertising competition affect the relative advantages of large and small firms? That is, how do scale economies from promotional expenditure interact with those in production to determine the overall advantages of size?[6]

To address the first of these issues, let us briefly compare models of advertising and price competition, respectively, in a market with product differentiation. For the first model, suppose that N firms agree to sell at a fixed price (P) and that all have constant unit cost (c).[7] If A_i and q_i are firm i's advertising spending and unit sales, respectively, suppose that demands (with fixed, equal prices) are given by

$$q_i = K \left[\sum_{j=1}^{N} (A_j)^\rho \right]^{\alpha/\rho} \left[(A_i)^e / \sum_{j=1}^{N} (A_j)^e \right], i = 1, \ldots, N. \quad (1)$$

Here ρ and α are constants between zero and one, with larger values of ρ indicating greater substitutability among firms' advertising in affecting market demand, and α being the elasticity of demand of the total market with respect to advertising. The positive parameter e measures the sensitivity of firms' market shares to differences among their advertising outlays, and K is a positive scale factor. Profits are given by

$$\pi_i = (P - c)q_i - A_i, \qquad i = 1, \ldots, N. \quad (2)$$

Note the formal similarity between this model and static models of technological competition that are not of the patent race, winner-take-all variety. (See, for instance, Dasgupta in this volume and the references he cites.)

At a symmetric Nash equilibrium in the A_i, the following relation holds:

$$A_i/(P - c)q_i = 1 - \pi_i/(P - c)q_i$$
$$= e + (\alpha - e)/N, \qquad i = 1, \ldots, N. \quad (3)$$

Following the analysis in Schmalensee (1976), one can show that:

(a) No oligopoly equilibrium with non-negative profits exists unless $e \leqslant (2 - \alpha)$;
(b) If $(2 - \alpha) \geqslant e > 1$, profits are eliminated by entry at a finite N;
(c) If $e = 1$, profits are eliminated by entry only in the limit as N increases without bound;
(d) If $e < 1$, profits remain positive even in the limit.

In order to compare price and advertising competition, let us now consider a model in which products are differentiated, advertising outlays are collusively set (to zero for convenience), and price is the instrument of rivalry. Let P_i be firm i's price, and let unit sales be given by the following equation, which has an obvious formal resemblance to (1):

$$q_i = K \left[(1/N) \sum_{j=1}^{N} (P_j)^{-\rho} \right]^{E/\rho} \left[(P_i)^{-e} / \sum_{j=1}^{N} (P_j)^{-e} \right],$$

$$i = 1, \ldots, N. \tag{4}$$

As before, K and ρ are positive constants relating to the scale of the market and the substitutability among products. E is the market price elasticity of demand, and the positive constant e measures the sensitivity of firms' market shares to differences in their prices.[8] Profits are given by

$$\pi_i = (P_i - c)q_i, \qquad i = 1, \ldots, N, \tag{5}$$

where c is unit production cost, as before. At a symmetric Nash equilibrium in the P_i, the following relation holds:

$$(P_i - c)/P_i = \pi_i/P_i q_i = 1/[e + (E - e)/N], \qquad i = 1, \ldots, N, \quad (6)$$

In both (3) and (6), the parameter e is a major determinant of equilibrium profitability. If market share is sensitive either to advertising or to price, firms' attempts to expand their shares using either variable will serve to erode profits. The formal differences between (3) and (6) flow from the different ways in which the corresponding instruments of rivalry enter the profit functions in the two models. Those differences do *not* suggest that advertising competition is less effective than price competition in eliminating excess profit. Note in particular that (6) indicates that Nash equilibria in prices always involve positive excess profit for all N, while increasing N drives profits to zero through intensified advertising rivalry in (3) as long as $e \geq 1$. Moreover, the argument that collusion on price is more likely than collusion on advertising for small N (Schmalensee, 1976) suggests that comparisons between (3) and (6), both of which assume non-collusive conduct, are likely to understate the relative impact of advertising rivalry on excess profits in oligopoly.

There is none the less a presumption in much of the relevant literature that advertising competition (and, indeed, non-price competition in general) is 'softer' than price competition, in the sense of being less of a threat to excess profits. The analysis above suggests as a rough generalisation that in order for this to be true, the value of e

in (4) must exceed its value in (1). That is, speaking loosely, market shares must be more sensitive to price differences than to differences in advertising outlays. While this may indeed describe many markets, if consumers' brand choices in some particular market are strongly affected by advertising and only weakly affected by price, these models lead one to expect that price competition will be 'softer' in that market than will advertising competition. (If e is absolutely small for both price and advertising, of course, neither form of rivalry will effectively eliminate excess profits.)

Two limitations of the above analysis deserve explicit mention. First, we examined only polar-case patterns of perfect but incomplete collusion, with strictly non-cooperative behaviour determining the non-collusive variable. More generally, one might find collusion to be imperfect as regards both price and advertising. In models involving rivalry along two dimensions, cross-effects in the demand equation, like the effect of lower prices on advertising elasticities, assume central importance. (This is nicely illustrated by Dehez and Jacquemin (1975), though in a slightly different context.) Little evidence on such effects is available, however.[9]

Second, the analysis above, like almost all related theoretical work, deals only with single-stage models, in which producers sell directly to consumers. In fact, for most advertised products, rivalry occurs among producers *and* among retailers, and the two levels interact. Steiner (1973), for instance, has argued persuasively that the availability of network television advertising, and its intensive use by US toy manufacturers beginning in the mid-1950s, transformed the nature of the corresponding retail competition. Toys became 'convenience goods' rather than 'shopping goods' (Porter, 1976) as consumers ceased relying on sales staff for information about product attributes, and retail margins fell sharply as competition shifted from non-price to price dimensions. Very little rigorous theoretical exploration of two-stage models, involving both producers and retailers, has been done; more work here would seem especially worthwhile.

Let us now turn to the second of the general issues raised above: the relation between scale economies in advertising and the overall advantages of size. Even though Bain (1956, pp. 117–20) discussed this relation over a quarter-century ago, the first satisfactory formal analysis was only recently provided by Spence (1980). In the remainder of this section, I present a slight generalisation of the Spence model and discuss some of its implications.

Consider a market with N sellers in which profits can be written as

$$\pi_i = B(m)y(a_i, q_i) - c(q_i) - h(a_i), \qquad i = 1, \ldots, N. \tag{7}$$

Here q_i denotes firm i's unit sales, with the corresponding production cost being $c(q_i)$, and a_i denotes that same firm's real advertising, with the corresponding advertising expenditures being $h(a_i)$.[10] Thus the function $h(a)$ reflects the technology and input prices relevant to the production and dissemination of advertising messages. The function $y(a,q)$ is assumed to be increasing in both its arguments, $B(m)$ is a decreasing function, and

$$m = \sum_{i=1}^{N} y(a_i, q_i). \tag{8}$$

Restrictions must be imposed on the demand functions of both the firm and the market in order for (7) to hold. If firm i's revenue is to be increasing with respect to a_i, for instance, (7) implies that the elasticity of B with respect to its argument must exceed $(-m/y_i)$. For this to hold for all possible sets non-negative y_i, that elasticity must exceed -1. But this in turn implies that the market-demand function is price-elastic, in the sense that increases in any q_i increase total market revenue. Still, (7) is a tractable special case that yields considerable insight.

Spence observes that, in this case, one can decompose the firms's profit maximisation into two stages. First, compute the function $\phi(y)$, which gives the minimum value of total cost, $c(q) + h(a)$, associated with each value of y. Then select y so as to maximise $[B(m)y - \phi(y)]$, taking into account rivals' behaviour in whatever fashion is appropriate. The first stage is simply cost minimisation with two inputs. In whatever equilibrium results, large firms will have a larger ratio of profit to sales revenue than will small firms, if $\phi(y)/y$ is decreasing in (y) over the relevant range. Thus the elasticity of $\phi(y)$ with respect to its argument gives a (local) indicator of the advantages of size which incorporates scale effects in both advertising and production.

To see how these effects interact, we can follow Spence and consider functional forms involving constant elasticities:

$$y(a, q) = y_0 a^\gamma q^\alpha, \qquad c(q) = c_0 q^{1/\beta}, \qquad h(a) = h_0 a^{1/\delta}, \tag{9}$$

where y_0, γ, α, c_0, β, h_0 and δ are positive constants.[11] Following the development made by Spence (1980), one can show that if (9) holds, the elasticity of $\phi(y)$ with respect to its argument, is given by

$$\theta = \phi'(y)y/\phi(y) = 1/(\alpha\beta + \gamma\delta). \tag{10}$$

If θ is less than (greater than) one, there are overall advantages (disadvantages) of size. That is, firms with larger y's, and thus greater sales revenues, will have higher (lower) ratios of profit to sales revenue than will others.

Equation (10) makes clear that any technical change which alters returns to scale in either production (β) or advertising (δ) will affect the net advantage of size (θ). Thus if, as many have argued, there are economies of scale in the use of network television advertising in the USA, the coming of television will have served to raise δ in many industries and thus to increase the net advantages of size across the board.[12] Equation (10) shows that the impact of a change of this sort varies directly with the demand parameter γ. Roughly, the larger is γ, then: the more responsive is sales revenue to an increase in advertising; the greater is the optimal degree of reliance on advertising to generate revenue; and the more likely it is that scale economies in advertising will produce overall advantages of size. Similarly, scale economies in production are more likely to imply a θ less than one the larger is α. It is difficult to relate the demand parameters γ and α to observable demand elasticities, however, since the net response of revenue to changes in (a) and (q) depends on the function $B(m)$, and neither y_i nor $B(m)$ are directly observable. (Spence (1980) relates these parameters to *m-constant* elasticities of demand.)

If (9) holds, the problem of selecting (a) and (q) to minimise the cost of producing (y) can be immediately reformulated as an ordinary two-input Cobb–Douglas cost minimisation exercise, with inputs $q^{1/3}$ and $a^{1/\delta}$. The exponents of these inputs in the resulting production function are easily seen to be $\alpha\beta$ and $\gamma\delta$, respectively. Equation (10) shows that the sum of these exponents determines returns to scale in exactly the ordinary way. It follows directly from this that the ratio of advertising expenditure to total (advertising plus production) cost must equal $\gamma\delta/(\alpha\beta + \gamma\delta)$ in equilibrium, for all values of y. Scale economies in advertising in this model do not imply a decline in the ratio of advertising to total cost as market share increases. If θ is less than one, the ratios of *both* advertising expenditures *and* production cost to sales revenue decline with market share.

In interpreting or applying this model, one must be careful to distinguish between y, which is not directly observable, and sales revenue, which is $R = yB(m)$. Let ψ be the ratio of profit, given by equation (7), to sales revenue. Consider the difference in ψ between two firms that in equilibrium have revenues differing by a small amount, ΔR. Differentiating the expression for ψ, and treating m as fixed in order to compare two firms in the same market equilibrium, one obtains

$$\Delta \psi \simeq (1 - \psi)(1 - \theta)(\Delta R/R). \tag{11}$$

If rivalry is intense, so that ψ is generally close to zero, profitability differences will be larger than if rivalry is restrained, with the consequence that ψ is generally near one. Hence even if θ is constant, any observable net advantages of size will depend on the exact nature of market equilibrium; the cost minimisation exercise that yields $\phi(y)$ does not provide complete information. If θ is not constant, the intensity of rivalry may be even more important. If $\phi(y)/y$ is U-shaped, for instance, one might observe advantages of size where there is a collusive equilibrium (with small y_i) and disadvantages of size when rivalry is more intense (and the y_i are larger).

While these analyses serve to deepen our understanding of advertising as a form of non-price competition, they obviously do not answer – or even address – all the interesting questions. Since the relevant literatures do not suggest deep uncertainty as to the nature of sensible models in this area, further theoretical work on non-price competition along the lines discussed here seems likely to be productive.

III ADVERTISING AND EFFICIENCY

Given basic conditions and market structure, do sellers provide the optimal amount of advertising? This question has attracted a good deal of attention over the years.[13] In this section, I discuss four important recent contributions to the optimality literature, each of which deals with a different polar-case model. The first two assume that advertising is purely informative: it provides information that directly enhances efficiency. In the model of Butters (1977), all sellers offer the same product, and advertising merely provides price information. In the analysis of Grossman and Shapiro (1984), however, products are differentiated and advertising also conveys information about product attributes. Dixit and Norman (1978), by contrast, assume that advertising is purely persuasive; it merely changes behaviour and has no direct impact on welfare or on the efficiency of resource allocation. Finally, Nelson (1974) considers uninformative advertising that may not be persuasive either. He argues that such advertising may enhance efficiency by providing consumers with a signal about product quality.

In Butters' model, all consumers have the same reservation price, (m), for some product. Sellers send out advertisements at random to buyers; these give price and location. In Butters' simplest model, consumers buy one unit of the product at the lowest price for which they receive an advertisement, so long as that price does not exceed (m). If they receive no advertisements, or if they receive only those with prices above (m), they buy nothing. Advertising thus creates social gain by allowing mutually-beneficial trades to occur.

Let (c) be unit production cost, let (h) be the cost of sending one advertisement to one (randomly-selected) consumer, and assume that (c) and (h) are constant for all sellers, with $c + h < m$. If A advertisements are sent at random to a population of B consumers, and both A and B are large, the fraction of consumers receiving no advertisement is approximately $\exp(-A/B)$. Let $a = A/B$. If all consumers who receive advertisements make purchases, net surplus per buyer is given by

$$W = (1/B)[B(1 - e^{-a})(m - c) - hA] = (1 - e^{-a})(m - c)ha. \quad (12)$$

It is easy to see that W is maximised when

$$a = a^* = \ln[(m - c)/h]. \quad (13)$$

In a free-entry competitive equilibrium, Butters shows that all prices between $c + h$ and m will be advertised. (There are no fixed costs in this model, so a continuum of firms can exist.) Let $z(p)$ be the probability that an advertisement sent out announcing the price (p) will generate a sale. Free entry implies zero expected profit, which in turn implies that

$$(p - c)z(p) - h = 0; \qquad z(p) = h/(p - c) \quad (14)$$

Since an advertisement that announces $p = m$ will produce a sale only if it reaches a buyer who has received no other advertisements, it must be that $z(m) = \exp(-a)$. Setting $p = m$ in (14), equating the two expressions for $z(m)$, and solving for (a), one finds that in a free-entry competitive equilibrium, $a = a^*$. In this special case, the market generates exactly the optimal amount of advertising.

This turns out to be a very delicate result. When Butters (1977) modifies his simplest model to allow consumers who receive no advertisements to engage in search, he finds that equilibrium involves too much advertising and not enough search. It is not intuitively clear why this occurs. This over-advertising result at least shows, by example, that the polar-case assumption that advertising is purely informative does not suffice to establish the optimality of market-determined advertising expenditures. At least it does not do so where there are information sources not directly under sellers' control.

In a recent study, Grossman and Shapiro (1984) also assume that advertising is purely informative, but they allow for real product differentiation. They consider a model of the sort analysed by Salop (1979), in which a continuum of buyers and a finite number of sellers are spread around a circle in product-attribute space. Buyers are interested in at most one unit of the product considered. They incur transport costs, which stand as proxies for utility losses, proportional to the distance between their location (ideal product) and the location of which ever seller they elect to patronise. Grossman and Shapiro modify the Salop model by assuming buyers to be initially ignorant of sellers' prices and locations (product attributes). Sellers are permitted to use a generalised verion of the Butters (1977) advertising technology to send price and location information to buyers. Grossman and Shapiro consider symmetric Nash equilibria for locations, prices, and advertising outlays. And they do so both with and without the assumption of free entry (zero profits). They note that advertising is pro-competitive in their model, in the sense that reductions in the cost of advertising reduce equilibrium price–cost differences, and they obtain a large number of interesting comparative-static results.

Grossman and Shapiro demonstrate that equilibria in their model do not involve optimal levels of advertising spending. With the number of brands fixed, there is too much advertising per brand. Grossman and Shapiro interpret this to reflect wasteful competition for market share. In free-entry equilibrium, there are too many brands (as in the original Salop (1979) paper). Apparently as a consequence, there is too little advertising per brand as compared with first-best optimum. While it seems likely that a number of the definite Grossman–Shapiro results are sensitive to their assumptions about functional forms, their work does again show that even if advertising is purely informative (and pro-competitive), the market need not generate optimal levels of advertising spending.

In contrast to Butters and also to Grossman and Shapiro, Dixit and Norman (1978) assume that advertising alters consumer behaviour, but has no direct effect on welfare or efficiency.[14] Advertising can be efficiency-enhancing in their model only if it encourages the consumption and production of goods that are over-priced because of the exercise of irremovable monopoly power.

The core of their argument can be easily outlined in partial-equilibrium terms. Let (q) be a monopoly's total output, (p) its price, and (a) its level of real advertising. Let q (a,p) be the market demand function, increasing in its first argument and decreasing in its second, and let the increasing function $V(q)$ give the true, social value placed on different quantities of this product.

Without advertising, it is customary to assume that behaviour maximises individual welfare and so to treat $V'(q)$ as equal to the observed inverse demand function. (This neglects income and distributional effects.) Dixit and Norman instead take $V'(q)$ to be the inverse demand function corresponding to some *fixed* value of (a). If advertising provided information that made the monopoly's product objectively more valuable or useful, (V) would logically be an increasing function of (a), but this sort of effect is assumed away. Similarly, advertising might directly increase utility by raising the subjective value of a given consumption vector, but Dixit and Norman argue that it is improper to take account of such effects.

With (c) and (h) defined as above, the level of net surplus generated by the monopoly is given by

$$W = V[q(a,p)] - cq(a,p) - ha$$
$$= \{V[q(a,p)] - pq(a,p)\} + \pi(a,p), \tag{15}$$

where $\pi(a, p)$ is the seller's profit. Setting $p = p^*(a)$, the price that maximises profit for a given level of advertising, we can treat both W and π as functions of (a) alone. Differentiating, we obtain

$$dW/da = (V' - p)(dq/da) - q(dp^*/da) + d\pi/da. \tag{16}$$

If dW/da is negative at a monopoly equilibrium it follows that an exogenously forced reduction in advertising, with the monopoly adjusting (p) to maximise profit, would lead to an increase in welfare.

At a monopoly equilibrium, the third term on the right of (16) is zero. In the second term, the sign of dp^*/da is not clear *a priori*. In the natural case of multiplicative separability, $q(a,p) = f(a)g(p)$, this derivative is zero. It will be positive if more advertising makes demand less elastic and negative if more advertising raises demand elasticity. Having little convincing evidence on this factual issue,[15] let us suppose that this second term is zero. This leaves us with the first term on the right of (16). Under almost any plausible assumptions, dq/da will be positive. (Recall that this is the total derivative, taking into account the optimal reaction of (p) to exogenous changes in (a).

We thus reach the conclusion that if demand is multiplicatively separable, dW/da has the sign of ($V' - p$).

A necessary and sufficient condition for monopoly advertising to be excessive in the separable case, is thus that V' (q) should be less than the corresponding equilibrium value of (p).[16] If one takes 'true' tastes to be those reflected in demands with $a = 0$, this condition is satisfied; the conclusion of excessive advertising is immediate. But this reasoning is circular: the *conclusion* that there is too much advertising rests on the *assumption* that advertising inflates demand beyond what 'true' tastes would justify. If one instead took 'true' tastes to be those corresponding to demands with infinite advertising, so that increasing (a) merely moves market behaviour closer to welfare-maximising behaviour, it would be equally immediate that monopolies spend too little on advertising. Thus, even if advertising is assumed to be purely persuasive, it appears that one cannot conclude that it is generally excessive. To reach this conclusion, one has to make the explicit value judgement that (in equilibrium) advertising generates *demand* which is excessive, when judged by the 'true' tastes embodied in the social-valuation function.

Finally, Nelson (1974) argues that advertising that is neither informative nor persuasive may none the less enhance welfare by serving as a signal through which high-quality brands can inform consumers of their superiority. Nelson is concerned with 'experience goods', the quality of which (by assumption) cannot be ascertained prior to purchase. All else (including price) being equal, he argues plausibly, consumers are more likely to repurchase a high-quality brand than a low-quality brand. Thus firms selling high-quality brands, he contends, are willing to spend more to persuade buyers to sample their wares, and they will consequently have larger advertising budgets, in equilibrium, than will low-quality brands. Buyers may then select brands to sample on the basis of advertising budgets, *either* because they are sophisticated and can unscramble quality signals, or because they are naïve and do what they are most often told to do. If they behave in this way, high-quality brands will receive an advantage and efficiency will be enhanced.

Nelson's analysis is informal, and cannot support any claims of optimality. If several qualities remain on the market at the same price, the situation is clearly not optimal. Cheaper signals (if any could be devised) would dominate advertising in this framework. Further, since one expects lower-quality brands to have lower costs of production, they would be expected to have higher mark-ups, all else equal. This tends to enhance the value of initial purchases of such brands and thus to raise their optimal amount of advertising. Under extreme conditions, this second force can overwhelm that stressed by Nelson and produce 'perverse' equilibria, in which the lowest-quality brands are the most heavily advertised (Schmalensee, 1978a). More important, the existence of this second force rules out the generic optimality of market equilibria in this context. Thus, while Nelson (1974) may have identified a mechanism by which uninformative advertising can generate gross benefits, he has not shown that the amount of such advertising is optimal in equilibrium, or even that it generates net benefits.

While further theoretical work on the optimality of market-generated levels of advertising may add to our store of models and insights, it is not likely to contribute to the formation of public policy. For tractability, the effects of advertising must apparently be simplified to the point of caricature, and even then general welfare results are not always easily obtained. Since imperfect information or monopoly power must be assumed in order to rationalise the presence of advertising, welfare analysis, even in polar-case models, must involve comparisons among imperfect, distorted equilibria. The information requirements of such second-best analysis make the derivation of workable, quantitative policy prescriptions unlikely – and would do so even if there were agreement as to the most relevant caricature of advertising to employ. There is a strong resemblance to the literature on product variety in these respects.[17]

IV ADVERTISING AS A DETERMINANT OF MARKET STRUCTURE

How do sellers' decisions about advertising spending affect the evolution of market structure, and particularly conditions of entry? Discussions of this question in the literature of industrial economics have been dominated by two extreme views. The critics of advertising stress its persuasive nature and contend that it is generally anti-competitive. They often point to markets for liquid bleach and other products in which heavily-advertised brands command substantial price premia over physically-identical alternatives (Scherer, 1980, pp. 381–3). Advertising's defenders emphasise its informative role and argue that it is generally pro-competitive. They frequently cite Benham (1972), who finds that state laws prohibiting eyeglass (spectacle) advertising are associated with higher-than-average eyeglass (spectacle) prices.

Since advertising is an aspect of seller conduct, which in turn is affected by market structure, it is not surprising that it has been difficult to choose empirically between these two positions. Moreover, measurement problems in this area are severe.[18] At a more fundamental level, as I have argued elsewhere (Schmalensee, 1982b, Section 4), it is likely that neither of the two extreme views is correct. As the examples in the preceding paragraph might suggest, the impact of advertising on market structure probably depends on product attributes, the nature of advertising, and consumer information.[19]

The classical elements of market structure are seller concentration, product differentiation and conditions of entry. The first of these can be dealt with briefly. Seller concentration is generally thought to be positively related to the importance of economies of scale. The model of Spence (1980), already discussed in Section II, is apparently the first to relate scale economies in advertising to overall advantages of size. Lynk (1981) explores this relation with a sharply-different model, and he presents some tests based on an analysis of the effects of the introduction of television advertising in the USA in the mid-1950s. There is clearly a great deal of room for further work in this area.

Product differentiation exists whenever rival brands are not viewed as perfect substitutes. It is more important the smaller, on average, are (brand-specific) own-price and cross-price elasticities of demand. Those who contend that advertising primarily changes tastes often argue that it must enhance product differentiation, though this is clearly not a logical necessity. It is not implausible, for instance, that wine advertising on balance encourages comparative tasting. Similarly, those who feel that advertising mainly provides information commonly argue that it must reduce differentiation and increase brand-specific demand elasticities by making buyers aware of available alternatives. But when buyers are heterogeneous, information can reduce brand-specific demand elasticities by making buyers aware that some alternatives are not satisfactory. To an uninformed individual, for example, Coca Cola and Pepsi Cola are likely to be perfect substitutes, while many regular cola drinkers strongly prefer one or the other.[20] The presence of this sort of matching effect does not imply that increased advertising *must* reduce demand elasticities; the model of Grossman and Shapiro (1982) discussed in Section III provides a counter-example. One would like to know, in general, when purely informative advertising either enhances or reduces differentiation on balance: it would also be interesting to examine this issue with two-stage models of the sort discussed briefly in Section II.

Actual advertising is, however, rarely adequately described by either of the two extreme cases. In order to analyse, in a persuasive fashion, the effects of actual advertising on demand elasticities, it would be necessary to employ a tractable, generally accepted micro-model of the effects of actual advertising on buyer behaviour. No such model now exists, though the empirical literature on consumer behaviour may be rich enough to permit its construction. (See, in particular, Engle, *et al.*, 1978.)

A great deal has been written on the possible effects of advertising on conditions of entry. Most of this work is empirical and is apparently motivated by Bain's (1956, p. 216) empirically-based assertion that the advantages of established brands in terms of product differentiation are the most important source of barriers to entry. Some of the literature that supports Bain's assertion argues that such advantages derive from the longevity of the effects of advertising on consumer behaviour. But the fact that investment in advertising gives long-term benefits does not by itself seem to be any more of a barrier to entry than is the durability of investment in plant and equipment (Schmalensee, 1974).[21]

Bain (1956, p. 143), himself, does not argue that advertising is the basic source of the advantages of product differentiation. A number of his observations point to the importance of uncertainty about product quality (Bain, 1956, pp. 116, 140, 142). I have recently constructed a model that is consistent both with these observations and with some recent empirical work (Schmalensee, 1982a). In that model, 'pioneering' brands of subjectively uncertain quality have a permanent advantage over later entrants of equally uncertain quality. Buyers who have invested in learning about the pioneer product, and are satisfied with it, are rationally less willing to experiment with later entrants than they were with the pioneer. If scale economies are present, the pioneer can use its advantage to deter later entry. Farrell (1982) analyses a similar model where there are more sophisticated and knowledgeable buyers, and finds that the pioneer can deter later entry even in the absence of scale economies. Advertising does not appear in either model. It may be that there are similar irreversible changes, associated with exposure to advertising, that give early entrants a long-lived advantage, but I know of no persuasive theoretical or empirical explorations of such phenomena.

In the usual situation – with one incumbent firm and one potential entrant – the latter's entry decision may be influenced by his expectations about the incumbent's post-entry advertising or, directly, by the incumbent's actual pre-entry spending. Post-entry advertising generally matters because it is a form of rivalry, and the more intense is the rivalry that a potential entrant expects to encounter, the less attractive is entry. If advertising can be used as an instrument of rivalry, expectations about post-entry advertising will thus play a role in entry deterrence.

Cubbin (1981) provides a general discussion of this effect. Pre-entry advertising by the incumbent seems to matter in his analysis only because it is arbitrarily assumed to determine expectations about post-entry spending. Spence (1980) shows how a binding commitment by an incumbent to heavy post-entry advertising can deter entry in the presence of scale economies, though he does not explore how such a commitment might be made. Kotowitz and Mathewson (1982) assume that the potential entrant expects the incumbent to adopt a non-co-operative advertising policy if entry occurs. They examine conditions under which this deters entry when the incumbent enjoys an information-based demand advantage of the sort treated by Schmalensee (1982a). If, as in these models, advertising is involved in entry deterrence *only* through the potential entrant's expectations of the incumbent's post-entry spending, it seems odd to say that advertising creates a barrier to entry. After all, entry deterrence in homogeneous-product models without advertising is accomplished through the potential entrant's expectations of the incumbent's post-entry production level. Yet nobody would say that *production* creates a barrier to entry in such models.

It seems preferable to say that advertising creates a barrier to entry only if increased pre-entry spending by an established firm acts directly (not just through expectations) to make entry less attractive. This seems the more interesting effect empirically, since we generally observe what amounts to pre-entry advertising spending. Recent work on barriers to entry in general has found that it may be optimal for an established seller to make irreversible pre-entry commitments, where these affect its post-entry incentives in such a way as to deter potential entrants (Dixit, 1982). Suppose an incumbent decides to incur sunk costs by investing in long-lived production capacity, for instance. Its future short-run cost function is then generally shifted in such a way that marginal cost is lowered at relatively high levels of output. Such investment is thus likely to increase the potential entrant's (rational) expectation of the incumbent's post-entry output and thereby to make entry less attractive. Several studies have found that it may be optimal for an incumbent seller to over-invest in capacity (relative to the optimal level when entry is impossible) in order to deter entry, especially in the presence of scale economies in production.[22] It thus seems natural to ask whether over-investment in pre-entry advertising can play a similar role, especially in the presence of overall scale economies.

This question was clearly posed by Spence (1977b), though he did not present a complete model to answer it. Baldani and Masson (1981) have recently constructed a model in which pre-entry over-advertising credibly and optimally deters entry. Their particular result is a bit forced, however, since under their assumptions a monopolist protected from entry would not find it optimal to adver-tise at all. If the incumbent advertises in advance of entry, this is assumed to create durable 'goodwill' that forces the entrant to advertise in order to sell anything.[23] The greater the incumbent's 'goodwill', the lower the entrant's sales at every advertising level. If entry does not occur, on the other hand, the incumbent's 'goodwill' is assumed not to affect the demand for his output. The assumed properties of 'goodwill' are not related to a model of the behaviour of individual buyers, and post-entry equilibrium is not fully modelled. Still, the central mechanism in the Baldani–Masson model is the ability of the incumbent to depress the entrant's demand by increas-ing its own pre-entry advertising. It seems likely that it will often be optimal for incumbents to exploit such a mechanism when it is available.

An alternative to the 'goodwill' approach is to focus on introduc-tory advertising, which is undertaken when a brand is launched in order to make buyers aware of its existence. Such advertising is clearly a sunk cost, and its effects on demand can be reasonably assumed to be long-lived. If a large, fixed amount must be spent on such introductory advertising, regardless of subsequent sales, a non-convexity is present that can deter entry. (See Schmalensee (1978b) for an application of this point.) In fact, the amount that a seller invests in introductory advertising is not fixed: the more he chooses to spend the more people are informed, and the greater is his product's sales poten-tial. By analogy with investment in production capacity, one might conjecture that in the presence of scale economies in advertising, over-investment in introductory advertising could be used to deter entry.

I have recently constructed a model (Schmalensee, 1983) in which this conjecture turns out to be false. A brief examination of a greatly simplified version of that model will serve to indicate how this can occur. It should also serve to emphasise the dangers of relying on apparent analogies between investment in advertising and investment in production capacity.

Consider two firms, A and B, capable of producing identical brands of some new product. There are two possible buyers, 1 and 2. If informed of the existence of the product, both buyers have flow demand functions $q = 1 - p$. There are zero production costs. In order to inform one or both buyers, a fixed cost (F) must be incurred. It then costs c_1 to inform buyer 1 and c_2 to inform buyer 2, with $c_1 < c_2$. To capture the general inability of late entrants to avoid informing some buyers who know of earlier entrants, suppose that buyer 1 must be informed before an advertisement can be sent to buyer 2.

If A enters first, informs only buyer 1, and charges the monopoly price ($p = \frac{1}{2}$) thereafter, the present value of firm A will be $[(1/4r) - c_1 - F]$, where r is the relevant discount rate. Suppose that $F + c_1 < 1/4r < c_2$, so that this is optimal behaviour if there is no threat of future entry. (Note that this implies diseconomies of scale: the necessary non-convexity derives from buyer 'lumpiness'. In Schmalensee (1983) there are economies of scale over a range and a continuum of buyers.) Under these assumptions, I want to argue that it is never optimal for A to over-invest in advertising, by informing buyer 2 in order to deter B's entry.

Let us consider the results of B's entry. Suppose that B informs only buyer 1. No Bertrand equilibrium exists here or in the cases examined below. We thus assume a Cournot post-entry equilibrium. Both sellers would then have present values of $[(1/9r) - c_1 - F]$. Now suppose that A has informed both buyers and that B enters and informs only buyer 1. Whatever the quantities offered by the two sellers, buyer 1 will clearly never pay a higher price than buyer 2. Since buyer 2 is unaware of B, it can only demand A's output. Let Q_A and Q_B be the outputs of the two sellers. If $Q_A \geqslant Q_B$, buyer 1 can perform an arbitrage function, and a single price equal to $[1 - (Q_A + Q_B)/2]$ prevails in the market. If $Q_A < Q_B$, however, the constraint that 2 does not buy from B is binding. Then 2 pays $(1 - Q_A)$ per unit for A's output, while 1 obtains B's output at a lower price of $(1 - Q_B)$. With these demand functions, it is straightforward to show that, in Cournot equilibrium, A sells only to buyer 2, B sells only to buyer 1, and the same price prevails as in the preceding case. The two firms divide the larger market created by A's advertising: customer 1's perfect information disciplines both sellers. B's present value in this case is $[(2/9r) - c_1 - F]$. A's over-investment in advertising would *raise*, not lower, B's post-entry profits, and such over-investment can obviously not be used to deter entry. Because $c_2 > 1/9r$, if A informs only buyer 1, B's best strategy (if it elects to enter) is also to inform only buyer 1. Whether or not it deters entry, A's best policy prior to B's appearance is the unconstrained monopoly strategy. Similarly, in the more complicated model of Schmalensee (1983), it is never possible to make entry less attractive by over-advertising.

This analysis suggests that the strategic implications of investments in introductory advertising may differ dramatically from those of investments in productive capacity. Two reasons come to mind. First, investment in productive assets affects the relation between cost and total output, while investment in advertising fundamentally acts on individuals' demand curves. When individual buyers can vary the number of units they purchase, this formal difference may have serious strategic implications. Second, investment in productive capacity serves to discourage entry by making high levels of output and thus low market prices relatively more attractive to the incumbent. But investment in advertising that provides the incumbent with a set of customers that would not be tempted by an entrant's wares may make it *less* eager to cut price in response to entry, since that involves giving up secure profits that could be earned on sales to those loyal customers. With price discrimination ruled out, an incumbent's investment in advertising may thus make entry more attractive by guaranteeing the entrant a friendlier welcome. This second effect has a close relationship to the 'judo economics' of Gelman and Salop (1982). They find that a potential entrant that can credibly limit its output may be able to enter profitably against an established monopoly, despite demand and cost disadvantages. Incomplete introductory advertising would seem to function here much as output limits do in the Gelman–Salop analysis.

The results obtained above and in Schmalensee (1983) seem to depend critically on properties of the Cournot post-entry equilibria. This equilibrium concept is not fully satisfactory when some buyers are imperfectly informed, however. In addition, a number of the results obtained in Schmalensee (1983) run counter to intuition and to the findings of other studies. This analysis clearly must be treated as exploratory.

We lack satisfactory models of the impact of advertising on important elements of market structure. Theoretical work to date seems to raise as many questions as it answers. Additional effort is clearly called for. In order to be persuasive, it should rest on empirically-defensible assumptions about the effects of advertising on consumers. Moreover, as Section I sought to indicate, the traditional exclusive focus on advertising, to the neglect of other marketing decision variables and other forces affecting purchase behaviour, may produce misleading results.

NOTES

1. I am indebted to the National Science Foundation for Research support, to Severin Borenstein for excellent research assistance, and to Alexis Jacquemin, Steven Salop, Jesus Seade and Joseph Stiglitz for helpful comments on an earlier version.
2. For introductions to the marketing literatures on firm decision-making and buyer behaviour, see Kotler (1980) and Engle, Blackwell and Kollat (1978), respectively.
3. Important work on product selection has been done by Dixit and Stiglitz (1977), Salop (1979), Spence (1976), and others, and Porter (1976) has stressed the importance of non-advertising information sources in some markets.
4. For international comparisons, see *Advertising Age* (1980) and Simon (1970, ch. 7).
5. This is clear in the Line-of-Business data compiled by the US Federal Trade Commission; see *Advertising Age* (1981).
6. Among the more interesting of the areas that will not be covered here is the theory of optimal advertising under dynamic conditions; see Sethi (1977) for an informative survey and an extensive list of references.
7. This model is a slight generalisation of the one used in Schmalensee (1976); see also Schmalensee (1977). For alternative approaches, see Stigler (1968) and Spence (1977a).
8. This differs from the demand structure in Dixit and Stiglitz (1977) in that E is assumed locally constant here, while the restriction $e = 1 + \rho$, derived from *individual* utility maximisation, is imposed on *market* demand there.
9. Lambin (1976, pp. 138–40) suggests that increases in advertising are most likely to lower brand-specific price elasticities. But his evidence is hardly conclusive, and there have been few other relevant empirical studies.

10. Spence (1980) does not employ this distinction, so that $h(a) = a$ in his analysis and the function y embodies both consumer behaviour and the cost function for advertising messages. For more on this distinction, see Schmalensee (1972, esp. pp. 231–7).

11. Spence (1980) sets $\delta = 1$, and his β and γ are the reciprocals of those here.

12. Caution is required here. If (9) holds and there are economies of scale in advertising, there must be everywhere increasing *marginal* returns to advertising spending. But Simon and Arndt (1980) conclude from their survey of the massive evidence on this point that everywhere diminishing marginal returns are in fact the norm. It seems likely that network television's scale effects derive instead from the indivisibility of the large audience it reaches at low average cost. The minimum expenditure necessary to advertise on network television is simply very large relative to the minimum outlays necessary to employ other media.

13. Important earlier contributions include Kaldor (1950), Telser (1964, 1966) and Steiner (1966).

14. For additional discussion of this paper, see comments by Fisher and McGowen (1979) and Shapiro (1980) and replies by Dixit and Norman that follow them.

15. Dixit and Norman (1978) assume that advertising is most likely to lower price elasticities; see note 9, above.

16. Dixit and Norman (1978) find that this is a sufficient but not necessary condition for oligopoly with a fixed number of sellers. Oligopolies carry advertising beyond the profit-maximising point, so that the third term on the right of equation (16) is negative. I have not been able to develop an intuitive understanding of the Dixit–Norman analysis of monopolistic competition; I suspect that results for this case are highly dependent on choices of functional forms.

17. See note 3, above. In order to determine policy it is not enough to know that there is too much advertising or too many products, one must be able to derive in quantitative terms what should be done about it. But it is hard to imagine a policy-maker ever knowing enough about even a single industry to do this with great confidence.

18. For discussions of the empirical literature, see Comanor and Wilson (1979), Demsetz (1979) and Scherer (1980, ch. 9 and 14).

19. For discussions of this sort of heterogeneity, see Nelson (1974), Porter (1976) and Comanor and Wilson (1979).

20. This example is from Salop and Stiglitz (1979), where the effects of information on demand elasticities are explored in a search model. I am indebted to Joe Stiglitz for a valuable discussion of the implications of this work and recent (as yet unwritten) extensions of it.

21. Moreover, most investments in advertising may not be very long-lived; see Comanor and Wilson (1979, pp. 462–7).

22. The seminal work is Spence (1977b). Dixit (1980) and Schmalensee (1981) assume different post-entry behaviour and highlight economies of scale.

23. See Sethi (1977) on dynamic advertising models involving stocks of 'goodwill'.

REFERENCES

Advertising Age (1980) 'Free World Ad Total Topped $70 Billion in 1977', vol. 51, p. 39.

Advertising Age. (1981) 'Advertising as Per Cent of Sales, By Industry', vol. 52, 19 October, p. 42.

Bain, Joe S. (1956) *Barriers to New Competition* (Cambridge: Harvard University Press).

Baldani, Jeffrey and Masson, Robert T. (1981) 'Economies of Scale, Strategic Advertising and Fully Credible Entry Deterrence', mimeographed, December.

Benham, Lee (1972) 'The Effects of Advertising on the Price of Eyeglasses', *Journal of Law and Economics*, vol. 15, October, pp. 337–52.

Butters, Gerard R. (1977) 'Equilibrium Distribution of Prices and Advertising', *Review of Economic Studies*, vol. 44, October, pp. 465–92.

Coen, Robert J. (1982) 'Industry Revenues Outpace GNP in '81', *Advertising Age* vol. 53, Mar. 22, pp. 10, 66.

Comanor, William S. and Wilson, Thomas A. (1979) 'Advertising and Competition: A Survey', *Journal of Economic Literature*, vol. 17, Jun. pp. 453–76.

Cubbin, John (1981) 'Advertising and the Theory of Entry Barriers', *Economica*, vol. 48, Apr. pp. 289–98.

Dasgupta, Partha (1985) 'The Theory of Technological Competition', in this volume.

Dehez, Pierre and Jacquemin, Alex. (1975) 'A Note on Advertising Policy under Uncertainty and Dynamic Conditions', *Journal of Industrial Economics*, vol. 24, Sept. pp. 73–8.

Demsetz, Harold (1979) 'Accounting for Advertising as a Barrier to Entry', *Journal of Business*, vol. 52, Jul. pp. 345–60.

Dixit, Avinash K. (1980) 'The Role of Investment in Entry Deterrence', *Economic Journal*, vol. 90, Mar. pp. 95–106.

——. (1982) 'Recent Developments in Oligopoly Theory', *American Economic Review*, vol. 72, May, pp. 12–17.

—— and Norman, Victor (1978) 'Advertising and Welfare', *Bell Journal of Economics*, vol. 9, Spring, pp. 1–18.

—— and Stiglitz, Joseph E. (1977) 'Monopolistic Competition and Optimum Product Diversity', *American Economic Review*, vol. 67, Jun. pp. 297–308.

Engle, James F., Blackwell, Roger D. and Kollat, David T. (1978) *Consumer Behavior*, 3rd ed. Hindsdale, IL: Dryden.

Farrell, Joe (1982) 'Introductory Offers and Entry with Rational (but uninformed) Buyers', mimeographed, March.

Fisher, Franklin M. and McGowan, John J. (1979) 'Advertising and Welfare: Comment', *Bell Journal of Economics*, vol. 10, Autumn, pp. 726–7.

Gelman, Judith R. and Salop, Steven C. (1982) 'Judo Economics, Entrant Advantages, and the Great Airline Coupon Wars', mimeographed, March.

Grossman, Gene M. and Shapiro, Carl (1982) 'Informative Advertising with Differentiated Products', mimeographed, July.

Kaldor, Nicholas (1950) 'The Economic Aspects of Advertising', *Review of Economic Studies*, vol. 18, pp. 1–27.

Kotler, Phillip (1980) *Marketing Management*, 4th ed. (Englewood Cliffs, NJ: Prentice-Hall).

Kotowitz, Yehuda and Mathewson, Frank (1982) 'Advertising as a Barrier to Entry', mimeographed, May.

Lambin, Jean Jacques (1976) *Advertising, Competition, and Market Conduct in Oligopoly over Time* (Amsterdam: North-Holland).

Lynk, William J. (1981) 'Information, Advertising, and the Structure of the Market', *Journal of Business*, vol. 54, Apr. pp. 271–303.

Nelson, Phillip (1974) 'Advertising as Information', *Journal of Political Economy*, vol. 82, Jul./Aug. pp. 729–54.

Porter, Michael E. (1976) *Interbrand Choice, Strategy and Bilateral Market Power* (Cambridge: Harvard University Press).

Salop, Steven C. (1979) 'Monopolistic Competition with Outside Goods', *Bell Journal of Economics*, vol. 10, Sprin, pp. 141–56.

—— and Stiglitz, Joseph E. (1979) 'Information, Welfare, and Product Diversity', mimeographed.

Scherer, Frederic M. (1980) *Industrial Market Structure and Economic Performance*. 2nd ed. (Chicago: Rand McNally).

Schmalensee, Richard (1972) *The Economics of Advertising* (Amsterdam: North-Holland).

—— (1974) 'Brand Loyalty and Barriers to Entry', *Southern Economic Journal*, vol. 40, Apr. pp. 579–88.

—— (1976) 'A Model of Promotional Competition in Oligopoly', *Review of Economic Studies*, vol. 43, Oct. pp. 493–507.

—— (1977) 'Comparative Static Properties of Regulated Airline Oligopolies', *Bell Journal of Economics*, vol. 8, Autumn, pp. 565–76.

—— (1978a) 'A Model of Advertising and Product Quality', *Journal of Political Economy*, vol. 87, Jun. pp. 485–504.

—— (1978b) 'Entry Deterrence in the Ready-to-Eat Breakfast Cereal Industry', *Bell Journal of Economics*, vol. 9, Autumn, pp. 305–27.

—— (1981) 'Economies of Scale and Barriers to Entry', *Journal of Political Economy*, vol. 89, Dec. pp. 1228–38.

—— (1982a) 'Product Differentiation Advantages of Pioneering Brands', *American Economic Review*, vol. 72, June. pp. 349–65.

—— (1982b) 'The New Industrial Organization and the Economic Analysis of Modern Markets', in Werner Hildenbrand (ed.), *Advances in Economic Theory* (Cambridge: Cambridge University Press).

—— (1983) 'Advertising and Entry Deterrence: An Exploratory Model', *Journal of Political Economy*, vol. 91, Aug., pp. 636–53.

Seithi, Suresh P. (1977) 'Dynamic Optimal Control Models of Advertising: A Survey', *SIAM Review*, vol. 19, Oct. pp. 685–725.

Shapiro, Carl (1980) 'Advertising and Welfare: Comment', *Bell Journal of Economics* vol. 11, Autumn, pp. 749–52.

Simon, Julian L. (1970) *Issues in the Economics of Advertising* (Urbana, IL: University of Illinois Press).

—— and Arndt, John (1980) 'The Shape of the Advertising Response Function', *Journal of Advertising Research* vol. 20, Aug. pp. 11–28.

Spence, A. Michael (1976) 'Product Selection, Fixed Costs, and Monopolistic Competition', *Review of Economic Studies*, vol. 43, Jun. pp. 217–35.

_____ (1977a) 'Non-Price Competition', *American Economic Review*, vol. 67, Feb. pp. 255–9.

_____ (1976b) 'Entry, Capacity, Investment and Oligopolistic Pricing', *Bell Journal of Economics* vol. 8, Autumn, pp. 534–44.

_____ (1980) 'Notes on Advertising, Economies of Scale, and Entry Barriers', *Quarterly Journal of Economics*, vol. 95, Nov., pp. 493–508.

Steiner, Peter O. (1966) 'The Economics of Broadcasting and Advertising – Discussion', *American Economic Review*, vol. 56, May, pp. 472–75.

Steiner, Robert L. (1973) 'Does Advertising Lower Consumer Prices?' *Journal of Marketing* vol. 37, Oct., pp. 19–26.

Stigler, George J. (1968) 'Price and Non-Price Competition', *Journal of Political Economy*, vol. 76, Jan./Feb., pp. 149–54.

Telser, Lester G. (1964) 'Advertising and Competition', *Journal of Political Economy*, vol. 72, Dec., pp. 537–62.

_____ (1966) 'Supply and Demand for Advertising Messages', *American Economic Review*, vol. 56, May, pp. 457–66.

Discussion of the Paper by Richard Schmalensee

Lucena and *Seade* both took issue with Schmalensee's attempt to examine price competition and advertising competition as polar cases. For example, advertising might alter price elasticities and therefore pricing policy by firms. Lucena suggested that there were few markets where both types of competition did not exist simultaneously while Seade thought that interactions between price and advertising as strategic variables would be particularly important. Schmalensee responded that he was in agreement that the polar cases did not describe actual markets so much as permit comparative statements on the effects that flow from each of pricing and advertising policies. Seade also questioned Schmalensee's interpretation of advertising as something that increased demand for the whole industry. Seade alluded, as well, to the arguments in the paper about whether high-quality or low-quality producers might do more advertising. He suggested that high-quality firms might be able to rely on repeat purchases and word-of-mouth to generate demand. Low-quality firms would have to rely on advertising to generate demand in the absence of these advantages. Finally, Seade suggested that, to the extent that advertising altered tastes, the question of whether *ex ante* or *ex post* preferences should be used in doing welfare analysis was critical.

Nelson remarked that, in the past, economists had focused on the idea that advertising fooled consumers, and should therefore be regulated. He noted that many modern works on advertising assumed that promises were kept. He suggested that this represented a certain consensus in the modern literature, that advertising conveyed information. He wondered whether that consensus was justified, and raised a question about the information value of the slogan – 'Coca Cola is coke.'

Thomas von Ungern-Sternberg added that one of the additional arguments put forward in favour of advertising was that, to the extent that it increased demand, it would permit firms to take advantage of economies of scale. Schmalensee agreed with this argument, but wondered to what extent it corresponded to situations that one might encounter in real markets.

Schmalensee felt that prior to writing in textbooks that advertising caused barriers to entry, we needed a theoretical justification for this alleged affect. This was something not currently available, but an effort might be found in Schmalensee (1982). The principal result in this paper was that in contrast to investment deterrence, the incumbent firm foreclosed entry or reduced the market share of the entrant by *under-investing* in advertising. In turn, this forced the entrant to be small, perhaps sufficiently small to deter entry. In general, 'sensible' assumptions on consumer choice were capable of yielding such curious results. In Schmalensee's view, this further pointed out the need to model carefully the impact of advertising on consumer choice.

REFERENCE

Schmalensee, R. (1982) 'Advertising and Entry Deterrence: An Exploratory Model', Working Paper, no. 1309–82, Sloan School of Management, Massachusetts Institute of Technology.

14 Theory of Competition, Incentives and Risk[1]

Joseph E. Stiglitz

PRINCETON UNIVERSITY, USA

I INTRODUCTION

It is now widely recognised that the nature of competition in market economies is far more complex (and more interesting) than the simple representation of price competition embodied in, say, the Arrow–Debreu model. Not only are there alternative *objects* of competition: firms compete not only about price but also about products and R & D. But, also, the *structure* of competition, the 'rules' which relate the pay-offs to each of the participants to the actions they undertake, may differ markedly from that envisioned in the standard model.[2]

Not only is the central result of standard competition theory, the fundamental theorem of welfare economics, not valid for these more general forms of competition, but this paradigm also fails to provide insights into when the market will, in some sense, work well and when it will not; and, as a consequence, it fails to provide much guidance for policy decisions which relate to R & D and industrial structure. I should emphasise that it is not simply the case that the standard development of the theory has failed to integrate R & D into the analysis. Rather, it is that the natural assumptions concerning the structure of R & D (and, more generally, information) are *inconsistent* with the basic structure of the Arrow–Debreu model.

In earlier studies, I have investigated alternative objects of competition, both product competition (Dixit–Stiglitz, 1977) and R & D competition (Dasgupta–Stiglitz, 1980a, b; Gilbert–Stiglitz, 1979; Dasgupta *et al.*, 1982 and 1983; Fudenberg *et al.*, 1983), and alternative

399

structures (Stiglitz, 1980; Nalebuff–Stiglitz, 1983a, b). In this chapter, I bring these two strands together. Competition for R & D is often (but not always) much like a contest with a large first prize, and small (zero) prizes to the other participants. In my previous studies, I considered the *design* of the *contract*. Associated with each contract there is a particular pay-off structure. Different contracts are thus characterised by the different levels of risk which the participants have to bear; the different incentives which they face; and the different degrees of *flexibility* – the responsiveness of the (implied) pay-off matrix to changes in the environment.[3]

One of the central results of this analysis was that it was, in general, desirable to employ reward functions which related compensation to relative performance rather than simply to the individual's own performance. Indeed, even when one restricted oneself to simple reward structures – contests with compensation depending simply on rank – competitive reward structures could be preferable to individualistic reward structures. Indeed, this would always be the case if there was sufficient uncertainty about the nature of the environment. This provides us with a new insight into the function of competition: when only one firm is engaged in a particular activity, it may be very difficult for an outsider to ascertain whether the firm is doing a good or a bad job. Since the firm has more information about the difficulty of the task than does the outsider, the outsider is somewhat at a disadvantage in designing effective reward structures. When there are several firms, we can get some information from the performance of the different firms. We can, implicitly, use this information to adjust the reward structure, so that individuals have incentives to adjust their behaviour in response to changes in environmental conditions.[4]

As I have said, competitive markets provide reward structures which, under certain conditions, look very much like the prizes of a contest. But in our previous studies we were concerned with *optimising* — choosing the best reward structure (contest prize structure) from among a set of feasible prize structures. Here, we are concerned with *describing*: ascertaining the nature of the prizes which are implicit in various market structures, and the consequences of these prize structures for: (1) the risks which the firms must bear; (2) the incentives of firms not only to engage in R & D but to choose among alternative research projects; and (3) the responsiveness of the incentives to changes in the environment.

Our concern, however, is more than just descriptive: changes in policy have effects on the implicit prize structure, and these consequences need to be taken into account in evaluating the desirability of any such policy change.

The central question, then, which we address in our analysis is whether 'competition' or 'monopoly' provides a greater spur to innovation and, more generally, whether there are particular biases in the *direction* of innovation undertaken under these alternative market structures.

I should emphasise my view that market structure itself should be taken as endogenous, a view which, in a more restricted context, Dasgupta and I developed earlier (Dasgupta–Stiglitz (1980a, b)). The implications of the analysis of this for the evolution of market structures is a question which we hope to pursue on another occasion.

Competition and Innovation

In spite of the long-standing concern about the relation between competition and innovation, there is no consensus. One view holds that monopolies have too little incentive to engage in R & D; without the spur of competition, monopolies will simply enjoy their monopoly rents. The other view holds that, without some degree of monopoly power, firms will be unable either to support R & D programmes or to appropriate the returns from research. As is so often the case, there is undoubtedly a grain of truth in both views: the question is; under what conditions, under what circumstances, is each view appropriate?

It is not, however, easy to translate these commonly expressed views into well-formulated hypotheses, let alone testable models. The view that monopolies have too few incentives can be put in at least two different ways. The first, and more traditional, way is to show that the increment in profits from R & D is less than the social returns and, indeed, less than the increment of profit in a competitive market. We argue that the sign of the differences is somewhat problematical; for instance, there may be more or less technical progress in a 'competitive' economy than in one in which each industry is dominated by a single monopolist. Indeed, under some circumstances, the monopolists may undertake an 'efficient' level of R & D (in a sense to be defined more precisely below).

This traditional formulation does not, however, capture well the distinction between monopoly and competitive markets. There is something in the notion of 'the spur of competition' in contrast to the slack (or X-inefficiency) associated with monopolies. To some extent, the notion that competition provides a spur to innovation can be translated into an analysis of how competition alters the pay-off matrix from undertaking research. But a detailed analysis of the effect of competition on the pay-off matrix suggests that the effects of competition are ambiguous.

To understand the role of competition in R & D markets, then, requires the abandonment of the simple model of the unitary firm maximising its (expected utility of) profits. Since the returns to managers (or workers) seldom coincide with the returns to the firm, it is seldom rational (i.e., in their own self-interest) for individuals to take the actions which maximise the (expected) profits of the firm. The original shareholder of the firm can attempt to design incentive structures which lead managers to take actions which are more in accord with the interests of the firm (profit-maximising). The set of feasible incentive structures is, however, limited by what information is available, and it is this which is affected in a marked way by the presence of competition.

Moreover, there is little reason to believe that firms employ incentive structures which lead to efficiency in general or to profit-maximising levels of R & D in particular. Whether an incentive structure is 'good' or is not is often revealed only by the consequences; the consequences of 'bad' incentive structures become apparent more readily in competitive environments than in monopolistic markets. Even if the owner-managers of firms fail to respond of their own accord to evidence concerning their inefficiency, the market may force them to do so: these firms will fail and control of their assets will pass to others. It should be emphasised, however, that there is no welfare theorem concerning the optimality of these evolutionary processes. Indeed, we conjecture that there may be systematic biases towards excessively myopic policies, at least in the presence of the kinds of capital market imperfections commonly observed[5] (which themselves may be endogenous, and related to costly information).

There is a final, quite distinct role that competition plays: while in traditional economic models (as well as those presented in this chapter), individuals' actions (and welfare) are determined completely by the *outcomes*, the (expected) utility which they receive, in fact, individuals are affected, in an important way, by *processes*; the competitive process itself may indeed provide a spur for action, a spur which cannot adequately be explained by the magnitude of the difference between the winner's and loser's prizes.[6]

The explanation of why individuals respond in particular ways to competition (other than in terms of the direct consequences) is of no direct concern for our argument; we do not need to consider, for instance, whether competition provides an outlet for aggressive instincts, which themselves might be explained in terms of vestigial traces from an earlier era in which such behaviour had survival value. So long as individuals do respond to the competitive process, it will be in the interests of firms (entrepreneurs) to take account of this behaviour in the design of the compensation schemes which they employ to pay their managers.

Thus, I am contending that to make sense of the commonly expressed views concerning the virtues of competition in spurring R & D and innovation – views which I find persuasive – one needs to do more than simply incorporate R & D into the traditional theory of the profit maximising firm; one needs to do more than understand the (fairly complex) ways in which competition affects the pay-off matrix from undertaking R & D. One needs to understand the behaviour of the managers and workers in these organisations, the rules by which they behave and the incentives which they face, and the circumstances under which the rules, the incentive structures, and ultimately, the managers, get changed.

It is the aim of this chapter to go a little way towards this goal. In Section II we present the standard comparison of the incentives for R & D of a monopolist, of a competitive firm, and of a social planner. Section III discusses, in an intuitive way, what is wrong with the standard argument that monopolists engage in too little research, while Section IV presents a simple general-equilibrium model within which one can compare the level of R & D expenditures under different market structures. Sections V–VII analyse the incentives for risk taking. Section V demonstrates that a variant of the traditional model can be used to show that monopolists undertake too much risk (do not spend enough resources to reduce risk), while Section VI uses the same framework to compare the incentives for undertaking more than one independent research project. In both sections, however, we assume only a single research project. Section VII considers the far more important case of competition among researchers. Finally, in Section VIII, we analyse innovation in the new theory of the firm.

II A SIMPLE MODEL

The object of Sections II to IV is to show that there is no presumption that an economy which is characterised by monopolies in its different sectors will do too little research; that technical progress will be less rapid than in a competitive environment.

We begin by reviewing the traditional analysis. This argues that the monopolist will engage in too little research, less than is socially optimal and less than would occur in a competitive industry.

Consider an industry with a demand curve

$$p = p(Q) \qquad p' < 0. \tag{1}$$

(A) MONOPOLY

If there is a single (monopoly) firm in the industry, it would have set marginal revenue equal to marginal cost, c_o, which, for simplicity, we assume is constant. Defining

$$R(Q) = p(Q)Q \tag{2}$$

we obtain

$$R'(Q) = c_o, \tag{3}$$

generating profits for the firm of

$$P(c_o) \equiv \max_Q \{R(Q) - cQ\}$$

$$= R(R'^{-1}(c_o)) - c_o R'^{-1}(c_o). \tag{4}$$

Assume an R & D project lowers the cost to c_1. Then the value of the innovation is given by[7,8]

$$V^m = (P(c_1) - P(c_o))/r \tag{5}$$

where r is the rate of interest. The change in the flow of monopoly profits is represented diagrammatically in Figure 14.1 by the area AEDF. (AHDF is the increment in profits at the old output; it is simply the savings in costs; DHE is the increment in profits resulting from increasing output from Q_0^m to Q_1^m).

R & D will be undertaken if

$$\pi V^m \geq x,$$

where π is the probability of success of the R & D project and x is its cost.

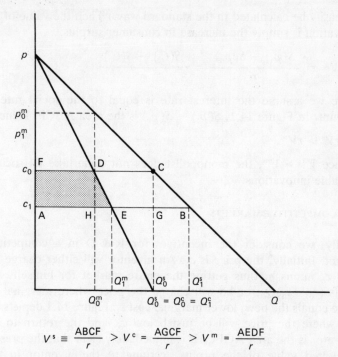

$$V^s \equiv \frac{ABCF}{r} > V^c = \frac{AGCF}{r} > V^m = \frac{AEDF}{r}$$

FIG. 14.1 Monopolies engage in less research than occurs in a competitive market which, in turn, is below the socially-optimal level of R & D.

Social Pay-off to Innovation

We now analyse the conditions under which it is socially desirable to undertake the R & D project, and compare this with the monopoly equilibrium, which we have just described.

Output both before and after the innovation will, of course, be larger than with monopoly. Social optimality requires that

$$p_o^s = c_o,$$

while

$$p_1^s = c_1,$$

where p_o^s (p_1^s) is the price before (after) the innovation (in the socially-optimal allocation).[9] Denote by S the consumer surplus associated with cost c (when price is chosen to equal the cost c). ($S(C)$

can easily be calculated in the standard way.) Then the value of the innovation is simply the increase in consumer surplus:

$$V^s \equiv \frac{S(p_1) - S(p_o)}{r} = \frac{S(C_1) - S(C_0)}{r}$$

where we assume the interest rate is equal to the social rate of discount. In Figure 14.1, $S(p_1) - S(p_o)$ is the area ABCF. Hence,

$$rV^s > rV^m.$$

Since $V^s > V^m$, the monopolist does not undertake all socially desirable innovations.

(B) COMPETITIVE MARKETS

Finally, we consider the incentives for R & D in a competitive market. Initially, the price is c_o. An inventor will either charge the price c_o minus ε, thus getting the entire market for himself, and profits $(c_o - c_1)Q_o$; or he will charge the price where marginal revenue equals the new, lower marginal cost c_1. Figure 14.1 depicts the case where the price will be just below c_o, and the return to the innovator is the area AGFC. It is immediately clear that the present discounted value of the profits accruing to the inventor in this regime,[10] V^c, lies between V^s and V^m.

This analysis suggests that monopolies do engage in too little research, and in less research than that of a competitive market.[11]

III DEFICIENCIES IN THE TRADITIONAL ANALYSIS OF THE EFFECT OF MARKET STRUCTURE OF R & D

The analysis of the preceding section, which provides a comparison of the level of R & D under alternative market structures, has a number of important limitations. When appropriate account of these is taken, some conclusions become problematical: for example, that monopolies engage in too little research and that economies that are dominated by monopolies will have a lower rate of technical progress than more-competitive economies. In any case, the differences in the levels of R & D may be much smaller than the previous analysis suggested. In this Section, we outline some of the more important deficiencies and explain, in a fairly intuitive way, how the conclusions are altered when the analysis is changed to take into account these criticisms.

1. The earlier analysis assumes that research projects exist in discrete sizes; if firms can reduce their costs by spending more on R & D, the above analysis does not tell us anything about the *marginal* incentives for cost reduction.

2. It is a very partial equilibrium analysis. It does not provide an answer to the question: 'Will there be more innovation in an economy in which all industries are competitive than in one in which each industry is monopolised?' When we modify the simple analysis to take account of these two factors, we get drastically different conclusions; in one central case, monopoly and competition are identical.

Consider an economy in which all sectors have the same constant-elasticity demand curves, and where each is monopolised by a single firm. There is a single factor of production, labour, which is inelastically supplied. Labour is also the only input into R & D. We postulate that all individuals (inventors and workers) have the same, homothetic indifference maps, so that an increase in national income of z per cent shifts the demand curve out by z per cent.

To analyse the equilibrium level of R & D, we need first to analyse the general equilibrium of the economy, both before and after the innovation.

Consider first the competitive market. For simplicity, assume that initially there are no profits; assume that, in each industry, there is then an invention which lowers the input required per unit of output by z per cent. Thus, the new demand curve will be shifted out by z per cent, leading to an increase in the demand for output (and hence for labour) by z per cent in each industry; this exactly countervails the decrease in the demand for labour in each industry resulting from the innovation. Thus, if the wage of production workers remains unchanged, but the inventor charges $(c_o - c_i)w_o$ for the use of his patent (per unit output), the demand for production workers will remain equal to the supply.[12] If the demand for research workers remains unchanged, then if the labour market was in equilibrium prior to the innovation, it will still be in equilibrium (see Figure 14.2).

By contrast, real wages will rise in the monopoly equilibrium by the same percentage as the reduction in labour input required to produce each unit of output; the marginal costs of production in the post-invention era are thus identical to the marginal costs of production in the initial period. To see this note that, in this case, the real income of workers will have risen by z per cent. Assume that the demand curve shifted out by z per cent. Then monopoly output will have increased by z per cent, with prices and marginal costs unchanged.

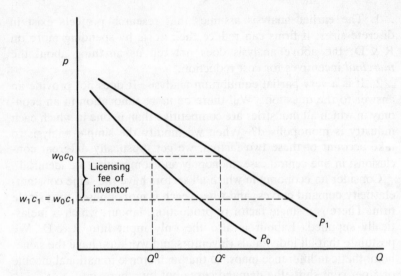

FIG. 14.2 In a competitive economy, with a patent holder in each sector, with all sectors of the economy experiencing an increase in productivity of z per cent, the demand curve shifts out by z per cent, prices and wages remain unchanged, and output increases by z per cent in each sector.

Hence, profits will have increased by z per cent. Hence, national income will also have increased by z per cent, confirming the postulated proportional shift in the demand curve. Since the output of each commodity has increased by z per cent, while the labour requirement per unit of output had decreased by z per cent, the demand for production labour remains unchanged (see Figure 14.3).

Thus, workers and firms both benefit from innovations under monopoly (in the same proportion as their original share in national income): under competition, all of the gains are reaped by the inventor.

So far, we have contrasted the equilibrium before and after the innovations under the two market structures. We also need to compare the monopoly and competitive equilibria with each other. If the supply of production (non-research) workers is the same, then output in each industry must be the same under the two regimes. For the profit-maximising output of a monopolist to be the same as under competition, the wage under monopoly must be lower, by a factor of $1 - 1/\eta$ (the degree of monopoly), where η equals the elasticity of demand; thus, if w_o is the wage in the pre-invention period,

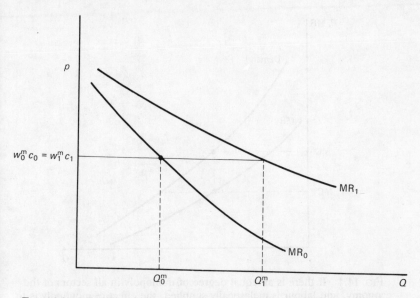

FIG. 14.3 With a monopoly, the wage rises by the same percentage that productivity increases, so that the marginal cost of production remains unchanged; the demand and marginal revenue curves shift out proportionately, and hence the equilibrium level of output increases proportionately.

$$w_o^m = \left(1 - \frac{1}{\eta}\right) w_o^c.$$

If we postulate, further, that the demand for research workers in the post-invention period is the same as in the pre-invention period, our earlier analysis has established that:

$$w_1^m = (1 + z)w_o^m, \text{ and}$$
$$w_1^c = w_o^c$$

(see Figure 14.4).

Assume now that increasing the input of labour into R & D in the ith sector, ℓ_i^r, reduces the labour required to produce each unit by $C_i'(\ell_i)$;[13] the savings in *costs* on an output of Q_o is $Q_o C' w_1$ in the post-innovation period. The equilibrium labour input into research thus satisfies the equation:[14]

$$\frac{Q_o C' w_1^j}{1 + r} = w_0^j \qquad j = m, c. \tag{6}$$

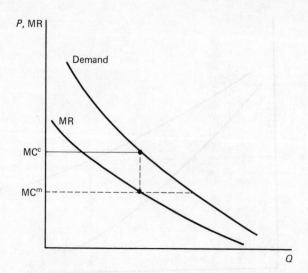

FIG. 14.4   If there is an equal degree of monopoly in all sectors of the economy, and labour is inelastically supplied, the effect of monopoly is to lower the real wage, leaving output and R & D in all sectors unchanged.

That is in the monopoly equilibrium,

$$(1 + z)Q_o^m C' = 1 + r;$$

while for the competitive equilibrium,

$$Q_o^c C' = 1 + r.$$

What is crucial about (6) is that it is not the level of wages which determines the equilibrium expenditure on R & D, but *changes* in these wages. The fact that, with monopoly, real wages are lower makes no difference.[15] The degree of monopoly thus has no effect on the equilibrium. Similarly, the differences in output between the monopoly and competitive equilibrium, (on which the earlier partial equilibrium analysis focused) disappear in this general equilibrium formulation; with a constant degree of monopoly in all sectors, and an inelastic labour supply, output in each sector must be the same.[16] (If the labour supply curve is backward-bending, as some have maintained, then

$$Q_o^m > Q_o^c.$$

The lower real wage will elicit a higher labour supply and hence, in equilibrium, a higher level of output in each sector.) The fact that in a monopoly equilibrium real wages will be rising as a result of innovation provides an incentive for monopolies to engage in more research.

This result should not be taken too seriously: it derives from an anomaly of the two-period model we have formulated. In a more dynamic model, it is reasonable to postulate that eventually the increase in productivity will be reflected in wages. Assume that labour requirements at time t are given by $C_t = C_{t-1}/[1 + z(l_{t-1}^r)]$. Then, expenditures on research at time t will improve labour productivity at all subsequent dates, and a monopolist would take this into account. In a competitive market, the inventor would take into account only the cost reductions during the period in which his patent remained effective. Thus, *if* the level of research in the two economies were the same, then the steady-state rate of wage increase would be the same. The differences between the two equilibria would then reside in the fact that while the monopolist appropriates all of the marginal returns, in the competitive régime the inventor only appropriates the return during the effective life of the patent.[17]

We thus again obtain the result that the incentives to carry out R & D are smaller in the competitive market than with monopoly, but our explanation focuses on the traditional problems of appropriability.[18]

3. The traditional analysis does not ask the correct welfare questions. Given that there is a distortion in the economy (e.g., a monopolised sector), then there is no reason to believe that the level of R & D in the monopolised sector 'should' be the same as it would be if that sector were not monopolised. Since the benefits which accrue from research are related to the scale of output, then, if the scale of output is lower, the benefits will be lower. There is therefore some presumption that R & D 'should' be lower.

Moreover, the previous analysis assumed that the government could raise revenues to finance R & D costlessly, and could easily and costlessly identify the beneficiaries of the lower prices resulting from R & D. A patent is like a benefit-excise tax.[19] Those who pay for the R & D in a sector are those who consume the product. In fact, almost all taxes imposed by the government cause distortions. There are other instances, besides R & D (e.g., highway programmes) where the government resorts to benefit-excise taxes because they represent the only way of ensuring that the beneficiaries of a programme pay for it.

The 'correct' welfare question depends on what are perceived to be the relevant constraints. There are plausible constraints under which the market can be viewed as (constrained) Pareto-efficient; and other cases where the distortions in the market allocation may be far smaller (and possibly of different sign) than the Arrow analysis suggests.

The importance of this can be seen most clearly by considering the marginal incentives for R & D in the competitive régime, by contrast with social optimality. By spending more on research, the firm can lower its cost of production further. Let $c_i(x_i)$ be the marginal cost of production to the ith firm, if it spends x_i on R & D. Then, for small innovations,[20] the return from additional expenditures is just $-c'Q_o$.

Assume now that the government can subsidise or tax the R & D of this research firm, but cannot control its pricing and output decisions. It is easy to see that the government would not wish to intervene. Given that it cannot affect output, the government knows that it will remain at Q_o (limiting our attention still to small innovations). And given that output remains at Q_o, the returns to cost reduction are just $-c'Q_o$. The firm that has the monopoly on R & D does an efficient amount of research.

Assume that the government is not in the position of breaking up a monopoly, forcing it to act competitively, or nationalising it.[21] Then, the question the government needs to ask is: 'Should we encourage or discourage research in that sector?' If the government could directly finance a monopolist's research, raising the required revenue by a lump sum tax, it would want to increase the level of R & D, but by an amount which was less than the earlier analysis suggested.

The marginal social return from the monopolist's carrying out additional research is the increase in consumer surplus plus the increase in producer surplus. Assume that the demand curves in each sector have constant elasticity (and are independent). Then an additional expenditure on R & D reduces marginal cost by c' and hence price by c'/ρ (where $\rho \equiv 1 - 1/\eta$, the markup). If $v(p, I)$ is the representative consumer's indirect utility function, a function of all prices and of income (I), then the lowering of price increases consumer welfare by $-v_p = v_I Q^m$ (where Q^m is the equilibrium output). The monopolist ignores this gain to consumers, and thus will do too little research. The 'error' is *not* related to the difference in output between the competitive and monopolistic regimes, but simply to the change in prices at the monopoly output.[22]

But assume that the government must raise the revenue required to finance the research by a tax on the sector, at the rate t per unit output. Then, monopolies have appropriate incentives for engaging in R & D, under our constant-elasticity assumption. To see this, recall that now price p is given by:

$$p = \frac{c + t}{\rho} ; \tag{7}$$

where research expenditures are given by

$$x = tQ(p) = tQ \left(\frac{c + t}{\rho} \right) , \text{ and} \tag{8}$$

where $Q(p)$ is the demand curve. Profits (P) are given by

$$P = (p - c - t)Q = (c + t) \frac{(1 - \rho)}{\rho} Q. \tag{9}$$

We can decompose the effect of a change in t into two parts:

(a) A price effect. Profits change by $Q \, dp$, while consumer welfare changes by $v_p \, dp = - v_1 Q \, dp$. Assuming that the marginal (social) utility of a dollar is the same to consumers and capitalists, these effects just cancel out.

(b) An output effect[23] on profits, given by

$$(c + t) \frac{(1 - \rho)}{\rho} \frac{dQ}{dt} = (c + t) \frac{(1 - \rho)}{\rho} \frac{dQ}{dp} \frac{dp}{dt} \tag{10}$$

$$= \frac{(c + t)}{\rho} \frac{(1 - \rho)}{\rho} \frac{dQ}{dp} \frac{d(c + t)}{dt}$$

$$= - \frac{(1 - \rho)}{\rho} Q\eta \frac{d(c + t)}{dt} .$$

Thus, social optimality requires setting

$$\frac{d(c + t)}{dt} = c' \frac{dx}{dt} + 1 = 0.$$

But, from (8),

$$\frac{dx}{dt} = \frac{Q + \dfrac{tQ'}{\rho}}{1 - tQ'c'/\rho} .$$

Substituting, we obtain after some manipulation,

$$c'Q + 1 = 0.$$

This is, precisely, the monopolist's first-order condition for R & D expenditure. (As we shall see in Section IV, the monopoly equilibrium may still not be a constrained Pareto optimum; the level of expenditures on R & D depends on Q as well and, to determine this, we need to analyse the full equilibrium of the economy.)

This list of objections to the earlier analyses is not meant to be exhaustive. In earlier work (Dasgupta and Stiglitz, 1980a, b), we dealt with two further objections.

4. The earlier analysis fails to distinguish between competition in the product market and competition in R & D. The argument that there is too little research under competition implicitly assumes that there *is* competition (originally) in the product market, but that there is *not* competition in R & D.

5. It treats the market structure as exogenous, rather than en-dogenous.

In our earlier work, we showed, for instance, that if there is competition in R & D, the level of R & D expenditures in the market equilibrium may exceed the socially-optimal level.

In Section IV we present a simple general-equilibrium model illustrating some of the propositions we have put forward in a heuristic way in this section.

IV   A SIMPLE GENERAL EQUILIBRIUM MODEL

In this section, we construct a simple general-equilibrium model illustrating the basic propositions established in the preceding sec-tion. The model is an adaptation of the Dixit–Stiglitz general equilib-rium model (1977), in which there are (n) industries, each with a single firm, facing a downward sloping demand curve of constant elasticity, and one competitive industry (labour). To make our wel-fare calculations simple, we assume that everybody has the same utility (demand) functions. The demand curves are derived from utility functions of the form[24]

$$U = U[Q_o, \{\Sigma_i Q_i^\rho\}^{1/\rho}], \tag{11}$$

where Q_o is the numeraire, Q_i is the ith commodity, and we assume that (U) is homothetic.

The budget constraint is,

$$Q_o + \sum_{i=1}^n p_i Q_i = I \tag{12}$$

where p_i are the (consumer) prices. I is the income (of the representa-tive individual) in terms of the numeraire.

$$I = 1 + \sum_{i=1}^{n} P_i - T, \tag{13}$$

where we have set the value of the endowment of Q_o, the numeraire, equal to unity. P_i is the net profit of the ith firm distributed to consumers, and T is the lump-sum tax, imposed to cover the losses of the firms.

This gives rise to demand curves of the form:

$$Q_i = y \left[\frac{v}{p_i} \right]^{1/1-\rho} , \quad Q_o = I(1 - s(v)), \tag{14}$$

where y and v are dual quantity and price indices:

$$y = \left\{ \sum_{i=1}^{n} Q_1^{\rho} \right\}^{1/\rho}, \quad v = \left\{ \sum_{i=1}^{r} p_i^{-1/\beta} \right\}^{-\beta}. \tag{15}$$

Here, $\beta = (1 - \rho)/\rho$, and $(1 - s(v))$, the share of full income spent on the numeraire commodity, depends simply on the form of the utility functions.

Changing p_i affects the demand for Q_i directly, and indirectly through v. The indirect effect is of the order $1/n$ (provided only that the prices of the products in the group are not of different orders of magnitude). We assume that n is reasonably large, and accordingly ignore this indirect effect. Thus, the elasticity of demand is (approximately)

$$- \frac{\partial \ln Q_i}{\partial \ln p_i} = \frac{1}{1 - \rho} = \frac{(1 + \beta)}{\beta}.$$

It is immediately clear that price will show a constant mark-up over marginal costs, c_i:

$$p_i = c_i(1 + \beta) = c_i/\rho. \tag{17}$$

We assume that the marginal cost, c_i, is a convex decreasing-function of the level of expenditure on R & D (but independent of the scale of production):

$$c_i'(x) < 0, \quad c_i''(x) > 0. \tag{18}$$

We focus our analysis on the symmetric equilibrium where

$$p_i = p. \quad Q_i = Q, \quad P_i = P, \qquad \text{all } i \tag{19a}$$

$$y = n^{1/\rho}Q, \quad v = n^{-\beta}p \tag{19b}$$

$$P \equiv (p - c)Q - x = \frac{(p - c)}{p} pQ - x \qquad (20)$$

$$= \frac{\beta}{1 + \beta} \frac{s(v)}{n} (1 + nP - T) - x$$

$$= \frac{\{(1 - \rho)s(v) (1 - T)/n\} - x}{1 - (1 - \rho)s(v)},$$

since

$$Q = \frac{sI}{np} . \qquad (21)$$

Using (13), (17) and (21), we obtain

$$Q_i = \frac{\rho s}{cn}\left(1 - T + \frac{(1 - \rho)s(v) (1 - T) - nx}{1 - (1 - \rho)s}\right) \qquad (22)$$

$$= \frac{\rho s(n^{-\beta} c/\rho)}{cn}\left(\frac{1 - T - nx}{1 - (1 - \rho)s(n^{-\beta} c/\rho)}\right)$$

Market equilibrium is described by (22) (with $T = 0$) and the first order condition for (x)

$$-c_i'(x)Q_i = 1. \qquad (23)$$

$(-c'(x)Q_i$ is the marginal savings in variable cost resulting from increasing R & D).[25] This provides us with two equations in two unknowns. The graphical solution for the case where $s' = 0$ (constant shares) is given in Figure 14.5.

(1) CONSTRAINED PARETO OPTIMALITY

Assume now the government cannot break up the monopoly, and finances the R & D out of profits taxes. (It gives a direct grant to each firm, and ensures that the funds are used to carry out R & D.) Would it support more research than the private sector does on its own?

The equations describing the equilibrium outputs and prices, for each level of expenditure, remain exactly as before. To ascertain the optimal levels of research, we employ the indirect utility function, giving the representative individual's level of utility as a function of the vector of prices p and income I:

$$V = V(p\ I).$$

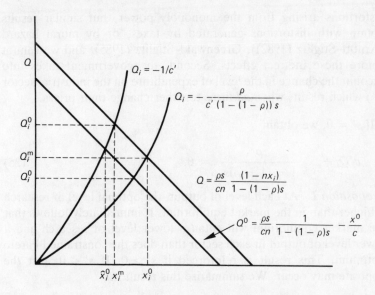

FIG. 14.5 Comparison of market equilibrium with constrained optimality.

$\{Q_i^o, x_i^o\}$ Constrained optimality: profits taxes.
$\{\hat{Q}_i^o, \hat{x}_i^o\}$ Constrained optimality: excise taxes.

Differentiating, and making use of (20), we obtain[26]

$$\frac{dv}{dx} = \sum_i \frac{V_{pi}}{\rho} c_i' + V_I \frac{dI}{dx} \tag{24}$$

$$= \frac{-v_I n}{\rho} \left(c_i' Q_i + \frac{1}{1 - (1 - \rho)s} \left(\rho - \frac{(1-\rho)s' c_i' n^{-\beta}(1-nx)}{n(1 - (1-\rho)s)} \right) \right) = 0.$$

Equilibrium is described by (24) and (22). In two limiting cases, this approximates the market equilibrium given by (22) and (23): if $s' = 0$ (so that the share of 'full income' spent on the commodity group is in variant to the price) and either (i) $s \approx 1$, the industrial sector is relatively large; or (ii) $\rho \approx 1$, i.e., demand curves are (almost) infinitely elastic. There are two reasons why the market equilibrium deviates from constrained Pareto optimality: first, the government takes into account the multiplier effects of the income effects associated with the increased expenditures on R & D; these are of the same nature as the kind of externalities which we normally ignore, in the absence of other distortions in the economy. Here, we have distortions arising from the monopoly power, but similar results obtain with distortions generated by taxes, or by moral hazard (Arnott–Stiglitz (1982)), Greenwald–Stiglitz (1985), and we cannot ignore these indirect effects. Second, the government takes into account the change in the level of expenditure on the industrial sector (s') which results when *all* firms together change their prices.

If $s' = 0$, we obtain

$$c_i'Q_i + \frac{\rho}{1 - (1 - \rho)s} = 0. \tag{25}$$

Proposition 1 At each level of output, the optimal level of research is higher than in the market equilibrium. It immediately follows that the market equilibrium will entail a lower level of research and a lower level of output in each sector than does the constrained Pareto optimum. This result is reinforced if $s' > 0$. If $s' < 0$, just the opposite may occur. We summarise this result in:

Proposition 2 The market equilibrium, with each sector controlled by a monopolist, may entail either more or less R & D than does the constrained Pareto optimum, where the government is not allowed to intervene directly in the production decisions of the monopolists, but can control the level of R & D, and where it finances the R & D expenditure by a profits tax. The market equilibrium will entail too little R & D provided $s' \geq 0$.

(2) AN ALTERNATIVE FORMULATION OF CONSTRAINED PARETO OPTIMALITY: EXCISE TAXES

Assume now that government must finance R & D in the *i*th industry by imposing a specific tax, at rate t, on the *i*th industry:

$$x_i = t_i Q_i. \tag{26}$$

Now,

$$p_i = (c_i + t_i)/\rho \tag{27}$$

and (20) becomes (in the symmetric equilibrium)

$$nP = \frac{(1 - \rho)s[n^{-\beta}(c + t)/\rho]}{1 - (1 - \rho)s[n^{-\beta}(c + t)/\rho]} \tag{28}$$

Hence, (22) becomes

$$Q_i = \frac{\rho s}{(c + t)n} \quad \frac{1}{1 - (1 - \rho)s} . \tag{29}$$

Using the indirect utility function, $V = V(p, I)$, we obtain

$$\frac{dv}{dt} = \frac{nv_p}{\rho} \frac{d(c + t)}{dt} + V_I \frac{dI}{dt}$$

$$= \frac{nv_I}{\rho} \left[Q_i - \frac{(1 - \rho)s'n^{-\beta-1}}{(1 - (1 - \rho)s)^2} \right] \frac{d(c + t)}{dt} .$$

This is maximised when $d(c + t)/dt = 0$, i.e.,

$$1 + c' \left(Q_i + t \frac{dQ}{dt} \right) = 0. \tag{31}$$

But at the point where $d(c + t)/dt = 0$,

$$\frac{dQ_i}{dt} = 0 \tag{32}$$

(since Q_i is simply a function of $c + t$). Hence, constrained Pareto optimality entails

$$-c'(x)Q_i = 1, \tag{33}$$

which is identical to (23). The difference between the market equilibrium and constrained optimality lies in the determination of Q_i. Substituting (26) into (29), we obtain

$$\hat{Q}^\circ = \frac{\rho s}{nc} \frac{1}{1 - (1 - \rho)s} - \frac{\hat{x}^\circ}{c} . \tag{34}$$

This should be constrasted with (22), which we rewrite as

$$Q^m = \frac{\rho s}{nc} \frac{1}{1 - (1 - \rho)s} - \frac{x^m \rho s}{c(1 - (1 - \rho)s)} \tag{35}$$

If s were fixed, at each value of nx,

$$Q^m > \hat{Q}^\circ \quad \text{since} \quad \frac{\rho s}{1 - (1 - \rho)s} < 1. \tag{36}$$

Hence, if s were fixed,

$$x^m > \hat{x}^o. \tag{37}$$

The level of research in the monopoly equilibrium exceeds the constrained Pareto-optimal level. On the other hand, s itself may be variable. Since, at any x,

$$s^m \gtrless s^o \quad \text{as} \quad s' \gtrless 0,$$

and since

$$\frac{d[s/(1 - (1 - \rho)s)]}{dv} = \frac{s}{[1 - (1 - \rho)s]^2} \gtrless 0 \text{ as } s' \gtrless 0,$$

$$Q^m > \hat{Q}^o \tag{38a}$$

and

$$x^m > \hat{x}^o \tag{38b}$$

provided $s' \geq 0$.

When the government finances R & D through an excise tax, the tax is shifted, raising the price of the goods in the sector. There is thus an additional distortion associated with each increase in R & D expenditures; this should be contrasted with the market solution, where R & D expenditures are taken as fixed costs, and increases in expenditures on R & D affect price only through their effect on direct-production costs. It is not surprising then that, in general, this constrained Pareto-optimum entails less expenditure on R & D than in the market equilibrium.

Proposition 3 The monopoly equilibrium entails more research than the constrained Pareto optimum when: the government is not allowed to intervene directly in the production decisions of the monopolist; it can control the level of R & D; but it must finance the R & D by a specific excise tax, provided $s' \geq 0$.

(3) CONSTRAINED OPTIMALITY: FREE DISTRIBUTION OF KNOWLEDGE

The final constrained Pareto optimum which we consider here is that where the government imposes a specific tax, to finance R & D; the knowledge produced by this R & D is then distributed freely. Thus

$$p = c + t, \quad x = tQ \tag{39}$$

and $I = 1$ (since there are no profits or lump-sum taxes). Hence,

$$Q = \frac{s(n^{-\beta}(c+t))}{n(c+t)}, \tag{40}$$

$$\frac{dv}{dt} = \sum \left\{ \frac{dv}{dp_i} \frac{dp_i}{dt} \right\} \tag{41}$$

$$= -v_i n Q \frac{d(c+t)}{dt} = 0,$$

or

$$c' \left[Q + t \frac{dQ}{dt} \right] + 1 = 0. \tag{42}$$

But $dQ/dt = 0$ when $d(c+t)/dt = 0$. Hence,

$$c'Q + 1 = 0. \tag{43}$$

Rearranging (40), we obtain

$$\hat{Q}^\circ = \frac{s}{nc} - \frac{x}{c}.$$

It immediately follows that (using the fact that $P^m \geqslant 0$, or $nx \leqslant (1-\rho)s$ for each level of x,

$$\hat{Q}^\circ - Q^m = \frac{(1-s)\,[(1-\rho)s - nx]}{c(1 - (1-\rho)s)n} = P_i \frac{(1-s)}{c}. \tag{44}$$

The constrained Pareto-optimum output exceeds the market equilibrium output, and hence the level of research in the constrained Pareto optimum situation exceeds that in the market equilibrium. However, the magnitude of the difference will be small, provided that the level of pure rents (profits, after paying for R & D) is small. In particular, this implies that

Proposition 4 In the monopolistically-competitive equilibrium, where entry occurs until profits are (approximately) zero, not only will the number of commodities being produced be the same as in the constrained Pareto optimum; the level of research in each sector will also be the same.

The analyses of this and the preceding section have established that the widespread presumption that monopolies will be characterised by too little research is, at best, questionable. Depending on the set of instruments available to the government, the monopoly equilibrium

may entail just the right amount of research, too little research, or
too much research.

In the following section, we explore another potential source of
inefficiency in the market allocation: will there be too little risk-
taking in R & D?

V   RISK TAKING IN R & D

So far, we have assumed that all research endeavours are successful.
In fact, one of the most important characteristics of R & D is that the
outcome of any expenditure is uncertain. The results of any research
programme can be described by the probability distribution of production costs. We simplify the analysis by assuming that there are
only two outcomes. Either the research project fails – and costs
remain at their original level; or it succeeds – with costs lowered to c_1.
By spending more resources, the probability of success may be
increased:

$$\pi = \pi(x, c) \quad \text{with} \quad \pi_x > 0, \pi_c > 0, \pi_{xx} < 0 \tag{45}$$

Firms may be risk-averse, and this may induce them to undertake
less-risky research projects than a risk-neutral government might
desire. But the inefficiencies with which we are concerned in this
chapter arise from other sources as well; to focus on these other
sources of inefficiency, we assume in this section that firms are
risk-neutral. Thus, for any given c, x is chosen by a monopolist to
maximise

$$\pi\{V^m(c_1) - V^m(c_0)\} - x,$$

where V^m is the present discounted value of the monopolist's profits,
when (marginal) costs are c. Hence x is chosen so that:

$$[V^m(c_1) - V^m(c_0)]\pi_x = 1.$$

By contrast, social optimality with lump-sum taxation entails

$$[S^m(c_1) - S^m(c_0)]\pi_x = 1,$$

while the single researcher in an otherwise competitive market sets

$$(c_1 - c_0)Q_0\pi_x = 1.$$

The differences between these different market allocations correspond to those discussed in Section II:

$$\pi^m < \pi^c < \pi^o,$$

That is, of the three, the monopolist undertakes the most risk (has the smallest probability of success), while social optimality entails undertaking the least risk (the highest probability of success). But the qualifications we raised earlier apply here as well, with two major modifications.

First, we noted earlier that when we focused our attention on a *marginal* analysis, where the firm could lower its costs slightly more by spending slightly more on R & D, the value of incremental cost saving was simply proportional to output; if output under alternative market structures were the same, then R & D would be the same. This is not true for our analysis of risk taking, even when we can change the probability of success slightly by spending slightly more on R & D. Even if output under two régimes were the same, the incentives for R & D would be different.

Second, in the earlier discussion, in analysing the symmetric equilibrium, we assumed that all firms had their costs reduced by an equal amount. Now, even when all firms expend the same amount of resources on R & D, some will be successful, and others not.

To see how this changes the analysis of Section III, consider the limiting case where π is very small. Then the demand curve facing the industry in the next period will shift out by a negligible amount, and the wage will change a negligible amount. This implies that

$$w_0^m = w_1^m \qquad w_0^c = w_1^c.$$

At each value of π, the incentives for spending more on R & D to reduce costs further are the same under monopoly as they are in the market equilibrium. However, since the incentives for increasing the probability of success are greater with the market equilibrium, i.e., since $\pi^m < \pi^c$, it follows that,[27] if output in the two regimes were identical,

$$c_1^m \lessgtr c_1^c \quad \text{as} \quad \frac{\partial c_1}{\partial x} + \pi \; \frac{\partial (\partial c_1/\partial x)\,\bar{\pi}}{\partial \pi} \gtrless 0. \tag{46}$$

It is only through this indirect route that the traditional presumption that monopolies spend too little on R & D may be restored. (Offsetting this effect are the concerns raised earlier, that while the monopolist appropriates all of the future returns to R & D, at least those which are internal to the industry, this is not true in the competitive market structure; overall, there may be more or less research under monopoly.)

VI   THE NUMBER OF INDEPENDENT RESEARCH
PROJECTS

A third important characteristic of the research programme of a
firm, or an economy, is the number of independent research programmes undertaken. When the probability of success of a particular
line of enquiry is less than one, there may be some gains from
attempting simultaneously two (or more) alternative research strategies. The answer, quite clearly, depends on the correlation between
the success of the two projects. With a perfect correlation, it is
obvious that if the first project failed, so too would the second
project. Therefore, it would never be socially-optimal to undertake
two projects. If the two projects are not perfectly correlated, it may
be desirable to undertake two (or more) projects.

The first project will be unsuccessful with the probability $1 - \pi_1$,
and it is only in that state that the second project has a social return.
Thus, the expected social return from the second project is:

$$\pi_{2f}(1 - \pi_1)V^s,$$

where π_{2f} is the probability of success for the second project, given
that the first fails. An exactly parallel analysis applies to the monopolist's decision to undertake two (or more) projects. His marginal
return to the second project is

$$\pi_{2f}(1 - \pi_1)V^m.$$

Thus, the distinction between the behaviour of a monopolist and
social optimality depends simply on the difference between V^s and
V^m, a difference which, in the general equilibrium, we suggested
might not be very large.[28]

This is not, however, true of the incentives for two or more
independent researchers; that is, in situations where there is competition in the R & D market (as opposed simply to competition in the
product market).

Before turning to this, in the next section, we comment briefly on a
closely-related question: Should one wait to find out whether the first
project is a failure before beginning the second project? The cost is
the possible waste from unnecessary duplication; the gain is that, if
the first project is unsuccessful while the second is successful, the
fruits of the research project will be enjoyed earlier than if the two
projects are undertaken sequentially. Obviously, if the interest rate is
zero, then there is no gain from discovering the invention earlier, and it

is never optimal to pursue the two research projects simultaneously.

More generally, when the interest rate is positive, there is some gain from making the discovery earlier. But whether the interest rate is zero or positive, the private and social returns to undertaking a second project simultaneously differ markedly. When both projects are successful, the private return is half of the (patentable) value of the invention, even though the marginal social return is zero. There is a systematic bias towards 'too fast' research.[29]

VII COMPETITION AND RISK

Though the prevalent view among economists is that competition is good, that it stimulates innovation and economic efficiency, businessmen are often less enthusiastic about its virtues. One of the central concerns expressed by businessmen is that competition forces upon them a high level of risk; there is uncertainty both about whether their own research will be successful and about what research programme their rivals are undertaking. And that is exacerbated by each firm's attempt to keep its strategies secret. Economists tend to treat their concerns as being self-serving attempts to acquire monopoly rents.

In this section, we shall see that competition actually reduces risk if the research strategies of rivals are known, but that it may force upon entrepreneurs a high degree of risk when they are not; as a result, if they are risk-averse, there may be less innovation than there is with monopoly.

The simplest 'competitive' environment is that of duopoly and, accordingly, that is what we focus on here. The consequences of engaging in R & D in a duopoly depend critically on the way the duopoly functions. Before considering any particular set of assumptions, however, it is useful to provide the general structure.

The decision tree facing the firm can be represented as in Figure 14.6. There are six distinct outcomes. (Contrary to the old adage, it is *not*, in general, better to have tried and failed than never to have tried at all: one loses the amount x.) We use the following notation:

V_{ss} = the present discounted value of profits when both firms are successful;

V_{fs} = the present discounted value of profits when the rival succeeds in developing the new technology, but you fail;

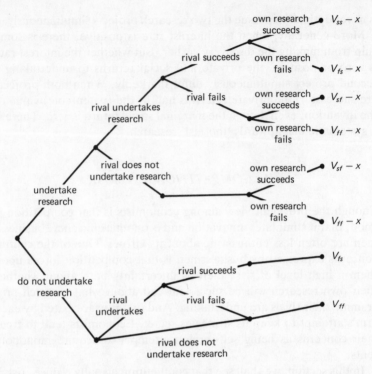

Fig. 14.6

V_{sf} = the present discounted value of profits when you succeed in developing the new technology, but your rival fails; and

V_{ff} = the present discounted value of profits when neither succeeds in developing the new technology.

Clearly

$$V_{sf} > V_{ff},$$

while

$$V_{sf} > V_{ss}$$

and

$$V_{ss} > V_{fs}.$$

The firm is better off when it is successful and its rival is not than when it is not successful and its rival is not; the firm is better off when it is successful and its rival is not than when both are successful; and the firm is better off when it is successful and its rival is successful than when it is a failure and its rival is successful. Success pays. The question is, does it pay enough.

Without detailing the nature of the interactions between the two duopolists, we can still say something about the nature of the pay-offs.

The increment in profits of a duopolist, if he alone is successful, can be divided into two parts:

(a) The increment in his profits, assuming his rival keeps his output constant. This, in turn, can be broken down into two parts:
    (i) The increment in profits, assuming he keeps his output constant; and
    (ii) The increment in profits from a change (increase) in his output.
(b) The change in his profits resulting from the response of his rival to his changed circumstances.

The return to the duopolist may be greater or less than that to the monopolist.

To see this, we focus on the case where one duopolist has already decided to undertake a given research project (the outcome of which is still uncertain), which will lower its costs from c_o to c_1 with a probability of π_1. The return to the second firm undertaking a research project which will lower its costs from c_o to c_1 is

$$R^d \equiv \pi_{2s}V_{ss}\pi_1 + \pi_{2f}V_{sf}(1 - \pi_1) + [(1 - \pi_{2s})V_{fs}\pi_1 + (1 - \pi_{2f})V_{ff}(1 - \pi_1)] - (V_{fs}\pi_1 + V_{ff}(1 - \pi_1)).$$

Here π_{2s} (π_{2f}) is the probability of success of the second research project given that the first project is a success (failure). To contrast this with the social return, we consider the limiting case of a Bertrand duopolist, for which

$$V_{ss} = V_{ff} = V_{fs} = 0 \quad \text{and} \quad V_{sf} = (c_o - c_1)Q_o.$$

Then

$$R^d = (c_o - c_1)Q_o\pi_{2f}(1 - \pi_1) = V^c\pi_{2f}(1 - \pi_1).$$

The only difference between social and private returns arises from the difference between V^c and V^s, a difference which we argued is likely to be small.

But this is the limiting case. With less-fierce competition,

$$V_{sf} > V_{ss} > V_{ff} > 0.$$

Profits are higher if the first duopolist is successful, but they are also higher if the first duopolist is *not* successful. As a result, it is possible for R^d to be either larger or smaller than with the Bertrand (price-setting) equilibrium. We consider two limiting cases:

Perfect correlation Here $\pi_{2f} = 1 - \pi_{2s} = 0$ and $R^d = 0$ with the Bertrand solution. On the other hand, with the Cournot (quantity-setting equilibrium),

$$V_{ss} > V_{ff}$$

and hence

$$\hat{R}^d = \pi_1(V_{ss} - V_{fs}) > x,$$

provided that π_1 is large enough.

Perfect negative correlation Here, $\pi_{2f} = 1 \ \pi_{2s} = 1$. Now for the Bertrand duopolists,

$$R^d = (V_{sf} - V_{ff}) (1 - \pi_1) = V^c(1 - \pi_1),$$

while for the Cournot duopolists

$$\hat{R}^d = (1 - \pi_1) (V_{sf} - V_{ff}),$$

which is positive for sufficiently small π_1. Clearly,

$$V_{sf} - V_{ff} - V^c < 0$$

implies

$$\hat{R}^d < R^d.$$

But our concern is not just with the mean (average) return, but with the riskiness of R & D. When the mean return to both the monopolist and the duopolist from undertaking the second project is identical, the monopolist's return is unambiguously riskier (in the sense of Rothschild–Stiglitz (1971)). For the monopolist, there is only one state in which the second project has a payoff; that is, when the first project is a failure and the second project is a success. But, for the duopolist, there are four possible states, with the highest profits (when the rival's project is a failure and his is a success) still being less than the monopolist's (so long as the first continues to produce), provided max $(V_{ss} - V_{fs}, V_{sf} - V_{ff}) < V^n$; if this inequality is not satisfied, as it may be, the results may be reversed.

It is thus apparent that if firms are sufficiently risk averse the second research project might not be undertaken by a monopoly, even though a duopolist would have undertaken it.

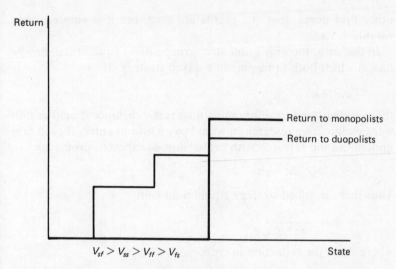

FIG. 14.7 When there is no uncertainty about rival's research strategy, competition induces less risk.

(1) UNCERTAINTY ABOUT RIVALS' RESEARCH STRATEGIES

The analysis thus far in Section VII has assumed that the second firm knows that the first firm has undertaken a research project. We have thus eliminated one of the most important sources of uncertainty about which businessmen complain. In Section VII(1), by contrast, we assume that firms do not know whether their rivals have undertaken research. We shall show that, even when firms are risk-neutral, equilibrium under duopoly may be characterised by a slower pace of technical progress than with monopoly.

For simplicity, we limit ourselves to the case where research projects yield a perfectly correlated return, and where there is fierce competition (Bertrand price-competition).

If the returns to research are perfectly correlated, there cannot exist an equilibrium in which both firms always undertake research. For they will both either be successful (profits zero) or a failure (profits zero), and in either case the research yields no returns: competition (even in this limited form) seems inconsistent with innovation.

There exists an asymmetric non-competitive equilibrium, in which one firm always engages in research, making a profit of $\pi V_{sf} - x$. The other firm never does (its profits are zero, but if it entered, they would be $-x$).

In this case, the only symmetric (competitive) equilibrium may be one in which both firms pursue a mixed strategy. If

$$\pi V_{sf} > x,$$

there is clearly no equilibrium with no research, since if neither firm were undertaking research, it would pay a firm to enter. If each firm undertakes the research with probability ϕ, expected profits are

$$(1 - \phi)\pi Q_o \, \Delta c - x.$$

Thus there is mixed strategy equilibrium with

$$1 - \phi = \frac{x}{\pi Q_o \, \Delta c}$$

where Δc is the reduction in costs

With only two firms, competition is so keen that the expected profits from R & D are driven down to zero. All the (producer) surplus generated by innovation is dissipated in the form of duplicative research. Moreover, there will now be instances when the monopolist undertakes cost-reducing innovation, but where this will not be undertaken (with probability $(1 - \phi)^2$) by either of the duopolists.[30]

The results that we have just derived, are that there may not be a symmetric Nash equilibrium in pure strategies in R & D markets (see Dasgupta and Stiglitz, 1980a), and that the level of technical progress (but not the level of R & D expenditures) may decline with an increase in competition. They are of more general significance than this simple example implies. Gilbert and Stiglitz (1979), for instance, consider a situation where, by spending more on research, the invention may be discovered at an earlier date. The first firm to make the discovery gets the patent, and reaps the entire return. The authors show that if the R & D process is non-stochastic,[31] then there will be no pure-strategy equilibrium; that there is a mixed-strategy equilibrium; competition again is sufficiently fierce for expected profits to be zero; and, as the number of firms engaged in research increases, the expected date of discovery is later (not earlier).

In this and the preceding sections of this chapter, we cast considerable doubt on the widespread presumption that competition serves as a spur to innovation; or, more accurately, we showed that the traditional argument was unpersuasive, when put into a general equilibrium context. We showed that there were other arguments, e.g. that competition increased riskiness and led to duplicative research, which suggested that competition might serve to discourage technical progress.

We believe, however, that there is considerable truth in the widespread presumption that competition is a spur to innovation. In Section VIII, we present an alternative view of the economy, in which the traditional presumptions concerning the desirability of competition can be shown to be valid.

VIII INNOVATION IN THE NEW THEORY OF THE FIRM

In the analysis of Section VII, we assumed that firms maximised their profits; this assumption was maintained both for the competitive and non-competitive environments.

For decades, there have been competing theories of the firm, asserting that most large enterprises were controlled by their managers. Managers did not, in general, act in the interests of shareholders, and did not maximise the firm's profits. These theories, regardless of their empirical validity, were usually dismissed on *a priori* grounds: it was impossible for rational firms not to be profit maximising. The shareholders would quickly dismiss any manager who refused to profit maximise; and if they failed to do so, some entrepreneur would take over the company, ensuring that all firms would in fact be profit maximising (or, more accurately, value maximising). Supporters of the managerial theory of the firm questioned the efficacy of these devices, which were intended to ensure that all firms value-maximised; more recently it has become clear that, if there is imperfect information, these mechanisms will not, in general, be effective: shareholders have only limited information concerning the performance of managers; it is costly for them to obtain additional information and there is, effectively, a public good involved in the management of any enterprise. It is not in the interests of any small shareholder to ensure that the company is well managed.

The same problems imply that the take-over mechanism will be ineffective in maintaining discipline. Thus, the central problem facing the 'founder' of a firm is how to devise incentive structures which ensure that his managers (workers) pursue policies which are in accord with the objectives of the entrepreneur.[32] That is, the entrepreneur must find an appropriate *compensation* scheme.[33] This is precisely the problem which we posed in our earlier study (Nalebuff–Stiglitz); while there the output (the number of widgets produced) was observable, the difficulty of the task was not. Similar considerations apply here. All that the firm's owner observes is whether the project was or was not successful. He does not generally have the information needed to judge whether the project should or should not have been undertaken. (Indeed, if he had had the information, he would not have needed to hire the manager to make the decision about undertaking the project; he could simply have directed the manager whether to undertake the project or not.)

The problem with which we are concerned in this Section, inducing the manager to act in the interests of the owner, is the standard problem in the principal agent literature. Our analysis differs from the standard analysis of such problems in several respects: first, we allow the principal to make use of information provided by other firms (thus this problem is closely related to the principal multiple-agent problem, studied, e.g., by Nalebuff and Stiglitz, Holmstrom and Farrell). But it differs in that the information which is used as a basis of comparison is the result of agents working for *other* principals. Second, we are concerned with analysing an (admittedly simple) market equilibrium, in which the pay-offs depend on – and simultaneously determine – the actions taken by all of the 'agents' in the market. Third, we have limited ourselves to analysing a much more restricted class of actions, undertaking or not undertaking a research project, which will either be, or not be, successful.

As we noted in the Introduction, the design of an optimal compensation scheme entails a balancing of considerations of risk, incentive and flexibility. Because managers are risk averse, compensation schemes will entail the manager's compensation having less variability than output; because incentive problems are important compensation schemes will, in general, have the manager's rewards increase to some extent with the profits of the firm.

The nature of the optimal compensation scheme depends critically on the economic environment of the firm, e.g., on the degree of competition, for two reasons:

(a) As we argued in Section II, the degree of competition will affect the riskiness of the returns to undertaking an R & D project. If the returns are less variable then the optimal compensation scheme will, in general, entail the manager bearing a larger fraction of the risks; he will then have better incentives.

(b) The set of feasible compensation schemes depends critically on what information is available. When there is more than one firm in the industry, it is at least possible to glean some information from the performance of the given firm relative to that of other firms in the industry. When there is only a single firm, such information simply is not available.

In the limiting case where the returns to the two firms (for any given level of inputs, such as effort, by the manager) are perfectly correlated, then the presence of the second firm in the industry makes possible the design of an incentive structure which simultaneously provides perfect incentives and eliminates all risk.

That is, we simply make the pay of the manager of the ith firm

$$Y^i = P^i(e, \theta) - P^j(e, \theta) + w, \tag{47}$$

where θ is some random variable which affects both firms equally, and where P^i is the profits of the ith firm – a function of θ and of the level of effort, e_i, of its manager (an unobservable variable). (If it were observable, the manager could be given direct compensation based on his level of effort.)

Thus, the manager who maximises his utility simply maximises

$$U(Y^i) - D(e_i),$$

where $D(e)$ is the disutility of supplying effort $(D' > 0, D'' > 0)$. Here, $U(Y)$ is the utility of income, $U' > 0$, $U'' < 0$, reflecting the risk aversion of managers. When the two firms are symmetric,

$$P^i(e, \theta) \equiv P^j(e, \theta)$$

and Y^i is not random: the manager faces no risk. However, the manager sets

$$U'(w) \quad \frac{\partial \bar{P}^i}{\partial e_i} = D'(e_i). \tag{48}$$

The manager behaves as he would do if he obtained all the returns of the firm:[34] he has perfect incentives.

Thus, the extent to which the firm behaves as an owner-managed firm (the extent to which there is a divorce between ownership and control) should be viewed as an endogenous variable. It is to be explained, at least partly, by the nature of the risks faced by the firm and by the availability of information on which one could base a compensation scheme which both reduced the risk of the manager and provided him with appropriate incentives.[35] (For a further development of this, see Nalebuff and Stiglitz (1983a).) Accordingly, monopolies will be characterised by the fact that their managers have incentive structures in which they appropriate only a small fraction of the increase in the profit of the firm. This is what gives rise to the widely observed phenomenon of *managerial slack* in monopolistic organisation.

For managers in competitive environments, in which the returns are perfectly correlated (for each level of output), there can be compensation schemes which provide perfect incentives and eliminate all risk. This means that competitive industries will appear to be much more 'efficient'.

Matters are somewhat more complicated if the outcomes of the research projects undertaken by the two duopolists are not perfectly correlated. For then the manager must still bear some risk, even in a symmetric equilibrium: there is some probability that his rival will be successful and he will not. This reduces the advantages from using comparative compensation schemes, but does not totally vitiate them.

(1) CHOICE OF PROJECTS

Thus far, this Section has shown how, even with a limited degree of competition we could, under certain circumstances, design compensation schemes which ensured that the manager undertook the correct level of effort. it also showed that managers of monopolies put forth too little effort (even where we had designed the 'best' incentive schemes we could making use of the available data).

Managers often have a choice among a variety of projects; some, for instance, may be riskier than others. Ensuring that the manager undertakes the 'correct' project (from the perspective of the owner of the firm) is a difficult matter. In sub-section VIII(1) we compare the incentives, say, for risk taking in competitive and non-competitive environments.[36]

We first consider the incentives of a manager of a monopoly whose compensation is a linear function of the profits of the firm, but which depends on whether the manager undertakes a project:

$$Y = \begin{cases} \alpha P + w_1 \text{ if a research project is undertaken} \\ \alpha P + w_2 \text{ if no research project is undertaken} \end{cases} \quad (49)$$

$$w_1 \geqslant w_2$$

The firm must decide whether to undertake a research project, which is characterised by V the value of the project if successful, x, the cost of the project, and π the probability of success.[37] Assume that the owner of the firm knows V and x, but does not know π; only the manager knows π. Can the owner of the firm provide the manager with an incentive structure such that he will undertake the project if, and only if, it is in the interests of the owner for him to do so?

The manager will undertake the project if and only if[38] (assuming profits in the absence of a successful project are zero)

$$U(w_1 + \alpha(V - x))\pi + U(w_1 - \alpha x)(1 - \pi) > U(w_2) \tag{50}$$

i.e., if

$$\pi \geq \pi^m \equiv \frac{U(w_2) - U(w_1 - \alpha x)}{U(w_1 + \alpha(V - x)) - U(w_1 - \alpha x)}. \tag{51}$$

The risk neutral owner wishes the manager to undertake the project if

$$\pi > \pi^o \equiv \frac{x}{V} + \omega/(1 - \alpha)V, \tag{52}$$

where

$\omega = w_1 - w_2$, is the reward for undertaking the risk.

The two decisions coincide if and only if

$$\pi^m = \pi^o.$$

We now show that for any $\alpha > 0$ there exists an $\omega > 0$ such that $\pi^m = \pi^o$, so that the two decisions coincide.

We first prove that if $\omega = 0$,

$$\pi^m > \pi^o.$$

This follows[39] from concavity of the utility function, which enables us to write

$$\pi^m = \left\{ \frac{U(W) - U(W - \alpha x)}{\alpha x} \middle/ \frac{U(W - \alpha x + \alpha V) - U(W - \alpha x)}{\alpha V} \right\} \frac{x}{V}$$

$$> \frac{x}{V} \equiv \pi^o.$$

Thus, a compensation scheme which rewards individual managers only on the basis of success or failure will always have a higher cut-off probability than the owner would choose. To correct this bias, the manager must be rewarded for undertaking the project, whether it succeeds or fails, i.e., $\omega > 0$.

Since an increase in ω increases π^o and decreases π^m, it is apparent that for a sufficiently large value of ω, the interests of the two can be made to coincide. Even so, the manager does not do what the owner would have liked him to do, if he could have costlessly motivated him to undertake the right action, and the manager's decisions will not maximise expected (national) income. (And the optimal contract will not, in general, have $\pi^o = \pi^m$.)

Unfortunately, the critical value of π (and hence the compensation scheme, $[\omega, \alpha]$, which induces managers to make the correct decision), depends on the values of the parameters V and x. The assumption that we previously employed, that the owner knows V and x, but not π, and that he can adjust the compensation scheme as circumstances (i.e., as V and x) change, is obviously not completely plausible.

Assume, by way of contrast, that the owner must specify a compensation scheme prior to knowing V (for simplicity, we assume throughout that x is fixed); the owner has a (subjective) probability distribution over the set of possible projects which the manager will have to consider in the next period. He chooses a compensation scheme which, on average, is correct. (We now show that a risk averse manager will accept some small projects which the owner would like rejected and will reject some large projects which the owner would like accepted. There appears, in other words, to be a systematic bias in the manager's incentives towards accepting 'conservative' projects.)

To see this, we plot (the logarithms of) π^m and π^o as functions of (the logarithm of) V, in Figure 14.7. From (52) it is clear that

$$\frac{d \ln \pi^o}{d \ln V} = -1$$

as depicted. Straightforward differentiation of (51) with respect to V yields

$$\frac{d \ln \pi^m}{d \ln V} = V\alpha U' (w_1 + \alpha[V - x])/[U(w_1 + \alpha[V - x]) - U(w_1 - \alpha x)]$$

But the concavity of the utility function implies that

$$0 > \frac{d \ln \pi^m}{d \ln V} > -1.$$

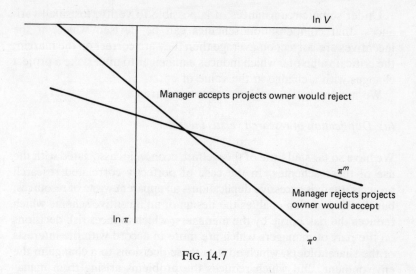

ln V

Manager accepts projects owner would reject

π^m

Manager rejects projects owner would accept

ln π

π^o

FIG. 14.7

(2) DUOPOLY

Consider, by contrast, the situation where there are two duopolists. Then a compensation scheme can be based on relative as well as absolute performance.

We consider the polar case of perfectly-correlated outcomes. Assume the firm compensates its manager by paying him a fixed wage plus a multiple k of the difference between his profits and those of the rival. In that case, by choosing the multiple correctly, to offset the effects of risk aversion, the manager will always do precisely what the owners of the firm would like. At the same time, however, provided that there is a symmetric equilibrium, no risk is imposed upon the manager. This is the critical advantage of competition and of compensation schemes based on relative performance.

Under some circumstances, it is possible to verify, for small variances, that compensation schemes can be devised which, if the incentives are correct on average then they are correct on the margin; the critical value of π which induces a manager to undertake a project changes with a change in the value of π°.

We now make two remarks about welfare:

(a) Duplication of research versus incentives

We have so far said little of the welfare economics associated with the use of these schemes. In the case of perfectly correlated research projects, there is excessive duplication – an apparent waste of resources; but this duplication enables the design of an incentive scheme which reduces the risk borne by the managers, which induces risk decisions on the part of managers which are more in accord with the interests of the shareholders, which adjusts these decisions to a change in the environment, and which reduces the problems arising from managerial slack.

(b) Correlation among research projects

At the same time, we noted in previous sections that the pay-off function for the firm need not coincide with the social pay-off function. This may be particularly evident with compensation schemes based on relative performance, when there is a choice of research projects to be undertaken. Assume there are two projects, both of which pay off with probability 1/2, and one of which will pay off if the other does not. Assume that the first firm undertakes project A. The manager of the second firm will undertake project A provided[40]

$$U(W) > \frac{U(W + kx)}{2} + \frac{U(W + k[V_{fs} - V_{sf} + x])}{2}$$

where the manager receives a fixed wage (W) plus a multiple (k) of the difference between his profits and those of his rival. Note that *not* undertaking the project is risky.

By contrast, the expected utility from undertaking project (B) is

$$\frac{U(W + k\,[V_{sf} - V_{fs}])}{2} + \frac{U(W + k[V_{fs} - V_{sf}])}{2}.$$

Thus, undertaking project (B), when his rival undertakes project A, imposes considerable risk. Since the expected return is zero, he will not do so. A compensation scheme which is designed to work well when managers do not have a choice over the correlation of their research projects, may not do so (at least from the social point of view) when managers do have some choice over it: there may be a bias towards excessively-high correlation. (It is also apparent that there may be multiple equilibria, one of which Pareto-dominates the others.)[41]

IX CONCLUDING REMARKS

The traditional comparison between incentives for innovation under monopoly and competition (best represented, perhaps, by Arrow's (1962) study) entails a partial-equilibrium comparison, with no uncertainty. And regardless of the nature of the competition in the product market, there is no competition for the development of the new product. The central issues revolve around: (a) the ability of the firm to appropriate some of the returns from the innovation; e.g., if the innovation can be imitated, it is clear that the firm will not have incentives to innovate;[42] and (b) the relationship between the returns to the firm and the *marginal* social return to innovation; in the case of a non-discriminating monopolist, for instance, the social returns from lowering the price, as a result of a lower marginal cost, are not appropriated by the firm.[43]

This analysis gave rise to the view that: (a) since both in competitive and non-competitive markets there were insufficient incentives for R & D, there should be government subsidies for research; and (b) since competition (provided the returns to innovation could be appropriated) was more conducive to innovation than monopoly, it was important for the government to encourage competition (e.g., through anti-trust policy).

Although the issues of appropriability and of the relationship between marginal social returns and expected private returns from engaging in R & D are clearly central, the traditional analysis has been shown to be faulty on several accounts. Among the most important of these are the following:

(i) It is partial-equilibrium rather than general-equilibrium analysis. The analysis might be correct for an isolated sector; that is, it might provide the correct answer to this question. If all sectors of the economy but one were competitive, and that one was the only one in which R & D could occur, would there be too much or too little research? This is hardly the question of interest: we are concerned with comparing two economies, one of which is characterised by 'monopolistic' industries, the other by 'competitive' industries. Which of these two economies would be characterised by more R & D is not clear. In one simple case, we showed that whether more or less research is undertaken with monopoly depends on whether the elasticity of labour supply is greater or less than zero.

(ii) It ignores the distortions which have to be introduced in order to raise the revenues required to finance any government subsidies for R & D. Indeed, the patent system can be viewed as a special tax system designed to raise revenues for paying for R & D.

(iii) Competition affects, in an important way, the risks associated with undertaking R & D. In some cases, it may be less risky to undertake research, given that one's rival does, than not to undertake it. These risk effects are important, not only in determining whether an R & D project will be undertaken, but also the nature of the R & D strategy. We suggested, for instance, that there might be a bias towards excessive correlation in research strategies.

As a consequence of the factors described above, we have reached this conclusion: there is no clear presumption that economies in which firms maximise profits (or the expected utility of profits) and which are dominated by monopolised industries have more or less R & D than more-competitive economies.

The critical difference, we suggest, lies in the impact on incentive structures for managers: with competition, compensation schemes based, at least in part, on relative performance can be employed and these will, in fact, be more effective in inducing managers to undertake risky research projects. They have the further advantage of 'flexibility' by inducing managers to make 'correct' decisions over a wider range of parameters than would the incentive schemes which a monopolist might employ. Our model also provides some insights into the widely-observed phenomenon of managerial slack in monopolistic sectors.

Though our analysis has focused on the comparison between the level of R & D under monopoly and under (at least some degree of) competition, if does provide some insights into the welfare economics of market allocations to R & D. Most important, we have emphasised that the appropriate comparison between the market and alternative solutions must take into account the costs of raising revenues, e.g., for R & D subsidies, as well as the difficulties met with in identifying the beneficiaries from any particular research project. We have identified circumstances in which the market, if not a constrained optimum, is probably not too far from it; R & D expenditures may be greater or less than at the constrained optimum; while the information required to design an optimal set of corrective taxes makes such schemes probably not feasible.

Two critical limitations in the analysis here – as in much of the earlier analysis – have been that we have not allowed for free entry, particularly into R & D, and we have treated the degree of monopoly in the product market (the number of firms) as exogenous. In fact, it should be viewed as endogenous (see Dasgupta and Stiglitz, 1980). This is important, because policies which might, in the short run, lead to more competitiveness (say, in reducing the patent life) could, through reduced incentives for entry into R & D, lead to less competitiveness in the long run. Moreover, in some circumstances a monopolist's attempt to deter entry may induce it to engage in more R & D (thus potential competition may lead to faster technical progress, even if it does not lead to more competitive markets (see Dasgupta and Stiglitz, 1980; Gilbert and Newbery, 1979). In other circumstances, however, it may have little effect on R & D (Gilbert *et al.*, 1979). With free entry into R & D, competition may not only result in excessive expenditures on R & D, relative to the social optimum (in contrast with the cases discussed here, where there is no significant difference), welfare may be even lower than in the monopoly situation (see Gilbert and Stiglitz, 1979); Stiglitz, 1981).

It is clear that the threat of entry affects the riskiness of alternative research strategies for existing firms (whether presently monopolies or competitors); and risk considerations clearly affect the incentive for entry. The implications of this for the nature of the market equilibrium, the design of managerial incentive structures and, more generally, for the level of R & D and the rate of technical progress are questions which we hope to pursue on another occasion.

NOTES

1. Research support from the National Science Foundation is gratefully acknowledged. I am indebted to Barry Nalebuff, Joe Farrell, Steve Salop, Partha Dasgupta, Richard Gilbert and Paul Klemperer for their helpful comments.

2. Most of us are familiar with sports competitions. There are a variety of rules of the game under which these competitions are conducted. Only a single prize may be awarded, or alternatively, the difference between the winning prize and the losing prizes (besides the 'recognition' of being first) may be relatively small. There may be handicaps, and almost any contest imposes a variety of restrictions on the set of 'feasible' actions which the participants can undertake; for instance, in sailing, the size of the mainsail is regulated; in boxing, the characteristics of the glove are regulated.

3. That is, we assumed that the contract had to be signed before all relevant properties of the environment were known; what would be a good contract for one environment might be a bad contract for another. The ability to adapt automatically to changes in the environment is what we refer to (somewhat roughly) as flexibility.

4. We are not, of course, claiming that they adjust their behaviour to what they would have done had the information about the state of the environment been available prior to the signing of the contract.

5. See Stiglitz (1975a).

6. In some contexts, e.g., in small-group interactions, competition may, in the same sense, be unproductive. See Nalebuff–Stiglitz (1982).

7. For simplicity, we shall assume that there will be no subsequent innovations which will decrease the value of the patent. Also, patents are assumed to be infinitely lived.

8. Throughout, the superscript m will denote the value of a variable in the monopoly equilibrium.

9. The superscript s will be used to denote variables in the socially-optimal allocation.

10. The superscript c will be used to denote the competitive market equilibrium. We use the term 'competitive' to cover a much broader range of economic environments than just that which has come to be associated with the Arrow–Debreu model.

11. The above analysis is due to Arrow (1962). This exposition is developed further in Dasgupta and Stiglitz (1980b).

12. Which, by hypothesis, is assumed to be unchanged.

13. $c_i(x_i)$ gives the marginal cost as a function of the expenditures on R & D; $C_i(\ell_i')$ gives the marginal input requirements (in physical units) as a function of inputs (in labour units) into R & D. The functions $c_i(x_i)$ can easily be derived from the functions $C_i(\ell_i')$ once factor prices are known.

14. Here, as elsewhere, we will drop the subscripts i when no confusion results.

15. This obviously is no longer true if both labour and goods enter the R & D process.

16. If the elasticity of demand differs among sectors, in the monopoly régime there will be relatively less output in the sectors with relatively low demand elasticities, and hence relatively less research in those sectors. Conversely for the sectors with high demand elasticities.

17. The effective life of the patent is often much shorter than the legal life; a subsequent discovery may make the original patent obsolete; even though the subsequent discovery would not have been made had the

original invention not occurred, the original invention will receive no compensation for this.

18. We have not provided a complete analysis of the comparison of equilibria between the two régimes. Because the incentives for engaging in research will be greater with monopoly, this will increase the demand for research workers; this will bid up the wage, so that $w_o^m > (1 - 1/\eta)w_o^c$.

19. The relationship between patents and excise taxes is discussed in Stiglitz (1969).

20. That is for those where, after the invention, the price remains the same.

21. Or there may be large costs associated with each of these actions.

22. If demand curves are linear, then (assuming we are considering an isolated monopoly, so wages in the two régimes are the same), $Q^m = \frac{1}{2}Q^s$ and $dp/dc = \frac{1}{2}$. Hence, assuming the marginal (social) utility of income to consumers and to capitalists is the same, constrained optimality entails setting $- \mid 3/2 \mid c'Q^m = 1$, while the monopolist sets $-c'Q^m = 1$, and unconstrained social optimality entails $-Q^s c' = -2Q^m c' = 1$.

23. Making use of the fact that $\rho = 1 - 1/\eta$.

24. For concavity, we require that $\rho < 1$. To ensure that the elasticity of demand exceeds unity, we assume $\rho > 0$.

25. Our model should be contrasted with Dixit–Stiglitz, who took x as exogenous, but n as endogenous.

26. We are calculating the effect of a simultaneous increase in the input of resources into R & D in all sectors.

27. That is, the first-order condition for c now becomes, for the monopolist,

$$\pi^m \frac{\partial V^m}{\partial c_1} \frac{\partial c_1}{\partial x \mid_{\bar{\pi}}} = 1,$$

while social optimality entails

$$\pi^o \frac{\partial S^m}{\partial c_1} \frac{\partial c_1}{\partial x \mid_{\bar{\pi}}} = 1,$$

Inverting (45), to express R & D expenditures as a function of c and π,

$$x = x(c, \pi),$$

(46) can be rewritten as

$$c_1^m \gtrless c_1^o \text{ as } \frac{\pi x_{\pi c}}{x_c} \gtrless 1.$$

28. Precisely analogous results hold for a *single* researcher undertaking a second research project in a market in which there is a competitive supply at the price c_o.

29. The problem is analogous to the dynamic inefficiencies which arise in common resource situations; each owner of an oil well may extract oil from the well too quickly, since he believes if he does not take the oil, the other owners of wells will.

30. For large innovations, where it pays a (non-discriminating) monopolist to lower his price, not all the expected social return to the innovation will be dissipated; some will accrue to consumers.

31. Or, more generally, if the uncertainty in the R & D process is sufficiently small.

32. For a more extensive discussion of these issues, see, e.g., Grossman and Hart (1980) and Stiglitz (1982).

33. The general problem is somewhat broader: the corporate charter includes provisions which affect take-overs, managerial discretion in changing the incentive structure, etc., all of which would, in principle, affect the price at which the original entrepreneur can sell his shares.

34. This is slightly imprecise: if the individual obtained all the returns, his income would be random, and he would act in a risk averse manner. (48) is equivalent to the individual's receiving the marginal increase in the average returns to the firm.

35. It is important to realise that what we are concerned with here is not only 'formal' compensation schemes, contracts which specify the pay of the manager for each level of performance of his firm, relative to the performance of his rivals, but also informal compensation schemes. A manager whose firm is losing market share, or whose profits are low relative to others in the industry will find himself under intense pressure, and if the company's relative performance remains poor, he will be fired or forced to resign.

36. We focus here only on incentive issues, in the absence of 'selection' or screening problems. One of the reasons that managers may work hard is so that they will be thought to be 'good', i.e., their performance conveys information about their characteristics. See Stiglitz (1975b).

37. We are not addressing here the question of how α is chosen. Presumably, $\alpha > 0$ because the firm wishes the manager to exert effort. In that case, changes in the terms of the contract alter the characteristics of the project. We shall ignore these effects throughout this section.

38. The actual expected return to the owner from undertaking the project is not πV but $(1 - \alpha)V\pi - (w_1 - w_2)$, but he has to pay only $(1 - \alpha)$ of the costs of research. So a risk neutral owner would wish the firm to undertake the research if and only if $(1 - \alpha)V\pi > (1 - \alpha)x + (w_1 - w_2)$. The compensation scheme we investigatge here is special for at least two reasons.

    First, it is linear: many firms employ highly non-linear compensation schemes. Second, it assume the manager must bear the same fraction of the costs that he receives of the returns. The manager may bear a smaller or larger fraction of the costs than he receives of the output. There are both effort costs and financial costs. Typically the manager bears all of the former, but a relatively small fraction of the latter. See Braverman–Stiglitz for a discussion of alternative cost sharing rules, and the design of the optimal cost sharing rule.

39. I am indebted to Paul Klemperer for pointing out a mistake in an earlier draft of this chapter.

40. We assume here that the manager's pay depends not on his own performance, but only on relative performance:

$$Y = W + k \, (\Delta P)$$

where ΔP is the difference in profits. When both undertake the research, then in the Bertrand equilibrium, either both are successful or both are failures; in either case,

$$\Delta P = 0$$

and hence the manager receives just W.

If the manager does not undertake the research project, then with probability 0.5, the other's research project is a failure, in which case

$$\Delta P = kx$$

(the other firm has spent x dollars on research, for which it has obtained no return); or the project is a success, in which case

$$\Delta P = V_{fs} - (V_{sf} - x)$$

41. Similar observations have been made in the context of regulatory authorities' use of comparative performance as a basis of rate setting: see Stiglitz *et al*. For a further discussion of this, see Nalebuff and Stiglitz (1983a).

42. The returns to R & D are often not patentable. Even an unsuccessful R & D programme yields information; e.g., about the non-feasibility of a certain production process, and the returns to this kind of information can often not be appropriated.

43. Similarly, some of the returns may represent the appropriation of rents on previously discovered knowledge which become embodied in the new innovation. See Barzel (1968) and Dasgupta and Stiglitz (1980b).

REFERENCES

Arnott, R. and Stiglitz, J. E. (1982) 'Equilibrium in Competitive Insurance Markets: The Welfare Economics of Moral Hazard' mimeo, Princeton University.

Arrow, K. J. (1962) 'Economic Welfare and the Allocation of Resources for Invention'. In *The Rate and Direction of Inventive Activity: Economic and Social Factors* (ed. Nelson, R.). (NBER) (Princeton University Press).

Barzel, Y. (1968) 'Optimal Timing of Innovation', *Review of Economics and Statistics*, Aug., pp. 348–55.

Braverman, A. and Stiglitz, J. E. (1983) 'Cost Sharing Arrangements under Sharecropping: Moral Hazard, Incentive Flexibility, and Risk', World Bank, mimeo, November 1983.

Dasgupta, P. and Stiglitz, J. E. (1980a) 'Industrial Structure and the Nature of Innovative Activity', *Economic Journal*, June, pp. 266–93.

Dasgupta, P. and Stiglitz, J. E. (1980b) 'Uncertainty, Industrial Structure, and the Speed of R & D', *Bell Journal of Economics*, Spring, pp. 1–28.

Dasgupta, P., Gilbert, R. and Stiglitz, J. E. (1982) 'Invention and Innovation Under Alternative Market Structures: The Case of Natural Resources', *Review of Economic Studies*, pp. 567–82.

Dasgupta, P. S., Gilbert, R. and Stiglitz, J. E. (1983), 'Strategic Considerations in Invention and Innovation: The Case of Natural Resources', *Econometrica*, pp. 1439–448.

Dixit, A. K. and Stiglitz, J. E. (1977) 'Monopolistic Competition and

Optimum Product Diversity', *American Economic Review* vol. 67, pp. 297–308.

Farrell, J. (1980) 'A Sufficient Statistic Theorem', mimeo, Dept of Economics, MIT.

Fudenberg, D., Gilbert, R., Stiglitz, J. E. and Tirole, J. (1983) 'Preemption, Leapfrogging, and Competition in Patent Races', *European Economic Review*, June, pp. 3–31.

Gilbert, R. J. and Newbery, D. (1982) 'Pre-emptive Patenting and the Persistence of Monopoly', *American Economic Review*, June, pp. 514–26.

Gilbert, R. and Stiglitz, J. E. (1979) 'Entry, Equilibrium and Welfare', mimeo.

Greenwald, B. and Stiglitz, J. E. (1985) 'Externalities in Economics with Imperfect Information and Incomplete Markets' *Quarterly Journal of Economics*.

Grossman, S. and Hart, O. (1980) 'Takeover Bids, the Free-Rider Problem, and the Theory of the Corporation', *Bell Journal of Economics*, April.

Holmstrom, B. (1982) 'Moral Hazard in Teams', *Bell Journal of Economics*, vol. 13, Autumn, pp. 324–40.

Levin, R. C. (1978) 'Technical Change, Barriers to Entry and Market Structure', *Economica*, vol. 45, no. 80, pp. 347–62.

Loury, G. (1979) 'Market Structure and Innovation', *Quarterly Journal of Economics*, vol. 93, pp. 395–410.

Nalebuff, B. and Stiglitz, J. E. (1983a) 'Information, Competition, and Markets', *American Economic Review*, vol. 73, pp. 278–83.

Nalebuff, B. and Stiglitz, J. E. (1983b) 'Prizes and Incentives: Towards a General Theory of Compensation and Competition', *Bell Journal of Economics*.

Nelson, R. R. and Winter, S. (1977) 'Forces Generating the Limiting Concentration Under Schumpeterian Competition', *Bell Journal of Economics*, vol. 9, no. 2, Autumn, pp. 524–48.

Rothschild, M. and Stiglitz, J. E. (1970) 'Increasing Risk: I. A Definition', *Journal of Economic Theory*, Sept., pp. 225–43.

Stiglitz, J. E. (1969) 'Discussion of the Theory of Innovation', *American Economic Review*, May.

Stiglitz, J. E. (1975a) 'Information and Economic Analysis'. In *Current Economic Problems* (eds Parkin and Nobay) (Cambridge, England: Cambridge University Press) pp. 27-52.

Stiglitz, J. E. (1975b) 'Incentives, Risk, and Information: Notes Towards A Theory of Hierarchy', *Bell Journal of Economics*, Autumn, pp. 552–79.

Stiglitz, J. E. (1980) 'Competition and Cooperation: Towards a General Theory of Compensation', mimeo.

Stiglitz, J. E. (1981) 'Potential Competition May Reduce Welfare', *American Economic Review*, May, pp. 184–9.

Stiglitz, J. E. (1982) 'Ownership, Control, and Efficient Markets: Some Paradoxes in the Theory of Capital Markets', in *Economic Regulation: Essays in Honor of James R. Nelson*, ed. Kenneth D. Boyer and W. G. Shpeherd (Ann Arbor: Michigan State University Press).

Stiglitz, J. E. and Gilbert, R. G. (1978) *Effects of Risk on Prices and Quantities of Energy Supplies* (Electric Power Research Institute, May).

Stiglitz, J. E. (forthcoming) *Information and Economic Analysis*.

Discussion of the Paper by Joseph Stiglitz

Salop attempted to put Stiglitz's paper into perspective by relating it to previous work by Stiglitz and others on 'relative-performance compensation schemes'. This literature pointed out that in a compensation problem with one principal and many agents, the principal could sometimes improve the sum of pay-offs by making each agent's pay-off depend upon information about other agents' efforts. To illustrate this, he referred to the contracting problem. 'Cost-plus, contracts eliminated all the risk for the contractor, but gave no incentive for the contractor to minimise costs. 'Fixed-fee' contracts had appropriate incentives for cost minimisation, but forced the contractor to bear all the risk. This problem could be partly resolved if two contracts were awarded simultaneously. Each contractor would be paid the other contractor's costs-plus. Since the other contractor's costs were beyond his control, each contractor had an incentive to reduce costs. In the case in which the costs of each contractor were positively correlated, dependence of the pay-off on the other contractor's costs would tend to limit the risk faced by each contractor. Salop pointed out that such schemes were common. He cited bonuses for top salesman and grading on the curve as examples. Competitive markets also compensated according to relative rather than absolute performance. For example, in perfect competition, the firm with the lowest marginal cost curve earned the highest profit. If all firms reduced costs equally, the profits of each firm might fall instead of rising, according to the elasticity of demand. He suggested that the contribution of the Stiglitz paper was the observation that the patent system represented a contest, or relative-performance compensation scheme. Society, in the role of the principal, should benefit from competition for the prize. This led to a presumption that more innovation would occur with competition than with monopoly, where the benefits of the relative performance compensation scheme could not, by definition, be realised.

Joseph Stiglitz pointed out that the motivation for his paper was an evaluation of the performance of the market in arriving at compensation schemes given a belief that the market did not choose the optimal compensation scheme. Further, the inappropriateness of the old partial equilibrium analyses of the problem in the context of invention came as somewhat of a surprise to Stiglitz.

He emphasised that there were three properties of contests and relative-performance schemes that made them desirable. First, these schemes often reduced the risk borne by the entrepreneur. For example, when there was a signal on the difficulty of making the invention that affected all participants in the contest in the same way, a contest extracted that signal through adjustment in effort by all the participants.

Second (related to the first feature), these schemes might be flexible. For example, when the environment was changing, a desirable contest should adjust to such changes. In general, a contract should allow for different degrees of risk taking and motives within alternative environments. However, the contract might have to be specified *ex-ante*. Flexibility in the contract, however, permitted the incentive structure to adjust implicitly. A contest was one way to accomplish this for all contestants would adjust their effort to respond to the environment in a way that was impossible to achieve with individualistic schemes.

Finally, contracts should have an incentive property, namely flexibility in adjusting the ratio of marginal to average returns. Marginal returns determined incentives; average returns determined total compensation and risk. Contests had such flexibility.

Seade pointed out that the usual way that R & D was modelled was to posit that there was a single target for research, which was attained with some positive probability. He suggested that uncertainty about the end results, or the target that was attained, as well as uncertainty about by-products that might be produced as a result of research might also be important. He suggested that this sort of uncertainty would require an explicit recognition of the temporal aspects of the R & D problem since a firm that did not reach the stated target might attain alternative achievements that would permit it to compete in R & D again. In this sense, more than one firm could win the R & D race, both in the short and long run.

Walroos asked whether incorporating a market for information about effort would alter the results on relative performance compensation schemes. Stiglitz responded that it would not provided perfect information could not be acquired.

Gilbert suggested that in some circumstances it might be desirable to create a compensation scheme that allowed firms to come in last, without penalising them too severely. As an example, he talked about electric power utilities trying to decide whether to research oil or nuclear power. If nuclear power were very risky, and all other utilities were researching oil, a risk-averse utility would be forced to research oil to avoid the large possible losses associated with nuclear research. Stiglitz responded that relative performance compensation schemes might lead to excessive duplication of research effort for precisely this reason. Schmalensee suggested that a resolution to this problem might require relative performance schemes that are not discontinuous.

White added that in the context of a patent system, the losers in the race for the patent made investments that were essentially lost. This was not true in the case of firms' managers since all of their efforts were translated into outputs. In this respect, a patent system run as a contest might be wasteful. *Partha Dasgupta* added that this might be especially true if R & D 'outputs' were perfectly correlated. Stiglitz responded that even though effort appeared to be duplicated, and therefore wasted, the additional incentive that this duplication generated made everyone better off than they would be if all R & D were done by a single firm. *Reinhard Selten* added that contests might create a situation where managers would expend resources in an attempt to make others in the contest look bad. This, he suggested, was the worst form of organisational slack, since it involved no consumption at the workplace.

15 Evolutionary Modelling of Economic Change

Richard R. Nelson

YALE UNIVERSITY, USA

I BASIC THEORETICAL PREMISES

This chapter provides an overview of the evolutionary economic theory which Sidney Winter and I have been developing, and describes several particular models. (For a more comprehensive treatment see our book, *An Evolutionary Theory of Economic Change* (1982) (Cambridge, Mass.: Harvard University Press).

The style of modelling we advance differs in important respects from that described at one level in the standard textbooks of economic theory, and found at another level in most articles aimed to advance the frontier of theory. We believe that the profession will ultimately be driven to adopt our approach, or something much like it, if it attaches high priority to characterising and explaining significant unforeseen economic change. The unforeseen change we have in mind here includes that induced by large unpredicted shocks to prevailing market conditions, as with the two oil price shocks of the last decade. We also include significant technological innovations that arise within the system, such as the revolution in computer technology that also marked the last decade.

The intellectual problem is simple to state, and familiar to most theorists. Over the years, economists have fashioned a set of tools designed for modelling situations where it can be presumed that the individual actors know the best things that they could be doing under different circumstances and that the circumstances themselves are known (perhaps subject to probabilistic uncertainty). The former presumption is modelled in terms of maximising decision-rules possessed by the economic actors. The latter condition then defines an equilibrium. The exact nature of the equilibrium, of course, depends on exogenous market forces and technological opportunities, or (correctly) predicted time-paths of these. Since the equilibrium concept is roomy enough to encompass a time path along which the salient variables change in a predictable manner, change can be treated as an aspect of moving equilibrium. Many models that admit technological advance treat it in such a way. Alternatively, one can do 'comparative statics' and examine how the equilibrium varies under different market and technological regimes. Much of the standard theory about the effects of changes in market conditions is, in fact, such comparative statics.

The issue is the adequacy of these two modes of dealing with change — either through comparative statics, *or* as an aspect of a moving equilibrium — in analyses of changes like those wrought by the oil price shocks, or the computer revolution. We are not the first to note that orthodox theory deals in an *ad hoc* way with the effects of unexpected shocks, and treats radical technological advance quite mechanically. The difficulties are not unconnected.

Orthodox comparative-static analysis is mute about how the system gets from one equilibrium to another, and even about whether the destination ever will be reached. Further, along the path (that may or may not lead) from one equilibrium to another, the behavioural assumptions of standard equilibrium theory have little bite. The argument that economic actors can be presumed to be doing the best they can, which has considerable (if falsifiable) explanatory and predictive power if the context is equilibrium, does not have much power out of equilibrium. Along the path actors may not know where they are going, or even where they are. According to orthodox theory, their beliefs about these matters are an important factor influencing what they do. That theory, however, says little about beliefs, except in equilibrium.

It is unclear just why this problem, while widely understood, keeps being ignored. Perhaps it is because many economists believe that the system always is close to equilibrium and that it tracks changes in equilibrium rapidly and accurately. If this is the argument it is a matter of faith; we know of no empirical work that persuasively supports it. The responses to the oil-price shocks make these assumptions highly dubious.

The above remarks hold even if well-defined 'best' decision rules can be presumed to exist, so long as firms do not know where they should be relative to the rules. The problem with the theory is compounded, obviously, if firms have not thought through the full range of possible actions they might take for any particular set of circumstances. Yet, we propose that this a common situation. Firms know that there must be better ways of doing things, but they are not sure just what they are. Firms know that resources will be required to explore the possibilities, and that the outcomes of such search will not be tightly predictable. Surely this was the way the situation was viewed by most firms in the wake of the energy-price shock. And, indeed, technological change – the identification, testing, and winnowing of new ways to save fuel costs – was an important part of the response. While some of the broad directions of the induced technological change could have been predicted in advance, the details could not have been. They had to be discovered through a process that involved considerable trial and error, luck and creativity.

We do not think that orthodox theory recognises adequately the central role played by technological innovation in responding to, and generating, economic change. Perhaps that is the reason why technological innovation is treated so mechanically by orthodox theory; if it were only a small side show, there would be no need to model it sensitively. But it is not a small side-show. As suggested, technological innovation is an important part of the response to changed market conditions. It is also a powerful force, in its own right, that lies behind changing market conditions. Computers, aircraft and pharmaceuticals are important industries. Competition in these industries operates largely through the introduction of new designs. Innovation in these industries has influenced the rest of the economy profoundly, and somewhat unpredictably. Our position is that to deal with technological advance adequately requires abandoning the idea of the well-defined choice set and, thus, the idea that prevailing decision-rules are truly optimising in the mathematical sense of that term.

We have viewed our task as being to develop a way of modelling which does not rely on a presumption that the system is in equilibrium, and that treats innovation as a way of exploring a choice-set that is not fully known. Many years ago Schumpeter remarked:

While in the accustomed circular flow every individual can act promptly and rationally because he is sure of his ground and is supported by the conduct, as adjusted to the circular flow, of all other individuals who in turn expect the accustomed activity from him, he cannot simply do this when he is confronted by a new task.

He also stated that:

> Carrying out a new plan and acting accordingly to a customary one are things as different as making a road and walking along it.

Those, indeed, are the problems as we see them. And we have found Schumpeter's words as relevant to our own endeavours to lay down a new intellectual road as to our understanding of the problems with the old, familiar one.

In our evolutionary models, as in orthodox ones, the actors are viewed as purposive and intelligent and as operating according to a set of decision rules. As in orthodox theory, these are the best rules the actors know about, and (metaphorically at least) some thought has been given to the matter. However, in our evolutionary theory we stress another aspect of decision rules. They are carried out as a matter of 'routine'.

In our perspective, a firm is at any time characterised largely in terms of the routines it has. At any time the firm simply *has* a set of routines, and if the analysis is pointed forward in time this is all the analyst need know. From another perspective, prevailing routines can be understood as having arisen in the firm through a series of past actions, which can be interpreted as 'searches' to find better ways of doing things. However, no search is exhaustive and, in limited time, only a fraction of the set of possible routines can be examined. Further, our firms are not viewed as possessing perfect memory; and a routine considered and rejected in the past, because it was not appropriate to the circumstances then, will not automatically be reconsidered and implemented at a later time if the circumstances are appropriate.

Firms that have better routines – production technologies, procedures for choosing alternative mixes of inputs and outputs, pricing rules, investment-project screening rules, mechanisms for allocating the attention of management and the operations research staff, R & D policies, etc. – will tend to prosper and to grow relative to those firms whose capabilities and behaviour are less-suited to the current situation. But there are limits (as in orthodox theory, when friction or adjustment costs are admitted) to the rate at which a firm can expand or contract.

In the discussion above, I have mentioned three analytically-separable kinds of 'routines'. First, there are those that might be called 'standard operating procedures'. In the standard theory of the firm, these would be those that in the short run (fixed capital stock) determine inputs and outputs. Second, there are routines that determine the investment behaviour of the firm, the equations that govern its growth or decline (measured in terms of its capital stock). Third, the deliberative processes of the firm, its 'search' behaviour, is also viewed as guided by routines. In principle, within our models, search-effort could be focused on any one of a firm's prevailing routines – its technology, its input- and output-determination rule, its investment rule, or even its R & D policy. In practice, in all the models we have built, search was assumed to uncover new technologies. We have taken the other 'routines' as constants.

The firm, or rather the collection of firms in the industry, perhaps involving new firms coming into the industry and old firms exiting it, is viewed as operating within an exogenously-determined environment modelled in terms of the demand curve for the product of the industry and the supply curves of the inputs purchased by firms in the industry. In all of our modelling to date we have taken these two kinds of markets as being in period-by-period equilibrium.

The logic of the model defines a dynamic and stochastic system. We often have modelled it as a complex Markov process. A standard iteration can be described as follows. At the existing moment of time all firms can be characterised by their capital stocks and their prevailing routines. Decision rules keyed to market conditions look to those conditions in the last period. Inputs employed and outputs produced by all firms then are determined. So, in turn, are input and output prices for this period. Given the technology and the other routines used by each firm, each firm's profitability is determined as well. The investment rule then determines how much each firm expands or contracts. Search routines focus on one or another aspect of the firm's behaviour and capabilities and (stochastically) come up with proposed modifications which the firm may, or may not, adopt. The system is now ready for next period's iteration.

The system may or may not have a steady state. If it has a unique one, it may or may not be globally stable. We (particularly Sidney Winter in earlier work) have given considerable attention to the question of the assumptions required if the behaviour of the system is to settle into a selection equilibrium; and also to the similarities and possible differences between behaviour in a selection equilibrium and behaviour in an equilibrium of a more-orthodox economic model.[1] But our models are perfectly usable, even if they have no steady states at all. Our models define equations of motion.

In the following sections I briefly describe three topics we have explored with models of this sort. Section II covers the response of firms and the industry to changed market conditions. Section III considers long-run growth fuelled by technological advance, and Section IV discusses the modelling of competition in the sense of Schumpeter. These all are topics that have been addressed, using orthodox models, and with success considerably greater toward the beginning of the list than towards the end. In each case, however, our approach sheds a different light. In the (concluding) Section V, I attempt to place our theoretical venture in the stream of the history of economic thought.

II FIRM AND INDUSTRY RESPONSE TO CHANGED MARKET CONDITIONS

A central question of micro-economic theory texts is this: how will industry inputs, output and price respond to a rightward shift in the demand curve for the product of the industry; or to changes in the terms under which different factors of production are available? Of course, as noted above, 'how will industry respond?' is not precisely the question that contemporary theory analyses. Rather the analysis compares equilibrium configurations under the two market conditions. In this section, I sketch how Winter and I address the question within our evolutionary theory. Important issues are at stake here. I suspect that most economists, if asked where economics has been most successful as a positive science, would point to explanations and predictions of the way in which industry output, inputs, and price respond to changing product and factor-market conditions – the stuff of textbook positive economics. To be credible as a general theory of firm and industry behaviour, an evolutionary theory must show itself capable of similarly predicting the standard responses.

In this section, I do not present a particular model, but rather a way of 'accounting for' the effects of a shock in prices that highlights the difference between an orthodox and an evolutionary perspective. Specific models of course can be, and have, been developed.[2]

Within our evolutionary theory, as within orthodox theory, a firm is viewed as having decision rules that determine its inputs and outputs, as a function of market conditions. For simplicity, assume that all techniques have the same fixed, capital-output ratio, but that variable input-proportions are flexible. Assume that, at time t, firm

i's decision rule governing variable inputs has the following general form:

$$\left(\frac{X}{K}\right)^t_i = D(P, d_i^t) \tag{1}$$

Here X_i is a vector of the firm's variable inputs, K_i the size of the firm's capital stock, P is the vector of input prices, and d_i is a vector of decision rule parameters. In orthodox theory, the decision rule would be viewed as the best of all possible ones, given a firm's objectives and its (well-defined) production set. In our evolutionary theory the firm just has that rule.

Let X equal the ΣX_i and K equal ΣX_i. Then, for the industry at time t:

$$\left(\frac{X}{K}\right)^t = \sum D(P, d_i^t) \left(\frac{K_i}{K}\right) \tag{2}$$

Even if all input prices remain constant, there is no assurance that X/K or, equivalently, X/Q (where Q is industry output), will be constant over time. Even with constant input prices, input proportions may change because of R & D, or operations research, which will result in a change in firms' routines (decision rules). The relative capital weight attached to different rules may change as some firms grow and others decline. At some time beyond t, say T, $(X/K)^T_0$ will be:

$$\left(\frac{X}{K}\right)^T_0 = \sum D[P_0, d_i^t] \left(\frac{K_i}{K}\right)^t$$

$$+ \sum \left(D[P_0, d_{i0}^T] - D[P_0, d_i^t] \right)\left(\frac{K_i}{K}\right)^t$$

$$+ \sum D[P_0, d_{i0}^T] \left(\left(\frac{K_i}{K}\right)^T_0 - \left(\frac{K_i}{K}\right)^t\right) \tag{3}$$

The superscripts T and t identify the time at which the variables are measured. The subscript zero has been used to tag variables that might be different at time T if the price regime were different. Given this notation, the first term is, of course $(X/K)^t$. The second term accounts for the effects of the evolution of rules between t and T weighted by capital stocks initially (at time t). The final term accounts for selection effects that change share weights for the final rules.

The canonical question of comparative statics is – what happens when (input) prices change. In the formulation here the comparison might be between a regime of constant input prices (P_0) and one in which, at time t, one of the prices (that of oil) jumped and thereafter remained at the higher level. Call this regime P_1. One can devise an equation, similar to (3), to show what (X/K) will be at time T, under this different regime.

$$\left(\frac{X}{K}\right)_0^T = \sum D[P_1, d_i^t]\left(\frac{K_i}{K}\right)^t$$

$$+ \sum \left(D[P_1, d_{i1}^T] - D[P_1, d_i^t]\right)\left(\frac{K_i}{K}\right)^t$$

$$+ \sum D[P_1, d_{i1}^T]\left(\left(\frac{K_i}{K}\right)_1^T - \left(\frac{K_i}{K}\right)^t\right) \tag{4}$$

By subtracting equation (3) from equation (4), one can 'account for' the *difference* in X/K at time T under the two market regimes.

$$\left(\frac{X}{K}\right)_1^T - \left(\frac{X}{K}\right)_0^T = \sum \left(D[P_1, d_i^t] - D[P_0, d_i^t]\right)\left(\frac{K_i}{K}\right)^t$$

$$+ \sum \left(D[P_1, d_i^T] - D[P_1, d_i^t] - D[P_0, d_0^T]\right.$$

$$\left. + D[P_0, d_i^t]\right)\left(\frac{K_1}{K}\right)^t$$

$$+ \sum \left(D[P_1, d_i^T]\left(\left(\frac{K_i}{K}\right)_1^T - \left(\frac{K_i}{K}\right)^t\right)\right.$$

$$\left. - D[P_0, d_0^T]\left(\left(\frac{K_i}{K}\right)_0^T - \left(\frac{K_i}{K}\right)^t\right)\right). \tag{5}$$

The first term (or, properly, the terms under the first summation) can be viewed as the result of firms' moving along the decision rules at time t in response to a change in price from P_0 to P_1. The second term reflects the fact that decision rules may evolve differently under the two regimes. The final term accounts for the difference in selection effects.

The above decomposition of the difference made by a price change could be regarded as merely a matter of accounting, without causal significance. We believe, however, that the separation we propose is useful analytically, because the three terms correspond to the operation of analytically-distinguishable mechanisms. Although what is essential to the theorising is that separable mechanisms are involved, we put forth as a tentative empirical proposition that the three effects occur at different speeds and that it is convenient to think of the along-the-rule effect as occurring promptly; followed by the appearance of differential innovation effects; followed, in turn, by differential selection effects. Our discussion of the individual mechanisms is relevant, however, whether the different mechanisms are assumed to operate in this sequence, some other sequence, or – realistically – concurrently.

In any case, the prototypical question of positive economic theory is: What is the sign of the difference analysed in equation (5) – say, the sign of the response of the intensity of use of an input to a rise in its price? In deference to tradition and the weight of empirical evidence, we shall call results that accord with orthodox qualitative predictions 'standard' and results that fail to accord 'perverse'.

Orthodox theory derives its 'standard' results from the assumption of profit maximisation over a given choice set. In terms of the accounting framework above, orthodox theory may be interpreted as a theory about responses governed by decision rules. The second and third terms are not considered. Our analysis involves both rejection of the orthodox view of the derivation of decision rules, and emphasis on the likely importance of the second and third terms.

For the overall response of an industry to be standard, it would be sufficient for each of the three terms in our accounting to carry the sign of standard response. Or, more modestly, the hope is that the expectations can plausibly be argued to be standard. But this is not hard.

One does not have to accept the view that a firm's sole objective is profit – and that its built-in decision rules are 'optimal' – to be comfortable with the presumption that firms *do* pay attention to profitability and *have* given some thought to whether their policies serve that objective. If firms have any routines at all for shifting among inputs in response to changes in input prices, one would expect the sign of that 'along-the-rule' effect to be standard. It also is plausible that if innovation is affected at all by the changes in factor prices, it ought to be nudged in a standard direction. Even if prices did not affect the kinds of R & D activities undertaken, but if firms screened their completed R & D endeavours to see if these new technologies would save on total costs, a jump in oil prices would have a standard effect on innovation. Actually, one would expect significant changes in the price of an input to focus effort specifically on doing something to economise on that particular input, or substitute away from it. The third term in the decomposition captures the effect of different price regimes on the growth or decline of firms that have different (time-T) decision rules. Again, under a variety of assumptions, selection effects will be standard. One can prove that this is the case, for example, if 'along-the-rule' and search responses occur very rapidly, so that the capital stock can be considered in effect constant while these changes are going on; and if firms' growth rates are linearly related to their profit rates.

Thus, models within an evolutionary theory are quite capable of explaining, and predicting, the standard kind of response of firms and industries to changes in market conditions. Further, I propose that, while somewhat more complicated, the richer formulation provided by an evolutionary theory corresponds much better to what economists really believe happens than does the characterisation of the streamlined, orthodox theory. For example, consider analysis of the effects of the rise of oil prices in the 1970s. Most economists recognise that most firms did not have pre-existing plans for coping with a large jump in oil prices. A few did – notably certain public utilities that had, in the past, the practice of switching among alternative fuel sources in response to changes in prices – but for most this was a situation not faced before, and not thought about much. Not all firms would be equally successful in thinking through what to do, or in carrying out R & D to discover or create ways to substitute or conserve. Part of the process of responding would involve induced innovation, and part of it a winnowing-out of firms on the basis of who coped effectively and who did not. This relatively complex verbal story is not well made abstract be discussed in terms of 'picking a different point along an isoquant'. Models within an evolutionary theory come much closer to characterising it.

The perspective provided by evolutionary theory opens up some issues that tend to be ignored under the orthodox formulation. As a prominent example, consider a concept like 'elasticity of substitution' or 'elasticity of supply'. Contemporary formalism takes these as 'technologically-determined data' and not as variables that themselves can be 'explained' by a deeper structural analysis that may also reveal them to be manipulable. An evolutionary theory of the response of firm and industry would suggest that substitution-and supply-responsiveness would be functions of the quantity and quality of 'searching' and 'innovating' that higher prices drew forth. Some of the key parameters of orthodox theory thus become endogenous in evolutionary theory.

Suppose that the policy question is how to induce desirable patterns of substitution. From an orthodox perspective, the inclination is to propose to: 'let the market work'. From an evolutionary point of view, where the elasticities of supply and substitution are not taken as given, the analyst can begin to think about how they can, and perhaps should, be influenced by government policies. In particular, the question of the appropriate role of government in facilitating or guiding the R & D effort might become a topic of enquiry. Questions such as whether certain important R & D projects generate significant externalities, or whether they require support on a scale beyond the resources of firms in the industry, are naturally called forth. This is not to say that these issues are easy to think through. But one of the advantages of evolutionary theory is that they are signalled. A serious indictment of the orthodox perspective is that, in almost all analyses of the energy policy question by economists, they are ignored.

III LONG RUN ECONOMIC GROWTH FUELLED BY TECHNICAL ADVANCE

Contemporary orthodox theory of the behaviour of the firm and industry focuses mainly on the behaviour of firms operating with given technologies. In view of the history of Western economics, this is something of a puzzle. Much of Adam Smith's *The Wealth of Nations* is about what today would be called technical change and economic growth. These were the concerns of many of the great classical economists. It is not easy to understand exactly why microeconomic theory was purged of serious concern with long-run change. One reason certainly was that it proved easier to provide a satisfactory mathematical statement of static theory then of a dynamic one. It also was the case that, during the period when these intellectual developments were occurring, economists tended to lose their interest in economic growth, although it is hard here to separate cause and effect.

In any case, the consequence was that in the 1950s when many economists again became interested in patterns of long-run economic growth they found themselves without a well-developed growth theory. First attempts at constructing one involved the Harrod–Domar extensions of Keynesian analysis. However, these models, which repressed factor substitution, proved poor tools for facilitating thinking about rising capital–labour ratios and increasing incomes per head, which were obviously salient features of observed growth patterns. By the late 1950s, growth theorists had responded to the need to understand these features by borrowing heavily from the intellectual tool-kit of static, neo-classical microeconomics.[3]

The result was a model identical in spirit to those in the standard price theory text book, but with accommodations in two ways to the different task. Factors of production, particularly capital, were seen as growing in quantity over time. Technical advance, in the form of a 'shift' in the production function, was allowed. The latter was a necessary accommodation to the fact that the observed patterns of growth seemed inexplicable if the economy were viewed simply as moving along a constant production function. By the late 1950s it had become apparent that technical advance, measured as the 'residual', was as large as that portion of the growth of total output which was explained by growth of conventional factors of production.

This would not be an embarrassment if what scholars learned about technical change turned out to be consistent with the basic assumptions of the model. These included, prominently, literal maximising behaviour on the part of the firm's managers, and (moving) equilibrium of the system as a whole. But observations about the micro-economics of technical change would appear to be grossly inconsistent with these assumptions. We have, for example, much evidence about the role of insight in the invention process, and of significant differences in the ability of inventors to 'see things' that are not obvious to all who are looking. Yet, once one inventor has made a breakthrough, others may see how to do similar, perhaps even better, things. Relatedly, there are considerable differences among firms, at any time, in terms of the technology used, productivity and profitability. Although these studies clearly show that purpose and calculation play an important role, the observed differences among persons and firms are hard to reconcile with simple notions of maximisation – that is, unless some explicit account is taken of differences in knowledge, maximising capabilities and luck. And the Schumpeterian competition process, involving 'creative destruction', is hard to reconcile with any notion of moving equilibrium.

Yet, clearly, neo-classical growth theory has been a useful instrument for studying and interpreting the macro-economic variables. The challenge for an evolutionary theory is to be as good as (maybe better than) neo-clasical theory in dealing with aggregates, but to be more consistent with (and perhaps even explain) the micro-economic patterns. Much of our early work was aimed at achieving just these objectives.

A model we employed contained the following elements. All feasible 'techniques' were assumed to be of the Leontief variety, employing a fixed amount of labour and a fixed amount of capital per unit of output. The firm's output rule was always to operate at full capacity. Its investment rule was, essentially, to plow back all profits into gross investment, (existing capital stocks were subject to depreciation). Firms engaged in two different kinds of 'search'. One kind, which we called 'internal' search, involved their sampling of the population of feasible techniques. Such search was 'local' in the sense that a firm was more likely to find a technique 'close' to its current technique than one that was far away. The other kind of search involved looking at what competitor firms were doing. If a newly-found technique was more profitable than the prevailing one, a firm switched over all its capital to the new technique. In so doing, it established, of course, a new location for local search. The context was a macro-economy with Say's law assumed. At any time, the economy faced an upward-sloping labour supply curve; over time, this curve shifted to the right as the labour supply grew. Any growth in the quantity of capital was, of course, endogenous to the analysis.

This model has the Markovian structure which most of our evolutionary models possess. We may start the system with a number of firms, each with a capital stock, and each possessing a particular technique. The 'operate-at-capacity' rule determines, for each firm, and for the industry, output and employment. The labour supply curve is then consulted to determine the wage rate. The 'profits' of each firm is simply output minus the wage bill. (Output price is the numeraire.) The next period's capital stocks are then generated. Firms adopt, probabilistically, new techniques which they find through local search; or they imitate techniques of others, if others come up with a technique that is more profitable than the one they have. The techniques associated with each firm in the next period are then determined. The labour supply curve shifts to the right. The process begins anew.

Since we wanted to see how well such a model would perform in tracking the macro-economic time path that Solow attempted to explain in his original article, we set initial conditions so that the overall constellation was roughly 'right' for the year 1909. We then ran the model for forty periods, the length of time which Solow explored. We did this in a large number of runs, varying a number of the key, model parameters. We aimed to get a set of parameters which tracked the real data reasonably well, but in no way did we try to get a 'best' fit.

Some of our time paths were way off the actual ones, others fitted the data quite well. It turned out to be relatively easy to set up the model so that the macro-economic time path generated by it would reveal a rising output per worker, a rising capital labor ratio, a rising wage rate, a roughly-constant rate of return on capital and a similarly constant share of capital in total income. Table 15.1 presents both data from one of our simulations and Solow's actual data.

We think, regarding the macro-economic data, that the contest should be regarded a 'tie'. The time paths of the central macro-economic variables are explained just as well by an evolutionary model, as by a neo-classical one.

An econometrician looking at the macro-economic data generated by virtually any of our runs would have a hard time in rejecting the hypothesis (Solow's) that the time series were generated by a Cobb–Douglas, neutral-technical-change, process; although they obviously were not.

We think, however, that our model provides a more plausible explanation of the macro-economic time paths than does the Cobb–Douglas model. Once the parameters (basic institutions?) are set in a way that encourages capital to grow faster than labour supply then, in our model, as in the orthodox one, wage rates rise. In our model, as in the orthodox one, rising wage rates make previously-unprofitable, capital-intensive techniques profitable to adopt; and they make unprofitable labour-intensive techniques which used to be profitable. Innovation is nudged in a labour-saving direction, and both the capital–labour ratio and output per worker rise. This is the neo-classical account also, but within our theory we are able to express the logic without assuming maximisation or equilibrium: only profit-oriented calculating behaviour, and competitive selection-pressure. It is a much more plausible story.

Even if the contest were viewed as a tie at the macro-economic level, at the micro-economic level there is no contest. As stated,

TABLE 15.1   SELECTED TIME SERIES FROM SIMULATION RUN
0001, COMPARED WITH SOLOW DATA, 1909–49

Year	Q/L Sim.	Q/L Solow	K/L Sim.	K/L Solow	W Sim.	W Solow	S_A Sim.	S_A Solow	A Sim.	A Solow
1903	0.66	0.73	1.85	2.06	0.51	0.49	0.23	0.34	1.000	1.000
1910	0.68	0.72	1.84	2.10	0.54	0.48	0.21	0.33	1.020	0.933
1911	0.69	0.76	1.83	2.17	0.52	0.50	0.25	0.34	1.040	1.021
1912	0.71	0.76	1.91	2.21	0.50	0.51	0.30	0.33	1.059	1.023
1913	0.74	0.80	1.94	2.23	0.51	0.53	0.31	0.33	1.096	1.054
1914	0.72	0.80	1.86	2.20	0.61	0.54	0.15	0.33	1.087	1.071
1915	0.74	0.78	1.89	2.26	0.56	0.51	0.24	0.34	1.103	1.041
1916	0.76	0.82	1.89	2.34	0.60	0.53	0.21	0.36	1.136	1.076
1917	0.78	0.80	1.93	2.21	0.59	0.50	0.23	0.37	1.159	1.005
1918	0.78	0.85	1.90	2.22	0.62	0.56	0.21	0.34	1.169	1.142
1919	0.80	0.90	1.96	2.47	0.57	0.53	0.29	0.35	1.199	1.157
1920	0.80	0.84	1.94	2.58	0.64	0.58	0.19	0.32	1.192	1.069
1921	0.81	0.90	2.00	2.55	0.61	0.57	0.25	0.37	1.208	1.116
1922	0.83	0.92	2.02	2.49	0.65	0.61	0.21	0.34	1.225	1.183
1923	0.83	0.95	1.97	2.61	0.70	0.63	0.17	0.34	1.243	1.126
1924	0.86	0.98	2.05	2.74	0.64	0.66	0.25	0.33	1.274	1.245
1925	0.89	1.02	2.19	2.81	0.59	0.68	0.33	0.34	1.293	1.254
1926	0.87	1.02	2.07	2.87	0.74	0.63	0.15	0.33	1.288	1.244
1927	0.90	1.02	2.16	2.93	0.67	0.69	0.25	0.32	1.324	1.235
1928	0.91	1.02	2.18	3.62	0.70	0.68	0.23	0.34	1.336	1.226
1929	0.94	1.05	2.27	3.06	0.68	0.70	0.28	0.33	1.370	1.251
1930	0.93	1.03	2.47	3.30	0.62	0.67	0.37	0.35	1.394	1.197
1931	0.49	1.06	2.46	3.38	0.70	0.71	0.29	0.33	1.403	1.226
1932	1.62	1.03	2.57	3.28	0.69	0.62	0.32	0.40	1.435	1.108
1933	1.02	1.02	2.46	3.40	0.85	0.65	0.46	0.36	1.452	1.214
1934	1.04	1.08	2.45	3.00	0.85	0.70	0.19	0.36	1.486	1.298
1935	1.05	1.10	2.44	2.87	0.87	0.72	0.17	0.35	1.500	1.349
1936	1.06	1.15	2.51	2.72	0.82	0.74	0.22	0.36	1.499	1.429
1937	1.06	1.14	2.55	2.71	0.83	0.75	0.22	0.34	1.500	1.415
1938	1.11	1.17	2.74	2.78	0.76	0.73	0.32	0.33	1.543	1.445
1939	1.10	1.21	2.66	2.66	0.88	0.79	0.20	0.35	1.540	1.514
1940	1.13	1.27	2.75	2.63	0.84	0.82	0.25	0.36	1.576	1.590
1941	1.16	1.31	2.77	2.58	0.90	0.82	0.23	0.38	1.618	1.660
1942	1.18	1.33	2.78	2.64	0.95	0.86	0.20	0.36	1.641	1.665
1943	1.49	1.38	2.79	2.62	0.93	0.91	0.22	0.34	1.652	1.733
1944	1.20	1.48	2.80	2.63	0.97	0.99	0.20	0.33	1.672	1.856
1945	1.21	1.52	2.82	2.66	0.97	1.04	0.20	0.31	1.683	1.895
1946	1.23	1.42	2.88	2.50	0.96	0.93	0.22	0.31	1.694	1.842
1947	1.23	1.40	2.89	2.50	0.93	0.94	0.21	0.33	1.701	1.791
1948	1.23	1.43	2.87	2.55	1.01	0.95	0.18	0.33	1.698	1.809
1919	1.23	1.49	2.82	2.70	1.04	1.01	0.15	0.33	1.703	1.852

Q/L   Output (1929 dollars per man-hour; Solow data adjusted from 1939 to 1929 dollars by
       multiplying by 1.171 = ratio of implicit price deflators for GNP).
K/L   Capital (1929 dollars per man-hour).
W   Wage Rate (1929 dollars per man-hour; Solow data adjusted from 1939 to 1929 dollars.
S_A Capital share (= 1 – labour share)
A   Solow technology index. Recalculation on the basis of figures in other columns will not
       check exactly, because of rounding of those figures. Solow figures shown for 1944–49
       are correct: the values originally published were in error.)

much of the micro-economic observation about technical change, and related phenomena, is flatly inconsistent with the standard formulation, even when this is doctored to admit things like different vintages of capital. Our model generated distributions – across firms – of variables like productivity level and firm-sizes. The productivity distributions are reminiscent of those published by the BLS and studied some time ago by Salter. I propose that they are much more-consistent with the mechanisms assumed in our model, than with those in his. The distribution of sizes of firm generated by the model is also reminiscent of actual, empirical observations.

Our model produced data about the spread of new techniques among the firms in the industry. The shapes of these 'diffusion' curves were similar to those found by scholars studying diffusion, except that in most cases the use of a new technique eventually began to fall off, as still-newer techniques superseded it.

We think we have met the challenge. Our account of economic growth and of technical change is simultaneously consistent both, in quantitative terms, with the broad features of macro-economic time series and, qualitatively, with such micro-economic phenomena as cross-section dispersions in capital–labour ratios and inefficiency, and with patterns of diffusion of techniques. While the neo-classical account can achieve the former, it is flatly inconsistent with the micro-economic phenomena associated with technical change.

IV   MODELLING COMPETITION IN THE SENSE OF SCHUMPETER

For many sectors of the economy, Schumpeter's characterisation of competition seems much more to the point than the view presented in orthodox textbooks. In electronics, pharmaceuticals and many other industries, and even without playing down the role of pricing strategies and wars, it is plain that competition among firms centrally involves their R & D policy – its successes and failures. And, as Schumpeter stressed, in the long run the gains to society from continuing innovation are vastly greater than those associated with competition in pricing.[4]

In articulating this view of competition, Schumpeter also put forth what has been called the 'Schumpeterian hypothesis': that a market structure, involving firms with a considerable degree of market power, is the price that society must pay for rapid technological advance. Thus, there is a trade-off between static efficiency, in the sense of prices close to marginal production cost, and dynamic progressiveness. It is not clear how much choice Schumpeter thought society actually had regarding the mix between static efficiency and dynamic progressivity, but many contemporary economists clearly write as if they think that market structure is a variable potentially under tight public control.

I should like to distinguish between Schumpeter's general propositions about the nature and social value of competition in technically-progressive industries, and his specific hypothesis about market structure and technical change. One can accept the right-headedness of the former while remaining open-minded or sckeptical about the latter. For many reasons, it is of high priority to get a better theoretical grip on the nature of Schumpeterian competition. One of these reasons is to explore what trade-offs, if any, there are: but there are many other interesting questions. It is difficult to fashion models based on orthodox theory that can come to grips with Schumpeterian competition; the assumptions of maximisation and equilibrium get in the way. The basic concepts of evolutionary theory seem much better-fashioned to the task.

In Schumpeterian competition there are winners and losers; but it is unlikely to be clear, before the fact, which player will be first, or last. Winning is partly a matter of having a good strategy. But it is not easy to judge, *ex-ante*, what the best strategies are likely to be. Different firms make different bets. Only actual experience will tell whose bet were right and whose wrong. One cannot adequately explore this process with a model which assumes that the contest is over and that it has resulted in a tie.

Once one thinks about Schumpeterian competition from the viewpoint of evolutionary theory, it is plain that the causal connections between technical change and market structure flow both ways. Large firms may, or may not, be good at innovation, but firms that are good at innovation will tend to be profitable, to grow and so to become large. If both luck and size contribute to innovation, there is the possibility here for competition to destroy itself as a successful innovator comes to dominate the industry. On the other hand, if innovation is costly and imitation relatively easy, firms that try to innovate may be able to survive only if they are large. There is clearly a rich set of dynamic possibilities here, which cannot possibly be attacked with orthodox tools.

We have attempted to attack them with a model similar, in many respects, to the one discussed in the preceding section, but one tailored for analysis of Schumpeterian competition. The principal differences between the present model and the former one are as follows. First, differences (among techniques) in the capital–labour ratio are repressed; techniques are assumed to differ only in their 'total efficiency'. Efficiency is defined in terms of output per unit of capital. Second, the R & D policies of firms are assumed to link the total quantity of R & D that they carry out with their size. The size of a firm's R & D budget determines the probability that the firm will find an element in the urn where it is searching. Thus, large firms, who spend more R & D, have a greater chance of successfully-drawing from the relevant distributions. Third, by contrast with the model of Section III, in the one discussed here the investment of a firm is linked not only to its profits, but also to its market share. Unlike small firms, firms whose sales account for a significant fraction of the market may hold back their own growth in order to avoid spoiling the market. Fourth, this is a 'sectoral' model, with a down-ward-sloping demand curve; the wage rate is an exogenous parameter.

The following formulation simplifies, in certain respects, our actual simulation mode, but it displays the basic logic.

$$Q_{it} = A_{it} K_{it} \qquad (6)$$

The output of firm i, at time t, equals its capital stock times the productivity of the technique it is using. In addition,

$$P_t = D(\Sigma Q_{it}) \qquad (7)$$

and

$$\Pi_{it} = P_t A_{it} - c - r_i. \qquad (8)$$

Profit on capital equals revenues minus production costs minus R & D costs, all per unit of capital.

$$K_i(t + i) = I \left(\Pi_{it}, \frac{Q_{it}}{\Sigma Q_{it}} \right) K_{it}. \qquad (9)$$

That is, the relative growth, or decline, of a firm's capital is determined by its profit rate and its market shares.

$$P_r (\text{draw} = 1) = a r_i k_{it} \qquad (10)$$

The probability that a firm will get a 'draw' (successful innovation) from a relevant population of alternative technologies is proportional to its total R & D spending. The populations which are drawn from include the population defined by the technologies employed by other firms; and that defined by the 'technological opportunities' facing the firm (which we specify in several different ways). For a firm that has both an *imitation* draw A^m, and an *innovation* draw, A^n, the productivity level next achieved is given by

$$A_{i(t+i)} = \text{Max} (A_{it} A_{it}^m A_{it}^n) \tag{11}$$

Of course, a firm may not have so rich a set to choose from.

Such a model is well-designed to examine the conditions under which competition will and will not tend to destroy itself. In our model, at least, three factors make an important difference. The first is the magnitude of the efficiency-edge that the average innovation yields the innovating firm over its competitors. The second is the ease, or difficulty, of imitation, in the sense of the expected amount of R & D resources that will need to be applied before a successful innovation of one firm can be copied by another. Third, there is the extent to which profitable, large firms continue to press their advantage through further growth. In circumstances where innovation does not give a major advantage, and where imitation is relatively easy, an initial competitive structure tends to be preserved. By contrast, where significant advantages go to the innovator, where imitation is difficult, and where investment behaviour is aggressive, there is a high likelihood that a dominant firm will emerge.

Once a firm with a superior technology comes to account for a large share of the industry's output, the competitive fringe is unlikely to recover. In competition against the dominant firm, small firms are at a disadvantage because of their smaller R & D spending. If a small firm produces a profitable innovation, that firm can expect only a limited time for its exploitation before the dominant firm copies its new techniques or devises something better. The limits on a firm's growth rate mean that, in that sheltered interval, the smaller innovator is likely to be able to make up for only a small portion of its disadvantage in size, and R & D spending.

In the model summarised above, we assumed that all firms spend both on R & D aimed at innovation and on R & D aimed at imitation. In another model, we assumed that some firms chose to spend both on innovative and imitative R & D, and others on imitative R & D only. The natural question then arises – under what conditions will the innovators thrive and prosper: and under what conditions will innovation be driven from the industry? The above discussion suggests that this depends on whether innovation, if achieved, is likely to give a significant advantage; and on how costly it is to imitate an innovation. Where a successful innovation is likely to give only a small advantage, and where imitation is relatively easy, innovators do not fare so well. Imitators will tend to lag somewhat technologically, but in these circumstances this is not a serious penalty. Moreover it is often more than offset by the fact that imitators spend less on R & D. Where large, profitable imitators are aggressive in their investment behaviour, innovators tend to be run out of the industry.

Indeed, even if innovations when they occur are relatively major, and if imitation is quite costly, where for some reason a large imitator arises in the industry, the innovative firms are likely to be in trouble. The trouble may be very serious if that large imitator continues to expand his capacity aggressively whenever he is profitable. As he grows, and as the innovators shrink, the latters' chances of innovating again decline; and the expected advantages to them if they do identify a new innovation diminish as well.

What difference does this make for the overall productivity growth of the industry? Of course, this ought to depend on the relationship between the amount of innovative R & D spending in the industry, and the overall rate of technical advance in it. One can think of several different possibilities. One is that innovative R & D in the industry may consist largely of exploiting new ideas created by outside science, or by making use of a flow of new materials and components created by their supplier-industries. In this case a low level of innovative R & D activity in the industry itself would result in there being a jerkier time path for best practice and a somewhat lower overall track to it then would exist if internal innovative R & D higher were, but not necessarily a slower rate of growth of productivity. On the other hand, if technical change in the industry results largely from its own internal R & D expenditure and if today's R & D efforts build on yesterday's R & D successes, a lower level of internal R & D spending might be expected to translate itself into a slower rate of advance of best- and average-practice technology.

Our models of Schumpeterian competition tend to confirm these conjectures. Or, rather, working with our models got us to think about them. Whereas Schumpeterian competition has proved very difficult terrain to explore with models built along orthodox lines, the subject seems to represent natural turf for the implementation of ideas drawn from evolutionary theory.

V   EVOLUTIONARY THEORY: RADICAL NEW DEPARTURE, OR RETURN TO AN OLD PATH?

The general theoretical framework, and the specific models, that Winter and I have been developing are certainly heterodox, and would be regarded by some as heresy. Yet, from another point of view, what we are doing is not radical at all. Our endeavour can be regarded as an attempt to build models consonant with the verbal theories that economists put forth, when they are not bound by their formal theories. Our evolutionary theory also may be interpreted as an attempt to shift formal economic theory back to the path defined by the great nineteenth- and early twentieth-century economists. These are the views we hold.

In our discussion of the response of a firm and industry to changed market conditions, we called attention to a disjunction between the verbal account of the phenomena which most economists would give, and the characterisation given by prevailing, formal theory. We argue that this is a widespread phenomenon in contemporary economics. The verbal story is not only more elaborated and more complex than the cleaner, simpler formal theory; it is structurally different. Put another way, the tension is not to be understood as simply the natural difference between attempts at description and attempts at abstraction. The verbal story often is quite abstract. The tension is between two different theories.

Many economists recognise this, though most of them not clearly enough. What lies behind this self-inflicted schizophrenia? Winter and I propose that it has been the widespread acceptance within the profession, since the 1950s, of maximisation-cum-equilibrium as the only respectable behavioural assumptions for *formal* theorising.

Yet, until the post-Second World War era, economists did not force themselves to live by these theoretical canons. The current intellectual schizophrenia did not afflict the great economic theorists of yesteryear. Smith saw businessmen and traders as greedy and clever, and after a buck (or a pound) wherever they saw the opportunity. He stressed that profit opportunities called out for someone to come and seize them, and that the call seldom went unheeded. But while economic man of Smith's theory is purposive and clever, Smith never said that he was literally a maximiser. And, while for Smith opportunities drew action, Smithian economics is not about systems in equilibrium in any meaningful sense. So, with Mill, so with Marshall, Pigou, Taussig, and most of the landmark figures of Western economics, until about the Second World War. For these scholars there was far less of a gap between their descriptive accounts and their formal analyses than is common, and accepted, today. These earlier scholars seemed more interested in achieving a theory that fitted the economic reality as they saw it neither than one that was, simply, elegant.

It is true that the earlier generations of theorists held mathematical rigor as less-important than does this generation. However, mathematical formalisation of the great unifying ideas of Western economics need not translate human rationality into maximisation: and competition among firms into the contemporary concept of equilibrium. Herbert Simon has elaborated the limitations and difficulties of the first translation. Joseph Schumpeter has provided an important alternative to the second. Advances in the theory of stochastic processes, and the coming of age of the computer, give the economist a far-wider range of mathematical tools to exploit in constructing theory than were available until recently.

The evolutionary models that Winter and I have been developing are somewhat crude and clumsy. Their first-generation vintage stands out all over them. But, with a little reflection, the ideas behind them can be recognised as venerable. Also, they appear to be abstract versions of those which are economists commonly employ when we explain to laymen what is going on in a particular economic context. Surely, there is some advantage in working with a formal theory that abstracts from the real world what we think 'really is going on out there'.

NOTES

1. For example, see his 'Satisficing, Selection and the Innovating Remnant', *Quarterly Journal of Economics*, vol. 85, pp. 273–281.
   In Chapter 6 of our new book we deal more broadly with the question.
2. The following discussion draws from 'Firm and Industry Response to Changed Market Conditions: An Evolutionary Approach', *Economic Inquiry*, vol. 18, pp. 179–202. See also Chapter 7 of our book.
3. The following discussion draws from 'Neoclassical vs. Evolutionary Theories of Economic Growth: Critique and Prospectus', *Economic Journal*, vol. 84, pp. 886–905 and 'Technical Change in an Evolutionary Model', *Quarterly Journal of Economics*, vol. 90, pp. 90–118. See also Chapters 8 to 11 of our book.
4. We deal with Schumpeterian competition in our 'forces generating and limiting concentration under Schumpeterian competition', *Bell Journal of Economics*, vol. 9, pp. 524–48 and 'The Schumpeterian Tradeoff Revisited', *American Economic Review* vol. 72, pp. 115–32. See also Chapters 12 to 14 of our book.

Discussion of the Paper by Richard R. Nelson

Brouwer began by questioning Nelson's conclusion that technical advance occurred as a result of technological shock or other exogenous forces. To illustrate her point she cited that recent history of the automobile industry in the US, which did not respond to increases in oil process by developing energy-saving technology until forced to do so by Federal Government regulations. The same objection applied to the introduction of labour-saving devices by firms seen as a response to the relative increase of the supply of capital and of the price of labour. Causality may also run the other way, in which the introduction of labour saving innovations were responsible for rising wages. On the question of whether small or large firms would be more likely to undertake research, she argued the appearance of new products and technologies involved a two-stage process. The investment in R & D must be distinguished from the investment in new production capacity that was required to make (successful) innovations to the R & D results. Even if large firms did spend more on research, it did not follow that these firms necessarily led in development. In fact, development of new products and procedures was an aspect of entrepreneurship that was often supplied by smaller and new firms.

Nelson responded that it was inappropriate to characterise the Nelson–Winter models as presuming that technological innovation was generally the result of 'shock'. He commented, similarly, that the connections between firm size and R & D upon which Brouwer commented were built into some of the models, but not others. He suggested the real issues lay in evolutionary modelling as a general flexible art form, rather than the adequacy of a particular model.

Schmalensee suggested that Nelson's paper involved three innovations: a focus on the dynamics of an economic system rather than on the steady state of that system; a reliance on the computer to analyse complex economic models; and an acceptance of bounded rationality in decision making. He questioned, however, whether dynamic systems which had been designed specifically to track data, like the Nelson and Winter system, could ever be tested. Further, he wondered whether new policy prescriptions based on models of this kind would be saleable if they did not agree with prescriptions of received economic theory.

Gilbert argued that the principal contentious issue involved in this sort of modelling was that the search rules used by people were not endogenous. One attempt to endogenise search rules was the paper by Akerloff and Dickens (1982) on cognitive dissonance. Cognitive dissonance led people to discount information that would otherwise cause them to change their decision rules. In this case, rules changed slowly. Gilbert also argued that the Nelson paper ignored the important distinction between technical progress and substitution of capital for labour. Low measured rates of technical progress that occurred after the oil embargo seem to contradict the plausible conjecture that technical progress would be positively correlated with factor-price changes. If technical progress was interpreted as a substitution of capital for labour, however, this empirical fact was perfectly natural.

In *Horvat's* view, at the macro level, the usual production function could be used, at most, for the measurement of technological change. The elasticities of, for example, Cobb–Douglas function had no relation whatsoever to actual changes of output in response to changes in capital and labour. This was primarily due to the fact that technological change was mostly embodied and the function which did not take this into account could not serve as a *production* function. It could be shown that the Cobb–Douglas function with disembodied technical change was simply a different name for geometric aggregation in the global productivity measurement.

Phlips argued that there was not a contradiction between maximisation theories and the new behavioural theories. For example, it was possible to incorporate consumer inertia directly in maximising models of consumer choice. Similarly, many of the results generated by Nelson could also be rationalised by maximising models by considering specific dynamics.

Joseph Stiglitz raised three issues for future research in evolutionary modelling. First, he proposed that a difficult problem for this theory would be welfare analysis. Since the choice set available to the agents and to the economy was not well defined, it would be difficult to derive a welfare concept like Pareto optimality to evaluate the consequences of actions in evolutionary models. It might be possible to compare the probability distribution over outcomes generated by different policy prescriptions without asking whether there was a best policy. Second, Stiglitz wondered how strategic interactions could be incorporated into evolutionary models. Finally, Stiglitz suggested that in contrast to the spirit of evolutionary modelling, psychological research suggested that people actually used simple models to explain the way in which the world behaved. These simple models yielded behaviour on the part of economic agents. The models could thrown out (and replaced) when they predicted very poorly. Therefore, it was the choice of (simple) models by individuals that evolved through time.

REFERENCE

Akerloff, G. A. and Dickens, W. T. (1982) 'The Economic Consequences of Cognitive Dissonance', *American Economic Review*, Jun. pp. 72–73.

16 Cost Reduction, Competition and Industry Performance[1]

Michael Spence

HARVARD UNIVERSITY, CAMBRIDGE, MASS., USA

I INTRODUCTION

In many markets, firms compete over time by expending resources with the purpose of reducing their costs. Sometimes the cost-reducing investments operate directly on costs. In many instances, they take the form of developing new products that deliver what customers need more cheaply. Therefore product development can have the same ultimate effect as direct cost reduction. In fact, if one thinks of the product as the services it delivers to the customer (in the way that Lancaster pioneered), then product development often is just cost reduction.

Let me make this relationship between cost reduction and product development a little more precise. Suppose that products deliver services to consumers. Let s be the services and $P(s)$ be the inverse demand. Services are delivered through goods. Let x be the quantity of goods, and $c(x)$ be the cost function. Let $f(q)$ be the quantity of services per unit of the good. Then $s = f(q)x$, and the cost of delivering services s is $c(s/f(q))$. If $f'(q) > 0$, and q is raised through R & D of the product-development kind, then the effect is to reduce the costs of the service. Thus, formally, this kind of product development is equivalent to cost reduction.

The subject of R & D and industry performance has a long and distinguished history in economics. It is well known that there are at least three sorts of problems associated with industry performance.

475

And they occur simultaneously – making the problem of the overall assessment of performance quite complicated. The problems are these. Cost-reducing expenditures are largely fixed costs. In a market system, the criterion for determining the value of cost-reducing R & D is profitability, or revenues. Since revenues may understate the social benefits both in the aggregate and at the margin, there is no *a priori* reason to expect a market to bring about optimal results. Second, and related to this, because R & D represents a fixed cost, and because, depending upon the technological environment, it can sometimes be a large one, market structures are likely to be concentrated and imperfectly competitive. This has consequences for prices, margins and allocative efficiency.[2]

These two problems are not unique to R & D. They would and do characterise markets with product differentiation and with the fixed costs associated with the sale of a differentated product. The fact that the relevant economies of scale are dynamic is of interest, and worthy of exploration. But it is not unique to R & D.[3]

What is distinctive about R & D is that to these problems of differentiation and of scale economies is added what are often referred to as appropriability problems — sometimes referred to as externalities problems. These are really two versions of the same problem. If the R & D for the single firm is not appropriable, i.e., the benefits flow without payment to other firms, the initial incentives to do the R & D are reduced. On the other hand, the price of the results of the R & D, namely zero, is close to or at the correct price, namely marginal cost. The marginal cost is the cost of transmitting it to other firms. Restoring appropriability is sometimes regarded as a second-best solution to the problem of providing incentives, because it creates monopoly or monopoly power. It may do that. But it is important to note that it also prices incorrectly the good that the R & D has created. And that by itself has its social costs. An alternative effect of near-perfect appropriability (whether created by circumstances or policy) is not to eliminate competition, but rather to lead to redundant (and hence excessive) levels of R & D at the industry level. That is to say, the levels of cost reduction that obtain may be achieved at an excessively high cost. Thus there appears to be an unpleasant trade-off between incentives on the one hand and the efficiency with which the industry achieves the levels of cost reduction it actually does achieve, on the other.

II COMPETITIVE BEHAVIOUR AND MARKET
PERFORMANCE

My purpose here is to explore the interaction of these forces on competitive behaviour and on market performance. The qualitative propositions that will emerge are of the following kind.

(1) TECHNICAL EFFICIENCY

Let me focus first on market structure and dynamic technical efficiency. It is argued below that monopoly firms do relatively little R & D compared with the optimum, because of the absence of pressure to do so. A monopoly does increase its profits by reducing its costs. But those incentives are generally insufficient. What a monopoly lacks is exogenous downward price pressure of the type that could be created by either competition or regulation.

Assume for the moment that there are no spillovers or externalities, so that R & D is appropriable. That is to say, each firm's R & D influences only its own costs. Competition has two conflicting effects on R & D and technical efficiency. It creates downward price pressure for individual firms: that has the effect of increasing the incentives to carry out R & D and hence of improving technical efficiency. But, as the number of firms increases, market shares fall. Reduced sales dilute the incentive to reduce costs because the cost-reduction expenditures are fixed given the rate of cost decline; while the benefits decline as market share falls. Competition is then of limited value. It does improve market performance for small numbers of competitors. It is relatively easy to establish that in some cases dynamic efficiency increases and then falls, as concentration declines from monopoly levels.[4] The reason, however, is only partly that profitability declines. One can, in fact, observe the effect even when margins are constant. The reason is that mentioned above. The benefits to the individual firm decline as its share declines, regardless of whether industry profits hold up under increased potential competition. Of course, if margins decline, the effect is exacerbated.

The differences between market outcomes and optimal outcomes in the cost-reduction dimension are quite large in certain market environments. It is easy to find plausible examples in which costs ought to decline 40 per cent over some reasonable period of time like ten years, while the decline in the 'best' market outcome is 15 per cent.

As we shall see, it is possible to restore the dynamic efficiency of the market by subsidising R & D. It is shown late in this chapter that, with subsidies, dynamic technical efficiency can be restored completely. But pursuing such a policy is far from optimal. Remember that we are still discussing cases in which there are no externalities (R & D benefits are appropriated perfectly and influence only the costs of the firm that makes the expenditures). In the absence of externalities (or what might be termed spill-overs), the costs of achieving a given rate of cost reduction rise linearly with the number of firms. Thus in markets with low concentration, which are desirable from a static competitive standpoint, dynamic technical efficiency is achievable (through subsidies that reduce the marginal and total cost to the firm of R & D) but at a high cost. The reason is that the knowledge generated by the R & D of the individual firm is priced incorrectly. The correct price is the cost of the transmitting it to other firms (which we can assume is near zero for this discussion). With complete appropriability, the implicit price of the output of R & D eliminates the market in such transfers.

(2) SPILL-OVERS

Now suppose that there are substantial spill-overs, so that a significant part of the cost-reducing effects of a single firm's R & D accrue to other firms.[5]

There is then a reduced incentive for individual firms to engage in R & D. It does not automatically follow that industry cost reduction is less than it would be with effectively complete appropriability. While individual firms may do less R & D, the collective efforts of all of them are more productive with spill-overs; that is, a given level of industry expenditure on R & D will result in more cost reduction when there are spill-over effects of one firm's R & D on another's cost. Spill-overs thus have a formally ambiguous effect on the actual rate of cost reduction in the market.

But, more importantly, spill-overs involve at least a partial transfer of the results of R & D to other firms at no cost. At the level of the industry, aggregate R & D costs for achieving a *given* level of cost reduction are therefore lower. This brings me to what I regard as the most important point of this analysis. With spill-overs, subsidies can be used to restore damaged incentives, without incurring the high costs associated with redundancy in the non-appropriable case. And thus the *potential* performance of a market with significant spill-overs is greater than it is with complete appropriability.

Since this theme is at the centre of what I want to argue in the following pages, let me state the fundamental points in a slightly different way. The term 'market structure' will, for the moment, be used to refer to both the number and the size-distribution of firms (i.e., concentration), and also to the extent of spill-overs. The latter range from none at all, to complete, where complete means that R & D done by the firm is essentially a public good. It is available to everyone.

All market structures have potential incentive problems with respect to R & D. There is a pronounced tendency for the rate of cost reduction to fall short of optimal levels. By lowering the cost of R & D to the firm, through a variety of kinds of subsidy, incentives can be restored. That is to say, there is a policy instrument that operates directly on the incentive problem. But its efficacy as an instrument in improving the dynamic aspects of performance depends critically on the second element of structure, namely spill-overs or appropriability. Subsidising R & D essentially will not work as a performance-improving device in the absence of spill-overs, because any cost reduction achieved will be purchased at too high a cost.

One is tempted to think that the part of the incentive problem that is attributable to unpriced positive externalities can be solved institutionally. This might be achieved through patents, copyrights and other features of the legal system that have as their purpose the restoration of the incentives for investment in R & D. That thought is technically correct. But it is also misleading. First, policy-induced appropriability may not restore the incentives to the requisite level. And more important (and to the extent that it does not) it renders subsidies, the other policy instrument that operates on incentives by changing the costs to the firm of R & D, essentially useless. I do not mean to suggest that this problem arises in every market. My aim is rather that it would be recognised as a significant feature of the underlying problem, and not as an accident or an economic fluke. Appropriability whether present *de facto* or induced by the policy- and legal-environment, has the effect of establishing high prices for things (pieces of knowledge) which, once required by someone, have a social marginal cost that is small or zero. It is not, therefore, surprising that in circumstances where those prices are far from zero, the potential performance of the system when it is so constrained is less good than it would otherwise be.

There are of course numerous qualifications to this, and matters of detail also influence these trade-offs and outcomes. As I explained in Section I, I want to pursue them in this chapter through the use of models in which the R & D is all done very early, so that the models are reducible to static models. Then, in the Appendices, I shall develop the more-realistic models in which there are diminishing returns to R & D expenditure, so that R & D and cost reduction are spread out over time. And, in those models, I shall argue that the issues just discussed – and which the 'static' models illustrate – are also features of the dynamic competitive process. As was mentioned earlier, the dynamic analysis was carried out first. But the technical details are so numerous that they tend to obscure the economic intuition.

IV THE MODELS

Before developing such models, I call the reader's attention to Figure 16.1 which may help in setting out the features of structure and performance that the models attempt to capture.

Figure 16.1 highlights the important interactions among structure, competitive interaction and performance. Concentration increases margins and profits and also reduces allocative efficiency and these higher profits and margins increase R & D spending. Concentration by itself has an ambiguous effect on R & D. Generally, R & D by an industry will be a humped-shaped function of concentration. Appropriability increases incentives to do R & D, but it also lowers the industry's rate of cost reduction for a given level of R & D expenditures. Or, to put it the other way round, appropriability increases the industry's R & D cost for a given rate of cost reduction. That is the central ambiguity associated with appropriability or its absence – spill-overs. Subsidies increase incentives. R & D expenditures and the achieved rate of cost reduction together constitute dynamic technical efficiency (the amount of cost reduction and the resources required to achieve it). Finally, allocative efficiency and dynamic technical efficiency together constitute overall performance.

In certain market environments, subsidies should be used to solve the incentive problem (even if the solution is approximate). Spill-overs should be allowed or encouraged or even co-operative R & D permitted and encouraged, in order to lower the dollar R & D cost per percentage point of decline in other costs. In at least some of our industries where costs are declining rapidly, I believe that the policy environment, perhaps partially inadvertently, has been close to this in approach. And, in other countries, this approach is used with what

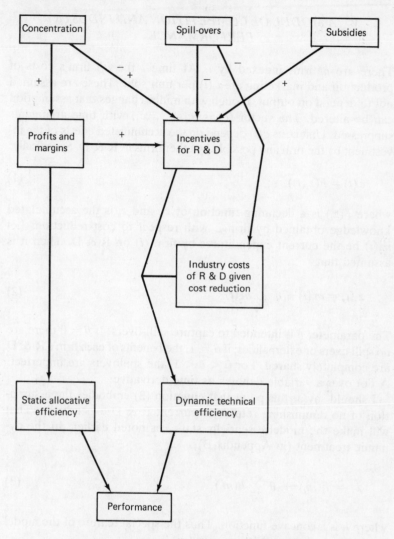

FIG. 16.1   R & D market structure relationships

seem to me to be effective results for both dynamic performance and for the establishment of the country's international competitive position. Part of my goal here is to begin the process of providing a conceptual structure for the debate that has already begun in these areas of economic policy.

V   A MODEL OF COMPETITION AND INDUSTRY PERFORMANCE

There are n firms indexed by i. At time t the *ith* firm's costs of production and marketing are $c_i(t)$ per unit sold. These are assumed not to depend on output, though with minor changes that assumption can be altered. The vector (c) is $(c_1, \ldots, c_n)$ with time arguments suppressed. Unit costs $c_i(t)$ depend on the accumulated effects of the investment by the firm and possibly by other firms in R & D. Specifically:

$$c_i(t) = F(z_i(t)), \tag{1}$$

where $F(z_i)$ is a declining function of z_i, and z_i is the accumulated knowledge obtained by firm i, with respect to cost reduction. Let $m_i(t)$ be the current expenditures by firm (i) on R & D. Then it is assumed that

$$\dot{z}_i(t) = m_i(t) + \theta \sum_{j \neq i} m_j(t). \tag{2}$$

The parameter θ is intended to capture spill-overs. If $\theta = 0$ there are no spill-overs or externalities; if $\theta = 1$, the benefits of each firm's R & D are completely shared. For $0 < \theta < 1$, the spillovers are imperfect. A dot over a variable denotes its time derivative.

I should say at this point that equation (2) embodies the assumption of no diminishing returns to current R & D expenditure. That will make the model essentially static, as noted earlier. In the dynamic treatment (in Appendix B),

$$\dot{z}_i = h(m_i) + \theta \sum_{j \neq i} h(m_j) \tag{3}$$

where h is a concave function. Thus the special feature of the model used here is that $h(m)$ is linear in (m).[6]

The goods produced by each firm are the same (the product is homogeneous). This, again, is an easily altered assumption.[7]

The inverse demand for the good is $P(x)$, where x is the quantity available in the market. The amount produced by firm i is x_i; thus $x = \Sigma_i x_i$. The profits of firm i are

$$\pi^i = x_i P(x) - c_i x_i. \tag{4}$$

It is assumed that there is an equilibrium at each point of time in the market, which depends on the costs $c = (F(z_1), \ldots, F(z_n))$, or on $z = (z_1, \ldots, z_n)$. It could be a Nash equilibrium in quantitites x_i, or some other equilibrium. All that we require is that it is unique, given c or z. Let $x_i(x)$ and $x(z) = \Sigma_i x_i(z)$, be the equilibrium.

The consumer surplus is then:

$$cs = \int_0^{x(z)} p(v) \, dv - x(z)P(x(z)). \tag{5}$$

The earnings (gross of R & D expenditures) for firm i are

$$E^i(z) = x_i(z)P(x(z)) - c_i(z_i)x_i(z). \tag{6}$$

We turn now to the R & D investment decisions. In the following discussion, it is assumed that there is a subsidy of s for R & D so that, of each dollar of R & D undertaken, the firm's cost is $(1 - s)$. Clearly $s = 0$ is one possibility. Firm i maximises the present value of its profits net of R & D costs:

$$V^i = \int_0^\infty [E^i(z) - (1 - s)m_i]e^{-rt} \, dt. \tag{7}$$

It knows and accepts the constraint

$$\dot{z}_i = m_i + \theta \sum_{j \neq i} m_j \tag{8}$$

$$z_i(0) = 0.$$

And it takes the investment path of its rivals (presumed optimal) as given. The other constraint is that $m_i(t) \geq 0$. In solving the problem, it is convenient to change the state variables from $z_i(t)$, $i = 1, \ldots, n$ to $M_i(t)$, $i = 1, \ldots, n$ defined as follows:

$$M_i(t) = \int_0^t m_i(\tau) \, d\tau \tag{9}$$

Then, with these new variables,

$$z_i = M_i + \theta \sum_{j \neq i} M_j. \tag{10}$$

The individual firm maximises

$$\int_0^\infty (E^i(z(M)) - (1-s)m_i)e^{-rt} \, dt \tag{11}$$

subject to $M_i = m_i$

$\qquad\qquad\quad M_i(0) = 0$

$\qquad\qquad\quad m_i(t) \geqslant 0.$

and takes the time paths of $M_j(t)$ as given.

It can be established that the joint solution to these optimisation problems has the property that each firm goes to some equilibrium level of z_i or M_i immediately or as fast as possible, and stays there. (To avoid a digression here, I present the argument in Appendix A.) This is a well known property of certain optimisation problems that are linear in the derivative of the state variable. We assume this property, which Raskeen established, and let z and M be the vectors of stationary values that are achieved immediately. The present value of the profits of firm i is

$$V^i = \frac{1}{r} E^i(z) - (1-s)M_i, \tag{12}$$

where $z_i = M_i + \theta \sum_{j \neq i} M_j.$

Maximising V^i with respect to M_i, we have the first-order condition

$$\frac{1}{r} \left[E_i^i + \theta \sum_{j \neq i} E_j^i \right] = (1-s), \qquad i = 1, \ldots, n. \tag{13}$$

The solution to these equations determines the market outcome. Here E_j^i is the derivative of $E^i(z)$ with respect to z_j.

One can calculate the consumer surplus, profits and the magnitude of government subsidies, and hence the total net surplus, from the equilibrium z or M. One can also find the maximum potential surplus by maximising

$$\text{TS} = \frac{1}{r}\left[\int\limits_{0}^{x(z)} P(v)\,dv - c\,(z)x(z) \right] - M, \qquad (14)$$

where from static optimisation $P(x(z)) \equiv c(z)$, and of course $z = M$. As in the market outcome, the solution to the problem of maximising the surplus involves doing all the R & D at the start. It also involves a single firm, unless $\theta = 1$, in which case the number of firms is irrelevant.

(1) THE SYMMETRIC CASE

I should like to focus for the most part on the symmetric case.[8] Except for possible issues of entry deterrence arising from negative profits or strategic behaviour, the symmetric case will result naturally from symmetry in the costs facing firms. We have symmetry if

$$E^i(z) \equiv E^j(z + (z_j - z_i)e_i + (z_i - z_j)e_j), \qquad (15)$$

where e_j is a vector with a one in the jth place and zeros elsewhere. When there is symmetry, it is easily established, by differentiation, that

$$E^i_i(z) \equiv E^j_j(\bar{z}), \qquad (16)$$

where $\bar{z} = z + (z_j - z_i)e_i + (z_i - z_j)e_j$. Furthermore, also by differentiating, we have

$$E^i_j(z) = E^j_i(\bar{z}) \qquad (17)$$

and

$$E^i_k(z) = E^j_k(\bar{z}) \qquad (18)$$

For $i \neq k, j \neq k$, let (e) be a vector of ones. If $z = ve$ for some scalar (v), then $\bar{z} = z = e$. Now consider

$$E^i_j(ve) + \theta \sum_{k \neq i} E^i_k(ve)$$

$$= E^j_i(ve) + \theta \sum_{k \neq j} E^j_k(ve), \qquad (19)$$

from the relationships above.

Recall that the conditions for a market equilibrium are

$$E^i_i(z) + \theta \sum_{k \neq i} E^i_k(z) = r(1 - s). \qquad (20)$$

If (for some i) we solve

$$E_i^i(ve) + \theta \sum_{k \neq i} E_k^i(ve) = r(1 - s) \tag{21}$$

for v, then ve is a symmetric equilibrium — from equation (13). Define a new function

$$R(v) \equiv \int_0^v [E_i^i(\psi e) + \theta \sum_{k \neq i} E_k^i(\psi e)] \mathrm{d}\psi \tag{22}$$

From the preceding remarks, $R(v)$ is independent of (i). Moreover, its derivative is

$$R'(v) = E_i^i(ve) + \theta \sum_{k \neq i} E_k^i(ve). \tag{23}$$

Thus we can write the equation summarising the symmetric equilibrium in the following term

$$\frac{1}{r}R'(v) = (1 - s). \tag{24}$$

Thus, the market acts as if it were maximising

$$\frac{1}{r}R(v) - (1 - s)v. \tag{25}$$

In the symmetric case, $M_i = M$, and hence

$$v = [1 + \theta(n - 1)] = kM, \tag{26}$$

where

$$k = 1 + \theta(n - 1). \tag{27}$$

Proposition The market in a symmetric equilibrium maximises

$$\frac{1}{r}R(v) - (1 - s)v, \tag{28}$$

where

$$R(v) \equiv \int_0^v [E_i^i(\psi e) + \theta \sum_{k \neq i} E_k^i(\psi e)] \mathrm{d}\psi \tag{29}$$

The R & D expenditures for each firm are $M = v/k$, where $k = 1 + \theta(n - 1)$.

Let $E^i(ve) = E(v, n)$. The total surplus is

$$TS(v) = \frac{B(v, n)}{r} + \frac{nE(v, n)}{r} - (1 - s)nM - snM$$

$$= \frac{B(v, n)}{r} + \frac{nE(v, n)}{r} - nM \tag{30}$$

where $M = v/k(\theta, n)$. Thus the performance of the market is measured by

$$T(v, \theta, n) = \frac{B(v, n)}{r} + \frac{n}{r} E(v, n) - \frac{n}{k}v \tag{31}$$

and the market acts so as to maximise

$$\frac{R(v, n, \theta)}{r} - (1 - s)v. \tag{32}$$

I have reintroduced the variables and parameters that affect the functions B, R and k. The variable v will henceforth be replaced by (z). It is the accumulated knowledge created by the R & D of all the firms: $z = k(\theta, n)M$. And costs are a declining function of z or v, so that $B(z, n)$ and $B(z, n) + nE(z, n)$ are increasing functions of z.

(2) PROPERTIES OF THE MARKET EQUILIBRIA

The function $R(z, n, \theta)$ captures the market incentives with respect to R & D investment. From the definition of R and knowing that $E^i_j < 0$ $i \neq j$, one can see that $R_\theta < 0$ and $R_{z\theta} < 0$. Thus an increase in the spill-overs reduces the incentives for R & D and cost reduction, and will reduce the amount of cost reduction in the market equilibrium.

The dependence of R on n is somewhat complicated. Let me defer a discussion of that until a specific example is introduced.

For a given level of z and $n > 1$, the R & D costs for the achieved-amount of cost reduction decline as θ increases. The R & D costs at the industry level are

$$\text{R \& D} = \frac{n}{z_k}$$

$$= z \frac{n}{1 + \theta(n-1)} \tag{33}$$

If e = 0, the costs are proportional to the number of firms. With $\theta > 0$, the unit costs have an upper limit of $1/\theta$. For example if $\theta = 0.05$, the unit costs cannot exceed 2, which is what they would be with two firms and no spill-overs. And if $\theta = 1$, the unit costs are independent of the number of firms and are equal to one.

Thus while spill-overs reduce the incentives for cost reduction, they also reduce the costs (at the industry level) of achieving a given amount of cost reduction. The incentives can be restored through subsidies. It can be shown that $R_z > 0$, provided that $dc/dz = F'(z) < 0$, so that subsidies are sufficient to determine the industry costs or cost reduction. It is therefore possible to maximise the surplus (for a given n and θ)

$$T(z, n, \theta) = L(z, n) - \psi(n, \theta)z \tag{34}$$

with respect to z, where

$$L(z,n) = \frac{B(z, n) + nE(z, n)}{r} \tag{35}$$

and

$$\psi(n,\theta) = \frac{n}{k(n, \theta)} = \frac{n}{1 + \theta(n-1)} \tag{36}$$

Let

$$D(n, \theta) = \max_z [L(z, n) = \psi(n, \theta)z]. \tag{37}$$

Since $\psi_\theta < 0$,

$$D_\theta = -\psi_\theta z \geq 0. \tag{38}$$

Thus spill-overs improve the performance of the market with the incentive appropriately restored. Or, to put it another way, with appropriability the achievable surplus is smaller because a high rate of cost reduction be can achieved only with a large R & D investment.

(2) AN EXAMPLE

It may be clearer if, at this point, we explore the model in the context of an example. Suppose, then, that the demand is of the constant-elasticity variety so that $x = Ap^{-b}$. And assume further that the static equilibrium is a Nash equilibrium in quantity of output, given unit costs. Let $c = g_0 + c_0 e^{-fz}$ be the unit costs in the symmetric case. Let $w = 1 - 1/bn$, where n is the number of firms and $b > 1$ the price-elasticity of demand. In the constant elasticity case

$$R(z, n, z) = \frac{A}{n(b-1)} \; w^{b-1}$$
$$\left[2w + \frac{k}{n} ((b-1)(1-w) - 2w) \right] c^{1-b} \tag{39}$$

where $k = 1 + \theta(n-1)$.[9] The earnings for the individual firms are

$$E = Ab \frac{w^{b-1}}{n} (1-w) c^{1-b}. \tag{40}$$

The consumer surplus is

$$CS = \frac{A}{b-1} w^{b-1} c^{1-b}. \tag{41}$$

The total surplus is

$$T = \frac{A}{r} w^{b-1} \left[\frac{1}{b-1} + 1 - w \right] c^{1-b} - \frac{n}{k z}. \tag{42}$$

The market acts so as to maximise

$$Q = \frac{1}{r} R(z) - (1-s)z \tag{43}$$

$$= \frac{A \, w^{b-1}}{rn(b-1)} \left[2w + \frac{P_z}{n} ((b-1)(1-w) - zw) \right] c^{1-b}$$
$$- (1-s)z.$$

These two functions $Q(z, n, \theta, x)$ and $T(z, n, \theta)$ provide us with a complete summary of symmetric equilibria and market performance. In some instances, a profitability constraint, which would take the form

$$Ab \frac{w^{b-1}}{n} (1-w) c^{1-b} - \frac{(1-s)}{k} z \geq 0, \tag{44}$$

might be binding.

The coefficient of k/n in $R(z, n, \theta)$ is negative. Thus an increase in θ increases (k) for $n > 1$, and hence reduces R and R_z. Other things being equal, that increase in spill-overs reduces the cost reduction, because $R(z, \theta, n)/1-s$ is the function that is implicitly maximised as the market equilibrates.

I should like at this point to describe some calculations which I made in order to provide a more-quantitative picture of the incentives under various market structures, and of the consequent performance. My example is chosen so that there are significant cost-reduction possibilities, but these require significant R & D investments to achieve them. The example has the following parameters: $A = 5, r = 0.1, b = 2.0$, $q_0 = 1, c_0 = 1$ and $f = 0.5$. In this model, what matters is c_0/q_0, and the magnitude of $A/(r)q_0^{1-b}$. Given c_0/q_0, any combination of A, r and c_0 that keeps $A/(r)q_0^{1-b}$ constant will give the same results. In this case, $A/(r)q_0^{1-b} = 50$.

In this model, if $f = 0$ (so that there are no cost reduction possibilities), then the optimal surplus (with price equal to marginal cost) is 25. With $f = 0.5$, the optimal surplus is 41.6456. R & D expenditures are 6.25 and costs after the R & D is completed are 1.04394.

Now consider market equilibria. With $s = 0$ so that there is no intervention, the market maximises $R(z,n,\theta)/(r) - z$. The optimal surplus is the maximum of

$$\frac{A}{r(b-1)} c^{1-b} - z. \tag{45}$$

Therefore the market incentives for cost reduction relative to the optimum are summarised by the ratio

$$I = \frac{R(z,n,\theta) \cdot (b-1)}{Ac^{1-b}}. \tag{46}$$

This ratio does not depend on c^{1-b} and hence does not depend on (z) either. For the numerical values above, Table 16.1 gives this ratio as a percentage for various values of θ and n. The following points should be noted. For $\theta = 0$ (no spill-overs) $I(n,\theta)$ rises as n goes from 1 to 2 and then falls. The same is true for $\theta = 0.25$. For $\theta > 0.25$, $I(n,\theta)$ declines with n. If you fix n and read across rows. $I(n, \theta)$ declines with θ for each n. Thus spill-overs reduce R & D and cost reduction. When spill-overs are small, some competition increases the amount of cost reduction. But the fragmentation of the market then overcomes the incentive provided by the downward price pressure and R & D falls.

TABLE 16.1   INCENTIVES FOR R & D: $I(n, \theta)$

	n		θ		
—	0	0.25	0.50	0.75	1.0
1	25	25	25	25	25
2	32.8	26.9	21.1	15.2	9.4
3	32.4	25.4	18.5	11.6	4.6
4	29.4	22.7	16.1	9.4	2.7
5	26.3	20.2	14.0	7.9	1.8
6	23.6	18.0	12.4	6.8	1.3

What is striking about Table 16.1, however, is the smallness of the numbers. The largest value for $I(n,\theta)$ is 32.8, which means that the implicit objective function of the market attaches benefits to R & D that are less than one-third of the appropriate ones.

It is not therefore surprising that the performance of the market is not particularly good under any market structure. For the same combinations of θ and n, Table 16.2 reports the ratio of the

TABLE 16.2   PERFORMANCE WITH NO POLICY INTERVENTION

			θ		
n	0	0.25	0.5	0.75	1.0
1	65.4	65.4	65.4	65.4	65.4
—	(19.8)	(19.8)	(19.8)	(19.8)	(19.8)
2	79.3	80.6	77.0	56.3*	56.3*
—	(11.7)	(17.0)	(28.6)	(91.6)	(91.6)
3	74.2	80.3	74.4	58.4*	58.4*
—	(12.0)	(19.0)	(39.8)	(91.6)	(91.6)
4	67.5	77.9	61.8	59.1*	59.1*
—	(14.5)	(24.1)	(80.3)	(91.6)	(91.6)
5	61.4	74.7	59.4*	59.4*	59.4*
—	(18.0)	(31.6)	(91.6)	(91.6)	(91.6)
6	56.3	70.5	59.6*	59.7*	59.7*
—	(22.2)	(44.1)	(91.6)	(91.6)	(91.6)

The upper number in each box is the percentage of the optimal surplus achieved. The lower number is the percentage by which achieved unit cost exceeds the optimum.

*Means that there is no R & D and hence no cost reduction.

surplus actually achieved in the market, to the first-best optimal surplus, as a percentage. Underlying these calculations is the fact that allocative efficiency is increasing with n), because margins are falling. The highest value for the performance ratio is 80.3, and it occurs when $n = 2$ and $\theta = 0.25$. The modest spill-overs reduce the industry's R & D costs without excessively removing incentives. But, even here, there is a 19.7 per cent loss of potential surplus. For monopoly the loss is 35 per cent. When n is large, there is no cost reduction. And, while allocative efficiency is high, 40 per cent of the surplus is lost because of the failure to reduce costs. In Table 16.2, the number in parentheses is that percentage by which equilibrium costs exceed the optimal unit costs. The smallest number is 11.7 for $\theta = 0$ and $n = 2$. The reason is that that is the case for which the R & D incentives are highest.

The appropriate conclusion seems to be that a market with this type of underlying structure will have performance problems.

Since spill-overs have a pronounced negative effect on cost reduction and performance, it may seem appropriate to conclude that where possible they should be eliminated. That would be mistake. First, the absence of spill-overs does not eliminate performance problems, as these calculations illustrate. Second, as discussed earlier, appropriability *increases* the R & D costs for an industry that are associated with a given level of cost reduction. Thus, if one wants to operate on incentives through subsidising R & D, it is better to do so in the lower-cost (i.e., higher spill-over) environment.

These points are illustrated with the same numerical example. Given (n) and (θ), the surplus is

$$T - \frac{A}{r} w^{b-1} \left[\frac{1}{b-1} + 1 - w \right] c^{1-b} - \frac{n}{k^z} \tag{47}$$

Let $W = T + n/(k)^z$. The market maximises

$$\frac{R}{r} - (1 - s)z. \tag{48}$$

Therefore, if the subsidy is set so that

$$1 - \frac{nk}{rkW}, \tag{49}$$

then the market will maximise $T(z, n, \theta)$ with respect to z and hence to cost reduction. Now increasing n raises w and hence reduces price-cost margins. But it also increases n/k, except when $\theta = 1.0$. Moreover, the rate of increase of n/k with (n) is a declining function of θ. Thus if the optimal subsidies are in place we should observe the following. Performance will increase with θ. As θ rises, the desirable number of firms will increase since, with high spillovers, adding further firms raises industry R & D costs less. We could, of course, introduce a fixed cost to having a firm undertake R & D and then actually perform the optimisation with respect to n, given θ. With the data in the tables that follow, one can do so by eye for any chosen level of fixed cost.

Table 16.3 is the analogue of Table 16.1. It is the ratio of the benefits implicitly recognised by the market to the optimal surplus. But here the market is, for each n and θ, provided with the optimal subsidy. As the reader can see, incentives rise with θ, reading across rows. They rise and fall with n (reading down columns). When $\theta = 1$, they simply increase with n, because of the absence of the redundancy problem.

TABLE 16.3   INCENTIVES WITH OPTIMAL SUBSIDIES

			θ		
n	0	0.25	0.5	0.75	1.0
1	75	75	75	75	75
2	46.9	58.6	70.3	82.0	93.8
3	32.4	48.6	64.8	81.0	92.7
4	24.6	43.1	61.5	79.9	98.4
5	19.8	39.6	59.4	79.2	99.0
6	16.6	37.2	57.9	78.6	99.3

The incentives are significantly greater, except when $\theta = 0$. When $\theta = 0$, the subsidies are essentially impotent. They do raise incentives for $n = 2$ (cf. Table 16.1). Beyond that, the redundancy costs overwhelm the competitive effect on margins. Table 16.4 provides the figures for the performance relative to the first-best optimum in percentage terms. The figures in Table 16.4 (A) are the amounts by which unit costs in the equilibrium exceed the optimally-reduced unit costs.

With $\theta = 0$, subsidies have little power to alter performance. With $\theta = 0.25$ and $n = 2$, performance is up to 85 per cent. With $\theta = 0.5$ and $n = 3$, performance is over 90 per cent. And with $\theta \geqslant 0.75$

TABLE 16.3(A)   OPTIMAL SUBSIDIES IN PERCENTAGE TERMS

n	θ				
	0	0.25	0.5	0.75	1.0
1	66.7	66.7	66.7	66.7	66.7
2	30	54	70	81.4	90.0
3	0	47.6	71.4	85.7	95.2
4	−19.4	47.2	73.9	88.2	97.2
5	−32.7	49.1	76.4	90.0	98.2
6	−42.3	51.7	78.6	91.3	98.7

TABLE 16.4   PERFORMANCE WITH OPTIMAL SUBSIDIES

n	θ				
	0	0.25	0.5	0.75	1.0
1	71.4	71.4	71.4	71.4	71.4
2	80.2	84.8	88.2	90.8	92.8
3	74.2	84.0	89.9	93.9	96.8
4	67.9	82.3	90.0	94.9	98.2
5	62.9	80.7	89.8	95.3	98.8
6	59.9	79.4	89.4	95.4	99.2

TABLE 16.4(A)   COST REDUCTION WITH OPTIMAL SUBSIDIES

n	θ				
	0	0.25	0.5	0.75	1.0
1	1.6	1.6	1.6	1.6	1.6
2	5.8	3.4	2.0	1.0	0.30
3	12.0	5.3	2.6	1.1	0.12
4	20.5	6.9	3.0	1.1	0.05
5	33.3	8.2	3.3	1.2	0.03
6	63.0	9.1	3.5	1.3	0.014

performance is over 95 per cent and one can tolerate relatively large numbers of firms. But the increases in benefits at the margin derived from adding further firms are relatively small for $n \geq 5$ or 6.

These results are, of course, perfectly consistent with what the theory led us to expect. What may be new is the magnitude of the performance problems in the markets where there is no type of intervention.

One could repeat these calculations for many examples, though lack of space makes an exhaustive presentation of the results for different uses impossible. The conclusions do not change. If one makes f small, of course, the relative importance of allocative efficiency versus dynamic technical efficiency increases and those elements of structure that influence the latter become less critical as determinants of performance. Similarly, if f is larger, so that the R & D investment required to achieve substantial cost reduction is small, then the qualitative effects are the same, but most market structures perform reasonably well on cost reduction. And thus their *differentials* are more closely related to margins and to allocative efficiency.

None of this is surprising. If R & D is either ineffective in reducing costs or very effective and hence relatively cheap, markets perform well. But in cases where the opportunities for cost reduction are substantial, and the costs of achieving them are also substantial, but not prohibitive, there are potential performance problems of considerable quantitative significance. The numerical example was selected to illustrate this last case.

It is worth noting that the optimal subsidies do not depend on f in this model. Hence, one does not need to take a view in advance about the magnitudes just discussed in order to be able to proceed with the problem of how to approximate reasonable policy environments.

One might ask how profitable these markets are. With no spillovers, profits become negative at $n = 4$. With $n = 2$ and $\theta = 0$, the internal rate of return on the initial investment in R & D is 22.4 per cent. With $n = 3$ and $\theta = 0$, the internal rate of return is 11.1 per cent. With $\theta = 0.25$ and $n = 2$, the interal rate of return is 31.8 per cent. With $\theta = 0.25$ and $n = 3$, that rate is 19.7 per cent. When there are spill-overs, profits do not become zero and entry is not blocked, at least not at once.

The incentives in the market, as summarised by $R(z, n, \theta)$, do depend on b. For $n = 3$ and $\theta = 0.25$, Table 16.5 shows how $I(n, \theta)$ varies with the elasticity b.

TABLE 16.5   INCENTIVES FOR $n = 3$, $\theta = 0.25$

b	I
1.1	22.95
1.5	24.5
2.0	24.46
3.0	26.34

The incentives increase with a rise in the price elasticity, but not dramatically. This qualitative feature holds for the other values of n and θ.

In view of this relative insensitivity to the change in elasticity, one might ask how markets would perform with a subsidy of 70 per cent to R & D. The motivation for this question lies in the fact that the optimal subsidy varies with n, θ and the price elasticity. Neither b nor θ are likely to be directly observable. A 70 per cent-subsidy policy is likely to improve performance in most cases, except when θ is zero or small. Table 16.6 gives the performance in an equilibrium as a percentage of the first-best outcome for the flat 70 per cent subsidy policy. Performance under this policy is quite good relative to market outcomes except at the extremes for θ. When $\theta = 0$, there is far too much R & D: the cost reduction is too expensive. With $\theta = 1$, and for $n \geq 3$, the disincentives created by the public-good character of the R & D are too great for the 70 per cent subsidy to overcome them.

TABLE 16.6   PERFORMANCE WITH A 70 PER CENT SUBSIDY

	$n\theta$				
	0	0.25	0.5	0.75	1.0
1	71.4	71.4	71.4	71.4	71.4
2	77.3	84.1	88.1	89.9	87.3
3	65.8	82.6	89.9	91.4	58.3*
4	53.3	80.6	89.9	90.2	59.1*
5	41.3	79.0	89.5	87.9	59.4*
6	30.3	77.9	88.9	84.8	59.6*

*Means that there is no incentive to carry out R & D and there is none.

At this point, it would be possible to deluge the chapter with numbers from different cases. But that would be pointless. The use of the example here is intended to illustrate propositions that are already, I hope, intuitively clear from the theory. It is also intended to show that there are some market structures which experiences performance problems of sizeable dimensions.

The reader may have concluded that in circumstances such as these, where redundancy is a problem, co-operative R & D might be useful. This idea may be reinforced by the fact that while co-operative R & D is not common in the US, it is used in other countries. Co-operative R & D is easily analysed in this framework.

Fully co-operative R & D, with n firms, produces results identical to those for a monopolist with price–cost margins constrained to $p/c = 1/w$. The reasons are: (i) that margins are set by competitive interaction, and (ii) that each firm's profits gross of R & D costs are $1/n$th of industry profits, while its R & D costs are $1/n$th of industry R & D costs. Therefore the firm wants to maximise $1/n$th of industry profits net of R & D costs. All firms agree, and maximise net industry profits.

As we have seen, that will not produce very good performance without a subsidy. But, with subsidies, the results are quite good. A monopolist with constrained margins has profits of $Aw^{b-1}(1 - w)c^{1-b}$. With $\theta = 1$,

$$R(z, n, \theta) = \frac{1}{n}Aw^{b-1}(1 - w)c^{1-b} .$$

(50)

Thus the objective which the monopolist pursues is n times as large as the objective implicitly maximised. Therefore if s^* is the optimal subsidy for n firms and $\bar{s}$ is the optimal subsidy for the margin-constrained monopolist,

$$\frac{n}{1-\bar{s}} = 1 - s^*$$

(51)

or

$$\bar{s} = 1 - n(1 - s^*).$$

(52)

Thus, with $\bar{s}$, a margin-constrained monopolist or firms engaging in co-operative R & D will duplicate exactly the results of the market with $\theta = 1$ and the subsidy of s^*. Table 16.4 gives the performance for various values of (n) when $\theta = 1$. The subsidies s^* are those in Table 16.3 (A). The corresponding required subsidies for the co-operative R & D case are in Table 16.7.

TABLE 16.7 OPTIMAL SUBSIDIES WITH CO-OPERATIVE R & D

n	Subsidy
1	66.7
2	80.0
3	85.7
4	88.8
5	90.9
6	92.3

There are interesting further questions concerning the desirability
of having co-operation on parts of the R & D and competition on the
remainder. An adequate treatment would take us beyond the scope
of the this chapter.

VI A REGULATED SINGLE FIRM

An unregulated monopoly performs relatively poorly, because its
margins are too high and because it lacks the incentives to do R & D
(Tables 16.1 and 16.2). On the other hand, a single firm does not
duplicate R & D and hence produces cost reductions efficiently at the
industry level. A monopoly that is subsidised performs better (Tables
16.3 and 16.4), but still has high margins.

Regulating margins without subsidising R & D is counter-
productive. With $p/c = 1/w$, the profits of the single firm are

$$\pi = \left[\frac{A}{r^{wb-1}} (1 - w) \right] c^{1-b} - z. \tag{53}$$

The term in square brackets has a maximum at $\bar{w} = 1-(1/b)$. That is
the profit-maximising price-cost margin and it provides the maximum
incentives for R & D. As (w) increases so that margins fall, the
investment in R & D falls. The effect of constraining margins is to
further reduce the dynamic technical efficiency. An individual
margin-constrained firm will under-invest in R & D unless the latter
is subsidised at the levels shown in Table 16.7, for the example.

Regulating price has a quite different effect. The profits of the
single firm are then

$$\pi = \frac{A}{r} (p - c)p^{-b} - z. \tag{54}$$

If the price is regulated, and if the firm is required to meet the
demand at that price, it will set z so as to minimise total costs

$$c = \frac{A}{r}p^{-b} c + z. \tag{55}$$

Given p, that is the optimal level of z. Thus a price-regulated
single firm will set R & D optimally, given that price. Now, if the
price corresponds to the optimum, then the optimal $p = c(z)$. Under
these conditions, the firm would have profits of $\Pi = -z < 0$.

Figure 16.2 provides a visual representation of the incentive structure of this situation. The line $p = c$ is the optimal price given cost,

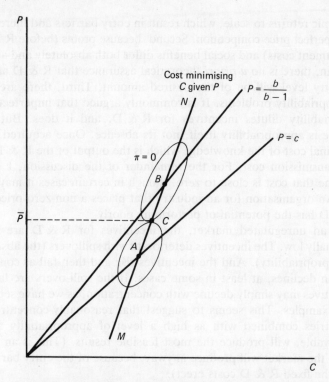

FIG. 16.2 Price-regulated monopoly. A = First-best outcome,
B = Unregulated monopoly, C = Second best with $\pi = 0$ and market
outcome with regulated price p^-

while $p = (b/b-1)^c$ is the profit-maximising price, given cost. The
line MN is the total-cost minimising c, given p. That is both the
surplus and the profit-maximising c, if cost is given p. Point B is
the monopoly outcome. Point A is the optimum. Iso-profit contours
and iso-surplus contours are vertical and hence tangent to each other
along MN. Therefore, at a point like C, $\Pi = 0$ and $p = \bar{p}$, the
outcome has two properties. This is the maximum surplus subject to
$\Pi \geqslant 0$. And this is the point which the firm would choose if p were set
equal to $\bar{p}$. Thus a monopoly confronted with the price that emerges
from the second-best optimum calculation, will invest the second-
best optimum amount of R & D.

VII CONCLUSIONS

R & D has proved a complex subject because there are three inter-
acting and simultaneous market failures. First, there will generally be

dynamic returns to scale, which result in entry barriers and therefore in imperfect price competition. Second, because profits (before R & D investment costs) and social benefits differ both absolutely and at the margin, there is no *a priori* theoretical assurance that R & D at the industry level will be of the desired amount. Third, there are the appropriability problems. It is commonly argued that imperfect appropriability dilutes incentives for R & D: and it does. But the failure is appropriability itself, not its absence. Once acquired, the marginal cost of the knowledge which is the output of the R & D, is its transmission cost. For the remainder of the discussion, I shall assume that cost is close to zero, though in certain cases it may not be. An organisation for an industry that places a non-zero price on R & D has the potential of performing poorly.

In an unregulated market, the incentives for R & D are sub-optimally low. The incentives deteriorate with spillovers (the absence of appropriability). And the incentives rise and then fall as concentration declines, at least in some cases. If the spill-overs are large, incentives may simply decline with concentration, as we have seen in the examples. This seems to suggest that reasonably-concentrated industries combined with as high a level of appropriability as is achievable, will produce the most feasible results. (This is an outcome the market will produce anyway, because of the entry barriers that the fixed R & D costs erect).

I hope the preceding discussion casts doubt on this view. Appropriability involves implicitly an incorrect pricing decision, so that concentration plus appropriability will not solve the problem. Market performance is not adequate.

The theory tells us to price the output of R & D at its marginal cost once it has been carried, that is at zero, and hence to view spill-overs as a positive attribute. The result is an incentive problem. The most direct way to deal with that problem is to subsidise the activity for which the market provides sub-optimally low incentives. This has the added benefit of lowering entry barriers, increasing competition, lowering margins and improving allocative efficiency. But, mainly, it makes the transformation from the input (R & D expenditures) to the output (cost reduction) efficient at the industry level. Therefore it is not surprising that, in the examples cited here and in any others that one might examine, high performance by the market occurs in the context of high spill-overs and appropriate subsidies. If high spill-overs or low appropriability are hard to achieve, co-operative R & D with appropriate subsidies will also lead to better performance.

It is interesting that spill-overs and appropriability are the source of confusion. The fact that the producer of knowledge does not appropriate all its social benefits leads to the conclusion that he should at least be rewarded for the benefits which R & D confers on other firms. And even that falls short of the social benefits. But it does not follow that other firms should pay for R & D. If they do pay for it, they are paying more than its marginal cost. There is a direct analogue with public goods. The output of R & D has the character of a public good. The incentives are weak for individuals to supply it. But we do not generally approach a solution to problems of a public good by contriving to have the beneficiaries pay for it where possible, because that leads to under-consumption and sub-optimal use. It is preferable to supply the public good publicly, or to subsidise the private supplier without collecting the subsidy by charging the users of the good on the basis of use. The R & D problem is essentially the same. The mistake is to attempt to solve the problem by having the price paid to the supplier made equal to the price paid by the recipient of the benefits.

APPENDIX A   THE PROPERTY OF THE MOST-RAPID APPROACH PATH

The objective function for the firm is

$$V^i = \int_0^\infty [E^i(z(M)) - (1 - s)\dot{M}_i]e^{-rt}dt.$$

Integrating the second term by parts, the objective is

$$V^i = \int_0^\infty [E^i(z(M)) - (1 - s)rM_i]e^{-rt}dt.$$

Since the integrand depends only on M_i, the firm will set M_i so as to maximise $E - (1 - s)rM_i$ at each time t. The constant $\dot{M}_i \geq 0$ could force it away from this strategy if E_i^i were to decline over time. each i. I shall assume there is only one vector M^* that satisfies these equations. Thus the only outcome that can be an equilibrium is the one in which M_i goes to M_i^* immediately and stays there. Once there, of course, there is no incentive to move.

Thus the market outcome is as if each firm set M_i so as to maximise the present value of its earnings net of R & D:

$$V^i - \frac{1}{r} E^i(z(M)) - (1-s)M_i.$$

APPENDIX B   THE DYNAMIC VERSION OF THE MODEL

Since much of the notation for the dynamic version of the model is the same as for static, I shall be brief in laying out the model. The firm has earnings (gross of R & D) of $E^i(z)$, where $z = (z_1, \ldots, z_n)$. It maximises

$$V^i = \int\limits_0^\infty [E^i(z) - (1-s)m_i]e^{-rt}dt,$$

subject to $\dot{z}_i = h(m_i) + \theta\Sigma_{j\neq i}h(m_j)$. Here s is the subsidy to R & D and θ is the spill-over parameter. It takes the paths $m_j(\cdot)$ as given for $j\neq i$. Define

$$H_i = \int\limits_0^\infty \mu\ (m_i(\tau)\ d\tau.$$

It follows that

$$z_i = H_i + \theta \sum_{j\neq i} H_j$$

The problem facing the firm is to maximise

$$V^i = \int\limits_0^\infty [E^i(z(H)) - (1-s)m_i]e^{-rt}dt$$

subject to $\dot{H}_i = h(m_i)$.

The conditions for an optimum are $1 - s/\lambda_i = h'(m_i)$, $[\dot{H} = h(m_i)]$ and

$$\dot{\lambda}_i - r\lambda_i = - [E^i_i + \theta \sum_{j \neq i} E^i_j].$$

Assuming the functions $E^i(z)$ are symmetric, in the sense described in the chapter, then there will be a symmetric equilibrium with $z_i = z, m_i = m, \lambda_i = \lambda$. Its path is described in the following way. Let

$$R(z) = \int\limits_0^z [E^i_i(ve) + \theta \sum_{j \neq i} E^i_j(ve)]dv.$$

$R(z)$ is independent of i by symmetry. The conditions describing the optimum and the evolution in the market in the symmetric case are $1/\lambda = h'(m)$, $\dot{H} = h(m)$, and $\dot{\lambda} - r\lambda = -R'(z)$. Alternatively, they are $1-s/\lambda = h'(m)$, $\dot{z} = kh(m)$, and $\dot{\lambda} - r\lambda = -R'(z)$, where $k = 1 + \theta(n - 1)$ and n is the number of firms.[1] Now suppose that there were a firm with earnings of $R(z)$, with R & D costs (before subsidies) of km, and such that $z = kh(m)$. Such a firm would maximise

$$\int\limits_0^\infty [R(z) - (1-s)km] \, e^{-rt}dt$$

subject to $\dot{z} = kh(m)$.

The conditions describing its optimal path are $1-s/\lambda = h'(m)$, $\dot{z} = kh(m)$ and $\dot{\lambda} - r\lambda = -R'(z)$. These are the same as the conditions describing the evolutions of the symmetric equilibrium.

Proposition   The symmetric equilibrium as described is the path that maximises

$$\int\limits_0^\infty [R(z) - (1-s)km] \, e^{-rt}dt$$

subject to $\dot{z} = kh(m)$.

That is to say, it is as if there were a single firm, with earnings R(z), R & D costs (km) and cost-reducing technology ż = kh(m).

All the comments made earlier about the function $R(z)$ apply to this case, since they are the same functions. Note that if $h(m) = m$, then $h'(m) = 1$, $\lambda = (1 - s)$, $\dot{\lambda} = 0$ and $R'(z) = r(1 - s)$. That is, when there are no diminishing returns to R & D expenditure, the market acts so as to maximise $R(z)/(r) - (1 - s)z$. When $h(m) = m$, the objective function is

$$\int_0^\infty [R(z) - (1 - s)\dot{z}]\, e^{-rt} dt$$

$$= \int_0^\infty [R(z) - (1 - s)rz]\, e^{-rt} dt.$$

Since the solution is to set z so as to maximise the integrand initially, say at $z = \bar{z}$, the solution maximises

$$\frac{R(\bar{z})}{r} - (1 - s)z .$$

This is the result used in the body of the chapter.

There is a special case which I should like to highlight. Suppose $r = 0$ and the time horizon is finite and equal to T. The first-order conditions are $\dot{\lambda} = -R'(z)$ and $\lambda = 1 - s/h'$. It follows that $\dot{\lambda} = -(1 - s)/(h'^2)h''\dot{m}$, and hence that

$$-(1 - s)k\, \frac{h\, h''}{(h')^2}\, h''\dot{m} = -R'(z)\dot{z} ,$$

since $\dot{z} = kh(m)$.

It is easily seen that

$$\frac{h\, h''^{\cdot}}{(h')^{2^m}} = \frac{d}{dt}\left[m - \frac{h}{h'} \right].$$

Thus integrating the optimising conditions with respect to t, we have:

$$\left[m - \frac{h}{h'}\right] = \frac{R(z)}{(1-s)k} + \text{a constant.}$$

Let $h(m) = m^{\alpha}$. Then $h/h' = 1/\alpha^{m}$, and thus

$$m = D - \frac{\alpha R(z)}{(1-\alpha)(1-s)k}$$

where D is a constant. By going back to the calculus-of-variations solution, one can establish that the boundary condition, $m(T) = 0$ must hold.[11] That determines the constant D. One can see that on an optimal path $m(t)$ declines monotonically to zero as $t \to T$. The single-equation description of an optimal path is

$$\dot{z} = \left[D - \frac{\alpha R(z)}{1 - \alpha(1-s)}\right]^{\alpha},$$

where D is set so that $\dot{z}(T) = 0$.

For $n = 1$, $R(z)$ is simply the earnings of the single firm. For $n > 1$, $R(z)$ depends on demand elasticities and spill-over effects.

But the point of this theoretical development is that the techniques used in the chapter for the case $h(m) = m$, also apply here.

INCENTIVES

In the linear cases ($h(m) = m$) we were able to study market incentives by looking at $R(z, n, \theta)$ or, more precisely, at one ratio of $R(z, n, \theta)$ to the consumer surplus at z. Here, the situation is complicated, because the cost-reducing technology depends on k. We do know that $R_z < 0$ for $n > 1$.

Thus, increasing spill-overs might appear to reduce incentives. But they also affect the implicit costs of achieving cost reduction, which was not true in the linear case. Consider the following problem.

Suppose for the moment that $\dot{z} = A$ is a constant, and let $f(x) = h^{-1}(x)$: $f(x)$ is convex because h is concave and $h(0) = 0$. Under these conditions, the recognised costs in the market's implicit objective are

$$\text{costs} = (1-s)kf\left(\frac{A}{k}\right).$$

The derivative of these costs with respect to k is

$$\frac{\text{d costs}}{\text{d}k} = (1 - s)\left[f\left(\frac{A}{k}\right) - \frac{A}{k} f'\left(\frac{A}{k}\right)\right] < 0$$

because f is convex. Thus even from the market's standpoint, cost reduction is achieved at a lesser cost.

The point then is that, in the dynamic case, the ratio of $R(z, n, \theta)$ to the consumer surplus is not an accurate measure of market incentives with respect to changes in either θ or n. This is so, unless $\theta = 0$, which means $k = 1$. The simple summary of incentives is not available to us in the dynamic case.

COST REDUCTION AND SPILL-OVERS

When there are diminishing returns to the R & D of the individual firm, then the R & D cost of achieving a given cost reduction may fall with a fall in the number of firms – as long as there are positive spill-overs. This complicates the welfare analysis slightly. Let $f(x) = h^{-1}(x)$ as before and let $\dot{z} = A$. Then the industry's costs of achieving $\dot{z} = A$ are

$$I = nF\left(\frac{A}{k}\right).$$

It follows that

$$\frac{\text{d}T}{\text{d}n} = f\left(\frac{A}{k}\right) - \frac{n\,\theta\,A}{k\,k}\, f'\,\frac{A}{k}.$$

Let $x = A/k$. Then for $\theta \neq 0$,

$$\frac{\text{d}I}{\text{d}n} = \left[\frac{k}{n\,\theta} - \frac{xf'}{f}\right]\frac{n\,\theta}{k}$$

$$= \left[\frac{1 - \theta}{n\theta} + 1 - \frac{xf'}{f}\right]\frac{n\theta}{k}.$$

Since $f(0) = 0$ and f is convex, $xf'/(x) > 1$. For $\theta = 1$, $\text{d}I/(\text{d}n) < 0$. For $\theta < 1$, $1 - \theta/(n\theta) > 0$ but declines as n increases. Also, as n increases $x \to 0$. Thus if $\lim_{x \to 0} xf'/f > 1$, then eventually, as n becomes large, $\text{d}I/(\text{d}n) < 0$. If $\lim_{x \to 0} xf'/f = 1$, then $\text{d}I/\text{d}n \to 0$ as $n \to 0$ and it is possible that $\text{d}I/(\text{d}n) > 0$ everywhere. Clearly, the smaller θ is, the greater will be the costs, I. And when $\theta = 0$, $\text{d}I/\text{d}n = f(A) > 0$. In examples when $h(m) = m^a, f(x) = 1/x^a$, and

$$\frac{dI}{dn} = \left[\frac{1 - \theta}{n \theta} + 1 - \frac{1}{\alpha} \right] \frac{n \theta}{k} .$$

Here costs eventually decline with n, since $\alpha < 1$. Thus costs decline for $n \geqslant \bar{n} = \alpha(1 - \theta)/\theta(1 - \alpha)$. I shall use $\alpha = 0.8$ in subsequent calculations. Then $\bar{n}$ as a function of θ is $\bar{n} = 4(1/\theta - 1)$.

TABLE B.1

θ	$\bar{n}$
0	∞
0.25	12.00
0.50	4.00
0.75	1.33
1.00	0.00

To summarise briefly, the preceding calculations indicate that when spill-overs are positive, the costs to the industry of achieving a given rate of cost reduction may diminish as the numbers of firms falls. They will certainly decline when $\theta = 1$. The analysis depends on $h(m)$ being everywhere concave. Presumably, in reality, there are fixed costs associated with a research establishment that cause the assumption of the strict concavity of $h(m)$ to fail: and if there are no fixed costs, at least something that creates economies of scale at low levels of (m), I have not modelled these explicitly, but rather have shown how the optimum depends on spill-overs and on numbers, in various cases.

NUMERICAL RESULTS

I turn now to some examples, to illustrate that the qualitative properties of the linear model persist in the dynamic setting.

The assumptions are that there is constant elasticity of demand: $x = ap^{-\beta}$. Unit costs are $c = q_o + c_o e^{-fz}$. Both these assumptions were made earlier. The assumption concerning R & D and cost reduction is $\dot{z}_i = m_i^\alpha + \theta \Sigma_{j \neq i} m_j^\alpha$, where $\alpha < 1$.

Finally, for ease of calculation, I take $r = 0$ and the finite horizon (T). The reader will find expressions for the $R(z, n, \theta)$ function in the chapter, as well as expressions for the firm's profits and for the consumers' surplus. These are unaltered here.

For these calculations, $\beta = 2$, $\alpha = 0.8$, $q_o = c_o = f = 1.0$, and

$T = 10$ years. Spill-overs and the number of firms vary. Price–cost margins are those that result from a Nash equilibrium in quantities. They depend on n and β. When $\beta = z$ they are as in Table B.2.

TABLE B.2

$\bar{n}$	Margin
1	0.50
2	0.25
3	0.17
4	0.125
5	0.10

I allow n to vary from 1 to 5 and θ to vary from zero to one. Table B.3 shows the surplus, with no subsidies. The absolute numbers are not relevant, but rather their relative sizes. Performance improves as (n) increases; except when $\theta = 0$, when $n = 3$ is optimal; and when $\theta = 0.25$, when $n = 4$ is optimal. As a reference point, the surplus is 5 when price equals unit cost and there is no cost reduction. Table B.3 gives the surpluses when the optimal subsidies are employed. As in the linear case, the optimal subsidy achieves the second-best optimum given n and θ. The optimal subsidies are those reported in Table 16.3 (A) in the main chapter. They depend on n, θ, and the elasticity β, but not on the cost-reducing technology. Hence they are the same as in the linear case.

TABLE B.3   SURPLUS WITH NO SUBSIDY

Number of firms	Spill-over parameter				
	0.00	*0.25*	*0.50*	*0.75*	*1.00*
1	3.88	3.88	3.88	3.88	3.88
2	4.97	4.91	4.79	4.85	4.93
3	4.99	5.07	5.01	5.14	5.35
4	4.94	5.09	5.13	5.32	5.62
5	4.93	5.07	5.22	5.48	5.85

Table B.4 gives the optimum given n and θ. This is different from the linear case. In the linear case the optimum occurs when $n =$ or $\theta = 1$. Here, the costs of cost reduction fall with n for higher values of θ, provided that there are no fixed costs. Note that

TABLE B.4   SURPLUS WITH OPTIMAL SUBSIDY

Number of firms	Spill-over parameter				
	0.00	0.25	0.50	0.75	1.00
1	4.62	4.62	4.62	4.62	4.62
2	5.12	5.48	5.83	6.13	6.39
3	4.99	5.48	6.03	6.48	6.84
4	4.96	5.44	6.11	6.64	7.05
5	4.97	5.41	6.16	6.75	7.18

TABLE B.5   SURPLUS WITH GIVEN n AND θ

Number of firms	Spill-over parameter				
	0.00	0.25	0.50	0.75	1.00
1	6.63	6.63	6.63	6.63	6.63
2	5.54	5.95	6.32	6.64	6.91
3	5.15	5.68	6.24	6.70	7.07
4	5.05	5.55	6.23	6.77	7.18
5	5.02	5.47	6.24	6.83	7.26

TABLE B.6   PERFORMANCE WITH NO SUBSIDY RELATIVE TO OPTIMUM GIVEN n AND θ

Number of firms	Spill-over parameter				
	0.00	0.25	0.50	0.75	1.00
1	58.52	58.52	58.52	58.52	58.52
2	89.78	82.58	75.80	73.01	71.41
3	96.84	89.22	80.26	76.66	75.61
4	97.78	91.85	82.42	78.65	78.31
5	98.15	92.53	83.71	80.23	80.47

performance declines with n for small values of θ, and rises with n for $\theta \geq 0.5$. The same is true of the optimal-subsidy figures in Table B.5.

Table B.6 gives the ratio of actual to potential surplus given n

and θ, in percentage terms. This contains the same message as we found earlier. The spill-overs damage incentives, causing market performance to deteriorate relatively to potential. But, of course, potential is increasing with θ. Thus, although performance is relatively poorer with a higher θ, absolutely the position is the reverse. (Cf. Table B.3.)

Table B.7 gives the second-best performances as a percentage of the potential, given n and θ. The message is that, unless there is monopoly, the subsidies permit a substantial fraction of the potential surplus to be realised.

TABLE B.7   PERFORMANCE WITH OPTIMAL SUBSIDY RELATIVE TO OPTIMUM GIVEN n

Number of firms	Spill-over parameter				
	0.00	0.25	0.50	0.75	1.00
1	69.61	69.61	69.61	69.61	69.61
2	92.40	92.16	92.21	92.33	92.43
3	96.76	96.53	96.56	96.61	96.69
4	98.30	98.09	98.09	98.15	98.20
5	98.90	98.79	98.81	98.86	98.90

Table B.8 gives the market performance as a percentage of the second best (i.e., the surplus achievable with optimal subsidies). Generally, the percentage loss of surplus is greater the larger is θ. But, as was discussed earlier, and is evident in the preceding calcu-

TABLE B.8   PERFORMANCE WITH NO SUBSIDY RELATIVE TO OPTIMAL SUBSIDY

Number of firms	Spill-over parameter				
	0.00	0.25	0.50	0.75	1.00
1	84.07	84.07	84.07	84.07	84.07
2	97.17	89.60	82.20	79.08	77.26
3	100.00	92.43	83.13	79.34	78.20
4	99.48	93.64	84.02	80.13	79.75
5	99.23	93.66	84.71	81.16	81.36

TABLE B.9   PERFORMANCE WITH NO SUBSIDY, RELATIVE TO
FIRST-BEST PERFORMANCE ($n = 5$, $\theta = 1$)

Number of firms	Spill-over parameter				
	0.00	*0.25*	*0.50*	*0.75*	*1.00*
1	53.41	53.41	53.41	53.41	53.41
2	68.43	67.59	65.93	66.71	67.92
3	68.69	69.73	68.97	70.75	73.58
4	67.98	70.13	70.66	73.29	77.41
5	67.83	69.73	71.86	75.41	80.47

TABLE B.10   PERFORMANCE WITH OPTIMAL SUBSIDY, RELATIVE
TO FIRST BEST ($n = 5$, $\theta = 1$)

Number of firms	Spill-over parameter				
	0.00	*0.25*	*0.50*	*0.75*	*1.00*
1	63.53	63.53	63.53	63.53	63.53
2	70.43	75.44	80.20	81.36	87.91
3	68.64	75.44	82.97	89.17	94.09
4	68.34	74.89	84.10	91.46	97.07
5	68.35	74.45	84.83	92.92	98.90

lations, the conclusion that a small value of θ is desirable is not warranted.

In order to give some idea of performance relative to a fixed standard, I took the first-best situation (with $n = 5$ and $\theta = 1$) as the standard. This is the largest surplus in Table B.9. Table B.10 reports market performance (with no subsidies) as a percentage of that first-best outcome. Performance is roughly-constant across θ for $n = 1,2$. It increases slightly with θ for large n.

In Table B.10, one sees the performance-improving effects of spill-overs once appropriate incentives are restored. With modest numbers and with high spill-overs, performance is quite good.

Table B.11 shows the optimum (given n, θ) as a percentage of the first-best standard. The point here is that potential performance increases with n and θ together.

TABLE B.11 PERFORMANCE OF OPTIMUM, GIVEN n AND θ
RELATIVE TO FIRST BEST ($n = 5$, $\theta = 1.0$)

Number of firms	Spill-over parameter				
	0.00	0.25	0.50	0.75	1.00
1	91.27	91.27	91.27	91.27	91.27
2	76.23	81.86	86.98	91.37	95.11
3	70.94	78.15	85.93	92.29	97.32
4	69.52	76.35	85.74	93.19	98.84
5	69.11	75.36	85.85	94.00	100.00

A brief summary of the figures may be useful. Let

$A(n, \theta)$ = market surplus with no subsidies;
$S(n, \theta)$ = market surplus with optimal subsidies;
$T(n, \theta)$ = surplus with $p = c$ and optimal R & D;
$T^* = \max_{n, \theta} T(n, \theta)$.

The figures in the tables are as set out in the Summary Table.

SUMMARY TABLE

B.3	$A(n, \theta)$
B.4	$S(n, \theta)$
B.5	$T(n, \theta)$
B.6	$A(n, \theta)/T(n, \theta)$
B.7	$S(n, \theta)/T(n, \theta)$
B.8	$A(n, \theta)/S(n, \theta)$
B.9	$A(n, \theta)/T^*$
B.10	$S(n, \theta)/T^*$
B.11	$T(n, \theta)/T^*$

Most of these results are quite similar in sign and magnitude to the
static case. The surplus losses in the market are substantial because of
the incentive problem and are of the order of 30 per cent. In the static
case $T(n, \theta)$ declines with n unless $\theta = 1$, in which case $T_n(n, 1) = 0$.
Here $T(n, \theta)$ increases with n for θ in the higher ranges. Hence
spill-overs increase potential performance. But the principal conclusion is the same. Potential performance is limited with $\theta = 0$ (see
Table B.10).

As in the linear case, if the parameter (f) is made either very large (cost-reduction is cheap) or very small (it is prohibitively expensive), then performance in the product-development or cost-reducing dimension declines in importance, and one gets results that depend primarily on allocative efficiency. These results are well known: performance depends largely on concentration. The example I have used here, like the one in the main chapter was selected to illustrate the problems for the intermediate cases, when R & D is expensive but not prohibitively so.

NOTES

1. This research was supported by the National Science Foundation.
2. Allocative inefficiency refers to losses associated with prices in excess of or below marginal costs.
3. For discussions of the welfare economics of product differentiation see Dixit and Stiglitz (1977), Spence (1976).
4. This qualitative proposition is due to Schumpeter, and has been subject to empirical tests. See Scherer (1975) for example.
5. In discussing the model of Section III, the nature of the spill-over effects is made more precise.
6. A fuller discussion of the implications of a concave $h(m)$ for competitive strategy and performance are contained in Appendix B.
7. For example, one can let the inverse demand for the ith firm's differentiated product be $\partial/(\partial x_i)G(\Sigma\phi(x_i))$. Then if we let $y_i = \phi(x_i)$, and express costs in terms of y_i, as $C_i\phi^{-1}(y_i)$, we have something that is formally equivalent to a homogeneous product model, but with convex costs. The latter have little or no effect on the models that follow.
8. Asymmetry is more likely and more interesting in the case in which $h(m)$ is concave. In that case, firms may fall behind, or find it optimal to stop investing and allow their relative costs to rise.
9. The argument is as follows. Given the assumptions, firm i maximises its profits with respect to x_i so as to satisfy the equation

$$s_i = \frac{1}{b}\left(1 - \frac{c_i}{p}\right)$$

where s_i is its market share. As a result, since $\Sigma s_i = 1$, $p = c/w$ where $w = 1 - 1/bn$, and $c = \Sigma c_i/n$. The profits of firm i are this

$$E^i = \frac{1}{b}\left(1 - \frac{c_i}{c^2}\right)^2 aw^{b-1}c^{1-b}.$$

where $c_i = q_0 + c_0 e^{-fz_i}$, and $z_i = M_i + \theta \sum_{j \neq i} M_j$.

If one differentiates E^i with respect to c_i and c_j, $j \neq i$, and then sets $c_j = c$ and $z_j = z$ for all j, the result is

$$\left(\frac{\partial c}{\partial z}\right)\left(E_i^i + \theta \sum_{j \neq i} E_j^i\right) = \frac{Aw^{b-1}c^b}{n}\left[-2w - \frac{k}{n}(b-1)\right.$$

$$\left. (1 - w) - 2w \right]fc_0e^{-fz}.$$

This is $R_z(z, n, \theta)$. Integrating with respect to z gives

$$R(z, n, \theta) = \frac{Aw^{b-1}c^b}{n(b-1)}\left[2w + \frac{k}{n}(b-1)(1-w)\right.$$

$$\left. - 2w) \right]fc_0e^{-fz}.$$

10. Warning about existence of equilibria.
11. The argument is as follows. With $r = 0$, the firm maximises

$$\int_0^\infty [E^i - (1 - s)m_i]dt$$

subject to $\dot{H}_i = h(m_i)$.

If at t, $m_i(t)$ is increased by ε on $(t, t + dt)$, then on $(t, t + dt)$, H_i is increased by $h'(m_i(t))\varepsilon$. Hence on (t, T) H_i is increased by $h'(m_i)\varepsilon dt$. If $m_i(t)$ is optimal, the marginal benefits must equal to costs or

$$\left[\int_t^T (E_i^i + \theta \sum_{j \neq i} - d\dot{\varsigma})\right]\left[h'(m_i(t))\varepsilon \, dt\right] \leq (1 - s)\varepsilon \, dt$$

or

$$\left[h'(m_i)\int_t^T E_i^i + \theta \sum_{j \neq i} E_j^i\right]d\dot{\varsigma} \leq (1 - s)$$

and if the inequality holds then $m_i = 0$. As $t \to T$, the integral approaches zero. If $h'(m_i)$ is finite then $m_i(t)$ will be zero before $t = T$. If $h'(0) = \infty$, then $m_i(t) \to 0$ as $t \to T$.

REFERENCES

Arrow, K. J. (1971) 'Economic Welfare and the Allocation of Resources for Invention', in K. J. Arrow, *Essays in the Theory of Risk Bearing* (Markham).

Dasgupta, P. and Stiglitz, J. (1980) 'Market Structure and the Nature of Innovative Activity', *Economic Journal*, vol. 90.

Dasgupta, P. and Stiglitz, J. (1980) 'Uncertainty, Industrial Structure and the Speed of R & D', *Bell Journal of Economics*.

Dixit, A. and Stiglitz, J. (1977) 'Monopolistic Competition and Optimum Product Diversity', *American Economic Review*, vol. 67, Jun.

Fisher, F. M. and Temin, P. (1973) 'Returns to Scale in Research and Development: What Does the Schumpeterian Hypothesis Imply?', *Journal of Political Economy*.

Kamien, Morton I. and Schwartz, Nancy L., (1975) 'Market Structure and Innovation: a Survey', *Journal of Economic Literature*, Mar.

Nelson, R. and Winter, S. (1982) *An Evolutionary Theory of Economic Change* (Cambridge, Mass: Harvard University Press).

Scherer, F. M., (1975) 'Firm Size, Market Structure, Opportunity and the Output of Patended Inventions', *American Economic Review*, vol. 65, Dec.

Schumpeter, J. A. (1950) *Capitalism, Socialism and Democracy*, (New York: Harper and Row).

Spence, M. (1976) 'Product Selection, Fixed Costs and Monopolistic Competition', *Review of Economic Studies*, Jun.

Discussion of the Paper by Michael Spence

Willig characterised the Spence analysis in terms of trade-offs across three operative features of R & D. First, the traditional characteristic of R & D was that the more appropriable was R & D, the greater was the private incentive to conduct R & D. (Appropriability had positive incentive features.) Second, however, the more appropriable (private) was the R & D, the greater the required amount of R & D replication for all firms to be technically efficient. Further, a specialist R & D firm selling the outcome of R & D to other firms was not efficient, for once the research was completed, the costs of an additional sale was virtually zero so any positive price was inefficient and if zero prices were set, we again had an appropriability problem. Finally, more firms were needed simply from the view point of the state of competition in the product market. That was, the greater the number of firms competing in the product market, the closer was product price to marginal cost. So, the trade-offs involved private incentives, wasteful industry-wide replication of R & D, and competition (pricing behaviour) in the product market.

Willig summarised the central features of the Spence model as follows: The post-invention game could be represented as a static oligopoly in inputs (outputs were homogeneous) yielding a rent flow to firm i of $E^i(Z) \equiv X_i^* P(\Sigma X_j^*) - C_i(Z_i) X_i^*$, where X_i^* was the equilibrium output of firm i and Z_i was the state of technological knowledge held by firm i. In turn, $Z_i \equiv M_i + \theta \Sigma M_j$ ($j \neq i$) where M_i was the expenditure of resources (\$) by firm i and θ was a non-appropriability parameter. The prior R & D decision was to maximise the flow of rents from invention $V^i(M) \equiv E^i(Z_i)/r - (1 - s)M_i$ where $E^i(Z_i)/r$ was the capitalised rent stream and s was a subsidy parameter. The first-order condition on R & D expenditures was $[\partial E^i/\partial Z^i + \theta \Sigma \theta E^i/\partial M_j]/r = 1 - s$. From this as $\partial E^i/\partial M_j < 0$, the incentive effect of appropriability was obvious. Symmetry yielded the total expenditure on R & D by the industry as $Z[n/(1 + \theta(n - 1))]$ where ∂ (total expenditures)$/\partial n > 0$ (the replication effect). Finally, within this problem, each firm faced increasing returns to scale as $AC_i/MC_i = 1 + M_i/C_i X_i$ so there were only a few firms in this industry (the number-of-firms effect on competition). Willig then summarised both the positive and normative features of the Spence model.

In commenting on the R & D problem, Willig suggested that the degree of appropriability of the output of research could be increased if more creative ways were designed to sell R & D output. He wondered what might happen if firms could give up the output of R & D research in exchange for a percentage of the profits that this research would generate. He also argued that many of the results presented by Spence depended on his assumption that equilibrium in the output market involved quantity-setting rather than price-setting strategies by firms. For example, if R & D output was not appropriable in the sense that results were shared equally among all firms, expenditures that reduced costs for one firm, reduced costs for all firms. With Bertrand equilibrium, prices would fall by the full extent of the cost reduction. In this type of world, there would be no incentive at all for firms to do research. On the other hand, if results were perfectly appropriable, development of a cost-saving technology would not cause the equilibrium price to fall. Incentives to do research would be large. He suggested that more attention should be given to alternative equilibrium concepts.

Schmalensee argued that many of the policy options considered by Spence should be considered as illustrations rather than serious options. For example, subsidisation of R & D expenditures would cause firms to over-report R & D expenditures. The government would have to expend resources to verify expenditures as R & D expenditures before subsidy payments could be made. He added that he felt that many of the broader conclusions of Spence's paper could be generalised in the direction of more general functional forms.

Von Ungern-Sternberg wondered why the sorts of spill-overs that occurred in R & D models might not also be applied to situations with learning curves. The idea was that one firm learnt from its rival's mistakes. *Spence* responded that, in fact, spill-overs could be applied. Spence suggested that, unlike the R & D problem where spill-overs increased efficiency and reduced incentives at the same time, spill-overs in a learning curve model would have only beneficial effects.

Nelson referred to his unpublished co-authored study of government R & D policies in seven different industries. The results suggested that in industries where research results were not appropriable, there had been significant government involvement in research. He cited agriculture as an example. On the other hand, when results were appropriable, as in computers and pharmaceuticals, there had been great resistance to government involvement in R & D and great efforts made to prevent the degree of appropriability from falling.

Selten remarked that the dynamic solutions computed by Spence involved open-loop equilibria. Closed-loop equilibria might give different results.

Gabszewicz criticised the Spencian approach because the results of R & D expenditures were always certain. He suggested three ways that R & D output might generate uncertainty: first, the timing of discovery; second, the effect that the discovery had on costs; and third, to the extent that the research generated a new product, the level of demand that would prevail once the product was introduced. These considerations would be especially relevant to the issue of centralisation of R & D expenditures, since centralisation would allow pooling of these risks.

Panzar viewed the model as one in which firms undertake investment which was, from the social viewpoint, a pure public good but from the private viewpoint, only a quasi-public good. The functional form chosen for costs was chosen such that the industry was a natural monopoly. In these circumstances the welfare effects of wasteful competition would always be mixed up with the welfare impacts of the R & D itself. He wondered whether there might not be a functional form for costs that would keep the industry from being a natural monopoly.

Stiglitz argued that if the returns to R & D were uncertain, and imperfectly correlated, then, from a social viewpoint it would be optimal for a number of firms to engage in R & D. This, in itself, would tend to eliminate the natural-monopoly situation. He also questioned Spence's concentration on symmetric equilibria and asked what the nature of asymmetric equilibria might be. *Spence* responded that in the models he had analysed, the dominant firm tended to improve industry performance. The reason was that the dominant firm tended to deter entry by smaller rivals, so that output and R & D were produced more efficiently by the single large firm. The efficiency benefits outweighed the misallocation that occured because there was a single firm.

17 The Theory of Technological Competition

Partha Dasgupta

UNIVERSITY OF CAMBRIDGE

I THE SCHUMPETERIAN HERITAGE

It is not self-evident that economists ought to engage in the task of explaining the characteristics of technological innovations. It is even less evident that development and inventive activities are related to the structure of economic organisations. Or so it would seem from the near-complete absence of a discussion of such issues in resource-allocation theory.[2] So would it seem, as well, from the sheer volume of effort that has been spent over the past quarter of a century in trying to demonstrate that economic forces are a prime architect of technological change.[3] If there is a single driving force behind these empirical investigations, it is the writings of Joseph Schumpeter (most especially perhaps his *Capitalism, Socialism and Democracy*, Schumpeter, 1976). Since recent developments in the theory of technological competition have addressed a few of the empirical findings, they reflect this heritage as well.

Economists are prone to having hero-figures. In the economics of technological change, Joseph Schumpeter continues to reign as the undisputed godfather. As with all such personalities, there is much discussion about what he actually *meant*. Nevertheless, it is clear that the several components of his scheme of thought are not all equally persuasive and some, it can be argued, have been downright detrimental to further developments of the subject. Thus, for example, Rosenberg (1976), Chapter 4, has shown how Schumpeter's obsession with the act of *innovation*, and the dominant role he gave to charismatic entrepreneurs at the vanguard of clusters of innovation, has

519

deflected attention from economic aspects of *inventive* and *development* activity. But the Schumpeterian view that there are periodic appearances of clusters of innovation (and this forms an important ingredient in his theory of business cycles) should be distinguished from his beliefs about the influence of the size of firms and the concentration of industries on technological change. And it is the latter which has had much the greater influence on recent thinking. Here too, his influence – or, to be more precise, the influence of what economists *thought* he meant – has not been entirely beneficial.[4]

The point is that, like other system-builders, Schumpeter did not write with the utmost clarity. It is easy enough to be beguiled into thinking that one understands the Schumpeterian vision until, that is, one attempts to formalise it. Take, for example, Schumpeter's claim that monopolistic firms *supply* more innovations than do competitive firms.[5] On this he says:

> there are superior methods available to the monopolist which either are not available at all to a crowd of competitors or are not available to them readily: for there are advantages which, though not strictly unattainable on the competitive level of enterprise, are as a matter of fact secured only on the monopoly level, for instance, because monopolization may increase the sphere of influence of the better, and decrease the sphere of influence of the inferior, brains, or because the monopoly enjoys a disproportionately higher financial standing. (Schumpeter, 1976, p. 101).

Here Schumpeter seems to be saying that large size has distinct advantages, whereas elsewhere on the same page he recognises that monopoly and large size are not synonymous. Now, someone interested in the structure of *industries*, but not so much in the internal organisations of *firms*, would be justified in treating an assertion about the relationship between the size of firms and their research and development (R & D) opportunities as a *hypothesis*. In this sense, Schumpeter's belief that there are increasing returns to scale in R & D – both to the size of R & D establishment and to the size of the firm engaged in R & D – *is* a hypothesis.[6] But the same status must not be awarded to claims about the relationship between *monopolistic* firms and their supply of innovations, for such claims ought to be derivable propositions within any theory which purports to embrace the structure of industries.

Here Schumpeter is less than clear. His famous chapter on the process of creative destruction (Schumpeter, 1976, ch.7) suggests strongly that he regarded the *threat* of entry by rival innovators as providing the essential spur to a sitting monopolist to innovate. But I have found no passage in which he asks whether the incentives for innovation would be greater or less in a competitive industry if the innovator had the guarantee of some form of patent protection. One can argue that recent propositions on pre-emptive patenting provide some partial support for the Schumpeterian view on the relationship between monopoly and the supply of innovations (see Dasgupta and Stiglitz, 1980b and Gilbert and Newbery, 1982). But these are derived propositions, not hypotheses. (See Section V.)

The lack of clarity in Schumpeter's writings is most conspicuous when one reflects that an entire generation of researchers has interpreted his views on market structure and innovative activity in *causal* terms: *from* market structure *to* innovative activity. Admittedly it has been customary to note in passing that the influence is not unidirectional, but the theoretical literature in which both market structure and innovative activity are endogenous remains sparse.[7] Most theoretical treatments of the subject take industrial structure as a datum. What is possibly more disturbing is that empirical observations on the relationship between innovative activity and the structure of industries have consistently been given a causal interpretation. (See Nelson *et al.*, 1967 and Kamien and Schwartz 1975, 1982 for references. An important exception is the work of Levin and Reiss, 1984.) The policy implications of such interpretations are rather obvious. For example, if it is held that industrial concentration is a *reason* for the intensity of innovative activity, then presumably anti-trust legislation will be called into question. The question is whether industrial structure ought to be raw data in a theory of technological competition. Quite obviously, except in the short run, it ought not. It would seem then that innovative activity and industrial structure both in turn depend on such ingredients as technological 'opportunities', demand conditions, the nature of capital markets and the legal structure.[8] At least some of the empirical explorations have tested hypotheses about such dependence. It is of not inconsiderable interest to know whether simple theoretical considerations can accommodate such empirical findings. In Section II I shall present a set of such empirical findings. The remainder of the chapter will be devoted to an examination of theoretical constructions that can cope with them. In Section III I review a model of *process* innovation and look at the nature of a particular form of technological competition. Section IV briefly discusses the issue of imitative research. A central feature of the models in Sections III and IV is that firms make their moves *simultaneously*. In Section V, therefore, I consider situations where it is natural to have firms move *sequentially*. The issue of pre-emptive patenting, which is the subject of Section V, is best discussed in this way. One of my purposes is to locate conditions under which a sitting monopolist pre-empts *all* potential patents. I shall be able to report only some limited results on this question. But they are suggestive. Finally, in Section VI, I attempt to classify models of technological competition. I argue that an essential distinction is based on whether the game describing the form of technological competition is *continuous* or *discontinuous*. This depends, quite obviously, on the form of rewards to innovators under the social organisation in question and, in particular, whether or not the competition is in the form of *tournaments*. The models developed in Sections III and V are examples of these two forms of competition.

II EMPIRICAL OBSERVATIONS

Before presenting one of his growth theories, Professor Kaldor, in a now classic article, began by listing a set of 'stylised facts' which, he felt, a growth model ought to generate as implications (see Kaldor, 1961). I rather doubt that the empirical observations that I shall list below can *all* be elevated to the status of stylised facts; 'academic rumours' would be a more accurate description. In the field of technological change there is often some ambiguity about what hypothesis the investigator has in fact tested (see Fisher and Temin, 1973). Moreover, economists attempting to test the same hypothesis have in several cases obtained conflicting results (see Kamien and Schwartz, 1975, 1982). In addition, one is often forced – due to data limitations – to use vastly imperfect surrogates for variables one wants to measure (e.g. the number of patents as a measure of the output of R & D effort). Unquestionably, we are in treacherous terrain. A theorist has to have gall to follow Professor Kaldor's deep footprints even at the best of times. Here it is positively foolhardy. I feel that I have to soften my pose by saying that it is no *disgrace* if a theory of technological competition accommodates the empirical observations that I shall list below.[9]

I want to separate these empirical observations into two categories. The first are those that should influence the choice of hypotheses on which a model of technological competition is based. The second are those that the theory should explain.

I begin with the first set:

(1) Over a wide range of industries it has been observed that there is a positive association between R & D effort (i.e. research inputs) and innovative output. (See e.g., Comanor, 1965; Schmookler, 1966; Mansfield, 1968; and Comanor and Scherer, 1969.)

(2) The cost associated with developing something seems to increase more than proportionately with a shortening of the period of development. That is, the transformation possibilities between time and cost are convex to the origin. (See Mansfield *et al.*, 1971.)

(3) In general, the technological possibilities linking R & D inputs and innovative outputs do not display any economies of scale with respect to the size of the firm in which R & D is undertaken. (See Kamien and Schwartz, 1975, pp. 8–11 for detailed comments on this observation.)

(4) Technological opportunities for making inventions and undertaking innovations are not independent of advances in basic scientific knowledge. Phillips, 1966 and Rosenberg, 1974, in particular, have emphasised the importance of progress in the underlying scientific base for making innovative possibilities easier.

(5) Success breeds success. Phillips, 1971, in particular, has argued that because learning involves costs, successful firms possess an advantage over their rivals in enjoying greater possibilities for further successes.

(6) A principal goal of R & D activity is the creation of entry barriers. The nature of inventive activity by existing firms defines limits to entry by new firms; that is, research and development can be a major element of interfirm rivalry. (See e.g., Comanor, 1964, 1967 and Freeman, 1965.)

Observation (1) may appear banal. But it is good to have actual evidence for it. If it were otherwise, the *economics* of technological change would be an uninteresting subject. In any event, I would not be writing this chapter now.

Observation (2) is interesting, because it suggests that in the construction of formal models one would want to assume some degree of diminishing returns to R & D effort. I hasten to add that this does *not* imply that the theory of technological competition will be similar to the theory of price competition. In particular, I shall note subsequently that (2) in itself does *not* rule out significantly increasing returns to scale in the relationship between a firm's R & D effort and its *economic* benefits.

Observation (3) has been much discussed and I shall not comment on it. (4) may appear self-evident. It has required emphasis by various authors (in particular Rosenberg, 1974) because there are theories that regard basic science today as so versatile that its progress, or so it is claimed, does not influence the *direction* of R & D activity (see Schmookler, 1966). (5) is interesting because it provides a direct reason for the persistence of monopoly. It is related to Professor Arrow's notion of learning-by-doing (see Arrow, 1962b). I shall look at the implications of this when I come to discuss preemptive patenting in Section V.

Observation (6) is of great importance. It provides a central distinctive characteristic of technological competition. One would clearly want a model of technological competition to blend with conventional price competition if the possibilities of entry barriers through R & D activity are negligible. In Section III I shall review a model of technological competition which has precisely this feature.

I now come to the second list of empirical observations:

(1*) A considerable body of research evidence suggests that larger firms do *not* engage in more R & D activity *relative* to their size than smaller firms. (See Kamien and Schwartz, 1975, pp. 16–18 for an assessment of this.)

(2*) There is a positive association between the degree of concentration in an industry and innovative activity within it, so long as concentration is not too great. That is, measures of R & D input relative to the industry's sales achieve their maximum at 'moderate' levels of concentration (see Scherer, 1967b). It has also been suggested (see Comanor, 1967), that concentration is associated with innovative activity in those cases where technological and innovative opportunities are weak.

(3*) Industries facing greater technological and innovative opportunities tend to be more concentrated (see Scherer, 1967b).

(4*) Growth in demand for the products of an industry stimulates R & D activity within it (see Schmookler, 1966).

(5*) There is some evidence that earlier R & D successes lead to greater current R & D effort on the part of successful firms. It has been argued that, from this, one might expect these firms to produce further innovations and thus to widen the gap between themselves and their rivals (see Grabowski, 1968).

(6*) Research activity appears to be strongest in industries where entry barriers are neither too high, nor too low; that is, it is strongest in industries where, say, rapid imitation is not possible but where entry has not been effectively foreclosed (Comanor, 1967).

(7*) Recent work by Professor Zvi Griliches and his associates suggests that there is a positive relationship between a firm's R & D activity and its stock market value (see, e.g., Pakes, 1984).

(8*) Imitative research is a pervasive phenomenon. Mansfield *et al.*, 1981 have reported that 60 per cent of the patented innovations in a sample of 48 industries studied by them were imitated within four years.

Observations (1*) and (3), though related, are nowhere near to being the same. Even if one uses (3) as an ingredient in a model, one would still need to check whether those firms that *become* larger in the process of technological competition spend more on R & D relative to their size. (2*) has been much discussed in the literature and it has been customary to impute a *causal* explanation to it. I shall come back and comment on this interpretation in Section III. The latter half on (2*) and (3*) have had several interpretations. For example, Comanor, 1967 interprets 'innovative opportunities' as the ease with which firms can engage in product differentiation. There are others, and I shall provide a natural one for the model that I discuss in Section III.

Observation (4*), chiefly associated with the works of Jacob Schmookler, has been widely discussed (see e.g. Rosenberg, 1976, and Dasgupta and Stiglitz, 1981). It provides the basis for a demand-led view of technological change and is, quite naturally, appealing to economists.

Observations (5) and (5*) are clearly related, in that (5) may be used as an immediate explanation for (5*). I shall attempt to probe this issue with some care when discussing pre-emptive patenting in Section V. (6*) may appear to be rather obvious and readily explainable. Nevertheless, it merits theoretical clarification. (7*) is interesting and can be addressed properly only in a model with an explicit stock market. I shall not do that here. Instead, I shall use the crude device of regarding a firm's profit level as a surrogate for its stock market value. (8*) has long been suspected of being true through casual empiricism. But it is only recently that systematic work has been done on the matter. Mansfield *et al.* (1981) have chided theorists for not incorporating technological imitation into their models, without bothering to ask what it is that the theorists they cite were *trying* to do.

A theoretical model does not become more virtuous by having additional complexities thrown in. I take it that the idea is not to have more and more 'real' features of the world introduced into the same model. The model would not then illuminate. It seems to me that the thing that has plagued theoretical work in the economics of technological competition is precisely a denial of this. For example, it is patently the case that the outcome of inventive and development activity is uncertain and that R & D decisions are not the 'once and for all' variety; that is, a firm *phases* its R & D programme over time.[10] In fact much has been made of this. The question is whether it is ridiculous to ignore either or both. The answer, quite obviously, is to what end the model is constructed. One can hardly avoid introducing uncertainty if, say, it is the relationship between the size of firm and the choice of the degree of risk-taking in R & D strategy that is under investigation. But no significant additional insight is obtained if results are restricted to those relating, say, the *expected* date of the completion of R & D work to other variables, when the same kind of relation has been obtained in a model devoid of uncertainty.

A slight unease about such methodological issues is also reflected in the recent monograph by Kamien and Schwartz (1982), where they catalogue modern *approaches* to theories of market structure and innovation according to whether they are *decision*-theoretic or *game*-theoretic. It transpires that by the former they mean investigations that study a firm's response to an exogenously given (or evolving) market environment and by the latter those which allow firms to interact strategically. But these are not different *approaches* at all. The former simply asks a more restricted set of questions. To say they are different approaches is rather like saying that the chapter on the competitive firm in, say, Debreu (1959) represents a different approach to a study of price-taking behaviour from that in the chapter on competitive equilibrium in the same book.

I emphasise these rather obvious methodological points because it is my intention in the remainder of this chapter to discuss theoretical constructs that can accommodate the empirical observations that I have listed, and I want *only* to consider the most 'economic' constructs that will do the work for me. An appeal to Occam's dictum is particularly important here. That the models which follow are 'simplistic' and do not capture many 'real world' features is not a confession, it is an assertion.

III NON-TOURNAMENT FORMS OF TECHNOLOGICAL COMPETITION

(1) PRELIMINARIES

The construction I shall discuss in this section has been presented in detail in Dasgupta and Stiglitz, 1980a, Section II. Here I want to have the model face the empirical observations listed in the previous section. The model is timeless and devoid of uncertainty. I study a market for a homogeneous product and I assume away income effects. Technological competition takes the form of *process innovation*.[11] I imagine that firms cannot manufacture the product without engaging in R & D activity, but that technological opportunities and the patent structure are such that if a firm spends x on R & D it can manufacture the commodity at unit cost $c(x)$, where $c(x)$ is twice continuously-differentiable; is declining in x; and displays diminishing returns to R & D expenditure: that is, $c(0) = \infty; c'(x) < 0$; and $c''(x) > 0$. The model therefore captures the features embodied in observations (1) to (3).[12]

Let $p(Q)$ be the market demand function, where Q is the total output of the commodity in question. I assume it to be twice continuously-differentiable and downward-sloping. Often, I shall specialise and consider the iso-elastic forms:

$$p(Q) = \sigma Q^{-\varepsilon}, \qquad \sigma, \varepsilon > 0 ;$$

and

$$c(x) = \beta x^{-\alpha}, \qquad \beta, \alpha > 0.$$

(2) EXOGENOUSLY-GIVEN ENTRY BARRIERS

To fix ideas, I begin with the case where there are precisely n firms in the industry – which in this case means that it is only these n firms that can engage in R & D and final production. Firms are indexed by i and j $(i, j = 1, \ldots ,n)$; and $x_i (\geq 0)$ and $Q_i (\geq 0)$ denote respectively the R & D expenditure and output level of firm i. All firms, by hypothesis, choose their R & D expenditure and output levels *simultaneously*. It follows that profit earned by i, which I denote by π_i, is of the form:

$$\pi_i = \left(p \left(\sum_{j \neq i} Q_j + Q_i \right) - c(x_i) \right) Q_i - x_i. \tag{3}$$

I am interested in a non-co-operative outcome. It is then natural to look at Nash–Cournot equilibria. Since the game is symmetric (output is homogeneous and firms face the same innovation opportunities, $c(x)$) we look for a symmetric equilibrium (i.e., where all firms pick the same strategy). I am not interested only in an existence theorem; I want also to be able to characterise equilibria so as to confront the model with empirical observations. Towards this we specialise and suppose that $p(Q)$ and $c(x)$ satisfy equations (1) and (2) respectively. It is then a simple matter to prove:

Theorem 1 If $p(Q)$ and $c(x)$ satisfy (1) and (2) respectively, and if n is a positive integer, then a symmetric Nash–Cournot equilibrium amongst n firms exists if:

(i) $\varepsilon < n \leqslant \varepsilon(1 + \alpha) / \alpha$,   and (ii) $\varepsilon(1 + \alpha) /\alpha > 1$. \tag{4}

Proof See Dasgupta and Stiglitz, 1980a, Appendix 1.[13]

In fact, one can explicitly compute the symmetric Nash–Cournot equilibrium which, as it happens, is unique. Routine calculations show that if $p(Q)$ and $c(x)$ satisfy (1) and (2) respectively, and if we denote R & D expenditure and output level of the representative firm at the symmetric equilibrium by x^* and Q^*/n respectively, then:

$$x^* = [\sigma(\alpha/n)^\varepsilon \beta^{\varepsilon-1} (1 - \varepsilon/n)]^{1/(\varepsilon - \alpha(1 - \varepsilon))}, \tag{5}$$

and

$$Q^*/n = (1/\alpha\beta)[\sigma(\alpha/n)^\varepsilon \beta^{\varepsilon-1} (1 - \varepsilon/n)]^{(1 + \alpha)/(\varepsilon - \alpha(1-\varepsilon))}. \tag{6}$$

Notice that $x^*(n + 1) < x^*(n)$ and $Q^*(n + 1) > Q^*(n)$; that is, if *inter-firm rivalry* is increased, equilibrium R & D effort per firm decreases, but market-output increases (see also Loury, 1979).[14]

The central limitation of this construct, for my purposes here, is that industrial structure is not explained; it is not endogenous. That is, the number of firms in the industry is given in advance of the analysis. But I need this model in order to confront observation (7*) of Section II for reasons that will become clear later.

I want to see the relationship between a firm's profit level and the level of its R & D activity. Both are endogenous to the construct, of course. So I shall have to vary some parameter of the model and see whether the equilibrium values of the two move in the same direction.

Using (1), (2), (5) and (6) in equation (3), it is a routine matter to check that:

$$\pi_i^* = [((\varepsilon(1+\alpha)-n\alpha)/\alpha)/(n-\varepsilon)][\sigma(\alpha/n)^\varepsilon \beta^{\varepsilon-1}(1-\varepsilon/n)]^{1/(\varepsilon-\alpha(1-\varepsilon))}, \quad (7)$$

where π_i^* denotes the *equilibrium* level of profit. Obviously, I want to assume that $\varepsilon(1+\alpha) > n\alpha$ (see condition (i) of (4)). Thus $\pi_i^* = \pi^* > 0$ in (7).

From (5) and (7) we obtain:

Corollary 1.1 If the conditions of Theorem 1 are satisfied, $\partial x^*/\partial\sigma$, $\partial\pi^*/\partial\sigma > 0$; $\partial x^* \partial\beta, \pi^*/\partial\beta \geqslant (<) 0$ as $\varepsilon \geqslant (<) 1$; and $x^*(n) > x^*(n+1)$, $\pi^*(n) > \pi^*(n+1)$. That is, in a cross-section study of industries differing solely by σ (the size of the market) *or* by β (the underlying scientific base; see observation (4)), *or* by n (the number of firms), one would find a positive association between a firm's R & D activity and its profit level (see 7^*). However, there is no causal direction in this relationship.

(3) ENDOGENOUS ENTRY BARRIERS

I come now to the central issue I wish to look at in Section III – the implications for the theory of technological competition when industrial structure is endogenous; that is, when the number of firms in the industry is *not* a datum. I suppose that there is a very large number of *potential* firms. The number of active firms is determined within the model. It is simplest to assume that the decision on whether or not to enter as well as decisions on how much to spend on R & D and how much to produce are made simultaneously by all firms.[15] It is clear from equation (3) both that R & D expenditure is a form of *fixed cost* and that it is a strategic variable. It creates entry barriers for rival firms by enabling a firm to produce the commodity at low unit cost (see observation (6)).

The obvious equilibrium notion is the Nash–Cournot one. I state it formally as:

Definition[16] $(n^*, (x_1^*, Q_1^*), \ldots, (x_i^*, Q_i^*), \ldots, (x_{n^*}^*, Q_{n^*}^*))$ is an equilibrium (with free legal entry) if for $i = 1, \ldots, n^*$,

$$\left(p\left(\sum_{j \neq i} Q_j^* + Q_i^* \right) - c(x_i^*) \right) Q_i^* - x_i^*$$

$$\geq \left(p\left(\sum_{j \neq i} Q_j^* + Q_i \right) - c(x_i) \right) Q_i - x_i \qquad \text{for all } x_i, Q_i \geq 0, \qquad (8)$$

and

$$\left(p\left(\sum_{i=1}^{n^*} Q_i^* + Q \right) - c(x) \right) Q - x \leq 0 \qquad \text{for all } x, Q \geq 0. \qquad (9)$$

As before, I am interested not only in an existence theorem but also in the characteristics of equilibria. Towards this, I specialise and suppose that $p(Q)$ and $c(x)$ satisfy (1) and (2). Then one has the following theorem:

Theorem 2 If $p(Q)$ and $c(x)$ satisfy (1) and (2) respectively there then exists $\bar{\alpha}(\varepsilon, \beta, \sigma)$ (> 0) such that if $0 < \alpha \leq \bar{\alpha}(\varepsilon, \beta, \sigma)$, there is a symmetric Nash–Cournot equilibrium with free entry.

Proof This comprises slight variations on the arguments in Novshek (1980) and Dasgupta and Stiglitz 1980a.

Looking at equation (2), one notes that α is the elasticity of the invention–possibility curve. The smaller is α, the fewer are 'innovational opportunities'. Therefore, I shall use α as the index of 'innovational opportunities' in the industry. Theorem 2 says that a symmetric equilibrium – under technological competition with free legal entry – exists if innovational opportunities are not excessive. But the problem is that even symmetric-equilibrium need not be unique. I therefore take a hint from condition (i) in Theorem 1 and consider the following selection mechanism (see Dasgupta and Stiglitz, 1980a, Appendix 2). Denote by $[y]$ the largest positive integer not in excess of the real number y. Now consider the number $\varepsilon(1 + \alpha) / \alpha$, (see condition (i) in Theorem 1). If we choose $n = [\varepsilon(1 + \alpha) / \alpha]$, then $\varepsilon(1 + \alpha) / n\alpha \simeq 1$ if α is small enough. Theorems 1 and 2, and equation (7), imply that if α is small enough a symmetric equilibrium with free entry exists and that the equilibrium profit level per firm is negligible if the number of active firms selected is $[\varepsilon(1 + \alpha) / \alpha]$. It follows that, provided α is small enough, we can suppose that profit per firm in equilibrium is negligible. I assume this. If we use an asterisk to denote the equilibrium values of economic variables, it is a routine matter to show that:

$$\varepsilon/n^* = n^*x^*/p(Q^*)Q^* , \tag{10}$$

$$n^*x^*/p(Q^*)Q^* = \alpha/(1 + \alpha) , \tag{11}$$

and

$$p(Q^*)/c(x^*) = 1 + \alpha \tag{12}$$

(See Dasgupta and Stiglitz, 1980a, Section II.)

In fact, one can easily solve these equilibrium conditions and express n^*, x^* and Q^* explicitly as:

$$n^* = \varepsilon(1 + \alpha)/\alpha, \tag{13}$$

$$x^* = [\sigma\alpha^{2\varepsilon} \beta^{\varepsilon-1} \varepsilon^{-\varepsilon} (1 + \alpha)^{-(1 + \varepsilon)}]^{1/(\varepsilon-\alpha(1-\varepsilon))} \tag{14}$$

and

$$Q^* = [\varepsilon(1 + \alpha)/\alpha^2\beta] [\sigma\alpha^{2\varepsilon} \beta^{\varepsilon-1} \varepsilon^{-\varepsilon} (1 + \alpha)^{-(1+\varepsilon)}]^{(1+\alpha)/(\varepsilon-\alpha(1-\varepsilon))} \tag{15}$$

I now proceed to analyse this equilibrium in the light of the empirical observations that I listed in Section II.

First, notice from equation (13) that n^* does not depend on σ and β.[17] From equation (10) we may therefore conclude with

Corollary 2.1 In a cross-section study of industries differing solely by way of σ (the size of the market) and β (the underlying scientific base), firms will be found to spend the same amount on R & D relative to their size; that is, $n^*x^*/p(Q^*)Q^*$ is independent of σ and β (See (1*).)

I come now to (2*). Since the equilibrium being studied is symmetric, any declining function of n^* can be used as a measure of industrial concentration. Here, of course, concentration is endogenous. I take the index of industrial concentration to be $1/n^*$. Note that the equilibrium conditions that I am studying are valid only if σ is small; that is, if 'innovative opportunities' are weak. From (13) we conclude that equilibrium concentration is 'low'. We now take note of equation (10) to obtain

Corollary 2.2 In a cross-section study of industries characterised by the same ε but differing α, one would observe a positive, linear relationship between industrial concentration $(1/n^*)$ and R & D expenditure as a fraction of sales $(n^*x^*/p(Q^*)Q^*)$; and this relation would hold only if innovative opportunities were weak. (See (2*).)

But no causality should be imputed to this relationship, since both variables are simultaneously determined.

We may, next, quickly confirm from equation (13) the following corollary.

Corollary 2.3 $\partial n^*/\partial\alpha < 0$, so that industries facing greater innovative opportunities are more concentrated. (See (3*).)

Next, equations (13) and (14) imply

Corollary 2.4 $\partial n^*/\partial\sigma = 0$ and $\partial x^*/\partial\sigma > 0$. Therefore an increase in the size of the product market leads to an increase in the equilibrium level of R & D activity per firm, as well as in that for the industry as a whole. (See (4*).) (Notice that the $c(x)$ function can be given the more conventional interpretation of a menu of technologies characterised by less or more 'specialisation' in production. The result, $\partial x^*/\partial\sigma > 0$, can then be used to substantiate the classical claim that the 'division of labour' varies with the size of the market and that, in particular, the greater the size of the market, the greater is the division of labour.)

Observation (5*) obviously cannot be accommodated by the model under discussion, not so much because it demands an explicit intertemporal structure, as much because it demands that we distinguish between firms. A model in which firms are *ex ante* identical cannot obviously broach (5*). I shall look at (5*) in Section V.

It is obvious that, as it stands, (6*) can be given several interpretations. Comanor, 1967 was concerned among other things with the spill-over of knowledge acquired through R & D and the possibilities of imitative research. Since I have prohibited any spill-over of knowledge in my model, I cannot discuss this interpretation. But Comanor, 1967 was also concerned with barriers to entry created by innovative opportunities. For the model under study, the parameter which reflects the possibilities for the creation of entry barriers is α, the elasticity of the innovation-locus. I remind the reader that the zero-profit approximation (which we have maintained so far) is valid only if α is 'small'; that is, if innovative opportunities are 'small'. From equations (13) and (14), we note that $x^* \to 0$ and $n^* \to \infty$ as $\alpha \to 0$, but that $n^*x^* \to 0$ as $\alpha \to 0$. In addition, equation (12) tells us that $p(Q^*)/c(x^*) \to 1$ as $\alpha \to 0$. So we have

Corollary 2.5 If innovative opportunities are weak, so that barriers to entry are weak, then the weaker are innovative opportunities the smaller is R & D effort in the industry. In particular, if innovative opportunities are vanishingly small, technological competition is vanishingly small and we would expect price competition to prevail; that is equilibrium under technological competition tends to a Walrasian equilibrium. (See (6*).)[18]

It should now be clear why I was forced to look at (7*) by way of the model of Section III.2. For computational ease, I have assumed α to be small enough in this section (III 3) for equilibrium-profit per firm to be 'negligible'. Quite obviously, I cannot test (7*) in such a context.

IV IMITATION

Imitative innovation would appear to be pervasive. The valuable recent work by Mansfield *et al*. (1981) suggests that, as one might expect, imitators usually *do* save on innovation costs. (In a sample of 48 new products they found that, on average, the ratio of imitation cost to innovation cost was 0.65.) But, of course, by definition the imitator *follows*, and so does not enjoy the profits that the innovator makes in the interim period. It is not unusual to hear the opinion that some firms are congenital imitators, while others are leaders. There may well be something in this, though it would be an error to think that from the *economic* point of view imitative research has less to commend it (see Rosenberg, 1976, ch. 4).[19] From an analytical point of view, it seems therefore that a preliminary question of some importance is whether it is possible that it is strategically convenient for one firm to be the innovator and for another to be the imitator, even when the two are *ex ante* similar. The answer must undoubtedly be 'yes', for we are familiar with such phenomena in what are called 'games of co-ordination', (also called 'mixed-motive' games; see Schelling, 1960).

Thus, consider a game characterised by two firms, each of which has two choices: innovate *now* (N) or *later* (L). Suppose the pay-off matrix of the game is the one given in Table 17.1.

The game is symmetric; implying that neither firm has an advantage. It has two pure-strategy Nash equilibria, (N, L) and (L, N). At such a Nash equilibrium, one is the innovator (N) and the other the imitator (L). Moreover, each firm has a preferred equilibrium.[20] It

TABLE 17.1

		$i = 1$	
$i = 2$		L	N
	L	(8, 8)	(5, 10)
	N	(10, 5)	(4, 4)

remains to construct a simple economic model which gives flesh to this pay-off matrix.[21]

Assume, as in the foregoing game, that there are two firms ($i = 1$, 2). A firm can adopt a new technology either now ($t = 0$) or at date T (> 0). The present value of expenditures involved in being an innovator is a constant, C^* (> 0); that of being an imitator is C^{**} (with $0 < C^{**} < C^*$). So long as neither has innovated, each earns profits at the rate π_0 (> 0). So long as one firm has adopted, but not the other, the innovator earns profits at the rate π_1 (> 0) and the other at the rate π_2 (> 0). After both have adopted, each earns profits at the rate π_3 (> 0). Naturally, one wants to assume that $\pi_1 > \pi_0 > \pi_2$.[22] The capital market is assumed perfectly competitive, and the rate of interest is a constant r (> 0). Each firm is interested in the present value of its profits.[23] A firm's strategy is its date of adoption of the new technology. By hypothesis, a firm can choose either $t = 0$ or $t = T$. Let $V_1 (t_1, t_2)$ be the present value of profits earned by firm 1 if firm i chooses t_i ($i = 1, 2$). The game is symmetric. Therefore, $V_1 (t_1, t_2) = V_2 (t_2, t_1)$. Finally, we may compute the pay-off matrix explicitly as:

$$
\begin{aligned}
V_1(0, 0) &= \pi_3 \int_0^\infty e^{-rt}\, dt - C^* \\[2mm]
V_1(0, T) &= \pi_1 \int_0^T e^{-rt}\, dt + \pi_3 \int_T^\infty e^{-rt}\, dt - C^* \\[2mm]
V_1(T, 0) &= \pi_2 \int_0^T e^{-rt}\, dt + \pi_3 \int_T^\infty e^{-rt}\, dt - C^{**} \\[2mm]
V_1(T, T) &= \pi_0 \int_0^T e^{-rt}\, dt + \pi_3 \int_T^\infty e^{-rt}\, dt - C^*.
\end{aligned}
\tag{16}
$$

We have supposed that $\pi_1 > \pi_0 > \pi_2$. From (16) it is then simple to check that if

$$(\pi_0 - \pi_2)\, e^{-rT} > r(C^* - C^{**}) > (\pi_3 - \pi_2)e^{-rT},$$

the pay-off matrix of this game has the same form as the one in Table 17.1: in particular, there are two pure-strategy Nash equilibria $(0, T)$ and $(T, 0)$ and a symmetric mixed-strategy equilibrium.

V PRE-EMPTIVE PATENTING

(1) TOURNAMENTS AS DISCONTINUOUS GAMES

The model of technological competition that I analysed in Section III has three features worth emphasising. First, it assumes implicitly that there is a large number of research strategies – strictly speaking an infinite number of research strategies. Each active firm picks a niche for itself amongst them. Stated another way, the model assumes a continuum of possible patents to be won. (In equilibrium, of course, only a finite number are awarded.)

Second, the pay-off functions of firms are all continuous. Thus the model does not distinguish winners and losers sharply: if a firm alters his action slightly, his net reward changes slightly. Put another way, the reward schedules faced by the competitors are not of the form of a *tournament*, where performance is rewarded on the basis of its *rank* within the set of all realised performances.

Third – and this is not an essential feature – it was assumed that firms moved simultaneously: that is, there was no firm which was distinctive in being allowed to move first.

The essence of patent races is that they *are* races, and the reward structure is such that *ex-post* pay-offs are discontinuous. In the absence of uncertainty, technological competition in the form of patent races leads to *discontinuous games*. Fortunately, the nature of the discontinuities from which patent races suffer is such that such games *do* possess equilibria, provided that competitors choose mixed strategies (see Dasgupta and Maskin, 1982a, b).[24]

The essence of a patent race among competitors enjoying complete and perfect information both about the world and about one another, can be distilled if we analyse the following bidding game: N players ($N \geq 2$) bid for an indivisible object valued by each at V (> 0). All bids are forfeited. The highest bidder wins the object. If there are K ($\leq N$) highest bidders each of these (K) players wins the object, with probability $1/K$.

Let a_i ($i = 1, \ldots ,N$) be player i's bid. Then we may as well suppose that $0 \leq a_i \leq V$. Notice that i's pay-off function is discontinuous at the set of points $a_i = \max \{a_j , j \neq i \}$. Suppose the players bid simultaneously. It is then simple to check that the game does not have a Nash equilibrium in pure strategies. But, if players mix their bids, there is an equilibrium. In particular, the symmetric outcome in which each player chooses the cumulative distribution function $(a/V)^{1/(N-1)}$, for $0 \leq a \leq V$, is a Nash equilibrium. Notice, first, that in equilibrium each player expects zero net profit; that is, all rents are dissipated if there are N (≥ 2) bidders. Notice also that, at this equilibrium, each player expects to bid V/N. Suppose we now interpret a forfeited bid as a sunk-cost in R & D; that firms face the same (deterministic) function relating the date of invention to R & D expenditure; and that this function is monotonically-decreasing. We may then conclude that the greater is competition (i.e. the larger is N) the more distant is the expected date of invention; that is, the slower is the rate of technological progress. (Note the corresponding result in Section III.2.)

In what follows, I want to study games of this type. I shall vary the number of players and the number of objects to be bid for, I shall also vary the player's pay-offs, with a view to analysing the issue of pre-emptive patenting.

(2) THE PRE-EMPTIVE MONOPOLIST: A SINGLE PATENT RACE

Suppose there are two firms, $i = 1, 2$. Firm 1 is the sitting monopolist, his past success being protected by a patent. The race is for the next patent. If the monopolist wins, his profit is $\check{V}$. But if Firm 2 wins, then the profits to the two players 1 and 2 are V^* and V^{**} respectively. Naturally, I shall assume that $\check{V} > V^* + V^{**}$. This is the precise sense in which the monopolist has a greater incentive to win the next patent, and it captures observation 5 in Section II in an indirect manner – for it abstracts the idea that a monopolist's pay-off, *relative* to its R & D effort in obtaining the patent, exceeds that of its rivals.

By definition, the sitting monopolist is already in the industry. Thus I let the monopolist make the first move. This is followed by a bid from Firm 2. The monopolist is therefore a Stackelberg leader. If the monopolist bids V^{**} (plus a tiny amount, to be precise) he will win the patent. This is because V^{**} is Firm 2's reservation price for the patent. If the monopolist bids less than V^{**}, he will be beaten in the race and will forfeit his bid. His choice therefore boils down to either bidding V^{**} or not bidding at all. If he chooses the former, his pay-off is $\bar{V} - V^{**}$; if the latter, it is V^*. He will therefore choose the former. This is the pre-emption result in its simplest form.[25]

Notice at once that the patent may be for a technology which is *strictly inferior* to the one which the monopolist holds. The pre-emption argument goes through, but the monopolist will not actually *use* the new patent. His incentive for winning it is simply to prevent his rival from using it. In this case, the monopolist will take pre-emptive action and hold a sleeping patent.[26]

Matters are somewhat complicated if the monopolist faces more than one rival for the new patent. Consider the general case of N ($\geqslant 2$) rivals (i = 1, . . . ,N) who are all identical. I label the monopolist as $i = 0$ and I assume, as before, that he bids first. At the second move, the rivals bid simultaneously. Now suppose the monopolist bids a_0. (Obviously $0 \leqslant a_0 \leqslant V^{**}$.) We have already seen that there is no equilibrium in pure strategies at the second stage of the game if $a_0 < V^{**}$. It is now an easy matter to check that, at the second stage, there is a symmetric mixed-strategy equilibrium in which *each* of the N rivals (i = 1, . . . ,N) chooses the following mixed strategy: 'no bid' with probability $(a_0/V^{**})^{1/(N-1)}$, and for $a_0 \leqslant a \leqslant V^{**}$ the cumulative distribution function $(a/V^{**})^{1/(N-1)}$ (see Section V.1).

I now return to the monopolist's choice of a_0. The monopolist will obviously win the patent if *all* rivals bid less than a_0 which, as we have just seen, means that *each* rival bids nothing (i.e. does not enter the race). The chance of that is $(a_0/V^{**})^{N/(N-1)}$. The monopolist loses if at least one of the rivals bids in excess of a_0. Now, the chance of this happening at the second stage of the game is $1 - (a_0/V^{**})^{N/(N-1)}$. It follows that if the monopolist selects a_0, his expected profit is:

$$(a_0/V^{**})^{N/(N-1)} [\bar{V} - V^*] + V^* - a_0. \tag{17}$$

By hypothesis, $\bar{V} > V^* + V^{**}$. From (17) we may therefore conclude that the monopolist will choose $a_0 = V^{**}$ and thus take pre-emptive action.

(3) THE PRE-EMPTIVE MONOPOLIST: MULTIPLE PATENT RACES

Quite obviously, a monopolist cannot guarantee pre-emption if there are uncertainties in the possibilities of invention, and if firm's uncertainties are not perfectly correlated. The reason why one wants, here, to study models with no uncertainty in the invention process is that it enables one to distil the relative incentives that firms may have for entering patent races. The question I want to ask now is whether a sitting monopolist will wish to pre-empt *all* potential discoveries, if there are several of them. Presumably not, unless he expects increasing returns to his profits from the acquisition of patents. The analysis that follows makes this precise.[27]

For tractability, I assume that the monopolist ($i = 1$) faces a single rival ($i = 2$). There are N (≥ 1) patents to be won, which are identical in their economic effects. The pay-off for the monopolist in winning K ($0 \leq K \leq N$) patents is $\bar{V}(K)$; and for the rival it is $V^{**}(K)$. By assumption

$$\bar{V}(K + 1) > \bar{V}(K) > 0 \qquad \text{for } 0 \leq K \leq N - 1, \qquad (18)$$

$$V^{**}(K + 1) > V^{**}(K) \qquad \text{for } 0 \leq K \leq N - 1, \qquad (19)$$

$$\bar{V}(K) > V^{**}(K) \qquad \text{for } 0 \leq K \leq N \qquad (20)$$

and

$$V^{**}(0) = 0. \qquad (21)$$

Consider, first, the case where the rival's pay-off is *superadditive*:

$$V^{**}(K)/K \geq V^{**}(J)/J \qquad \text{for } J < K. \qquad (22)$$

If the monopolist intends to win precisely K ($0 \leq K \leq N$) patents in such a situation, he should bid nothing for ($N - K$) and $H(K)$ for *each* of the rest, where

$$H(K) = [V^{**}(N) - V^{**}(N - K)]/K. \qquad (23)$$

If he does this, the pay-off to him (in obtaining (K) patents) is

$$M(K) \equiv \bar{V}(K) - KH(K)$$

or

$$M(K) = \bar{V}(K) - V^{**}(N) + V^{**}(N - K) \qquad (24)$$

The monopolist's problem is to choose K so as to maximise $M(K)$. A *sufficient* condition for complete pre-emption is therefore $M(K + 1) \geq M(K)$ for all K; or

$$\left.\begin{array}{l} \bar{V}(K + 1) + V^{*}(N - (K + 1)) \geq \bar{V}(K) + V^{**}(N - K) \\ \qquad\qquad\qquad\qquad\qquad \text{for all } K \end{array}\right\} \qquad (25)$$

(25) is intuitively appealing, for it says that the *total* profits of the industry are rising with the number of patents captured by the monopolist. But it does not say directly whether the *monopolist* enjoys increasing or decreasing returns in the acquisition of patents. However, note that (25) is guaranteed if

$$\bar{V}(K + 1) - \bar{V}(K) > \bar{V}(K) - \bar{V}(K - 1) \qquad \text{for } K \geq 1, \qquad (26)$$

and if

$$\bar{V}(1) - \bar{V}(0) \geq V^{**}(N) - V^{**}(N - 1). \qquad (27)$$

It follows that (22), (26) and (27) are together sufficient for complete pre-emption.

Suppose instead the other extreme to (22), that is, that the rival's pay-off is *subadditive*, i.e.

$$V^{**}(K)/K < V^{**}(J)/J, \qquad \text{for } J < K. \qquad (28)$$

This case does not allow us to obtain as clean a set of sufficient conditions for complete pre-emption on the part of the monopolist.

First, note that if the monopolist decides to win precisely K patents, then under (28) he will bid nothing for $N - K$ of them and $L(K)$ for *each* of the remaining ones, where

$$L(K) = V^{**}(N - K + 1) - V^{**}(N - K). \qquad (29)$$

In this event, his pay-off $M(K)$ is:

$$M(K) = \bar{V}(K) - KL(K)$$

or

$$M(K) = \bar{V}(K) + KV^{**}(N - K) - KV^{**}(N - K + 1). \qquad (30)$$

It follows immediately from (30) that a *sufficient* condition for complete pre-emption ($M(K) \geq M(K - 1)$ for $1 \leq K \leq N$) is:

$$\bar{V}(K) - \bar{V}(K - 1) \geq (2K - 1)$$
$$(2K - 1) [V^{**} (N - K + 1) - V^* (N - K)]$$
$$\text{for } 1 \leq K \leq N. \qquad (31)$$

The conditions linking the monopolist's pay-off and that of the rival that have been stressed here suggest the kind of increasing returns in the profitability of inventions that are sufficient for complete pre-emption. It seems to me, also, that the formulation adopted here for studying patent races is suggestive for another reason. The question can be asked whether it really is advantageous for the monopolist to move first. John Vickers of Oxford University has pointed out to me (in his comments on this chapter) that if the monopolist's pay-off is superadditive it would win *all* patents at zero cost if the sequence of moves were to be reversed. One concludes, then, that there may be serious disadvantages in having to move first.

VI   A CLASSIFICATION OF TECHNOLOGICAL COMPETITION

Models attempting to capture the phenomenon of technological competition have been of two broad kinds. There are those that are continuous games and there are those that are discontinuous. If this classification appears excessively mathematical, that is a deception. The classification is based on the manner in which models postulate the structure of rewards that firms in an industry expect to get if they engage in R & D activity. The economic organisation which I analysed in Section II is one which generates a continuous game. Much technological competition displays this feature. (It has this feature when, for example, there is a continuum of potential discoveries to choose from.) The models that I studied in Section V were discontinuous games. They arise in those social organisations where competition assumes the form of a tournament; that is, roughly speaking, where the 'winner' is clearly identifiable; where the winner 'takes all'; and where there is no 'neighbouring' race for rivals to move to. One can have a tournament when there is only a discrete number of potential discoveries. Patent races are a pristine form of tournament. They remain so in the face of imitation. Imitation typically dilutes the innovator's profits; it does not alter the fact that competition for the (imperfectly-protectable) patent is essentially a tournament. It is for this reason that theorists usually concentrate on patent races where the winner literally 'takes all'. The analysis of Section IV hopefully clarifies this.

But I want now to argue that such discontinuous games as I have presented in Section V are really rather spurious. They *hint* at something, but they are also misleading. Tournaments distinguish winners and losers sharply, but on their own they do not make for discontinuous games. One requires, in addition, the hypothesis that firms face uncertainties that are perfectly correlated.[28] This is really hard to swallow. If they are not then, in general, no firm can be certain of being the winner – no matter how much effort it puts in – unless it can make it unprofitable for rivals to enter the race. Firms in such circumstances will choose probability distributions whose parameters are affected by R & D effort. Typically their *expected* profits (or pay-offs) will be continuous functions. The resulting games, reflecting technological competition, are therefore continuous. (See Loury, 1979, and Dasgupta and Stiglitz, 1980b.) The theory of pre-emptive patenting should not be taken too literally. It merely highlights relative incentives among firms. The second purpose of this chapter has been to distinguish these two broad classes of models capturing technological competition, by means of two sets of examples (Sections III and V). [29] Not surprisingly, the two sets display somewhat different features. My first purpose has been to look at a number of empirical observations on technological competition, and to produce models that can explain them. I re-emphasise that these observations are still the subject of controversy among applied economists. But, many years ago, a distinguished physicist advised the world never to trust an experimental result until it is confirmed by theory. So perhaps we should now start believing in them.

NOTES

1. An earlier version of this paper was delivered as lectures at the Norwegian School of Economics and Business Administration, Bergen, and at the Stockholm School of Economics. My greatest debt is to Joseph Stiglitz with whom I have discussed and written on technological competition over several years. In writing this paper I have had the benefit of conversations with Vincent Crawford, Tracy Lewis, Jonathan Liebenau, Eric Maskin, Dilip Mookherjee, Barry Nalebuff, Jesus Seade and in particular the comments of John Vickers.
   It is dedicated to the memory of Nancy Schwartz.
2. Leading graduate texts on microeconomics, such as Malinvaud (1972), Layard and Walters (1978) and Varian (1978), contain absolutely no discussion of these matters.
3. Excellent documentations of this empirical research are in Kamien and Schwartz (1975) and (1982), Chapter 3, and Boylan (1977). Rosenberg, ed. (1971), continues to be the best collection of essays on the subject.
4. For different illustrations of this, see Fisher and Temin (1973) and Dasgupta and Stiglitz (1977, 1980a).
5. His claim that a monopolistic firm will have a greater *demand* for innovations (because its market power enables it to benefit more from innovations) has been shown to be false by Arrow (1962a).

6. Fisher and Temin (1973) provide a powerful critique of a large body of literature that has attempted to test this hypothesis.

7. Dasgupta and Stiglitz (1977, 1980a, b, 1981), Levin (1978), Loury (1979) and Futia (1980) are examples of this small literature. Nordhaus (1969) is an important precursor. Scherer (1967a), Barzel (1968) and Kamien and Schwartz (1972, 1978) have suggestive features. But they are not comprehensively explored. Von Weizsäcker (1980), Chapters 8 and 9, contains interesting, elaborate constructions. But he does not model industrial structure explicitly, and in any case, he is for the most part concerned with *biases* in R & D activity in a market economy relative to a socially-managed one. Nelson and Winter (1977, 1978) represent part of an impressive research programme on Schumpterian competition. Theirs *is* a somewhat different approach to these issues. But it would appear that *analytical* results are hard to come by in this approach. A serious defect in Futia (1980) and Dasgupta and Stiglitz (1981) is that in order to admit 'realistic' features into their models of competition, *ad hoc* assumptions had to be imposed on what firms attempt to achieve and what they can or cannot do. In what follows, I want to avoid *ad hoc* assumptions (such as the precise form of bounded rationality) very strongly.

8. J. K. Galbraith has consistently emphasised that demand conditions are significantly influenced by expenditures on persuasion. (See e.g. Galbraith, 1974). This can be accommodated in the models that I shall discuss subsequently. Spence (1980) provides an analysis of advertising as a barrier to entry. Levin and Reiss (1984) have used an extended version of the model presented in Section III.3 to test the hypothesis that R & D investment and industrial structure are a jointly-determined outcome of the competitive process. Their findings provide some support for the view that they are.

9. Kamien and Schwartz (1982), Chapter 3, has an excellent and detailed documentation of these empirical findings and I have gained much from this. Unfortunately they do not do much with the findings in the remainder of their book.

10. Examples of models incorporating both features are Dasgupta *et al.* (1977), Kamien and Schwartz (1978) and Reinganum (1981a). Models containing the latter feature are often called 'dynamic' which, in economics, invariably carries approbation.

11. The model can easily be adapted to a market for (potentially) differentiated products where firms are engaged in *product* innovation. Since the model then becomes a tiny bit more complicated, I refrain from adapting it here.

12. We can allow for a spill-over in the acquisition of knowledge by having the R & D expenditures of *other* firms influence the unit cost of production of a given firm. The implications of such a modified model are precisely the ones that one would expect from a model of incomplete appropriability of knowledge. I do not therefore present this extension. (For such extensions see Leung, 1982, and Levin and Reiss, 1984). In any event, the issue of *imitative* research is more delicate, and requires an explicit inter-temporal formulation. I discuss this briefly in Section IV.

13. As there is an extensive discussion of the theorem in Dasgupta and Stiglitz (1980a) I shall not elaborate on it here. Condition (ii) in fact guarantees that a firm's *profit* level, as a function of its R & D expenditure, faces diminishing returns at high levels of R & D expenditure.

14. However, one should note that $(n + 1)x^*(n + 1) > nx^*(n)$. The model captures in a sharp form the wastes of duplication of R & D under technological competition. A socially-managed industry in this model would have only *one* R & D laboratory, of course.

15. It is an easy enough matter to give a sequence to the decisions by having firms first decide whether or not to enter and then decide on R & D expenditure and output levels simultaneously. As regards the features I wish to highlight here (subgame) perfect equilibria in such a model are no different from the equilibria I shall be studying in the text. It is a great deal more complicated to characterise (subgame) perfect equilibria if firms first decide whether or not to enter and then decide on R & D expenditures and then on output levels. I do not know whether perfect equilibria in such a model have the features I wish to highlight below.

16. For discussions of this equilibrium concept, see Novshek (1980); Dasgupta and Stiglitz (1980a); von Weizsäcker (1980), Chapter 4 and the Symposium on large economies in the *Journal of Economic Theory*, August, 1980. Dasgupta and Ushio (1981) and Guesnerie and Hart (1981) consider a special case of this model by eschewing R & D activity: they assume that there exists $\bar{x}$ (> 0) such that $c(x) = \infty$ if $0 \leqslant x < \bar{x}$ and $c(x) = \beta > 0$ if $x \geqslant \bar{x}$.

17. This is clearly a mathematical artefact, depending severely on the parametrisation (1) and (2). Since nothing much would be gained by moving away from this parametrisation and *then* locating conditions under which the following corollaries hold, I refrain from doing this.

18. Tandon (1982) has investigated welfare losses under oligopoly when α is not negligible.

19. Contrast this with Schumpeter's obsession with the periodic emergence of the daring and charismatic leader who innovates, only to be followed by a cluster of further innovations by others (see Schumpeter, 1939). Dasgupta and Stiglitz, 1981 construct a model in which the periodicity of innovations is explained by sunk-costs involved in R & D. It is an implication of this model that a competitive industry is characterised by over-frequent, but 'small', innovations as compared to a socially-managed industry.

20. There is also a symmetric mixed-strategy Nash equilibrium, where each firm chooses L with probability 1/3. But, even at this equilibrium, there is a chance of 4/9 that the two will not innovate simultaneously.

21. That is, in what follows, I restrict myself to an economic game in which players face binary choice. This is for expositional ease only. I shall return to infinite games in Section V since I want to highlight the discontinuous structure of patent races under certainty. If cast as an infinite game, a model of imitation will also be discontinuous. I want to avoid the issue of discontinuity in this section.

22. Reinganum, 1981b discusses an infinite economic game which can be suitably modified to capture the idea of imitative possibilities. I am restrict-

ing myself to this finite (binary-choice) game for expositional ease.

23. I am, of course, side-stepping important features of capital markets. In an interesting paper Bhattacharya and Ritter (1984) have analysed a model in which firms are required to finance R & D from external sources and in which to improve their borrowing terms they must disclose technological information directly useful to their rivals.

24. Imitation games are also typically discontinuous. We avoided this issue in Section IV by restricting ourselves to a finite game. But it should be emphasised that an essential form of uncertainty is eschewed here, that firms face uncorrelated risks in R & D. See Section VI on this.

25. See Dasgupta and Stiglitz (1980b) and Gilbert and Newbery (1982). In other contexts pre-emptive behaviour has been discussed by Eaton and Lipsey (1979, 1980) and Dixit (1980) among others.

26. The phenomenon of sleeping patents is very similar to the maintenance of excess capacity as an entry-deterring device, which has been analysed by Spence (1977) among others. These models, being timeless, cannot identify situations where 'excess capacity' is maintained only for a finite period. For illustrations of cases where it is strategically convenient to hold an unused patent for only a finite period, see Dasgupta *et al.* (1982).

27. In a splendid recent paper, Eswaran and Lewis (1982) have addressed this question in the context of firms bidding for oil reserves. Their arguments depend heavily on the characteristics of inter-temporal oligopolistic markets for exhaustible resources. It would be good to have results on partial pre-emption for less-structured markets. The example in the text is designed to study this.

28. The models analysed in Section V assume no environmental uncertainty and so satisfy this condition trivially.

29. I am therefore arguing implicitly that, at the analytical level, the customary classification – consisting of product and process innovations – is unilluminating.

REFERENCES

Arrow, K. J. (1962a) 'Economic Welfare and the Allocation of Resources for Inventions', in Nelson R. R. (ed.), *The Rate and Direction of Inventive Activity* (Princeton University Press). Reprinted in N. Rosenberg, *The Economics of Technological Change* (1971).

Arrow, K. J. (1962b) 'The Economic Implications of Learning by Doing', *Review of Economic Studies*, vol. 29, pp. 155–73.

Barzel, Y. (1968) 'Optimal Timing of Innovations', *Review of Economics and Statistics*, vol. 50, pp. 348–55.

Bhattacharya, S. and Ritter, J. R. (1983) 'Innovation and Communication: Signalling with Partial Disclosure', *Review of Economic Studies*, vol. 50, pp. 331–46.

Boylan, M. G. (1977) 'The Sources of Technological Innovations', in Gold. B. (ed.), *Research, Technological Change, and Economic Analysis* (Lexington, Massachusetts: Lexington Books)

Comanor, W. S. (1964) 'Research and Competitive Product Differentiation in the Pharmaceutical Industry in the United States', *Economica*, vol. 31, pp. 372–84.

Comanor, W. S. (1965) 'Research and Technical Change in the Pharmaceutical Industry', *Review of Economics and Statistics*, vol. 47, pp. 182–90.

Comanor, W. S. (1967) 'Market Structure, Product Differentiation and Industrial Research', *Quarterly Journal of Economics*, vol. 81, pp. 639–57.

Comanor, W. S. and Scherer, F. M. (1969) 'Patent Statistics as a Measure of Technical Change', *Journal of Political Economy*, vol. 77, pp. 392–8.

Dasgupta, P., Heal, G. and Majumdar, M. (1977) 'Resource Depletion and Research and Development', in Intriligator, M. (ed.), *Frontiers of Quantitative Economics*, vol. IIIB (Amsterdam: North-Holland).

Dasgupta, P., Gilbert, R. and Stiglitz, J. (1982) 'Invention and Innovation under Alternative Market Structures: the Case of Natural Resources', *Review of Economic Studies*, vol. 49, pp. 567–82.

Dasgupta, P. and Maskin, E. (1982a) 'The Existence of Equilibrium in Discontinuous Economic Games, I: Theory' (mimeo., London School of Economics), forthcoming, *Review of Economic Studies*.

Dasgupta, P. and Maskin, E. (1982b) 'The Existence of Equilibrium in Discontinuous Economic Games, 2: Applications', (mimeo., London School of Economics), forthcoming, *Review of Economic Studies*.

Dasgupta, P. and Stiglitz, J. (1977) 'Market Structure and Research and Development', Paper presented at the World Congress of the *International Economic Association* on *Economic Growth and Resources*, Tokyo, Aug. (mimeo., London School of Economics).

Dasgupta, P. and Stiglitz, J. (1980a) 'Industrial Structure and the Nature of Innovative Activity', *Economic Journal*, vol. 90, pp. 266–93.

Dasgupta, P. and Stiglitz, J. (1980b) 'Uncertainty, Industrial Structure and the Speed of R & D', *Bell Journal of Economics* Spring, pp. 1–28.

Dasgupta, P. and Stiglitz, J. (1981) 'Entry, Innovation, Exit: Towards a Dynamic Theory of Oligopolistic Industrial Structure', *European Economic Review*, vol. 15, pp. 137–58.

Dasgupta, P. and Ushio, Y. (1981) 'On the Rate of Convergence of Oligopoly Equilibria in Large Markets: an Example', *Economic Letters*, vol. 8, pp. 13–17.

Debreu, G. (1959), *Theory of Value*, Cowles Foundation Monograph (New Haven, Connecticut: Yale University Press).

Dixit, A. (1980) 'The Role of Investment in Entry Deterrence', *Economic Journal* vol. 90, pp. 95–106.

Eaton, B. C. and Lipsey, R. (1979) 'The Theory of Market Pre-emption: the Persistence of Excess Capacity and Monopoly in a Growing Spatial Market, *Economica*, vol. 46, pp. 149–58.

Eaton, B. C. and Lipsey, R. (1980) 'Exit Barriers and Entry Barriers to Entry', *Bell Journal of Economics*, vol. 11, pp. 721–9.

Eswaran, M. and Lewis, T. R. (1982) 'Evolution of Market Structure in a Dominant Firm Model with Exhaustible Resources' (mimeo, Department of Economics, University of British Columbia).

Fisher, F. M. and Temin, P. (1973) 'Returns to Scale in Research and

Development: What Does the Schumpeterian Hypothesis Imply?', *Journal of Political Economy*, vol. 81, pp. 56–70.

Freeman, C. (1965) 'Research and Development in Electronic Capital Goods', *National Institute Economic Review*, vol. 34, pp. 40–91.

Futia, C. A. (1980) 'Schumpeterian Competition', *Quarterly Journal of Economics*, vol. 94, pp. 675–95.

Galbraith, J. K. (1974) *Economics and the Public Purpose* (London: André Deutsch).

Gilbert, R. and Newbery, D. (1982) 'Pre-emptive Patenting and the Persistence of Monopoly', forthcoming, *American Economic Review*.

Grabowski, H. G. (1968) 'The Determinants of Industrial Research and Development: A Study of the Chemical, Drug and Petroleum Industries', *Journal of Political Economy*, vol. 76, pp. 292–306.

Guesnerie, R. and Hart, O. (1981) 'Notes on the Rate of Convergence of Cournot-Nash Equilibria ' (mimeo., University of Cambridge).

Kaldor, N. (1961) 'Capital Accumulation and Economic Growth', in Lutz, F. A. and Hague, D. C. (eds), *The Theory of Capital* (Macmillan: London).

Kamien, M. I. and Schwartz, N. L. (1972) 'Market Structure, Rival's Response, and the Firm's Rate of Product Improvement', *Journal of Industrial Economics*, vol. 20, pp. 159–72.

Kamien, M. I. and Schwartz, N. L. (1975) 'Market Structure and Innovation: a Survey', *Journal of Economic Literature*, vol. 13, pp. 1–37.

Kamien, M. I. and Schwartz, N. L. (1978) 'Potential Rivalry, Monopoly Profits and the Pace of Inventive Activity', *Review of Economic Studies*, vol. 45, pp. 547–57.

Kamien, M. I. and Schwartz, N. L. (1982) *Market Structure and Innovation* (Cambridge University Press).

Layard, R. and Walters, A. A. (1978) *Microeconomic Theory* (New York: McGraw-Hill)

Leung, H. M. (1982) 'Industrial Structure and R & D Spill-Overs' (mimeo., London School of Economics).

Levin, R. C. (1978) 'Technical Change, Barriers to Entry and Market Structure', *Economica*, vol. 45, pp. 347–61.

Levin, R. C. and Reiss, P. C. (1984), 'Tests of a Schumpeterian Model of R & D and Market Structure', in Griliches, Z. (ed.) *R & D Patents and Productivity* (University of Chicago Press).

Loury, G. (1979) 'Market Structure and Innovation', *Quarterly Journal of Economics*, vol. 93, pp. 395–410.

Malinvaud, E. (1972) *Lectures on Microeconomic Theory* (Amsterdam: North-Holland).

Mansfield, E. (1968) *Industrial Research and Technological Innovation – An Econometric Analysis* (New York: W. W. Norton).

Mansfield, E. *et al.* (1971) *Research and Innnovation in the Modern Corporation*, (New York: W. W. Norton).

Mansfield, E., Schwartz, M. and Wagner, S. (1981) 'Imitation Costs and Patents: An Empirical Study', *Economic Journal* vol. 91, pp. 907–18.

Nelson, R. R., Peck, M. J. and Kalachek, E. D. (1967), *Technology, Economic Growth and Public Policy* (Brookings Institution, Washington, DC).

Nelson, R. R. and Winter, S. G. (1977) 'Dynamic Competition and Technical Progress', in Balassa, B. and Nelson, R. R. (eds), *Economic Progress, Private Values and Public Policy: Essays in Honour of William Fellner* (Amsterdam: North-Holland).

Nelson, R. R. and Winter,S. G. (1978) 'Forces Generating and Limiting Concentration under Schumpeterian Competition', *Bell Journal of Economics*, vol. 9 pp. 524–48.

Nordhaus, W. D. (1969) *Invention, Growth and Welfare* (Cambridge, Mass: MIT Press).

Novshek, W. (1980) 'Nash-Cournot Equilibrium with Entry', *Review of Economic Studies*, vol. 47, pp. 473–86.

Pakes, A. (1984) 'Patents, R & D and the Stock Market Rate of Return', in Griliches, Z. (ed.) *R & D, Patents and Productivity* (University of Chicago Press).

Phillips, A. (1966) 'Patents, Potential Competition and Technical Progress', *American Economic Review*, vol. 56, pp. 301–10.

Phillips, A. (1971) *Technology and Market Structure: a Study of the Aircraft Industry* (Lexington, Massachusetts: Lexington Books).

Reinganum, J. F. (1981a) 'Dynamic Games of Innovation', *Journal of Economic Theory*, vol. 25, pp. 21–41.

Reinganum, J. (1981b) 'On the Diffusion of New Technology: a Game Theoretic Approach', *Review of Economic Studies*, vol. 48, pp. 395–406.

Rosenberg, N. (ed.) (1971) *The Economics of Technological Change* (Harmondsworth: Penguin Modern Economic Readings).

Rosenberg, N. (1974) 'Science, Innovation and Economic Growth', *Economic Journal* vol. 84, pp. 90–108.

Rosenberg, N. (1976) *Perspectives in Technology* (Cambridge University Press).

Schelling, T. C. (1960) *The Strategy of Conflict* (Cambridge, Massachusetts: Harvard University Press).

Scherer, F. M. (1967a) 'Research and Development Resource Allocation under Rivalry', *Quarterly Journal of Economics*, vol. 81, pp. 359–94.

Scherer, F. M. (1967b) 'Market Structure and the Employment of Scientists and Engineers', *American Economic Review*, vol. 57, pp. 524–31.

Schmookler, J. (1966) *Invention and Economic Growth* (Cambridge, Mass.: Harvard University Press)

Schumpeter, J. (1939) *Business Cycles*, (New York: McGraw-Hill)

Schumpeter, J. (1976) *Capitalism, Socialism and Democracy*, 5th ed (London: Allen and Unwin).

Spence, A. M. (1977) 'Entry, Capacity, Investment and Oligopolistic Pricing', *Bell Journal of Economics*, vol. 8, pp. 534–44.

Spence, A. M. (1980) 'Notes on Advertising, Economies of Scale and Entry Barriers', *Quarterly Journal of Economics*, vol. 94, pp. 493–504.

Tandon, P. (1982) 'Innovation, Market Structure and Welfare' (mimeo., Department of Economics, Boston University).

Varian, H. (1978) *Microeconomic Analysis* (New York: W. W. Norton).

von Weizsäcker, C. C. (1980) *Barriers to Entry: A Theoretical Treatment* (Berlin: Springer-Verlag).

Discussion of the Paper by Partha Dasgupta

In discussing this paper, *Seade* first made several specific comments. He noted that Dasgupta's models were not dynamic (i.e., there was no time structure to R & D) and contained no uncertainty about returns to R & D. Though these were strong assumptions, he remarked that they were not uncommon in the literature. He questioned the relationship established in the paper between profit rates and investment in R & D. He commented that since these were both endogenous variables, the only way to establish a relationship was to change some third parameter and observe whether the response of the two endogenous variables was the same or different. In a general model, he suggested that the answer to this question should depend upon the chosen third variable. A simple relationship would be very hard to establish without strong assumptions that would ensure homogeneity of response.

More generally, Seade observed that R & D expenditures had been modelled in such a way that they behaved exactly like investment in capital produced internally by the firm. This specification was particularly advantageous since it permitted the application of a long literature on capital accumulation. One particular extension immediately apparent involved setting up external markets for R & D where firms specialised in producing research which they subsequently sold. Known results on capital markets would then be applied to research markets. The limitation of the approach was that it ignored the essential distinction between capital and R & D which was the ability to appropriate all the returns associated with the investment. Seade felt that the 'continuous' model (e.g. pay-offs were a continuous function of investment) studied by Dasgupta in the first part of the paper, belonged to a class of well-developed models. Research into discontinuous models (e.g., contests where there was a single winner), examined in the second part of the paper, was, however, still in its infancy. Discontinuities become particularly important when patents existed, a common situation. Finally, Seade suggested that being first in the R & D market, or first to make a discovery, conveyed a very important advantage. The implications of this advantage should be studied in greater detail.

While *Gilbert* thought Dasgupta's paper contained a first rate synthesis of the new Schumpeterian uprising, he observed that the empirical regularities cited by Dasgupta should be used with caution. They resulted either from gross aggregation, in which case the implications were unclear, or extreme industry specificity, in which case the generality of the results could be questioned. He suggested as well that the time had come to attempt to integrate the specialised knowledge about industry structure, gained by studying research and development, with knowledge about industry structure gained from other sources.

Gilbert further suggested that an important distinction should be made between research and development. The lack of uncertainty and complete appropriability of returns made Dasgupta's model appropriate as a model of development rather than a model of research. Finally, he suggested that the reported link between opportunities for innovation and concentration might be misleading. He referred to the paper by Dasgupta and Stiglitz (1980) which he interpreted as giving the opposite result. He suggested that the tendency towards concentration might be the result of scale economies built into the model.

Walroos observed that the problem of modelling the process of entry, and the transition from the short to the long run was critical. He felt uncomfortable with the specific functional forms chosen for costs and wondered about the robustness of the results with respect to changes in the specification of costs. Finally, he suggested that the results in the discontinuous case depended critically on the assumption of certainty of returns. Stiglitz responded that in discontinuous games with certainty, equilibrium often existed in mixed strategies only, if it existed at all. Adding uncertainty will often give equilibrium in pure strategies with the exogenous uncertainty taking the roll of the randomisation involved with mixed strategies.

Michael Spence wondered how cross-industry data could be understood since variation arose because of variation in unobservable parameters. Stiglitz agreed but suggested that this problem was common to all empirical work. *Von Ungern-Sternberg* suggested that work should be done on what determined the types of R & D projects that would be chosen by industries. For example, what determined when basic research, rather than applied research, would be undertaken.

REFERENCE

Dasgupta, P. and Stiglitz, J. (1980) 'Uncertainty, Industrial Structure and the Speed of R & D', *Bell Journal of Economics*, vol. 11, no. 1, pp. 1–28.

Index

Entries in **bold type** under the names of participants in the conference indicate their Papers or Discussions of their Papers. Entries in *italic type* indicate contributions by participants to the Discussions.